Smith and Keenan's
Mercantile Law

Smith and Keenan's Mercantile Law

Sixth Edition

Denis Keenan

LL.B. (Hons.), F.C.I.S., D.M.A., Cert. Ed.
of the Middle Temple, Barrister-at-Law, formerly Head of the Department of Business Studies and Law, Mid-Essex Technical College and School of Art (now the Chelmer Institute of Higher Education)

Pitman

PITMAN PUBLISHING LIMITED
128 Long Acre, London, WC2E 9AN

PITMAN PUBLISHING LIMITED
1020 Plain Street, Marshfield, Massachusetts 02050

Associated Companies
Pitman Publishing Pty Ltd, Melbourne
Pitman Publishing New Zealand Ltd, Wellington
Copp Clark Pitman, Toronto

First published in Great Britain 1985

British Library Cataloguing in Publication Data
Smith, Kenneth, *1910–1966*
Smith and Keenan's mercantile law.—6th ed.
1. Commercial law—England
I. Title II. Keenan, Denis III. Smith, Kenneth, *1910–1966*. Mercantile law
344.206′7 KD1629

ISBN 0-273-02207-5

Typeset by BAS Printers, Over Wallop, Hampshire
Printed and bound in Great Britain at Pitman Press, Bath

Contents

Preface to sixth edition

This edition has been substantially rewritten and updated, on the basis of advice received from lecturers who have used the book over the years and have from time to time responded to the publisher's enquiries of various kinds.

The chapter on registered companies has been dropped because the subject has now become so extensive, being based on five Companies Acts (soon to be consolidated) and ever-expanding case law, that to encapsulate it in one chapter and still do any sort of justice to the subject is truly impossible. Company law is now studied as a separate subject and seldom, if ever, forms merely a part of a business law syllabus. Where it does a separate text is required.

The chapter on bankruptcy has also been omitted. The law relating to insolvency of persons and companies is now often studied as a separate subject and is regarded by many as too specialised for inclusion in a general course on business law.

The chapter on guarantees and indemnities was dropped because it really forms part of a specialised and separate subject of the law of securities, and the chapter on arbitration has been omitted because it is in essence part of legal procedure.

It is hoped that the book will now be even more suitable for a variety of business law courses and the space provided by the changes referred to above has been used in some measure to improve the appendix of cases. Each case, or sometimes a group of cases, has introductory material which leads to the possibility of studying the case appendix along with or separately from the text. It is hoped that the book will now be even more effective as a text and case book combined.

In addition, a chapter on the law of employment protection has been added. This confines itself largely to the statute law on the subject since a knowledge of this area is a major requirement for practitioners in the field of company administration, accountancy, and general management. Other aspects of employment law are of less importance to the non-lawyer.

A few cases on the subject of employment law have been included by way of illustration of the legal principles involved. However, it would have been impossible in a general book of this kind to give a complete coverage of employment protection cases. There are so many of them that even to have included 100 would have been merely to have scratched the surface. In addition, a knowledge of case law in the field of employment protection is not of the same importance as in other branches of law since industrial tribunals and even the Employment Appeal Tribunal are less and less inclined to follow precedent, being more concerned to look at cases on an individual basis according to the circumstances.

Once again, graded questions and tutorial problems appear in an appendix. Answers have not been supplied as before because lecturers felt that this limited the general use of the questions in courses where, inevitably the lecturer was supplementing the text with other material and would prefer to give his or her own answer; regrettably, also, some students do copy answers if they are easily to hand.

Only a minor amount of updating is required. This is set out below.

Hire Purchase and Consumer Credit (p. 191 of text)

SI 1984/436 brings into force on 19 May 1985 ss 123–125 of the Consumer Credit Act 1974. These sections restrict the use of negotiable instruments in 'regulated' consumer credit agreements and consumer hire agreements. SI 1984/435, which is also in force from 19 May 1985, exempts leasing agreements entered into by a UK company with a foreign company from the above restrictions on taking or negotiating negotiable instruments.

Partnerships (p. 222 of text)

The references to the Companies Act 1981 in regard to business names are currently part of a consolidation of company and related law which is before Parliament. When the relevant legislation is passed the law referred to, whilst unchanged, will appear in the Business Names Act 1985.

Generally

The references in various parts of the text to Companies Acts, eg Companies Act 1948, will change when consolidating legislation currently before Parliament is passed. So far as this text is concerned, the law is substantially unchanged but the references will be to the Companies Act 1985. There will also be changes in the section numbers quoted.

In the preparation of this edition the publishers and I have once again received the invaluable assistance of my wife in terms of the preparation and editing of the typescript, indexes, and proofs, together with general organisation of sources of new material since the last edition.

I must also express my thanks to Eric Dalton of Pitman Publishing Ltd for his help throughout and also to the printers for their assistance in processing the typescript and the proofs.

In conclusion I must, once again, mention the contribution of my students. The questions which they raise often provoke a rethink of certain matters and improve understanding of the areas involved which, hopefully, reflect upon the text and improve it as a means of exposition.

For the errors and omissions I am, of course, solely responsible.

Maenan, Gwynedd
January 1985

DENIS KEENAN

Table of Statutes

Table of Cases

NOTE. The number of the case in the Appendix is printed in bold type; the page on which the case is cited is printed in ordinary type.

1 The law of contract

A contract may be defined as an *agreement* enforceable by the law between two or more persons to do or abstain from doing some act or acts, their intention being to create legal relations and not merely to exchange mutual promises.

The formation of contract

In order to decide whether a contract has come into being it is necessary to establish that there has been agreement between the parties. In consequence it must in general be shown that an offer was made by one party (called the offeror) which was accepted by the other party (called the offeree).

OFFER

An offer may be made to a particular person, or in some cases, to the public at large. An offer to the public at large can only be made where the contract which eventually comes into being is a unilateral one, i.e. where there is a promise on one side for an act on the other. An offer to the public at large would be made, for example, where there was an advertisement offering a reward for services to be rendered, such as finding a lost dog. (And see also *Carlill* v *Carbolic Smoke Ball Co.* 1893).[1]

OFFER DISTINGUISHED FROM INVITATION TO TREAT

An offer capable of being converted into an agreement by acceptance must consist of a definite promise to be bound provided that certain specified terms are accepted, and not a mere offer to *negotiate*. The distinction is sometimes expressed in judicial language by the contrast of an 'offer' with that of an 'invitation to treat'. The distinction may be considered under the following headings—

(1) *Auctions*. The advertisement of an auction is not an offer to hold it. (*Harris* v *Nickerson* 1873.)[2] At an auction the bid is the offer; the auctioneer's request for bids is merely an invitation to treat. The sale is complete when the hammer falls and until that time any bid may be withdrawn. (S.57(2), Sale of Goods Act 1979.) However if *dicta* in

Warlow v *Harrison* (1859) 1 E. & E. 309 are correct, the addition to the advertisement of an auction sale of the two words 'without reserve' converts it into an offer, presumably to the public at large, that the sale will in fact be subject to no reserve price. If in these circumstances the sale is actually held and a prospective purchaser makes a bid, he accepts the offer of a sale 'without reserve'. The auctioneer, if he then puts a reserve price on any of the lots, is liable to an action for breach of his undertaking that the sale would be without reserve, though it should be noted that the goods in question will not have been sold unless the auctioneer's hammer has fallen.

(2) *Price lists, catalogues.* The issue of tradesman's circular or catalogue advertising goods for sale is usually regarded as a mere attempt to induce offers, not an offer itself. The same is true of advertisements to sell goods inserted in newspapers or periodicals. (*Partridge* v *Crittenden* 1968.)[3]

(3) *Price tickets.* The display of an article with a price on it in a shop window, or on the shelves of a self-service store, is merely an invitation to treat. It is not an offer for sale, the acceptance of which makes a contract. (*Pharmaceutical Society of Great Britain* v *Boots Cash Chemists Ltd* 1953.)[4]

(4) *Negotiations for the sale of land.* The same principles are applied, with perhaps this difference, that in the case of a sale of land which involves the adjustment of so many matters of detail, e.g. finding out whether the seller is the owner, the court is likely to regard a communication as an invitation to treat unless the intention to contract is very clear and not in the least casual. (*Harvey* v *Facey* 1893.)[5]

(5) *Company prospectus.* A prospectus issued by a company in order to invite the public to subscribe for its shares (or debentures) is an invitation to treat so that members of the investing public offer to buy the securities when they apply for them and the company, being the acceptor, will only accept that proportion of public offers which matches the shares or debentures which the company wishes to issue. If there are more offers than shares the issue is said to be over-subscribed.

ACCEPTANCE

Once the existence of an offer has been proved the court must be satisfied that the offeree has accepted otherwise there is no contract. The problems arising are considered under the following headings—

(1) *The person who accepts must have seen the offer.* Thus if B has found A's lost dog and, not having seen an advertisement by A offering a reward for its return, returns it out of goodness of heart, B will not be able to claim the reward. However, as long as the acceptor is aware of the making of the offer his motive in accepting it is immaterial. (*Williams* v. *Carwardine* 1843,[6] and see *Carlill's case.*[1])

(2) *Effect of acceptance 'subject to contract'.* Acceptance must be absolute and unconditional. One important form of conditional assent is a acceptance 'subject to contract'. The law has placed special significance on these words and they are always construed as meaning that the parties do not intend to be bound until a formal contract is prepared. (*Winn* v *Bull* 1877.)[7]

(3) *Counter offer.* A counter offer is a rejection of the original offer and has the effect of cancelling the original offer. (*Hyde* v *Wrench* 1840.)[8] However, the communication must amount to a counter offer. Thus where it appears that the offeree is merely seeking further information before making up his mind, his request for information will not destroy the offer. (*Stevenson* v *McLean* 1880.)[9]

It should be noted, however, that the counter offer may be accepted by the original offeror. The above principles of contract law are of increasing importance because of the modern commercial practice of making quotations and placing orders with conditions attached, so that the terms and conditions of the contract which may eventually be made may not be those which the original offeror put forward, since these may have been changed as a result of a 'battle of forms' between the parties. For an illustration see *Butler Machine Tool Co. Ltd* v *Ex-Cell-O Corporation (England) Ltd* (1979).[10]

(4) *Acceptance in the case of tenders.* It is essential to understand what is precisely meant by 'accepting' a tender since different legal results are obtained according to the wording of the invitation to tender. If the invitation by its wording implies that the potential buyer *will* require the goods, acceptance of a tender sent in response to such an invitation results in a binding contract under which the buyer undertakes to buy all the goods specified in the tender from the person who has submitted it. On the other hand, if the invitation by its wording suggests that the potential buyer *may* require the goods, acceptance of a tender results in a standing offer by the supplier to supply the goods set out in the tender as and when required by the person accepting it. The use of the word *may* indicates a vagueness in the requirements of the purchaser which prevents a contract for the whole of the goods coming into being. Under the standing offer each time the buyer orders a quantity there is a contract confined to that quantity; but if the buyer does not order any of the goods set out in the tender, or a smaller number than the supplier quoted for, there is no breach of contract. If the person submitting the tender wishes to revoke his standing offer he may do so except insofar as the buyer has already ordered the goods under the tender. These must be supplied or the tenderer is in breach of contract. (*Great Northern Railway* v *Witham* 1873.)[11]

(5) *Inchoate contracts.* A contract will not be enforced unless the parties have expressed themselves with reasonable clarity on the matter of essential terms. A situation may, therefore, exist in which there is

sufficient assent to satisfy the basic requirements of offer and acceptance and yet the contract is in complete (or inchoate) as to certain of its terms. (*Scammell* v *Ouston* 1941.)[12] The court will not make up a contract for the parties and enforce it so that the contract will remain unenforceable unless—

(*a*) the vague term is meaningless and can be ignored (*Nicolene* v *Simmonds* 1953),[13] or

(*b*) the contract itself provides a method of clarifying the contract (*Foley* v *Classique Coaches Ltd* 1934),[14] or

(*c*) the court can complete the contract by reference to a trade practice or course of dealing between the parties. (*Hillas* v *Arcos* 1932.)[15]

The communication of acceptance

An acceptance may be made in various ways. It may be made in writing or orally but it must in general be communicated. (*Felthouse* v *Bindley* 1862.)[16] The decision in *Felthouse* provides some protection against inertia selling as where a firm sends a book to a person. A, at his home stating that if no reply is received within seven days it will be assumed that A has accepted the offer to sell the book and is bound in contract. Silence cannot amount to acceptance in this way.

However, the matter is also covered by the Unsolicited Goods and Services Act 1971 (as amended by the Unsolicited Goods and Services (Amendment) Act 1975). Under this legislation a person who receives, e.g. unsolicited goods, is entitled to treat them as if they had been given to him unless the sender takes them back within six months, or, if the recipient gives notice to the sender that he wants them taken back, within 30 days of the notice being given.

WAIVER OF COMMUNICATION

There are some cases in which the offeror is deemed to have waived communication of the acceptance. This occurs, for example, in the case of unilateral contracts, such as a promise to pay money in return for some act to be carried out by the offeree. Performance of the act operates as an acceptance and no communication is required. (*Carlill* v *Carbolic Smoke Ball Co.* 1893.)[1] In addition, acceptance need not necessarily be communicated if the post is used. (See below.)

MODE OF COMMUNICATION PRESCRIBED BY OFFEROR

The offeror may stipulate the mode of acceptance, e.g. to be by letter so that there will be written evidence of it. In such a case, however, the offeror could still waive his right to have the acceptance communicated in a given way and agree to the substituted method.

In addition, an acceptance made in a different way may be effective if there is no prejudice to the offeror, as where the method used is as quick and reliable as the method prescribed. (*Yates Building Co.* v *R. J. Pulleyn & Sons (York)* 1975.)[17]

ORAL ACCEPTANCES

If the offeror has not stipulated a method of acceptance the offeree may choose his own method, though where acceptance is by word of mouth it is not enough that it be spoken, it must actually be heard by the offeror. As regards the use of the telephone and teleprinter, these are methods of instantaneous communication and it has been held that the contract is not complete unless the offeror hears the acceptance. (*Entores Ltd.* v *Miles Far Eastern Corporation* 1955.)[18]

USE OF THE POST AND TELEGRAMS

If the post is a proper and reasonable method of communication between the parties, then acceptance is deemed complete immediately the letter of acceptance is posted, even if it is delayed or is lost or destroyed in the post so that it never reaches the offeror. (*Household Fire Insurance Company* v *Grant* 1879.)[19]

The better view is that in English law an acceptance cannot be recalled once it has been posted, even though it has not reached the offeror at the time of recall.

A telegram is effective as an acceptance when it is given to an employee of the Post Office such as a counter clerk. (*Cowan* v *O'Connor* (1880) 20 Q.B.D. 640.)

CROSS OFFERS

There is some controversy as to whether agreement can result from cross offers. Suppose after discussions between X and Y regarding the sale of X's watch, X by letter offers to sell his watch to Y for £50 and Y by means of a second letter which crosses X's letter in the post offers to buy X's watch for £50. Can there be a contract? The matter was discussed by an English court in *Tinn* v *Hoffman* (1873) 29 L.T. 271 and the court's decision was that no contract could arise. However, the matter is still undecided and it is possible to hold the view that a contract could come into being where it appears that the parties have intended to create a legally binding agreement on the same basis.

Termination of offer

It is now necessary to consider the ways in which an offer may be terminated or negatived.

REVOCATION—GENERALLY

The general rule is that an offer may be revoked at any time before acceptance. If there is an option attached to the offer as where the offeror agrees to give seven days for acceptance, the offeror need not keep the offer open for seven days but can revoke it without incurring legal liability unless the offeree has given some consideration for the option. Where consideration has been given by the offeree the offeror may still revoke his offer and sell the property which was the subject-matter of the offer to someone else. He will, however, be liable to an action for damages for breach of option. It was thought at one time that where the option to buy property was not supported by consideration, the offer could be revoked merely by its sale to another. However, in modern law it is necessary for the offeror to communicate the revocation to the offeree himself or by means of some other reliable person. (See *Stevenson* v *McLean* 1880,[9] the facts of which make this point.)

To be effective revocation must be communicated to the offeree before he has accepted the offer. (*Byrne* v *Van Tienhoven* 1880.)[20] When revocation is by letter the question arises as to whether it is effective when delivered or when the offeree has read it. The latter solution seems unreasonable because the offeree may delay reading the letter until he has accepted the offer. A better solution would be to regard revocation as effective when the offeree has had a reasonable time or opportunity to read the letter after delivery. Indeed, in *Eaglehill Ltd* v *J. Needham (Builders) Ltd* [1972] 3 All E.R. 895 (see further p. 555), the House of Lords when discussing notice of dishonour of a bill of exchange, said that an offer would be revoked when the letter of revocation 'was opened in the ordinary course of business or would have been so opened if the ordinary course of business was followed'.

Communication may be made directly by the offeror or may reach the offeree by some other reliable source. (*Dickinson* v *Dodds* 1876.)[21]

REVOCATION—UNILATERAL CONTRACTS

Where the offer consists of a promise in return for an act, as where a reward is offered for the return of lost property, the offer, although made to the whole world, can be revoked as any other offer can. It is thought to be enough that the same publicity be given to the revocation as was given to the offer, even though the revocation may not be seen by all the persons who saw the offer. A more difficult problem arises when an offer which requires a certain act to be carried out is revoked after some person has begun to perform the act but before he has completed it. For example, X offers £1000 to anyone who can successfully swim the Channel and Y, deciding he will try to obtain the money, starts his swim from Dover. Can X revoke his offer, e.g. from a helicopter when Y is half way across the Channel? The better view is that he cannot on the grounds that an offer of the kind made by X is two offers in one, namely—

(1) to pay £1000 to a successful swimmer, and

(2) something in the nature of an option to hold the offer open for a reasonable time once performance has been embarked upon so that a person trying to complete the task has a reasonable chance of doing so.

A similarly fair result can be achieved by regarding Y as accepting the offer when he enters the water, making effective revocation impossible thereafter. However, Y would not qualify for the prize of £1000 unless and until he had provided the consideration by actually swimming the Channel. It would have been necessary to consider the application of one or other of these solutions in *Carlill's case*[1] if the company had revoked the offer *after* Mrs Carlill had started to use the ball.

The matter also came before the Court of Appeal in *Errington* v *Errington* [1952] 1 All E.R. 149. In that case a father bought a house for his son and daughter-in-law to live in. He paid the deposit but the son and daughter-in-law made the mortgage payments after the father gave the building society book to the daughter-in-law, saying 'Don't part with this book. The house will be your property when the mortgage is paid.' The son left his wife who continued to live in the house. It was held by the Court of Appeal that neither the father nor the plaintiff, his widow, to whom the house was left by will, could eject the daughter-in-law from the property. As Lord Denning said: 'The father's promise was a unilateral contract—a promise of the house in return for their act of paying the instalments. It could not be revoked by him once the couple entered on the performance of the act, . . .' The Court went on to decide that the son and daughter-in-law would be fully entitled to the house once they had made all the mortgage repayments.

LAPSE OF TIME

If a time for acceptance has been stipulated then the offer lapses when the time has expired. If no time has been stipulated then acceptance must be within a reasonable time, and this is a *matter of fact* for the judge to decide on the circumstances of the case. (*Ramsgate Victoria Hotel Co.* v *Montefiore* 1866.)[22]

CONDITIONAL OFFERS

An offer may terminate on the happening of a given event if it is made subject to a condition that it will do so. Thus, an offer to buy goods may terminate if the goods offered for sale are seriously damaged before acceptance. Such a condition may be made expressly in the contract but may also be implied from the circumstances. (*Financings* v *Stimson* 1962.)[23]

EFFECT OF DEATH

The effect of death would appear to vary according to the type of contract in question, whether the death is that of the offeror or offeree and whether death takes place before or after acceptance.

(1) *Death of offeror before acceptance.* If the contract envisaged by the offer involves a personal relationship, such as an offer to act as an agent, then the death of the offeror prevents acceptance. If the contract envisaged by the offer is not one involving the personality of the offeror, there are two points of view. In *Dickinson* v *Dodds* 1876[21] Mellish, L.J., in an *obiter dictum* expressed the opinion: 'that if a man who makes an offer dies the offer cannot be accepted after he is dead.' However, the decision in *Bradbury* v *Morgan* 1862[24] suggests that the offer can be accepted until the offeree is notified of the offeror's death. The matter is, therefore, unresolved pending a further decision.

(2) *Death of offeree before acceptance.* Once the offeree is dead there is no offer which can be accepted and his executors cannot, therefore, accept the offer in his stead. The offer being made to a living person can only be accepted by that person and assumes his continued existence. The rule applies whether the proposed contract involves a personal relationship or not. (*Re Cheshire Banking Co., Duff's Executors' Case* 1886.)[25]

(3) *Death of parties after acceptance.* Death after acceptance has normally no effect unless the contract is for personal services when it is discharged. Thus if X sells his car to Y and before the car is delivered X dies, it would be possible for Y to sue X's personal representatives for breach of contract if they were to refuse to deliver the car. But if X agrees to play the piano at a concert and dies two days before the performance, the contract is discharged and his personal representatives are not expected to play the piano in his stead.

Offer and Acceptance not identifiable

Before leaving the topic of formation of contract it should be noted that the court may from time to time infer the existence of a contract from the words and acts of the parties in a situation where there has been *no offer and acceptance.*

Examples are provided by collateral contracts, so called because they derive from another main contract. (See *Rayfield* v *Hands* 1958.)[26]

However, there are also other cases which are not collateral contracts in which it is difficult to see where offer and acceptance lie. (See, for example, *The New Zealand Shipping Co. Ltd* v *A.M. Satterthwaite & Co. Ltd* 1974 (see p. 13).)

Consideration

Consideration is essential to the formation of any contract not made under seal.

Definition and related matters

The definition given by Sir Frederick Pollock is to be preferred—

> 'An act of forbearance of one party *or the promise thereof* is the price for which *the promise* of the other is bought and the promise thus given for value is enforceable.'

This definition, which was adopted by the House of Lords in *Dunlop v Selfridge* [1915] A.C. 847, is preferred because it properly describes executed consideration by including acts and forbearances and executory consideration by referring to the fact that a promise to do something in the future also amounts to consideration.

EXECUTED AND EXECUTORY CONSIDERATION

Consideration may be *executory* where the parties exchange promises to perform acts in the future. For example, C promises to deliver goods to D and D promises to pay for the goods; or it may be *executed* where one party promises to do something in return for the act of another rather than for the mere promise of future performance of an act. Here the performance of the act is required before there is any liability on the promise. Where X offers a reward for the return of his lost dog, X is buying the act of the finder and will not be liable until the dog is found and returned. (And see *Carlill's case.*)[1]

Consideration in relation to formation of contract

The main rules governing consideration in *formation* of contract are set out below.

PAST CONSIDERATION

Sometimes the act which one party to a contract puts forward as consideration was performed before any promise of reward was made by the other. Where this is so the act in question is regarded as past consideration and will not support a contractual claim. This somewhat technical rule seems to be based on the idea that the act of one party to an alleged contract can only be regarded as consideration if it was carried out in respect to some promise of the other. Where this is not so the act is regarded as gratuitous, being carried out before any promise of reward was made. (*Re McArdle* 1951.)[27] However, there are exceptions to this rule as follows—

(1) Where services are rendered at the express or implied request of the promisor in circumstances which raise an implication of a promise to pay. (*Re Casey's Patents, Stewart* v *Casey* 1892.)[28] This exception is not entirely a genuine one since the promisor is assumed to have given an implied undertaking to pay at the time of the request, his subsequent promise being regarded as deciding merely the actual amount to be paid. In this situation the act which follows the request but precedes the settling of the reward is more in the nature of executed consideration which, as we have seen, will support a contract.

(2) Section 27 of the Bills of Exchange Act 1882 provides that an 'antecedent debt or liability' will support a bill of exchange. This genuine exception was probably based on pre-existing commercial custom designed to give a bill of exchange the maximum possible negotiability.

Most cheques are given after a contract, e.g. for the sale of goods, has been made and are therefore given in most cases for past consideration. Nevertheless s.27 renders them valid but would not apply in the *McArdle* situation if a cheque had been given to Mrs McArdle because there was no 'antecedent debt or liability' in that case.

CONSIDERATION MUST MOVE FROM THE PROMISEE—THE DOCTRINE OF PRIVITY OF CONTRACT

If A wishes to sue successfully upon a promise made by B, it is essential for A (as the recipient of the promise—the promisee) to show that he gave consideration to B (the promisor). The concept is based upon a fundamental assumption of English law that a contract is a bargain. If a person furnishes no consideration he takes no part in a bargain; if he takes no part in a bargain he takes no part in a contract. (*Dunlop* v *Selfridge* 1915.)[29]

There has been much discussion as to whether the doctrine is based on consideration or whether it is a matter of privity, i.e. not being a party to the contract. It is now settled that consideration is the crucial matter in English law. Thus, if A and B contract to benefit C, C cannot sue because he has not supplied consideration and also because he is not a party. However, it is also clear that if A contracts with B and C to benefit C, C still cannot sue unless he has supplied consideration or unless the contract is under seal where consideration is not required. In all cases B, or his executors, can sue on behalf of C. (*Beswick* v *Beswick* 1967,[30] and *Jackson* v *Horizon Holidays* 1975.)[31]

There are, however, some exceptions to the rule, the most important of which are as follows—

(1) A principal may sue on a contract made by an agent. This exception is perhaps more apparent than real because in fact the principal

is the contracting party who has merely acted through the instrumentality of the agent.

(2) The holder for value of a cheque can sue prior parties. Thus, if A buys goods from B and pays by cheque which B then endorses over to C, his son, as a birthday present, then C can sue A although no consideration moved from him to A. C cannot sue B because as between immediate parties absence of consideration makes a claim impossible.

(3) The law of insurance also provides a number of exceptions to the doctrine of privity. These will be considered in more detail in Chapter 8.

(4) Under the Resale Prices Act 1976, s.26, the supplier of goods is given a statutory cause of action so that he may enforce against a person not a party to the contract of sale a condition as to resale price. However, the resale price agreement must have been approved under the provisions of the Resale Prices Act 1976, otherwise there can be no enforcement of it.

The section has effect upon the decision in *Dunlop* v *Selfridge* 1915[29] in the sense that although the rules relating to privity of contract at common law are still valid, Dunlop may now have had a statutory cause of action in the particular circumstances. The object of s.26 is to allow a manufacturer to bring a cut-price retailer before an ordinary court of law which was not possible before 1956 unless the retailer had bought the goods direct from the manufacturer. Consequently, manufacturers not having access to the ordinary courts of law often brought the retailer before a secret and possibly unjust trade association tribunal which might put the retailer quite unreasonably on a stop list so that he was denied supplies.

However, it is unlikely that the court would have approved Dunlop's arrangements, and in fact most minimum resale price maintenance agreements were regarded as void by the courts and cannot be enforced against anyone.

(5) The position in land law is that benefits and liabilities attached to or imposed on land may in some circumstances follow the land into the hands of other owners. (*Smith and Snipes Hall Farm Ltd* v *River Douglas Catchment Board* 1949[32] and *Tulk* v *Moxhay* 1848.)[33]

(6) Bankers commercial credits also present problems in the field of privity. It is common practice for an exporter, E, to ask the buyer of the goods, B, to open with his banker a credit in favour of E, the credit to remain irrevocable for a specified time. B agrees with his banker that the credit should be opened and in return promises to pay the banker and usually gives him a lien over the shipping documents. The banker will also require a commission for his services. B's banker then notifies E that a credit has been opened in his favour and E can draw upon it on presentation of the shipping documents.

It will be seen that E and B's banker are not in privity of contract. It might be thought that this could give rise to problems in the unlikely event that the banker did not pay. However, this is not so. In fact the buyer/customer of the bank cannot stop payment. In *Malas (Hamzeh)* v *British Imex* [1958] 1 All E.R. 262 the plaintiffs, who were buyers of goods, applied to the Court for an injunction restraining the sellers, who were the defendants in the case, from drawing under a credit established by the buyer's bankers. The Court of Appeal refused to grant this injunction and Jenkins, L.J., said: 'The opening of a confirmed letter of credit constitutes a bargain betwen the banker and the vendor of the goods which imposes on the banker an absolute obligation to pay. . .'. Sellers, L.J., said that there could well be exceptions where the court would exercise a jurisdiction to grant an injunction, as where there was a fraudulent transaction. However, in other situations the binding nature of the bankers' commercial credit is an exception to privity of contract.

There are similar developments rendering performance bonds enforceable by commercial custom, so that where a bank guarantees performance of an export contract by the supplier the bank must pay the buyer if the contract is not performed. (See *Edward Owen Engineering Ltd* v *Barclays Bank International Ltd* [1978] 1 All E.R. 976.)

Adequacy of consideration

The courts do not exist to repair bad bargains and though consideration must be present, the parties themselves must attend to its value. Under this principle it would be possible to enforce a contract to purchase a Rolls Royce for half a new penny. Obviously inadequate consideration gives rise to suspicion of fraud, duress or undue influence, and possibly unsoundness of mind, but if these are not proved the contract is good.

Thus in *Thomas* v *Thomas* [1842] 2 Q.B. 851, the plaintiff's husband had expressed the wish that the plaintiff, if she survived him, should have the use of his house. He left a will of which his brothers were executors. The will made no mention of the testator's wish that his wife should be given the house. The executors knew of the testator's wish and agreed to allow the widow to occupy the house on payment of £1 per year for as long as she remained a widow. The plaintiff remained in possession of the house until the death of one of the executors, Samuel Thomas. The other executor then turned her out. She sued him for breach of contract. It was held that the plaintiff's promise to pay £1 a year was consideration and need not be adequate. The action for breach of contract succeeded.

However, what is offered by way of consideration must be capable of expression in terms of value. Thus a parent who makes a promise to induce his son to refrain from boring him with complaints cannot be sued upon it since the essential elements of a bargain are lacking. (*White* v *Bluett* 1853.)[34] That apart, acts or omissions, even of a trivial nature, may be sufficient to support a contract. (*Chappell & Co. Ltd* v *Nestle Co. Ltd* 1959.)[35]

Although there were once arguments to the contrary, it is now accepted that forbearance to sue may be adequate consideration. It is not necessary to show that the action would have succeeded but merely that if it had been brought to trial it might have done. (See *Horton* v *Horton* 1960.)[36] Thus, the court would be unlikely to accept that a bookmaker could supply consideration by forgoing a claim against a client for stake money. Such an action, being based upon an illegal transaction, could have no hope of success.

Existing duties and consideration

Under this heading we consider whether a person can provide consideration by doing or promising to do something he is already bound to do. Three situations should be noted, as follows—

(1) The discharge of a public duty imposed by law is not consideration. (*Collins* v *Godefroy* 1831.)[37] However, where the contractual duty is not precisely coincident with the public duty but is in excess of it, performance of the contractual duty may provide consideration. (*Glasbrook Bros.* v *Glamorgan County Council* 1925[38] and *Ward* v *Byham* 1956.)[39]

(2) The performance of a contractual duty already owed to the defendant is not consideration. (*Stilk* v *Myrick* 1809.[40] Contrast *Hartley* v *Ponsonby* 1857.)[41]

(3) The actual performance of an outstanding contractual obligation may be sufficient to support a promise of a further payment by a third party. (*Shadwell* v *Shadwell* 1860.)[42]

An interesting application of the problems of consideration is to be found in *The New Zealand Shipping Co. Ltd* v *A.M. Satterthwaite & Co. Ltd* [1974] 1 All E.R. 1015. In that case the makers of an expensive drilling machine entered into a contract for the carriage of the machine by sea to New Zealand. The contract of carriage (the bill of lading) exempted the carriers from full liability for any loss or damage to the machine during carriage and also purported to exempt any servant or agent of the carrier, including independent contractors employed from time to time by the carrier. The machine was damaged by the defendants, who were stevedores, in the course of unloading, and the question to be decided was whether the defendant stevedores, who had been employed by the carrier to unload the machine, could take advantage of the exemption clause in the bill of lading since they were not parties to the contract. It was decided by the Privy Council that they could. The stevedores provided consideration and so became parties to the contract when they unloaded the machine. (*Carlill* v *Carbolic Smoke Ball Co.* 1893[1] applied.) The performance of services by the stevedores in discharging the cargo was sufficient consideration to constitute a contract, even though they were already under an obligation to the carrier to perform those services because the actual performance of an outstanding contractual obligation was sufficient to support the promise of an exemption from liability given by the makers of the drill, i.e. the shippers, who were in effect, third parties to the contract between the carrier and the stevedores. (*Shadwell* v *Shadwell* 1860[42] applied.)

It is not easy to see when and where the relevant offers and acceptances were made in this case, but as we have already noted, a court can construe a contract from the circumstances without a precise application of the offer and acceptance formula.

Consideration viewed in relation to the discharge of a contract

All that has so far been said in regard to consideration relates to the *formation* of a contract. As we have seen, there must be offer, acceptance, consideration and intention to create legal relations in order to bring a contract into existence. The rules are rather different where a contract is to be *discharged*. There are a number of ways in which a contract may be discharged, all of which will be dealt with later. However, the one with which we are now concerned is *discharge by agreement* under which contract A is to be discharged by a new contract, B, the question being to what extent does contract B require consideration? The attitude of the common law is different from that equity, as we shall see.

COMMON LAW—THE DOCTRINE OF ACCORD AND SATISFACTION

At common law if A owes B £10 and wishes to discharge that obligation by paying B £9 he must—

(1) obtain the agreement (accord) of B; and
(2) provide B with some consideration (satisfaction) for giving up his right to £10 unless the release is under seal.

This is the common law doctrine of accord and satisfaction. The doctrine is an ancient one and an early example of it is to be found in the judgement of Brian, C.J., in *Pinnel's Case* (1602) 5 Co. Rep. 117a. Pinnel sued Cole in debt for what would now be £8.50 which was due on a bond on 11 November 1600. Cole's defence was that at Pinnel's request he had paid him £5.12½ on 1 October and that Pinnel had accepted this payment in full satisfaction of the original debt. Although the court found for Pinnel on a technical point of pleading, it was said that—

(*a*) payment of a lesser sum on the due day in satisfaction of a greater sum cannot be any satisfaction for the whole; but
(*b*) payment of a smaller sum at the creditor's request before the due day is good consideration for a promise to forgo the balance for it is a benefit to the creditor to be paid before he was entitled to payment and a corresponding detriment to the debtor to pay early.

The first branch of the rule in *Pinnel's Case* was much criticized but was approved by the House of Lords in *Foakes* v *Beer* 1884[43] and the doctrine then hardened because of the system of binding precedent. However, the practical effect of the rule is considerably reduced under common law by the following—

(1) *Where there is a dispute as to the sum owed.* If the creditor accepts less than he thinks is owed to him the debt will be discharged.

(2) *Where the creditor agrees to take something different in kind*, e.g. a chattel, the debt is discharged by substituted performance. Thus, if A gives B a watch worth £5 and B is agreeable to taking it, then the debt of £10 will be discharged. In this connection it should be noted that a cheque for a smaller sum no longer constitutes substituted performance. (*D. & C. Builders Ltd* v *Rees* 1965.)[44]

(3) *The payment of a smaller sum before the larger is due* gives the debtor a good discharge. This is the second branch of the rule in *Pinnel's Case*.

(4) *If a debtor makes an arrangement with his creditors* to compound his debts, e.g. by paying them 85p in the £1, he is satisfying a debt for a larger sum by the payment of a smaller sum. Nevertheless, it is a good discharge, the consideration being the agreement by the creditors with each other and with the debtor not to insist on their full rights. (*Good* v *Cheesman* 1831.)[45]

(5) *Payment of a smaller sum by a third party* operates as a good discharge. (*Welby* v *Drake* 1825.)[46]

EQUITY—THE DOCTRINE OF PROMISSORY ESTOPPEL

There has always been some dissatisfaction with the common law rule of accord and satisfaction. After all, if A owes B £10 and B agrees to take £9, as he must before there can be any question of discharging the obligation on A to pay £10, why should B be allowed afterwards to break his promise to take £9 and succeed in an action against A simply because A gave him no consideration?

It was to deal with this sort of situation that the equitable doctrine of promissory estoppel was propounded, first by Lord Cairns in *Hughes* v *Metropolitan Railway* (1877) 2 App. Cas. 439 and later by Denning, J. (as he then was), in the *High Trees Case* 1947.[47] It was affirmed by the house of Lords in *Tool Metal Manufacturing Co. Ltd* v *Tungsten Electric Co. Ltd* 1955.[48]

The doctrine of estoppel is basically a rule of evidence under which the court, surprisingly enough, is not prepared to listen to the truth.

It occurs at common law out of physical conduct. Suppose A and B go into a wholesaler's premises and A asks for goods on credit. The wholesaler, who knows that B is creditworthy, but has no knowledge of A, is not prepared to give credit until A says, 'Do not worry, you will be paid, B is my partner.' If B says nothing and A receives the goods on credit and does not pay, then B could be sued for the price, even though he can produce evidence that he was not in fact A's partner. This evidence will not be admitted because the wholesaler relied on a situation of partnership created by B's conduct.

Promissory estoppel in equity is very little different except that the estoppel arises from a *promise*, not *conduct*. The common law does not recognize an estoppel arising out of a promise, or about *future conduct*.

As a result of the above decisions and others (as indicated) the doctrine of promissory estoppel has the following ingredients—

(1) It arises from a promise made with the intention that it should be acted upon.

(2) It was once thought that the person who had received the promise must do something to show that he had relied on it. If A, a landlord, said B could pay only half his usual rent while he was unemployed, it was thought that B would have to show, for example, that he had spent what should have been the rent money on travelling expenses to find work in the district. Reliance upon the promise in this way is not, it would appear, a necessary requirement. (*Alan* v *El Nasr* 1972.)[49]

(3) It relates only to variation to discharge of contract by agreement and does not affect the requirement of consideration on formation of contract. (*Combe* v *Combe* 1951.)[50]

(4) So far as the rule has been developed in cases, it merely *suspends* rights but does not totally preclude enforcement of the original contract after reasonable notice has been given. (*Tool Metal Manufacturing Co. Ltd* v *Tungsten Electric Co. Ltd* 1955.)[48]

(5) The promise must be freely given and not extorted by threats, for if it is then it is not inequitable to allow the promisor to go back on his promise. (*D. & C. Builders Ltd* v *Rees* 1965.)[44]

(6) Of considerable importance is a *dictum* by Lord Denning in *D. & C. Builders* v *Rees* 1965[44] that the rule could be developed to the point at which it operated, not merely to suspend rights, but to preclude enforcement of them. If this point is reached, then if A owes B £10 and B agrees to take £9, A will be discharged from his obligation to pay £10 without the need for consideration.

Such a situation would involve a virtual overruling of *Foakes* v *Beer* 1884[43] and would put an end to the first branch of the rule in *Pinnel's Case* which is that payment of a lesser sum on the due day in satisfaction of a greater sum cannot be any satisfaction for the whole. Although in the past a number of *dicta* by Lord Denning have been incorporated into the *ratio* of subsequent decisions, the position outlined in (*f*) above has not as yet been reached.

DISCHARGE OF CONTRACT BY PERFORMANCE—RELEVANCE OF *HIGH TREES* CASE

The rule of equitable estoppel has relevance in discharge of a contract by performance. (See p. 79.) Although the agreed date of delivery must usually be complied with in a contract of sale, the buyer may waive the condition relating to the date of delivery and accept a later date. Such a waiver may be binding on him whether made with or without consideration. It was held by Lord Denning in *Charles Rickards Ltd* v *Oppenhaim* 1950 (see p. 79) that the binding nature of a waiver without consideration might be based on the *High Trees Case*[47] (i.e. a promissory estoppel to accept a later delivery date). Alternatively, the seller may rely on s.11(2) of the Sale of Goods Act 1979 which states: 'Where a contract of sale is subject to any condition to be fulfilled by the seller, the buyer may waive that condition.'

Intention to create legal relations

The law will not necessarily recognize the existence of a contract enforceable in a court of law simply because of the presence of mutual promises. The subject can be considered under two headings as follows.

(I) CASES WHERE THE PARTIES HAVE NOT EXPRESSLY DENIED THEIR INTENTION TO CREATE LEGAL RELATIONS

Advertisements

Most advertisements are statements of opinion and as such are not actionable. Thus unless the advertisement makes false statements of specific verifiable facts, which is rare, the court will not enforce the claims made for the product on a contractual basis. However, where a company deposits money in the bank against possible claims then the court is likely to hold that legal relations were contemplated. (*Carlill* v *Carbolic Smoke Ball Co.* 1893.)[1]

Family agreements

Many of these cannot be imagined to be the subject of litigation but some may be. The question is basically one of construction and the court looks at the words and the surrounding circumstances. The two basic divisions of family agreements are set out below.

(1) *Husband and wife.* With regard to agreements between husband and wife, it is difficult to draw precise conclusions. However, the following situations have appeared in decided cases—

(*a*) Where husband and wife were living together in amity when the agreement was made, then the agreement is not enforceable as a contract because legal proceedings are an inappropriate method of settling purely domestic disputes. (*Balfour* v *Balfour* 1919.)[51]

(*b*) Where husband and wife were living together but not in amity or were separated altogether when the agreement was made, the court may enforce it. (*Merritt* v *Merritt* 1969.)[52]

(*c*) If the words used by the parties are uncertain, then the agreement will not be enforced, the uncertainty leading to the conclusion that there was no intention to create legal relations. Thus in *Gould* v *Gould*, [1969] 3 All E.R. 728, a contractual intention was negatived where a husband on leaving his wife undertook to pay her £15 per week 'so long as I can manage it'. The uncertainty of this term ruled out a legally binding agreement.

Agreements of a non-domestic nature made between husband and wife are enforceable, e.g. in *Pearce* v *Merriman* [1904] 1 K.B. 80 it was held that a husband may be his wife's tenant and as such could be made to pay the rent.

(2) *Other family agreements.* Wherever the contracting parties are members of a family group or friends, the question of intention to create legal relations arises.

However, intention to create legal relations is more readily assumed in these cases, particularly where the transaction is not of a domestic nature (*Simpkins* v *Pays* 1955),[53] or where one of the parties has altered his position to his detriment in reliance on the promises of the other. (*Parker* v *Clark* 1960.)[54]

However, *uncertainty* as to the terms of the agreement normally leads to the conclusion that there was no contractual intent. (*Jones* v *Padavatton* 1969.)[55]

Other cases

There may well be other areas where intention to create legal relations is doubtful but which have not been the subject of cases in court. Again, the matter is one of fact for the court. However, in the case of clubs and societies many of the relationships which exist and promises which are made are enforceable only as moral obligations. They are merely *social agreements.* For example, the decision in *Lens* v *Devonshire Club, The Times*, 4 December 1914, would suggest that if a person competes for a prize at a local golf club and is the winner, he or she may not be able to sue for the prize which has been won if it is not otherwise forthcoming.

However, in *Peck* v *Lateu, The Times*, 18 January 1973 two ladies attended bingo sessions together and had an arrangement to pool their winnings. One of them won an additional 'Bonanza' prize of £1107 and claimed it was not covered by the sharing arrangments. Pennycuick VC *held* that there was an intention to create legal relations and to share all prizes won. The plaintiff was entitled to a share in the prize.

(II) CASES WHERE THE PARTIES EXPRESSLY DENY ANY INTENTION TO CREATE LEGAL RELATIONS

By contrast with family arrangements, agreements of a commercial nature are *presumed* to be made with contractual intent. Furthermore, the test applied by the court is an *objective* one so that a person cannot escape liability simply because *he did not* have a contractual intention. The presumption is a strong one and it was held in *Edwards* v *Skyways Ltd* [1964] 1 All E.R. 494 that the use of the word *ex gratia* in regard to an airline pilot's contractual redundancy payment did not displace the presumption, so that the airline had to make the payments and did not have a discretion whether to make them or not.

Some agreements where the court would normally assume an intention to create legal relations may be expressly taken outside the scope of the law by the parties agreeing to rely on each other's honour. This is a practice which appears to be allowable to pools companies who are especially subject to fraudulent entries (*Jones* v *Vernons Pools Ltd* 1938)[56], but should not be allowed to spread into other areas of *standardized contracts*, i.e. contracts where the consumer has no choice of supplier as where he requires electrical services laid on which can only be provided by a state corporation.

There is no such objection where businessmen reach agreements at arm's length, and if the parties expressly declare, or clearly indicate, that they do not wish to assume contractual obligations, then the law accepts and implements their decision. (*Rose and Frank Co.* v *Crompton & Brothers Ltd* 1925.)[57]

Statutory provisions

Sometimes an Act of Parliament renders an agreement unenforceable. Thus under s.1 of the Law Reform (Miscellaneous Provisions) Act 1970, a contract of engagement which is, in effect, an agreement to marry, is not enforceable at law since there is a statutory presumption that there was not intention to create legal relations. Thus actions for breach of promise are no longer possible.

In addition, under the Post Office Act 1969, the acceptance of ordinary letters and packets for transmission does not give rise to a contract between the Post Office and the sender.

Finally, under s.18 of the Trade Union and Labour Relations Act 1974, collective agreements between trade unions and employers (or employers' associations) concerning industrial conditions such as hours, wages, holidays, procedures in disputes, and so on, are presumed *not* to be intended to be legally enforceable unless they are in writing and contain a provision to that effect.

Formalities

In most cases a contract made orally (or by parol, which is an alternative expression) is usually just as effective as a written one. Exceptionally, however, written formalities are required as follows—

Contracts which must be made by deed

A lease of more than three years should be made by deed otherwise no legal estate is created. (See s.52 and s.54(2), Law of Property Act 1925.) If there is no deed then there is in equity a contract for a lease. This is an estate contract under s.2(3)(iv), Law of Property Act 1925. It is enforceable against third parties who acquire the freehold from the landlord only if it has been registered at the Land Registry. Registration gives notice to the whole world. Failure to register makes the contract void against a later purchaser of the freehold from the landlord for a consideration, even though in fact the purchaser *knows* the lease exists (s.199(1), Law of Property Act 1925.) The purchaser could turn out the tenant if the lease was not registered. However, where it is registered the tenant is protected.

Contracts which must be in writing

For example, the following simple contracts are required by statute to be in writing otherwise they are affected in various ways—

(1) Regulated consumer credit agreements, including hire-purchase agreements under which the amount of credit does not exceed £7500. (Consumer Credit Act 1974, s.61.) If these agreements are not in appropriate written form they cannot be enforced by the dealer. (See further p. 195.)

(2) Contracts of marine insurance, which must be embodied in a written policy otherwise the contract is not effective, being inadmissible in evidence unless embodied in a written policy signed on behalf of the insurer. (Marine Insurance Act 1906, s.22.)

Contracts which must be evidenced in writing

In two cases writing, though not essential to the formation of a contract, is needed for evidential purposes and in its absence the courts will not enforce the agreement. These two special cases are—

(1) contracts of guarantee (under the Statute of Frauds 1677), and

(2) contracts for the sale or other disposition of land or any interest in land. (s.40, Law of Property Act 1925.)

The provision in the Statute of Frauds applies to guarantees and not to indemnities. It is therefore necessary to distinguish between these two. In a contract of indemnity the person giving the indemnity makes himself primarily liable by using such words as 'I will see that you are paid'.

In a contract of guarantee the guarantor expects the person he has guaranteed to carry out his obligations and the substance of the wording would be: 'If he does not pay you, I will'. An indemnity does not require writing because it did not come within the Statute of Frauds; a guarantee requires a memorandum. (*Mountstephen* v *Lakeman* 1871.)[58]

An additional distinction is that it is an essential feature of a guarantee that the person giving it is totally unconnected with the contract except by reason of his promise to pay the debt. Thus a *del credere* agent who, for an extra commission, promises to make good losses incurred by his principal in respect of the unpaid debts of third parties introduced by the agent, may use the guarantee form 'if they do not pay you I will' but no writing is required. Such a promise is enforceable even if made orally because even where a person does promise to be liable for the debt of another that promise is not within the Statute of Frauds where it is, as here, an incident of a wider transaction, i.e. agency.

THE MEMORANDUM

The memorandum in writing to satisfy the court in the two cases where it is now required need not be made when the contract is made but must exist before the action is brought. There are four requirements as follows—

(1) It must identify the parties, usually by containing their names.

(2) The subject-matter of the contract must be described, e.g. '12 Acacia Avenue', so that it can be identified and all the material terms of the contract must be stated. (See *Tweddell* v *Henderson* 1975.)[59]

(3) The consideration must appear, except in contracts of guarantee. In the latter case s.3 of the Mercantile Law Amendment Act 1856 dispenses with the necessity of setting out the consideration, but it must exist. The consideration for a guarantee is normally the extension of credit and for this reason it is not necessary to state it.

(4) The memorandum must contain the signature of the party to be charged or his agent properly authorized to sign. However, the law is not strict and initials or a printed signature will do. In this connection the party to be charged is the defendant and there may be cases where one party has a sufficient memorandum to found an action whereas the other may lack the necessary signature.

It should also be noted that the memorandum need not be in a single document but may consist of a number of connected documents. Oral evidence will be admitted to connect separate documents if—

(*a*) one refers to the other or to the transaction details of which are contained in the other document. (*Timmins* v *Moreland Street Property Ltd* 1957.)[60]; or

(*b*) the documents are *prima facie* connected, since in this case proof of connection is not entirely oral. (*Pearce* v *Gardner* 1897.)[61]

EFFECT OF ABSENCE OF MEMORANDUM

At common law the contract is not void but is unenforceable. The language of the relevant statues is 'no action shall be brought . . .' so that the contract is only affected by absence of writing, if a person wishes to *sue upon it*. It may be proved and raised as a *defence to an action* without the need for written evidence. Thus, if X orally agrees to let Y dig for gravel on X's land, Y would not commit a trespass if he entered on the land to dig. If, however, X asked him to leave and Y refused then he may become a trespasser in spite of the contract since it was at best a licence which has now been withdrawn. Furthermore, since the contract is not void, money paid or property transferred under it cannot be recovered unless there is total lack of consideration. (*Monnickendam* v *Leanse* 1923.)[62]

Equity will grant specific performance of the contract where there has been *part performance* by the plaintiff, under an oral contract.

Thus, if A has purchased a shop from B under an oral contract and B has allowed A to go onto the premises to fit new counters and shelves, it would be unfair to allow B to take the benefit of A's work and yet refuse to convey the shop to A, which is what he could do at common law. Equity will, however, grant specific performance to A, thus ensuring that the shop is conveyed by B who will be in contempt of court if he refuses to complete the transaction.

The following conditions must exist before the doctrine can operate—

(1) The contract must be one which is enforceable by specific performance. This confines the remedy to land because equity will not specifically enforce a guarantee.

(2) The acts of part performance must suggest a contractual relationship. (*Wakeham* v *MacKenzie* 1968.[63] Contrast *Re Gonin* 1977.)[64]

(3) There must be adequate oral evidence of the terms of the contract.

(4) The acts of part performance must be those of the plaintiff.

(5) It is said that a mere payment of money is not a sufficient act of part performance because money has no exclusive nature; such a payment raises no equity except the right to recover the money. This is certainly true of the payment of purchase money in a sale of land. In other situations a payment of money, e.g. an instalment of rent due under a lease, may be enough. (*Steadman* v *Steadman* [1973] 3 All E.R. 977.) Occupation of property is usually considered a sufficient act of part performance and is the most common one.

(6) The contract which is partly performed must not be made 'subject to contract'. Thus in *Cohen* v *Nessdale Ltd* [1982] 2 All E.R. 97, the plaintiff brought an action against the defendants seeking specific performance of a lease sold to him in a letter from the landlord for £20,000 'subject to contract' on the basis that he had partly performed the contract by making the first payment of rent. The Court of Appeal held that the trial judge had been right to refuse the plaintiff specific performance

because the landlord's letter did not constitute a final contract.

Capacity to contract

Adult citizens have full capacity to enter into any kind of contract but certain groups of persons and corporations have certain disabilities in this connection. The most important groups for our purposes are dealt with below.

Minors

The Family Law Reform Act 1969, s.1, reduced the age of majority from 21 to 18 years. A minor's contracts may be valid, void, voidable or unenforceable.

VALID CONTRACTS

These are as follows—

(1) *Executed contracts for necessaries.* These are defined in s.3(3) of the Sale of Goods Act 1979 as 'Goods suitable to the condition in life of the minor and to his actual requirements at the time of sale and delivery.'

If the goods are deemed necessaries the minor may be compelled to pay a reasonable price which will usually, but not necessarily be, the contract price. The minor is not liable if the goods, though necessaries, have not been delivered. This, together with the fact that he is only required to pay a reasonable price, illustrates that a minor's liability for necessaries is only quasi-contractual.

If the goods (or services) have a utility value, such as clothing, and are not merely things of luxury, e.g. a diamond tiara, then they are basically necessaries. Whether the minor will have to pay a reasonable price for them then depends upon—

(*a*) The minor's income which goes to his condition in life. If he is wealthy then quite expensive goods and services may be necessaries for him provided they are useful.

(*b*) The supply of goods which the minor already has is also relevant. If the minor is well supplied with the particular articles then they will not be necessaries even though they are useful and are well within his income. (*Nash* v *Inman* 1908.)[65]

(2) *Contracts for the minor's benefit.* These include contracts of service, apprenticeship, and education. (*Roberts* v *Gray* 1913.)[66] However, the modern tendency is not to restrict the concept of the beneficial contract to these particular categories, but to interpret the word 'benefit' more broadly, and to include contracts which are analogous to contracts of service in that they enable the minor to make a living, e.g. as an author.

(*Chaplin* v *Leslie Frewin (Publishers)* 1965.)[67] However, trading contracts of minors are not enforceable no matter how beneficial they may be to the minor's trade or business. (*Mercantile Union Guarantee Corporation* v *Ball* 1937.)[68] The theory behind this rule is that when an infant is in trade his capital is at risk and he might lose it, whereas in a contract of service there is no likelihood of capital loss.

It should be noted that the subject-matter of the contract is not decisive. A contract, which as regards its subject-matter, is in the category of contracts for the minor's benefit, will not be enforced if its terms are onerous and the court will look at the whole contract, not merely at isolated terms, and will arrive at its decision on the total effect of the agreement. (*De Francesco* v *Barnum* 1890[69] and *Clements* v *L. & N.W. Railway* 1894.)[70]

VOID CONTRACTS

These are as follows—

(1) *Those under s.1 of the Infants' Relief Act 1874*, of which the most important are—

(*a*) Contracts for repayment of money lent or to be lent. (*Coutts & Co.* v *Browne-Lecky* 1946).[71]

(*b*) Contracts for goods supplied or to be supplied other than necessaries.

Although the Infants' Relief Act provides that the above contracts are 'absolutely void', the minor obtains property in non-necessary goods supplied to him and can give a good title to third parties who buy from him. (*Stocks* v *Wilson* 1913.)[72]

(2) *S.5 of the Betting and Loans (Infants) Act 1892*. This Act renders *void* any agreement made by a person after he comes of age to pay a loan contracted during minority.

(3) *S.22 of the Bills of Exchange Act 1882*. A minor cannot be held liable on a cheque or other bill of exchange, even though given in payment of a debt incurred for necessaries supplied and delivered. So far as the actual supplier is concerned, there would be an action in quasi-contract on the consideration, i.e. for a reasonable price, not necessarily the contract price, but third parties to whom the bill had been negotiated would have no claim whatever on the minor, though other parties to the instrument would be fully liable in accordance with the rules relating to liability on negotiable instruments.

VOIDABLE CONTRACTS

These are usually contracts by which the minor acquires an interest of a permanent nature in the subject-matter of the contract. Such contracts bind the minor unless he takes active steps to avoid them, either during his minority or within a reasonable time thereafter. Examples of voidable contracts are shares in companies (see *Steinberg* v *Scala* 1923),[73] leases of property (see *Davies* v *Benyon-Harris* 1931),[74] and partnerships (see *Goode* v *Harrison* 1821.)[75]

UNENFORCEABLE CONTRACTS

These do not bind the minor and he need not take any steps to repudiate them. The other party is bound, however. Nevertheless, the minor cannot recover property or money which has passed under the contract unless there is total failure of consideration. A contract of insurance with a minor would fall into this class. In addition, under s.2 of the Infants' Relief Act 1874 there can be no ratification after age of a *debt* incurred during minority, e.g. for non-necessaries. The section also prevents a fresh promise made after age from being enforced, even if it is supported by new consideration as where a lender makes a fresh advance after majority as consideration for a promise to pay that advance and one made during minority.

Section 2 of the Infants' Relief Act 1874 was not entirely effective in the case of loans. As we have seen, it rendered certain promises unenforceable against the minor, but although the promise to repay the loan was unforceable, the lender could sell any security the minor had used to secure the loan because here he was pursuing a real remedy against the security and was not suing the former minor on his contractual promise.

The Betting and Loans (Infants) Act 1892 was therefore passed rendering *loans*, as distinct from *debts*, void so that any security taken is also void and the lender can neither enforce the minor's promise nor proceed against any security the minor may have given to secure the loan.

Consequences of the contracts of minors

As we have seen, contracts entered into by minors will, if defective, be void, voidable or unenforceable. The effect of the terms 'void' and 'voidable' in this context is untypical and must be considered here.

RECOVERY BY MINOR OF MONEY PAID UNDER A VOID OR VOIDABLE CONTRACT

When a minor has paid money under a void or voidable contract, although he can repudiate the contract and disclaim all future liability, he cannot recover money paid unless he can prove a total failure of consideration, i.e. that he has received no benefit at all under the contract. In this sense, therefore, repudiation is not retrospective. The court is reluctant to find that no benefit has been received and this can be seen in the context of a *void* contract in *Pearce* v *Brain* 1929[76] and a *voidable* contract in *Steinberg* v *Scala* 1923.[73] However, if there has really been no consideration at all a minor will be able to recover his money. (*Corpe* v *Overton* 1833.)[77]

EFFECT OF PURCHASE BY MINOR OF NON-NECESSARY GOODS

As we have seen, although the Infant's Relief Act 1874 states that contracts for goods other than necessaries are 'absolutely void' yet the minor acquires a title to the goods and can give a good title to a third party who takes them *bona fide* and for value. (*Stocks* v *Wilson* 1913.)[72] The tradesman who sold the goods to the minor cannot recover them from the third party and it is doubtful whether he can recover the money paid by the third party to the minor. In *Stocks* v *Wilson* 1913,[72] Lush, J., *held* that there could be recovery but the Court of Appeal in *Leslie* v *Sheill* 1914[78] suggested *obiter* that Lush, J., was wrong. Thus, although the matter is still at large, it is generally thought that *Leslie* v *Sheill* 1914[78] represents the better view and that there can be no recovery.

Where a minor has committed a fraud, e.g. deliberately overstated his age (not merely failed to give it), in order to obtain non-necessary goods, then the equitable doctrine of restitution of the goods is available to the tradesman. The remedy of restitution exists so long as the minor still has the goods in his possession and they can be identified. If the goods are not in the possession of the minor then there is no remedy, either against the minor or a third party who may have taken them *bona fide* and for value. It is well established that a tradesman cannot sue a minor on the tort of decit which occurs when the fraud is committed, since this would be using the law of torts to circumvent the Infants' Relief Act. (*Leslie* v *Sheill* 1914.)[78] Apart from circumstances such as this a minor may be liable in tort, e.g. for trespass.

Mental disorder and drunkenness

Where the property and affairs of a mental patient are placed under the management of the court by order under Part VII of the Mental Health Act 1983, the mental patient has no capacity to contract as regards that property. However, the other party is bound should the patient's representatives wish to regard him as bound. (*Re Walker* [1905] 1 Ch. 160.)

Apart from the above, the position is governed by the common law as follows—

(1) A contract made by a person who by reason of mental disease or drunkenness is incapable of understanding what he is doing is valid unless he can prove—

(*a*) that he did not understand the nature of the contract; and

(*b*) that the other party knew this to be the case. (*Imperial Loan Co.* v *Stone* 1892.)[79]

(2) A contract made by such a person is binding on him if he afterwards ratifies it at any time when the state of his mind is such that he can understand what he is doing. (*Matthews* v *Baxter* 1873.)[80]

(3) *Where necessaries are sold and delivered* to a person who by reason of mental incapacity or drunkenness is incompetent to contract, he is bound to pay a reasonable price. (Sale of Goods Act 1979, s.3(2).)

(4) *Necessaries are* 'goods suitable to the condition in life of such person and to his actual requirements at the time of the sale and delivery'. (S.3(3) *ibid.*) Therefore the principle of 'necessaries' is applied to persons with mental incapacity and drunkards in the same way as it is to minors.

Corporations

Regardless of the method by which it is formed, a company on incorporation becomes a *legal person* and acquires an identity quite separate and distinct from its members (*Salomon* v *Salomon & Co.* 1897)[81] and carries on its activities through agents.

At common law contracts made by corporations had to be under seal unless they were of trifling importance or daily necessity. That rule has been amended by statute, the Companies Act 1948 providing in s.32 that a registered company need not contract under seal except where an ordinary person would have to do so. The Corporate Bodies Contracts Act 1960 extends this privilege to all companies no matter how formed.

As regards powers, charter corporations have the same powers as ordinary persons and may act legally even though the transaction concerned is not provided for in the charter. However, if a charter corporation does act beyond its powers the Crown may forfeit the charter or a member of the corporation may ask the court to restrain it by injunction from doing acts which are *ultra vires* (i.e. beyond its powers). (*Jenkin* v *Pharmaceutical Society* 1921.)[82] The activities of statutory and registered corporations are limited by the powers conferred upon them by the creating Act or by the memorandum of association respectively. An act in excess of the powers given is *ultra vires* and void.

ULTRA VIRES RULE

The powers of statutory corporations, as we have seen, are contained in the statute setting them up and these powers are sometimes increased by subsequent statutes or by delegated legislation. As we have seen, acts beyond these powers are *ultra vires* and *void.*

The powers of registered companies are determined by the objects clause of the memorandum of association and an act in excess of the powers given in this clause is *ultra vires* and *void.* (*Ashbury Railway Carriage & Iron Company* v *Riche* 1875[83] and *Re Jon Beauforte* 1953.)[84]

RESPONSE OF THE COURTS AND PARLIAMENT TO THE PROBLEMS OF *ULTRA VIRES*

Lawyers, the courts, and Parliament have responded as follows in order to deal with some of the problems created by the *ultra vires* rule—

(1) *Drafting the objects clause.* It has become customary for legal draftsmen to draft objects clauses which are extremely wide in scope and in addition include a provision that each part of the objects clause should be considered separate and distinct from, and in no way ancillary to or dependent upon, the main object. The House of Lords conceded in *Cotman* v *Brougham* 1918[85] that such a provision was not illegal and that under it each of the objects set out in each sub-clause could be pursued separately.

However, some limit has been placed on this device, the court deciding in *Introductions Ltd* v *National Provincial Bank Ltd* 1969[86] that the borrowing or raising of money cannot be an independent object but must be read as a back-up or ancillary power to other activities since money is never borrowed for its own sake.

(2) *Acts fairly incidental* to the specified objects are valid. (*Deuchar* v *The Gas, Light & Coke Co.* 1925.)[87]

(3) *The decision of the Court of Appeal in Bell Houses Ltd* v *City Wall Properties Ltd* 1966.[88] In this case the Court of Appeal made a decision which in effect allows the directors of a company to decide what is reasonably incidental to the company's stated objects and furthermore allows them through ignorance or mistaken intention to bind the company to an activity which cannot conveniently be combined with the existing objects and is therefore in real terms *ultra vires.*

(4) *The European Communities Act 1972.* This Act, which came into force on 1 January 1973, is the United Kingdom's response to the first directive issued by the Council of the European Communities for the harmonization of company law in the member states. As regards the *ultra vires* rule, s.9(1) is relevant and provides that in favour of a person dealing in good faith with a company, any transaction *decided on by its directors* shall be deemed to be within the capacity of the company to enter into validly and the other party to the transaction shall not be bound to enquire about the capacity of the company to engage in it and shall be presumed to have acted in good faith unless the contrary is proved. The subsection does not abolish the *ultra vires* rule but merely allows the other party to an *ultra vires* transaction with a company to enforce it against the company if the necessary conditions are fulfilled. Thus the subsection does not—

(*a*) prevent a member of the company from obtaining an injunction to restrain the company and its directors from entering into an *ultra vires* transaction; or

(*b*) absolve the directors from liability for any loss which is caused to the company if, for example, the *ultra vires* contract is unprofitable; or

(*c*) make the transaction enforceable by the company but only against it; thus the other party can raise the defence of *ultra vires* if sued by the company. (*Bell Houses Ltd* v *City Wall Properties Ltd* 1966.)[88] However, if the other party sues the company it can plead defences and make counter claims. Furthermore, if the other party accepts benefits under the transaction or allows the company to incur expense in connection with it, he may be estopped from denying the validity of the transaction.

PRACTICAL EFFECT OF SECTION 9(1)

Unfortunately, the effect of s.9(1) on the *ultra vires* rule appears limited. The subsection applies only if the transaction has been 'decided on by the directors'. Not all transactions of a *public* company are formally resolved upon at board meetings and the subsection would seem to apply only where the transaction has been authorized, effected or ratified by a resolution of a board meeting or by all the directors assenting to it. In addition, transactions which the directors do not decide upon but which are, for example, approved by the members of the company in general meeting, or decided on by an executive other than a director of the company, are also outside the protection of the section. However, it does extend to a 'dominant director', i.e. a sole effective director to whom all authority has in the circumstances of the case been delegated. (*International Sales and Agencies Ltd* v *Marcus* 1982.)[89] Nevertheless not all *ultra vires* transactions of public companies will be validated by s.9(1). Some will remain invalid and be covered by the common law rules described above. In *private* companies, which may have only one director, the Act should make *ultra vires* transactions enforceable because most transactions and the details thereof will be decided on by the board.

In this connection it is interesting to note that the Conservative Government's Companies Bill of 1973 provided in Clause 5 that a transaction between a company and another party should not be repudiated by the company on the ground that it was beyond the capacity of the company or the powers of the directors, unless the other party had actual notice of that fact. Such a provision would have been much more effective in validating *ultra vires* transactions with companies, since it did not rely on the transaction being decided on by the directors.

Reality of consent

A contract which is regular in all respects may still fail because there is no real consent to it by one or both of the parties. There is no *consensus ad idem* or meeting of the minds. Consent may be rendered unreal by mistake, misrepresentation, duress and undue influence.

It is particularly important to distinguish between mistake and misrepresentation because a contract affected by mistake is void, whereas a contract affected by misrepresentation is only voidable. As between the parties themselves, this makes little difference since in both cases goods sold and money paid can be recovered. However, the distinction can be vital so far as third parties are concerned. If A sells goods to B under circumstances of mistake and B resells them to C, then C gets no title and A can recover the goods from him or sue him for damages in conversion.

If, on the other hand, the contract between A and B was voidable for misrepresentation, then if B sold the goods to C who took them *bona fide* and for value before A had rescinded his contract with B, then C would get a good title and A would have a remedy only against B.

Mistake

Mistake, to be operative, must be of *fact* and *not of law*. (*Sharp Bros and Knight* v *Chant* 1917.)[90] Furthermore, the concept has a technical meaning and does not cover, for example, errors of judgment. Thus, if A buys an article thinking it is worth £100 when in fact it is worth only £50, the contract is good and A must bear the loss if there has been no misrepresentation by the seller. This is what is meant by the maxim '*caveat emptor*' (let the buyer beware).

DOCUMENTS MISTAKENLY SIGNED

If a person signs a contract in the mistaken belief that he is signing a document of a different nature, there may be a mistake which avoids the contract. He may be able to plead *non est factum* ('it is not his deed'). This is a defence open to a person who has signed a document by mistake. At one time the defence was available only where the mistake referred to the *kind* of document it was and not merely the *exact* content. Now the defence is available to a person who has signed a document having made a *fundamental* mistake as to the kind of document it is or as to its contents. Furthermore, the defendant must prove that he made the mistake despite having taken all reasonable care. If he is negligent he will not usually be able to plead the defence.

The charge of negligence might be avoided where a person was told he was witnessing a confidential document and had no reason to doubt that he was. Thus the decision in the old case of *Lewis* v *Clay* (1898) 77 L.T. 653 would probably be the same under modern law. In that case Clay was asked by Lord William Neville to witness a confidential document and signed in holes in blotting paper placed over the document by Neville. In fact he was signing two promissory notes and two letters authorizing Lewis to pay the amount of the notes to Lord William Neville. The court held that the signature of Clay in the circumstances had no more effect than if it had been written for an autograph collector or in an album and he was not bound by the bills of exchange.

As between the immediate parties to what is always in effect a fraud, there is, of course, no difficulty in avoiding the contract or transaction mistakenly entered into. The rules set out above are relevant only where the contract or transaction mistakenly entered into has affected a third party, as where he has taken a bill of exchange *bona fide* and for value on which the defendant's signature was obtained under circumstances of mistake (*Foster* v *Mackinnon* 1869)[91] or has lent money on an interest in land obtained by a fraudulent assignment under circumstances of mistake. (*Saunders* v *Anglia Building Society* 1970.)[92] The principles set out in *Saunders' Case* apply also to those who sign blank forms as well as to those who sign completed documents without reading them. (*United Dominions Trust Ltd* v *Western* [1975] 3 All E.R. 1017.)

UNILATERAL MISTAKE

Unilateral mistake occurs when one of the parties, X, is mistaken as to some fundamental fact concerning the contract and other party, Y, knows, or ought to know, this. (*Legal and General Assurance Society* v *General Metal Agencies* 1969.)[93] This latter requirement is important becuase if Y does not know that X is mistaken the contract is good. (*Higgins* v *Northampton Corporation* 1927.)[94]

The cases are mainly concerned with mistake by one party as to the *identity* of the other party. Thus a contract may be void for mistake if X contracts with Y thinking that Y is another person, Z, and if Y knows that X is under that misapprehension. Proof of Y's knowledge is essential but since in most cases Y is a fraudulent person, the point does not present great difficulties. (*Cundy* v *Lindsay* 1878.)[95]

It is also essential that at the time of making the apparent contract the mistaken party regarded the identity of the other party as vital and that he intended to deal with some person other than the actual person to whom in fact he addressed the offer, as in *Cundy* v *Lindsay* 1878.[95] The mistake must be as to *identity*, not *attributes*, e.g. credit-worthiness. As between the parties the result is much the same since a mistake as to attributes may make the contract *voidable*, but the difference may vitally affect the interests of third parties. (*King's Norton Metal Co. Ltd* v *Edridge, Merrett & Co. Ltd* 1897.)[96]

There were difficulties where the parties contracted face to face because in such a case the suggestion could always be made that whatever the fraudulent party was saying about his identity, the mistaken party must be regarded as intending to contract with the person in front of him, whoever he was. Thus in this situation, the court might find on the facts of the case that the contract was voidable for fraud or sometimes void for mistake. (*Ingram* v *Little* 1961.)[97]

However, the position is now a little clearer as a result of the decision in *Lewis* v *Averay* 1971[98] where it was said that if the parties contracted face to face the contract will normally be voidable for fraud but rarely void for mistake.

EFFECT OF UNILATERAL MISTAKE IN EQUITY

If the plaintiff is asking for an equitable remedy, such a rescission of the contract or specific performance of it, then equitable principles will apply. As far as unilateral mistake is concerned, equity follows the principles of the common law and regards a contract affected by unilateral mistake as void and will therefore rescind it or refuse specific performance of it. (*Webster* v *Cecil* 1861.)[99] Rectification of the contract is also available. (See p. 33.)

BILATERAL, IDENTICAL (OR COMMON) MISTAKE

This occurs when the two parties have reached agreement but have made an identical mistake as to some fundamental fact concerning the contract. Suppose, for example, that X sells a particular drawing to Y for £5000 and all the usual elements of agreement are present, including offer and acceptance and consideration, and the agreement concerns an identified article. Nevertheless, if both X and Y think that the drawing is by Rembrandt when it is in fact only a copy worth £25, then the agreement is made in circumstances of common mistake.

EFFECT OF IDENTICAL BILATERAL (OR COMMON) MISTAKE AT COMMON LAW

At common law a mistake of the kind outlined above has no effect on the contract and the parties would be bound in the absence of fraud or misrepresentation. (*Bell* v *Lever Bros.* 1932[100] and *Leaf* v *International Galleries* 1950.)[101]

There are, however, two categories of case in which the common law regards a common mistake as rendering the contract void. These are as follows—

(1) *Cases of res extincta.* Here there is a common mistake as to the existence of the subject-matter of the contract. Thus, if S agrees to sell his car to B and unknown to them both the car had at the time of the sale been destroyed by fire, then the contract will be void because A has innocently undertaken an obligation which he cannot possibly fulfil. (*Couturier* v *Hastie* 1856.)[102]

(2) *Cases of res sua.* These occur where a person makes a contract to buy something which already belongs to him. Such a contract is void at common law. (*Cochrane* v *Willis* 1865.)[103]

EFFECT OF IDENTICAL BILATERAL (OR COMMON) MISTAKE IN EQUITY

The position in equity is as follows—

(1) *Cases of res extincta and res sua.* Equity treats these in the same way as the common law, regarding the agreement as void. The equitable remedy of specific performance is not available for such an agreement which may also be rescinded. (*Cooper* v *Phibbs* 1867.)[104]

(2) *Other cases.* Equity will apparently regard an agreement affected by common mistake as *voidable* even though the case is not one of *res extincta* or *res sua*. (*Solle* v *Butcher* 1950.)[105] The remedy is a discretionary one and the parties seeking it may be required to accept other solutions to the problem put forward by the court. Thus in *Solle* v *Butcher*[105] to set aside the lease without more would have been inequitable to the tenant since this would require his immediate dispossession. Therefore he was given the choice of surrendering the lease entirely or of remaining in possession at the full rent that would have been permissible under the Rent Acts had the landlord served the statutory notice upon him within the proper time limit. The way in which the court set out to achieve this appears in the summary of the case.

(3) *Rectification.* If the parties are agreed on the terms of their contract but by common mistake write them down incorrectly, the court may order equitable rectification of the contract so that it properly represents what the parties agreed. Thus if A orally agrees to give B a lease of premises for 99 years and in the subsequent written contract the term is expressed as 90 years by mistake, then if A will not co-operate to change the lease, B may ask the court to rectify if by substituting a term of 99 years for 90 years. In order to obtain rectification it must be proved—

(*a*) that there was complete agreement on all the terms of the contract or at least a continuing intention to include certain terms in it which in the event were not included. It is not necessary to show that the term was intended to be legally binding prior to being written down (*Joscelyne* v *Nissen* 1970)[106];

(*b*) that the agreement continued unchanged until it was reduced into writing. If the parties disputed the terms of the agreement then the written contract may be taken to represent their final position;

(*c*) that the writing does not express what the parties had agreed. If it does then there can be no rectification. (*Rose* v *Pim* 1953.)[107]

Rectification is also available in cases of unilateral mistake. (*Thomas Bates & Son Ltd* v *Wyndham's (Lingerie) Ltd* 1981.)[108]

NON-IDENTICAL BILATERAL (OR MUTUAL) MISTAKE

If X offers to sell car A and Y agrees to buy, thinking X means car B, there is a bilateral mistake which is non-identical. It will be remembered that in the previous category the mistake was bilateral but both parties had made an identical mistake. Confusion of this kind generally exists in the mind of one party only and may therefore have no effect on the contract. (See below.)

EFFECT OF NON-IDENTICAL BILATERAL (OR MUTUAL) MISTAKE AT COMMON LAW

The contract is not necessarily void because the court will try to find the 'sense of the promise', i.e. the sort of bargain which the reasonable man looking at the dealings of the parties would have thought had been made. This results in the contract being enforced on the terms understood by one of the parties. (*Wood* v *Scarth* 1858.)[109]

If the court cannot find the 'sense of the promise', as where a reasonable man looking at the dealings of the parties would still be confused as to the intention, then the contract is void. (*Raffles* v *Wichelaus* 1864.)[110]

EFFECT OF NON-IDENTICAL BILATERAL (OR MUTUAL) MISTAKE IN EQUITY

Equity also tries to find the 'sense of the promise', thus following the law. (*Tamplin* v *James* 1880.)[111] However, equitable remedies are discretionary and even where the 'sense of the promise' can be ascertained equity will not necessarily grant specific performance if it would cause hardship to the defendant. (*Wood* v *Scarth* 1858.)[109]

Misrepresentation

Misrepresentation is an expression used to describe a situation in which there is no genuineness of consent to a contract by one of the parties. The effect of misrepresentation on a contract is less serious than that of mistake because the contract becomes *voidable and not void.* This means that the party misled can ask the court to rescind the contract, i.e. to put the parties back into the positions they held before the contract was made. Thus in a sale of goods the goods would be returned to the seller and the money to the buyer.

However, the effect on third parties is more fundamental because if A sells goods to B under circumstances of misrepresentation by B and before A has a chance to rescind the contract B sells the goods to C, who takes them for value without notice of the misrepresentation, C has a good title and A cannot recover the goods or sue him in conversion.

His remedy is against B and the type of remedy available will depend upon the nature of B's misrepresentation, i.e. whether it was fraudulent, negligent or innocent.

REPRESENTATION—MEANING OF

A representation is an inducement only and its effect is to lead the other party merely to make the contract. A representation must be a statement of some specific existing and verifiable fact or past event. It becomes a misrepresentation, of course, when it is false.

Thus there are three ingredients as follows—

(1) *There must be a statement.* In consequence silence or non-disclosure has no effect except—

(*a*) Where the statement was true when made but became false before the contract was concluded. Here there is a duty on the party making the statement to disclose the change and if he does not do so his silence can amount to an actionable misrepresentation. (*With* v *O'Flanagan* 1936.)[112]

(*b*) *Where the contract is uberrimae fidei* (of utmost good faith), such as a contract of insurance. This matter will be dealt with more fully in Chapter 8.

(*c*) Where there is a confidential or fiduciary relationship between the parties, as where they are solicitor and client. Here the equitable doctrine of constructive fraud may apply to render the contract voidable.

Although this branch of the law is closely akin to undue influence, which will be considered later, there is a difference in the sense that in undue influence the person with special influence, such as a solicitor over his client, is often the prime mover in seeking the contract. Constructive fraud, however, could apply where the client was the prime mover in seeking a contract with his solicitor. In such a case if the solicitor remains silent as regards facts within his knowledge material say, to the contract price, then the client could rescind the contract for constructive fraud.

(*d*) Where statute requires disclosure, as does s.38 of the Companies Act 1948 under which a number of specified particulars must be disclosed in a prospectus issued by a company to invite the public to subscribe for shares or debentures. However, the sole remedy for failure to disclose is damages and not rescission. (*Re South of England Natural Gas Co.* [1911] 1 Ch. 573.) (See further p. 41.)

(2) *Specific existing and verifiable fact or past event.* The representation must be a statement of some specific, existing and verifiable fact or past event, and in consequence the following are excluded—

(*a*) Statements of law. Everyone is presumed to know the law which is equally accessible to both parties and on which they should seek advice and not rely on the statements of the other party. Thus, if A has allowed B, a tradesman, to have goods on credit and C has agreed orally to indemnify A in respect of the transaction, then if A enters into a second contract with B under which A is to receive two-thirds of the price of the goods from B in full settlement on B's representation that C's indemnity is unenforceable at law because it is not in writing, then the second contract would be good because A cannot deny that he knows the law because of the maxim 'ignorance of the law is no excuse'.

(*b*) Statements as to future conduct or intention. These are not actionable, though if the person who makes the statement has no intention of carrying it out, it may be regarded as a representation of fact, i.e. a misrepresentation of what is really in the mind of the maker of the statement. (*Edgington* v *Fitzmaurice* 1885.)[113]

(*c*) Statements of opinion. Again these are not normally actionable unless it can be shown that the person making the statement held no such opinion whereupon the statement may be considered in law to be a misstatement of an existing fact as to what was in the mind of the maker of the statement at the time. (*Smith* v *Land and House Property Corporation* 1884.)[114] However, in *Bissett* v *Wilkinson* [1927] A.C. 177 it was held that a vendor of land was not liable for stating that it could support 2000 sheep, because he had no personal knowledge of the facts, the land having never been used for sheep farming. The buyer knew this so that it was understood by him that the seller could only be stating his belief.

(*d*) Sales talk, advertising, 'puffing' (or what is called these days 'hype'). Not all statements in this area amount to representations. The law has always accepted that it is essential in business that a seller of goods or services should be allowed to make some statements about them in the course of dealing without necessarily being bound by everything he says. Thus, if a salesman confines himself to statements of opinion such as 'This is the finest floor polish in the world' or 'This is the best polish on the market', there is no misrepresentation. However, the nearer a salesman gets to a statement of specific verifiable fact, the greater the possibility that there may be an action for misrepresentation. Thus a statement such as 'This polish has as much wax in it as Snooks' wax polish' may well amount to a misrepresentation if the statement is not in fact true.

(3) *The statement must induce the contract.* It must therefore—

(*a*) be addressed to the person claiming to have been misled; (*Peek* v *Gurney* 1873.)[115]

(*b*) have been relied upon by the person claiming to have been misled who must not have relied on his own skill and judgment; (*Redgrave* v *Hurd* 1881.)[116]

(*c*) have been material in the sense that it affected the plaintiff's judgment; (*Smith* v *Chadwick* 1884.)[117]

(*d*) have been known to the plaintiff. The plaintiff must always be prepared to prove that an alleged misrepresentation had an effect on his mind, a task which he certainly cannot fulfill if he was never aware that it had been made.

Thus in *Re Northumberland and Durham District Banking Co, ex parte Bigg* (1858) 28 L.J. Ch. 50 a person who bought shares in a company asked to have the purchase rescinded because the company had published false reports as to its solvency. Although these reports were false, the claimant failed because, among other things, he was unable to show that he had read any of the reports or that anyone had told him what they contained.

TYPES OF ACTIONABLE MISREPRESENTATION AND REMEDIES

Innocent misrepresentation. A purely innocent misrepresentation is a false statement made by a person who had reasonable grounds to believe that the statement was true, not only when he made it but also at the time the contract was entered into. As regards reasonable grounds, the representor's best hope of proving this will be to show that he himself had been induced to buy the goods by the same statement. (See *Oscar Chess Ltd* v *Williams* 1957, p. 423.) The party misled can ask the court to rescind the contract but has no right to ask for damages. However, the court may at its discretion award damages instead of rescission. (Misrepresentation Act 1967, s.2(2).)

Rescission in effect cancels the contract and the court may in some cases regard this as a drastic remedy, particularly where there has been misrepresentation on a trival matter, such as the quality of the tyres on a car. Suppose the seller of a car says: 'the previous owner fitted new tyres at 26,000 miles'. If that statement is false but the seller was told this by the previous owner, then the court could award damages instead of recission, thus leaving the contract intact but giving the party misled monetary compensation.

Negligent misrepresentation. A negligent misrepresentation is a false statement made by a person who had no reasonable grounds for believing the statement to be true. The party misled may sue for recission and/or damages and the onus of proving that the statement was not made negligently but that there were reasonable grounds for believing it to be true is on the maker of the statement (or representer). (Misrepresentation Act 1967, s.2(1).) (See *Gosling* v *Anderson* 1972.)[118]

The subsection rcognizes only a claim for damages and says nothing as to rescission. However, in *Mapes* v *Jones* (1974) 232 E.G. 717 a property dealer contracted to lease a grocer's shop to the plaintiff for 21 years but in fact did not have sufficient interest in the property himself to grant such a lease, the maximum period available to him being 18 years. Despite constant requests no lease was supplied as originally promised and the plaintiff shut the shop and elected to treat the contract as repudiated. Willis, J., *held* that the plaintiff was entitled to rescission for misrepresentation under s.2(1) of the 1967 Act. He also found that the defendant's delay in completion was breach of condition allowing the plaintiff to repudiate the contract.

Fraudulent misrepresentation. A fraudulent misrepresentation is a false representation of a material fact made knowing it to be false, or believing it to be false, or recklessly not caring whether it be true or false. Mere negligence is not enough. (See *Derry* v *Peek* 1889.)[119] The party misled may sue for rescission and/or damages. As regards the action for damages, the plaintiff sues not on the contract but on the tort of deceit.

AGENT'S BREACH OF WARRANTY OF AUTHORITY

Under the law of Agency where an agent represents himself as having authority he does not possess, the third party will not obtain a contract with the principal and if he suffers loss as a consequence he may sue the agent for breach of warranty of authority, the action being for damages and brought in *quasi-contract*. Quasi-contract is based on the idea that a person should not obtain a benefit or unjust enrichment or cause injury to another with impunity merely because there is no obligation in contract or another established branch of law which will operate to make him account. The law may in these circumstances provide a remedy by implying a *fictitious promise* to account for the benefit of enrichment or to compensate for damage caused.

COMPENSATION UNDER S.43, COMPANIES ACT 1948

Under this section, where the directors of a company publish a prospectus containing false statements made innocently they may have to pay a form of damages called compensation.

There are a number of special defences available under the Act. For example, a director may deny responsibility for the prospectus, as where he ceased to be a director before it was issued. Assuming, however, that he does admit responsibility for the prospectus, the defences are that—

(1) he had reasonable grounds for believing the statement true;
(2) the statements were made on the authority of an expert who was thought to be competent; or
(3) the statements were a copy of an official document.

Experts, such as accountants, are also liable under the section for false statements in their reports which are included in the prospectus. Again, the defence of lack of responsibility is available, as where the expert has not consented to the inclusion of his report in the prospectus. However, given that he accepts responsibility for the inclusion of his report, he has a defence if he can show that he had reasonable grounds for believing the statement to be true. Presumably, he could sustain this defence by showing, amongst other things, that the false statement came from an official document.

NEGLIGENCE AT COMMON LAW

Where the parties concerned were *not in a pre-contractual relationship* when the statement was made, s.2(1) of the Misrepresentation Act 1967 will not apply. However, an action for damages for negligence will lie in tort, provided the false statement was made negligently (*Hedley Byrne & Co. Ltd* v *Heller & Partners Ltd* 1963.)[120]

In *Esso Petroleum* v *Mardon* [1976] 2 All E.R. 5, the court held that the principle in *Hedley Byrne* could apply even where the parties concerned were in a pre-contractual relationship and in addition that the person who had made the statement need not necessarily be in business to give advice, provided it is reasonable for one party to rely on the other's skill and judgment in making the statement. Mr Mardon was awarded damages for a negligent misstatement by a senior sales representative of Esso in regard to the amount of petrol he could expect to sell per year from a petrol station which he was leasing from Esso. The facts of *Mardon* pre-dated the 1967 Act and the court could not use it. The decision is obviously important but where the facts have occurred since 1967 the Misrepresentation Act is likely to prove more popular to plaintiffs since they can ask the representor to show he was not negligent. In *Hedley Byrne* claims the burden of proof is on the plaintiff to prove negligence.

Finally, as regards actions against directors and experts under prospectus, the court is likely to insist that the claim he brought under s.43 of the Companies Act 1948. As we have seen, special defences are available to these people under that section and they would be denied the defences if a claim was brought against the company under the Misrepresentation Act or under *Hedley Byrne.* The matter is not, however, free from doubt and there is no judicial decision on which we can rely. However, there are advantages in suing under the Misrepresentation Act because a claim under that Act is made against the company for damages in respect of the false statements of its agents, whereas the action under s.43 is a personal action against those who actually made the statement. In addition, the principle in *Hedley Byrne* would apply to statements of opinion, whereas under s.43 we are concerned with statements of fact. Furthermore, under *Hedley Byrne,* the company could presumably be sued for damages on the basis of vicarious liability for the torts of its agents. (See further p. 117.)

REMEDY OF RESCISSION

As we have seen, this remedy is available to a party misled by innocent, negligent, or fraudulent misrepresentation. It restores the *status quo,* i.e. it puts the parties back to the position they were in before the contract was made. However, the remedy may be lost—

(1) *By affirmation.* If the injured party affirms the contract he cannot rescind. He will affirm if with full knowledge of the misrepresentation he expressly affirms the contract by stating that he intends to go on with it or if he does some act from which an implied intention may properly be deduced. (*Long* v *Lloyd* 1958.)[121]

(2) *By lapse of time.* This is a form of implied affirmation and applies as follows—

(*a*) In innocent and negligent misrepresentation the position is governed by equity and the passage of a reasonable time, even without knowledge of the misrepresentation, may prevent the court from granting rescission. (See *Leaf* v *International Galleries* 1950.)[101]

(*b*) In fraudulent misrepresentation the position is governed by s.32 of the Limitation Act 1980 and lapse of time has no effect on rescission where fraud is alleged as long as the action is brought within six years of the time when the fraud was, or with reasonable diligence, could have been discovered.

(3) *Where status quo cannot be restored.* Rescission is impossible if the parties cannot be restored to their original positions as where goods sold under a contract of sale have been consumed. (See also *Clarke* v *Dickson* 1858.)[122]

(4) *Where a third party has acquired rights in the subject-matter of the contract.* Thus if X obtains goods from Y by misrepresentation and pawns them with Z, Y cannot rescind the contract on learning of the misrepresentation in order to recover the goods from Z. Nor can he sue Z in conversion. (See *Lewis* v *Averay* 1971.)[98]

Contracts *uberrimae fidei*

Silence does not normally amount to misrepresentation. However, an important exception to the rule occurs in the case of certain contracts where from the circumstances of the case one party alone possesses full knowledge of all the material facts and in which therefore the law requires him to show utmost good faith. He must make full disclosure of all the material facts known to him otherwise the contract may be rescinded. The contracts concerned are as follows—

(1) *At common law.* Contracts of insurance provide the only true example of a contract *uberrimae fidei*. There is a duty on the person taking up the insurance to disclose to the insurance company all facts of which he is aware which might affect the premium or acceptance of the risk. Failure to do so renders the contract voidable at the option of the insurance company. In addition, most proposals for insurance require the proposer to sign a declaration in which he warrants that the statements he has made are true and agrees that they be incorporated into the contract as terms. Where this is so any false statement which the proposer makes will be a ground for avoidance of the contract by the insurance company, even though the statement was not material in terms of the premium. (See *Dawsons Ltd* v *Bonnin*, 1922.)[123]

(2) *By statute.* As regards contracts to take shares in a company under a prospectus, there is a duty on the directors or its promoters, under s.38 of the Companies Act 1948, to disclose the various matters set out in the fourth schedule to that Act. The list of matters set out in the fourth schedule is sufficiently long to cover most of the representations and non-disclosures that may mislead an applicant for shares. For example,

the interest of each director of the company in any property which the company is to purchase must be disclosed. This would reveal, for example, a situation in which a director might be selling property belonging to him to the company at an exorbitant price. Failure to make the disclosures required by the fourth schedule does not mean that a shareholder can rescind the contract to take shares if the omission makes the prospectus misleading. (*Re Wimbledon Olympia Ltd* [1910] 1 Ch. 630.) Nevertheless, those responsible for the prospectus, e.g. promoters or directors, have a liability in damages to persons misled if the omission is material, i.e. important to the investor, as in the case of the contract described above. (*Re South of England Natural Gas Co.* [1911] 1 Ch. 573.) Certain defences appear in s.38(4), e.g. that non-compliance or contravention arose from an honest mistake of fact.

(3) *In equity–fiduciary relationships*. In contracts between members of a family, partners, principal and agent, solicitor and client, guardian and ward, a trustee and beneficiary, the relationship of the parties requires that the most ample disclosure should be made. (See *Gordon* v *Gordon* 1819.)[124]

The duties of disclosure arising from the above fiduciary relations recognized by equity are not situations of *uberrimae fidei*. In contracts *uberimmae fidei* it is the nature of the contract, i.e. insurance, which requires disclosure regardless of the relationship of the parties. In the fiduciary situation it is the relationship of the parties and not the particular contract which gives rise to the need to disclose.

Duress

Duress will affect all contracts and gifts procured by its use. Duress, which is a common-law concept, means actual violence or threats of violence to the person of the contracting party or those near and dear to him. The threats must be calculated to produce fear of loss of life or bodily harm. (*Welch* v *Cheesman* 1974.)[125]

A contract will seldom be procured by actual violence but threats of violence are more probable. The threat must be illegal in that it must be a threat to commit a crime or tort. Thus to threaten an imprisonment, which would be unlawful if enforced, constitutes duress, but not, it is said, if the imprisonment would be lawful. However, the courts are unlikely to look with favour on a contract obtained by threatening to prosecute a criminal. A contract procured by a threat to sue for an act which was not a crime, e.g. trespass, would not be affected by duress.

The concept is not applicable to threats to property. Thus in *Skeate* v *Beale* (1840) 11 Ad. & El. 983, a tenant owed £19.10s. and agreed to pay £3.7s.6d. immediately and the remaining £16.2s.6d. within a month if his landlord would withdraw a writ of distress under which he was threatening to sell the tenant's goods. The tenant later disputed what he owed and the landlord tried to set up the agreement and sued for the remaining £16.2s.6d. It was held that the landlord was entitled to £16.2s.6d. under the agreement which was not affected by duress since the threat was to sell the tenant's goods. However, more recently the courts have been moving away from the view that threats to property cannot invalidate contracts. In *The Siboen and the Sibotre* [1976] 1 Lloyd's Rep. 293 it was said that duress could be a defence if a person was forced to make a contract by the threat of having a valuable picture slashed or his house burnt down.

Duress probably renders a contract *voidable*. This, at least, is the view of Cheshire, though other writers have argued that the effect of duress is to render a contract void. However, the judgments of the Privy Council in *Barton* v *Armstrong* [1975] 2 All E.R. 465 suggest that duress has the same effect as fraud, i.e. it renders a contract voidable. The issue is an important one for third parties, since if B procures goods from A by duress and sells the goods to C, who has no knowledge of the duress, A will be able to recover the goods from C if the contract is void, but will not be able to do so if it is voidable.

Undue influence

The doctrine of undue influence was developed by equity. The concept of undue influence is designed to deal with contracts or gifts obtained without free consent by the influence of one mind over another.

If there is no special relationship between the parties undue influence may exist, but must be proved by the person seeking to avoid the contract.

Where a confidential or fiduciary relationship exists between the parties, the party in whom the confidence was reposed must show that undue influence was not used, i.e. that the contract was the act of a free and independent mind. It is desirable, though not essential, that independent advice should have been given.

There are several confidential relationships known to the law, *viz.* parent and child, solicitor and client, trustee and beneficiary, guardian and ward. There is no presumption of such a relationship between husband and wife, nor, according to the Court of Appeal in *Mathew* v *Bobbins* (1980) 256 E.G. 603, between employer and employee. The fiduciary relationship between parent and child ends usually, but not necessarily, on reaching 18 or on getting married (but see *Lancashire Loans Ltd* v *Black* 1934.)[126] However, there may be a presumption of undue influence even though the relationship between the parties is not in the established categories outlined above. In *Re Craig Dec'd* [1970] 2 All E.R. 390, Ungoed Thomas, J., ruled that presumption of undue influence arose on proof—

(1) of a gift so substantial or of such a nature that it could not on the face of it be accounted for on the grounds of the ordinary motives on which ordinary men acted; and

(2) of a relationship of trust and confidence such that the recipient of the gift was in a position to exercise undue influence over the person making it. This principle was applied in *Hodgson* v *Marks* 1970.[127]

EFFECT ON THE CONTRACT

Undue influence renders the contract voidable so that it may be rescinded. However, since rescission is an equitable remedy, there must be no delay in claiming relief after the influence has ceased to have effect. Delay in claiming relief in these circumstances may bar the claim since delay is evidence of affirmation. (*Allcard* v *Skinner* 1887.)[128]

EFFECT ON THIRD PARTIES

A contract between A and B procured by undue influence cannot be avoided by rescission against third parties who acquire rights for value without notice of the facts. Where this has happened the party suffering the undue influence, say, A, will have to rely on tracing the proceeds of sale into the original purchaser's, i.e. B's, assets. The contract may be avoided and the property recovered from third parties for value with notice of the facts and also against volunteers (i.e. persons who have given no consideration) even though they were unaware of the facts.

Economic duress and unconscionable bargains

Apart from the old concepts of duress and undue influence, the courts are developing in modern terms wider rules to protect persons against improper pressure and inequality of bargaining power as it affects contracts. This development was perhaps best described by Lord Denning in *Lloyds Bank* v *Bundy* [1974] 3 All E.R. 757 at p. 765 where he said, having discussed duress and various forms of undue pressure in contract:

> 'Gathering all together, I would suggest that through all these instances there runs a single thread. They rest on "inequality of bargaining power". By virtue of it, the English law gives relief to one who, without independent advice, enters into a contract on terms which are very unfair or transfers property for consideration which is grossly inadequate, where his bargaining power is grievously impaired by reason of his own needs or desires, or by his own ignorance or infirmity. Coupled with undue influence or pressures brought to bear on him by or for the benefit of the other.'

Ecomonic duress is within this concept. Suppose A agrees to build a tanker for B by an agreed date at an agreed price and B enters into a contract with C under which the tanker is to be chartered to C from the agreed completion date or shortly afterwards. If A then threatens not to complete the contract by the agreed date unless B pays more and B makes an extra payment because he does not want to be liable in breach of contract to C, then the extra payment may be recovered from A by B on the grounds of economic duress. (See the judgment of Mocatta, J., in *North Ocean Shipping Co. Ltd* v *Hyundai Construction Co Ltd, The Atlantic Baron* [1978] 3 All E.R. 1170.)

The decision of the House of Lords in *Universe Tankships Inc. of Monrovia* v *International Transport Workers' Federation* [1982] 2 All E.R. 67 is instructive in that it affirms the existence of the doctrine of economic duress. In that case a ship called the *Universe Sentinel*, which was owned by Universe Tankships, was 'blacked' by the respondent trade union, the ITF, which regarded the ship as sailing under a flag of convenience. ITF was against flag-of-convenience ships and refused to make tugs available when the ship arrived at Milford Haven to discharge her cargo. The blacking was lifted after Universe Tankships had made an agreement with ITF regarding improvements in pay and conditions of the crew and had paid money to ITF which included a contribution of $6480 to an ITF fund known as The Seafarers' International Welfare Protection and Assistance Fund. Universe Tankships sued for the return of the $6480 on the basis of economic duress, and the House of Lords held that they were entitled to recover it. It appears from the judgments that the effect of economic duress is to make the contract voidable and to provide a ground for recovery of money paid as money had and received to the plaintiff's use—a form of quasi-contractual claim.

Further examples of inequality of bargaining power may be found in *Clifford Davies Management* v *W.E.A. Records* [1975] 1 All E.R. 237 where A, an experienced manager, obtained a contract with a pop star, B, who had little or no business experience, under which B gave A the copyright in all his compositions for a period of years. It was held that B could avoid the contract because A had exploited his superior bargaining power. The concept has also applied to a guarantee of a bank loan obtained from the borrower's father by a bank manager in whom the father placed his trust. (*Lloyds Bank* v *Bundy* 1974.)[129]

However, there is no rule of law which states that a fair price must be paid in *all* transactions and some unfair contracts will be held binding provided the parties were of equal bargaining strength. In *Burma Oil Ltd* v *The Governor of the Bank of England, The Times*, 4 July 1981, Burma was in financial difficulties and sold a large holding of shares which it had in British Petroleum to the Government at a price below the Stock Exchange price. Burma then brought an action to set the contract aside. The Court refused to do so. Although there was authority to set aside a transaction where one party had acted without independent advice, or where the bargaining strength of one party was grievously impaired, neither of those situations existed in this case. The relationship was purely commercial and the contract for the sale of shares must stand.

The contents of the contract

Even where it is clear that a valid contract has been made it is still necessary to decide precisely what it is the parties have undertaken to do in order to be able to say whether each has performed or not performed his part of the agreement.

In order to decide upon the terms of the contract it is necessary to find out what was said or written by the parties. Furthermore, having ascertained what the parties said or wrote, it is necessary to decide whether the statements were mere inducements (or representations) or terms of the contract, i.e. part of its actual contents. The distinction in diagrammatic form together with an indication of remedies appears on p. 47.

The distinction is less important than it was since the passing of the Misrepresentation Act 1967. Before the Act became law there was often no remedy for a misrepresentation which was not fraudulent, and in such a case the plaintiff's only hope of obtaining a remedy was to convince the court that the defendant's statement was not a mere inducement but a term of the contract of which the defendant was in breach. As we have seen, under the Misrepresentation Act of 1967 rescission is not now so easily lost and the new form of negligent misrepresentation which did not exist before will now give rise in many cases to an action for damages even in respect of a mere misrepresentation or inducement.

Nevertheless, it is still necessary to consider the main tests applied by the courts in order to distinguish between mere misrepresentation and terms of the contract, bearing in mind always that the question whether a statement is an inducement or a term and, if a term, whether a condition or warranty *is a matter of fact for the judge.* Fact decisions of this sort vary widely according to the circumstances of each case, so that it is virtually impossible to predict with absolute accuracy what the outcome of a particular case will be. However, by way of illustration it may be said that—

(1) The court is always concerned to implement the intentions of the parties as they appear from statements made by them. Where in a contract the parties have indicated that a particular undertaking is to be a term of the contract, the courts will in general abide by the wishes of the parties. However, the court will not slavishly follow the parties' statements and where, for example, the parties appear to have regarded a trivial matter as a vital term of the agreement, the court may still take the view that it is not.

Thus so far as a written contract is concerned, the court may disregard a statement by the parties that a particular undertaking is a condition and say instead that it is a warranty. So far as wholly oral contracts are concerned, the court may ignore the statements of the parties and decide that a particular undertaking is a condition, a warranty, or a mere inducement.

Thus in *L. Schuler A.G.* v *Wickham Machine Tool Sales* [1973] 2 All E.R. 39, the plaintiffs entered into a contract for four years with the defendants giving them the sole right to sell panel presses in England. A clause of the contract provided that it should be a condition of the agreement that the defendants' representative should visit six named firms each week to solicit orders. The defendants' representatives failed on a few occasions to do so and the plaintiffs claimed to be entitled to repudiate the agreement on the basis that a single failure was a breach of condition giving them an absolute right to treat the contract as at an end. The House of Lords said that such minor breaches by the defendants did not entitle the plaintiffs to repudiate. The House of Lords construed the clause on the basis that it was so unreasonable that the parties could not have intended it as a condition, giving Schuler a right of repudiation but rather as a warranty. Thus Schuler were themselves in breach of contract leaving Wickham with a claim for damages against Schuler.

This case is also an example of the court trying to give redress in regard to an unconscionable bargain and to correct unscrupulous commercial conduct.

So in modern law there are terms which the parties call conditions and where the breach has *in fact* had a serious result on the contract. The court will then agree that the breach should be treated as a breach of condition and the contract can be repudiated. There are also terms which the parties call warranties and where the breach has *in fact* not been serious. The court will then agree that the breach shall be treated as a breach of warranty and the contract cannot be repudiated. The parties must go on with it though the person injured by the breach has an action for damages.

In addition there are what are called *intermediate terms* which the parties may have called conditions or warranties. The effect of these on the contract will depend upon how serious the breach has turned out to be *in fact*. If the breach has turned out to be serious the court will then treat the term as a condition, even if called a warranty by the parties, so that the contract can be repudiated. If *in fact* the breach has not had a serious effect on the contract the court will treat it as a breach of warranty, even if called a condition by the parties, so that the parties must proceed with the contract, though the injured party will have an action for damages. (*Cehave NV* v *Bremer Handelsgesellschaft mbH* 1975.) (See p. 496.)

(2) A statement is likely to be an inducement rather than a term if the person making the statement asks the other party to check or verify it, e.g. 'The car is sound but I should get an engineer's report on it.'

(3) A statement is likely to be a term rather than a mere inducement if it is made with intention of preventing the other party from looking for defects and succeeds in doing this, e.g. 'The car is sound, you need not look it over.'

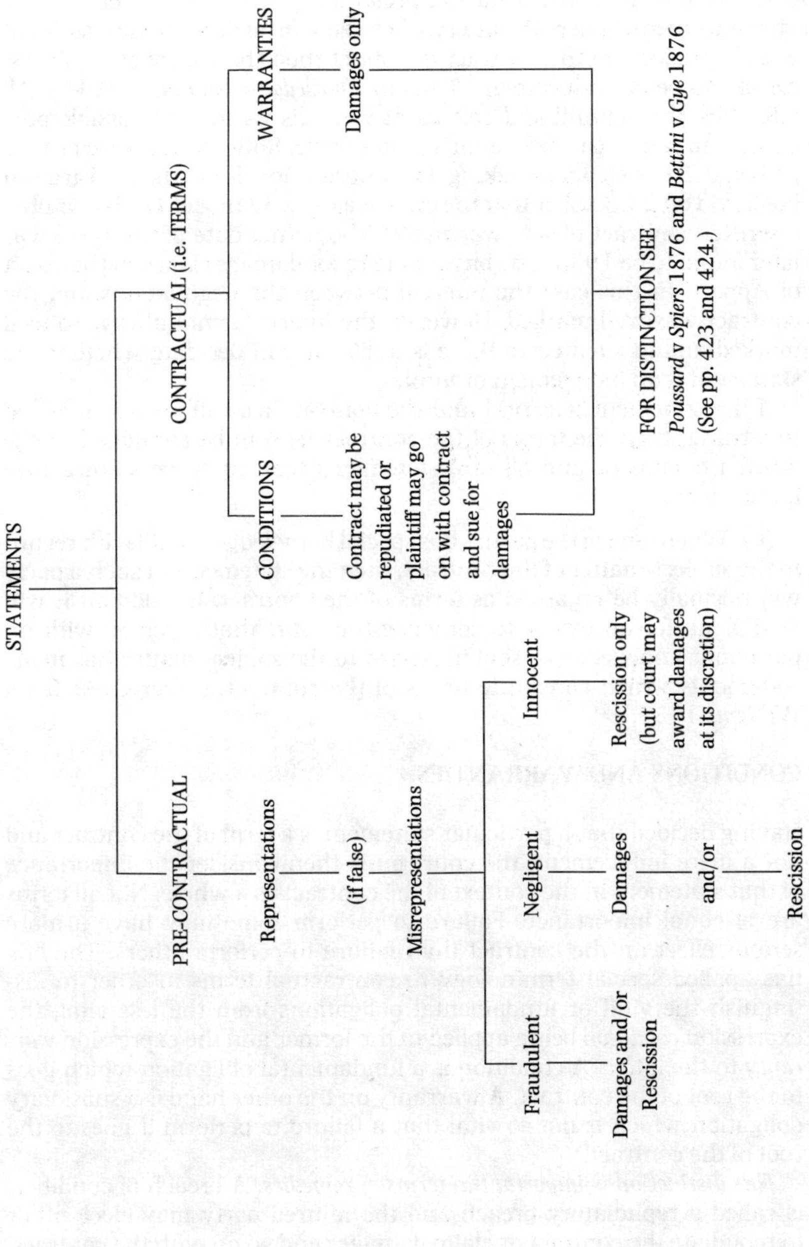
STATEMENTS
CONTRACTUAL (i.e. TERMS)
CONDITIONS
Contract may be repudiated or plaintiff may go on with contract and sue for damages
WARRANTIES
Damages only
FOR DISTINCTION SEE
Poussard v Spiers 1876 and Bettini v Gye 1876
(See pp. 423 and 424.)
PRE-CONTRACTUAL
Representations
(if false)
Misrepresentations
Fraudulent
Damages and/or Rescission
Negligent
Damages
and/or
Rescission
Innocent
Rescission only (but court may award damages at its discretion)

(4) If the statement is such that the plaintiff would not have made the contract without it, then the statement will be a term of the contract and not a mere inducement. (*Bannerman* v *White* 1861.)[130]

(5) A statement made during preliminary negotiations tends to be an inducement. Where the interval between the making of the statement and the making of the contract is distinct then the statement is almost certain to be an inducement. Thus in *Routledge* v *McKay* [1954] 1 All E.R. 855, the plaintiff and defendant were discussing the possible purchase and sale of the defendant's motor cycle. Both parties were private persons. The defendant taking the information from the registration book said on 23 October that the cycle was a 1942 model. On 30 October a written contract of sale was made. The actual date of the cycle was later found to be 1930. The buyer's claim for damages failed in the Court of Appeal. In this case the interval between the negotiations and the contract was well marked. However, the interval is not always so well marked and in such cases there is a difficulty in deciding whether the statement is an inducement or term.

If the statement was oral and the contract was afterwards reduced to writing, then the terms of the contract tend to be contained in the written document and all oral statements tend to be pre-contractual inducements.

(6) Where one of the parties has special knowledge or skill with regard to the subject-matter of the contract, then the statements of such a party will normally be regarded as terms of the contract. In addition it will be difficult for an expert to convince the court that a person with no particular knowledge or skill in regard to the subject-matter has made statements which constitute terms of the contract. (*Oscar Chess Ltd* v *Williams* 1957.)[131]

CONDITIONS AND WARRANTIES

Having decided that a particular statement is a term of the contract and not a mere inducement, the court must then consider the importance of that statement in the context of the contract as a whole. Not all terms are of equal importance. Failure to perform some may have a more serious effect on the contract than failure to perform others. The law has applied special terminology to contractual terms in order to distinguish the vital or fundamental obligations from the less vital, the expression *condition* being applied to the former and the expression *warranty* to the latter. A condition is a fundamental obligation which goes to the root of the contract. A warranty on the other hand is a subsidiary obligation which is not so vital that a failure to perform it goes to the root of the contract.

This distinction is important in terms of remedies. A breach of condition is called a repudiatory breach and the injured party may elect either to repudiate the contract or claim damages and go on with the contract.

It should be noted that the plaintiff must go on with the contract and sue for damages if he has affirmed the contract after knowledge of a breach of condition. He may do this expressly as where he uses the goods, or by lapse of time as where he simply fails to take any steps to complain about the breach for what in the court's view is an unreasonable period of time. A breach of warranty is not repudiatory and the plaintiff must go on with the contract and sue for damages.

Whether a term is a condition or warranty is basically a matter for the court which will be decided on the basis of the commercial importance of the term. As we have seen, the words used by the parties are, of course, relevant, but are not followed slavishly by the court which may still decide differently from the parties on the basis of the commercial importance of the term. An interesting contrast is provided in *Poussard* v *Spiers and Pond* 1876[132] and *Bettini* v *Gye* 1876.[133]

IMPLIED TERMS

Before leaving the topic of the contents of the contract it must be appreciated that in addition to the express terms inserted by the parties, the contract may contain and be subject to implied terms. Such terms are derived from custom or statute and in addition a term may be implied by the court where it is necessary in order to achieve the result which in the court's view the parties obviously intended the contract to have.

CUSTOMARY IMPLIED TERMS

A contract may be subjected to customary terms not specifically mentioned by the parties. (*Hutton* v *Warren* 1836.)[134]

STATUTORY IMPLIED TERMS

In a contract for the sale of goods or hire purchase the Sale of Goods Act 1979 and the Supply of Goods (Implied Terms) Act 1973, ss.8–11 (as amended by Sch. 4, Part I, para, 35 to the Consumer Credit Act 1974, and s.17 of the Supply of Goods and Services Act 1982) deal with the matter of implied terms. These Acts are considered in Chapters 3 and 4.

JUDICIAL IMPLIED TERMS

The court may imply a term into a contract whenever it is necessary to do so in order that the express terms decided upon by the parties shall have the effect which was presumably intended by them. This is often expressed as the giving of 'business efficacy' to the contract, the judge regarding himself as doing merely what the parties themselves would *in fact* have done in order to cover the situation if they had addressed themselves to it. The operation of the doctrine is illustrated by *The Moorcock* 1889.[135]

Sometimes, however, the courts imply a term which is quite complex so that the parties would not, *in fact*, have addressed themselves to it. Here the judge is saying *as a matter of law* how the contract should be performed. This is illustrated by *Liverpool City Council* v *Irwin* [1977] A.C. 239, where the House of Lords held that it was an implied term of a lease of a masionette in a block of properties owned by the Council that the landlord should take reasonable care to keep the common parts of the block in a reasonable state of repair, although the obligation to do so would *not* have been accepted by the landlord.

When *Irwin*'s case was in the Court of Appeal, Lord Denning, in deciding that there should be an implied term regarding maintenance, rejected the business efficacy test as the only test, saying that the Court could imply a term whenever it was *just and reasonable* to do so, whether or not the term was strictly *necessary* to the performance of the contract or not. Although the House of Lords implied a term relating to maintenance, they did not go along with the view of Lord Denning that the test should be reasonableness regardless of necessity. The Court of Appeal returned to the 'necessary' approach in *Mears* v *Safecar Security* [1982] 2 All E.R. 865 and refused to imply a term into a contract of service that payment should be made to an employee during sickness. Stephenson, L.J., was of opinion that the term could not be implied because, although it might be *reasonable* to imply a term relating to sick-pay, it was not *necessary* in a contract of employment. The term relating to maintenance in *Irwin* was in a sense not absolutely vital to performance of the contract in that the tenants could have walked up the stairs, even in the dark, to their flats if lift and light maintenance had not be carried out, but it was much closer to being necessary to performance of the contract than was the sick-pay term in *Mears*.

Exclusion clauses

A contract may contain express terms under which one or both of the parties excludes or limits liability for breach of contract or negligence. Although such express terms are permissible, both the courts and Parliament have been reluctant to allow exclusion clauses where they have been imposed on a weaker party, such as an ordinary consumer, by a stronger party, such as a person or corporation in business to supply goods or services.

THE ATTITUDE OF THE COURTS

The judges have protected consumers of goods and services against the effect of exclusion clauses in two main ways, i.e. by deciding that the exclusion clause never became part of the contract, and by construing (or interpreting) the contract in such a way as to prevent the application of the clause.

WAS THE CLAUSE PART OF THE CONTRACT?

The court will require the person wishing to rely on an exclusion clause to show that the other party agreed to it at or before the time when the contract was made, otherwise it will not form part of the agreement. In this connection—

(1) *Where a contract is made by signing a written document* the signer will in general be bound by everything which the document contains, even if he has not read it (*L'Estrange* v *Graucob* 1934),[136] unless the signature was induced by misrepresentation as to the effect of the document. (*Curtis* v *Chemical Cleaning and Dyeing Co.* 1951.)[137]

(2) *Where the terms are contained in an unsigned document*, the person seeking to rely on an exclusion clause must show that the document was an integral part of the contract which could be expected to contain terms. (*Chapelton* v *Barry U.D.C.* 1940.)[138] However, if the document is contractual in the sense outlined above the clause will apply even though the plaintiff did not actually know about the exclusion clause in the sense that he had not read it. Communication may be constructive so long as the document adequately draws the attention of a reasonable person to the existence of terms and conditions. (*Thompson* v *L.M.S. Railway* 1930.)[139]

(3) *As regards previous dealings*, where the defendant has not actually given the plaintiff a copy of conditions or drawn his attention to them when making a particular contract, the doctrine of constructive notice will not apply, at least in consumer transactions, in order to enable the defendant to rely on previous communications in previous dealings. Thus in *Hollier* v *Rambler Motors* [1972] 1 All E.R. 399, it appeared that the plaintiff had had his car repaired a number of times by the defendants and had signed a form containing a clause stating 'the company is not responsible for damage caused by fire to customers' cars on the premises'. On the occasion in question the plaintiff was not required to sign a form when leaving his car for repair. In the event the car was damaged by fire caused by the defendants' negligence. In an action by the plaintiff the defendants pleaded the clause. It was held by the Court of Appeal that the plaintiff succeeded and that the clause did not apply. Previous dealings were not incorporated and in any case as a matter of construction the wording was not sufficiently plain to exclude negligence. However, where the parties are, for example, large corporations, terms used in previous dealings between the parties themselves *or in the trade generally* may be incorporated. Thus in *British Crane Hire Corporation Ltd* v *Ipswich Plant Hire Ltd* [1974] 1 All E.R. 1059, the defendants hired a crane from the plaintiffs who were the owners.

The agreement was an oral one, though after the contract was made the defendants received a printed form from the plaintiffs containing conditions. One of these was that the hirer of the crane was liable to indemnify the owner against all expenses in connection with its use. Before the defendants signed the form the crane sank into marshy ground, though this was not the fault of the defendants. The plaintiffs were put to some cost in repairing the crane and now sued the defendants for an indemnity under the contract. The defendants argued that the indemnity had not been incorporated into the oral contract of hire. It was held that the bargaining power of the defendants was equal to that of the plaintiffs and the defendants knew that printed conditions in similar terms to those of the plaintiffs were *in common use in the business*. The conditions had therefore been incorporated into the oral contract on the basis of the common understanding of the parties and the plaintiffs' claim for an indemnity succeeded.

(4) Any attempt to introduce an exclusion clause *after* the contract has been made is ineffective because the consideration for the clause is then past. (*Olley* v *Marlborough Court Ltd* 1949.)[140]

(5) The doctrine of privity of contract may also prevent the application of an exclusion clause. Thus, if A, the owner of a road haulage company, excludes his own and his employees' liability for damage to the goods of his business customers by a properly communicated clause, an employee who causes damage to the goods will be liable, although his employer will not be provided the clause is reasonable under the Unfair Contract Terms Act 1977, because the employee has not supplied consideration for the contract which is between his employer and the customers.

CONSTRUCTION OF EXCLUSION CLAUSES

Rules of construction (i.e. interpretation) of contract may, when applied, prevent the application of an exclusion clause. The major rules of construction are as follows—

(1) *The contra proferentem rule.* Under this rule if there is any ambiguity or room for doubt as to the meaning of an exclusion clause the courts will construe it in a way unfavourable to the person who put it into the contract. An example of the application of this rule is to be seen in *Hollier* v *Rambler Motors* (above) because the Court of Appeal, having decided that previous dealings were not incorporated, went on to use the rule by saying that the wording in the form was not sufficiently plain to exclude negligence. That ambiguity had therefore to be construed against the defendants who put it into the contract. (And see also *Alexander* v *Railway Executive* 1951.)[144]

(2) *The repugnancy rule.* This rule says in effect that the exemption clause is in direct contradiction to another term of the contract and is

therefore repugnant to it. Where such repugnancy exists the exemption clause can be struck out. Thus, if A makes a contract to supply oranges to B but includes a clause which allows him to supply any sort of fruit, the clause is repugnant to the main purpose of the contract and could be struck out. Thus, A would be liable in breach of contract if he supplied B with apples and could not rely on the clause to excuse his breach of contract. (See also *Evans* v *Merzario* 1976.)[141]

(3) *The four corners rule.* Under this rule exemption clauses only protect a party when he is acting within the four corners of the contract. Thus he is liable for damage which occurs while he is deviating from the contract and he would not be protected by the exclusion clause. (See *Thomas National Transport (Melbourne) Pty Ltd* v *May and Baker* 1966.)[142]

THE DOCTRINE OF FUNDAMENTAL BREACH

This doctrine was usually invoked where a plaintiff sought a remedy on a contract containing exemption clauses which had been adequately communicated. The doctrine said, in effect, that where one party had fundamentally broken his contract, that is, done something fundamentally different from what he contracted to do, an exclusion clause could not protect him, and that this was a *rule of law* and *not a rule of construction*, so that the court had no discretion in the matter. Examples of the application of the doctrine are to be found in *Karsales (Harrow) Ltd* v *Wallis* 1956[143] and *Alexander* v *The Railway Executive* 1951.[144]

Difficulties arose over the meaning of a fundamental breach and attempts were made to distinguish it from a condition (or repudiatory breach) so that an exemption clause excluding liability for breach of condition would be ineffective to exclude liability for fundamental breach.

The House of Lords had decided in the *Suisse Case* 1966[145] that there was *no rule of law* by which exclusion clauses had become inapplicable to exclude liability for a fundamental breach of contract, though the House or Lords agreed that the rules of construction of contract, already referred to, might prevent an exclusion clause from operating. This position was reaffirmed by the House of Lords in *Photo Production Ltd* v *Securicor Transport Ltd* 1980.[146]

The effect of this decision is, broadly speaking, as follows—

(1) *Non-consumer transactions.* Where the parties to a contract are of equal bargaining power, as in the *Photo Production Case*, then an exclusion clause, if appropriately worded, can exclude liability for a fundamental breach, though Viscount Dilhorne said in the *Suisse Case* that any provision that intends to give exemption from the consequences of a fundamental breach must be expressed in clear and unambiguous terms.

(2) *Consumer transactions and contracts based on standard terms.* Here

the Unfair Contract Terms Act of 1977 applies and exclusion clauses can only operate if it is just and reasonable to let them do so, and, indeed, certain terms implied into contracts of sale and hire purchase cannot be excluded at all in consumer transactions. (See further p. 55.)

As we have seen, the House of Lords has stated on a number of occasions that the rules of construction of contracts may be used legitimately to prevent an exclusion clause operating. Thus—

(*a*) Under the *contra proferentem* rule exclusion clauses are read strictly against those wishing to rely on them. The application of this rule would provide an alternative way of arriving at the decision in *Alexander* v *Railway Executive* 1951.[144]

(*b*) A court will strike out or modify an exemption clause which is repugnant to the main purpose of the contract. The application of this rule would provide an alternative way of arriving at the decision in *Karsales (Harrow) Ltd* v *Wallis* 1956.[143]

THE APPROACH OF PARLIAMENT TO EXCLUSION CLAUSES

Parliament has tried to prevent the widespread use of exclusion clauses by the passing of various statutes, the main one being the Unfair Contract Terms Act 1977.

The strongest protection is given by the Act to persons who deal as consumers (C), though those dealing otherwise than as consumers, e.g. where the goods are bought for use in a business, are covered. To be a consumer one must be dealing as a *private buyer* with a *person in business* (B). Thus a contract between a *private buyer* and a *private seller* is not a consumer deal.

CLAUSES RENDERED INEFFECTIVE BY THE UNFAIR CONTRACT TERMS ACT

These are as follows—

(1) Any exclusion clause contained in a contract or notice by which B tries to exclude or restrict his liability for death or personal injury resulting from negligence is wholly ineffective (ss.2 and 5).

(2) A manufacturer's guarantee cannot exclude or restrict the manufacturer's liability for loss or damage arising from defects in goods if used by a consumer which results from negligence in manufacture or distribution (s.5).

The section is concerned with actions either in negligence or on the collateral contract which the guarantee can create, against the manufacturer who is not the seller of the goods to the customer. The section is not concerned with a contractual relationship between the seller and the customer which is covered by ss.6 and 7. Thus a manufacturer's 12-month guarantee which said that the goods would, if defective, be replaced or repaired free of charge but ended with a phrase such as: 'This guarantee is in lieu of, and expressly excludes, all liability to compensate for loss or damage howsoever caused' would not prevent a claim by the purchaser against the manufacturer if he/she was electrocuted by the cleaner (see *Donaghue* v *Stevenson* 1932, p. 506) or possibly for defective performance not causing physical injury. (See *Junior Books Ltd* v *Veitchi Co Ltd* 1982. (See p. 506.)

(3) A clause under which B tries to exclude his liability, whether by guarantee or otherwise, to C for breach of the implied terms in the Sale of Goods Act 1979 (on a sale) or the Supply of Goods (Implied Terms) Act 1973 (as amended) (on a hire-purchase transaction), e.g. that the goods are fit for the purpose or of merchantable quality, is wholly ineffective, as is a clause which tries to exclude against the consumer the implied terms in the Supply of Goods and Services Act 1982 in a contract of pure hiring, e.g. of a car, or a contract for work and materials, as in the repair of a car (ss.6(2) and 7(2)).

Section 6 also applies to non-business liability. However, since the implied terms requiring merchantable quality and fitness for the purpose do not apply to non-business transactions, only s.13 (sale by description) can be implied. However, s.13 cannot be excluded in a non-business transaction with a consumer.

(4) The Consumer Safety Act 1978 makes it a criminal offence to market goods which do not comply with safety requirements imposed by regulations under the Act. Sometimes regulations only affect the manufacturer, e.g. those which are concerned with design. Other regulations may affect the manufacturer, the wholesaler, and the retailer, e.g. those which require safety information to be supplied with the goods. If a trader, whether a manufacturer, wholesaler, or retailer, infringes any of the regulations *provided that they apply to him* and causes damage or loss to a consumer by reason of the infringement, that person may sue for damages. It is not necessary to prove negligence. An action may be brought directly against the manufacturer even though the goods were not bought from him and even though the goods were not bought at all by the person injured, as where they were received as a gift. An exclusion clause which tries to exclude or restrict this liability is void (s.6(2), Consumer Safety Act 1978).

EXCLUSION CLAUSES APPLICABLE IF REASONABLE

These are as follows—

(1) Any clause by which B tries to exclude or restrict his liability for loss arising from negligence other than death or personal injury (s.2(2)).

Section 2(2) came up for consideration in two County Court cases which were brought under the Act. in *Woodman* v *Photo Trade Processing Ltd*, heard in the Exeter County Court in May 1981, Mr Woodman took to the Exeter branch of Dixons Photographic for processing a film which carried pictures of a friend's wedding. The film was of special value because Mr Woodman had been the only photographer at the wedding, and he had said he would give the pictures as a wedding present. Unfortunately, the film was lost and when Dixons were sued they relied on an exclusion clause which, it appeared was standard practice throughout the trade and had been communicated. The clause read as follows: 'All photographic materials are accepted on the basis that their value does not exceed the loss of the material itself. Responsibility is limited to the replacement of film. No liability will be accepted consequential or otherwise, however caused'. His Honour Judge Clarke found in the County Court that the customer had no real alternative but to entrust his film to a firm that would use such an exclusion clause and that, furthermore, Dixons could have foreseen that the film might be irreplaceable and although they could argue that the exclusion clause enabled them to operate a cheap mass-production technique, it could not be regarded as reasonable that all persons, regardless of the value of their film, should be required to take their chance of the system losing them. The judge therefore granted compensation of £75 to Mr Woodman and held that the exclusion clause was unreasonable.

In *Waldron-Kelly* v *British Railways Board*, which was heard in the Stockport County Court in 1981, the plaintiff delivered a suitcase to Stockport railway station so that it could be taken to Haverfordwest station. The contract of carriage was subject to the British Railways Board general conditions 'at owner's risk' for a price of £6.00. A clause exempted the Board from any loss, except that if a case disappeared then the Board's liability was to be assessed by reference to the weight of the goods, which in this case was £27.00 and not to their value, which in this case was £320.00. The suitcase was lost whilst it was in the control of British Rail. In the County Court Judge Brown *held* that the plaintiff succeeded in his contention that the exclusion clause was unreasonable and therefore of no effect. The judge held that in the case of non-delivery of goods the burden of proof to show what had happened to the goods was on the bailee. British Rail had failed to show that the loss was not their fault, and in any case the fault and loss were not covered by the exclusion clause because it did not satisfy the test of reasonableness.

Where there is no contract, as in the *Hedley Byrne*[120] situation where a bank used a 'without responsibility' disclaimer, s.2(2) of the Act applies the reasonable test to the disclaimer.

(2) Any clause by which B tries to exclude or restrict his liability to a non-consumer for breach of the implied terms in the Sale of Goods Act 1979, the Supply of Goods (Implied Terms) Act 1973, and the Supply of Goods and Services Act 1982 relating, e.g. to contracts of hiring and work and materials (s.6(3) and 7(3)). (*Mitchell (George)* v *Finney Lock Seeds Ltd* 1983.)[147]

(3) Any clause by which B tries to exclude his liability for breach of contract if the contract is with a consumer or, in the case of a non-consumer contract, the agreement is on B's written standard terms

(s.3(1) and (2)(*a*)).

There is no definition of 'written standard terms' in the 1977 Act but it obviously covers cases in which the seller requires that all (or nearly all) of his customers purchase goods on the same terms with no variation from one contract to another.

This section applies also to cases where the clause purports to allow B to render a substantially different performance, as where a tour operator tries to reserve the right to vary the accommodation or itinerary or reserves the right to render no performance at all (s.3(2)(*b*)).

(4) As regards *indemnity clauses in consumer transactions*, B may agree to do work for C only if C will indemnify B against any liability which B may incur during performance of the contract, e.g. an injury to X caused by B's work (s.4). B may, for example, be a builder who takes an indemnity from C, the owner of a property on which B is to do work in regard to any injuries which B's work might cause to third parties. Such an indemnity will be unenforceable by B unless reasonable. Such clauses are unlikely to be found reasonable and B will have to cover himself by insurance. The section does not cover non-consumer situations and the indemnity found in *British Crane Hire* (see p. 51) would still be enforceable.

(5) Any clause purporting to exclude liability for misrepresentation applies only if reasonable, whether the transaction is with C or a non-consumer. (S.3, Misrepresentation Act 1967, as substituted by s.8(1) of the Unfair Contract Terms Act 1977.) Thus an estate agent would not be able to exclude his liability for falsely representing the state of a house unless the court felt that it was reasonable for the agent to exclude his liability, as it might be if the property was very old and there had been no survey. (And see *Walker* v *Boyle* 1982.)[148]

Section 3 also applies to non-business liability. A private seller cannot exclude his liability for misrepresentation unless he can show that the exclusion clause concerned satisfied the test of reasonableness.

REASONABLENESS—THE BURDEN OF PROOF

The burden of proving that the clause is reasonable lies upon the party claiming that it is—usually B, the person in business. (S.11(5).)

REASONABLENESS—MEANING OF

Although the matter is basically one for the judge, the following guidelines appear in the 1977 Act—

(1) The matter of reasonableness must be decided on the circumstances as they were when the contract was made. (S.11(1).)

(2) Where a clause limits the amount payable regard must be had

to the resources of the person who included the clause and the extent to which it was possible for him to cover himself by insurance. (S.11(4).)

The object of this rule is to encourage companies to insure against liability in the sense that failure to do so will go against them if any exclusion clause which they have is before the court. However, in some cases it may be right to allow limitation of liability, e.g. in the case of professional persons such as accountants where monetary loss may be caused to an horrendous amount following negligence and be beyond their power to insure against.

(3) Where the contract is for the supply of goods, i.e. under a contract of sale, hire purchase, hiring, or work and materials, the criteria of reasonableness are laid down by s.11(2) and Sch.2 of the 1977 Act. They are—

(*a*) Strength of the bargaining position of the parties. Thus if one party is in a strong position and the other in a weaker in terms of bargaining power, the stronger party may not be allowed to retain an exclusion clause in the contract.

(*b*) Availability of other supplies. Again, if a seller is in a monopolistic position so that it is not possible for the buyer to find the goods readily elsewhere, the court may decide that an exclusion clause in the contract of a monopolistic seller shall not apply.

(*c*) Inducements to agree to the clause. If the goods have been offered for sale at £10 without an exemption clause but at £8 with the inclusion of the clause, the court may see fit to allow the clause to apply at the lower price because there has been a concession by the seller in terms of the price.

(*d*) Buyer's knowledge of the extent of the clause. If the clause had been pointed out to the buyer and he is fully aware that it reduces the liability of the seller, then this will be relevant in deciding whether the seller should be allowed to rely on the clause. If a buyer is reasonably fully informed and aware of the seller's intentions as regards exclusion of liability, then the buyer may have to accept the clause.

(*e*) Customs of trade and previous dealings. If, for example, exclusion clauses are usual in the trade or have been used by the parties in previous dealings, then the court may decide that an exclusion clause should apply. It should be noted that previous dealings do not seem relevant in consumer transactions but they are in this area where one is considering a non-consumer situation.

(*f*) Whether the goods have been made, processed or adapted to the order of the buyer. Obviously if the seller has been required by the buyer to produce goods in a certain way, then it may well be fair and reasonable for the seller to exclude his liability in respect of faults arising out of, for example, the buyer's design which he insisted was used.

Although the above criteria are strictly speaking confined to exclusion of statutory implied terms in, e.g. the Sale of Goods Act 1979, they are being applied in other situations. For example, Judge Clark in *Woodman* felt it was right to use them where what was at issue was a negligent service. The Supply of Goods and Services Act 1982 has not changed the law regarding the exclusion of liability of a supplier of services. Services are not specifically mentioned in the 1977 Act but they fall within the ambit of ss.2 and 3 which deal with negligence and breach of contract respectively.

PROVISIONS AGAINST EVASION

If an attempt is made to exclude or restrict liability in contract X by a clause in a secondary contract Y, then the clause in Y is ineffective (s.10).

For example, C buys a television set from B. There is an associated maintenance contract. The sale of a television would be within s.6 of the 1977 Act and so there could be no exclusion of B's implied obligations. Any attempt to exclude or restrict these obligations in the maintenance contract would also fail. If the transactions was a non-consumer one the 'reasonable' test would have to be applied.

Nor can the Act be excluded by a clause which states that the contract is to be governed by the law of another country which does not outlaw exclusion clauses, at least if it is part of an evasion scheme, or if the contract is with a United Kingdom consumer and the main steps in the making of the contract took palce in the UK. (S.27.)

The Act does not apply to insurance contracts, nor to contracts for the transfer of an interest in land. (S.1(2) and Sch.1, para. 1(*a*) and (*b*).) House purchase is therefore excluded. Nor does it apply to certain contracts involving the supply of goods on an international basis because these are covered by conventions. Furthermore, it should be noted that a written arbitration agreement will not be treated as excluding or restricting liability for the purposes of the 1977 Act and such an agreement is valid. (S.13(2).)

Fair Trading Act 1973. Under s.13 of this Act the Director-General of Fair Trading can in the course of investigating consumer trade practices deal in particular with 'terms and conditions on which or subject to which goods or services are supplied'. This, of course, concerns exemption clauses being used in consumer transactions. If after investigation the Director-General feels that a particular practice in terms of exemption clauses should cease he will make a report to the Minister who may pass a statutory instrument to stop the practice. For example, the Consumer Transactions (Restrictions on Statements) Order 1976 (No. 1813) as amended by S.I. 1978/127 makes it a criminal offence to sell or supply goods and purport that the implied terms in sale of goods and hire-purchase legislation can be excluded in a consumer sale since this might suggest to the customer that he has no rights so that he will not bother to try to enforce them.

Contracts and public policy

Freedom of contract must always be subject to overriding considerations of public policy. Public policy has been ascertained as follows—

(1) **At common law by the judiciary.** At one time the judiciary had wide powers of discretion in the matter of creating new categories of public policy but this view is now unacceptable. In *Fender* v *Mildmay* [1938] A.C.1, the House of Lords declared against the extension of the heads of public policy, at least by the judiciary. However, up to 1938 the judiciary had created a number of categories of public policy. These fell into two areas as follows—

(*a*) *Illegal contracts.* These involve some degree of moral wrong, and contracts to commit crimes or to defraud the Inland Revenue fall into this category.

(*b*) *Void contracts.* In these cases there is not in any strict sense blameworthy conduct but the contracts are rendered void because if enforced by the courts they could produce unsatisfactory results on society. Examples are contracts in restraint of trade, e.g. an agreement under which an employee covenants with his employer that on the termination of his contract he will not work for a rival firm or start a competing business, and contracts prejudicial to marriage, e.g. a contract under which a person promises not to marry at all.

(2) **By Parliament.** Parliament expresses its view as to what is public policy by Acts of Parliament and rules and orders made by ministers under Acts of Parliament. Again, statute law in this area falls into two categories as follows—

(*a*) *The creation of illegal contracts.* This happens where the Act of Parliament actually makes the contract *unlawful.* Thus s.1 of the Resale Prices Act 1976 declares unlawful all agreements between suppliers of goods to, e.g. withhold supplies of those goods from retailers who sell below the minimum resale price agreed by the suppliers.

(*b*) The creation of void contracts. Here there is no suggestion that the contract is unlawful in the strict sense or that moral blame attaches. There are two main areas as follows—

(i) wagering contracts, which will be dealt with later; and

(ii) the prevention of restrictive practices. Thus agreements by suppliers to fix prices or restrict supplies are void under the Restrictive Trade Practices Act 1976 unless the parties can prove to the Restrictive Practices Court that their agreement is beneficial and in the public interest.

PUBLIC POLICY—THE CONTRIBUTION OF THE JUDICIARY

Illegal contracts

These contracts involve some form of moral weakness which society in general seeks to control. They are as follows—

(1) *Contracts to commit crimes* (*see Dann* v *Curzon* 1911)[149] *or civil wrongs.* Thus a contract between an agent and his client whereby the agent was to receive a double commission would be illegal because it has as its object the commission of a fraud on the principal, since if the agent takes a double commission there is a conflict of interest.

(2) *Contracts involving sexual immorality.* Agreements for future illicit cohabitation are void, because the promise of payment might encourage immoral conduct in a person who otherwise would not have participated. However, a contract under which a person promises to pay another money in return for past illicit cohabitation is not illegal because it does not necessarily encourage future immorality between the parties. Such a contract will, however, be unenforceable unless made under seal because it is for past consideration. Furthermore, contracts which are on the face of it legal may be affected if *knowingly* made to further an immoral purpose. (*Pearce* v *Brooks* 1886.)[150]

(3) *Agreements hostile to a friendly nation.* This category includes contracts to carry out acts which are illegal by the law of a foreign and friendly country, since to enforce such contracts would encourage disputes. Thus in *Foster* v *Driscoll* [1929] 1 K.B. 470 a contract to smuggle whisky into the United States when prohibition was in force there was *held* illegal.

(4) *Contracts prejudicial to the administration of justice.* Thus, a contract tending to defeat the bankruptcy laws is illegal at common law. (See *John* v *Mendoza* 1939.)[151]

(5) *Contracts tending to corruption in public life.* A contract to procure a title of honour is illegal under this head. (See *Parkinson* v *College of Ambulance* 1952.)[152]

(6) *Contracts to defraud the Revenue.* This applies whether the fraud is in connection with local rates or national taxes. (See *Napier* v *National Business Agency Ltd* 1951.)[153]

Consequences

The consequences of illegality in the above cases depends upon whether the contract was unlawful on the face of it, i.e. there was no way in which lawful performance could be achieved, or whether the contract was lawful on the face of it, i.e. it could have been performed in a lawful manner.

(1) *Contract unlawful on face of it.* This includes all the categories mentioned above except some contracts involving sexual immorality. The consequences in this case are as follows—

(*a*) The contract is void and there is no action by either party for debt (*Dann* v *Curzon* 1911),[149] damages, specific performance or injunction.

(*b*) Money paid or property transferred to the other party under the contract is irrecoverable. (*Parkinson* v *College of Ambulance* 1925.)[152] Unless—

(i) The plaintiff is relying on rights other than those which are contained in the contract. Thus if A leases property to B for five years and A knows that B intends to use the property as a brothel, then A cannot recover rent or require any covenant to be performed without pleading the illegal lease. However, at the end of the term A can bring an action for the return of his property as *owner* and not as a landlord under an illegal lease. (See also *Bowmakers Ltd* v *Barnet Instruments Ltd* 1944.)[154]

(ii) The plaintiff is not in *pari delicto* (equal wrong). Where the contract is unlawful on the face of it, equal guilt is presumed but this presumption may be rebutted if the plaintiff can show that the defendant was guilty of fraud, oppression or undue influence. (See *Atkinson* v *Denby* 1862.)[155]

(iii) The plaintiff repents provided that the repentance is genuine (*Bigos* v *Bousted* 1951)[156] and performance is *partial* (*Taylor* v *Bowers* 1876)[157] and not *substantial* (*Kearley* v *Thomson* 1890).[158]

(2) *Contract lawful on face of it.* The result here is as follows—

(*a*) Where both parties intended the illegal purpose. There is no action by either party for debt, damages *specific performance or injunction* (*Pearce* v *Brooks* 1886)[150] or to recover money paid or property transferred under the contract.

(*b*) Where one party was without knowledge of the illegal purpose. The innocent party's rights are unaffected and he may sue for debt, damages, specific performance, or injunction, or to recover money paid or property transferred. Thus in *Clay* v *Yates* (1856) 1 H.&N. 73 it was held that a printer who had innocently printed libellous matter could recover his charges.

PUBLIC POLICY AND THE JUDICIARY—VOID CONTRACTS

These contracts do not involve any type of moral weakness but are against public policy because they are inexpedient rather than unprincipled. The contracts concerned are contracts to oust the jurisdiction of the courts, contracts prejudicial to the status of marriage, and contracts in restraint of trade. These are dealt with individually below.

CONTRACTS TO OUST THE JURISDICTION OF THE COURTS

A contract which has the effect of taking away the right of one or both of the parties to bring an action before a court of law is void. (*Re Davstone*

Estates Ltd 1969.)[159] This rule does not make void honourable pledge clauses (see, e.g. *Rose and Frank* v *Crompton Bros* 1925)[57] because in such cases the parties do not intend to be bound by the contract at all. If the contract is to be binding, however, then the parties cannot exclude it from the jurisdiction of the courts. Furthermore, arbitration clauses are not affected. Many commercial contracts contain an arbitration clause, the object being to provide a cheaper or more convenient remedy than a court action. An arbitration clause in a contract is not void if the effect of it is that the parties are to go to arbitration *first* before going to court. An arbitration clause which denies the parties access to the courts completely is, of course, invalid.

CONTRACTS PREJUDICIAL TO THE STATUS OF MARRIAGE

A contract in absolute restraint of marriage, i.e. one in which a person promises not to marry at all, is void. Partial restraints, if reasonable, are said to be valid, e.g. a contract not to marry a person of certain religious faith, or not to marry for a short period of time. However, there are no recent cases and it may be that even a partial restraint would be regarded as void today. Marriage brokage contracts, i.e. contracts to introduce men and women with a view to their subsequent marriage, are also void on the grounds that third parties should not be free to reap financial profit by bringing about matrimonial unions. As regards separation agreements, these are invalid if made for the future, as where a husband promises that he will make provision for his wife if she should ever live apart from him, unless the agreement is made as part of a reconciliation arrangement. In this case the agreement is valid, although it may make provision for a renewed future separation. If the parties are not living in amity or are actually separated, then a separation agreement is valid. Once it is apparent that the parties cannot live together in amity it is desirable that a separation which has become inevitable should be concluded upon reasonable terms.

CONTRACTS IN RESTRAINT OF TRADE—GENERALLY

Such contracts are *prima facie* void and will only be binding if reasonable. Thus the contract must be reasonable between the parties which means that it must be no wider than is necessary to protect the interest involved in terms of the area and time of its operation. It must also be reasonable as regards the public interest. (See *Wyatt* v *Kreglinger and Fernau* 1933.)[160] Finally, the issue of reasonableness is a matter of law for the judge on the evidence presented to him which would include, for example, such matters as trade practices and customs.

VOLUNTARY CONTRACTUAL RESTRAINTS OF TRADE

There are four categories of voluntary contractual restraints as follows—

(1) *Restraints imposed upon employees.* In this connection it should be noted that there are only *two* things an employer can protect—

(*a*) Trade secrets. A restraint against competition is justifiable if its object is to prevent the exploitation of trade secrets learned by the employee in the course of his employment. (See *Forster & Sons Ltd* v *Suggett* 1918.)[161]

In this connection it should be noted that the area of the restraint must not be excessive. Thus in *Empire Meat Co. Ltd* v *Patrick* [1939] 2 All E.R. 85, a restraint concerning a retail butcher's business was held to be invalid because, amongst other things, the area within which the employee agreed not to carry on or be employed in the business of butcher, although it was only five miles from the place where the employer carried on business, was too wide in view of the limited area of the employers' trade. Furthermore, a restraint may be invalid because its duration is excessive. The burden on the employer increases as the duration of the restraint is extended, though in rare situations a restraint for life may be valid. (*Fitch* v *Dewes* 1921.)[162]

(*b*) Business connection. Sometimes an employer may use a covenant against *solicitation* of persons with whom the employer does business. No problem of area arises in this type of covenant, though its duration must be reasonable. (*Home Counties Dairies* v *Skilton* 1970.)[163]

(2) *Restraints imposed on the vendor of a business.* Such a restraint will be void unless it is required to protect the business sold and not to stifle competition. (*British Reinforced Concrete Co.* v *Schelff* 1921.)[164]

It should be noted, however, that the protection of the business sold may in rare situations involve a worldwide restraint. (*Nordenfelt* v *Maxim Nordenfelt Guns and Ammunition Co.* 1894.)[165]

(3) *Restraints arising from agreements between manufacturers and traders.* This branch of law is now largely regulated by statute, i.e. the Restrictive Trade Practices Act 1976. Nevertheless, it is necessary to consider the common-law position because not all restrictive agreements are covered by the above legislation and where it does not apply, the common law on the topic may be invoked. For example, the restrictive agreement which was at the root of *Kores Manufacturing Co.* v *Kolok Manufacturing Co. Ltd* 1958[166] was not covered by the Act which is not concerned with agreements between traders in regard to their employees and was decided on common-law principles. These principles are that the agreement must be reasonable between the parties and reasonable in the public interest. Both of these points arose in *Kores*, the Court of Appeal holding that the agreement was unreasonable as between the parties and also that it was contrary to the public interest, though the ratio is based on the fact that the agreement was unreasonable as between the parties.

(4) *Restrictions accepted by distributors of merchandise.* A manufacturer

or wholesaler may refuse to make merchandise available for distribution to the public unless the distributor accepts certain conditions restricting his liberty of trading. This is the main purpose of the solus agreement used by petrol companies. Such agreements are void unless reasonable. (See *Esso Petroleum Co. Ltd* v *Harper's Garage (Stourport) Ltd* 1967.)[167] It should be noted that there is a distinction as regards the duration of the restraint between a garage proprietor who is already in possession of the land before he ties himself to the oil company and a person who is out of possession and is let in by the oil company. A longer period of restraint may be allowed against a garage proprietor who is let into possession by the oil company. (*Cleveland Petroleum Co. Ltd* v *Dartstone Ltd* 1968.)[168]

INVOLUNTARY RESTRAINTS OF TRADE

We have so far considered restrictions against trading contained in contracts. However, the doctrine is not confined to these voluntary restraints. It extends to involuntary restraints imposed by trade associations or professional bodies upon their members. Such restraints are void unless reasonable. (*Pharmaceutical Society of Great Britain* v *Dickson* 1968.)[169]

CONSEQUENCES WHERE THE CONTRACT IS CONTRARY TO PUBLIC POLICY

Where a contract is rendered void by the judiciary it is unenforceable only insofar as it contravenes public policy. Thus—

(1) money paid or property transferred is recoverable (*Hermann* v *Charlesworth* 1905);[170] and

(2) lawful promises may be severed and enforced. Thus a contract of service which contains a void restraint is not wholly invalid and the court will sever and enforce those aspects of it which do not offend against public policy. Thus an employee who has entered into a contract of service which contains a restraint which is too wide can recover his wages or salary. (*Wallis* v *Day* 1837.)[171]

The court will not add to a contract or in any way redraft it but will merely strike out the offending words. What is left must make sense without further additions otherwise the court will not sever the void part in order to enforce what is good.

ILLEGAL CONTRACTS—THE CONTRIBUTION OF PARLIAMENT

Some contracts are prohibited by statute in terms that they are illegal, the word 'unlawful' being used in the statute concerned. In this context 'statute' includes the orders, rules and regulations that ministers of the Crown and other persons are authorized by Parliament to issue.

The statutory prohibitions with which we ae concerned may be express or implied.

(1) *Implied prohibition.* In these cases the statute itself does not say expressly that contracts contravening its provisions are necessarily illegal. The statute may affect the formation of a particular contract as where a trader does business without taking out a licence. In some cases the statute may affect the manner of performance of the contract as where a trader is required to deliver to a purchaser a written statement such as an invoice containing, for example, details of the chemical composition of the goods.

In either case whether failure to comply with a statutory provision renders the contract illegal is a matter of construction of the statute and is for the judge to decide.

If, in the opinion of the judge, the Act was designed to protect the public then the contract will be illegal. Thus in *Cope* v *Rowlands* (1836) 2 M.&W. 149 an unlicensed broker in the City of London was held not to be entitled to sue for his fees because the purpose of the licensing requirements was to protect the public against possible shady dealers. Furthermore, in *Anderson Ltd* v *Daniel* [1924] 1 K.B. 138 a seller of artificial fertilizers was held unable to recover the price of goods which he had delivered because he had failed to state in an invoice the chemical composition of the fertilizers which was required by Act of Parliament.

On the other hand, if in the opinion of the judge the purpose of the legislation was mainly to raise revenue or to help in the administration of trade, contracts will not be affected. Thus, in *Smith* v *Mawhood* (1845) 14 M.&W. 452 it was held that a tobacconist could recover the price of tobacco sold by him even though he did not have a licence to sell it and had not painted his name on his place of business. The purpose of the statute involved was not to affect the contract of sale but to impose a fine on offenders for the purpose of revenue. In addition, in *Archbolds (Freightage) Ltd* v *Spanglett Ltd* [1961] 1 Q.B. 374 a contract by an unlicensed carrier to carry goods by road was held valid because the legislation involved was only designed to help in the administration of road transport.

(2) *Express prohibition.* In a book of this nature it would be inappropriate to deal in detail with all statutes which render contracts illegal but a modern example is found in the Resale Prices Act 1976, s.1. One particular type of agreement, namely an agreement for the collective enforcement of conditions regulating the price at which goods may be sold is prohibited and made unlawful.

Such agreements were not usually regarded as illegal at common law but the doctrine of privity of contract prevented enforcement of the resale price agreement by a manufacturer against a retailer. (See, e.g. *Dunlop* v *Selfridge* 1915.)[29] Consequently, manufacturers not having access to the ordinary courts of law often brought the retailer before a secret and possibly unjust trade association tribunal which might put the retailer quite unreasonably on a stop list so that he was denied supplies.

Under Part I of the Resale Prices Act 1976 *collective* agreements by two or more persons regulating the price at which goods may be resold are unlawful. There is no criminal penalty but the Crown may institute civil proceedings in the High Court and obtain, for example, an injunction to prevent the practice.

It is important to note that *individual* agreements between one manufacturer and his retailers are sanctioned by s.26 of the Resale Prices Act 1976 so that such a manufacturer now has access to the ordinary courts of law to enforce his agreement. The action may be for damages or an injunction, though it is important to note that s.26 only applies if the resale price agreement has been approved by the Restrictive Practices Court under the Resale Prices Act 1976. In fact very few such agreements have been approved although an example is the *Net Book Agreement* (1964) L.R. 4 R.P. 484, under which publishers can enforce resale price maintenance agreements in respect of books.

VOID CONTRACTS—THE CONTRIBUTION OF PARLIAMENT

There are certain classes of contracts which are expressly declared by statute to be void. It would not be appropriate in a book of this nature to deal with all of them and therefore only those with a commercial connotation are described.

WAGERING CONTRACTS

In essence for a wager to exist it must be possible for one party to win and one party to lose and there must be two persons or two groups opposed to each other in their views as to a future event. Thus, where X, Y and Z each put £5 into a fund to be given to the party whose selected horse wins a given race, there is no wager. The only commercial importance of the concept of wagering and the only reason why it is introduced in a book of this nature relates to insurance. A contract is not a wager if the person to whom the money is promised on the occurrence of the event has an interest in the non-occurrence of that event, e.g. where a person has paid a premium to insure his house against destruction by fire. Such an interest is called an *insurable interest* and is not a wager. However, to insure someone else's property would be a wager and not a valid contract of insurance.

The Gaming Act of 1845 renders wagering contracts void so that there is no action for the bet or for the winnings. However, it should be noted that if the bet or the winnings have actually been paid over they cannot be recovered. Payment operates as waiver of the Act and the payment over of the money confers a good title to that money upon the person to whom it is paid.

CONTRACTS AFFECTED BY THE RESTRICTIVE TRADE PRACTICES ACT 1976

Under the Act of 1976 collective agreements between two or more persons designed to fix prices and/or regulate supplies of *goods* must be registered with the Director General of Fair Trading. They are then presumed void unless the parties can prove to the Restrictive Trade Practices Court that the agreement is in the public interest. This might be done, for example, where the parties can show that the agreement is designed to maintain the export trade. If the parties attempt to operate the agreement in spite of the fact that it has not been approved by the Restrictive Practices Court, the Director General of Fair Trading may ask for an injunction to prevent the operation of the agreement. However, it is rare that such action has to be taken because in most cases the firms concerned have not attempted to operate an agreement if it has been rejected by the Court.

This Act also allows the Director General of Fair Trading to investigate restrictive practices in regard to services. If necessary the matter can be brought before the Restrictive Trade Practices Court which now has a jurisdiction in respect of restrictive agreements relating to services.

THE RESALE PRICES ACT 1976

This Act is concerned with arrangements (or agreements) under which a supplier *imposes* upon a buyer a restriction in regard to the price at which the buyer must resell the goods he has bought under that arrangement or agreement.

Resale price maintenance agreements are presumed void under the 1976 Act unless the supplier can prove to the Restrictive Practices Court that the restriction is in the public interest. This might be done, for example, by showing that after-sales service would be reduced or non-existent unless the resale price maintenance agreement was enforced. We have already seen that if a resale price maintenance agreement is approved by the Restrictive Practices Court it can be enforced regardless of the doctrine of Privity of Contract under s.26 of the Resale Prices Act 1976.

FAIR TRADING ACT 1973

This Act gives wide powers to the Office of Fair Trading under the Director General of Fair Trading by reason of which it can deal with monopolies, mergers, restrictive practices, and the protection of consumers against trading practices which are considered unfair. The Office of Fair Trading is perhaps best known for its duty to vet mergers between companies involving £15 million or more assets and to recommend to the Department of Trade and Industry whether they should be referred to the Monopolies and Mergers Commission. The Government is not bound to take the advice of the Office of Fair Trading regarding reference.

A review currently being made by the Department of Trade and Industry suggests that the level for scrutiny of mergers by the Office of Fair Trading should be lifted from £15 million to £25 million.

The Office of Fair Trading has, however, a much wider brief under the following main pieces of legislation: the Consumer Credit Act 1974 (see p. 206); the Competition Act 1980 (see below); the Estate Agents Act 1979 (see p. 108); and, as we have seen, the Restrictive Trade Practices Act 1976 and the Resale Prices Act 1976.

As regards consumer protection and surveillance of traders it works with local Trading Standards Consumer Protection departments and advice agencies and gives information on consumer rights. It can obtain assurances of future obedience to the law from traders under the Fair Trading Act 1973 and under the Consumer Credit Act 1974 it vets the fitness of traders offering credit and resolves disputes over the accuracy of information on people which is given by credit reference agencies.

The competition legislation brings monopolies and mergers and other trade practices which restrict, distort, or prevent competition in the UK under the surveillance and control of the Office of Fair Trading.

THE COMPETITION ACT 1980

The main significance of this Act is that it brings within the scope of investigation the practices of single firms which are neither monopolies in a statutory sense nor in collusion with other enterprises for the purposes of the Restrictive Trade Practices Act 1976.

The Act provides a two-stage inquiry process. First of all the Director General of Fair Trading can, under s.3 of the Act, initiate a preliminary inquiry into a practice of a firm or firms and is required to report publicly his findings as to whether it constitutes an anti-competitive practice and if so, whether he feels it is right to refer the matter for investigation to the Monopolies and Mergers Commission. A company may volunteer undertakings in regard to the abandonment of its restrictive or monopolistic practices to the Director General at this stage he and may accept them instead of taking the matter to the Monopolies and Mergers Commission.

If the matter goes to the Commission, the Commission must assess and report whether the practice is anti-competitive and, in addition, whether it has or may be expected to operate against the public interest.

Where the conclusion of the Commission is adverse the Secretary of State may make an order under s.10 requiring the company to desist from or amend the practice concerned, or ask the Director General of Fair Trading to seek undertakings from the company.

A number of s.3 investigations have been made by the Office of Fair Trading. For example, there was an investigation into certain practices within the Raleigh Group. The report of the Director General found certain anti-competitive practices by the company regarding the supply of their products to discount stores. These operated against the public interest. Accordingly, the company gave the Director General an undertaking not to refuse to supply certain makes of bicycle to discount stores and certain other retail outlets.

Section 13 provides for prices to be investigated by the Director General at the direction of the Secretary of State if the price is a matter 'of major public concern'. There are no follow-up powers by which any recommendations could be enforced.

Section 11 allows public bodies to be referred to the Monopolies and Mergers Commission for a review of efficiency and costs, sometimes known for short as an efficiency audit. Section 12 allows the relevant Minister to order the body concerned to prepare a plan to put matters right. A number of reports have been published, e.g. one dealing with the London and South Eastern commuter services of British Rail.

EUROPEAN COMMUNITY

Under Articles 85 and 86 of the Treaty of Rome all agreements between firms which operate to prevent or restrict competition in the Market are void. Under s.5 of the Restrictive Trade Practices Act 1976 the Director General of Fair Trading and the Restrictive Practices Court are to take Articles 85 and 86 into account—

(1) on the issue of registration of a particular agreement, and
(2) if the agreement comes before the Court for adjudication.

Restrictive trading agreements and the Treaty of Rome

We have considered above the position under English domestic law in regard to restrictive trading agreements. Some consideration must now be given to the position under Community Law.

POLICY AND SOURCE OF LAW

The provisions of the Treaty, which have been part of our law since January 1973, are based, as UK law is, on the protection of the public interest. The basis of the competition policy is to be found in Articles 85 and 86 of the Treaty. These ban practices which distort competition between members of the Community (Art. 85), and prohibit the abuse of a monopolistic position by an organization within the market (Art. 86). There is an additional aim of raising living standards.

The result of a breach of the Treaty is that the agreement or decision concerned becomes automatically void whether or not there has been a ruling of the Commission in Brussels or the European Court of Justice in Luxembourg, or a national court. Additionally, the Commission may impose fines.

POWERS OF INVESTIGATION

The Directorate-General for Competition is the Department of the European Commission which investigates suspected infringement of Articles 85 and 86 (the Competition Rules), and then if there is sufficient evidence prosecutes the organizations concerned and passes judgment upon them. There are powers of entry into premises for the purposes of an inquiry. There is also a power in the Treaty to ask for information from governments and from companies in order to pursue inquiries.

The development of the objectives of the Treaty can best be appreciated by looking at some of the major decisions which have been made under Articles 85 and 86.

ARTICLE 85

(1) *Use of trade marks to restrict competition.* One of the most famous decisions is that of *Consten and Grundig* [1966] C.M.L.R. 418. Grundig set up a network of exclusive distributors for its products throughout the Community and appointed a French firm, Consten to be its exclusive distributor in France. Consten, in common with all other Grundig distributors was not permitted to sell either directly or indirectly outside France, and, to make certain that none of the other distributors violated Consten's exclusive territorial rights, Consten was permitted to register the trade mark G.I.N.T. (which stands for Grundig International) as its French trade mark. A third party imported Grundig products into France and Consten brought an action against the importer for infringement of trade mark. The case went to the European Court of Justice and it was held that the purpose of the trade-mark agreement between Grundig and Consten was to guarantee complete territorial protection to Consten in the sale of Grundig products in France. That agreement was prohibited by Art. 85 as its purpose was to hamper the importing into France of Grundig products by other firms and in these circumstances the agreement was void.

(2) *Cartel arrangements.* A classic illustration of cartel arrangements is to be seen in the *Quinine* cartel [1969] C.M.L.R. D.41. In that case an agreement had been made between the six manufacturing companies holding a dominant position on European and world markets by which they agreed to charge the same prices for quinine and a drug extracted from quinine and also set up export quotas in respect of imports from other Member countries. The companies involved had received legal advice to the effect that their arrangements infringed Art. 85 but nevertheless they continued to apply it and took precautions to keep it secret, instructing their members to destroy any compromising documents. However, mainly as a result of an investigation by the US Senate Anti-Trust Monopolies Sub-Committee, the European Commission opened its investigations of the companies' headquarters in the Community and

this led them to impose fines ranging from $10,000 up to $210,000, the fines being set in relation to each company's market position and its responsibility for the arrangements.

In the *Dyestuffs* cartel [1969] C.M.L.R. D.23, the Commission's investigations were commenced on the basis of information which they received from trade organizations of industrial users. The investigations revealed that the 10 major manufacturers of dyestuffs had made uniform, and for all practical purposes, simultaneous price increases between 1964 and 1967 on the sale of their goods. This price-fixing agreement led to the imposition of fines of $50,000 on the companies involved.

(3) *The use of patent rights to restrict competition.* An illustration of the attitude of the European Court on this issue is to be found in *Parke-Davis* v *Probel* [1968] C.M.L.R. 47. The Parke-Davis company, based in Detroit, held certain Dutch patents for an antibiotic. Another company imported the drug into Holland without the permission of the patent holder, Parke-Davis, and they brought an action against the other company for breach of the patent. It appeared that the defendant company had purchased the drug in Italy, where there was no patent protection in medicines, and had then imported it into Holland. Thus Parke-Davis had been unable to take out patents in Italy in order to protect their rights because there was a gap in Italian law as regards patents. In these circumstances Parke-Davis took the only action they could by suing the defendant company. The defendant company pleaded that the action was in breach of competition rules and the Dutch court referred the matter to the European Court of Justice. The European Court recognized the existence of the patent rights and that the exercise of those rights to prevent goods being imported into Holland from a country where such patent rights did not exist was a wholly proper action and did not constitute a restriction to competition. However, if the goods had been imported from another country where patent rights were in existence, an attempt to prevent their importation would probably have constituted an infringement of Art. 85.

ARTICLE 86

In order that Art. 86 shall be applicable it must be shown firstly that a dominant position is held by some undertaking, and that secondly there had been an abuse of that domination and thirdly, that the abuse has had an effect on trade between member states. The attitude of the Commission and the European Court to the abuse of Art. 86 is illustrated by the *Continental Can Case* [1972] C.M.L.R. D.11. The Continental Can Company was an American company producing packing materials, e.g. meat tins, fish tins, and metal lids for glass jars. In 1969, through a Belgian subsidiary, it took control of the largest German producer of packaging and in 1970 followed this up by acquiring a majority holding in a Dutch company which was the leading manufacturer of packing materials in the Benelux countries. In the opinion of the Commission the situation arising from this concentration within the market of light packings in the North-West region of the Common Market constituted the necessary conditions for an abuse of dominant position within Art. 86. The finding of the Commission was set aside by the European Court on a technical ground that the Commission had failed to define which market was abused, whether it was that of meat tins, fish tins, metal lids for glass jars or all three. However, the Court stressed that Art. 86 would have been infringed on a definition of the market abused so that the mergers would have been void.

An illustration of the use of Art. 86 in an English court of law is provided by *Garden Cottage Foods Ltd* v *Milk Marketing Board* [1982] 2 All E.R. 292. Garden Cottage (the company) was a middle-man transferring butter from the Board to traders in the bulk market in Europe and the UK taking a cut of the price. In March 1982 following some packaging problems which the company appeared to have overcome, the Board refused to supply direct. It said that supplies must be obtained from one of four independent distributors nominated by the Board.

These distributors were the company's competitors. The company would have to pay more to them for its supplies than if it bought direct from the Board. Therefore it could not compete on price, and would be forced out of business.

The company alleged that the Board was in breach of Art. 86 of the Treaty of Rome. This provides: 'Any abuse by one or more undertakings of a dominant position when in the Common Market or in a substantial part of it, shall be prohibited as incompatible with the Common Market insofar as it may affect trade between Member States . . .'.

The Court of Appeal granted an interlocutory injunction, i.e. an injunction until the trial, restraining the Board from refusing to maintain normal business relations contrary to Article 86.

The Board appealed to the House of Lords (see *Garden Cottage Foods Ltd* v *Milk Marketing Board* [1983] 2 All E.R. 770) against the injunction. Interlocutory injunctions were considered by the House of Lords in *American Cyanamid Co.* v *Ethicon Ltd* [1975] A.C. 396. It was decided in that case that if when the trial came on damages were likely to be regarded as an adequate remedy, and the defendant could clearly pay any damages which might be awarded, then no interlocutory injunction should be granted.

That was the position here, said the majority of their Lordships. If the Board refused to supply the company direct, and this meant the suspension of its butter business, the loss would be monetary, i.e. its cut of the price as middle-man. There could hardly be a clearer case of damages being an adequate remedy, and no insuperable difficulty of estimation had so far appeared. The injunction was withdrawn. The House of Lords therefore thought that the eventual action would be for damages. However, it is in fact uncertain whether an infringement of

Art. 86 gives rise in English law to an action for damages in this way. Their Lordships thought it did, but the case shows that there are still problems in terms of defining English law remedies for breaches of EEC law.

RELATIONSHIP WITH UK LAW

National legislation on restrictive trade practices and monopolies applies alongside Community law unless it conflicts with Community law as interpreted by the Commission or the European Court of Justice. Therefore, if a restrictive agreement or merger threat affects only the UK market, the matter will remain subject exclusively to UK legislation. If such agreement affects trade between two or more Member States then to that extent national law is excluded by Community law. Furthermore, if there is an overlap between Community and national law, Community law predominates. Therefore, once an agreement with inter-Market effect has been exempted by the Commission under Art. 85, it will from then on be immune from attack under United Kingdom restrictive practices or resale prices legislation. If the agreement had already been regarded as invalid under that legislation the invalidation will cease to be effective if the Commission exempts it under Art. 85. Additionally, if the restrictive practice has been approved by a UK court its approval will lapse if the agreement turns out to infringe the provisions of Art. 85. This is why it is important for UK restrictive practices courts to decline or postpone exercising jurisdiction where the Treaty applies and the Commission has already initiated proceedings. The reader will recall that this is provided for in the Restrictive Trade Practices Act 1976.

PROCEDURE FOR NOTIFICATION OF POTENTIALLY RESTRICTIVE AGREEMENTS

If an agreement is thought to infringe Art. 85, the contracting parties may take one of three courses of action—

(1) The agreement may be amended by the deletion of the offending provisions thereby taking it outside the provisions of the Article altogether.

(2) The parties may leave the agreement as it stands and run the risk of the practice coming to the notice of the Commissions with the possible imposition of a fine.

(3) The parties may register or notify the agreement to the Head of the Competition Department (i.e. the Directorate-General for Competition) of the Commission in Brussels. Once registered the agreement obtains provisional validity and protection from fines until such time as the Commission declares it to be unlawful, or grants an exemption.

There is no need for notification of an agreement when all the parties are from one Member State and the agreement does not relate either to import or export between member states.

There is no need to notify agreements in which only two enterprises participate, regardless of the Member States to which they belong, provided the agreements are only concerned to fix prices or conditions of trading in the resale of goods which have been acquired by the other party to the contract; or where the restrictions are concerned with a licence to use industrial property rights of restrictions in terms of manufacturing processes or knowledge.

In addition, two-enterprise agreements which are concerned, for example, with joint research and development, need not be notified.

There is nothing to stop the parties in case of doubt from notifying agreements in order to satisfy their own minds as to their legality and to cover the possible risk of misinterpretation of the agreement.

Interpretation of community law generally

It was decided by the Court of Appeal in *Bulmer* v *Bollinger* [1974] 2 All E.R. 1226, that the High Court and the Court of Appeal have a jurisdiction to interpret Community law and that they are not obliged to grant a right of appeal to the European Court of Justice. However, if the case goes to the House of Lords on appeal, the House of Lords is bound on request to refer the matter to the European Court of Justice. The decision was based upon an interpretation of Art. 177 of the Treaty which gives a discretion whether to refer such questions to the European Court. In the case Bulmers had marketed products for many years under the name of 'Champagne Cider' and 'Champagne Perry'. Bollingers claimed that this was contrary to an EEC regulation which restricted the use of the word 'Champagne' to wine produced from grapes grown in the Champagne district of France. The Court of Appeal decided that since cider was made from apples and perry was made from pears, there was no infringement of the regulation. The Court also refused to refer the matter to the European Court.

In the course of his judgment Lord Denning, M.R., laid down certain guidelines to assist judges in deciding whether to refer a case to the European Court or not. These guidelines are as follows—

(1) The time to get a ruling. The length of time which may elapse before a ruling can be obtained from the European Court should always be borne in mind. The average length of time at present seems to be between six and nine months. It is important to prevent undue protraction of proceedings.

(2) The European Court must not be overloaded. In this connection it should be borne in mind that the European Court consists of nine judges. All nine must sit on a reference from a national court and they cannot split up into divisions of three or five judges. Thus, if there are too many references the Court would not be able to get through its work.

(3) The reference must be on a question of interpretation only of the Treaty. It is a matter for the national courts to find the facts and apply the Treaty, though the way in which the national court has interpreted the Treaty can then be a matter for reference.

(4) Difficulty and importance. Unless the point is really difficult and important, it is better for the English judge to decide it himself. If he does so much delay and expense will be saved.

(5) Expense. The expense to the parties of getting a ruling from the European Court should always be borne in mind.

(6) Wishes of the parties. If both parties want the point to be referred to the European Court, the English court should have regard to their wishes, but it should not give them undue weight. The English court should hesitate before making a reference against the wishes of one of the parties, seeing the expense and delay which it involves.

Lord Denning went on to deal with the principles of interpretation of the Treaty, saying in particular that English judges should follow the European pattern. They should not be concerned to examine the words of the Treaty in meticulous detail or argue about the precise grammatical sense of the words. They must look to the purpose or intent. If they find a gap in the Treaty they must fill it as best they can. They must do what the framers of the Treaty or instrument would have done if they had thought about it. The above principles are, of course, different from those adopted in England where if a gap is revealed Parliament must fill it in by another statute.

Discharge of contract

The discharge of a contract means in general that the parties are freed from their mutual obligations. A contract may be discharged in four ways: by agreement, by performance, by breach or by frustration.

DISCHARGE BY AGREEMENT

Obviously, what has been created by agreement may be ended by agreement. Discharge by agreement may arise—

(1) *Out of the original agreement.* Thus the parties may have agreed at the outset that the contract should end automatically on the expiration of a fixed time. This would be the case, for example, with a lease of premises for a fixed term. Alternatively, the contract may contain a provision entitling one or both parties to terminate it if they wish. Thus a contract of employment can normally be brought to an end by giving reasonable notice. This area of the law is, of course, subject to statutory minimum periods of notice laid down by s.49 of the Employment Protection (Consolidation) Act 1978. They are one week after four weeks' service, two weeks after two years' service and an additional week

for each year of service up to 12 weeks after 12 years' service. Section 49(2) (*ibid.*) provides that the employee must, once he has been continuously employed for four weeks, give at least one week's notice to his employer to terminate his contract of employment. This is regardless of the number of years of service. Individual contracts may provide for longer periods of notice both by employer and employee.

(2) *Out of a new contract.* If the contract is *executory*, i.e. a promise for a promise and there has been no performance, the mutual release of the parties provides the consideration and is called bilateral discharge. The only difficulty here is in relation to the form of the release. The position is as follows—

(*a*) written contracts may be rescinded or varied by oral agreement;
(*b*) deeds may be rescinded or varied orally;
(*c*) contracts required to be evidenced in writing may be totally discharged by oral agreement but variations must be in writing.

If the contract is executed as where it has been performed or partly performed by one party, then the other party who wishes to be released must provide consideration for that release unless it is effected by deed. This is referred to as unilateral discharge. In other words, the doctrine of accord and satisfaction applies. This matter has already been dealt with and is really an aspect of the law relating to consideration. (See p. 14.)

DISCHARGE BY PERFORMANCE

A contract may be discharged by performance, the discharge taking place when both parties have performed the obligations which the contract placed upon them. Whether performance must comply exactly with the *terms* of the contract depends on the following—

(1) *Construction of the contract.* According to the manner in which the court construes the meaning, the contract may be—

(*a*) An entire contract. Here the manner of performance must be complete and exact. (*Moore* v *Landauer* 1921.)[172]

(*b*) A divisible contract. Thus a contract of employment which provides for payment every week or month is divisible in terms that payment is due for any completed week or month as the case may be, even though the contract may be for an indefinite term or for a term of, say, three years. Another example is a building contract which usually provides for progress payments thus avoiding the unfortunate result arrived at in *Sumpter* v *Hedges* 1898.[174]

(*c*) Capable of being fulfilled by substantial performance. If the court construes the contract in such a way that precise performance of every term by one party is not required in order to make the other party liable to some extent on it, then the plaintiff may recover for work done, though the defendant may, of course, counter-claim for any defects in peformance. (*Hoenig* v *Isaacs* 1952.)[173] In this connection it should be noted that in construing a contract to see whether a particular term must be fully performed or whether substantial performance is enough, the court will refer to the difference between conditions and warranties. A condition must be wholly performed whereas substantial performance of a warranty is often enough. (*Poussard* v *Spiers and Pond* 1876[132] and *Bettini* v *Gye* 1876.)[133]

(2) *Whether partial performance has been accepted by one party.* If, for example, S agrees to deliver three dozen bottles of brandy to B and delivers two dozen bottles only, then B may exercise his right to reject the whole consignment. (S.30(1), Sale of Goods Act 1979.) But if he has accepted delivery of two dozen bottles he must pay for them at the contract rate. (S.30(1) (*ibid.*).)

However, the mere conferring of a benefit on one party by another is not enough; there must be evidence of acceptance of that benefit by the party upon whom it was conferred. (*Sumpter* v *Hedges* 1898.)[174]

(3) *Whether full performance has been prevented by one party.* Here the party who cannot further perform his part of the contract may bring an action on a *quantum meruit* against the party in default for the value of work done up to the time when further performance was prevented. (*De Barnardy* v *Harding* 1853.)[175]

TIME OF PERFORMANCE

Section 41 of the Law of Property Act 1925 provides that stipulations as to time in a contract are not construed to be of the essence of the contract unless equity would have regarded them as such. There are the following exceptional situations in which time was of the essence even in equity—

(1) The contract fixes a date and makes performance on that date a condition.

(2) The circumstances indicate that the contract should be performed at the agreed time. The sale of a reversionary interest would come into this category. Suppose property is left by will to X for life with remainder to Y. If Y sells his remainder, as he may do, it is obvious that the contract of sale should be completed at the agreed date, for delay will mean that the life tenant is growing older and the value of the remainder is therefore increasing above the price which Y has accepted. Similarly, in the sale of a business, equity will generally take the view that the contract should be completed on time so that uncertainties regarding a change of owner should not be prolonged and affect adversely the goodwill of the business. Mercantile contracts, such as contracts for the sale of goods where a time is fixed for delivery, are also in this category. (*Bowes* v *Shand* 1877.)[176]

(3) Where the time of performance was not originally of the essence of the contract or has been waived but one party has been guilty of

undue delay, the other party may give notice requiring that the contract be performed within a reasonable time. (*Chas. Rickards Ltd* v *Oppenhaim* 1950.)[177]

That a waiver of a date of delivery without consideration is binding can be based on promissory estoppel (as in *High Trees*), said Denning, L.J., in *Rickards*, or on s.11(2) of the Sale of Goods Act 1979 which states: 'Where a contract of sale is subject to any condition to be fulfilled by the seller, the buyer may waive that condition.' 'This section was used to justify a waiver without consideration by McCardie, J., in *Hartley* v *Hymans* [1920] 3 K.B. 475.

This is an example of the doctrine of promissory estoppel being used by a plaintiff, i.e. as a sword not a shield, because a seller may tender delivery after the originally agreed date relying on the buyer's promise to accept such delivery by reason of his waiver. If the buyer then refuses to accept the delivery the seller can claim damages and is in essence suing upon the waiver which is unsupported by consideration.

TENDER

With regard to the manner of performance, the question of what is good tender arises. Tender is an offer of performance which complies with the terms of the contract. If goods are tendered by the seller and refused by the buyer the seller is freed from liability, given that the goods are in accordance with the contract as to quantity and quality. As regards the payment of money, this must comply with the following rules—

(1) It must be in accordance with the rules relating to legal tender. By s.1(2) and (6) of the Currency and Bank Notes Act 1954 a tender of a note or notes of the Bank of England expressed to be payable to bearer on demand is legal tender for the payment of any amount. A tender of notes of a bank other than the Bank of England is not legal tender, though the creditor may waive his objection to the tender if he wishes. As regards coins, s.2 of the Coinage Act 1971, as amended by the Currency Act 1983, provides that coins made by the Mint shall be legal tender as follows—

(*a*) Gold coins for payment of any amount;

(*b*) coins of cupro-nickel or silver of denominations of more than 10 pence, for payment of any amount not exceeding £10;

(*c*) coins of cupro-nickel or silver of denominations of not more than 10 pence for payment of any amount not exceeding £5;

(*d*) coins of bronze, for payment of any amount not exceeding 20 pence.

There is power by proclamation to call in coins which then cease to be legal tender or to make other coins legal tender.

(2) There must be no request for change.

(3) Tender by cheque or other negotiable instrument is not good tender unless the creditor does not object. It should be noted that if a

proper tender of money is refused the debt is not discharged, but if the money is paid into court the debtor has a good defence to an action by his creditor and the debt does not bear interest.

APPROPRIATION OF PAYMENTS

In connection with performance it is important to consider the rules governing appropriation of payments. Certain debts are barred by the Limitation Act 1980 and money which has been owed for six years under a simple contract or 12 years under a speciality contract without acknowledgement may not be recoverable by an action in the courts. Where a debtor owes several debts to the same creditor and makes a payment which does not cover them all, there are rules governing how the money should be appropriated. These are as follows—

(1) The debtor can appropriate either expressly by saying which debt he is paying or by implication as where he owes £50 and £20 and sends £20.

(2) If the debtor does not appropriate the creditor can appropriate to any debt, *even to one which is statute-barred.*

(3) Where there is a current account, appropriation follows the rule in *Clayton's Case* (1816) 1 Mer. 572. The major example is bank current accounts where, under *Clayton's Case*, and in the absence of a contrary intention, the money first paid in is to be regarded as the money which is first withdrawn. (*Deeley* v *Lloyds Bank* 1912.)[178]

DISCHARGE BY BREACH

There are several forms of breach of contract as follows—

(1) Failure to perform the contract is the most usual form as where a seller fails to deliver goods by the appointed time or where, although delivered, they are not up to standard as to quality or quantity.

(2) Express repudiation which arises where one party states that he will not perform his part of the contract. (*Hochster* v *De la Tour* 1853.)[179]

(3) Some action by one party which makes performance impossible. (See *Omnium D'Enterprises and Others* v *Sutherland* 1919.)[180]

Any breach which takes place before the time for performance has arrived is called an *anticipatory breach.* Thus the situations described in (2) and (3) above are anticipatory breaches.

Where the breach is anticipatory the aggrieved party may sue at once for damages. (See *Hochster* v *De la Tour* 1853).[179] Alternatively, he can wait for the time for performance to arrive and see whether the other party is prepared at that time to carry out the contract. (*White and Carter (Councils) Ltd* v *McGregor* 1961.)[181] As regards the decision in *White and Carter (Councils) Ltd* v *McGregor*, it should be noted that the ruling of the House of Lords appears to conflict with the principle of *mitigation of loss.* (See Remedies.) In fact it does not because it has been laid down in a number of cases (e.g. *Shindler* v *Northern Raincoat Co. Ltd* [1960] 2 All E.R. 239) that there is no duty on a plaintiff to mitigate his damages before there has been any breach which he has accepted as a breach. In the *White and Carter* case the plaintiffs did not accept the first breach but preferred to wait until the date of performance. During that time they were, according to the law, not obliged to mitigate loss. However, the case could produce a most unfair result and the problem could probably have been dealt with differently by saying that although the plaintiffs were under no duty to mitigate their loss, they were surely bound not to aggravate the damage. If the House of Lords had taken the line that the plaintiffs' expense was self-imposed and not in fact caused by the breach of contract, then the defendants would not have been liable for it. This is the line taken in the more recent cases of *Attica Sea Carriers* 1976 and *Clea Shipping Corporation* v *Bulk Oil International* 1983 (see p. 450). The cases suggest that unless there is a 'legitimate interest' in preserving the contract the party preserving it could be forced to accept damages instead of the sums falling due under the contract.

Note also that it may be dangerous to wait for the time of performance to arrive since the contract may, for example, have become impossible of performance, thus providing the party who was in anticipatory breach with a good defence to an action. (*Avery* v *Bowden* 1855.)[182]

EFFECT ON CONTRACT

Not every breach entitles the innocent party to treat the contract as discharged. It must be shown that the breach affects a vital part of the contract, i.e. that it is a breach of condition rather than a breach of warranty (contrast *Poussard* v *Spiers*[132] with *Bettini* v *Gye*)[133] or that the other party has no intention of performing his contract as in *Hochster* v *De la Tour,*[179] or has put himself in a position where it is impossible to peform it as in *Omnium D'Enterprises and Others* v *Sutherland.*[180]

DISCHARGE BY FRUSTRATION

If an agreement is impossible of performance from the outset it is void. This is at the root of s.6 of the Sale of Goods Act 1979 which provides that where there is a contract for the sale of specific goods and the goods, without the knowledge of the seller, have perished at the time when the contract is made, it is void. (See further p. 124.) However, some contracts are possible of performance when they are made but it subsequently becomes impossible to carry them out in whole or in part.

The view of the early common-law judges was that such eventualities should be provided for in the contract and if this was not done the party liable for the performance of an impossible undertaking would be obliged to pay damages to the other party for such non-performance. Later the judges developed the doctrine of discharge by frustration, which applies, as the House of Lords decided in *Davis Contractors Ltd* v *Fareham UDC* [1956] 2 All E.R. 145, in the restricted set of circumstances where there has been such a change in the significance of the obligation that the thing undertaken would, if performed, be a different thing than that contracted for.

OPERATION OF THE DOCTRINE

The operation of the doctrine can be divided into two main sections as follows—

(1) Contracts for personal service. Such a contract is discharged by the *death* of the person who was to perform it; thus if A has agreed to play the piano at a concert and dies before the date on which the performance is due, his personal representatives will not be expected to go along and play in his stead.

Incapacity of a person who has to perform a contract may discharge it. However, temporary incapacity is not enough (*Storey* v *Fulham Steel Works* 1907)[183] unless it affects the contract in a fundamental manner. (*Poussard* v *Spiers and Pond* 1876.)[132]

The doctrine of frustration will usually only apply where there is no fault by either party. Where performance of the contract is prevented by the fault of one party, that party is in breach of contract and that is the proper approach to the problem. (*Norris* v *Southampton City Council* 1982.)[184]

(2) Other contracts. These may be frustrated in the following circumstances—

(*a*) Government interference. (*Re Shipton, Anderson & Co. and Harrison Bros' Arbitration* 1915.)[185]

(*b*) Destruction of the subject-matter. (*Taylor* v *Caldwell* 1863)[186]

(*c*) Non-occurrence of an event (*Krell* v *Henry* 1903)[187] but it must be shown that the contract will be substantially affected. (*Herne Bay Steamboat Co.* v *Hutton* 1903.)[188]

(*d*) Commercial purpose defeated, because peformance, though possible, would by reason of delay or other matters be of little value. (*Jackson* v *Union Marine Insurance Co.* 1874.)[189]

SITUATIONS IN WHICH THE DOCTRINE DOES NOT APPLY

The doctrine will not apply—

(1) where the parties have made express provision for the event which has occurred. In such a case the provisions inserted into the contract by the parties will apply. Thus in some of the coronation seat cases, e.g. *Clark* v *Lindsay* (1903) 19 T.L.R. 202, the contracts provided that if the procession was postponed the tickets would be valid for the day on which it did take place or that the parties should get their money

back with a deduction for the room owner's expenses. These took effect to the exclusion of the principles of frustration.

(2) where the frustrating event is self-induced (*Maritime National Fish Ltd* v *Ocean Trawlers Ltd* 1935.)[190]

(3) to leases and contracts for the sale of land; since these create an estate which survives any frustrating event. (*Cricklewood Property* v *Leighton's Investment Trust* 1945[191] and *Hillingdon Estates* v *Stonefield Estates* 1952.)[192] However, this presumably applies only where the land continues to exist. Thus it is thought that a lease of cliff land would be frustrated if the land slipped into the sea. In addition, the more recent judicial statements on this matter in *Amalgamated Investment and Property Co. Ltd* v *John Walker & Sons Ltd* 1976 and *National Carriers* v *Panalpina (Northern)* 1981 (see p. 455) should be noted.

THE LAW REFORM (FRUSTRATED CONTRACTS) ACT 1943

This important statute has laid down the conditions which will govern the rights and duties of the parties when certain contracts are frustrated.

(1) Before 1943. The common-law doctrine of frustration did not make the contract void *ab initio* (from the beginning) but only from the time when the frustrating event occurred. Thus money due and not paid could be claimed and money paid before the frustrating event was not recoverable. (*Chandler* v *Webster* 1904.)[193]

(2) After 1943. The position under the Act is as follows—

(*a*) Money paid is recoverable.

(*b*) Money payable ceases to be payable.

(*c*) The parties may recover expenses in connection with the contract or retain the relevant sum from money received, if any.

(*d*) It is also possible to recover on a *quantum meruit* a reasonable sum of money as compensation where one of the parties has carried out acts of part performance before frustration, provided the other party has received what the Act calls 'a valuable benefit' under the contract other than a money payment 'before the time of discharge', i.e. to the time of the frustrating event. There are difficulties in regard to the expression 'valuable benefit', particularly where the work is destroyed since the Act is not clear as to whether a sum can be recovered by the person conferring the benefit where there has been destruction of his work. In *Parsons Bros* v *Shea* (1965) 53 D.L.R. (2d) 86, a Newfoundland court, in dealing with an identical provision under the Newfoundland Frustrated Contracts Act 1956 held that the carrying out of modifications to a heating system in an hotel subsequently destroyed by fire could not be regarded as conferring any 'benefits' upon the owner. However, in *BP Exploration* v *Hunt* (No. 2) [1982] 1 All E.R. 125, the plaintiffs were engaged to develop an oil field on the defendant's land and were to be paid by oil from the wells. After the wells came on stream but before BP had received all the oil which the development contract provided they should have, the wells were nationalized by the Libyan Government which gave the defendant some compensation. The contract was obviously frustrated but Goff, J., who was later affirmed by the Court of Appeal and the House of Lords, gave BP a sum of 35 million dollars as representing the 'benefit' received by the defendant prior to the frustrating event.

Clearly, here there was a surviving benefit conferred before the frustrating event and at the time of it, e.g. the value of the oil already removed by Mr Hunt before nationalization and, of course, his claim for compensation against the Libyan Government. None of these things would have been available to him before BP's discovery and extraction of oil on his land. Since the benefit conferred up to the time of frustration clearly survived the frustrating event, i.e. the nationalization, the case does not resolve the problems posed by *Parsons Bros* v *Shea* (above) where the benefit did not survive the frustrating event.

Limitation of Actions

Contractual obligations are not enforceable for all time. After a certain period the law bars any remedy in the main because evidence becomes less reliable with the passage of time. The Limitation Act 1980 lays down the general periods within which an action may be brought. They are as follows—

(1) An action on a simple contract may be brought within six years from the date when the cause of action accrued.

(2) An action upon a contract under seal may be brought within 12 years from the date when the cause of action accrued.

However, where the plaintiff's claims include a claim for damages in respect of personal injuries, the period is three years.

However, a person may suffer personal injury the extent of which only comes to light more than three years after the breach of contract which caused it. For example, A is a passenger on B's coach and B's careless driving causes an accident as a result of which A suffers injury consisting of bruising of the face. Four years later A goes blind as a result of the accident. Under the Limitation Act 1980 A has three years from his knowledge of the blindness to sue B and the court's permission is not required. The court may extend this period at its discretion, though in this case application must be made to the court for the extension.

A right of action 'accrues' from the moment when breach occurs, not from the date when the contract was made. Thus if money is lent today for four years the creditor's right to recover it will not expire until 10 years from today.

If when the cause of action accrues the plaintiff is under a disability by reason of minority or unsoundness of mind, the period will not run until the disability is ended or until his death, whichever comes first. Once the period has started to run subsequent insanity has no effect.

If the plaintiff is the victim of fraud or acts under a mistake, the limitation period will not begin to run until the true state of affairs is discovered or should with reasonable diligence have been discovered. (See *Lynn* v *Bamber* 1930[194] which illustrates the common-law principles which are now contained in s.32 of the Limitation Act 1980.)

The Limitation Act does not truly discharge a contract, which is why it has been dealt with separately here. The Act merely makes the contract unenforceable in a court of law and if the defendant does not plead the statutes of limitation, the judge will enforce the contract. In addition, where the contractual claim is not for damages but for a debt or other liquidated (i.e. ascertained) demand, time for making a claim can be extended by a subsequent payment of money not appropriated by the debtor, because, as we have seen, the creditor can appropriate it, or by the debtor or his duly authorized agent making a written acknowledgement of the debt to the creditor or his agent. (S.29 (*ibid.*).) Time begins to run again from the date of the acknowledgement. However, once a debt is statute-barred it cannot be revived in this way. (S.29(7) (*ibid.*).)

Equitable remedies, i.e. specific performance or an injunction, are not covered by the ordinary limitation periods but will usually be barred much earlier under general equitable rules. An equitable remedy must be sought promptly and, according to the nature of the contract, a short delay of weeks or even days may bar the remedy.

Remedies for breach of contract

DAMAGES

This is the main remedy for breach and the principles on which damages are assessed are as follows—

(1) Damages are intended as compensation for the plaintiff's loss and not as punishment for the defendant. Thus where no loss has been suffered, as where a seller fails to deliver the goods but the buyer is able to purchase elsewhere at no extra cost, the court will award *nominal* damages of £2 to mark the breach. An additional example arises in actions for loss of earnings arising from a breach of contract where damages are reduced after taking into account the plaintiff's liability to taxation. (See *Beach* v *Reed Corrugated Cases Ltd* 1965.)[195]

Exemplary or punitive damages which exceed the actual loss suffered by an amount intended to punish the offending party are not awarded for breach of contract. The intention is that the plaintiff should be placed in the same situation as if the contract had been performed.

Contractual damages are certainly not intended to put the plaintiff in a better position than if the contract had been properly performed. (See *C & P Haulage* v *Middleton* 1983, p. 457.)

(2) Apart from the question of *assessment*, the matter of *remoteness of damage* arises. The consequence of a breach of contract may be far reaching and the law must draw a line somewhere and say that damages incurred beyond a certain limit are too remote to be recovered. Damages in contract must therefore be proximate. The modern law regarding remoteness of damage in contract is founded upon the case of *Hadley* v *Baxendale* 1854[196]. The case is authority for the statement that damages in contract will be too remote to be recovered unless they are such that the defendant as a reasonable man would have foreseen them as likely to result according to the usual course of things or because of special facts made known to him. Where damages do not arise naturally from the breach, they may be recovered only if the defendant was made aware of the possibility of such damage. (*Horne* v *Midland Railway Co.* 1873[197] and *Victoria Laundry Ltd* v *Newman Industries Ltd* 1949.)[198] There has been, however, a more recent development in *Koufos* v *Czarnikow Ltd* 1967[199] (better known as *The Heron II*).[199] In *The Heron II* the House of Lords commented on the foreseeability test laid down in *Hadley* v *Baxendale* 1854.[196] The view was taken that the word 'foreseeable' was not the best phrase to use since in a sense all the results of a breach of contract are foreseeable. The House of Lords, whilst not overruling *Hadley* v *Baxendale* 1854,[196] felt that the correct criterion of liability is not whether the loss is reasonably forseeable by the parties but whether it should have been within their reasonable contemplation at the time of the contract, having regard to their knowledge at that time. The difference between the two tests is slight, but in the view of the Law Lords 'foreseeability' and 'contemplation' are different concepts in the law and the former, which is wider than the latter, should be restricted to cases of tort.

(3) The injured party has a duty to *mitigate* or minimize his loss, i.e. he must take all reasonable steps to reduce it. Thus a seller whose goods are rejected must attempt to get the best price for them elsewhere and the buyer of goods which are not delivered must attempt to buy as cheaply as possible elsewhere. Loss arising from failure to take such steps cannot be recovered. (See also *Brace* v *Calder* 1895.)[200]

However, the plaintiff is not under a duty to mitigate his loss before there has been a breach of contract which the plaintiff has accepted as a breach. No doubt this is logical but it can produce startling results. (See *White and Carter (Councils) Ltd* v *McGregor* 1961.)[181]

(4) In some cases the parties foreseeing the possibility of breach may attempt in the contract to assess in advance the damages payable. Such a provision for *liquidated* damages will be valid if it is a genuine pre-estimate of loss and not a *penalty* inserted to make it a bad bargain for the defendant not to carry out his part of the contract. The court will not enforce a penalty but will award damages on normal principles.

Certain tests are applied in order to decide whether or not the provision is a penalty. Obviously, extravagant sums are generally in the nature of penalties. Where the contractual obligation lying on the defendant is to pay money then any provision in the contract which requires the payment of a larger sum on default of payment is a penalty because the damage can be accurately assessed. Where the sum provided for in the contract is payable on the occurrence of any one of several events it is probably a penalty for it is unlikely that each event can produce the same loss. (*Ford Motor Co. (England) Ltd* v *Armstrong* 1915.)[201] If the sum is agreed by the parties as liquidated damages it will be enforced even though the actual loss is greater or smaller. (*Cellulose Acetate Silk Co. Ltd* v *Widnes Foundry Ltd* 1933.)[202]

INTEREST ON DEBT AND DAMAGES

Under the provisions of s.15 of the Administration of Justice Act 1982 the court has power to award interest on debt or damages at the end of the trial or where judgment is obtained in default, i.e. where there is no defence and no trial. Interest may also be awarded where the defendant settles after service of writ but before judgment. Interest is not available where a person settles *before* service of writ no matter how long he has kept the other party waiting. The interest payable is at such rate as the court thinks fit or as rules of court may provide. The rate currently payable on judgment debts under s.17 of the Judgments Act 1838 which is likely to be a guideline is 12 per cent per annum. The interest is tax-free. (S.74, Administration of Justice Act 1982.)

CLAIMS ON A *QUANTUM MERUIT*

This remedy means that the plaintiff will be awarded as much as he has earned or deserved. The remedy can be used contractually or quasi-contractually as follows—

(1) Contractually. Here it may be used to recover a reasonable price or renumeration where there is a contract for the supply of goods or services but the parties have not fixed any precise sum to be paid.

(2) Quasi-contractually. A claim on this basis may be made where, for example, work has been done under a void contract. The plaintiff cannot recover damages for breach because no valid contract exists, but he may in some circumstances recover on a *quantum meruit* (*Craven-Ellis* v *Canons Ltd*1936.)[203]

A DECREE FOR SPECIFIC PERFORMANCE

This is an equitable remedy which is sometimes granted for breach of contract, where damages are not an adequate remedy or where specific performance is regarded by the court as a more appropriate remedy. (See *Beswick* v *Beswick* 1967.)[30] It is an order of the court and constitutes an express instruction to a party to a contract to perform the actual obligations which he undertook in a contract. For all practical purposes the remedy is now confined to contracts for the sale of land, though it may be a more appropriate remedy in the case of a contract to pay an annuity because the exact value of the annuity will depend on how long the annuitant lives and this cannot be known at the time of the breach. (See *Beswick* v *Beswick* 1967.)[30] It is not normally granted in the case of contracts for the sale of goods because other goods of a similar kind can be purchased and the difference assessed in money damages. In addition, it should be noted that specific performance will not be granted if the court cannot adequately supervise its enforcement. Thus contracts of a personal nature, such as employment, which rely on a continuing relationship between the parties will not be specifically enforced because the court cannot supervise performance on the day-to-day basis which would be necessary. Furthermore, specific performance will not be awarded either to or against a minor because a minor's contracts cannot be enforced against him and equity requires equality or mutuality as regards its remedies.

AN INJUNCTION

This is an order of the court used in this context to direct a person not to break his contract. The remedy has a somewhat restricted application in the law of contract and will be granted to enforce a negative stipulation in a contract where damages would not be an adequate remedy. Being an equitable remedy it is only ordered on the same principles as specific performance, so that it will not normally be awarded where damages are an adequate remedy. (See *Garden Cottage Foods Ltd* v *Milk Marketing Board* 1982, p. 73.) Its main use in the contractual situation has been as an indirect means of enforcing a contract for personal services (*Warner Bros Pictures* v *Nelson* 1937),[204] but a clear negative stipulation is required. (*Whitwood Chemical Co.* v *Hardman* 1891.)[205]

MAREVA INJUNCTION

This remedy, which can be of assistance to a party suing for breach of contract, has developed considerably over recent times. In general terms a court will not grant an injunction to prevent a person disposing of his property merely to assist a person suing, for example, for a debt, to recover his money. However, the Mareva injunction is an exception to that general rule and is granted to restrict removal of assets outside the jurisdiction, often by a foreign defendant, where this is a real and serious possibility. It is clearly a valuable addition to existing contractual remedies, particularly when business is now so often conducted on an international scale.

RESCISSION

This is a further equitable remedy for breach of contract. The rule is the same when the remedy is used for breach as it is when it is used for misrepresentation. If the contract cannot be completely rescinded it cannot be rescinded at all; it must be possible to restore the *status quo*.

REFUSAL OF FURTHER PERFORMANCE

If the person suffering from the breach desires merely to get rid of his obligations under the contract, he may refuse any further performance on his part and set up the breach as a defence if the party who has committed the breach attempts to enforce the contract against him.

Quasi-contractual rights and remedies

Quasi-contract is based on the idea that a person should not obtain a benefit or an unjust enrichment as against another merely because there is no obligation in contract or another established branch of the law which will operate to make him account for it. The law may in these circumstances provide a remedy by implying a fictitious promise to account for the benefit or enrichment. This promise then forms the basis of an action in quasi-contract.

In practice the following two areas are important—

(1) Claims on a *quantum meruit*. As we have seen, where the plaintiff has done work for the defendant but no specific sum is owing, the plaintiff can recover a reasonable sum on a *quantum meruit*. The rules relating to *quantum meruit* are in fact based on a quasi-contractual principle.

(2) Actions for money had and received. Of particular importance here is the action for total failure of consideration. A total failure will result in the recovery of all that was paid. A common reason for total failure of consideration arises where A, who has no title, sells goods to B and B has to give up the goods to the true owner. B can then recover the whole of the consideration from A, his action being based upon the quasi-contractual claim of money had and received. (See *Rowland* v *Divall* 1923.)[206]

It should be noted that the action is based on failure of consideration and not its absence. Thus money paid by way of a gift cannot be recovered in quasi-contract.

2 Agency

Agency is a relationship existing between two parties, called principal and agent, the function of the agent being to create a contractual relationship between the principal and third parties.

There is a similarity between agents and employees. An agent is, generally speaking, a person who is employed or appointed to make contracts, whereas many employees are not agents because they do not make contracts for their employers. Nevertheless one person may occupy both roles, e.g. an usherette in a theatre is an employee when she is showing patrons to their seats, but becomes an agent when she sells them programmes. Moreover an agent may be an employee or an independent contractor, i.e. an agent may be employed or self-employed. Thus an estate agent, engaged to sell a house, is both an agent and an independent contractor.

Capacity

The ordinary rules of contract apply to the contract of agency. It follows that—

(1) The third party must have capacity to contract in order that the contract which the agent makes with him on behalf of the principal may be enforceable.

(2) The agent must have capacity to contract if his contract with the principal is to be enforceable; otherwise agent and principal may not be able to enforce the rights and duties arising under the contract of agency.

(3) However, a person does not require contractual capacity merely to act as an agent, and a minor may so act. So also may a bankrupt unless his insolvency makes him unfit for the position of agent. Thus a company director who is a bankrupt cannot continue to act as such without the permission of the court which adjudicated him bankrupt. Where the company is governed by Art. 88 of Table A or a similar Article, a director vacates office on becoming bankrupt and cannot lawfully act even if the court has given him permission. The appointment of an insane person as agent would be invalid, and if an agent becomes insane, the appointment will be terminated. Furthermore, if the agent lacks capacity, this will affect a third party and may prevent an action for breach of warranty of authority.

(4) The principal must have capacity in order that the contracts between principal and third party and principal and agent shall be enforceable. A minor or person of unsound mind is bound by a contract made on his behalf by his authorized agent where the circumstances are such that he would be bound if he had made the contract himself. (Per Lord Denning in *G.* v *G.* [1970] 3 All E.R. 546) Thus the Infants' Relief Act 1874 will invalidate contracts made on behalf of a minor unless they are for his benefit or for necessaries. Furthermore, a registered company may not contract through an agent if the act is beyond the scope of the company's memorandum. (*Ashbury Railway Carriage and Iron Co.* v *Riche* 1875.)[83]

Creation of agency

The relationship of principal and agent may be created by an *express* agreement or an *implied* agreement, as in *Freeman & Lockyer* v *Buckhurst Park Properties Ltd* 1964 (see p. 92) where the person who made the contract on behalf of Buckhurst was *acting* as managing director of the company but without any express appointment. However, he did act with the wholehearted consent of the board of the company. It should be noted that persons who allow the agent to act as such must have authority to appoint him, as a board of directors may appoint a managing director, even though they may not, as in *Buckhurst*, have actually done so. Thus in *British Bank of the Middle East* v *Sun Life Assurance of Canada (U.K.) Ltd* [1983] 2 Lloyd's Rep 9 the House of Lords decided that a unit manager of the Sun Life had no authority to bind the company to a transaction concerning mortgage protection and life assurance with the appellants. The fact that his senior, a branch manager, had held him out as having authority did not affect the decision because the branch manager had no authority to bind the Sun Life either in the matters concerned. All matters relating to mortgage protection and life assurance had to be referred to head office. Thus a person without authority himself cannot make representations as to the authority of others.

No particular form of agreement is required, though the following special cases are worth noting—

(*a*) Where the agent is to contract under seal he must be appointed by deed, i.e. a power of attorney. Thus an agent appointed to grant leases of more than three years must be appointed under seal. It should be noted, however, that an agent not appointed by power of attorney can validly execute a deed if he does so in the presence and by the authority of his principal.

(*b*) Under s.41(1) of the Companies Act 1948, an agent who signs the prospectus of a company on behalf of a person named therein as a director, must be appointed in writing.

(*c*) An agent who is appointed orally may bind his principal by a written contract or a contract which requires a memorandum in writing, e.g. an agreement concerning land.

In addition, if the agent exceeds his authority thus stepping out of the four corners of the relationship of principal and agent, the principal may *ratify* the act and create the relationship of principal and agent in respect of it. The relationship may also be created by operation of law as where the principal becomes bound under the rules relating to apparent authority or agency by estoppel.

Authority

ACTUAL AUTHORITY

This may arise as follows—

(1) *Actual authority by express agreement.* The agent is entitled to exercise the powers actually given to him under the contract of agency and will bind the principal by the exercise of those powers.

(2) *Actual authority by implication or incidental authority.* While the court may be prepared to imply an authority not *expressly* contained in the contract of agency, it is, in general, reluctant to imply powers where the contract of agency is under seal. Where the contract is not sealed, there is greater latitude and the court may more easily imply that an agent has authority to do what is ordinarily or necessarily incidental to the proper performance of his *express* authority. (*Comber* v *Anderson* 1808;[207] *Australia and New Zealand Bank* v *Ateliers de Constructions Electriques de Charleroi* 1966.)[208]

(3) *Actual authority derived from usual or customary authority.* Where the agent is one of a class of agents, e.g. an auctioneer, estate agent, factor, solicitor, partner, managing director of a company or company secretary his actual authority may be extended to cover the powers which an agent of his class normally possesses. Thus in *Freeman & Lockerly* v *Buckhurst Park Properties Ltd* [1964] 1 All E.R. 630, a person acting as managing director without express authority of the board, but with their knowledge, employed on behalf of the company a firm of architects and surveyors for the submission of an application for planning permission which involved preparing plans and defining boundaries. It was held that the company was liable to pay their fees. The managing director had bound the company by his acts, because he had the usual powers of a managing director. Again, in *Panorama Developments (Guildford)* v *Fidelis Furnishing Fabrics* [1971] 3 All E.R. 16, the Court of Appeal held that a modern company secretary was not a mere clerk and must be regarded as having authority to sign contracts connected with the administrative side of the company's affairs, and in this case bound the company when he ordered taxis, some of which were used to take cus-

tomers of the firm to Heathrow Airport, but some of which he used for his own purposes.

It would also appear that a solicitor has usual authority to compromise a claim by his client. In *Waugh* v *H.B. Clifford & Sons* [1982] 1 All E.R. 1095 a claim by the plaintiff against the defendant builders for damages for alleged negligence in building a house was compromised by the defendant solicitor who agreed with the plaintiff's solicitor that the defendants should purchase the house. The defendants did not wish this compromise but their solicitor did not know this at the time that he made it. This action, in the Court of Appeal by the plaintiff to enforce the agreement to buy the house by specific performance, succeeded.

Thus, unless the third party knows that the usual powers have been withdrawn, the agent will bind the principal so long as the contract is one which an agent of the class has *usual* authority to make, even though the agent has exceeded his express authority. (*Watteau* v *Fenwick* 1893.)[209] It is a matter for the court to decide what the usual authority is any particular case.

Where the agent has actual authority the third party will obtain a contract with the principal; the agent will be able to enforce the contract of agency against the principal and recover his remuneration or claim indemnity for any losses incurred, and the principal cannot sue the agent for breach of the contract of agency and third party cannot sue the agent for breach of warranty of authority, except in the case of usual authority.

Where the principal has expressly withdrawn the usual powers of the agent, as in *Watteau* v *Fenwick* 1893,[209] the third party obtains a contract with the principal by virtue of the *usual authority* of the agent, but the principal can sue the agent for breach of the contract of agency, and the agent cannot claim either remuneration or indemnity.

APPARENT OR OSTENSIBLE AUTHORITY OR AGENCY BY ESTOPPEL

This arises where the principal holds out a person as his agent for the purpose of making a contract with a third party, and the third party relies on that fact. (*Spiro* v *Lintern* 1973.)[210] The third party will obtain a contract with the principal, but the principal can sue the agent for damages and the agent cannot recover remuneration or indemnity if he had in fact no authority. Such apparent authority often arises from the course of dealing between the parties. (*Dodsley* v *Varley* 1840;[211] *Povey* v *Taylor* 1966.)[212]

AGENCY OF NECESSITY

An agent of necessity is a person who, in an emergency, acquires, by operation of law, presumed authority to act as an agent. The topic may be considered under the following headings—

(1) *Ships' masters.* A ship's master may mortgage the ship or the cargo

in order to pay for repairs or other expenditure necessary to successfully complete the voyage. Where the ship's master mortgages the ship, he is an agent of necessity for the shipowner and, in the case of cargo, for the cargo owner. If the cargo is perishable, the ship's master can presumably sell it if it is going bad.

The authority of the ship's master is said to depend upon inability to communicate with the owner or his agent, and, if this is a basic requirement, then modern systems of communication make the situation less likely to occur today.

(2) *Salvors.* A person who aids a ship in distress at sea and saves life or property may claim a reward which is generally at the discretion of the court.

(3) *Carriers and other bailees.* Carriers and other bailees may do acts intended to preserve the things in their custody. (*Great Northern Railway* v *Swaffield* 1874.)[213] However, they cannot sell the things entrusted to them without facing an action for conversion unless there is (*a*) some emergency, e.g. where the goods are perishing; or where the agent's premises are destroyed and the goods are exposed to weather or possible theft; and (*b*) it is impossible to communicate with the owner in time to save the goods. (*Springer* v *Great Western Railway* 1921.)[214]

The doctrine of agency of necessity is rarely applied where the goods are not perishable (*Prager* v *Blatspiel Stamp and Heacock Ltd* 1924),[215] or where the goods are sold merely because they are an inconvenience to the bailee. (See e.g. *Sachs* v *Miklos* 1948.)[216] This is a harsh rule for bailees who are left with goods and are unable to find the owner, although where the bailees accept goods for repair or other treatment for reward the Torts (Interference with Goods) Act 1977 applies. Briefly, the Act in s.12 and Sch.1 provides for the sale of goods accepted for repair or other treatment or for valuation or appraisal, or for storage and warehousing, providing the bailee gives notice to the bailor specifying the date on or after which he proposes the sell the goods. The period between the notice and date specifying sale must be such as will afford the bailor a reasonable opportunity of taking delivery of the goods. This period must in general be at least three months. A bailee who sells the goods under s.12 must account to the owner for the proceeds of sale. He may, however, deduct the costs of sale and any money owing to him by the owners, e.g. for the work done on the goods.

A bailee who does not wish to sell under s.12 without more may apply to the court under s.13 for authority to sell under the direction of the court in order to gain protection from any subsequent complaint by the bailor. This would be particularly advisable where there was a dispute between the bailor and another as to who owned the goods.

It should also be noted that the High Court has a general discretion under Rules of The Supreme Court to order the sale of goods if it is reasonable to do so, as where the goods are perishable (and see *Larner* v *Fawcett* 1950).[217]

Thus the Unsolicited Goods and Services Acts 1971 and 1975 (see p. 4) regulate the position of a person who has unsolicited goods sent to him, while the 1977 Act deals with bailees who are left with uncollected goods on their premises.

It is doubtful whether the cases in which carriers and other bailees have been able to sell or dispose of the goods in their care are really true examples of agency of necessity, and it is perhaps better to regard their powers of disposition as an example of an implied term in the pre-existing contract of carriage or bailment.

Where a complete stranger deals with the goods of another, agency of necessity does not arise. (*Binstead* v *Buck* 1777[218] and *Nicholson* v *Chapman* 1793.[219] This rule seems to be based upon the fact that liabilities are not to be forced upon persons behind their backs.

SUBSEQUENT AUTHORITY OR RATIFICATION

Where an agent makes an unathorized contract on behalf of his principal, though purporting to act for him, the principal may afterwards expressly ratify or adopt the contract.

The principal may, alternately, make an *implied* ratification by his conduct. For example, if the agent makes an unauthorized contract to buy good, and his principal receives the goods and fails to return them or uses them, he has ratified by implication of law. No formal ratification is required. Again where an agent makes a contract for the supply of goods to be delivered in the future, then, if the principal delays unduly in repudiating it after he has notice that the agent has made it, he will be regarded as having ratified by his acquiescence.

The following rules govern whether ratification can take place.

(1) The agent must contract expressly as an agent for a principal, who must be named or so described as to make it possible for the third party to identify him. Thus an undisclosed principal cannot ratify. (See p. 113) (*Keighley, Maxsted* v *Durant* 1901.)[220]

(2) The principal must be in existence when the agent makes the contract. Thus a prospective agent, e.g. a company promoter, cannot enter into a contract on behalf of a company before incorporation, and the company cannot ratify the contract after its incorporation. The position is now governed by the European Communities Act 1972, s.9(2), which provides that a promoter is personally liable on a pre-incorporation contract, whether he makes it in the capacity of an agent for the company or not.

(3) A void contract cannot be ratified. Thus a company cannot ratify *ultra vires* contracts made by its agents on its behalf. (*Ashbury Railway Carriage Co.* v *Riche* 1875.)[83]

A voidable contract can be ratified but the principal becomes liable for the fraud or misrepresentation of the agent. For example, if an agent, acting without authority, sells P's house and represents that the drains are in good order when they are not, and P later ratifies the contract, P becomes liable along with the agent for fraud, if the agent knew that the drains were not in good order. If the agent's statement is made innocently, the third party can rescind the contract with P, or if made negligenly, sue P for damages. (*Gosling* v *Anderson* 1972.)[118] There is no action against the agent under s.2(1) of the Misrepresentation Act 1967. The agent will be liable in damages to the third party only if he is guilty of fraud or under the rule in *Hedley Byrne*[120] for negligence at common law. (See *Resolute Maritime Inc* v *Nippon Kaiji Kyokai* 1983, p. 415.)

(4) A forgery cannot be ratified. If X forges Y's signature on a document, Y cannot ratify the signature so as to make the document good. However, if the person whose signature is forged knows of the forgery and acts in such a way as to induce a third party to believe that the signature is genuine, he will be estopped from denying that it is his signature in any action between him and third party who has acted upon it. (*Greenwood* v *Martins Bank Ltd* 1933.)[221]

(5) Ratification must be based on full knowledge of the material facts. If the agent tells his principal: 'I have sold your house for £36,000', when he has only sold for £35,000, the principal can cancel the ratification.

(6) ratification must be of the whole contract. The court will not allow ratification of the beneficial parts only. To do so would be to impose on the third party a contract he did not make.

(7) ratification can only be retrospective. A principal cannot say to his agent in advance, 'I will ratify all your future contracts'.

(8) Where ratification of a contract is validly effected, it is retrospective in its operation, i.e. the parties are put in the position they would have occupied if the professed agent had, when the contract was made, the authority he purported to possess. (*Bolton Partners* v *Lambert* 1889.)[222]

The rule of retrospective ratification is subject to certain exceptions—

(*a*) The rule does not allow ratification of an insurance contract after loss has occurred unless it is marine insurance.(*Grover and Grover Ltd* v *Mathews* 1910.)[223]

(*b*) The rule does not apply where it would cause excessive hardship to the third party. (*Walter* v *James* 1871.)[224]

(*c*) The rule does not apply if the third party knows he is dealing with an agent who *requires* the ratification of his principal (*Watson* v *Davies* 1931.)[225], or where the third party has some intimation that this is so. (*Warehousing and Forwarding Co. of East Africa* v *Jafferali & Sons* 1963.)[226] In *Bolton Partners*[222] the third party believed that the agent had authority and did not require the ratification of his principal.

(*d*) Ratification must be within a reasonable time, and before the time fixed for performance has expired.

Where the contract between the agent and third party has been made under seal, the ratification must be under seal. (*Hunter* v *Parker* (1840)

7 M. & W.322.) Otherwise ratification may be made informally even where the contract between the agent and third party is in writing or requires a memorandum in writing. (*Maclean* v *Dunn* (1828) 4 Bing. 722.)

The principal must have capacity both when he ratifies and when the agent made the unauthorized contract, e.g. he must not be a minor or a person of unsound mind at either time. So if the principal was insane when his agent made the contract, he cannot ratify it if he regains his sanity. The Infants' Relief Act 1874, s.2, provides that, if an agent makes a contract for a minor, then the minor cannot ratify it after reaching his majority, unless the contract was for necessaries or beneficial services, or was a voidable contract, e.g. a contract to take shares in a company.

The agency of a wife

The subject may be considered under the following headings.

REAL AUTHORITY

This arises where the husband actually authorizes his wife to buy the goods needed by the family.

PRESUMPTION OF AUTHORITY DURING COHABITATION

This form of agency has no necessary connection with marital status and could just as well arise in the case of a common-law wife or housekeeper. However, arising from the fact of cohabitation in a domestic establishment there is a presumption that a wife has authority to order necessaries suitable to her husband's style of living for those departments of their household which a wife usually has under her control, and to pledge her husband's credit for that purpose.(*Jolly* v *Rees* (1864) 15 C.B.(N.S.) 628.)

The husband may rebut this presumption and avoid liability by showing that he has expressly warned the tradesmen, whether by a particular or a general notice, not to supply his wife with goods on credit, or that he has forbidden her to pledge his credit, or that she has already a sufficient supply of the goods in question, or that the order was, in view of the style in which the husband was living, excessive in terms of quantity or extravagant in terms of quality, or finally, that the wife was supplied with a sufficient allowance or sufficient means of obtaining the articles in question without pledging her husband's credit. However, if the husband relies upon an allowance which he makes to his wife it must be of a fixed amount and paid regularly. Certainly, the fact that the wife has an income of her own may negative her presumptive authority to pledge her husband's credit for her own, as opposed to household, necessaries.

If credit was not given to the husband but exclusively to the wife, the husband is not liable, even though the wife is living with her husband and he has seen her in possession of the goods received on credit.

AGENCY OF NECESSITY

Section 41 of the Matrimonial Proceedings and Property Act 1970, abolishes the concept of a deserted wife's agency of necessity. A wife cannot pledge her husband's credit for necessary goods while deserted.

Section 41 of the 1970 Act was repealed by the Matrimonial Causes Act 1973, s.54 and Sch.3, but not so as to revive the deserted wife's agency of necessity. (See Interpretation Act 1978, s.161(1), which provides that where an Act is repealed pre-existing law is not revived unless a contrary intervention appears.)

It is worth noting that there is no agency of necessity in a child to pledge its father's credit; there must be some evidence of assent by the father.

The duties of an agent

AS A GENERAL RULE THE AGENT MUST PERFORM HIS DUTIES IN PERSON

The maxim is *delegatus non potest delegare*. (A delegate cannot delegate.) The rule that an agent cannot delegate his authority without the express or implied assent of his principal arises out of the personal trust and confidence which must be reposed in an agent by his principal. The principal may, of course, give his agent authority to delegate, or may ratify the agent's act of delegation either expressly or by his conduct, and the maxim does not rule out the employment of clerks and assistants, i.e. persons who carry out their duties under some supervision. Clearly anyone can type letters for an agent so long as he dictates them.

Delegation is allowed in certain cases—

(1) Where delegation of authority is authorized by custom. It is the practice of country solicitors to employ town agents in the matter of litigation. (*Re Newen* [1903] 1 Ch. 812.)

(2) Delegation by implication may arise from the circumstances. Where the agent is a company, the company must obviously act through agents, and where the agent is a partnership, each partner may bind the firm.

(3) Delegation may be permitted in a sudden emergency, as where the agent is ill.

(4) Delegation may be permitted, even though it has not been expressly authorized, where the work of the agency is such that it does not require the discretion or particular skill of the agent. In this connec-

tion it was held by the Court of Appeal in *John McCann & Co.* v *Pow* [1975] 1 All E.R. 129 that the role of estate agents in advertising a property for sale and introducing prospective purchasers was a role involving particular skill, confidence or discretion, so that the estate agents in this case were not entitled to delegate their functions to sub-agents without the authority express or implied of the vendor principal. Furthermore, the vendor was under no liability to pay commission either to the agents or unauthorized sub-agents in respect of a sale to a purchaser introduced by the unauthorized sub-agents.

Where delegation is authorized expressly or by implication, or where the agent's conduct in delegating is known to the principal and is acquiesced in, or where the delegation is in the nature of a mere ministerial act, i.e. an act not requiring discretion or particular skill, the act of the sub-agent is effective and binding as between the principal and third party. Thus in *Allam & Co.* v *Europa Poster Services* [1968] 1 All E.R. 826, Allam and its subsidiary companies placed advertisements on sites owned by several persons. This arrangement could be terminated by the owners of the sites giving notice to Allam. Europa wished to place advertisements on the sites and the site owners authorized Europa to act as agents to serve the necessary notices. Europa asked their solicitors to write the letters giving notice, which they did. Allam later challenged the validity of the notices, i.e. had they been served by the site owners' agents or not? It was held by Buckley, J., that although a contract of agency normally involves a confidential relationship between principal and agent, the agent may nevertheless properly sub-delegate acts such as the writing of letters giving notice because such acts are purely ministerial and involve no confidential relationship.

The legal relationship of the principal and the sub-agent depends upon whether there is privity of contract between them—

(1) Where the sub-agent completely replaces the agent, there is privity of contract between the principal and the sub-agent, provided the agent has clear authority to create such privity. If he has, the principal can sue the sub-agent direct, e.g. for an account of profits made on the sale of the principal's goods. Thus in *De Bussche* v *Alt* (1878) 8 Ch.D. 286 the principal, De Bussche, appointed Gilman & Co. as his agents to sell a ship in China at a certain price. Gilman, not being able to sell the ship in China at the agreed price, obtained the approval of the principal, De Bussche, to the appointment by Gilman & Co. of a sub-agent, Alt, in Japan to sell the ship at the price required by the principal. It was held that De Bussche had a direct claim against Alt for the sale price of the ship.

(2) Where the sub-agent merely assists in the carrying out of the agency, but does not entirely replace the agent, there is no privity of contract between the principal and the sub-agent, and only the the agent can be sued by the principal in respect of the sub-agent's breaches of agreement. However, the sub-agent is under a fiduciary duty to the

principal to disclose secret profits, and probably also for negligence resulting in loss or damage to the principal's goods while in the sub-agent's possession. This liability arises from the law of bailment and is based upon cases concerning the liability of sub-bailees. (*Learoyd Bros* v *Pope* 1966.)[227] In a proper case of delegation where an agent exercises care in selecting the sub-agent, the agent is not liable to the principal for the sub-agent's fraud.

THE AGENT MUST CARRY OUT HIS WORK WITH ORDINARY SKILL AND DILIGENCE

Both gratuitous agents and paid agents are responsible to the principal for the negligent performance of their duties. (*Keppel* v *Wheeler* 1927[228] and *Kenney* v *Hall* 1976.)[229] A gratuitous agency arises where the agent renders the principal some friendly service for which there is no payment. In such cases there is no question of the principal suing the agent for breach of an agency contract because, without consideration, there is no contract to enforce. Nevertheless the fiduciary duties of principal and agent exist, so that a gratuitous agent must not make secret profits, and must act throughout with the same good faith as a paid one. A gratuitous agent will be held liable for negligent acts in the course of his work, but not for neglecting to act at all, i.e. for *misfeasance* but not for *nonfeasance*. Where he damages the principal's goods by negligent handling of them, he will be liable. Where he agrees to sell the principal's house for him without reward and makes no attempt to sell it, thus losing a favourable market, he will not be liable. A paid agent will be liable in both cases, i.e. for either misfeasance or nonfeasance.

As regards the standard of care, a person who acts as an agent for another without reward is bound to display such skill as he actually posesses and exercise such care as he would in his own affairs, i.e. comply with a subjective test. An agent for reward is under a more extensive obligation and must exhibit such a degree of skill and diligence as is appropriate to the performance of the duties he has accepted. This is, of course, an objective test. It should be noted in particular that a professional agent must show the degree of care to be expected of those in his profession and this will normally apply even where the professional agent is acting gratuitously.

THERE MUST BE NO CONFLICT OF INTEREST BETWEEN PRINCIPAL AND AGENT

The agent must acquaint his principal immediately with everything relating to the agency, and must obtain the best possible price on sale. The fiduciary duty which the agent owes to his principal is a high one.

The agent must not use his position for his personal benefit to the detriment of his principal, and he must not become a principal as against his employer. In other words there must be *no conflict of interest between principal and agent.* Therefore unless full disclosure exists between them, the agent cannot buy the principal's property, and it is immaterial that the contract is in all respects fair. Thus in *McPherson* v *Watt* (1877) 3 App. Cas. 254, the agent of two trustees who wanted to sell a house subject to a trust, bought it in the name of his brother so as to conceal that he was really buying it for himself. Specific performance of the contract of sale was refused and it was immaterial that the contract price was a fair one. Nor may an agent act for the two principals in the same transaction unless both agree. (*Anglo-African Merchants Ltd* v *Bayley* 1969.)[230] The fiduciary duty may continue to rest on an ex-agent (*Reiger* v *Campbell-Stuart* 1939[231] though only where the agency is confidential in its subject-matter or concerned with trade secrets. However, as a general rule the continued duty to observe the principal's interest can only be achieved by a contract in restraint of trade which is not against public policy or excessively wide.

There is also a fiduciary duty where the agent is self-appointed and is acting without authority. Thus in *English* v *Dedham Vale Properties* [1978] 1 All E.R. 382, A sold property to B without planning permission for development. Before contracts were exchanged B applied for planning permission for a detached house on the site in A's name as A's agent. Planning permission was given but contracts were exchanged at the original price. It was held by Slade, J., that B must account for the extra profit made as a result of the increase in price arising from planning permission, which was undisclosed.

THE AGENT MUST KEEP PROPER ACCOUNTS OF ALL TRANSACTIONS CONNECTED WITH THE AGENCY AND RENDER THEM TO THE PRINCIPAL ON REQUEST

This duty is very useful where the agent is a general agent carrying out a series of transactions for the principal, and enables the principal to see what profits have been made, what charges the agent has incurred, and whether the expenditure is legitimate. An agent must pay over to his principal all money received on the principal's behalf. This applies even though the transaction under which the money was received was void or illegal. Thus if an agent is employed to make bets he must pay over any winnings he receives as a result. (*De Mattos* v *Benjamin* (1894) 63 L.J.Q.B. 248.)

THE AGENT MUST HAND OVER ALL PROFITS RESULTING DIRECTLY OR INDIRECTLY FROM THE AGENCY

Unless the agent tells his principal that he has made a profit over and above his agreed commission or remuneration by the use of the principal's property or from the fact that he has acted as the principal's agent *and the principal consents*, then A must account to P for any profit made. (See *Hippisley* v *Knee Bros* 1905.)[232]

THE AGENT IS UNDER A DUTY TO OBEY THE LAWFUL INSTRUCTIONS OF HIS PRINCIPAL

Where an agent has specific instructions he must follow them (*Bertram, Armstrong & Co.* v *Godfrey* 1830),[233] unless they are unlawful. (*Bexwell* v *Christie* 1776.)[234] In the absence of instructions, and where matters are left to his discretion, the agent must act in good faith and to the best of his judgment for the benefit of the principal. If he does not do so, he is liable to his principal for loss incurred.

THE AGENT HAS A DUTY TO KEEP THE PRINCIPAL'S PROPERTY SEPARATE

The agent must keep his principal's property and money separate from his own. If he fails to do so and he is solvent, everything which he cannot prove to be his own will be presumed to belong to the principal, and there is a presumption that everything in a mixed account is the principal's, at least up to the amount that the principal alleges the agent owes him. The onus of proving otherwise is on the agent.

If the agent is bankrupt the matter is more complicated. Suppose A (the agent) owes P (the principal) £1000, being the proceeds of sale of P's goods which A has sold. A is bankrupt. Must P prove in the bankruptcy with A's other creditors for an equal dividend with them, or can he trace his money into A's funds and withdraw it from those funds by means of a charging order?

This depends upon whether the court considers that the relationship between A and P is *for the purpose of remedies* fiduciary, i.e. like that of trustee and beneficiary, or that of debtor and creditor. Certainly the relationship between A and P is fiduciary for some purposes, e.g. the agent must not make secret profits. However, the position with regard to remedies is not so clear. In *Lister & Co.* v *Stubbs* (1890) 45 Ch.D. 1 Stubbs was authorized by the plaintiff to buy materials for use in their business which was silk spinning, dyeing and manufacturing. In the course of this agency Stubbs secretly and wrongfully recovered from a trade customer, Varley & Co., large sums of money by way of double commision which he was liable to hand over to the plaintiffs. Instead he purchased investments for himself. In this action the plaintiffs tried to recover the investments. The Court of Appeal said that they only had an action for the money against Stubbs personally and not against the investments. The relationship was that of debtor and creditor. Lindley, L.J., said: 'But the relation between them (he refers to Lister and Stubbs) is that of debtor and creditor it is not that of trustee and *cestui que trust* (beneficiary). We are asked to hold that it is—which would involve consequences which, I confess, startle me. One consequence, of course, would be that, if Stubbs were to become bankrupt, this property acquired by him with the money paid to him by Messrs Varley would be withdrawn from the mass of his creditors and be handed over bodily to Lister

& Co. Can that be right? . . .' He went on to say that it was not right, the relationship being that of debtor and creditor.

By contrast in *Taylor* v *Plumer* (1815) 3 M.&S. 562 Sir Thomas Plumer had given money to Walsh, a stockbroker, for investment. Walsh improperly purchased American investments and bullion and hurried to Falmouth to take a ship to Lisbon and so to North America. He was apprehended while waiting for the ship to put to sea and the investments and bullion were seized. His trustee in bankruptcy claimed in this action to recover them from Sir Thomas Plumer. The action failed. In other words, Sir Thomas had a right to claim against Walsh the full value of the property in to which the money given to Walsh had been converted and not merely a dividend in the bankruptcy.

The true position may well be therefore that there is no tracing remedy in general commercial transactions such as *Lister* where the court may well hold that the relationship between agent and principal is one of debtor and creditor. However, if, as in *Taylor*, P entrusts money to A to hold or convert into specific property for the benefit of P, then a trust relationship may be created and the remedy of tracing could be used.

BRIBES

If the agent takes any bribe, i.e. a secret commission the principal has all the following rights—

(1) To dismiss the agent without notice.

(2) To refuse the agent his renumeration or commission, or to recover it if paid. (*Andrews* v *Ramsay & Co.* 1903.)[235]

(3) To recover the bribe—

(*a*) from the agent if he has received it (*Andrews* v *Ramsay & Co.* 1903;[235] or

(*b*) from the third party if it has not been paid but only promised.

(4) To sue the third party for damages. These are awarded without deduction of the amount of any bribe recovered by the principal. (*Salford Corporation* v *Lever* 1891.)[236] It should be noted, however, that the agent may be sued for the recovery of the bribe or in fraud but not for both. There can be no double recovery from the agent himself. Thus in *Maheson S/O Thambiah* v *Malaysia Government Officers' Cooperative Housing Society* [1978] 2 All E.R. 405, T bought land for 456,000 dollars and spent 45,000 on it. He then sold the land to P for 944,000 dollars, having bribed P's agent with the sum of 122,000 dollars. P wanted to sue A for recovery of the bribe of 122,000 dollars and for loss in fraud, i.e., 443,000 dollars. It was held by the Privy Council that they must elect and so P sued for their loss in fraud and recovered 443,000 dollars against A. The Privy Council disapproved *dicta* in the *Salford Case*[236] which suggested that there might be double recovery from the agent himself.

(5) The principal may repudiate the contract with the third party whether or not the secret payment had any effect on the agent. (*Shipway* v *Broadwood* 1889.)[237]

(6) The principal may prosecute the agent and the third party under the Prevention of Corruption Act 1906, with the consent of the Attorney-General or Solicitor-General. (See also the Public Bodies Corrupt Practices Act 1889, which operates where the agency occurs in a public service situation, e.g. local government.)

The rules relating to secret profits and bribes apply to an agent who is not receiving payment. (*Turnbull* v *Garden* 1869.)[238]

AN AGENT IS ESTOPPED FROM DENYING HIS PRINCIPAL'S TITLE TO MONEY OR GOODS ON THE GROUNDS THAT HE OR OTHERS HAVE SUPERIOR RIGHTS

If there are competing demands for property in the agent's possession, the agent must not deliver it to a third party who may be claiming for example that the principal has sold him the goods. This would constitute a denial of the principal's title which an agent cannot in general do. (*Lyell* v *Kennedy* (1889) 14 App. Cas. 437.) What the agent may do is to institute interpleader proceedings whereby the principal and the third party are brought into an action together to decide who has the right to the property. The agent can then hand over the property to the person entitled and will not be liable in conversion.

An agent may deny the principal's title to property where—

(1) at the time of taking possession the agent had no knowledge of other claims; and

(2) the agent is defending the third party's title with the latter's authority against the principal.

Thus if P (a landlord) takes T's (a tenant's) goods for non-payment of rent and gives them to A his agent to sell, then if in fact T had paid his rent so that P's taking of the goods was unlawful, A could refuse to sell them and defend T's title against P. (*Biddle* v *Bond* (1865) 6 B.&S. 225.) A could not take this action if he was aware of the unlawful taking when he received the goods for he is then virtually a party to the illegality himself and cannot stand aside from it. T could sue P for unlawful distraint.

As regards the receipt of money unlawfully obtained, the agent is not accountable to the third party unless he is involved in the wrongful act. Thus if P (a trustee) wrongfully takes trust money and gives it to A (his agent) to buy goods, then T (a beneficiary) cannot sue A unless A was involved in and had knowledge of the unlawful act of P. T could sue P for breach of trust. (*Carl-Zeiss Stiftung* v *Herbert Smith & Co.* (No. 2),

[1969] 2 All E.R. 367.)

Rights of the agent against his principal

THE AGENT'S LIEN

This is a special right under which the agent may retain the principal's goods which are in the agent's lawful possession where the principal has not satisfied his liabilities to the agent, e.g. his charges and commissions. The power is to retain in the hope of a settlement; there is not in general a power to sell.

Lien may be of two kinds—

(1) *A general lien.* Under a general lien the agent may retain goods of the principal even though the principal does not owe the agent money in respect of those goods, but in respect of other goods the agent has dealt with. Such a lien may be possessed by a general agent, i.e. an agent who carries out a series of transactions for the principal. However, the law does not favour general liens, and such a lien will only arise—

(*a*) by express agreement of the principal and agent; or

(*b*) By judicially recognized custom, e.g. a customary general lien is possessed by solicitors, bankers and factors. See p. 118.)

(2) *A particular lien.* A particular lien is favoured by the law and a lien, where it exists, is likely to be particular rather than general. Under such a lien the agent is entitled to retain a particular article until the principal pays him what he owes in respect of it and in addition, has the right to sue a purchaser in his own name for the whole purchase price, even though he has been paid his agent's commission, by reason of the contract between him and the purchaser which gives a lien on the goods for the whole purchase price. (*Chelmsford Auctions Ltd* v *Poole* 1973.)[239]

It was decided in *Woodworth* v *Conroy* [1976] 1 All E.R. 107 that an accountant has a particular lien over documents belonging to his client in respect of which the accountant has performed work for which he has not been paid the fee due. A lien would probably not be upheld in regard to the accounting records which a company must keep in order to comply with s.12 of the Companies Act 1976. These records are documents which must by reason of that section be kept by the company, at its registered office or at such other places as the directors of the company think fit and must at all times be open to inspection by the officers of the company. It would be difficult to comply with this section if an accountant were to be exercising a lien upon the accounting records of companies. In addition, of course, a long line of authority exists, e.g. *Re Capital Fire Insurance Association* (1883) 24 Ch.D. 408, in which the courts have held that no lien can exist over the books or documents of a registered company.

THE AGENT'S RIGHT TO REMUNERATION

The remuneration is generally specified in the agreement and may take the form of salary or commission or both. If no remuneration is specified, the court will imply a reasonable remuneration where the relationship is a commercial one and payment is usual. If the agent wishes to sue for remuneration under the contract, then it must comply with the general law of contract, and must not, for example, be illegal. (*Crouch and Lees* v *Haridas* 1971.)[240] The agent loses his right to remuneration if he acts without authority or is in breach of a fiduciary duty, though the court may grant relief. (See *Hippisley* v *Knee* 1905.)[232] The agent must also substantially perform his part of the contract before he is entitled to remuneration. (*Rimmer* v *Knowles* 1874.)[241]

Where the agent buys or sells goods on behalf of the principal he can generally ensure that a contract binding on the principal is made. The main difficulties with regard to remuneration have arisen in connection with commission agents, e.g. estate agents. Such an agent, being paid by commission, is not really paid for the work he does, but for the contracts he procures. If he does not procure a contract, he does not seem to be entitled to any payment, it being the common understanding of people that the agent's commission is payable out of the purchase price, unless he has made some provision regarding this in his agreement with the principal. Such agents have less control over the making of the contract than other agents. Estate agents merely introduce a possible purchaser to the principal and hope that a contract will be made between them.

The agent's right to commission can be considered under the following headings—

(1) *Where the transaction goes through*, i.e. where the third party and the principal actually make a contract. To obtain his commission the agent must show that the sale really and substantially proceeded from his acts. (*Coles* v *Enoch* 1939[242] and *Rolfe & Co.* v *George* 1968.)[243]

(2) *Where the transaction does not go through to completion*. The courts are not anxious to imply terms into the contract of agency in order to secure the agent's commission if no contract is made. (*Luxor (Eastbourne) Ltd* v *Cooper* 1941.)[244]

A term may be implied, however, if the principal has entered into a concluded contract with the third party which he does not then perform. (See *Alpha Trading Ltd* v *Dunnshaw-Patten Ltd* [1981] 1 All E.R. 482, p. 477.)

Estate agents tried to make commission payable on 'introducing a purchaser'. This formula could fail because it was construed by the courts as a 'willing purchaser', and a purchaser is not 'willing' if he accepts 'subject to contract'. (*Christie, Owen and Davies Ltd* v *Stockton* 1953.)[245] However, where the purchaser signs a contract and the seller will not sign it and go on with the contract, commission may be payable. (*Christie, Owen and Davies* v *Rapacioli* 1974.)[246]

The agent can find some answer to his dilemma by providing in his contract that he is appointed sole agent, *and* that he has the sole and exclusive right to sell. The sole agency protects him against sales by other agents and the sole and exclusive right to sell against sales by the owner and he may claim commission even if another agent or the owner sells. Thus in *Gross Fine & Krieger Chalfen* v *Gaynor* (1974) 233 E.G. 1015 it was held that the plaintiffs, who had been appointed sole agents to sell land by auction, were entitled to their commission although the land was sold by another agent by a private purchase before the auction. The agent may further provide that commission is payable when the prospective purchaser signs the agent's purchaser's agreement and the vendor signs the agent's vendor's agreement. In such a case it seems that commission is payable whether the sale takes place or not, depending as it does merely on the signing of the two agreements. (*Drewery & Drewery* v *Ware Lane* 1960.)[247] There is no right of action on a *quantum meruit* in these cases. The principle of *quantum meruit* does not apply if there is, as here, a specific contract fixing the way in which remuneration or commission is to be earned. (See p. 87.)

Where the property to be sold is in the hands of more than one agent then, on the assumption that none of the agents has a sole and exclusive right to sell, commission is payable to the agent who first finds a person who enters into a contract with the vendor. Thus in *A. A. Dickson & Co.* v *O'Leary* (1979) 254 E.G. 731, the estate agents, Dickson, had been instructed by Mr O'Leary in the sale of his flat. The terms of the agreement between the agents and O'Leary were: 'Should we be successful in either directly or indirectly introducing a person ready, able, and willing to purchase on terms authorized by you, we shall look to you for payment of our commission of 2½% of the purchase price.' Mr O'Leary had also instructed other agents and although Dickson produced a prospective purchaser, Mr O'Leary had exchanged contracts with another purchaser before the Dickson purchaser was ready to exchange contracts. Dickson unsuccessfully sued for the commission.

Where the agent misleads the purchaser so that the contract is voidable, commission will not be payable, since its payment depends upon the agent introducing a purchaser 'ready, willing and able' to enter into a binding contract, and a voidable contract is not binding. (*Peter Long and Partners* v *Burns* 1956[248] and *Blake & Co.* v *Sohn* 1969.)[249] However, *Scheggia* v *Gradwell* 1963[250] suggests that the third party need not be able to purchase so long as he is willing to sign the contract, though in *Wilkinson* v *Brown* 1966[251] it was said that the scope of this decision should not be extended and that normally the third party must be able to complete the purchase if he wishes to do so.

As regards deposits, a potential purchaser can generally recover any deposit paid if he does not continue with a 'subject to contract' purchase. (*Chillingworth* v *Esche* 1923.)[252] Additionally, it should be noted that if A employs B, an estate agent, to sell a property, then unless A actually authorizes B to receive a deposit from a purchaser, C, on his (A's) behalf, then A will not be liable to repay it to C if B receives it and misappropriates it. (*Sorrel* v *Finch* 1976.)[253]

Although *Sorrel* v *Finch* 1976[253] is still to be relied upon as regards the situation as between principal and agent where the agent misappropriates a deposit, under the Estate Agents Act 1979, s.13, any deposit received by an estate agent is held by that agent on trust for the person making the deposit. It does not form part of the agent's assets on insolvency and his trustee in bankruptcy is not entitled to it. Thus the deposit can be recovered in full in the bankruptcy of the agent but if it has been mixed with other funds it would be necessary to trace it as far as identifiable into those funds. This should not happen because s.14 requires that clients' money be paid into a separate client account which must be audited. In addition, under s.16 the estate agent is bound to take up an indemnity policy to cover loss of money deposited with him. Furthermore, the Act excludes from the function of estate agency those who are bankrupts, though bankrupts may work as employees of estate agents.

AGENT'S RIGHT TO AN INDEMNITY

The agent may in the course of his duty incur liabilities or make payments of money for the principal, and he has a right to be indemnified against such liabilities and to recover any money paid. (*Christoforides* v *Terry* 1924.)[254] He can enforce this right by action, by exercise of lien, or, if he is sued by the principal, by set-off.

The agent has no right to an indemnity if he acts without or against authority, unless the act is ratified by the principal, nor can he recover if, although obeying instructions, he commits a breach of a fiduciary duty or does not use skill and care. (*Davison* v *Fernandes* 1889.)[255]

Termination of agency

The contract between the agent and the principal may be terminated in many ways—

(1) *By mutual agreement* on terms acceptable to both parties.

(2) *By custom of trade* (*Dickinson* v *Lilwal* 1815.)[256]

(3) *By complete performance* of the contract, i.e. the completion of the business for which the agency was created. Thus an agent who is employed to sell a house determines his agency on selling it.

(4) *By expiration of time*, where the agency is entered into for a definite period.

(5) *By frustration*, which may arise—

(*a*) By impossibility of performance, as where the subject-matter of the agency is destroyed. Thus, if an agent is employed to sell a house, the agency terminates if the house is destroyed by fire.

(*b*) By illegality, as where the agency involves dealings with enemy aliens. (*Stevenson & Sons Ltd* v *A. G. für Cartonnagen Industrie* 1918.)[257]

(6) *By the death of either party.* Obviously the death of the agent will terminate the contract, since it is one of personal service. The agent's personal representatives could not be required to carry on the agency and the agent, being dead, cannot execute it. Similarly the agent's authority is terminated by the death of the principal, and this is so whether the agent or third party knows of the principal's death or not. Where the agent purports to contract on behalf of his principal after the principal's death, there is no contact with the principal's estate, and the agent can be sued for breach of warranty of authority. (*Blades* v *Free* (1829) 9 B.&C. 167.)

(7) *By insanity.* When the principal has become insane the agency itself is automatically terminated; and the same is true where the agent becomes insane, so long as the insanity is such as to render the principal or agent incapable of making a contract for himself. (*Yonge* v *Toynbee* 1910.)[258] However, where the principal is insane it seems that, if the agent purports to contract with persons who are ignorant of the fact of the principal's insanity and to whom the principal, when sane, had held out the agent as having authority, the principal cannot deny to those persons the continuation of the agent's authority. Thus it seems that, although actual authority is lost, apparent authority continues. (*Drew* v *Nunn* 1879.)[259]

The cases cited above are difficult to reconcile. The goods in *Drew* v *Nunn*[259] may have been necessaries but the report does not say so, and the court did not make its decision on that ground. If the liability of the principal is based on the ground of holding out the agent to the third party as having authority, the principal can only prevent liability from arising by giving it notice to the third party, and, since the principal is insane, it seems somewhat unjust to expect him to do this. On the other hand *Drew* v *Nunn*[259] may be an aspect of the agency of necessity of a wife, and may have more to do with family law as it then was than with the law of agency as such. However, it can be said that the question whether the third party must have notice or not of the insanity of the principal is not finally settled.

(8) *By bankruptcy or liquidation.* The principal's bankruptcy terminates the authority of the agent but the agent's bankruptcy does not of itself give the principal the right to dismiss him unless the insolvency affects the agent's fitness to act. By s.45 of the Bankruptcy Act 1914, where a principal becomes bankrupt, the agent has no liability for breaches of warranty of authority in respect of contracts which he makes before the date of the receiving order, but without notice of any act of bankruptcy. If the principal is a company, a winding-up order will

terminate the authority of its agents.

(9) *Revocation of the agent's authority by the principal.* The principal may terminate the agent's real or actual authority at any time. No special formalities are required and even an appointment by deed is revocable by parol notice. However, this may not terminate the contract and the agent will have an action for damages if the principal does not give him the period of notice specified in the contract, or, if none is specified, such notice is customary and reasonable. Nevertheless the agent's apparent authority continues until third parties with whom he has had dealings are notified of the agent's lack of authority.

Sometimes the continuation of apparent authority causes no difficulty, e.g. where the contract is one of service because managers of shops or clerks, when they are dismissed, normally disappear from the shop or office. The more difficult case is the agent who is an independent contractor, such as a broker, who may well continue to act as a broker even though a particular principal has terminated his authority. If the agent does contract on behalf of the principal in circumstances where he has apparent authority but after his actual authority is terminated, the principal will be bound by the contract but will have an action against his agent.

(10) *By renunciation.* The agent may renounce his authority and thus terminate the agency, but again the contract cannot be arbitrarily broken. The agent must give his principal the specified, or customary or reasonable notice, and, if he does not do so, the principal may sue the agent for breach of contract. The agent's apparent authority continues until third parties with whom he has had dealings are on notice of the agent's renunciation and, if the agent does make a contract on behalf of his principal after renouncing his authority, the principal will be bound to the third party, but will have an action against the former agent.

Limitations on principal's power to terminate the agency

The power of the principal to terminate the agent's authority is limited in certain circumstances.

(1) The principal cannot revoke the agent's authority where the agent has carried out, or is in process of carrying out, his instructions. Similarly the principal cannot terminate the agent's authority after a third party has started to act in reliance on the contract negotiated with the agent. (*Chappell* v *Bray* 1860.)[260]

(2) The principal cannot revoke where the agency is coupled with an interest. The interest of the agent must be more than a mere right to salary or commission and must amount to a form of security, as where P gives his creditor a power of attorney to collect P's debts and pay himself out of the proceeds. Furthermore, it was held in *re Olympic Fire &*

General Reinsurance Co Ltd [1920] 2 Ch. 341 that the authority to subscribe for shares which a sub-underwriter gives to a principal underwriter is an authority coupled with an interest and is irrevocable as between the two parties and the sub-underwriter and the company. An agency which is coupled with an interest is not termined by revocation, death or other incapacity of principal or agent.

(3) Irrevocable powers of attorney. The Powers of Attorney Act 1971 provides a type of irrevocable agency. For example, under s.4(1) of the Act a power of attorney which states that it is irrevocable and is given as a security for a proprietary interest of the person to whom it is given (the donee) or anyone deriving title to it from him, is not capable of being revoked so long as the interest remains unsatisfied—

(*a*) by the person giving it (the donor)—unless the donee consents; or

(*b*) by the death, unsoundness of mind, or bankruptcy of the donor including, where the donor is a corporation, winding-up or dissolution.

An example occurs where an equitable mortgage of a legal estate in land, e.g. a freehold, is made by deposit of title deeds, accompanied by what is known as a memorandum of deposit. The memorandum frequently contains a power of attorney authorizing the lender to sell the property if the borrower fails to repay the mortgage. Thus the lender has an interest in the land and the power cannot be revoked so long as that interest lasts, i.e. until the mortgage is repaid.

Powers of attorney which are not given as security may be revoked at any time by the donor and will be revoked automatically by his death, unsoundness of mind, or bankruptcy. (But see preface.)

However, the donee and persons dealing with him after the power has been revoked and whether given for security or not, will be protected by s.5 (*ibid.*) as follows—

(1) where the donee acts under the power at a time when it has been revoked he will not be liable to the donor or any other party if at the material time the donee was unaware of the revocation. A donee for security will normally only be in that position when his interest has been satisfied, since he should know that this has happened;

(2) where a power has been revoked and a person not knowing of the revocation deals with the donee, the transaction will be as valid as if the power had still been in being, though the donee may be liable to the donor if the donee knows of the revocation.

The Act abolishes the need to file copies of powers of attorney in the Central Office of the Supreme Court and at the Land Registry where appropriate. Copies filed before the Act may still be inspected. In this connection it was always difficult to see what real purpose filing served as the fact of a power being on file was not evidence that it was in force.

A power of attorney must be created by deed (s.1(1) (*ibid.*)) and properly signed and witnessed as in the case of a will.

Rights of third parties against principal and agent

Once there is a contract between the principal and the third party the agent normally drops out of the transaction and is no longer liable on it.

LIABILITY OF AGENT TO THIRD PARTIES

In exceptional cases the agent retains liability independently of or concurrently with the principal.

(1) *Bills of exchange.* The general rule is that an agent is liable on a bill of exchange if he signs it without making it clear that he is signing on behalf of a named principal, as where he does not sign 'for and on behalf of' a named person. The rule may be modified where the agent signs as acceptor, since a bill cannot be accepted by anyone other than the person on whom it is drawn, and an agent's signature is more likely to be considered as made in a representative capacity when the drawee is his principal who alone can accept the bill. (Bills of Exchange Act 1882, s.26(2).)

(2) *Contracts under seal.* Where the agent enters into a deed on behalf of the principal, it is the agent who must sue and be sued. Thus where a chartered accountant entered into an agreement under seal as liquidator of a company it was held that because the agreement was in the form of a deed the defendant was personally liable on it, though with an indemnity from the company's funds. (*Plant Engineers (Sales)* v *Davies* (1969) 113 S.J. 484.)

This will only happen where the liquidator has been given a power of attorney under the seal of the company and contracts under his own seal. He has power to use the company seal under s.245(2) (*b*) of the Companies Act 1948 and when he does he will not be personally liable. The moral is to use the company seal in all cases where sealing is required.

(3) *Custom.* The agent may retain liability by virtue of custom and an example of this can be seen in *Davison* v *Fernandes* 1889.[255]

(4) *Third party insistence.* There may be cases where the third party has insisted that the agent also accepts liability before he makes the contract. If the agent has agreed to do this, he will be liable along with the principal. In other cases the agent may have agreed to be the principal's guarantor.

(5) *Foreign principals.* A foreign principal is one who does not reside in England and Wales and does not carry on business there. There was a presumption of law in earlier times that the agent was liable, the rule being based on the jurisdiction problems involved in suing the principal. This presumption of law no longer applies (see *Teheran-Europe Co Ltd* v *S.T. Belton (Tractors) Ltd* [1968] 2 All E.R. 886) and it seems that the agent's liability is a matter of the intentions of the parties in each case.

The problem of suing foreign principals is to some extent solved by the use of *confirmatory agents* who act as sureties. A confirmatory agent takes the order from the foreign buyer and guarantees to the seller that the order will be accepted and paid for.

Another course open to an English seller is to require the foreign buyer to open an irrevocable credit with an English bank, the bank becoming liable to pay the seller when he tenders the shipping documents to it. However, the disadvantage of such an arrangement is that the banks are not usually prepared to accept liability for the buyer's non-acceptance or cancellation.

(6) *Undisclosed principal.* Suppose an agent contracts with a third party on behalf of his principal but does not inform the third party that he is an agent and appears to be himself a principal, then the doctrine of the undisclosed principal applies. The rights and liabilities of the parties are as follows—

(*a*) The third party can, at his election, sue either the principal or the agent. Thus in *Sika Contracts Ltd* v *Gill, The Times*, 27 April 1978, Mr Gill, a Chartered Civil Engineer, made a contract with Sika, a building company, on behalf of the owners of certain property. He did not mention to Sika the name of the owners or that he was acting on their behalf until after the contract was concluded. He had written and been written to in the style of 'B.L. Gill BE, MICE'. He had signed his letters 'Chartered Civil Engineer'. The question arose as to whether he was personally liable on the contract and it was held by Kerr, J., that he was personally liable. It was possible for a person who was in fact, an agent, to contract in such a way as to involve him in personal liability. It was uncommon to add a phrase 'Acting as agent' at the end of letters. However, as the correspondence stood, it was impossible to say that G was acting as an agent. Sika were therefore entitled to assume that he was personally liable upon the contract. It was not enough that he had signed the letters constituting the contract with his professional qualification.

(*b*) Election must be made within a reasonable time, otherwise only the agent can be sued.

(*c*) Having made his election, the third party cannot return to the other party and sue him.

(*d*) The undisclosed principal can sue the third party on the contract subject to certain qualifications which will be discussed later. This includes an undisclosed foreign principal who can sue and be sued on a contract except where the contract limits rights of action to the English agent and excludes the foreign principal. (*Teheran-Europe C.* v *S.T. Belton (Tractors)* [1968] 2 All E.R. 886.)

(*e*) Since the agent is the contracting party, he too can sue.

(*f*) If the undisclosed principal intervenes and brings an action against the third party, then the agent cannot sue, or must discontinue any action he has begun.

(*g*) The doctrine does not apply where the agent has expressly described himself as a principal.

If the third party sues the agent, this is not an irrevocable election unless he knows of the existence and identity of the principal. It is an election to prove or petition in the bankruptcy of the agent or the principal, but not merely to ask one or the other for payment. The question of election is one of fact and the institution of proceedings against either agent or principal does not amount, as a matter of law, to a binding election so as to bar proceedings against the other. In order to constitute an election the decision to initiate proceedings must have been taken with full knowledge of all the relevant facts and must be an unequivocal act (*Clarkson Booker Ltd* v *Andjel* 1964).[261] However, if the third party elects to sue and actually obtains judgment against the agent or principal, he cannot sue the other even if the judgment is unsatisfied. If the third party has a claim against the agent before he discovers the existence of the principal, the principal's right to sue is subject to the third party's right to set off the debt due from the agent.

There are certain limitations on the right of the principal to intervene.

(*a*) The principal cannot ratify unless the authority of the agent to act for him existed at the time the contract was made.

(*b*) Since the undisclosed principal is not identified, he can never ratify the unauthorized acts of his agent. (*Keighley Maxsted* v *Durant* 1901.)[220]

(*c*) If the personality of the agent is a matter of importance to the third party, the undisclosed principal is not allowed to intervene. (*Said* v *Butt* 1920.)[262] As Lord Denman said in *Humble* v *Hunter* (1848) 12 Q.B. 310: 'You have a right to the benefit you contemplate from the character, credit and substance of the party with whom you contract.'

Thus a promise by the third party to lend money to the agent cannot be enforced by a principal who was unknown, and contracts of personal service cannot be performed by an undisclosed principal. A landlord has an obvious interest in the substance and reputation of his tenant, and if a lease is granted to an agent, the undisclosed principal will not be able to intervene.

(*d*) The fact that no intervention is allowed may derive from the words in the contract, thus in *Humble* v *Hunter* 1848 (above) the agent was described as 'owner' of the property being dealt in, and it was held that evidence that the agent contracted on behalf of a principal was not admissable because it contradicted the words of the contract.

(*e*) Where there is actual misrepresentation by the agent, the undisclosed principal will not be able to intervene. If the third party says to the agent, 'Are you selling for a principal?' and the agent replies that he is not, the contract with the agent can be rescinded and the undisclosed principal cannot intervene.

(7) *Where the agent purports to contract for a principal who has not yet come into existence.* A person acting for a company prior to incorporation is not merely liable for breach of warranty of authority, but is personally liable on the contract unless the company, when incorporated, enters into a new contract, called a novation, with the third party. (S.9, European Communities Act 1972.) The company cannot ratify the acts of its 'agent' expressly or by conduct after its formation.

(8) *Principal's lack of capacity.* Where company directors make contract with a third party which is *ultra vires* the company, the contract will be void and the company cannot ratify it even if all the members agree to do so. (*Ashbury Railway Carriage Co* v *Riche* 1875.)[83] The directors may be liable in damages to the third party for breach of warranty of authority, though much depends upon whether the company is formed by special statute or registered under the Companies Acts.

If the company's powers are contained in a special Act of Parliament, a misrepresentation as to their extent is probably a matter of law and the third party cannot claim to have been misled. (Ignorance of the law is no excuse.)

Where the company is a registered company, misrepresentation of the contents of the objects clause is a matter of fact and unless the doctrine of constructive notice of the contents of the clause binds a third party, which is unlikely but which has not been subject to judicial decision, he may be able to sue the directors.

For the effect of s.9 of the European Communities Act 1972 on contracts of companies which are *ultra vires*, see p. 28.

(9) *Agent's lack of authority.* Where an agent exceeds his authority he is liable to the third party for breach of warranty of authority—

(*a*) if the third party does not know of the lack of authority; and

(*b*) if the third party suffers loss as a result of his lack of knowledge.

The agent's liability is strict and does not depend upon his fraud or misrepresentation. (*Starkey* v *Bank of England* 1903.)[263] Thus, where the agent enters into a contract and acts in all respects *bona fide*, without notice that his authority has been terminated (e.g. by the death or insanity of his principal or the dissolution of the company he represents), he will nevertheless be liable for impliedly warranting that his authority still exists. (*Yonge* v *Toynbee* 1910.)[258]

The action seems to be based on *quasi-contract*, for the agent is not liable on the contract as such and cannot be required to carry it out.

However, the measure of damages awarded against the agent will include compensation for the loss of the bargain with the principal, and damages will be awarded in the same way as if the third party had been suing the principal for breach of contract.

LIABILITY OF THE PRINCIPAL FOR THE AGENT'S WARRANTIES

Where the principal is a dealer, his agent wil generally be able to give warranties as to the quality of the principal's goods even though he is not authorized to do so. Where the principal is not a dealer in the goods in question, the agent is unlikely to be able to give warranties because he is probably a particular agent relying on a specific authority. (*Brady* v *Todd* 1861.)[264] Much also depends upon the type of agent appointed, i.e. whether or not he is the sort of agent who can give warranties, e.g. a factor.

However, an estate agent has no implied or ostensible authority to give a warranty that premises can be used for any particular purpose. (*Hill* v *Harris* 1965.)[265] It should also be noted that the possibility of a warranty may be expressly exluded. Thus in *Overbrooke Estates* v *Glencombe Properties Ltd* [1974] 3 All E.R. 511 the conditions of sale contained in an auction catalogue stated that neither the auctioneers nor any person in their employ, had any authority to make or give representations or warranty in relation to a particular property. Brightman, J., held that this clause was not rendered inoperative by s.3 of the Misrepresentation Act 1967 as substituted by s.8 of the Unfair Contract Terms Act 1977. Section 3 prevents a person excluding liability for statements amounting to misrepresentation made by his duly authorized agent in circumstances where the agent has authority to make the statement. It does not prevent persons cutting down the authority of their agents to make statements at all. Thus, if the agent has authority to make the statement and it is false, liability cannot be excluded by reason of s.3. If, however, the agent has no authority to make the statement at all s.3 does not apply and the principal will not be liable for what he says, at least to a person who knew, or ought to have known, that the agent had no authority to make the statement.

LIABILITY OF THE PRINCIPAL FOR THE AGENT'S FRAUDS AND MISREPRESENTATIONS

In general a principal is liable only for the fraud of his agent where the agent has committed the fraud in order to sell the principal's property. For example, if the agent, in selling the principal's house, states that the drains are sound when he knows they are not, principal and agent will be liable as joint tortfeasors.

Where, however, the agent's fraud is not committed in order to sell the principal's property, but in order that the agent may gain an advantage for himself, the principal will only be liable if the act which forms the basis of the fraud is within the agent's apparent authority. (*Lloyd* v *Grace Smith & Co.* 1912.)[266]

Where the agent makes an innocent misrepresentation in the course of selling the principal's property, the contract with the principal can be rescinded by the third party. A more difficult situation arises where the agent makes a representation which he believes to be true but which the principal knows to be false. Suppose the principal knows that the drains of a house are faulty but has not told his agent and the agent, who is selling it, states the drains are sound, believing this to be true. It might be thought that, in this sort of situation, the untrue statement of the agent could be added to the knowledge of the principal so as to make the principal liable in deceit. But in *Armstrong* v *Strain* 1952.[267] the Court of Appeal rejected this idea and, as the law now stands, the principal will not be liable in deceit unless it can be established that he kept his agent in ignorance of the truth in expectation and hope that he would make some false statement as to the quality of the article he was employed to sell. It is uncertain what effect *Hedley Byrne* v *Heller* 1963,[120] might have had on this situation. If the agent could be regarded as having made negligent misstatements because he might be regarded as under a duty to check their validity, he could be liable in negligence and his principal could be liable vicariously in the absence of an effective exemption clause. P is liable for A's negligent statements under s.2(1) of the Misrepresentation Act 1967. (*Gosling* v *Anderson* 1972.)[118] The agent is not liable under the 1967 Act (see *Resolute Maritime Inc.* v *Nippon Kaiji Kyokai* 1983, p. 415). The possibility of the giving of a warranty may be excluded (See *Overbrooke Estates Ltd* v *Glencombe Properties Ltd* 1974, p. 116)

AUTHORITY OF THE AGENT TO RECEIVE PAYMENT

Suppose that the third party pays money to the agent and the agent has no authority to collect it; must the third party pay again? It seems that, unless the agent has authority allowing him to receive payment on the principal's behalf, the third party will get a good discharge only if the agent has apparent authority, e.g. in the course of employment, to receive payment, as where the agent is a cashier in a bank or a salesman in a shop or a rent collector. It should be noted that authority to sell is not necessarily an authority to receive payment.

NOTICE TO AGENT

It is a matter of importance as to how far notice given to the agent operates as notice to the principal. The general rule is that notice to the agent is imputed to the principal in all matters which the agent is employed to carry out. If the agent is buying property for the principal and discovers an incumbrance, e.g. a mortgage, but does not inform the principal the principal cannot refuse to complete the transaction as the agent's knowledge is imputed to him. Furthermore, in a contract of insurance effected through brokers as agents, the insurance company cannot avoid the policy because of non-disclosure of a criminal record by the insured in his application for the insurance where the brokers know of that criminal record and have failed to inform the insurer. The knowledge of the brokers is imputed to the insurance company as principal. (*Woolcott* v *Excess Insurance Co.* [1979] 1 Lloyd's Rep. 231.) Notice will not be imputed where the agent acts contrary to the principal's interests and the third party knows this. (*Wells* v *Smith* 1914.)[268]

It is important that the agent received the notice while acting for the principal, and the principal is not generally affected by matters coming to the agent's notice in other agencies and employments. This applies more particularly to confidential relationships, e.g. solicitor and client, but in commercial situations it seems that the principal may sometimes be affected by the knowledge of the agent gained in another capacity. (*Dresser* v *Norwood* 1864.)[269]

Particular agents

THE MERCANTILE AGENT (OR FACTOR)

The Factors Act 1889, using the term mercantile agent for what is also known as a factor, defines him as follows: 'A mercantile agent having in the customary course of his business as such agent authority either to sell goods, or to consign goods for the purpose of sale, or to buy goods, or to raise money on the security of goods.' (S.1(1).)

The following points arise from the definition—

(1) *Mercantile agent.* An agent is a factor if, and only if, it is in the customary course of his business as such agent—

(*a*) to sell goods; or
(*b*) to consign goods for sale; or
(*c*) to buy goods; or
(*d*) to raise money on the security of goods.

A person who is not normally a factor may become one if he satisfies one of these four requirements, and a person may be a factor even though he acts for one principal only, or where he acts as a factor for the first time. (*Lowther* v *Harris* 1927.)[270] Conversely a person who is normally in business as a factor will not be one for any transaction outside the scope of these four categories. (*Staffs. Motor Guarantee Co.* v *British Wagon Co.* 1934.)[271] The term factor does not, however, include carriers, wharfingers, warehousemen or other mere bailees (*Kendrick* v *Sotheby & Co.* 1967),[272] nor does it include a person who is selling goods on behalf of himself and not for another, or a mercantile agent who is in possession of goods as a result of an illegal hire-purchase agreement as where statutory regulations as to deposit or period of payment have been infringed. (*Belvoir Finance* v *Cole* [1969] 2 All E.R. 904.)

(2) *Customary course of business.* An agent may be a factor although he is not normally in business as a factor, nor a known kind of commercial agent. For example, a man who normally sells secondhand furniture which he has previously bought on his own account, becomes a factor if he undertakes to sell a bedroom suite for a principal.

(3) *He must be authorized to sell the goods in his own name without saying that he is an agent.* Thus in *Rolls Razor* v *Cox* [1967] 1 All E.R. 397 the defendant was a self-employed door-to-door salesman of washing machines. The plaintiff company supplied him with stock and a van. The company went into liquidation owing the plaintiff money for commission on goods sold. He wished to keep the company's goods until he was paid in full rather than prove in the liquidation. He alleged he could do this by exercising a factor's right of general lien. (See p. 105.) He needed to do this because the company did not owe him money on the goods in his hands but on goods already sold. The Court of Appeal said that he was not a factor and not entitled to a factor's lien. Lord Denning said: 'The usual characteristics of a factor are these. He is an agent entrusted with the possession of goods of several principals, or sometimes only one principal, for the purpose of the sale in his own name without disclosing the name of his principal and he is remunerated by a commission. These salesmen lacked one of those characteristics. They did not sell in their own names but in the name and on behalf of their principals the Company. They are agents pure and simple and not factors'.

(4) *Goods.* This term includes all forms of merchandise, but does not include stocks and shares and negotiable instruments.

TITLE

The Factors Act 1889, s.2(1), makes an important amendment to the common-law rule *nemo dat quod non habet* (no one can give what he has not got) as regards agents who may properly be called factors. The section provides that 'where a mercantile agent is, with the consent of the owner, in possession of goods or of the documents of title to goods, any sale, pledge, or other disposition of the goods, made by him when acting in the ordinary course of business of a mercantile agent, shall, subject to the provisions of this Act, be as valid as if he were expressly authorized by the owner of the goods to make the same; provided that the person taking under the disposition acts in good faith, and has not at the time of the disposition notice that the person making the disposition has not authority to make the same.'

The main points of interest in the same section are as follows—

(1) *The mercantile agent must be in possession of the goods or documents of title in his capacity as a mercantile agent.* Thus the owner of a car who

leaves it for repair at a garage does not consent to possession by the garage as a dealer. The garage cannot therefore confer a good title if they sell it, even though they might from time to time sell cars.

(2) *The consent of the owner.* Consent is presumed in the absence of evidence to the contrary. (S.2(4).) Even where the mercantile agent obtains the goods by false pretence or fraud he has usually obtained them with the consent, however mistaken, of the owner, and will give a good title to a purchaser from him. Where, however, the agent had obtained the goods by the old offence known as larceny by a trick, he was not normally regarded as having the real consent of the owner, but the better view was that he could still give a good title. (*Pearson* v *Rose & Young Ltd* 1951.)[273] Many modern cases on consent have arisen in connection with the sale of motor vehicles by fraudulent agents. From these cases it seems clear that the owner must consent not only to the agent's possession of the vehicle but also to his possession of the vehicle registration document and ignition key, because the sale of a vehicle without these items is not a sale in the ordinary course of business. (*Pearson* v *Rose and Young Ltd* 1951;[273] *Stadium Finance* v *Robbins* 1962;[274] *George* v *Revis* 1966.)[275] Since the passing of the Theft Act 1968, the offence of larceny by trick has disappeared from English law and it likely that deceptions of the kind practised in *Pearson* and similar cases will no longer be regarded as preventing the consent of the owner, the new offence of obtaining property by deception being more akin to false pretences. Thus it may be easier to obtain a good title from the deceiver.

(3) *Regarding pledge.* The factor's power to pledge goods is statutory; there was no such power prior to the Factors Act. In order to obtain the protection of the section, the pledge must be for valuable consideration.

The principal can, of course, redeem the goods pledged by paying to the pledgee the amount of any loan or other consideration, e.g. goods given to the agent under the pledge. Where the consideration is goods and not money, the principal cannot be required to pay more than value at the time of the pledge, even if the goods which formed the consideration have since appreciated in value. Whatever the principal has to pay to redeem the goods pledged he may recover from the agent, subject to an offset by the agent for any rights he had over the goods pledged, e.g. for a lien he may have had over the goods for his charges when he pledged the goods.

(4) *Acting in the ordinary course of business.* The factor must make the sale, pledge or other disposition, within business hours and at some place of business, and generally in circumstances which do not give rise to suspicion. As we have seen, the sale of a vehicle without the registration document and ignition key is not a sale in the ordinary course of business.

A sale or pledge by a mercantile agent through a clerk or other person, authorized in the ordinary course of business to make contracts of sale or pledge on behalf of the mercantile agent, is considered to be an agreement with the mercantile agent. (S.6.)

(5) *Regarding notice and good faith*. The person taking from the factor must prove that he did so in good faith and without notice of lack of authority. This probably means actual knowledge, though there may be circumstances where the third party is put on inquiry, as where a car is sold without a vehicle registration document. If in such circumstances the third party fails to make further inquiries he may be fixed with notice of the factor's lack of authority.

DEL CREDERE AGENTS

In return for an extra commission, called a *del credere* commission, a *del credere* agent promises to guarantee the principal if the third party introduced by the agent fails to pay for the goods delivered to him, or if the third party becomes insolvent. As the contract with the *del credere* agent is part of the wider contract of agency no memorandum is required. This derives from the fact that a *del credere* agent is not totally unconnected in an economic sense with the transaction he is underwriting, as a guarantor must be. He receives some benefit from it by reason of the commission. The *del credere* agent is not liable for any other breach by the third party, e.g. where the third party refuses to take delivery of the goods; his liability, therefore, is not so extensive as that of the confirmatory agent mentioned earlier in the chapter.

3 The sale of goods

The law relating to the sale of goods is to be found in the Sale of Goods Act 1979. This is a consolidating measure bringing together a number of previous Acts but in particular the Sale of Goods Act 1893. Certain provisions of the Factors Act 1889 are also relevant, as are rules of the common law not dealt with by legislation. All section references are to the Sale of Goods Act 1979 unless otherwise stated.

Definition

A contract of sale of goods is a contract whereby the seller transfers or agrees to transfer the property in goods to the buyer for a money consideration called the price. (S.2(1).) The definition covers—

(1) *A contract of sale* in which the property in goods is transferred from seller to buyer.

(2) *An agreement to sell* in which the transfer of property takes place at a future time or on fulfilment of certain conditions. (S.2(5).) A contract for the sale of goods yet to be manufactured is an agreement to sell because the property in the goods cannot pass until they are manufactured and ascertained.

Unless the contract otherwise provides, the property in goods which are the subject of a contract of sale passes to the buyer when the contract is made. English law does not require actual delivery of the goods, and the contract of sale operates as the conveyance.

Property is defined as the general property in goods and not merely a special property (s.61), and therefore to say that the property passes to the buyer normally means that he gets ownership and not mere possession. A contract which does not pass ownership at all, e.g. a contract to rent a TV set, is outside the definition (but see Supply of Goods and Services Act 1982, Chapter 4).

However, under s.12(3) A may transfer goods to B on the basis of whatever title he or a third person may have. This may turn out to be a right of possession only. Nevertheless such a contract is a contract of sale of goods. A common example of the use of s.12(3) occurs where the sale is of goods taken in execution by the bailiffs to satisfy a judgment debt. Some of these goods, which are sold very cheaply, may not be owned by the debtor, as where he has them on hire purchase, although the bailiffs try to avoid this. If a finance company takes the goods away from the buyer he has no claim for breach of condition under s.12 but the warranties of quiet possession in s.12 apply. (See further p. 134.) Thus a purchaser has no claim unless the true owner repossesses the goods which he may not. Delivery is the voluntary transfer of possession from one person to another, and whether the property in the goods passes on delivery is a question to be decided from the contract or, where the contract is silent, from the circumstances.

Goods

Section 61 provides that goods includes all personal chattels but excludes all choses in action (e.g. cheques and share certificates) and money, although a coin which is a curio piece is goods for the purposes of a contract of sale. (*Moss* v *Hancock* [1899] 2 Q.B. 111.) The term also includes *emblements*, i.e. crops to be severed before sale or under the contract of sale. Products of the soil are generally sold with a view to severance and though they may sometimes be of the nature of land for the purposes of s.40 of the Law of Property Act 1925 (see p. 20), they are usually goods within the meaning of the Act of 1979. The Act does not apply to the sale of an interest in the land itself. The sale of gravel *in situ* under land would not be covered by the Act. Nor would crops sold with the land on which they are growing because they are not in such a case to be 'severed before sale or under the contract of sale' as s.61 requires.

Goods may be—

(1) *Existing goods*, i.e. goods actually in existence when the contract is made, though they need not be specific and may yet have to be appropriated to the contract. (S.5(1).)

(2) *Future goods*, i.e. goods yet to be acquired or manufactured or grown by the seller. (S.5(1).) See *Sainsbury* v *Street* 1972 (p. 493) where the seller agreed to sell to the buyers 'a crop of some 275 tons of barley' to be grown by him on his farm.

(3) *Specific goods*, i.e. goods identified and agreed upon at the time the contract of sale is made. (S.61(1)), e.g. the sale of a second-hand washing machine.

(4) *Unascertained goods* which consist of the following—

(*a*) goods to be made or grown by the seller, which are, of course, future goods;

(*b*) goods defined by description only; and

(*c*) an unidentified part of a specified whole.

If X sells to Y two hundred bags of flour from a stock of two thousand lying in X's warehouse, the flour is existing goods, but so far as the contract is concerned, the goods are not specific until a selection of bags has been made by Y. Generally, future goods are not specific, but if they can be sufficiently identified, they may be, and their destruction will frustrate the contract. (*Howell* v *Coupland* 1876).[276] Where X agrees to sell to Y 100 bags of coal, these are identified by description only and are unascertained, and X would perform his contract by delivering any hundred bags of coal he chose. Since such goods are not appropriated to the contract, they are also future goods.

The existence of goods

There is no provision in the Act that the seller warrants the existence of the goods, but s.6 provides that where there is a contract for the sale of *specific goods* and the goods without the knowledge of the seller have perished at the time when the contract is made, the contract is void.

Thus, if X sells his car to Y, and unknown to X the car has caught fire and burnt out an hour before the sale, the contract would be void and there would be no liabilities on either side.

As regards the meaning of the word 'perished', *Couturier* v *Hastie* 1856[102] illustrates that the goods may still *in fact exist*. If, however, they can no longer be sold as the goods described in the contract, they can be regarded as having perished.

The goods must be specific before s.6 can operate, and if X agrees to sell Y '100 tonnes of coal', X is still liable at common law to supply the coal or pay damages, even though he had a particular 100 tonnes in mind which have in fact perished.

Difficulties may arise where the goods are to some extent ascertained. For example, suppose X agrees to sell to Y 'Six dozen bottles of Grandiosa Port from the stock at present in my warehouse'. If, unknown to X, the stock is wholly destroyed before the sale, the contract would be void at common law. But if ten dozen bottles were left, i.e. if performance of the contract were still possible, presumably the seller X would be required to carry out his obligations. If there were only two dozen bottles left the contract would either be avoided or at common law the seller would have to offer the two dozen bottles to the buyer, though the latter would presumably not be obliged to accept them. (See *Sainsbury* v *Street* 1972 (below).)

Where, although the goods are specific, they exist only in part, the parties are, under s.6, released from their liabilities. (*Barrow, Lane & Ballard Ltd* v *Phillip Phillips & Co.* 1929.)[277] For the position at common law see *Sainsbury* v *Street* 1972.[278]

Section 6 does not apply if the goods have never existed. A contract about goods which have never existed is void at common law. (But see *McRae* v *Commonwealth Disposals Commission* 1951.)[279] This will depend upon the contract itself and the circumstances.

Section 7 provides that where there is an agreement to sell *specific goods*, which have subsequently perished, without any fault on the part of the seller or buyer, before the risk passes to the buyer, the agreement is thereby avoided. In other words, the contract is frustrated and the buyer is not liable for the price, and the seller is not liable to deliver the goods and consequently cannot be sued for non-delivery. If the goods have *already perished* when the contract is made, s.6 and not s.7 applies.

The application of the section is limited for the goods must be specific and the risk must not have passed, and in a contract for the sale of specific goods, property and risk usually pass when the contract is made. Once the ownership has passed the goods are at the buyer's risk and the contract cannot be frustrated. The section will apply to contracts of sale where the goods are not in a deliverable state, since in such a case the property will not have passed. In other words, to an agreement for sale and not a sale.

Section 7, like s.6, cannot apply if the goods have never existed. Thus a contract for the purchase of a crop of wheat to be grown on 'MacDonald's Farm' will not be avoided under s.7 if the crop fails. The contract will, however, be frustrated at common law. (See *Howell* v *Coupland* 1876.)[276]

The meaning of 'perished' in s.7 is thought to be the same as in s.6 and if this is so it seems that if only some, but not all, of the goods have perished the parties are released from their liabilities. (*Barrow, Lane & Ballard Ltd* v *Phillip Phillips & Co.* 1929.)[277] But if the contract is severable, presumably it is valid with regard to the goods which have not perished. However, this conclusion may not be sound in view of the decision in *Sainsbury* v *Street* 1972.[278] As we have seen, that case, although not coming within s.7, suggests that if part only of the goods perish the seller may be obliged to offer the remaining goods to the buyer, though the buyer may not be obliged to take them. (On the issue of frustration, see also p. 81.)

Contracts of sale and related transactions

CONTRACTS FOR SALE AND CONTRACTS FOR WORK AND MATERIALS

If the contract is for the sale of goods it is governed by the Sale of Goods Act 1979; a contract for work and materials is not. Hence the need to distinguish between the two. A contract for work and materials results in the transfer of goods but also involves the supply of skill and labour over and above what is required to produce the goods as an essential and significant part of the contract. Thus in *Cammell Laird & Co. Ltd* v *Manganese Bronze & Brass Co. Ltd* [1934] A.C. 402 the construction of two ship's propellers was held to be a contract of sale of goods; so, too, was a contract for the making of a fur coat from selected skins. (See *Marcel (Furriers) Ltd* v *Tapper* [1953] 1 All E.R. 15.)

Before 1983 contracts for work and materials were governed by common law only. The court would normally imply into those contracts terms which were similar to those implied into contracts of sale by the sale of goods legislation, e.g. that the goods were fit for the purpose and of merchantable quality. (*Myers & Co. Ltd* v *Brent Cross Service Co.* 1934.)[280] Now the Supply of Goods and Services Act 1982 applies, (See Chapter 4). However, as a matter of contrast between the two types of contract, some examples of work and materials must be given. In *Robinson* v *Graves* [1935] 1 K.B. 579 it was held that a contract to paint a portrait was a contract for work and materials and not a sale of goods, even though the property in the chattel, i.e. the portrait, was eventually to be transferred. In general terms, all forms of repair and maintenance contracts fall into the category of work and materials, e.g. repair of cars (as in *Myers*), the servicing of computers and X-ray and photocopying machines, roof repairs, painting and decorating, and the installation of double-glazing and air-conditioning and so on.

CONTRACTS FOR SALE AND BARTER OR EXCHANGE

Section 2(1) requires that the consideration be money, and contracts of pure exchange are not within the Sale of Goods Act. Difficulties arose where a seller took goods in part-exchange, as where a car dealer took in part-exchange the car of the purchaser in reduction of the purchase price of another car. Certainly the contract was a sale of goods so long as money was a substantial part of the consideration, and even if it was not the court might regard the transaction as a sale if the parties appeared to have done so. Thus where the difference in price between the car which was 'traded in' and the one which was purchased is marginal, there would most probably be a sale since that is what the parties envisaged.

Since the 1982 Act was passed the problem of sale or barter is of no real practical importance. Whether the contract is a contract of sale or an exchange of goods for goods, or goods for money and goods, almost identical terms will be implied in the contract under the 1979 Act (if a sale) or under the 1982 Act (barter and exchange).

SALE AND HIRE PURCHASE

A sale of goods differs from a hire-purchase transaction because a hire purchase contract gives the hirer a mere bailment of the goods, with an option to purchase them, an option which the hirer may or may not exercise after payment of the agreed instalments. There is a contract of sale when the hirer exercises his option to purchase, which he will normally do, since the purchase price is then nominal and the eventual sale of the goods is the object of the contract. However, because under a contract of hire purchase a person does not *legally* commit himself to purchase the goods, there is no contract of sale.

A further distinction is that, while a contract of sale normally involves two parties only, a hire-purchase contract generally involves three. The owner of the goods selected by the hirer sells them to a finance company which in turn hires them to the hirer. The Sale of Goods Act does not apply to the hiring contract, but certain terms are implied into that contract by ss.8–11 of the Supply of Goods (Implied Terms) Act 1973 (as substituted by the Consumer Credit Act 1974, Sch.4, para. 35 which made some changes in terminology in the original provisions of the 1973 Act), and are available against the finance company.

The distinction between a contract of sale and hire purchase is also important in the matter of title. If the contract is one of hire purchase it does not come within the provisions of s.25(1) of the Sale of Goods Act, under which a buyer in possession can give a good title to a purchaser if he sells the goods, because the hirer is not a person who has bought or agreed to buy the goods. He is hiring with an option to purchase and is under no obligation to buy. The hirer, therefore, cannot give a good title to a third party and, on the bankruptcy of the hirer, the owner of the goods can recover them subject to the doctrine of reputed ownership, ie, if used in the hirer's business.

Where the contract is one of sale, but payment is to be made by instalments, the contract may pass the property, in which case there is an unconditional contract of sale and the buyer, having ownership, can give a good title to a third party. On the bankruptcy of the buyer, his trustee takes the goods, and the seller must prove in the bankruptcy for the instalments.

If, although the goods have been delivered, the passing of the property is postponed until all instalments are paid, then there is a conditional contract of sale; such a contract is within s.25(1) and the buyer can give a good title to a third party if the total purchase price exceeds £15,000. If the total purchase price is £15,000 or under, the contract is governed by the Consumer Credit Act 1974, and the conditions and warranties implied will be those under the Supply of Goods (Implied Terms) Act 1973 and not those under the Sale of Goods Act, and the buyer cannot give a good title to third parties, though there are exceptions in the case of motor cars (see p. 204). In both cases, however, the seller can claim the goods on the bankruptcy of the buyer subject to the doctrine of reputed ownership. (Hire-purchase contracts are considered further on pages 191–206.)

SALE AND HIRE (OR LEASING)

Hire purchase and hire have a lot in common. However, the distinction between them is that a contract of hire is only a contract of bailment which gives the hirer the right to possess the goods. Hire purchase is, as its name suggests, hire *plus* purchase. The hirer has a right to possess plus an option to buy the goods when the instalments have been paid. Contracts of hiring were governed by the common law; now the Supply of Goods and Services Act 1982 applies. Examples of hiring agreements abound; office equipment, photocopying machines, typewriters, and cars are commonly hired. More modern expressions include 'leasing', 'contract hire', and 'rental agreements', but whatever called they are all contracts of hire and the rights and obligations of the parties are in the 1982 Act (see Chapter 4).

SALE AND AGENCY

Brief mention should be made of certain problems arising in agency. If the person who is selling the goods is an agent there will be privity of contract between the buyer and the supplier. If the seller is not an agent but, e.g. a distributor who has purchased the goods himself, no action could be brought against the supplier in respect of the condition and quality of the goods. (*Dunlop* v *Selfridge* 1915[29] but see now *Junior Books Ltd* v *Veitchi Co Ltd.* 1982, p. 508.)

Problems may arise in relation to title. If the seller is an agent he cannot pass a title in the goods to a buyer unless the sale is within the agent's actual or apparent authority (see pp. 92–3), or he has the goods on 'sale or return' terms. (*London Jewellers Ltd* v *Attenborough* 1934.)[281] (See also p. 160.)

Thus a contract under which F (a finder) transfers goods to a purchaser is not a contract of sale to which the Act applies. F is not the owner, nor is he the agent of the owner. (But see sales in market overt, p. 157.)

SALE AND LOANS ON SECURITY

If A, who is the owner of goods, borrows money by using the goods as security and gives a charge or mortgage over them but retains possession, the transaction resembles a sale in the sense that the lender has a right to take the goods if A does not repay the loan or interest. This is not, however, a sale, but in view of the fact that A retains the goods so that third parties might give him credit on the strength of his apparent absolute ownership of them, the transaction must be committed to writing as a bill of sale which must be registered under the Bills of Sale Acts 1878 and 1882. If the transaction is unregistered (which is often the case) the contract is void and the lender will not be able to seize the goods or even recover the agreed interest, although the actual loan itself is recoverable as money had and received. (*North Central Wagon Finance Co. Ltd* v *Brailsford* [1962] 1 All E.R. 502.)

The contract of sale

CAPACITY OF THE PARTIES

Capacity to buy and sell is regulated by the general law concerning capacity to contract and to transfer and acquire property. The problems relating to capacity have already been dealt with in the chapter on the law of contract (see p.23) and no further comment is necessary, other than to refer to the capacity problems which may arise in business from dealing with minors (see p. 23) and companies (see p. 27).

THE PRICE

Section 8 provides that the price may be—

(1) fixed by the contract; or

(2) left to be fixed in a manner provided by the contract, e.g. by a valuation or an arbitration; or

(3) determined by the course of dealing between the parties, e.g. previous transactions between them, or any relevant custom of the trade or profession. If the price is not so fixed, there is a presumption that the buyer will pay a reasonable price. What is a reasonable price is a question of fact dependent upon the circumstances of each case. Thus a contract of sale of goods should not be regarded as *inchoate* simply because the parties have not agreed a price. (For inchoate agreements see p. 3.)

Section 9 provides that where the price is to be determined by the valuation of a third party, and no such valuation is made, then the contract is avoided, but—

(1) If the goods or part thereof have been delivered to the buyer and he has appropriated them to his use, the buyer must pay a reasonable price for them.

(2) If the valuation is prevented by *either party* to the contract, the non-defaulting party must sue for damages against the party in default.

It is difficult to see how the buyer would be able to prevent valuation, but presumably the Act is concerned to cover all possibilities. Section 9 applies only if the agreement names a valuer. Thus a sale of 'stock at valuation' is an agreement to sell at a reasonable price, and s.8 will apply if the parties do not appoint a valuer or otherwise agree a price.

If the buyer pays part of the price when he makes the contract it may be a *deposit or a part payment*. If it is a deposit it will be forfeited if the buyer does not go on with the contract. A part-payment must be returned. Whether a payment is one or the other is a matter for the parties to decide in their contract. If they do not do so the court will have to discover as best it can what their intention was. In this connection the use of the word 'deposit' without more is a strong indication of a guarantee that the purchaser will complete and that the payment will be forfeit if he does not.

THE CONSIDERATION

It has already been mentioned that the consideration for a sale must consist wholly or in part of money; otherwise the transaction is an exchange or barter. Where goods are conveyed without consideration there is a gift, and any agreement to be enforceable must be under seal, though actual delivery of the goods will give the recipient or donee a good title.

FORMALITIES OF THE CONTRACT

Under s.4, contracts for the sale of goods can be made in writing (either with or without seal), or by word of mouth or partly in writing and partly by word of mouth, or may be implied from the conduct of the parties. By reason of s.32 of the Companies Act 1948, registered companies need not now contract under seal, except where an ordinary person would have to do so. The Corporate Bodies Contracts Act 1960 extends this privilege to all companies no matter how formed in respect of contracts made since 29 July 1960.

Nevertheless provisions in other statutes may affect a sale. For example, s.24 of the Merchant Shipping Act 1894 provides that the sale of a ship or a share in a ship must be in writing. Furthermore, since s.61 defines goods as including emblements, e.g. growing crops which are agreed to be severed before sale or under the contract of sale (which covers most cases). It may be that crops which are not to be severed are land under the Law of Property Act 1925, in which case the contract if made before severance may require a memorandum in writing under s.40 of the Law of Property Act 1925. (See p. 20.) Singleton L.J., seemed to think a memorandum in writing was required in such a case in *Saunders* v *Pilcher* [1949] 2 All E.R. 1097 where a person bought a cherry orchard 'inclusive of this year's fruit crop'. The crop was not severed before sale or under the contract of sale and Singleton was of the view that s.61 had no application and that the contract including the fruit crop was a sale of land.

In addition certain formalities are prescribed for credit sale agreements covered by the Consumer Credit Act 1974. (See p. 195).

The provisions of the Bills of Sale Acts may also affect the position regarding formalities. It is necessary to distinguish two situations—

(1) A straight sale—the seller retaining possession

(*a*) If the sale is and remains oral the Acts do not apply and the buyer takes the risk (subject to an action for breach of contract or non-delivery) that the seller may dispose of the goods either voluntarily (by subsequent sale) or involuntarily (by, e.g. execution of a judgment or on bankruptcy).

(*b*) If, as is usual, the buyer takes written evidence by means of a bill of sale this must be registered, though it need not be in any special form. If this is not done, the contract of sale is void in respect of involuntary dispositions, e.g. to a trustee in bankruptcy or a sherrif levying execution; but if the seller, while still in possession of the goods already sold, voluntarily transfers the property by way of sale to a third party, the latter may obtain a good title under s.24 of the Sale of Goods Act or under s.8 or the Factors Act 1889.

(2) A sale operating as a security—the seller retaining possession

(*a*) The Sale of Goods Act does not apply. (See s.62(4) of that Act.)

(*b*) The Bills of Sale Act 1882 covers the transaction and unless there is a registered bill of sale made out in the form required by ss.8–10 of the Act of 1882 the transaction is void altogether, even as between the parties, though money advanced on an unregistered bill may be removed in quasi-contract (see p. 89) as money had and received. (*North Central Wagon Finance Co. Ltd* v *Brailsford* [1962] 1 All E.R. 502.) Thus involuntary and voluntary dispositions by the seller are effective to give title.

The position where a seller of goods delivers them but provides in the contract that ownership is not to pass until the goods are paid for is considered at p. 150.

Conditions and warranties

In the chapter on the law of contract (pp. 48-9) we have discussed the problems relating to statements made in the course of negotiating an agreement, and we have seen that such statements may be—

Pre-contractual, i.e. representations; or

Contractual, i.e. terms of the contract which may be either conditions or warranties.

The importance of the distinction lies in the remedies which are available.

In the chapter on the law of contract we were concerned in the main with *express* statements made by the parties; here we are concerned with the conditions and warranties *implied* into contracts for the sale of goods by the Sale of Goods Act 1979, and with how those conditions and warranties are defined by the Act.

The Act does not define a condition, but a condition may be said to be a material term or provision which, while going to the root of the contract, falls short of non-performance. A condition is a contractual term of a major description.

A warranty is defined by s.61 as an agreement with reference to goods which are the subject of a contract of sale, but collateral to the main purpose of the contract, the breach of which gives rise to a claim for damages, but not the right to reject the goods and treat the contract as repudiated. Although s.61 uses the word 'collateral' which gives the impression that a warranty is a term outside the contract a warranty in the intention of s.61 is a term inside the contract but of a minor description which does not go to the root of the contract.

The Act does not say how we are to distinguish between conditions and warranties, and, although the words used by the parties are relevant, a stipulation may nevertheless be a condition though called a warranty in the contract. (S.11(3).) When in doubt as to the nature of a stipulation, the court will look at the contract and the surrounding circumstances, and decide what the intentions of the parties were, and whether those intentions can best be carried out by treating the statement as a condition or as a warranty.

This is in effect the doctrine of the 'intermediate term' laid down as regards contracts for the sale of goods in *Cehave NV* v *Bremer Handelsgesellschaft mbH*, 1975.[283]

With regard to the relationship of the Misrepresentation Act 1967 and the implied terms of the Sale of Goods Act 1979 the following matters should be noted—

(1) Claims based on negligent misrepresentation under s.2(1) of the 1967 Act will usually be joined with claims for damages for breach of condition or warranty. This is especially likely where the action is based on a misdescription of the goods under s.13 of the 1979 Act. (See p. 135.)

(2) Under the 1967 Act the burden of disproving that the misrepresentation was negligent is on the representor, which is helpful to the plaintiff. Nevertheless the best remedy for misdescription is still one based on the Act of 1979 because liability under that Act is strict and cannot be avoided by the seller showing he was not negligent.

It should also be noted that in addition to the various remedies for loss arising out of false pre-contractual representations and breaches of contractual terms an action for negligence may lie in tort provided the false statement is made negligently and a special relationship exists between the parties. (*Hedley Byrne Byrne & Co. Ltd* v *Heller and Partners Ltd* 1963.)[120] This action is probably of less importance in the context of contract since s.2(1) of the Act of 1967 provides a statutory course of action in negligence specifically designed for the contractual situation.

Thus a seller who makes a false statement about his goods may be liable at civil law in misrepresentation or for breach of an express or implied term. He may also be convicted of an offence under Trade Description legislation. (See p. 144.)

Terms implied by the Act

Some contracts of sale are very detailed; the parties have dealt with all or most eventualities. Many contracts of sale are not so detailed. The only thing the parties have dealt with is the goods to be sold and the price to be paid. The provisions of the Sale of Goods Act are designed in large measure to fill in the gaps by implied terms and other rules, e.g. as to the passing of the property and damages. We must now consider the question of implied terms.

TIME

Where this has not been dealt with expressly the following rules apply—

(1) *Payment.* The Act provides that, unless a different intention appears from the contract, stipulations as to the time of payment are not deemed to be of the essence of a contract of sale. Whether any other stipulation as to time is of the essence of the contract or not depends upon the terms of the contract. (Ss.10(1) and (2).)

Thus failure to pay on time is a breach of warranty rather than a breach of condition. The seller cannot repudiate the contract and resell the goods, but may sue the buyer for damages. However, where payment is delayed for an excessive time, the seller may treat the contract as abandoned and resell the goods. The seller can, of course, provide expressly for a right of resale in the absence of prompt payment, and this right is implied where the goods are perishable. (S.48(3).)

(2) *Delivery.* The Act does not lay down any rules regarding the time of delivery of the goods, but the decided cases show that, where the time of delivery is fixed by the contract, failure to deliver or allow collection on time is a breach of condition and the buyer can reject the goods even though they are not damaged or in any way affected by the delay. (*Bowes* v *Shand* 1877.)[176] Where the goods are unaffected the buyer will normally only reject if external circumstances such as a fall in the market price lead him to do so. Nevertheless his right to reject has in the past remained. However, in view of the decision in *Cehave NV* v *Bremer Handelsgesellschaft mbH*, 1975[283] it may be that the courts are not so fully committed to the principle that any breach of condition by the seller entitles the buyer to take advantage of a fall in the market to reject the goods. Where the seller is bound to send the goods to the buyer but no time of delivery is fixed by the contract, the seller is bound to deliver the goods within a reasonable time. (S.29(3).) Failure to deliver within a reasonable time may amount to breach of condition. (*Borthwick (Thomas) (Glasgow) Ltd* v *Bunge & Co. Ltd* [1969] 1 Lloyds' Rep. 17.) It is assumed that this rule applies also where the seller's duty is to have the goods ready for collection.

The time of delivery may be waived by the buyer even after the delivery date and such a waiver is binding even though the seller has given no consideration for it. The basis of this rule according to Denning, L.J., in *Rickards (Charles) Ltd* v *Oppenhaim*, 1950,[177] was equitable estoppel. (See further p. 17.)

Other rules relating to delivery will be considered when dealing with performance of the contract. (See p. 161.)

TITLE

The rules governing title are as follows—

(1) *Implied condition as to title.* Section 12(1) provides that, unless the circumstances show a different intention, there is an implied condition on the part of the seller that in the case of a sale he has the right to sell the goods, and that in the case of an agreement to sell, he will have the right to sell the goods at the time when the property is to pass. (*Rowland* v *Divall* 1923.)[206]

The decision in *Rowland*,[206] which has been applied in subsequent cases (see *Karflex Ltd* v *Poole* [1933] 2 K.B. 251), produces an unfortunate result in that a person who buys goods to which the seller has no title is allowed to recover the whole of the purchase price even though he has had some use and enjoyment from the goods before he is dispossessed by the true owner. It is thus difficult to suggest that there has been total failure of consideration. The Law Reform Committee (see 1966 Cmnd 2958, para. 36) has recommended that, subject to further study of the law relating to restitution, an allowance in respect of use and enjoyment should be deducted from the purchase price and the balance returned to the plaintiff. It should be noted that the 1979 Act does not deal with this matter.

Section 12(1) might be construed as meaning that the seller must have the power to give ownership of the goods to the buyer, but in *Niblett* v *Confectioners' Materials Co. Ltd* 1921,[284] it was decided that, if the goods can only be sold by infringing a trade mark, the seller has no right to sell for the purposes of s.12(1).

Under s.12(3), the sale of a limited interest is now possible. Where the parties intend only to transfer such a title as the seller may have, there is an implied warranty that all charges or encumbrances known to the seller and not known to the buyer have been disclosed to the buyer before the contract is made (s.12(4)), and an implied warranty that the buyer's quiet possession will not be disturbed. (S.12(5).) There is an action by the buyer for breach of these warranties. Furthermore, the seller is not able to contract out of this liability.

Sales under a limited title are common where the sale is of goods taken in execution by the bailiffs to satisfy a judgement debt.

(2) *Implied warranties as to title.* Section 12(2) provides that there is—

> An implied warranty that the goods are free, and will remain free until the time when the property is to pass, from any charge or encumbrance not disclosed or known to the buyer before the contract is made, and that the buyer will enjoy quiet possession of the goods except so far as it may be disturbed by the owner or other person entitled to the benefit of any charge or encumbrance so disclosed or known.

This does not apply where a limited interest is sold, but s.12(4) and (5) do and contain similar provisions. (See above.)

It is not easy to see what rights this subsection gives over those in s.12(1). The law does not recognize encumbrances over chattels unless the person trying to enforce them is in possession of the goods or in privity of contract with the person who is in possession. (*Dunlop* v *Selfridge* 1915.)[29] Thus if A uses his car as security for a loan from B then—

(*a*) if B takes the car into his possession the charge will be enforceable if necessary by a sale of the vehicle;

(*b*) the charge is equally enforceable against the car while it is still in A's possession, though if A sells it to C then B will be prevented by lack of privity of contract from enforcing any remedies against the vehicle once it is in the possession of C.

Thus if situation (*a*) above applied the subsection is unnecessary since A could not deliver the vehicle even if he sold it and would therefore be liable in damages for non-delivery to C. If situation (*b*) above applied then the encumbrances would not attach to the vehicle once C had taken possession. C would not, therefore, require a remedy.

However, the usefulness of s.12(2) is illustrated by the decision of the Court of Appeal in *Microbeads A.C.* v *Vinhurst Road Markings Ltd* [1975] 1 All E.R. 529. In this case A sold road-marking machines to B. After the sale C obtained a patent on the machines so that their continued use by B was in breach of that patent and C was bringing an action against B in respect of this. In a claim by A against B for the purchase price, B wished to include in their defence breach of ss.12(1) and (2). It was held by the Court of Appeal that they could include breach of s.12(2) but not breach of s.12(1). There had been no breach of s.12(1) at the time of the sale so that A had not infringed that section but since B's quiet possession had been disturbed after sale, A was in breach of s.12(2).

SALE BY DESCRIPTION

Section 13(1) provides that, where there is a contract for the sale of goods by description, there is an implied condition that the goods shall correspond with the description.

(1) A sale is by description where the purchaser is buying on a mere description having never seen the goods, e.g. a sale of future goods.

(2) A sale may still be by description even though the goods are seen or examined or even selected from the seller's stock by the purchaser, as in a sale over the counter (*Grant* v *Australian Knitting Mills* 1936, p. 499), because most goods are described if only by the package in which they are contained. Therefore a sale in a self-service store would be covered by s.13 though no words were spoken by the seller.

In addition, there may be a sale by description even in regard to a specific article which has been inspected where the description relates to something not apparent on that inspection. (*Beale* v *Taylor* 1967.)[285]

Section 13 is applied strictly, and every statement which forms part of that description is treated as a condition giving the buyer the right to reject the goods, even though the misdescription is of a minor nature, and might more properly have been regarded as a misrepresentation or warranty not giving the right to reject. Buyers have been allowed to reject goods on seemingly trivial grounds, e.g. misdescriptions of how the goods are packed, and regardless of the fact that no damage has been suffered. (*Moore & Co. Ltd* v *Landauer & Co. Ltd* 1921.)[172] Although the Sale of Goods Act applies in the main to sales by dealers, s.13 applies even where the seller is not a dealer in the goods sold. (*Varley* v *Whipp* 1900).[286]

There can be no contracting out of s.13 at all in a business or private 'consumer sale'. In a non-consumer sale contracting out is allowed to the extent that it is 'fair or reasonable'. (See further p. 58.)

Provided the goods correspond to their description there is no action under s.13 if they are of unmerchantable quality and/or unfit for the purpose, though s.14 could then apply. (*Ashington Piggeries Ltd* v *Chistopher Hill Ltd* 1971.)[287] Where the sale is by sample as well as by description, s.13(2) provides that the bulk must correspond with both the sample and the description. Thus in *Nichol* v *Godts* (1854) 10 Ex. 191 a purchaser bought by sample 'foreign refined rape oil'. It was held that the goods must correspond, not only with the sample, but must also be in fact 'foreign refined rape oil' and not a mixture of rape and hemp oil which was inferior.

IMPLIED CONDITIONS AS TO FITNESS AND QUALITY

These are as follows—

(1) *Fitness for purpose.* Section 14(3) lays down the following conditions—

Where the seller sells goods in the course of a business and the buyer (or debtor in a credit sale), expressly, or by implication, makes known—

(*a*) to the seller, or

(*b*) to the dealer in a credit sale any particular purpose for which the goods are being bought, there is an implied condition that the goods supplied under the contract are reasonably fit for that purpose whether or not that is a purpose for which such goods are commonly supplied, except where the circumstances show that the buyer (or debtor) does not rely, or that it is unreasonable for him to rely, on the skill or judgment of that seller or dealer.

There is no need for the buyer to specify the particular purpose for which the goods are required when they have in the ordinary way only one purpose. (*Priest* v *Last* 1903.)[288] The words 'any particular purpose' apply where the goods are sold for a variety of uses and are unsuitable for a particular use to which a particular buyer puts them. (*Ashington Piggeries Ltd* v *Christopher Hill Ltd* 1971.[287]

Reliance on the seller's skill and judgement will be readily implied even to the extent of saying that, at least in sales to the general public as consumers, the buyer has gone to the seller because he relies on the seller having selected his stock with skill and judgement. (Per Lord Wright in *Grant* v *Australian Knittng Mills Ltd* 1936.)[289] The onus is on the buyer to show that he has made known the purpose for which the goods are being bought. Reliance will then be presumed, unless it can be disproved, or if the seller can show that reliance was unreasonable.

The court has to decide what amounts to 'unreasonable reliance'. However, presumably the seller can disclaim reponsibility. For example, suppose B goes into S's general stores and sees some tubes of glue. If he then asks whether the glue will stick metal to plastic and S says:'I am not expert enough to say', then if B buys the glue and it does not stick metal to plastic it would surely be unreasonable for B to suggest that he relied on S's skill and judgment.

Where the buyer knows that the seller deals in only one brand of goods, e.g. where a public house sells only one brand of beer, there will not in general be any implication of such reliance. (*Wren* v *Holt* 1903,[290] but see *Manchester Liners Ltd* v *Rea* 1922.)[291] The section applies to non-manufactured goods. (*Frost* v *Aylesbury Dairy Co. Ltd* 1905.)[292] The section also applies to the containers in which the goods are packed. (*Geddling* v *Marsh* 1920.)[293] Cases such as *Geddling* have received statutory confirmation in the 1979 Act because s.14(3) expressly extends the implied conditions to the 'goods supplied under the contract'. Thus foreign matter which is supplied with goods would be covered since it would be within the term 'goods supplied under the contract'. (See *Wilson* v *Rickett, Cockerell & Co. Ltd* 1954.)[294] Where there are special circumstances of which the seller is unaware, s.14(3) does not apply. (*Griffiths* v *Peter Conway Ltd* 1939.)[295]

A majority of the Court of Appeal *held*, in *Hardwick Game Farm* v *Suffolk Agricultural and Poultry Producers Association Ltd* [1966] 1 All E.R. 309 (cited as *Kendall* v *Lillico* on appeal to the House of Lords) that the fact that the seller and the buyer were dealers did not in itself prevent a finding that the buyer relied on the seller's skill and judgment. However, there is no ground for assuming reliance in this sort of case and proof of it must be forthcoming. (See the judgment of Lord Reid in *Kendall* v *Lillico* [1969] 2 A.C. 31 at pp. 79–85.)

Liability under s.14(3) is strict and extends to latent defects which the seller could not have discovered even by the use of proper care and diligence. (*Frost* v *Aylesbury Dairy Co. Ltd* 1905.)[292]

If defects emerge fairly quickly after sale this is strong evidence that the goods were not reasonably fit at the time of sale. (*Crowther* v *Shannon Motor Company* 1975.)[297]

Before proceeding to consider merchantable quality, we must distinguish the two heads of liability, i.e. fitness and merchantable quality. Under s.14(2) an article is regarded as not merchantable because of a manufacturing defect so that a perfect article would have served the purpose, or in other words it is the right article but it is faulty. Under s.14(3) an article is regarded as not fit for the purpose because of its design or construction. It may be perfect in terms of its manufacture but its construction or design does not allow it to fit the purpose and consequently no amount of adjustment or repair will ever make it right. In other words, it is a perfect article but the wrong article for the purpose. This is illustrated by the case of *Baldry* v *Marshall* 1925.[296]

(2) *Merchantable quality*. By s.14(2) where the seller sells goods in the course of a business there is an implied condition that the goods supplied under the contract are of merchantable quality, except that there is no such condition—

(*a*) as regards defects specifically drawn to the buyer's attention before the contract is made; or

(*b*) if the buyer examines the goods before the contract is made, as regards defects which that examination ought to reveal.

If the seller does not normally deal in goods of the type in question, there is no condition as to fitness (nor as to merchantability unless the sale is by sample which is dealt with below). The *only* condition in such a case is that the goods correspond with the description. This arises because s.14(1) provides that except as provided by s.14 and s.15 (sale by sample), and subject to any other enactment, there is no implied condition or warranty about the quality or fitness for any particularl purpose of goods supplied under a contract of sale. If, therefore, S (who is not a dealer) sells a car to B with no express terms as to quality and fitness, the court is prevented by s.14 from implying conditions or warranties, even though S seems, from the circumstances, to have been warranting the car in good order.

The s.14 provision regarding merchantable quality applies where the sale is by a dealer who does not ordinarily sell goods of precisely the same description. Thus if B ordered an 'X' brand motor bike from S who has not formerly sold that make, s.14 applies if the motor bike is unfit or unmerchantable.

Section 14(5) is concerned with the problem of a private seller who sells through an agent. The subsection provides that the implied conditions of fitness and merchantability operate if the agent is selling in the ordinary course of business unless the principal is not acting in the course of business and the buyer is aware of this, or reasonable steps have been taken to bring it to his notice. Thus, for example, an auctioneer acting for a private seller could exclude these sections by making it clear that the principal was a private seller.

There is no need under s.14(2) for the buyer to show that he relied on the seller's skill and judgment, and the seller is liable for latent defects even though he is not the manufacturer and is merely marketing the goods as a wholesaler or retailer. Such a seller can, however, obtain an indemnity from the manufacturer if the buyer successfully sues him for defects in the goods.

If the buyer has examined the goods, there is no implied condition as regards defects which such an examination ought to have revealed. However, the law now contained in the 1979 Act has probably altered the decision in *Thornett & Fehr* v *Beers & Son* 1919[299] since the wording of s.14(2)(*b*) specifically refers to '*that* examination' which seems to suggest that there must be an actual examination of the goods and not a mere opportunity for examination which was not accepted.

The interpretation of the word 'merchantable' has often been discussed in the courts. Section 14(6) provides—

> Goods of any kind are of merchantable quality within the meaning of this Act if they are as fit for the purpose or purposes for which goods of that kind are commonly bought as it is reasonable to expect having regard to any description applied to them, the price (if relevant) and all the other relevant circumstances.

The price paid by the buyer is therefore a factor to be taken into account. Goods (provided they are not defective) are not unmerchantable simply because their resale price is slightly less than that which the buyer paid, though they may be if the difference in purchase and resale price is substantial. (*B.S. Brown & Son Ltd* v *Craiks Ltd* 1970.)[300] Even where the goods are not purchased for resale the purchase price may be relevant. Thus the sale of a car with a defective clutch would be a sale of unmerchantable goods but if the seller makes an allowance in the price to cover the defect it may not be. (*Bartlett* v *Sydney Marcus Ltd* [1965] 2 All E.R. 753.)

As regards the description applied to the goods, old cars or other mechanical items which are sold and described as scrap need not be merchantable. Furthermore, 'shop-soiled', 'fire-damaged', 'flood-salvage' and so on might imply non-merchantable lines. In addition, old items, such as antiques and curios would not presumably be required to be in perfect working order.

As regards the time during which the goods must be merchantable; the law is not clear. As regards perishable goods, the decision in *Mash and Murrell* v *Joseph I. Emmanuel* [1961] 1 All E.R. 485 is relevant. In that case potatoes, though sound when loaded in Cyprus, were rotten by the time the ship arrived in Liverpool, though there was no undue delay. It was held by Diplock, J., that the sellers were liable under s.14(2) because the goods should have been loaded in such a state that they could survive the normal journey and be in a merchantable condition when they arrived. In addition, the seller is liable for defects inherent in the goods when they are sold and will not escape merely because the defects do not become apparent until a later time. Circumstances such as those seen in *Crowther* v *Shannon Motor Co.* 1975[297] provide an illustration of this situation.

Where part only of the goods are unmerchantable it seems to depend on how much of the consignment is defective. In *Jackson* v *Rotax Motor and Cycle Co. Ltd* [1910] 2 K.B. 937 the plaintiffs supplied motor horns to the defendants and one consignment was rejected by the defendants who alleged they were unmerchantable. Half the goods were dented and scratched because of bad packing and the Court of Appeal held that the buyers were entitled to reject the consignment.

Section 14(6) does not create a susbstantial change in the concept of merchantable quality which has always been flexible. Whether goods are or are not merchantable is a matter of fact, not law, and it is a matter for the court to decide on the basis of the circumstances of each case.

Nevertheless, the test of merchantable quality is somewhat unsatisfactory. A buyer of goods has no rights at all where there are a number of minor defects such as small scratches and dents in a new car. The car is not necessarily unmerchantable because of these defects, nor is it unfit for the purpose. The Law Commission in Working Paper 85 suggest a new test as follows: 'The goods should be of such quality as would in all the circumstances of the case be fully acceptable to a reasonable buyer who had full knowledge of their condition, quality and characteristics'.

The rules as to fitness for purpose and merchantable quality do not apply to private sales of secondhand goods and there is still a fairly wide application of the maxim *caveat emptor* (let the buyer beware!). In practice only manufacturers, wholesalers, retailers and dealers in new or secondhand good will be caught by the implied conditions. The courts cannot imply conditions and warranties into private contracts similar to those implied by the Act into sales by dealers, because, as we have seen, s.14(1) forbids it.

Before leaving the topic of s.14 implied terms, it should be noted that if a retailer sells goods which are faulty and in breach of s.14 he is obliged to indemnify the purchaser if the faulty goods injure a third party to whom the purchaser is found liable. However, no such indemnity is payable if the purchaser has contined to use the goods having become aware that they are faulty and dangerous. (*Lambert* v *Lewis* 1981.)[298]

USAGE OF TRADE

Section 14(4) provides than an implied warranty or condition as to quality or fitness for a particular purpose may be annexed to a contract of sale by usage. Where the transaction is connected with a particular trade, the customs and usages of that trade give the context in which the parties made their contract and may give a guide as to their intentions. Thus in a sale of canary seed in accordance with the customs of the trade it was held that the buyer could not reject the seed delivered on the grounds that there were impurities in it. A custom of the trade prevented this but allowed instead a rebate on the price paid. (*Peter Darlington Partners Ltd* v *Gosho Co. Ltd* [1964] 1 Lloyd's Rep. 149.)

SALE BY SAMPLE

Section 15(1) states that a contract of sale is a contract of sale by sample where there is a term in the contract, express or implied, to that effect.

The mere fact that the seller provides a sample for the buyer's inspection is not enough; to be such a sale there must be either an express provision in the contract to that effect, or there must be evidence that the parties intended the sale to be by sample.

There are three implied conditions in a sale by sample—

(1) *The bulk must correspond with the sample in quality.* (S.15(2)(*a*).)

(2) *The buyer shall have a reasonable opportunity of comparing the bulk with the sample.* (S.15(2)(*b*).) The buyer will not be deemed to have accepted the goods until he has had an opportunity to compare the bulk with the sample, and will be able, therefore, to reject the goods, even though they have been delivered, if the bulk does not correspond with the sample. He is not left with the remedy of damages for breach of warranty. (See s.34, p. 147.)

(3) *The goods shall be free from any defect, rendering them unmerchantable, which would not be apparent on reasonable examination of the sample.* (S.15(2)(*c*).) (*Godley* v *Perry* 1960.)[301]

The effect of s.15(2)(*c*) is to exclude the implied condition of merchantability if the defect could have been discovered by reasonable examination of the sample whether or not there has in fact been any examination of the sample. This is presumably based upon the premise that the seller is entitled to assume that the buyer will examine the sample. The provision is in contrast with s.14(2) where the implied condition of merchantability is not excluded unless an examination has actually taken place. (See pp. 138–9.)

LIABILITY OF SELLER WHERE GOODS ARE IN A DANGEROUS CONDITION

Quite apart from any question of implied conditions or warranties, there is a duty lying upon a seller who knows of the dangerous character of the goods he is supplying, to warn the buyer of the danger. (*Clarke* v *Army & Navy Co-operative Society Ltd* 1903;[302] *Fisher* v *Harrods* 1966.)[303]

In addition, s.6 of the Health & Safety at Work Act 1974 imposes a criminal liability on manufacturers who fail to give adequate information to enable their products to be used properly and safely.

Liability of manufacturer

PRODUCT LIABILITY IN THE TORT OF NEGLIGENCE

Where the goods are purchased from a retailer, no action can be brought under the Sale of Goods Act by the purchaser against the manufacturer. The doctrine of privity of contract applies (see p. 10) with the result that there is no contract between them into which the warranties and conditions set out in the Act can be implied. However, the purchaser may have an action in negligence against the manufacturer in respect of *physical* injuries caused by defects in the goods. (*Donoghue* v *Stevenson* 1932.)[304]

The rule enunciated in *Donoghue* v *Stevenson*[304] has been widened since 1932, and now applies to defective chattels generally which cause injuries to purchasers. (*Grant* v *Australian Knitting Mills Ltd* 1936.)[289] However, although the above cases show that the manufacturer has a duty to take care, evidence may show that he was not in breach of that duty because he took proper precautions. (*Daniels* v *White & Sons* 1938.)[305]

In the cases mentioned above the question of inspection of the goods was raised. It was an important fact in the decision in *Donoghue* v *Stevenson* 1932,[304] that the bottle was made of dark glass, so that the snail could not be seen on external inspection of the bottle, and that normally no inspection of the goods would take place until they reached the consumer. It is not thought that in the developing law of negligence, a manufacturer can rely on an inspection revealing the defects in his product, except perhaps in a special case where it is known that an expert inspection normally takes place. If such an inspection does not take place, or fails to find the defect which it should have found, the manufacturer may regard this as a *novus actus interveniens* (a new act intervening) breaking the chain of causation between his negligence and the injury.

Further, it may not be enough for a manufacturer to prove a safe system of manufacture as in *Daniels* v *White & Sons* 1938,[305] because the fact that the goods are dangerous postulates negligence. The maxim *res ipsa loquitur* (the thing speaks for itself) may apply so that the manufacturer bears the burden of explaining the matter on grounds other than his own negligence. Since in these cases there is often no evidence or explanation as to how the dangerous substance got into the goods the manufacturer will rarely be able to discharge his burden of explanation and will lose the action, though the manufacturer did manage to satisfy the court that he was not negligent in the *Daniels* case where *res ipsa loquitur* was pleaded.

Product liability in negligence has, up to recent times, been confined to defective chattels which cause *physical injury* to purchasers as in *Donoghue*[304] and *Grant*.[289] However, in *Junior Books Ltd* v *Veitchi* 1982[306] the law seems to have taken a step forward. Product liability in negligence appears now to extend to complaints relating to defects in goods which have caused *economic loss*.

In the past the remedy for defective goods which have not worked properly has been against the seller in contract but this may no longer be the case. The remedy in tort is not affected by privity of contract (see p. 10) and therefore can extend, e.g. to an action directly against the manufacturer, without the need to find a collateral contract, as in *Carlill*.[1]

The ability to sue the manufacturer of defective goods directly does not take away the need for the Sale of Goods Act remedies against the retailer, because the manufacturer may, in these days of international trade, often be outside the jurisdiction of our courts and for that reason difficult to sue.

THIRD PARTY PROCEEDINGS

Strict liability under the Act of 1979 can, in effect, be imposed on a manufacturer by means of third (or fourth) party proceedings. Thus if the seller is sued by the buyer for breach of an implied condition under the Act, the seller may claim an indemnity from his own supplier which may be the manufacturer. If the retailer has purchased from a wholesaler the retailer may claim an indemnity from the wholesaler who may in turn claim an indemnity from the manufacturer who supplied the goods. In this way the manufacturer can be made to pay for defects affecting the quality or fitness of the goods. *Godley* v *Perry* 1960[301] provides an example of joinder of parties.

COLLATERAL CONTRACTS

The manufacturer may also be liable for defects in quality or fitness under a collateral contract. Thus in *Shanklin Pier Ltd* v *Detel Products Ltd* [1951] 2 All E.R. 471, Shanklin entered into a contract with A to paint the Pier and asked A to use paint made by Detel, the suitability of which had been communicated to Shanklin by Detel's agent. The paint was not suitable and Shanklin recovered damages against Detel for breach of a contract which the Court held was collateral to the main contract with A. This applies however, only where a specific and express undertaking has been given by the manufacturer to the seller and it is doubtful whether such a claim could be based on statements made in a manufacturer's public advertisements. There are no firm illustrations of this in English law, though *Carlill* v *Carbolic Smoke Ball Co.* 1893[1] could perhaps be developed. The Court did not in fact go for the collateral contract solution in *Lambert* v *Lewis* 1981.[298] The action against the manufacturer in that case was framed in negligence.

The Law Commission has recognized the need to provide some general form of action against the manufacturer but has felt that this cannot be done by a simple amendment to the Sale of Goods Act 1979. The Commission therefore recommends that a wider study of the problem be made before embarking upon legislative measures. (Exemption Clauses, First Report, para. 63.)

MANUFACTURERS' GUARANTEES

A manufacturers' guarantee (or warranty, as it is sometimes called) normally amounts to a warranty to repair or replace during a specified time with the addition in the case of vehicles of a mileage limit.

Such guarantees are presumably enforceable by the buyer as a collateral contract as in *Carlill* v *Carbolic Smoke Ball Co.* 1893.[1]

They cannot affect the purchaser's right to sue upon the implied conditions and warranties set out in the Sale of Goods Act 1979 or at common law for negligence because under s.5 of the Unfair Contract Terms Act 1977 a clause in a manufacturer's or distributor's guarantee cannot operate to exclude or restrict the manufacturer's or distributor's liability to the customer provided the goods are of a type ordinarily supplied for private use or consumption and prove defective whilst in consumer use, i.e. not used exclusively for the purposes of a business.

OTHER STATUTORY DUTIES

In addition to the Sale of Goods Act 1979 Parliament has passed a number of statutes all of which seek to provide some form of consumer protection. There is Food & Drugs and Weights & Measures legislation, and more recently the Trade Descriptions Acts 1968–72. These Acts, however, normally rely on criminal law for their enforcement and do not provide civil remedies. An exception is the Consumer Safety Act 1978. As we have seen, this legislation gives the Home Secretary power to make regulations regarding standards of manufacture of goods, and regulations have been made, for example, in relation to oil heaters. The Acts give a civil remedy for damages to the consumer for injury arising out of defects in the goods. (See further p. 55.)

FAIR TRADING ACT

The Fair Trading Act 1973 establishes the office of Director General of Fair Trading who is given wide powers to keep under review the whole field of sale of goods and supply of services to consumers.

The Director General is assisted in carrying out his functions by the Consumer Protection Advisory Committee. This Committee, which is staffed by experts on consumer sales generally, weights and measures and trade descriptions legislation and consumer protection groups, considers consumer trade practices referred to it by any minister or by the Director. These practices may under s.13 of the 1973 Act include—

(1) the terms and conditions and the manner as to which consumer goods are sold;

(2) promotion, advertising and salesmanship in relation to such goods;

(3) the methods of obtaining payment for such goods.

The Committee can recommend that orders be made to prevent undesirable practices continuing. Indeed, where the Director makes a reference to the Committee he can include a proposal for an order to be made. The Committee must report within three months of taking up a reference. This provision is designed to avoid delays which often occur in the administrative process where a committee is appointed and charged with duties.

Powers to make orders. The minister concerned has very wide powers under s.22 of the 1973 Act to make orders following a recommendation by the Committee. These can affect the relationship between supplier/seller and consumer. Schedule 6 of the Act sets out the basis of such orders and includes, for example, the prohibition of the inclusion in consumer contracts of terms or conditions excluding liability for specified matters. This provision would cover an order forbidding exclusion clauses in particular contracts.

Penalties. The Act specifically provides that a contract is not to be void or unenforceable merely because one of its terms contravenes an order, nor does the breach of an order confer the right of civil action. Criminal penalties are provided for contravention of the orders but there are some defences, e.g. a person will escape liability if he can show that he took all reasonable steps and acted with due diligence to prevent the commission of an offence.

Enforcement. The duty of enforcing orders is given to local Trading Standards/Consumer Protection departments and wide powers of entry into premises to search for and seize documents are given if reasonable grounds exist for believing an offence to have been committed.

Sanctions of the Director. If the Director considers that a business is being carried on which is detrimental to the interests of consumers and is unfair in the sense that it contravenes statutory or contractual conditions in regard to such business, then he can require an undertaking that such practices will cease. If no such undertaking is given he can bring proceedings against the defaulter before the Restrictive Practices Court. If after the hearing the Court is satisfied that there has been such business conduct as referred to above then it can make an order directing the defaulter to refrain from pursuing that course of conduct. A breach of such an order would, of course, be contempt of court for which the defaulter could be fined or imprisoned. Directors of companies may be asked for undertakings and be proceeded against if their companies are defaulters in the sense referred to above. The Director General has made a number of references to the CPAC in regard to consumer trade practices and the first Report of the Advisory Committee proposed an order, which, as we have seen, was made, prohibiting the use of advertisements or written clauses which contain void exemption clauses, and which may mislead consumers who do not appreciate that the clauses are void. (See further p. 59.)

Before leaving the topic of consumer protection it is worth noting that the remedies available to the consumer are in most cases restricted to an action in a court of law for damages. Since this postulates an involvement in the process of litigation, with all that that means in terms of consulting lawyers and paying fees, the remedy is not appropriate in the case of small claims. (But see below.)

REMEDIES OF THE CONSUMER

Since October 1973 the County Court Rules have been amended so that where no more than £500 is involved, arbitration instead of a trial is automatically ordered. The arbitrator is normally the Registrar of the County Court and the greater informality and lower cost involved make it much easier for small claims to be made. That the provision is having effect is illustrated by the Civil Judicial Statistics which are published annually and show a very significant increase in small claims brought before the County Court. In addition, many more disputes were apparently settled at a pre-trial review by the Registrar who was able to get the parties to compromise before going to a hearing of any kind.

An important point to note about arbitration proceedings is the 'no costs' rule. The plaintiff does not have to pay his opponent's lawyer's fees if he loses. However, he will have to pay his opponents other out-of-pocket expenses, including witness expenses. This might be quite a large sum, say, in excess of £100 if, for example, his opponent has called an expert witness to deal with some technical aspect of the dispute. It should also be noted that if the plaintiff wins he cannot get the other side to pay his lawyer's fees. The court fees to bring the proceedings must be paid. These are not prohibitive. They vary from £5 for claims up to £50 to £32 for claims between £300 and £500. For claims between £50 and £300 the fee is 10 per cent of what is being claimed.

In addition, many compensation orders are now being made under the Powers of Criminal Courts Act 1973, Section 35 of that Act enables a criminal court which has convicted an offender to order that offender to pay compensation to the victim and this can be done whether or not it was the victim who brought the prosecution. In Magistrates Courts the maximum amount which may be awarded is £2000 on any one occasion. Nevertheless, until the amount of money involved in the arbitration provisions can be increased, and this depends upon the provision of extra staff in the County Court, the consumer is not really able to enforce effectively the legal rights given to him by, e.g. the Sale of Goods Act.

Exclusion of seller's liability

The law relating to exclusion clauses has already been considered in Chapter 1. (See pp. 50–59.)

Treating a breach of condition as a breach of warranty

Section 11(2) provides that the buyer can waive a breach of condition altogether or may treat it as a breach of warranty. If he chooses to treat the breach of condition as a breach of warranty, then he may sue for damages but cannot reject the goods.

However, unless there is a contrary provision in the contract, a breach of a condition implied under the Sale of Goods Act *must* be treated as a breach of warranty *where the contract is not severable and the buyer has accepted the goods or part thereof.* (S.11(4).)

Problems of severability arise where the goods are delivered by instalments. Where the price is paid for the whole consignment and delivery is by instalments, the contract is probably not severable, and acceptance by the buyer of early instalments will prevent him from rejecting later instalments which are not in accordance with the contract.

However, if, under the terms of the contract, each instalment is to be paid for separately, the contract is probably severable (s.31(2)), and acceptance of earlier instalments will not prevent the buyer from rejecting later deliveries which are not in accordance with the contract.

A contract may, however, be regarded as severable in a number of other situations. Thus in *Longbottom & Co. Ltd* v *Bass Walker & Co. Ltd* [1922] W.N. 245, a contract for the sale of cloth was regarded as severable where delivery was by instalments but the price was paid as part of a monthly account and not separately for each delivery of cloth.

Section 11(4) does not come into force when the goods are merely delivered; there must be some act by the buyer indicating his acceptance of the goods. A buyer is deemed to have accepted the goods—

(1) when he informs the seller that he has accepted them; or

(2) where, after delivery, and provided he has had a reasonable opportunity to examine the goods to see if they comply with the contract, he acts in a manner inconsistent with the continued ownership of the seller, as where he uses or consumes the goods; or

(3) where, after the lapse of a reasonable time, he still retains the goods, without giving notice of rejection. (Ss.34 and 35(1).)

RESCISSION OF A CONTRACT OF SALE

It is useful at this point to compare the rules set out in s.11 of the Act of 1979 with the right to rescind a contract of sale for misrepresentation arising from a misstatement of fact. The rules relating to rescission are governed by separate principles. (See p. 39.) Since the Misrepresentation Act 1967, rescission of a contract of sale is barred only where there is affirmation, lapse of time, inability to make restitution or acquisition of rights by innocent third parties for value. It seems that a buyer's right to rescind for misrepresentation and his right to reject for breach of condition are now much the same in principle, since an act which amounts to acceptance under s.35(1) of the 1979 Act will almost always amount to affirmation so as to bar rescission. There may, however, be exceptional cases were rescission is available when rejection is not. For example, under s.35(1) if a buyer does not intimate his rejection of the goods within a reasonable time he is automatically deemed to have accepted them and cannot reject. In equity lapse of time is not in itself sufficient to prevent rescission unless it amounts to affirmation, or the person making the representation (i.e. the seller) is prejudiced. Thus if in spite of lapse of time there is no prejudice to the seller, equity may allow rescission although the right to reject has been lost under s.35(1).

Transfer of the property in goods

The provisions of the Act regarding the transfer of the property in the goods are important because the parties to contracts of sale do not usually express their intentions as to the passing of the property. In addition the risk normally passes when the property passes and the seller can in general terms only sue for the *price* as distinct from *damages* if the property has passed.

The following are the relevant statutory provisions—

WHERE THE GOODS ARE SPECIFIC

We will consider six cases.

(1) Section 17 provides that, where there is a contract for a sale of specific or ascertained goods, the property in them is transferred to the buyer at such time as the parties intend it to be transferred, and, for the purpose of ascertaining the intention of the parties, regard shall be had to the terms of the contract, the conduct of the parties, and the circumstances of the case. Thus, an obligation on one party to insure is an indication that he has the risk and, by inference, and in the absence of an express provision to the contrary, the property. (*Allison* v *Bristol Marine Insurance Co. Ltd* (1876) 1 App. Cas. 209.)

Section 17 is the overriding one, i.e. the intentions of the parties must be taken into account first. The following rules apply only if no different intention appears.

(2) Section 18, Rule 1, provides that, where there is an unconditional contract for the sale of specific goods, in a deliverable state, the property in the goods passes to the buyer when the contract is made, and it is immaterial whether the time of payment or the time of delivery, or both, be postponed. (*Underwood Ltd* v *Burgh Castle Brick & Cement Synd.* 1922.)[307]

However, since s.18 provides that the statutory rules do not apply if a contrary intention appears, it may be that *an agreement to the* postponement of payment or delivery would indicate that the parties do not want the property to pass. The mere fact that the buyer has not paid and the seller has not delivered does not prevent ownership passing. (See *Dennant* v *Skinner & Collom* 1948, p. 509.)

Other factors may indicate that there is no intention to pass the property. Thus in *Ingram* v *Little* 1961,[97] it seems to have been assumed that no property was to pass until the method of payment, i.e. cash or cheque, had been agreed by the parties, and in *Lacis* v *Cashmarts* [1969] 2 Q.B. 400 it was held that in a supermarket no contract was made until the price was actually paid.

(3) In the case of specific goods not in a deliverable state, s.18, Rule 2, provides that the property does not pass until the seller puts them into a deliverable state, and the buyer is notified thereof. It is assumed that 'notice' to the buyer means what it says and that if a letter of notification is posted to the buyer it is not effective on posting but only when it reaches him and would have been read in the ordinary course of business. (See *Holwell Securities* v *Hughes* 1974, p. 361.)

(4) In the case of conditional sales of specific goods, s.18, Rule 3, provides that, where there is a contract for the sale of specific goods in a deliverable state, but the seller is bound to weigh, measure, test, or do some other act or thing with reference to the goods for the purpose of ascertaining the price, the property does not pass until such act or thing is done, and the buyer has notice thereof. Rule 3 applies only to acts which must be done by the seller. Thus where X sold a consignment of cocoa to Y at an agreed price for 60 lb, the arrangment being that Y would resell the cocoa and weigh it in order to ascertain the amount owed to X, it was held that the fact that Y had to weigh the cocoa did not make the contract conditional. The property passed to Y before the price was arrived at. (*Nanka Bruce* v *Commonwealth Trust Ltd* [1926] A.C. 77.)

(5) In the case of sales on approval, or on sale or return, or other similar terms, s.18, Rule 4, provides as follows—

(*a*) The property passes to the buyer when he signifies his approval or acceptance to the seller, or does any other act adopting the transaction, such as pledging the goods with a third party. (*London Jewellers Ltd* v *Attenborough* 1934.)[281]

(*b*) If the buyer does not signify his approval or acceptance to the seller but *retains the goods without giving notice of rejection*, then the property passes on the expiration of the time, if any, fixed for the return of goods, or on the expiration of a reasonable time. What is a reasonable time is a question of fact. (*Poole* v *Smith's Car Sales (Balham) Ltd* 1962.)[308] This part of the rule applies only if it is the buyer who retains the goods. Thus if goods on sale or return are seized and retained by the buyer's unpaid creditors, the property will not pass under 4(*b*). (*Re Ferrier* [1944] Ch. 295.)

Where the goods are on approval and the seller has expressly provided in the contract that the property is not to pass until they are paid for, then Rule 4 will not operate because the express provision indicates a contrary intention. But if the buyer sells or disposes of the goods, a third party may still get a good title under the doctrine of estoppel, or under s.2 of the Factors Act 1889. (*Weiner* v *Harris* 1910.)[309]

(6) Section 19(1) provides that, where there is a contract for the sale of specific goods or where goods are subsequently appropriated to the contract, the seller may, by the terms of the appropriation or contract, reserve the right of disposal of the goods until certain conditions are fulfilled. In such a case, even if the goods are delivered to the buyer, or to a carrier or other bailee for the purpose of transmission to the buyer, the property in the goods does not pass until the conditions imposed by the seller are fulfilled.

The section does not safeguard the seller as much as might appear because the buyer, being a person who has bought or agreed to buy the goods, can give a good title to a third party under s.25(1) of the Act.

Section 19(3) provides that where the seller of goods draws a bill of exchange on the buyer for the price, and transmits the bill of exchange and bill of lading to the buyer together to secure acceptance or payment of the bill of exchange, the buyer is bound to return the bill of lading if he does not honour the bill of exchange, and if he wrongfully retains the bill of lading, the property in the goods does not pass to him.

Here again there is no complete safeguard for the seller. It is true that the passing of the property is conditional upon the bill of exchange being accepted and honoured, but a transfer of the bill of lading to a third party who takes it bona fide and for value gives the third party a good title under s.25(1) of the Sale of Goods Act, and prevents the seller from exercising his right of lien or stoppage *in transitu* against the third party under s.47(2) of the Sale of Goods Act and s.10 of the Factors Act 1889.

Reservation of title by seller

It has become fashionable in recent times for sellers of goods to try to protect themselves against the worst effects of a company receivership or liquidation by inserting retention clauses of one form or another into their contracts of sale. These are allowed by s.19(1) of the Sale of Goods Act 1979. (See above.)

These clauses have as their purpose the retention of the seller's ownership in the goods until the buyer has paid for them, even though the buyer is given possession of the goods and may use them in the manufacture of other goods which he will then resell.

If the clause works and the purchasing company goes into a receivership or liquidation because of insolvency, then the seller is able to recover the goods which the purchasing company still has and the proceeds of resale by the purchasing company. The seller will normally find such a procedure more advantageous than—

(*a*) proving in a liquidation for whatever he can get by way of dividend leaving his goods to be sold for the benefit of creditors generally, or (*b*) in a receivership leaving his goods with the receiver who may in law continue the company's business without paying its existing debts, including that of the seller.

Retention clauses have been used on the Continent for much longer than they have here. They are an understandable reaction by unsecured trade creditors to the increasing number of insolvencies in which a bank is found to hold a debenture giving a floating charge over the insolvent company's assets to secure an overdraft. The bank, being a secured creditor, takes the company's assets first, subject to certain preferential payments through the medium of a receivership or liquidation, leaving trade creditors unprovided for. There have been a number of legal decisions on the use of retention clauses. The following are among the most instructive.

(1) *THE ROMALPA CASE* (*Aluminium Industrie Vaassen B.V.* v *Romalpa Aluminium* [1976] 2 All E.R. 552.) This was the first case in a series of three which alerted the legal and accountancy professions to the problems which retention clauses might cause in insolvency practice.

The facts of the case were that AIV sold aluminium foil to Romalpa, the contractual conditions of sale being—

(*a*) that the ownership of the material to be delivered by AIV would only be transferred to the purchaser when he had met all that was owing to AIV, no matter on what grounds;

(*b*) that Romalpa should store the foil separately;

(*c*) that if the foil was used to make new objects, those objects should be stored separately and be owned by AIV as *security* for payment;

(*d*) that Romalpa could sell the new objects but so long as they had not discharged their debt they should hand over to AIV if requested the claims they had against purchasers from Romalpa.

Romalpa got into financial difficulties and was in debt to its bankers in the sum of £200,000. The bank had a debenture secured over Romalpa's assets and appointed a receiver under that debenture. At the time of the receiver's appointment Romalpa owed AIV £122,000 and in order to recover some of that money at the expense of the bank AIV sought, under their conditions of sale, to recover from Romalpa foil valued in round terms at £50,000 and the cash proceeds of resold foil of some £35,000. The proceeds had been received from third-party purchasers from Romalpa after the receiver was appointed and he had kept the fund of £35,000 separate so that it was not mixed with Romalpa's other funds and was therefore identifiable.

The Court of Appeal held that the foil was recoverable and so were the proceeds of sale since there was a fiduciary relationship between AIV and Romalpa. This arose because ownership in the goods had not passed to Romalpa so that Romalpa was a bailee of AIV's goods and AIV was the bailor. This relationship is fiduciary and allows the bailor to recover the goods from his bailee. In addition, the fiduciary duty stemming from the bailment includes the right to trace the proceeds of sale so long as the goods bailed have not been paid for. These rules derive from *Re Hallett's Estate* (1880) 13 Ch.D. 696.

Therefore Romalpa was accountable to AIV for the foil and the proceeds of its sale and AIV could trace the proceeds into the hands of the receiver.

As regards a claim by counsel for Romalpa that the retention clause created a charge which should have been registered under s.95 of the Companies Act 1948, and that the retention clause was inoperative because there had been no such registration, the Court decided that since ownership had not passed to Romalpa the charge was not over the property of Romalpa and so s.95 did not apply, that section being confined to charges over the property of a company. In addition, the Romalpa clause included a contractual charge over mixed objects. The Court did not give a decision as to the position in regard to this charge since there was no need in the case to use it. The claim was merely for foil remaining in the buyer's possession and for the proceeds of sale, and both of these items could be recovered on the basis of the bailor/bailee relationship.

(2) *THE BORDEN CASE* (*Borden (UK) Ltd* v *Scottish Timber Products Ltd* [1979] 3 All E.R. 961.) In this case Borden (B) supplied resin to Scottish Timber (S) which S used in making chipboard. B inserted the following retention clause in the contract under which the resin was supplied: 'Goods supplied by the company shall be at the purchaser's risk immediately on delivery to the purchaser or into custody on the purchaser's behalf (whichever is the sooner) and the purchaser should therefore be insured accordingly. Property and goods supplied hereunder will pass to the customer when: (*a*) the goods the subject of this contract, and (*b*) all other goods the subject of any other contract between the company and the customer which, at the time of payment of the full price of the goods sold under this contract, have been delivered to the customer but not paid for in full, have been paid for in full.'

S went into receivership and B sought to trace their resin into chipboard made from the resin and also to trace the proceeds of sale of chipboard made with the resin.

The Court of Appeal decided that S was not a bailee in spite of the clause. Bailment implied the right to redelivery of the resin and B must have known that there would be no true bailment because resin was supplied only in sufficient quantities for two days' production because that is all the resin which S had room to store. B must therefore have been taken to know that the resin would be mixed with goods belonging to S almost immediately. The resin had ceased to exist except as chipboard over which there was *no contractual charge.* Thus there was no fiduciary relationship; tracing was not available. If the clause had created a contractual charge over the board it would apparently, have been registrable, being created by S at least in part over its own property. The decision in *Romalpa* was not overruled but distinguished because nothing had been said in that case about the need to register contractual charges over mixed property.

(3) *THE PEACHDART CASE* (*Re Peachdart Ltd* [1983] 3 All E.R. 204.) Freudenberg Leather Co. Ltd supplied leather to Peachdart Ltd. It was used to make handbags. The leather was sold under a retention clause which provided that until payment was made in full Freudenberg retained the ownership in the leather and in any goods made from the leather, until they were sold by the company. Once the leather goods were sold Freudenberg was to have the right to trace the proceeds of sale of the handbags. Peachdart got into financial difficulties. Barclays Bank, who held a debenture over the company's assets appointed a receiver. Freudenberg were owed money by Peachdart and tried to make use of the retention clause. The receiver accepted that the ownership in the unused stock of leather remained with Freudenberg but argument centred upon the complete/incomplete handbags and the proceeds of sale arising before the receiver was appointed. The Court decided among other things that once the process of manufacture had begun the leather was converted through Peachdart's skill and use of other materials, such as handles and clasps, into other goods of a distinctive character. The ownership in those goods vested in Freudenberg only as a security for any outstanding balance of the price of the relevant parcel of leather. Since the charge had not been registered it was void under s.95 of the Companies Act 1948 and Freudenberg ranked only as an unsecured creditor.

It will be remembered that in *Romalpa*, aluminium foil, which was the subject of a retention clause, had not been used in a process of manufacture. In the *Borden case* resin, which was supplied under a retention clause, was used to make chipboard. It thus lost its identity as a separate substance. In the *Peachdart case* the process of manufacture did not have quite the same effect in that an expert might well have identified which handbags had been made from a particular parcel of leather. Clearly, however, *any* process of manufacture will put the application of a retention clause at risk; handles and clasps had been added, and the skill of the designer and workforce had been applied. All of this went to prevent the leather being the exclusive property of Freudenberg.

Borden and *Peachdart* do not overrule *Romalpa* on its own facts, though it is now clear that if AIV had tried to enforce the contractual security part of their clause over mixed products, had there been any mixed products, that aspect of their claim would have failed for lack of registration. However, a retention clause containing provisions on the *Romalpa* pattern should still be effective against a floating charge.

These provisions are that—

(1) the ownership of the goods must not pass to the buyer;
(2) the buyer must be stated to hold the goods as a bailee;
(3) where the goods are used in the manufacture of other products

it should be stated that those products are held by the buyer as *security* for payment of what is owed to the supplier, i.e. the clause should create a contractual charge over mixed goods;

(4) the goods and products made therefrom must be identifiable and kept separate.

Provided the clause contains the above terms and conditions, it should be effective and on a receivership or liquidation the goods or things made from them or proceeds of resale will be held for the supplier unless and until he is paid in full. However, in view of *Borden* and *Peachdart*, clause (3) above creates a registrable charge, and failure to register the charge within 21 days would result in that aspect of the clause, but not others, being void against a receiver or liquidator.

WHERE THE GOODS ARE UNASCERTAINED

Section 16 provides that, where there is a contract for the sale of unascertained goods, no property in the goods is transferred to the buyer unless and until the goods are ascertained. This is a commonsense rule because until the goods have been identified it is not possible to say in which goods the property is passing. Where an unidentified part of a bulk is sold there is no appropriation until there is severance of the goods sold from the rest. (*Laurie & Morewood* v *John Dudin & Sons* 1926.)[310]

There are many contracts for the sale of unascertained goods where the parties do not deal in their contract with the passing of the property. Where this is so s.18, Rule 5 applies. Rule 5(1), provides that where there is a contract for the sale of unascertained or future goods by description, and goods of that description and in a deliverable state are unconditionally appropriated to the contract (but see *Wait and James* v *Midland Bank* 1926)[311] either by the seller with the assent of the buyer, or by the buyer with the assent of the seller, the property in the goods thereupon passes to the buyer. Such assent may be express or implied and may be given either before or after the appropriation is made. (*Pignataro* v *Gilroy & Son* 1919.)[312]

The necessity for the buyer's assent to appropriation gives rise to difficulties where a consumer orders goods by post. Where under a commercial contract the seller is required to ship the goods to the buyer the shipping is regarded as an unconditional appropriation and the assent of the buyer is *assumed.* (*James* v *Commonwealth* (1939) 62 C.L.R. 339.) This rule seems inappropriate in the case of consumer sales by post. Though the law is not clear it is suggested that the posting of consumer goods should not pass the property otherwise the goods are, unknown to the buyer, at his risk during transit. There is no need to assume the consumer's consent to appropriation since in that sort of case he has agreed merely to dispatch of the goods and not to a particular appropriation.

An example of an unconditional appropriation, i.e. delivery to a carrier, is given in s.18, Rule 5(2), which provides that where, in pursuance of the contract, the seller delivers goods to the buyer or to a carrier or other bailee (whether named by the buyer or not) for the purpose of transmission to the buyer, and does not reserve the right of disposal, he is deemed to have unconditionally appropriated the goods to the contract. However, delivery to a carrier does not pass the property if identical goods destined for different owners are mixed (*Healey* v *Howlett & Sons* 1917).[313] nor if the seller is bound to weigh, measure or test the goods in order to ascertain the price. (*N.C.B.* v *Gamble* 1958.)[314]

The question of the transfer of property in goods is important, because risk generally passes with the property. The maxim is *res perit domino*. (A thing perishes to the disadvantage of its owner.)

Section 20 provides that, unless otherwise agreed, the goods remain at the seller's risk until the property therein is transferred to the buyer, but when the property in them is transferred to the buyer, the goods are at the buyer's risk whether delivery has been made or not, i.e. the rule applies, irrespective of who had possession of the goods at the time the property passed (see *Pignataro* v *Gilroy & Son* 1919.)[312] It seems that there may sometimes be a transfer of risk without transfer of the property (*Sterns Ltd* v *Vickers Ltd* 1923),[315] and a transfer of the property without risk. (*Head* v *Tattersall* 1870.)[316]

Of course, the goods may be despatched at the seller's risk, in which case s.33 provides that, where the seller of goods agrees to deliver them at his own risk at a place other than that where they are when sold, the buyer must, nevertheless, unless otherwise agreed, take any risk of deterioration in the goods necessarily incident to the course of transit.

In connection with this it is necessary to note two further provisions of s.20—

(1) where delivery has been delayed through the fault of either buyer or seller, the goods are at risk of the party at fault as regards any loss which might not have occurred but for such fault (*Demby Hamilton & Co. Ltd* v *Barden* 1949);[317] and

(2) nothing in s.20 shall affect the duties and liabilities of either seller or buyer as a bailee of the goods of the other party. (s.20(3).) Thus a seller must still take proper care of the goods even though the buyer is late in taking delivery of them. Thus the risk which passes with the property does not include damage due to the other party's regligence.

Transfer of title by non-owners

The sections in the Sale of Goods Act which will be discussed here are concerned with the circumstances in which a person who is not the owner of goods can give a good title to those goods to a third party.

The general rule of common law is expressed in the maxim *Nemo dat quod non habet.* (No one can give what he has not got.) It follows that, if the seller's title is defective, so is the buyer's. This rule of the common law is confirmed by s.21(1) which provides that, subject to certain other sections of the Act, where goods are sold by a person who is not the owner thereof, and who does not sell them under the authority or with the consent of the owner, the buyer acquires no better title to the goods than the seller had, unless the owner of the goods is by his conduct precluded from denying the seller's authority to sell.

There are, however, the following exceptions to the rule—

(1) *Encumbrances over chattels.* The law does not generally allow encumbrances to run with chattels. (*Dunlop Pneumatic Tyre Co. Ltd* v *Selfridge & Co. Ltd* 1915.)[29]

(2) *Estoppel.* Where the owner of goods, by his words or conduct, represents to the buyer that the seller is the true owner, the owner is precluded from denying the title of the buyer. (*Henderson & Co.* v *Williams* 1895.)[318] The doctrine of estoppel is preserved in the final words of s.21(1) of the Act, i.e. 'unless the owner of the goods is by his conduct precluded from denying the seller's authority to sell'.

Estoppel does not rise merely because the owner of goods allows another to have possession of them (*Mercantile Bank of India Ltd* v *Central Bank of India Ltd* [1938] A.C. 287), and attempts have been made to set up a doctrine of estoppel by negligence, the third party alleging that it is the negligence of the true owner which has given the non-owner the apparent authority to sell. However, in order to establish negligence, it is necessary to show the existence of a duty of care in the owner, and such a duty, which is a matter of law, does not seem to exist where the owner has even by negligence lost his property or facilitated its theft or other form of fraudulent disposition. (See for example *Cundy* v *Lindsay* 1878,[95] and *Ingram* v *Little* 1961.)[97] So, if X loses his watch, and Y finds it and sells it to Z, then X can still claim his property; and it is nothing to the point that X's negligence enabled Y to sell the watch to Z.

However, where the owner is face to face with the person who defrauds him when the contract is made, it would seem that an element of negligence in the owner will prevent him from recovering the property from a third party. (*Lewis* v *Averay* 1971.)[98] For the doctrine of estoppel to operate there must be a more deliberate act holding out the non-owner as a person having authority to sell. (*Eastern Distributors* v *Goldring* 1957.)[319]

(3) *Sale by a factor.* Section 21(2) provides that nothing in the Sale of Goods Act shall affect the provisions of the Factors Acts, or any enactment enabling the apparent owner of goods to dispose of them as if he were the true owner thereof. The Sale of Goods Act thus preserves the power of disposition in such cases. (See further p. 118.)

(4) *Sale by an agent under apparent or usual authority.* Section 62(2) provides that the rules relating to the law of principal and agent are to be preserved, and so a sale by an agent without actual authority will

give the purchaser a good title if the sale is within the agent's apparent authority or usual authority. (See further p. 92–3.)

(5) *Special powers of sale.* Section 21(2)(*b*) provides that nothing in the Act shall affect the validity of any contract of sale under any special common law or statutory power of sale, or under the order of a court of competent jurisdiction.

Thus a *pledgee* has a power to sell the goods pledged at common law and may give a good title to a purchaser from him. However, if the pledge is made under a 'regulated agreement', i.e. is taken by a person providing credit for a consumer, the new powers relating to pawns under the Consumer Credit Act 1974 apply. Under s.120 of this Act a pawn for under £15 can be forfeited at the end of the redemption period. The property in the pawn passes to the pawnee and so can be sold by him. A pawn for a sum exceeding £15 can only be realized in accordance with s.121 of the 1974 Act. This involves giving notice to the pawner of the sale and for information to be given to the pawner of the result of that sale. The pawner is entitled to challenge the price realized on sale or the expenses of sale and the burden is then on the pawnee to justify the price of the expenses as the case may be. It is not necessary for the sale to take place by auction.

A *sheriff* has power by statute to sell goods taken in execution under a writ of *fieri facias*, and under s.1 of the Innkeepers Act 1878, an *innkeeper's lien* over the goods of his guests for his charges may be converted into a power of sale. A sale giving a good title by a *bailee* who has carried out works on goods, e.g. a watch repairer, is possible under the provisions of the Torts (Interference with Goods) Act 1977, s.12. (See p. 94.)

The Rules of the Supreme Court give the court a jurisdiction to order the sale of goods which for any just and sufficient reason it may be desirable to have sold at once, as where they are perishable goods. (See also *Larner* v *Fawcett* 1950.)[217] The purchaser of the goods sold will obtain a good title in spite of the owner's lack of consent.

(6) *Market overt.* Section 22(1) provides that where goods are sold in *market overt*, according to the usuage of the market, the buyer acquires a good title to the goods, provided he buys them in good faith and without notice of any defect or want of title on the part of the seller. The sale of horses is not covered by this section and is not within the rules of market overt. Apart from this the Act preserves the ancient rule relating to sales in open market, and applies to markets throughout England so long as the market is open, public, and legally constituted either by grant of charter, longstanding custom, or statute, provided the goods are usually sold in the market. There are no markets overt in Wales or Scotland. The person who wishes so to protect his title must prove that the place in which the sale took place was market overt. Every shop within the City of London is market overt in respect of goods usually

sold in that shop. Thus a sale of a watch by a confectioner would not be a sale in market overt, even though the shop was within the market.

Market overt is held every day except Sunday and Bank Holidays in London, but elsewhere only on recognized market days. The rule does not apply to sales between traders in the same market; nor does it apply to dispositions other than sales, so that pledge would not be covered by the rule.

To obtain the protection of market overt, the sale must commence and finish in open market in full view of the public between sunrise and sunset, and be according to the usage of the particular market, (*Reid* v *Commissioner of Police of Metropolis* 1973.)[320] and the buyer must act in good faith and give value. A sale in the back room of a shop to which the public can only gain access by invitation is not a sale in market overt. (*Clayton* v *Le Roy* 1911.)[321]

A purchaser in market overt obtains a good title against the whole world, even though the seller had no title, except—

(*a*) where the purchaser is on actual notice that the seller has no title; or

(*b*) where the goods belong to the Crown.

In former times the title of a purchaser in market overt could be defeated if the person responsible for dispossessing the true owner was later convicted of false pretences or larceny. The Theft Act 1968, s.33(3), repeals this rule and there is no longer any question of a title acquired in market overt revesting in the true owner. Under s.28 of the Theft Act a criminal court can give a restitution order to a person who has been deprived of his property by theft but such an order does not lie against a *bone fide* purchaser of the goods. However, an action in conversion may be brought against the seller by the true owner because market overt does not protect the seller but only the buyer. (*Peer* v *Humphrey* (1835) 2 Ad.&El. 495.)

(7) *Sale under a voidable title.* Section 23 provides that, when the seller of goods has a voidable title, but his title has not been avoided at the time of the sale, the buyer acquires a good title to the goods, provided he buys them in good faith and without notice of the seller's defect of title. Thus, if B obtains goods from S by giving S a cheque which he knows will not be met, and B sells the goods to T, who takes them *bona fide* and for value, T obtains a good title, provided S has not avoided the contract with B before B sells to T. (*Car & Universal Finance Co. Ltd* v *Caldwell* 1964.)[322] The section only applies to sales, but pledges are subject to the same rule by virtue of the common law. Where the fraud is such as to render the original contract of sale void for mistake, the fraudulent buyer cannot give a good title to a third party. (*Cundy* v *Lindsay* 1878.)[95]

(8) *Sale by a seller in possession of the goods after sale.* Section 24, which is similar to s.8 of the Factors Act 1889, provides that, where a person, having sold goods, continues in possession of the goods, or of the doc-

ments of title to the goods, the delivery or transfer by that person or by a mercantile agent acting for him, of the goods or documents of title under any sale, pledge, or other disposition thereof, to any person receiving the same in good faith and without notice of the previous sale, shall have the same effect as if the person making the delivery or transfer were expressly authorized by the owner of the goods to make the same.

The section applies where the property in the goods has passed but the seller still retains possession. If the property in the goods has not passed, the seller gives a good title by virtue of his ownership and not by virtue of the section.

There are a number of decisions which suggest that it is not enough to prove that the seller was still in possession but that the third party must show that the seller was in possession as a seller and that he had not changed his legal position by some subsequent transaction, e.g. as where he had become a bailee under a hire purchase agreement. (See for example, *Eastern Distributors* v *Goldring* 1957.)[319] These decisions were put in doubt by the ruling of the Privy Council in *Pacific Motor Auctions* v *Motor Credits Ltd* [1965] 2 All E.R. 105. In that case dealers sold cars to the plaintiffs but remained in possession of them for display purposes. They were authorized to sell as agents for the plaintiffs. This authority was later revoked by the plaintiffs but the dealers sold to the defendants who were *bona fide* purchasers. It was held that the defendants had obtained a good title by reason of the provision in the New South Wales Sale of Goods Act which was identical to s.24 of the 1979 Act. The Privy Council decided that the words 'continues . . . in possession' in s.24 must be regarded as referring to the continuity of physical possession regardless of any private transaction between seller and buyer which might alter the legal title under which possession was held. This decision was followed later by the Court of Appeal in *Worcester Works Finance Ltd* v *Cooden Engineering Co. Ltd* [1971] 3 All E.R. 708, and it would seem that there is now no need to show that the seller was in possession as a seller.

The section only protects the title of third parties, and the original buyer can sue the seller either in conversion, or for breach of contract when he fails to deliver the goods, or may protect himself by means of a Bill of Sale.

(9) *Sale by a buyer in possession.* Section 25(1) of the Sale of Goods Act, which is similar to s.9 of the Factors Act 1889, provides that, where a person, having bought or agreed to buy goods, obtains, with the consent of the seller, possession of the goods or the documents of title thereto, the delivery or transfer by that person, or by a mercantile agent acting for him, of the goods or documents of title, under any sale, pledge, or other disposition thereof, to any person receiving the same in good faith and without notice of any lien or other right of the original seller in respect of the goods, shall have the same effect as if the person making the delivery or transfer were a mercantile agent in possession of the

goods or documents of title with the consent of the owner.

The section applies where the buyer has possession, but the property has not passed to him. If the buyer has the property in the goods, he can give a good title without the aid of the section.

The section does not apply to persons in possession under hire-purchase contracts, because a person who is hiring the goods is not a person who has agreed to buy them. A hire-purchase contract is a contract of bailment only, with an option to purchase. The section would apply to a person in possession under a credit sale agreement where the property had not passed, because such a person has bought or agreed to buy the goods. If, although the goods have been delivered, passing of the property is postponed until all instalments of the purchase price are paid, then there is a conditional contract of sale; such a contract is within s.25(1) and the buyer can give a good title to a third party if the total credit provided exceeds £15,000, or if the buyer is a corporation. If the total credit provided is £15,000 or under, the contract is governed by the Consumer Credit Act 1974, and the buyer cannot give a good title to third parties (Sch.4, para. 2, Consumer Credit Act 1974), though Part III of the Hire Purchase Act 1964 (as substituted by s.192 and Sch.4, para.22 of the Consumer Credit Act 1974 protects a *bona fide* private (not a trade) purchaser of a motor vehicle who has bought it from a person in possession under a hire-purchase or conditional sale agreement. (See p. 204.)

A person who has goods *on approval* cannot pass a good title under this section because he has not bought or agreed to buy the goods; he has a mere option. However, he may pass a good title by virtue of his ownership if, by selling the goods, he indicates his approval. (*London Jewellers Ltd* v *Attenborough* 1934.)[281]

It appears that the 'consent' of the seller may be sufficient to protect the title of a purchaser from the original buyer even if the latter obtained the goods by criminal fraud, as where he paid for them by a cheque which he knew would not be met. (*Du Jardin* v *Beadman Bros* [1952] 2 All E.R. 160.) Furthermore the fact that the seller withdraws his consent after he has given the buyer possession does not prevent s.9 of the Factors Act 1889 operating to protect the title of a purchaser from the buyer, since s.2(2) of the 1889 Act specifically provides for this situation.

It should be noted that where the buyer has possession of the documents of title but not of the goods complications can arise in respect to the seller's lien and right of *stopping in transitu* (See p. 166.)

Section 9 of the Factors Act states that the buyer is deemed to make delivery or transfer of the goods as if he were a mercantile agent. However, s.2(1) of the same Act provides, in effect, that the protection given to a person buying from a mercantile agent applies only where the agent is acting in the ordinary course of business. Thus where the buyer who resells is not in fact a mercantile agent, it is difficult to see how s.9 can have effect. The better view, which was supported by the Law Reform Committee (12th Report Cmnd 2958, 1966) is that the section should operate as if the buyer was a mercantile agent without the need to show that he acted like one.

Section 9 could also operate to validate the title of a purchaser from a thief because the purchaser could be regarded as in possession with the consent of the seller (i.e. the thief). This unfortunate result could be avoided if the court decided, as a matter of interpretation, that 'seller' meant 'owner' in this situation, though there is no English authority on this point.

(10) *The Hire Purchase Act 1964, Part III (as substituted by s.192 and Sch.4, para. 22, of the Consumer Credit Act 1974).* These provisions protect the title of a *bona fide* private purchaser of a motor vehicle from a seller in possession under a hire purchase or conditional sale agreement (See p. 204.)

Performance of the contract

DELIVERY

Section 61(1) defines delivery as the voluntary transfer of possession from one person to another. There are various forms of delivery as follows—

(1) by physical transfer as where the goods are handed to the buyer with the intention of transferring possession;

(2) by delivery of the means of control as where the key of a warehouse or store is handed to the buyer;

(3) by attornment as where the goods are in the possession of a third party, e.g. a warehouseman who acknowledges to the buyer that he holds the goods on his behalf. (S.29(4));

(4) by delivery of documents of title as where a bill of lading representing the goods is delivered. (S.29(4)). A vehicle registration document is not a document of title for this purpose;

(5) by constructive delivery as where the buyer already has possession of the goods as a bailee. Thus in a hire-purchase contract the character of possession changes when the instalments have been paid and the hirer becomes owner by constructive delivery. This form of delivery also applies where a seller agrees to hold the goods as a bailee or agent of the buyer.

PLACE OF DELIVERY

Section 27 provides that it is the duty of the seller to deliver the goods, and of the buyer to accept and pay for them, in accordance with the terms of sale. The seller's duty to deliver does not mean he must necessarily take or send them to the buyer.

Section 29(1) provides that whether it is for the buyer to take possession of the goods or for the seller to send them to the buyer is a question depending in each case on the contract, express or implied, between the parties.

The place of delivery, in the absence of express agreement to the contrary, is the place of business of the seller or, if he has no place of business, his residence. (S.29(2).) If the contract is for the sale of specific goods which to the knowledge of the parties when the contract is made are in some other place, then that place is the place of delivery. (S.29(2).) Thus, in the absence of a contrary intention, the buyer is under a duty to collect the goods.

Where the seller is, under a special contract, bound to deliver the goods, he discharges the duty by delivering them to a person who, being at the buyer's premises, appears respectable and likely to be authorized to take delivery, even if in the event he is not. (*Galbraith & Grant Ltd* v *Block* 1922.)[323]

Delivery of goods to the wrong address may amount to conversion by the carrier, thus providing the owner with a remedy in tort against him if the goods are not recovered.

PAYMENT AND DELIVERY ARE CONCURRENT CONDITIONS

Section 28 provides that, unless otherwise agreed, e.g. where the seller gives credit to the buyer, delivery and payment of the price are concurrent conditions. The seller must be ready and willing to give possession of the goods to the buyer in exchange for the price, and the buyer must be ready and willing to pay the price in exchange for possession of the goods.

Thus, if the buyer is suing the seller for non-delivery, he need not give evidence that he has paid, but merely that he was ready and willing to pay. In an action for non-acceptance of the goods, the seller need not prove that he has tendered delivery, but merely that he was ready and willing to deliver.

OTHER RULES AS TO DELIVERY

Where under the contract of sale the seller is bound to send the goods to the buyer, but no time for sending them is fixed, the seller is bound to send them within a reasonable time (s.29(3)) and at a reasonable hour. (S.29(5).) What is reasonable in both cases is a matter of fact.

QUANTITY OF GOODS DELIVERED

Where the seller delivers to the buyer a quantity of goods less than he contracted to sell, the buyer may reject them, but if he accepts them, he must pay for them at the contract rate. (S.30(1).)

Where the seller delivers to the buyer a quantity of goods larger than he contracted to sell, the buyer may accept the goods included in the contract and reject the rest, or he may reject the whole. If the buyer accepts the whole of the goods so delivered, he must pay for them at the contract rate. (S.30(3).)

If the goods delivered are mixed with goods of a different description not included in the contract, the buyer may accept the goods which are in accordance with the contract and reject the rest, or he may reject the whole. (S.30(4).) (*Moore & Co.* v *Landauer & Co.* 1921.)[172]

The above provisions are subject to any usage of trade, special agreement, or course of dealing between the parties (s.30(5)), and the buyer's right to reject may not exist if the differences are microscopic. (*De minimus non curat lex*—The law does not concern itself with trifles.) Thus, in *Shipton Anderson & Co. Ltd* v *Weil Bros* [1912] 1 K.B. 574, the sellers were to deliver 4950 tons of wheat and in fact delivered 4950 tons and 55 lb. The Court held that the buyers were not entitled to reject the whole consignment which they in fact did, since the excess of 55 lb was so trifling. The sellers were awarded damages for breach of contract by the buyers.

DELIVERY BY INSTALMENTS

Unless otherwise agreed, the buyer of goods is not bound to accept delivery by instalments. (S.31(1).) Thus the seller cannot excuse short delivery by undertaking to deliver the balance in due course. Where there is a contract of sale of goods to be delivered by stated instalments, which are to be separately paid for, and the seller makes defective deliveries in respect of one or more instalments, or the buyer neglects or refuses to take delivery of or pay for one or more instalments, it is a question in each case depending on the terms of the contract and the circumstances of the case, whether the breach of contract is a repudiation of the whole contract, or whether it is a severable breach giving rise to a claim for compensation but not a right to treat the whole contract as repudiated. (S.31(2).)

The main tests to be considered in applying s.31(2) are—

(1) the ratio quantitatively which the breach bears to the contract as a whole; and

(2) the degree of probability or improbability that such a breach will be repeated. (*Maple Flock Co. Ltd* v *Universal Furniture Products (Wembley) Ltd* 1934.)[324]

DELIVERY TO A CARRIER

Where the seller is authorized or required to send the goods to the buyer, delivery by the seller to a carrier is, in the absence of any evidence to the contrary, deemed delivery to the buyer. (S.32(1).) In the absence of a contrary agreement the seller is required to make a contract with a carrier which is reasonable in terms of the goods to be carried. If he does not and the goods are lost or damaged the buyer may refuse to regard delivery to the carrier as delivery to himself and may sue the seller for damages. (S.32(2).) Where the carriage involves a sea voyage where it is usual to insure, the seller must make it possible for the buyer to insure otherwise the goods are at the seller's risk during sea transit. (S.32(3).)

Where the seller of goods agrees to deliver them at his own risk at a place other than that where they are when sold, the buyer must, unless otherwise agreed, take the risk of accidental destruction or deterioration, but not the risk of damage caused by the fault of the seller. (S.33.) Where the goods are perishable, they are not considered merchantable unless they are sent off by the seller in time to reach their destination in saleable condition. (See *Mash & Murrell Ltd* v *Joseph I. Emmanuel Ltd* [1961] 1 All E.R. 485 (p. 139).)

THE BUYER'S RIGHT TO EXAMINE THE GOODS

A buyer who has not previously examined the goods is not deemed to have accepted goods deliverd to him unless and until he has had a reasonable opportunity of examining them for the purpose of ascertaining whether they are in conformity with the contract. (S.34(1).) Unless otherwise agreed, when the seller tenders delivery of goods to the buyer, he is bound, on request, to give the buyer a reasonable opportunity of examining the goods to see whether they are in conformity with the contract. (S.34(2).)

ACCEPTANCE OF THE GOODS

The buyer is deemed to have accepted the goods—

(1) when he intimates to the seller that he has accepted them; or

(2) when the goods have been delivered to him and he does any act in relation to them which is inconsistent with the ownership of the seller; or

(3) when after the lapse of a reasonable time, he retains the goods without intimating to the seller that he has rejected them. (S.35(1).)

Section 35(1) provides that s.34 is always to prevail over s.35 so that a buyer is not prevented from rejecting goods until he has examined them or at least has had a reasonable opportunity of examining them. It should be noted, however, that delay in rejection will still defeat a claim for repudiation for breach of condition, but not a claim for damages for breach of warranty.

The effect of this provision is, therefore, that persons who buy goods such as refrigerators, washing machines and radios will be able to examine and test them in their own homes. If the goods are faulty they will be able to repudiate the contract and return the goods demanding a refund of the purchase price. However, the goods must be returned within a reasonable time otherwise the buyer's only remedy will be an action for damages.

Where the buyer has the right to refuse to accept the goods and does so refuse he is not bound to return them but only to notify the seller of the refusal. (S.36.) If the seller is able to deliver the goods and requests the buyer to take delivery the buyer must do so within a reasonable time. If he does not do so he is liable to the seller for any resulting loss and also for a reasonable charge for the care and custody of the goods. If the buyer's refusal amounts only to a request to postpone delivery for a short time, the seller is still bound to deliver. If, however, the refusal is absolute or involves a long postponement it may amount to a repudiation of the contract which discharges the seller from liability to deliver and gives him a right of action in damages against the buyer. (S.37(2).)

Remedies of the seller

1. REAL REMEDIES AGAINST THE GOODS

The unpaid seller, in addition to his personal remedies, e.g. an action for damages, has, under Part V of the Act, certain real remedies against the goods.

Section 39(1) provides that, even if the property in the goods has passed to the buyer, the unpaid seller of goods, as such, has by implication of law—

(1) a lien on the goods or the right to retain them for the price while he is still in possession of them;
(2) in the case of the insolvency of the buyer, a right of stopping the goods *in transitu* after he has parted with possession of them;
(3) a right of resale as limited by the Act.

Section 39(2) provides that, where the property in goods has not passed to the buyer, the unpaid seller has, in addition to his other remedies, a right of witholding delivery similar to and co-extensive with his rights of lien and stoppage *in transitu* where the property has passed to the buyer.

The rights set out in s.39(1) may only be exercised by an unpaid seller, and s.38(1) provides that a seller of goods is deemed to be an unpaid seller—

(1) when the whole of the price has not been paid or tendered:
(2) when a bill of exchange or other negotiable instrument has been received as conditional payment, and the condition on which it was received has not been fulfilled by reason of the dishonour of the instrument or otherwise.

The terms seller includes in certain circumstances the agent of the seller. (S.38(2).) Thus where the goods are sold through an agent who has either paid the price to his principal, or has made himself liable to pay the price under the terms of his contract of agency, the agent can exercise any of the rights of the unpaid seller.

Lien

A lien is generally speaking the right of a creditor in possession of the goods of his debtor to retain possession of them until the price has been paid or tendered, or his debt has been secured or satisfied. *A lien does not normally carry with it a power of sale,* though the unpaid seller of goods has a statutory power, and will generally exercise his lien as a preliminary to resale.

The lien conferred by the Act is a particular lien, though a general lien may be conferred by an express contractual provision. This means that the unpaid seller can retain only the goods which are not paid for, and not other goods belonging to the buyer. However, where delivery is being made by instalments and an unpaid seller has made part delivery of the goods, he may exercise his lien on the remainder, unless such part delivery can, in the circumstances, be construed as a waiver of the right of lien by the seller. (S.42.)

Where the goods have been sold without any stipulation as to credit, the unpaid seller who is in possession of them is entitled to retain possession until payment or tender of the price. (S.41(1)(*a*).) A lien can also be claimed, even though credit has been given—

(1) where the goods have been sold on credit but the term of credit has expired (s.41(1)(*b*)); and

(2) where the buyer becomes insolvent (S.41(1)(*c*).)

A person is deemed to be insolvent within the meaning of the Act if he has either ceased to pay his debts in the ordinary course of business, or cannot pay his debts as they become due, whether he has committed an act of bankruptcy or not. (S.61(4).)

The effect of the insolvency provision is that the seller cannot be compelled to deliver the goods to an insolvent person and to prove for a dividend in the bankruptcy. However, a trustee in bankruptcy can have the goods if he tenders the whole price.

The seller's lien is a possessory lien. The seller must be in possession of the goods, but he need not be in possession as a seller and may exercise his right of lien even if he is in possession of the goods as agent or bailee for the buyer. (S.41(2).) The seller's lien is for the price of the goods, and cannot be exercised in respect of other costs, e.g. storage charges and the like. (*Soames* v *British Empire Shipping Co.* (1860) 8 H.L. Cas. 338.)

Loss of lien

The right of lien is lost—

(1) if the price is paid or tendered;
(2) if the right of lien has been waived by the seller;
(3) if the buyer or his agent lawfully obtains possession of the goods;
(4) if the unpaid seller delivers the goods to a carrier or bailee for the purpose of transmission to the buyer, without reserving the right of disposal of the goods. A right of *stoppage in transitu* may arise here, but only if the buyer is insolvent.

A *waiver* may be an express waiver under the contract between the parties, or may be implied from the conduct of the seller. For example, suppose B buys furniture on credit from S, and after the sale has taken place, S then asks B to lend him the furniture for a week until he can get more furniture to display in his shop. Here the conduct of S would imply that, although the property was B's, he held the furniture on a new contract of loan, and that his right of lien on the contract of sale was waived.

The exercise of a lien by the seller does not rescind the contract (s.48(1) and the right of lien is not lost when the seller obtains a judgment from the court for the price of the goods. (S.43(2).)

Stoppage in transitu

When the buyer of goods becomes insolvent, the unpaid seller who is not in possession of the goods has the right of stopping them *in transitu*, i.e. he may resume possession of the goods as long as they are in course of transit, and may retain them until payment or tender of the price. (S.44.)

The remedy is only available when the buyer is insolvent and, if exercised, means that the seller need not allow the goods to form part of an insolvent estate, leaving himself with a mere right to prove for a dividend for the price. Nevertheless, the exercise of stoppage *in transitu* does not rescind the contract of sale, nor does it vest the property in the goods in the unpaid seller. (*Booth SS. Co. Ltd* v *Cargo Fleet Iron Co. Ltd* [1916] 2 K.B. 570.) Thus if the buyer's trustee in bankruptcy tenders the price, the seller must deliver the goods or be liable for breach of contract. Three conditions must be satisfied before the right can be exercised: (1) the seller must be unpaid; (2) the buyer must be insolvent; and (3) the goods must still be in transit.

Section 45(1) provides that goods are deemed to be in course of transit from the time when they are delivered to a carrier by land or water, or other bailee for the purpose of transmission to the buyer, until the buyer, or his agent in that behalf, takes delivery of them from such carrier or other bailee.

We have seen that delivery to a carrier is *prima facie* deemed to be a constructive delivery of the goods to the buyer, and where the carrier is the agent of the buyer this constitutes actual delivery and there can be no stoppage *in transitu*. Where, however, the carrier is an independent contractor, the remedy is available until the goods are actually delivered to the buyer.

If the buyer or his agent obtains delivery of the goods before their arrival at the appointed destination, the transit is at an end. (S.45(2).) If, after the arrival of the goods at the appointed destination, the carrier or other bailee acknowledges to the buyer, or his agent, that he holds the goods on his behalf and continues in possession of them as bailee for the buyer or his agent, the transit is at an end, and it is immaterial that a further destination for the goods may have been indicated by the buyer. (S.45(3).) (*Kendall* v *Marshall Stevens & Co.* 1883.)[325]

If, however, the goods are rejected by the buyer, and the carrier or other bailee continues in possession of them, the transit is not deemed to be at an end, even if the seller has refused to take them back. (S.45(4). When goods are delivered to a ship chartered by the buyer, it is a question depending on the circumstances of the particular case, whether they are in the possession of the master as a carrier, or as an agent of the buyer. (S.45(5).) The ship's master will not normally be the agent of the buyer where the goods are shipped under a charter for one voyage. The master will be the buyer's agent where the ship belongs to the buyer, and may well be where the ship is chartered by the buyer for several voyages, as under a time charter.

Where the carrier or other bailee wrongfully refuses to deliver the goods to the buyer or his agent, the transit is deemed to be at an end. (S.45(6).)

Where part delivery of the goods has been made to the buyer or his agent, the remainder of the goods may be stopped in transit, unless such part delivery has been made under such circumstances as to show an agreement to give up possession of the whole of the goods. (S.45(7).)

The unpaid seller's right of lien or stoppage *in transitu* is not affected by any sale or other disposition of the goods which the buyer may have made unless the seller has agreed to it. However, where documents of title, e.g. bills of lading respecting the goods, have been lawfully transferred to the buyer, and he has transferred them to a third party, who takes them in good faith and for value by way of sale, the seller's right of lien or stoppage *in transitu* is defeated. (S.47.) Where the transfer is by way of pledge, however, the seller can exercise a lien or stop the goods in transit, but only subject to the rights of the pledgee. (*Leask* v *Scott Bros* 1877.)[326]

The unpaid seller may exercise his right of stoppage *in transitu* either by taking actual possession of the goods, or by giving notice of his claim to the carrier or other bailee in whose possession the goods are. Such notice may be given either to the person in actual possession of the goods or to his principal. In the latter case the notice, to be effectual, must be given at such time and under such circumstances that the principal, by the exercise of reasonable diligence, may communicate it to his servant or agent in time to prevent delivery to the buyer. (Ss.46(1), (2) and (3).)

When notice of stoppage *in transitu* is given by the seller to the carrier, or other bailee in possession of the goods, he must redeliver the goods to or according to the direction of the seller. The expenses of such redelivery must be borne by the seller. (S.46(4).) If the carrier delivers the goods after notice to the contrary, the unpaid seller has his remedy for what it is worth, against the buyer who will by definition be insolvent, *or* may sue the carrier in tort for conversion.

The carrier can refuse to redeliver if his charges have not been paid, and his lien overrides the seller's right of stoppage *in transitu*. However, unless a general lien is conferred by the contract, a carrier's lien is normally a particular lien so that he can only refuse to redeliver the actual goods in respect of which charges are outstanding, and not other goods dispatched by the seller.

The right of resale

The unpaid seller of goods has a right to resell, without being in breach of contract, in the following circumstances—

(1) Where the buyer repudiates the contract either expressly or by conduct, the seller can resell the goods, retain any profit made, returning to the buyer any part payments.

(2) Where the contract of sale expressly provides for resale in case the buyer should make default, and the seller resells the goods on default, the original contract of sale is rescinded, but without prejudice to any claim the seller may have for damages. (S.48(4).)

(3) Where the goods are of a perishable nature, or where the unpaid seller gives notice to the buyer of his intention to resell, and the buyer does not within a reasonable time pay or tender the price, the unpaid seller may resell the goods and recover from the original buyer damages for any loss occasioned by the breach of contract. (S.48(3).) The contract of sale is not rescinded by the seller's mere exercise of his right of lien or stoppage *in transitu*, but it is when the unpaid seller resells the goods or part of them, either under s.48(4), where the contract expressly provides for resale, or under s.48(3), which gives a right of resale even where there is no express provision in the contract.

In either event resale, whether of the whole or part of the goods, rescinds the contract and the property reverts to the seller, who has then no action for the price against the buyer. Thus if the unpaid seller resells at a profit he does not have to account to the original buyer for it. If the original buyer has made a payment for the goods the seller can keep this if it is a *deposit* to be forfeited if the contract does not proceed. If it is regarded as a *part payment* it must be returned to the original buyer. Which of these it is will be dealt with either by the contract or by the court in case of dispute.

If the seller sells at a loss he has an action for *damages* from which must be deducted *any payment* received from the buyer. (*R. V. Ward Ltd* v *Bignall* 1967.)[327]

Title

A seller has power to give a title, whether he has the right to sell or not, in the following circumstances—

(1) where, although the goods are sold, the property is still in the seller;
(2) under s.24 of the Sale of Goods Act 1979, or s.8 of the Factors Act 1889, if he is in possession;
(3) under s.48(2) of the Sale of Goods Act 1979, which provides that where an unpaid seller who has exercised his right of lien or stoppage *in transitu* resells the goods, the buyer acquires a good title thereto as against the original buyer.

Unless the seller resells in accordance with the rules laid down in ss.48(3) and 48(4) he will usually be liable in breach of contract to the original buyer, though in most cases the second buyer will obtain a good title to the goods.

2. PERSONAL REMEDIES OF THE SELLER

In addition to the real remedies discussed above, the seller has a personal action against the buyer either—

(1) for the price under s.49(1); or
(2) for damages for non-acceptance under s.50(1).

The passing of the property and the conduct of the buyer will determine the sort of action which the seller will bring, and the property may, of course, have passed before delivery.

If the property has passed and the buyer has accepted the goods, the seller has an action for the price. If the property has not passed and the buyer will not accept the goods, the seller has an action for damages. Finally, if the property has passed and the buyer will not accept the goods, the seller has an action either for the price or for damages. If the seller sues for the price he may also include a claim for losses or expenses, e.g. in storing the goods because the buyer would not take them. (S.37(1).) If the seller sues for damages, such losses will be taken into account. Where the price is due in foreign currency, it is now possible for an English court to give judgment for the debt in the foreign currency itself. (*Miliangos* v *George Frank Textiles Ltd.* [1975] 3 All E.R. 801.) A plaintiff may also claim in a foreign currency for *damages* for breach of contract (*The Folias* [1979] 1 All E.R. 421) and in *tort*, e.g. for conversion of goods. (*The Despina* [1979] 1 All E.R. 421.) *The Miliangos* rule does not apply to the claims of creditors in the winding up of a company. Here the claim in foreign currency must be converted into Sterling at the date of the winding up. (See *Re Lines Bros Ltd* [1982] 2 All E.R. 183.) This is to prevent the introduction of further complications in the administration of the assets of a company on winding up.

Section 49(2) provides that where, under a contract of sale, the price is payable on a certain day irrespective of delivery, and the buyer wrongfully neglects or refuses to pay such price, the seller may maintain an action for the price, although the property in the goods has not passed, and the goods have not been appropriated to the contract.

MEASUREMENT OF DAMAGES

In an action for damages the main problem is that of assessment. Section 50(2) provides that the measure of damages is the estimated loss directly and naturally resulting, in the ordinary course of events, from the buyer's breach of contract.

Section 50(3) further expands the concept by providing that, where there is an available market for the goods in question, the measure of damages is *prima facie* to be ascertained by the difference between the contract price and the market or current price at the time or times when the goods ought to have been accepted, or, if no time was fixed for acceptance, then at the time of the refusal to accept.

An available market exists where on the facts of the case the seller is in a position where the goods can be readily disposed of to a number of buyers, *all of whom want the identical article which is for sale*, e.g. as in the case of a new motor car. Given an available market then if the supply exceeds the demand the seller is entitled to the loss of profit on sale to a defaulting buyer. (*Thompson Ltd* v *Robinson (Gunmakers) Ltd* 1955.)[328] If, however the demand for the goods exceeds the supply so that the seller can readily sell every item he can obtain from the manufacturers, he is not entitled to loss of profits on the first sale where he has made the same profit on a substituted sale following the first buyer's default. (*Charter* v *Sullivan*) 1957.)[329]

Section 50(3) does not apply where there is no available market and damages must be assessed on general principles, i.e. what is the estimated loss directly and naturally resulting in the ordinary course of events from the buyer's breach of contract? (*Lazenby Garages* v *Wright* 1976.)[330]

Where there is an available market and the seller has sold the goods at the market price, then—

(1) if that price is less than the contract price, the seller can recover the balance by way of damages;

(2) if the market price is the same as or even higher than the contract price, the seller will only be entitled to nominal damages;

(3) if the seller sells for less than the market price, then he cannot recover the difference between the contract price and the resale price.

It is the seller's duty to mitigate or reduce the loss and not to aggravate it;

(4) even if the seller keeps the goods after the buyer's breach of contract, and the later sells them for more than the market price was at the date of the breach, the seller can still recover the difference between the contract price and market price at the date of the breach, if the market price was then lower than the contract price.

Thus in *R. Pagnan & Fratelli* v *Corbisa Industrial Agropacuaria* [1970] 1 All E.R. 165 Salmond, L.J., said: '. . . The innocent party is not bound to go on the market and buy or sell at the date of the breach. Nor is he bound to gamble on the market changing in his favour. He may wait if he chooses; and if the market turns against him this cannot increase the liability of the party in default; similarly, if the market turns in his favour, the liability of the party in default is not diminished.'

Suppose the contract price was £100 and the market price at the time of the breach was £80, then the seller is entitled to £20 damages.

(1) If he sells on the day of the breach for £60, the damages will still only be £20.

(2) If, hoping the market will improve, he delays the sale, he will still have the right to £20 damages and can retain the proceeds of the subsequent sale.

Where there is an anticipatory breach of contract, e.g. where the goods are to be delivered in May but the buyer tells the seller in February that he will not accept, then if the seller refuses to accept the breach but sues upon the actual breach date damages are assessed on the market price at the date when the goods were to be delivered and accepted, i.e. the May market price. Where the seller accepts an anticipatory breach and sues upon it immediately, the date for delivery having not yet arrived when the case is tried, the court will have to estimate the market price at the date of delivery as best it can.

As regards the matter of *mitigation*, where there is an anticipatory breach and the market is falling, there are two possible situations—

(1) If the seller does not accept the repudiation, he need not resell the goods at once but is entitled to wait until the delivery date. If the buyer refuses to take delivery, the seller may resell and may recover from the original buyer as damages the difference between contract and market price at that date. It should be noted that the seller cannot be required to accept an anticipatory breach. (*White and Carter (Councils) Ltd* v *McGregor* 1961.)[181]

(2) If the seller accepts the repudiation, he must do all that he reasonably can to decrease the damages when the market is falling. If he delays in selling the goods, he will only be able to recover as damages the difference between contract and market price at the date of repudiation.

However, he has only to act reasonably and need not get the highest price possible. Thus in *Gebrüder Metelman GmbH & Co. KG* v *NBR*

(London) Ltd, The Times, 25 January 1984 the sellers, having accepted the buyers' repudiation, sold sugar immediately to a terminal market which stored sugar for future sales, rather like a marketing board. A higher price could have been obtained by shopping around the physical market. Nevertheless, the Court held that the sellers had acted reasonably and their damages against the buyers could not be reduced by the higher price obtainable on the physical market.

Where there is no market for the goods, as where the goods were made or procured specially for the purposes of the contract and cannot be sold to another buyer (e.g. because they are highly specialized goods) then there are two possible situations—

(1) Where the seller has actually made or procured the goods, he can claim the whole contract price, that is to say the cost to him of procuring or making the goods plus his profit.

(2) Where the seller has not made or procured the goods, he can claim his profit only.

Remedies of the buyer

REJECTION OF THE GOODS

The buyer may repudiate the contract and reject the goods where the seller is in breach of a condition. The effect of this is that the buyer may refuse to pay the price, or recover it if paid, or sue for damages, basing the latter claim on the seller's failure to deliver goods in accordance with the contract.

If the buyer rejects the goods, the property revests in the seller, and the buyer has no lien on the goods for the return of money paid by him under the contract. Section 36 provides that, unless otherwise agreed, where goods are delivered to the buyer, and he refuses to accept them, having the right to do so, he is not bound to return them to the seller, but it is sufficient if he intimates to the seller that he refuses to accept them.

Obviously the right to reject the goods will be lost where the property in them has passed to the buyer, or where they have been accepted by him. A breach of condition will have to be treated as a breach of warranty and repudiation will not be possible. (The meaning of *acceptance* for the purpose of the Act has already been given.)

However, the buyer might ask for rescission of the contract on the grounds that the statements made regarding the goods were not conditions or warranties (i.e. terms) but were pre-contractual misrepresentations, and, if this is possible, the remedy of rescission of contracts of sale of goods has survived the Sale of Goods Act 1979, and a remedy may be given for a mere misrepresentation which is superior to that available for breach of a term.

AN ACTION FOR DAMAGES

The buyer may be able to bring an action for damages for non-delivery of the goods; or for breach of condition or warranty; or where the property has passed to the buyer, an action in tort for wrongful interference with goods.

(1) *Non-delivery*. Where the seller wrongfully neglects or refuses to deliver the goods to the buyer, the buyer may maintain an action against the seller for damages for non-delivery. (S.51(1).) The measure of damages is the estimated loss directly and naturally resulting, in the ordinary course of events, from the seller's breach of contract. (S.51(2).)

The buyer will, therefore, recover the difference (if any) between the market price and the contract price (s.51(3)), and if he can buy similar goods cheaper in the market, the damages will be nominal. Where there is an anticipatory breach by the seller, the market price for the purpose of damages is that ruling when delivery ought to have been made, though if the buyer accepts the breach, he must buy quickly if the market price is rising for he has a duty to mitigate loss.

In addition where a buyer has lawfully rejected goods under a contract and makes a new agreement with the seller for the sale and purchase of the same goods at a reduced price, then although the buyer can sue under the original contract, the principle of mitigation of damages allows the court to take account of any profit made by the buyer on the subsequent contract provided that the subsequent contract is a part of a continuous dealing between the parties. If, therefore, S delivers 100 tonnes of wheat at £30 per tonne to B, and B lawfully rejects the wheat because it is not up to standard, then according to s.51(3), B has an action for damages based on the difference between the contract price and the market price. If we suppose that the market price was £32 per tonne B should recover damages of £200. If, however, at a later date B agrees to accept the same wheat at £28 per tonne he has no loss which is claimable, s.51(3) being a mere guide to the assessment of damages which does not preclude other methods of assessment in appropriate cases. (*R. Pagnan & Fratelli* v *Corbisa Industrial Agropacuaria* [1970] 1 All E.R. 165.)

Loss of profit on resale by the buyer is generally ignored in assessing damages for non delivery. Thus in *Williams* v *Agius* [1914] A.C. 510, W agreed to buy from A a cargo of coal at a price of 16s 3d per ton. Later he agreed with X, a sub-purchaser, to sell him a similar cargo at 19s per ton. A failed to deliver the coal and W's damages were assessed at the difference between the contract price of 16s 3d and the market price on the date when the delivery should have been made, which in this case was 23s 6d.

However, in *R. H. Hall Ltd* v *W. H Pim & Co. Ltd* [1928] All E.R. Rep.

763, the House of Lords laid down exceptions to the rule that losses of profit on resale would be ignored. In general terms, a subsale will be taken into account where the first contract contemplates the creation of subsales so that the seller knows from the beginning that in the event of non-delivery the buyer could suffer loss in connection with such sales. In addition, the subcontract must be for the sale of *the same* goods as are to be supplied under the first contract and the subcontract must be created before the delivery date under the first contract and must not be an extravagant or unusual bargain. In *Hall* v *Pim* the buyers agreed to buy a cargo of wheat at 51s 9d per quarter and the contract clearly referred to the fact that goods might be resold. Later the buyers made a subsale of the same cargo at 56s 9d per quarter. When the seller refused to deliver the cargo the market price was 53s 9d per quarter and the buyers were awarded damages assessed at 5s per quarter and also damages which the buyers had to pay to their sub-buyer because they could not deliver.

(2) *Breach of condition or warranty*. Where there is a breach of warranty by the seller or where the buyer elects, or is compelled, to treat any breach of condition on the part of the seller as a breach of warranty, the buyer is not by reason only of such breach of warranty entitled to reject the goods. However, he may—

(*a*) set up against the seller the breach of warranty in diminution or extinction of the price; or

(*b*) maintain an action against the seller for damages for the breach of warranty. (S.53(1).)

When there is late delivery, damages will be assessed on the basis of the actual loss resulting from the breach. Thus, if X should have delivered goods to Y on 1 January when the market price was £3.50 a tonne, and in fact delivers them on 1 February when the market price is £2.50 a tonne, the measure of damages would appear to be £1 a tonne. But if Y in fact resells the goods at £3.25 a tonne, the damages will only be the difference between £3.25 and £3.50, i.e. 25p a tonne.

In the case of breach of warranty of quality the loss resulting is *prima facie* the difference between the value of the goods at the time of delivery to the buyer, and the value they would have had if they had answered to the warranty. (S.53(3).)

Losses incurred or damages paid by the buyer on subcontracts are, as we have seen, generally ignored in actions for breach of condition or warranty, as they are in actions for non- (or late) delivery (*Slater* v *Hoyle and Smith* 1920)[331] *unless the buyer can show either:*

(*a*) that the seller had actual notice of the subcontracts; or

(*b*) that from the circumstances the seller had constructive notice of the subcontracts. (*Pinnock Bros* v *Lewis and Peat Ltd* 1923.)[332]

(3) *Wrongful interference with goods*. Where the property in the goods has passed to the buyer he may bring an action for wrongful interference with goods. The action may be to recover possession or for damages.

SPECIFIC PERFORMANCE

Under s.52(1) in any action for breach of contract to deliver specific or ascertained goods the court may, if it thinks fit, on the plaintiff's application by its judgment or decree direct that the contract shall be performed specifically, without giving the defendant the option of retaining the goods on payment of damages.

It will be appreciated that the remedy of specific performance is discretionary and will only be granted where damages would be insufficient. Thus in *Behnke* v *Bede Shipping Co.* [1927] 1 K.B. 649 a shipowner agreed to buy a ship called *The City* which he required immediately and which satisfied all relevant shipping regulations in terms of equipment. There was only one other ship available. An order for specific performance was made since damages would not have been an adequate remedy in this case.

Until recent times it was thought that the court could not grant specific performance of a contract for the sale of unidentified goods, but see *Sky Petroleum* v *V.I.P. Petroleum* 1974.[333]

Special sales

AUCTION SALES

Where goods are put up for sale by auction in lots, each lot is *prima facie* deemed to be the subject of a separate contract of sale. (S.57(1).) A sale by auction is complete when the auctioneer announces its completion by the fall of the hammer, or in other customary manner. Until such announcement is made, any bidder may retract his bid. (S.57(2).

It seems also that, at an auction, each bid lapses when a new one is made. So, if X bids £10 for certain goods, and then Y bids £12, X's bid of £10 lapses. If Y withdraws his bid before the auctioneer has accepted it, the auctioneer cannot return to X's bid and accept that; X must be prepared to bid again.

A sale by auction may be notified to be subject to a reserve or upset price, and a right to bid may also be expressively reserved by or on behalf of the seller. (S.57(3).) Where a right to bid is expressly reserved, but not otherwise, the seller, or any person on his behalf, may bid at the auction. (S.57(4).)

(1) *Seller's right to bid.* If in a sale by auction the seller does not specifically reserve the right to bid, it is not lawful for the seller to bid himself or to employ any person to do so, or for the auctioneer knowingly to take any bid from the seller or any such person. Any sale contravening this rule may be treated as fraudulent by the buyer. (S.57(5).)

If there is no express statement as to the seller's right to bid, but he does bid, the buyer may repudiate the contract or sue for damages where he has paid a greater price than he would have had to pay because the seller has been bidding against him.

The seller is not allowed to bid merely because the sale is advertised to be without a reserve price. There must be some express notification of the seller's right to bid. Where the sale is subject to reserve price, and the seller bids without notification, the buyer may repudiate the contract or sue for damages, though, if the reserve price was not reached, the would-be buyer will not have suffered loss, since he would not have obtained the *goods* even if the seller had not made bids.

(2) *Significance of reserve price.* Where a sale is expressly notified to be subject to a reserve, the auctioneer has no power to sell below that reserve. (*McManus* v *Fortescue* 1907.)[334] Where there is no express statement as to a reserve price, the auctioneer is still entitled to refuse to accept any bid. Where an auction is expressly advertised to be without reserve, it is clear that there is no sale of the goods if the auctioneer refuses to accept a bid. (S.57(2).) It is, however, possible that the auctioneer may be personally liable for breach of warranty of authority on the ground that he has contracted to sell to the highest bidder. (*Warlow* v *Harrison* (1859) E.&E. 309.)

The Auctions (Bidding Agreements) Act 1927, as amended by the Auctions (Bidding Agreements) Act 1969, provides for certain criminal penalties designed to prevent illegal auction rings which involve the giving of consideration to a person to abstain from bidding. Of interest as regards the civil law is s.3 of the 1969 Act which provides that a sale at auction to any one party to an agreement with a dealer not to bid for the goods may avoid the contract. If the goods have been resold and cannot be handed back to the seller all the parties to the ring are liable to the seller to make good the loss he has suffered by selling at a lower price as a result of the activities of the ring.

Export and import sales

Certain special clauses have been used over the years in sales where delivery has involved carriage by sea. These clauses have given rise to certain main types of contract, the major terms of which have become largely standardized, though there are variations as regards detailed provisions. These contracts and their major terms are dealt with briefly below.

F.O.B. CONTRACTS

Under such a contract the seller must put the goods *free on board* a ship for despatch to the buyer. The buyer is generally responsible for selecting the port of shipment and the date of shipment of the goods. Where the contract provides for a range of ports from which the goods are to be shipped then it is the buyer's right and duty to select one of them and to give the seller sufficient notice of his selection. (*David T. Boyd & Co. Ltd* v *Louis Louca* [1973] 1 Lloyd's Rep. 209.) The seller pays all charges incurred prior to the goods being put on board, but the buyer is liable to pay the freight or insurance. Once the goods are over the ship's rail, they are normally at the buyer's risk.

It is a matter for the buyer to insure the goods and his risk if they are lost, damaged, delayed or uninsured *en route*. (*Frebold* v *Circle Products Ltd* [1970] 1 Lloyd's Rep. 499.) The seller may under a particular contract be responsible for shipping the goods and where this is so it is important to know whether the seller ships on his own account as principal or as an agent for the buyer. If he ships as principal the property in the goods will not normally pass on shipment, though it will usually do so if he ships as agent. (*President of India* v *Metcalfe Shipping Co.* [1969] 3 All E.R. 1549.)

Section 32(3) provides that, unless otherwise agreed, where the goods are sent by the seller to the buyer by a route involving sea transit, under circumstances in which it is usual to insure, the seller must give such notice to the buyer as may enable him to insure them during their sea transit, and, if the seller fails to do so, the goods shall be deemed to be at his risk during such sea transit. Thus delivery to the carrier will not necessarily pass the risk in f.o.b. contracts.

Nowadays the seller often makes the contract of carriage. It must be reasonable in terms of the nature of the goods and other circumstances. If not and the goods are lost or damaged in the course of transit, the buyer may decline to treat the delivery to the carrier as a delivery to himself or may hold the seller responsible in damages. (S.32(2).)

C.I.F. CONTRACTS

GENERALLY

A c.i.f. contract is one by which the seller agrees to sell goods at a price which includes the *cost* of the goods, the *insurance* premium required to insure the goods, and the *freight* (or cost) of transporting them to their destination.

DUTIES OF THE SELLER

(1) To ship goods of the description contained in the contract under a contract of affreightment which will ensure the delivery of the goods at the destination contemplated in the contract. Undertakings in the contract as to time and place of shipment are nearly always treated as conditions. Thus the buyer may reject the goods if they are shipped too late (*Aruna Mills Ltd* v *Dhanrajmal Gobindram* 1968)[335] or too soon (*Bowes* v *Shand* 1877).[176]

(2) To arrange for insurance which will be available to the buyer.

(3) To make out an invoice for the goods.

(4) To tender the documents to the buyer in exchange for the price, so that the buyer will know the amount of the freight he must pay, and so that he can obtain delivery of the goods if they arrive, or recover for their loss if they are lost on the voyage.

REFUSAL OF BUYER TO ACCEPT GOODS

In a c.i.f. contract the buyer or his agent may repudiate the contract—

(1) by refusing to accept the documents if they do not conform with the contract; and

(2) by rejecting the goods on delivery if following inspection they do not comply with the contract.

PASSING OF THE RISK

The risk passes in a c.i.f. contract when the goods are shipped, and the buyer will still have to pay for the goods if they are lost on the voyage, though he will have the insurance cover. The property in the goods does not pass until the seller transfers the documents to the buyer and the latter has paid for them. (*Mirabita* v *Imperial Ottoman Bank* (1878) 3 Ex. D. 164.) If the goods have been shipped, but the documents have not been transferred, there is a conditional appropriation of the goods to the contract which will not become unconditional until the buyer takes up the documents and pays for them. It will be seen, therefore, that a c.i.f. contract is in essence a 'sale of documents' the delivery of which transfers the property and the possession of the goods to the transferee. However, a c.i.f. contract is regarded as a sale of goods because it contemplates the transfer of goods in due course, and for this reason the Act of 1979 applies.

If the goods are damaged by the negligence of the carrier, the buyer can sue him in contract. A person who buys the documents after the damage has been done while the goods are at sea may sue the carrier in negligence only since he is not the owner at the time of the damage. The fact that the buyer may sell the documents to others is foreseeable so far as a claim in negligence by a person who was not owner at the time of the damage is concerned. (*Schiffahrt und Kohlen GmbH* v *Chelsea Maritime Ltd – The Irene's Success* [1982] 1 All E.R. 218.)

F.A.S. CONTRACTS

In a free alongside ship contract the seller is required to deliver the goods to the buyer at a named port of discharge and place them alongside the ship which is to carry them. If the ship cannot enter port the seller must pay for barges or lighters to take the goods alongside the ship. The buyer must concern himself with loading. If the seller does not make delivery, the buyer cannot be made to pay the price, or, if the price has been paid, it can be recovered on the basis of total failure of consideration. The property and the risk in the goods pass when the goods are delivered alongside the ship, and the seller is under no obligation to insure them; if he does so it is entirely for his own benefit.

F.O.R. CONTRACTS

The seller is responsible under an f.o.r. (free on rail) contract for all charges incurred in delivering the goods to an appropriate rail depot for transportation to the buyer.

F.O.T. CONTRACTS

The seller is responsible under an f.o.t. (free on truck) contract for all charges incurred in delivering the goods to a carrier by road and for the loading of these on to the lorry or truck which is to transport them.

EX-WORKS OR EX-STORE CONTRACTS

Here it is the duty of the buyer to take delivery of the goods at the works or store of the seller as the case may be. The property and risk usually pass when the buyer takes delivery. These sales are almost always of unascertained goods, the appropriation taking place when the goods are selected or handed over at the works or store. They are perhaps not ideally categorized as export sales because they consist of the mere collection of goods by the buyer who may then deal with them as he wishes. There need not in fact be any export involving carriage by sea.

4 The supply of goods and services

As regards the rights of those who purchase goods, we have seen that the Sale of Goods Act 1979 applies and that ss.12–15 of that Act imply terms to which a buyer may resort if the goods are faulty, defective or unsuitable. Conditional sales and credit sales come within the 1979 Act. Those who take goods on hire purchase are similarly protected by ss.8–11 of the Supply of Goods (Implied Terms) Act 1973.

As regards contracts for work and materials, the supply of goods (or the materials used) is governed by Part I of the Supply of Goods and Services Act 1982. The services supplied (or the work element) are governed by Part II of the 1982 Act.

Contracts of exchange or barter, hire, rental, or leasing, are governed by Part I of the 1982 Act, while contracts for services only, e.g. a contract to carry goods or advice from an accountant or solicitor are governed by Part II of the 1982 Act. The relevant provisions of the Act are dealt with in detail below.

The supply of goods

CONTRACTS FOR THE TRANSFER OF PROPERTY IN GOODS

The contracts concerned are dealt with in s.1(1) which provides that a contract for the transfer of goods means a contract under which one person transfers, or agrees to transfer to another, the property in goods, unless the transfer takes place under an excluded contract. These excluded contracts are set out in s.1(2). They are contracts for the sale of goods, hire-purchase contracts, and those where the property in goods is transferred on a redemption of trading stamps. (These are governed by the Trading Stamps Act 1964.) Transfer of property rights in goods by way of mortgage, pledge, charge, or other security are excluded, as are gifts.

There must be a contract between the parties. If not, the statutory implied terms cannot be relied upon if the goods supplied prove to be defective. Thus a chemist supplying harmful drugs under a National Health Service prescription will not come within the Act. This is because the patient does not provide consideration. The chemist collects the prescription charge for the Government and not for himself. The payment to the chemist does not come from the patient unless it is a private prescription where the patient has paid the full amount. Otherwise an action against the chemist would have to be framed in the tort of negligence.

As regards promotional free gifts, e.g. the giving away of a radio to a purchaser of a television set, the free gift would appear to be within the 1982 Act. In *Esso Petroleum Co. Ltd* v *Commissioners of Customs and Excise* [1976] 1 All E.R. 117, Esso supplied a 'World Cup' coin depicting a footballer with every four gallons of petrol. If the supply was a sale Esso were liable to pay purchase tax (now abolished). The House of Lords held that the sale of the petrol being for money was obviously a contract of sale. However, the coins were supplied under a collateral contract. The consideration for this was the making of a contract to buy four gallons of petrol. Thus it was not a money consideration and so not a sale of goods. However, since the House of Lords found that the coins were supplied under a collateral contract for which there was consideration, presumably the implied terms of the 1982 Act can be implied into that collateral contract. Thus normally the distributor of the goods will be liable under the Act if the goods are defective. If the manufacturer sells the goods direct he will be liable under a collateral contract in respect of the promotional gift.

THE CONTRACTS COVERED BY PART I

These are contracts for work and materials, exchange and barter, and hire.

CONTRACTS FOR WORK AND MATERIALS

Reference has already been made to the distinction between these contracts and contracts of sale of goods and some examples have been given. (See p. 125.) It is impossible to provide a complete list of contracts for work and materials but they fall under the three broad heads as follows—

(1) *Maintenance contracts*. Here the organization doing the maintenance supplies the labour and spare parts as required. An example would be a maintenance contract for lifts.

(2) *Building and construction contracts*. Here the builder supplies labour and materials. An example would be the alteration of an office or workshop involving the insertion of new windows and extending the central heating system.

(3) *Installation and improvement contracts*. Here the contractor does not have to build or construct anything but, e.g. fits equipment into an existing building or applies paint to it. Examples are the fitting of

an air-conditioning system, or painting and decorating an office or workshop.

THE TERMS IMPLIED

Title

Section 2 implies terms about title. Under s.2(1) there is an implied condition that the supplier has a right to transfer the property in the goods to the customer. Under s.2(2) two warranties are implied:

(*a*) that the goods are free from any charge or encumbrance which has not been disclosed to the customer; and

(*b*) that the customer will enjoy quiet possession except when disturbed by the owner or other person whose charge or encumbrance has been disclosed.

The customer would have an action here if he suffered loss as a result of the true owner reclaiming or suing in conversion where the materials fitted had been stolen. Section 2(3), (4) and (5) are concerned with sales under a limited title. If under the contract the supplier is to give only such title as he may possess, s.2(1) does not apply but warranties are implied that the supplier will disclose all charges and encumbrances which he knows about and that the customer's quiet possession of the goods will not be disturbed by, e.g. the supplier or the holder of an undisclosed charge or encumbrance.

Cases involving bad title have occurred not infrequently in the sale of goods but the problem seems to have arisen only rarely in contracts for work and materials.

Description

Under s.3 there is an implied condition that where a seller transfers property in goods by description, the goods will correspond with that description. If the goods are supplied by reference to a sample as well as a description they must correspond with the sample as well as the description. Section 3 applies even where the customer selects the goods.

Section 3 will operate for example where a person is having his house or business premises extended and agrees with the contractor a detailed specification which describes the materials to be installed. It will not operate in some types of maintenance contract where the materials to be replaced are unknown until the maintenance is carried out. The materials fitted in the course of such a contract will not be described *before* the contract is made but probably only in an invoice *after* it has been made, which is too late to apply s.3. It should be noted that ss.2 and 3 apply to supplies in the course of a business and to a supply by a private owner, provided there is a contract. They would not apply to a mere friendly transaction without consideration.

Quality and fitness

The first implied term in this area is in s.4 and it relates to *merchantable quality*. (S.4(2).) Merchantability is defined in s.4(9) which states that the goods must be as fit for the purpose for which they are commonly supplied as it is reasonable to expect, having regard to their description, price, and other relevant circumstances. This condition of merchantable quality does not apply to defects—

(1) drawn to the customer's attention before the contract is made; or

(2) which any prior examination the customer *has actually made* ought to have revealed.

Thus if the materials used are dangerous, unsafe, defective, or faulty, and will not work properly under normal conditions, the supplier is in breach of s.4(2).

However, if the materials are described as 'seconds' or 'fire-damaged' the customer cannot complain if the materials are of lower quality than goods not so described.

As regards defects which ought to have been revealed where the customer has examined the goods, it is not likely that materials used in a contract for work and materials will be identified before the contract or that the customer will examine them. If they are examined the customer should ensure that it is done properly so that obvious defects are seen and the goods rejected.

The second implied term in s.4 relates to *fitness for the purpose*. (S.4(5).) Where a customer makes known, either expressly or by implication, to the supplier any particular purpose for which the goods are being acquired, there is an implied condition that the goods are reasonably fit for the purpose. This condition does not apply where the customer does not rely on, or it is not reasonable for him to rely on, the skill or judgment of the supplier.

If, for example, a factory process requires a lot of water supplied under high pressure, e.g. to clean special equipment, and the factory owners ask for the installation of a system of pressure hoses and a pump, revealing to the contractor precisely what the requirements are, then the contractor will be in breach of s.4(5) if the pressure is inadequate. This will be so even though the pressure hoses and pump are perfectly merchantable and would have been quite adequate for use in a different type of installation.

Of course, the way out of the fitness problem for the supplier is for him to make it clear to the customer that he has no idea whether the equipment will be suitable for the customer's special requirements. In such a case he will not be liable, though he may put some customers off by his unhelpful attitude.

Sample

If under the contract there is a transfer of the property in goods by reference to a sample, then under s.5 there is an implied condition that—

(1) the bulk will correspond with the sample in quality;
(2) the customer will have a reasonable opportunity of comparing the bulk with the sample; and
(3) there will not be any defect making the goods unmerchantable which would not have been apparent on a reasonable examination of the sample.

Except as provided by ss.4 and 5, no conditions or warranties as to quality or fitness are to be implied into contracts for the transfer of goods. Sections 4 and 5 apply only to a supply of goods in the course of a business.

Remedies

Insofar as the implied terms are conditions and are broken by the supplier, then the customer can treat the contract as repudiated. The customer is discharged from his obligation to pay the agreed price and may recover damages. The breach of implied warranties gives the customer only the right to sue for damages.

EXCHANGE AND BARTER

The most likely transactions to emerge here are the exchange of goods for vouchers and coupons as part of promotional schemes. Part I of the 1982 Act applies and the retailer who supplies the goods under a contract to the customer is the one who is liable if they are in breach of, e.g. the implied terms of fitness and/or merchantable quality. The manufacturer will be liable to the retailer, of course.

An exchange transaction in which goods are simply exchanged is not a sale but is covered by the 1982 Act. Where part of the consideration is money, as in a part-exchange of an old car for a new one with a cash difference, the contract is presumably a sale of goods because money is at least part of the consideration. It does not really matter now whether it is a sale or a supply, because the implied terms are almost identical.

Often where there has been a sale of faulty goods the seller exchanges them for other goods of the same type, although he is under no legal duty to do so unless a particular contract expressly provides. What happens if the other goods are faulty? The substitute goods must comply with the implied terms as to title, description, quality, and fitness, and there is no longer any point in going into legal niceties as to whether the exchange is a sale or supply.

THE TERMS IMPLIED

The implied terms in exchange or barter are the same as those implied in contract for work and materials, i.e. s.2 (title), s.3 (description), s.4(2) (merchantable quality), s.4(5) (fitness), and s.5 (sample).

CONTRACTS FOR THE HIRE OF GOODS

The main areas of hiring (or renting or leasing) are as follows—

(1) *Office equipment*, e.g. office furniture and a variety of machines, including telephones.

(2) *Building and construction plant and equipment*, e.g. cranes and JCB's.

(3) *Consumer hiring*, e.g. cars, television and video.

Under s.6(1) a contract for the hire of goods means a contract under which one person bails, or agrees to bail, goods to another by way of hire. There must be a contract, so that when the next-door neighbour makes a free loan of his lawnmower the Act does not apply. Also excluded are hire-purchase agreements. A contract is a contract of hire whether or not services are also provided. This would be the case where a supplier rented a television to a customer and also undertook to service it.

THE TERMS IMPLIED

The title

Section 7 deals with title. It reflects s.2 except that being a contract of hire there is provision only for the transfer of possession and not ownership. There is an *implied condition* on the part of the supplier that he has the right to transfer possession of the goods to the customer by hiring for the appropriate period. *There is also a warranty* that the customer will enjoy quiet possession of the goods except where it is disturbed by the owner or other person entitled to the benefit of any charge or encumbrance disclosed to the customer before the contract was made.

If, for example, the undisclosed true owner retakes possession so that the supplier is in breach of s.7, then the customer will have an action for damages. These will reflect the value he had had under the contract before the goods were taken from him. Thus if C pays S £120 for the year's rent of a television but the undisclosed true owner takes it back after, say, two months, the damages would, on the face of it, be £100.

Neither of the terms in s.7 prevent the supplier from taking the goods back himself provided the contract allows this, as where it provides *expressly* for the repossession of the goods on failure to pay the rental or the court is prepared to *imply* that it does.

DESCRIPTION

Section 8 is the equivalent of s.3. Where the supplier hires or agrees to hire the goods by description there is an implied condition that the goods will correspond with the description. If the goods are hired by reference to a sample as well as by description, they must correspond with the description as well as the sample. Section 8 applies even where the customer selects the goods. If the goods do not match the description the customer will be able to reject them and recover damages for any loss.

QUALITY AND FITNESS

Section 9 enacts the same provisions for hiring contracts as s.4 does for contracts of work and materials and exchange and barter. Except as provided by ss.9 and 10 (hire by sample), there are no implied terms regarding quality or fitness for any purpose of goods hired.

There are two terms in s.9 as follows—

(1) *An implied condition that the goods hired are of merchantable quality.* There is no such condition where a particular defect has been drawn to the customer's attention before the contract was made or to defects which he should have noticed *if he actually examined* the goods.

This condition relates to the state of the goods at the beginning of the hiring and a for a reasonable time thereafter. It does not impose upon the supplier a duty to maintain and repair. This must be provided for separately in the contract.

(2) *An implied condition that the goods hired are reasonably fit for any purpose to which the customer is going to put them.* The purpose must have been made known to the supplier, expressly or by implication. The condition does not apply if the customer does not rely on the skill of the seller or if it is unreasonable for him to have done so.

Once again, where goods are to be hired for a special purpose, the supplier should make it clear that the customer must not rely on him if he wishes to avoid the implied condition of fitness. This has rather special application to those who supply DIY equipment on hire. A supplier in this area should certainly not overestimate the capacity of, e.g. power tools, in order to get business. If he does he certainly faces s.9 liability.

Where the goods are leased by a finance house, it is responsible for breach of the implied terms in the hiring contract. It is in effect the supplier. This is also true of hire purchase where the implied terms of the Supply of Goods (Implied Terms) Act 1973 apply against the finance company.

As regards fitness for the purpose, it is enough to involve the finance company in liability if the customer has told the distributor of the purpose. Generally, of course, the finance house will have an indemnity against the distributor under which it may recover any damages it has to pay, so it will all get back to the distributor in the end.

As with s.4 (above) the terms of s.9 are implied only into contracts for hiring entered into in the course of a business. Thus if there is a hiring for value with a private owner, or a mere friendly lending without consideration, s.9 of the Act would not apply. Incorrect and express statements by a private owner would be actionable in the common law of contract provided that there was consideration. In a friendly lending there could be an action for negligent mis-statements made by the owner about the goods if they cause damage. (See *Hedley Byrne* v *Heller & Partners* 1963.)[120]

SAMPLE

Section 10 applies and is in line with s.5 (above). Section 10 states that in a hiring by sample there is an implied condition that the bulk will correspond with the sample in quality; that the customer will have a reasonable opportunity to compare the bulk with the sample; and that there will be no defects in the goods supplied rendering them unmerchantable which would not have been apparent on a reasonable examination of the sample.

EXCLUSION CLAUSES

Section 11 of the 1982 Act applies the provisions of the Unfair Contract Terms Act 1977 to exclusion clauses in work and materials barter and exchange, and hiring contracts. The effect of this is set out below.

(1) *Consumer transactions.* In a contract covered by Part I of the Act, the rights given by the implied terms under ss.3–5 and ss.8–10 of the 1982 Act cannot be excluded or restricted. We have already described the circumstances in which a person deals as a consumer. (See p. 54.)

(2) *Business contracts.* In these circumstances the supplier can only rely on an exclusion clause if it is reasonable. However, the obligations relating to title in s.2 of the 1982 Act cannot be excluded in a business dealing relating to work and materials and barter and exchange any more than they can in a consumer dealing. (See s.7, Unfair Contract Terms Act 1977, as amended by s.17(2) of the 1982 Act.)

However, the term in s.7 relating to the right of possession in the case of a hiring can be excluded in a consumer or business contact if reasonable.

The supply of services

The main areas of complaint in regard to services have been the *poor quality of service*, e.g. the careless servicing of cars; *slowness in completing work*, where complaints have ranged over a wide area from, e.g. building contractors to solicitors; *the cost of the work*, i.e. overcharging. Part II of the Act is concerned to deal with these matters.

THE CONTRACTS COVERED

Under s.12(1) a contract for the supply of a service means a contract under which a person agrees to carry out a service. A contract of service (i.e. an employment contract) or apprenticeship, is not included, but apart from this no attempt is made to define the word 'service'. However, the services provided by the professions, e.g. accountants, architects, solicitors, and surveyors, are included.

Section 12(4) gives the Secretary of State for Trade and Industry power to exempt certain services from the provisions of Part II. Of importance here is the Supply of Services (Exclusion of Implied Terms) Order 1982 (SI 1982/1771) which retains the common-law liability in negligence of lawyers by exempting barristers and solicitors when acting as advocates before various courts and tribunals. It also exempts services rendered by a director to his company, thus retaining existing common-law liability in this area, too. This is largely because more time is needed to consult the relevant interests and and decide what sort of liability there should be in the areas referred to.

Part II applies *only to contracts*. If there is no contract there cannot be implied terms. This will exclude work done free as a friendly gesture by a friend or neighbour. If, however, injury is caused to a person who is not in a contractual relationship with a supplier as a result of the negligence of the supplier, there may be an action in the tort of negligence at common law. (See *Junior Books Ltd* v *Veitchi Co. Ltd* 1982.)[306]

DUTY OF CARE AND SKILL

This duty applies to contracts which are purely for service, e.g. advice from an accountant or solicitor, and also to the service element of a contract for work and materials. Section 13 provides that where the supplier of a service is acting in the course of a business there is an implied term that the supplier will carry out that service with reasonable skill and care. This means that the service must be performed with the care and skill of a reasonably competent member of the supplier's trade or profession. In other words, the test is objective, not subjective. Thus an incompetent supplier may be liable even though he has done his best. A private supplier of a service will not have this duty.

There is no reference to conditions and warranties in regard to this implied term. Generally, therefore the action for breach of the term will be damages. In a serious case repudiation of the contract may be possible. This is rather like the intermediate term concept discussed at p. 46.

Cases such as *Woodman* v *Photo Trade Processing Ltd* and *Waldron-Kelly* v *British Railways Board*, which were brought on the basis of the common-law tort of negligence, would now be brought under the 1982 Act. (See further p. 55.)

TIME FOR PERFORMANCE

Section 14 provides that the supplier will carry out the service within a reasonable time. This term is only implied where the time for performance is not fixed by the contract, left to be fixed in a manner agreed by the contract, or determined by the dealings of the parties. Section 14 states that what is a reasonable time is a question of fact. A plaintiff can claim damages for unreasonable delay. Of course, if a time for performance is fixed by the contract, it must be performed at that time and the question of reasonableness does not arise. Time is of the essence in commercial contracts unless the parties expressly provide otherwise or there is a waiver. (See further p. 78.)

THE CHARGES MADE FOR THE SERVICE

Under s.15 the customer's obligation is to pay 'a reasonable charge' which is again a matter of fact. This matter is not implied where the charge for the service is determined by the contract, left to be determined in a manner agreed by the contract, or determined by the dealings of the parties. The section in essence enacts the common-law rule of *quantum meruit* (see p. 87); it protects both supplier and the customer.

EXCLUSION CLAUSES

Section 16 of the 1982 Act applies the provisions of the Unfair Contract Terms Act 1977 to exclusion clauses in regard to services. Section 2 of the 1977 Act is, as we have seen, concerned with liability for negligence. There can be no exclusion of liability if death or personal injury is caused. In other cases an exclusion clause may apply if reasonable.

Section 3 of the 1977 Act is concerned with liability for breach of contract. Broadly speaking, as we have seen, there can be no exclusion of liability for breach of contract, or a different performance or non-performance unless reasonable. The terms implied by the 1982 Act cannot be excluded in a consumer transaction. They can in a non-consumer deal if reasonable. The criteria relating to bargaining power and so on apply only to the exclusion of implied terms in a non-consumer transaction relating to goods, but they will no doubt be applied by analogy to contracts under the 1982 Act.

5 Hire purchase and consumer credit

A hire-purchase contract takes the form of bailment under which the goods are hired. This contract of bailment is accompanied by an option to purchase the goods, subject to the conditions of the agreement being complied with. The law derived from two sources as follows—

(1) the common law, where the total credit is £50 or less or exceeds £15,000 or the hirer is a corporation; and

(2) the Consumer Credit Act 1974, which applies where the total credit exceeds £50 but does not exceed £15,000 and the hirer is not a corporation. This is known as regulated agreement.

Under s.189(1) of the 1974 Act the operation of the above rules is to be calculated by reference to the balance of the price which is financed and not to the total price of the goods. If the cash price of the goods is £17,000 and the hirer (being an individual) pays a deposit of £4000, the agreement is a consumer credit agreement within the Act. The balance financed, i.e. £13,000 does not exceed £15,000.

Throughout this chapter section references are to the 1974 Act unless otherwise indicated. The whole of the Consumer Credit Act 1974 is now in force (see SI 1983/1551), with the exception of ss.123–125. These sections prevent a creditor from taking bills of exchange and promissory notes in discharge of sums payable by a debtor or hirer under a regulated agreement. Cheques can be taken but can only be paid into a bank and not indorsed over to another. The object of this is that holders in due course cannot arise. They would be entitled to payment of the instrument from the debtor or hirer, even though the contract between the debtor or hirer and the dealer was affected, e.g. by fraud as to the quality of the goods hired. A holder in due course can overcome defects of this kind. (See further p. 271.)

Subject to that exception, the Act now replaces previous legislation in dealing with moneylenders, pawnbrokers, and hire-purchase traders and their transactions by the provisions of the 1974 Act.

A connected lending agreement is one in which a credit supplier (the creditor, e.g. a bank or finance house), advances money by way of loan or makes a quasi-loan, e.g. through a credit card, to a purchaser (the debtor) so that he can buy goods from a supplier. There must be an arrangement between the creditor and the supplier regarding this, e.g. an agreement between a finance house and car dealer to finance his credit sales of cars.

A direct loan by a finance house to a customer which was not made in this way but happened to be used for the purchase of a car would not be a connected lending agreement.

The liability of the parties

1. HIRE PURCHASE AND CONDITIONAL SALE AGREEMENTS

Financial institutions conducting business in these areas are liable under the contract in their own right and not jointly and severally with the supplier, under ss.8–11 of the Supply of Goods (Implied Terms) Act 1973. Thus the conditions and warranties as to title, description, merchantable quality, fitness and sample, apply. They have an indemnity against the supplier under the Sale of Goods Act 1979 if they are sued by the debtor because there is a contract of sale between them and the supplier.

In addition, they are liable under s.56(4) of the 1974 Act for misrepresentation and breach of terms by the supplier arising from the negotiations leading to the hire-purchase or conditional sale agreement. For this purpose the supplier is the agent of the financial institution. The action is brought directly against the finance house under s.56(4). There is no need to construe a collateral contract as in *Andrews* v *Hopkinson* 1957. (See below.) This liability cannot be excluded (s.56(3)) but the finance house has an indemnity against the supplier. (*Porter* v *General Guarantee Corporation* 1982, see p. 526.)

The agreement must be a regulated agreement. That is an agreement in which the credit is more than £50 but not more than £15,000 (SI 1983/1878). There is no limit to the range of *cash* prices as there is under s.75. (See below.)

2. CONNECTED LENDING AGREEMENTS

Section 75 equates the rights of those involved in these agreements with those involved in hire-purchase and conditional sale agreements. Under this section the debtor has all the remedies against the creditor that he would have if the transaction was one of hire purchase or conditional sale, i.e. the implied terms and liability for misrepresentation of the supplier apply.

The liability of the creditor and supplier is joint and several. This means they can be sued together or individually. In either event s.17(2) gives the creditor an indemnity (rather than a contribution) against the supplier if the creditor incurs loss as a result of an action brought against him by the debtor. (*Porter* v *General Guarantee Corporation* 1982, see p. 526.) If the creditor is sued by the debtor any defence available to the supplier is available to him. The credit extended must be to an individual or partnership or unincorporated association for business or non-business purposes, but not to a company. It must also be for more than £50 but not more than £15,000 (see SI 1983/1878). For the purpose of s.75 *only* agreements are excluded from the section if the *cash* price of the goods is below £100 or above £30,000 (see SI 1983/1878). Non-commercial agreements, i.e. agreements not made by the supplier in the course of a business (s.189(1)) are not within s.75. (S.73(3) (*b*).) An example of the use of s.75 is provided by *United Dominion Trust* v *Taylor* 1980.[336]

RETAILER AND HIRER

There is no contract between the supplier and the debtor under a hire-purchase transaction financed by a finance house. If there is anything wrong with the goods there is no straightforward contractual claim against the retailer (*Drury* v *Victor Buckland Ltd* [1941] 1 All E.R. 269.) The law on this matter has not been changed by the 1974 Act.

The supplier may, of course, become liable to indemnify the finance company if the latter has been held liable for what are, in effect, the supplier's breaches. (*Porter* v *General Guarantee Corporation* 1982, see p. 526.)

However, a debtor may have an action against the retailer or supplier in *negligence* where the goods are in a dangerous condition or by establishing a separate contract with the supplier, the consideration for which is the debtor's agreement to enter into a hire-purchase contract with the finance company.

Thus in *Andrews* v *Hopkinson* [1956] 3 All E.R. 422 a dealer, during the sale of a car, told the customer: 'It's a good little bus, I would stake my life on it.' Following this remark the customer made a hire-purchase contract with a finance company. However, soon after taking delivery of the car he had an accident in it because of its defective steering mechanism. The Court held that the dealer was liable in damages to the customer on two grounds—(i) There was a contract between the dealer and the customer. This consisted of the dealer promising that the car was a 'good little bus' in return for the customer agreeing to apply to a finance company to acquire the car on hire-purchase terms. The dealer was therefore liable for breach of his warranty as to the car's condition. (ii) the defect in the steering mechanism was due to lack of inspection and proper servicing by the dealer who was therefore liable, regardless of contract, to anyone foreseeably injured by his negligence under the neighbour principle in *Donoghue* v *Stevenson* 1932.[304]

As we have seen, the action against the finance company is based on s.56. There is no need to construe a collateral contract. However, it is necessary to construe such a contract for a claim against the supplier.

FINANCE COMPANY AND RETAILER

The relationship is basically that of buyer and seller. However, under ss.56(2) and 69(1) of the 1974 Act the retailer is also made an agent of the finance company for two purposes, i.e. as regards the making of representations about the goods whether these are terms of the contract or not, and also in regard to receiving notices of cancellation under the 'cooling-off' provisions of the 1974 Act. The above sections apply only where the agreement is a regulated agreement and is protected by the 1974 Act but where they are applicable they cannot be excluded by the agreement. (S.173.) Finally, as we have seen, under s.75(2) the finance company has a statutory right to indemnity from the dealer where the finance company has been made liable for a breach of the hire-purchase agreement which is a result of the dealer's acts.

FINANCE COMPANY AND GUARANTOR

The supplier may give a guarantee of payment by the debtor to the finance company. This is, of course, to protect the finance company, but in order to protect the supplier it is usual to ask the debtor to obtain his own guarantor. The contract of guarantee usually allows the finance company, for example, to extend the period of credit without discharging the guarantor. Such a discharge would occur if there was no special provision in the contract. If the debtor terminates the agreement, e.g. under s.99 (see p. 203), then if he discharges his liability (see p. 203) the guarantor is also discharged. Section 113 makes it clear that the guarantor can in no situation be liable to a greater extent than the debtor is. Section 113 is designed to prevent evasion of the Act by the use of a security.

A guarantor who pays the finance company because the debtor does not do so stands in the finance company's place and may use its remedies against the debtor. The better view is that this includes the right to seize the goods.

There are a number of provisions in the 1974 Act which relate to guarantors. These are as follows—

(1) a guarantor, along with the debtor, is not liable if an agreement controlled by the Act does not comply with the statutory formalities. (See below);

(2) a guarantor is entitled to a copy of the contract of guarantee and to the agreement together with a statement of account. (Ss.107–9);

(3) a guarantor and the debtor are discharged from liability if the owner seizes the goods without a court order when a third of the price has been paid. (Ss.91 and 113);

(4) the statutory provisions relating to guarantees apply also to contracts of indemnity. (S.189(1).)

There is one situation where s.113 allows a security to be enforced, even though the regulated agreement itself is not enforceable. This occurs where the security is an indemnity and the only reason that the regulated agreement cannot be enforced is that the debtor or hirer is not of full age or capacity. The reason for this is that tradesmen will often not give credit to a person under 18 unless an indemnity is given by an adult. The exception referred to above means that the indemnity will not be valueless if the minor debtor or hirer defaults. The exception is contained in s.113(7).

Formalities

The 1974 Act gives certain formalities for regulated agreements, i.e. agreements under which a person is given credit not exceeding £15,000.

Under s.55 the pre-contractual requirements are left to be made by regulation. SI 1983/1555 applies and, e.g. the debtor must be told in writing what the cash price of the goods is, as was the case under hire purchase legislation.

Regulations set out in SI 1983/1555 also provide for the form and contents of regulated agreements and cover the following—

(1) the names of the parties to the agreement and their addresses;

(2) the amounts of all payments due under the agreement and when and to whom they are payable;

(3) the total charge for the credit, i.e. the cost to the debtor of having the credit;

(4) the true annual rate of the total charge for credit, expressed as a percentage rate per annum;

(5) the debtor's right to pay off his debt earlier than agreed.

Furthermore, the agreement and every copy of it must—

(6) contain all the terms of the agreement, and

(7) contain details of the debtor's rights to cancel the agreement. (See p. 203.)

As regards the signing of the agreement, this must, under s.61(1), be by the debtor *personally* who consequently cannot sign through an agent. The creditor may sign personally or through an agent.

The debtor must not be given blank forms to sign, the details in them being filled in at a later date by the creditor or supplier.

If the requirements relating to form are not complied with the creditor is unable to enforce the agreement unless the court so orders. If it does not so order the creditor cannot reposses the goods, even where the debtor has stopped payment of instalments.

The parties and their duties

The duties of the parties to a hire-purchase agreement must now be dealt with.

DUTIES OF OWNER

Sections 8–11 of the Supply of Goods (Implied Terms) Act 1973 (as substituted by Sch. 4 Part I, para. 35, of the Consumer Credit Act 1974) lay upon the owner duties identical to those of a seller of goods. The implied conditions and warranties are the same and exclusion clauses are under the Unfair Contract Terms Act forbidden in consumer sales, though allowed if reasonable in non-consumer sales. All of this applies in all the credit agreements under consideration with no financial limit and is applicable also even if a corporation is a party to the contract.

DUTIES OF DEBTOR

These depend upon the agreement and regulations made under the 1974 Act. However, it can be said that—

(1) the debtor must pay the instalments while the agreement is in force;

(2) if the debtor terminates the agreement then if it is covered by the 1974 Act he is liable to pay—

(*a*) instalments in arrear;

(*b*) an additional sum to make up the total payments to 50 per cent of the total price (unless they already reach or exceed that figure). Thus, if the total price is £520 and the debtor terminates after he has paid £180 and owes £20 in unpaid instalments, he must pay the £20 and a further £60 so as to bring his total payments up to one-half of the total price. But if he has paid, or becomes liable to pay, more than one-half of the total price before the termination, he cannot recover or be relieved from, the excess. By s.100(3) the court may make an order for the payment of a sum less than one-half of the total price where it is satisfied that a sum less than half would equal the loss sustained by the creditor. Thus the one-half minimum payment is in practice the maximum amount recoverable by the creditor;

(*c*) damages if he has not taken reasonable care of the goods.

(3) The debtor must take reasonable care of the goods and, e.g. in the case of cars, take out a comprehensive insurance policy for the full value.

Finally, the agreement will usually contain prohibitions on the debtor under which he cannot move the goods from the place where they are normally kept or garage a car in other than its usual place. There are also commonly provisions preventing resale, pledge and parting with the possession of the goods. Regulations made under the Act control any additional prohibitions which can be inserted into agreements.

Under s.80(1) the debtor has a duty to inform the owner if requested where the goods are kept and breach of this requirement is a criminal offence triable summarily.

Section 86 contains provisions designed to prevent or inhibit the creditor or owner under a regulated agreement from, e.g. terminating the agreement or accelerating payment by reason only of the death of the debtor.

Remedies of the creditor

These will depend upon whether the agreement is *regulated* by the 1974 Act, or not.

AGREEMENTS WHICH ARE NOT REGULATED

Here we must consider claims for instalments and general damages and seizure of the goods.

Claims for instalments and general damages

The agreement may provide that where the debtor has accepted delivery of the goods failure to pay an instalment when due renders the whole amount due and payable immediately. A provision of this kind may be valid in a non-regulated agreement unless it is an extortionate bargain for the purposes of the 1974 Act (see p. 201) or a penalty. (See p. 86.)

Terms such as those outlined above have increasingly been regarded by the courts as in the nature of a penalty (see p. 86) and unenforceable. (*Bridge* v *Campbell Discount Co. Ltd* 1962.)[337] In consequence a creditor may decide now to rely on an action for damages.

The amount recoverable will depend upon the following—

(1) Where the debtor is in serious breach which amounts to repudiation of the contract. If, for example, a debtor has repeatedly refused to pay instalments, the creditor may accept that as repudiation of the contract and sue for general damages. This will be, according to the decision in *Yeoman Credit* v *Waragowski* [1961] 3 All E.R. 145, the total hire-purchase price, subject to the following deductions—

(*a*) the value of the goods if and when repossessed;
(*b*) payments already made;
(*c*) arrears of instalments due before termination which the court will award separately to the finance company.

The *Waragowski* formula will in most cases mean that the finance company recovers virtually the whole of the hire-purchase price.

(2) Where the debtor's breach is not sufficiently serious to be regarded as a repudiation but the creditor exercises his right to terminate the contract, as where there has been an occasional failure to pay instalments by the debtor, then the measure of damages is as follows—

(*a*) the instalments in arrears at the date of the commencement of the action, or if the goods have been repossessed, to the date of repossession (*Financings Ltd* v *Baldock* [1963] 1 All E.R. 443);
PLUS
(*b*) damages for failure to keep the goods in proper repair if, as is com-

monly the case, the agreement contains a provision to that effect. (*Brady* v *St. Margaret's Trust Ltd* [1963] 2 All E.R. 275.)

If the debtor refuses to accept delivery of the goods the creditor may sue for damages for non-acceptance which appears to be his only remedy, whatever a particular contract may provide. (*National Cash Register Co. Ltd* v *Stanley* [1921] 3 K.B. 292.)

The amount of the damages will depend upon the market situation as follows—

(1) if the supply of goods is greater than, or matches demand, the loss is—

(*a*) the total amount which would have been paid under the contract if it had run its full term *less*

(*b*) deductions, e.g. in regard to depreciation of the goods which will not arise if they were not accepted.

(2) If demand exceeds supply the creditor may be regarded, as in the case of a sale, as having no loss (*Charter* v *Sullivan* 1957)[329] or at most as having lost rental, less deductions, e.g. for lack of depreciation, between the time of repudiation and the finding of a new debtor.

Seizure of goods

Under hire-purchase agreements this normally occurs on breach by the debtor, e.g. failure to pay instalments, or on the death of the debtor, or where another creditor is taking the debtor's goods to pay a judgment debt (execution).

In an unregulated agreement it is a matter for the contract itself to decide what the rights of seizure are. If the contract so provides a creditor can, so far as the common law is concerned, seize goods even though, say nine-tenths of the purchase price has been paid. However, relief may be obtainable under those provisions of the 1974 Act which relate to extortionate bargains. (See p. 200.)

REGULATED AGREEMENTS

As regards claims for instalments or damages, s.129 of the 1974 Act gives the court power to make a 'time order' under which the debtor is given more time to pay.

As regards awards of money, s.129 gives the court absolute discretion in the matter, whether the debtor has repudiated the agreement or not and whether the goods have been delivered or not. In short, however he may frame his action, the creditor is at the mercy of the court.

As regards seizure of the goods, where a debtor is not a company and the credit does not exceed £15,000 (i.e. where the agreement is regulated) the right to retake the goods is much modified by the 1974 Act. The restrictions are as follows—

(1) Under s.87 the creditor is unable to terminate the agreement or recover possession of the goods, or exercise any other remedy except possibly sue for instalments due, unless he has served a *default notice* on the debtor giving the debtor at least seven days in which to remedy any breach of the agreement. This gives the debtor fair warning that action may be taken against him.

(2) Under s.90 if one-third of the total price has been paid by the debtor the creditor has no right to take possession of the goods without a court order unless the debtor has terminated the agreement himself. Should a creditor retake the goods in defiance of this section, s.91 states that the debtor is released from all liability under the agreement and may recover from the creditor all sums paid by him under the agreement. The 1974 Act seems to confirm that there is no breach of these provisions if the hirer abandons the goods, as where he leaves a damaged car at a garage and disappears, so that they are no longer in his possession.

(3) Under s.92 the creditor has no right without a court order to enter the debtor's premises to retake possession of any goods let to him under a hire purchase agreement. This section applies whether or not one-third of the price has been paid, but again, the debtor may consent to the creditor's entry for the purpose of retaking the goods.

If the creditors bring an action to recover possession of the goods, the court has wide discretionary powers under ss.129–136 to make reasonable orders regardless of the terms of the contract. The court may, for example, make an order for delivery but postpone its coming into force so that the debtor may have an opportunity to pay the balance due in such a way as the court thinks fit in terms of the number of instalments and their amount and the times on which they shall be payable. This is the most usual order for the court to make and in practical terms it means that the hirer will obtain additional time to pay and that the instalments will be reduced in amount, based on his ability to pay.

MINIMUM PAYMENTS AND FORFEITURE CLAUSES

Some agreements may contain express provisions relating to forfeiture of payments made and additional minimum payments by the debtor if the contract is terminated, either voluntarily by the debtor himself, or by the creditor seizing the goods for non-payment of the rental. For example, a particular contract may provide—

(1) that all payments made up to the termination of the contract are to be forfeited (a forfeiture clause); and

(2) that the debtor is to bring his total payments up to a certain percentage (generally ranging between 50 per cent and 75 per cent) of the full price if his payments do not reach that figure (a minimum payments clause). Forfeiture of payments can produce an inequitable result, as where a contract involving the credit purchase of a car priced at

£3000 is terminated when the hirer has paid £2500. Even so forfeiture clauses are permissible, except as regulated by statute, and no form of relief, either in law or equity, is available.

A minimum payments clause may, however, be avoided if it is not regarded by the court as a genuine pre-estimate of loss but in the nature of a penalty. (See p. 86.) Avoidance on this ground applies, however, only to a situation in which the debtor has broken the contract as where he is refusing to make the agreed payments. If the debtor voluntarily returns the goods he may be regarded as exercising a right to terminate given by the contract, the 'fee' for this 'privilege' being the minimum payment provided in the contract. The courts are, however, inclined to regard voluntary termination by the debtor as, in effect, a breach of contract except where the debtor was obviously fully aware of his rights and appears to have been exercising them. (See *Bridge* v *Campbell Discount Co. Ltd* 1962.)[337]

The above provisions are now of less practical importance. The Consumer Credit Act has two sets of rules relating to the enforcement of clauses of this kind, the first being general and applying to all credit agreements, and the second being applicable to regulated agreements only.

GENERAL PROVISIONS

Wide powers are given to the court under ss.137–140 to re-open credit agreements so as to do justice between the parties. The power is not confined to regulated consumer credit agreements as 'credit agreements' means any agreement between a debtor and a creditor and there are no maximum financial limits or other exemptions.

The power is available if the credit bargain is extortionate, i.e. the payments are grossly exorbitant, or it otherwise grossly contravenes ordinary principles of fair dealing. (S.138.) The section gives a number of factors to be taken into account, including prevailing interest rates, the debtor's age, experience, business capacity, state of health and financial pressure upon him, and the degree of risk accepted by the creditor, his relationship to the debtor and whether an inflated cash price was quoted for goods or services.

If the court finds that the agreement is extortionate it may re-open the transaction and has sweeping powers to adjust the rights and duties of the parties under s.139(2). In particular, the court may set aside or reduce any obligation which has been imposed on the debtor or may require the creditor to repay any sums which the debtor has already paid.

The number of cases brought before the courts have been few and it is therefore interesting to note the case of *Barcabe Ltd* v *Edwards* (1983) 133 New L.J. 713. Here, the borrower, a low-paid working man with four children and little business capacity, answered the lender's advertisement in a newspaper. The lender's credit reference check showed no money judgments against him. He took an unsecured loan of £400 at a flat rate in interest of £100 per annum. Judge Gosling, of the Birmingham County Court, reduced the flat rate of interest to 40 per cent per annum. There was evidence that the money could have been obtained elsewhere at a flat rate of 20 per cent per annum. The Office of Fair Trading is of the opinion that the reason there are so few cases is that borrowers may be too scared to come before the courts. However, this case illustrates that the law can be of assistance if only borrowers will invoke it.

These provisions will also cover minimum payments and forfeiture clauses. It is difficult to say how the courts will operate such wide powers but it is to be expected that the courts will generally regard a minimum payments or forfeiture agreement as extortionate if it contains provisions which would give the creditor significantly more than the repayment of his capital together with interest at the agreed rate on the assumption that the rate of interest itself is not extortionate. Thus minimum payments and forfeiture clauses will normally be unenforceable unless they provide solely for sufficient payments to make good any loss to the creditor caused by the debtor's breach or other act.

REGULATED AGREEMENTS–ADDITIONAL PROVISIONS

So far as regulated agreements are concerned, the 1974 Act provides additional safeguards against minimum payments and forfeiture clauses. As regards forfeiture, clauses, the debtor's protection lies in provisions under which the creditor cannot retake possession of the goods without a court order when one-third of the price has been paid. If the court does allow a creditor to retake the goods, it will give the debtor every chance to pay the balance and avoid forfeiture. If the debtor has not paid one-third of the price the Act does not prevent the creditor from retaking the goods but he must first serve a notice of default and cannot enter the debtor's premises to recover the goods. In this situation there is nothing to prevent forfeiture of the amounts paid by the debtor other than the provisions relating to extortionate agreements. These are not likely to apply since the amounts paid by the debtor, i.e. less than one-third of the price, will not normally be sufficient to cover the drop in the value of the goods, unless they were second-hand.

In connection with minimum payments clauses, s.99 entitles the debtor to terminate the agreement at any time before the final payment falls due and then the Act provides for its own minimum payments clause. The debtor in this situation is liable to pay enough to bring his total payments up to one-half of the total price, but if the creditor's loss is less than that, then his actual loss is the maximum of the debtor's liability.

Remedies of the debtor

TO REJECT THE GOODS

The debtor may reject the goods for breach of condition by the creditor. The conditions are those set out in the Supply of Goods (Implied Terms) Act 1973 (as substituted by the Consumer Credit Act).

As regards the right to reject, the provisions of s.11(4) and ss.34 and 35 of the Sale of Goods Act 1979, which deal with acceptance and the right of examination of the goods, do not apply to hire-purchase contracts and the courts have to decide the question of the debtor's right to repudiate on the general principles of the law of contract. If, for example, the debtor has affirmed the contract the right to repudiate will have been lost. It should, however, be noted that the right to repudiate is not necessarily lost simply because there has been considerable use of the goods.

Thus in *Farnworth Finance Facilities* v *Attryde* [1970] 2 All E.R. 774, Mr Attryde bought a motor cycle on hire purchase. The machine had many faults and although Mr Attryde always complained about them he did drive the machine for some 4000 miles before deciding to repudiate the contract. He was then sued by the finance company. It was held by the Court of Appeal that Mr Attryde had not affirmed the contract by using the machine. He had always complained about the defects and had indicated that he would only finally accept the machine if they were remedied.

DAMAGES

The debtor is not likely to claim damages. If the goods are defective he will normally stop paying the instalments and wait for the creditor to sue him. Consequently there is little authority on the law relating to damages in this area. However, if an action was brought by the debtor for damages, the position would appear to be as follows—

(1) If the debtor keeps the goods and has them repaired, the cost of repairing the goods is the appropriate measure of damages, together with damages for loss of use while they are being put right. (*Charterhouse Credit Co.* v *Tolley* [1963] 2 All E.R. 432.)

(2) If the debtor elects to treat the contract as repudiated and rejects the goods there is some doubt as to the measure of damages which he is entitled to recover. However, it would seem that he can claim the return of all monies paid by him at the time of the termination of the agreement, plus any sum actually spent on repairing the goods bailed to him, less a deducation for the use of the goods during the period they have been in his possession. (*Charterhouse Credit Co.* v *Tolley* [1963] 2 All E.R. 432.)

TO TERMINATE THE CONTRACT

Under s.99 in a regulated credit agreement the debtor can terminate the agreement at any time before the final payment falls due merely by giving notice to the creditor. The debtor is not obliged to return the goods to the creditor but must make them available when the creditor calls to collect them. The same rules apply to a conditional sale agreement in which the price is payable by instalments. The buyer can determine the agreement even after the property has passed to him, but not if he has sold the goods to a third party.

COOLING-OFF

The 1974 Act in ss.68–73 substantially reproduces the cooling-off provisions of the old Hire Purchase Act. Under these provisions the debtor can cancel the agreement *not later than five days after service on him of a second copy of the agreement as required by s.63*, if the agreement has not been signed at the premises of the creditor, or the supplier or some associated party. Thus the exact cooling-off period depends upon how much time elapses between the debtor signing the agreement and his receipt of the second copy. Certainly it will be in most cases more than five days.

The 'cooling-of' period is designed to prevent high-pressure salesmanship being carried out on the debtor's doorstep or in his home and not to affect transactions in shops. The provisions do not apply where the transaction takes place on 'appropriate trade premises'. This means premises at which goods of the description to which the contract relates or goods of a similar description, are normally offered or exposed for sale in the course of the business carried on at those premises.

In order to exercise the right to cancel the agreement the debtor can give 'notice of cancellation' to the creditor or his agent (which includes the supplier of the goods). The notice need not be in any particular form so long as the intention to cancel is clearly indicated. It may be sent by post and to assist service by this method the agreement must give the name and address of the person to whom the notice may be sent.

When the notice is served it operates to cancel the agreement as to the provision of credit and also any 'linked transaction', e.g. an agreement to maintain the goods which was entered into at the same time as the hire-purchase agreement.

Once the notice has been served the debtor must take reasonable care of the goods (if they have been delivered to him) for 21 days. He is not under a duty to return the goods but must allow the creditor to collect them, though he may insist on being repaid anything he has paid under the agreement before he allows the owner to retake the goods. Where the debtor has traded in goods in part-exchange to the supplier, these must be returned to him or an amount equal to the part-exchange allowance repaid to him.

It should be noted that under the Consumer Credit Act the cooling-off provisions are no longer restricted to hire-purchase agreements but extend to a wider variety of consumer transactions. Thus a loan of an amount not exceeding £15,000 will be subject to cancellation under the cooling-off provisions if the agreement is signed at the debtor's own house. In the event of cancellation the money must be repaid.

EARLY PAYMENT

The Consumer Credit Act, ss.94 and 95 provide that the debtor may pay off the whole amount due under a hire-purchase, or other credit agreement, at any time. Regulations made under the Act give the debtor a right to a rebate on the credit charges where he has paid early.

Provisions relating to motor vehicles

Formerly, if the hirer of a motor vehicle sold the vehicle whilst it was bailed to him under a hire-purchase or conditional sale agreement, the purchaser did not get a good title and the true owner of the vehicle, usually a finance company, could recover the vehicle from the purchaser or sue him in conversion. This was so even though the hirer had all the appearances of ownership, including the registration book. Part III of the Hire Purchase Act 1964, i.e. ss.27–29 (as substituted but not repealed by s.192 and Sch.4, para. 22, of the Consumer Credit Act 1974), is all that remains of the 1964 Act. It is designed to protect *bona fide* purchasers for value of motor vehicles where the seller is a mere bailee under a hire-purchase or conditional sale agreement and where he disposes of the vehicle before the property is vested in him. The provisions do not apply unless the vehicle has been let under a hire-purchase agreement or there is an agreement to sell under a conditional sale agreement. Thus they do not apply to an ordinary hiring, nor to situations such as those in *Central Newbury Car Auctions Ltd* v *Unity Finance Ltd* [1956] 3 All E.R. 905, where a dealer allowed a fraudulent person to take possession of a vehicle after he had signed hire-purchase forms which were then rejected by the finance company. It was held that a purchaser from the fraudulent person was not protected because the vehicle was not let under a hire purchase agreement.

PRIVATE PURCHASERS

A private purchaser is a purchaser who at the time of the disposition is not a motor vehicle dealer or a person engaged in financing motor vehicle deals.

Where the disposition is to a private purchaser who takes the vehicle in good faith and without notice (see *Barker* v *Bell* 1971)[338] of the hire-purchase or conditional sale agreement, that disposition shall have effect as if the title of the owner or seller of the vehicle had been vested in the hirer or buyer immediately before that disposition. Thus a private purchaser gets a good title and the owner or seller must pursue his remedies against the hirer or buyer.

TRADE OR FINANCE PURCHASERS

Where the disposition is made to a trade or finance purchaser, i.e. a person who deals in motor vehicles or finances such transactions, then the trade or finance purchaser does not get a good title.

In this connection it should be noted that a person who carries on a part-time business of buying and selling motor cars is a 'trade or finance purchaser' under the Hire Purchase Act 1964 and is not within the protection given to a 'private purchaser' by that Act, even where he acquires a vehicle in his private capacity for personal use. (*Stevenson* v *Beverley Bentinck* 1976.)[339]

However, if a private purchaser buys the vehicle from a trade or finance purchaser, either by paying cash for it or as a result of paying up all the instalments under a hire-purchase or conditional sale agreement, then the trade or finance purchaser is deemed to have had a good title in order that the private purchaser shall obtain one.

FACTORS

The provisions of the Act operate without prejudice to the provisions of the Factors Acts or of any other act enabling the apparent owner of goods to dispose of them as if he were the true owner. Thus a person may still claim a title because the person from whom he bought the goods was a factor. However, the provisions of the 1964 Act are wider than those of the Factors Act in that they protect a purchaser even though the goods have not been *delivered* to him, in the sense that he has bought the vehicle but not taken delivery. Under the Factors Act delivery is an essential part of the protection of title.

LIABILITIES AFTER UNLAWFUL DISPOSAL

The liability of the hirer (or debtor) who has unlawfully disposed of the vehicle is not affected by the 1964 Act. Thus he may still be guilty of theft at criminal law and liable in conversion at civil law, provided that the creditor has served a default notice under ss.87–89 of the Consumer Credit Act 1974 on the debtor so that the creditor has a right to immediate possession. Where the sale is by auction the auctioneer may similarly be liable in conversion. (*Union Transport Finance* v *British Car Auctions* [1978] 2 All E.R. 385.) The liability of any trade or finance purchaser to whom the hirer disposes of the vehicle is also unchanged, and such a person could be sued in conversion. The first private purchaser is not liable in conversion and subsequent purchasers from him are not liable, even though they may be trade or finance purchasers.

PRESUMPTIONS

In order to assist a purchaser to establish his title in any action, the 1974 Act provides that certain presumptions shall be made which will apply unless evidence is brought to the contrary.

(1) If the purchaser who seeks to establish his title can show that the vehicle he has acquired was let to someone under a hire-purchase or conditional sale agreement and that a private purchaser acquired the vehicle in good faith and without notice of the letting agreement, it is presumed that the hirer or buyer made the original disposition and that the Act applies to perfect the purchaser's title.

(2) If it is proved that the hirer or buyer did not in fact make the disposition, but that a purchaser from him did so, then it is presumed that the said purchaser was a private purchaser in good faith and without notice so that the present purchaser's title is again perfected by the Act.

(3) If it is proved that the purchaser from the hirer or buyer was not a private purchaser but a trade or finance purchaser, then it is presumed that the purchaser from the trade or finance purchaser was a private purchaser in good faith and without notice and that the present purchaser's title is again perfected under the Act. A disposition for the above purposes includes any sale or contract of sale, including a conditional sale agreement, any letting under a hire-purchase agreement, or the transfer of the property to the hirer on payment of agreed instalments.

Credit cards and consumer credit generally

The 1974 Act does not refer to credit cards as such but refers instead to credit tokens. These are defined so as to cover both a store credit card issued by a retailer to the holder of an 'option' or 'budget' account facility, and also bank credit cards, such as Barclaycard or Access. A 'credit token agreement' is defined by the Act as 'a regulated agreement for the provision of credit in connection with a credit token'.

The definition excludes American Express and Diners Club cards because they require accounts to be settled in full monthly. Both cards are credit tokens but the agreement covering the use of them is not a credit token agreement. Both American Express and Diners Club are subject to the prohibition on sending unsolicited credit tokens discussed below, but they are not otherwise governed by the Act.

Cheque guarantee cards are not credit tokens within the Act because they cannot be used by the debtor to obtain cash or services or goods on credit.

PROHIBITION OF UNSOLICITED CREDIT TOKENS

Section 51(1) of the 1974 Act states: 'It is an offence to give a person a credit token if he has not asked for it'. A credit token is defined in s.14(1) of the Act as follows: 'A credit token is a card, voucher coupon, stamp, form, booklet or other document or thing given to an individual by a person carrying on a consumer credit business, who *undertakes*—(*a*) that on the production of it (whether or not some other action is also required) he will supply cash, goods and services . . . on credit'. It is thus an offence to send a credit token to any person without a request in a document signed by him. (See *Elliott* v *Director General of Fair Trading* 1980.)[340]

Section 66 of the 1974 Act deals with the situation in which a credit token, e.g. a credit card, is intercepted before it reaches the person for whom it was intended and is used to obtain credit. The section, which applies whether the token was unsolicited or requested, provides that the person for whom it was intended shall not be liable for its wrongful use unless he has accepted it. He accepts it, not when it reaches him, but when he signs it or signs a receipt for it or uses it.

Section 84 of the 1974 Act deals with a situation in which there is unauthorized use of a token after the debtor has accepted it. The debtor may be made liable for the unauthorized use but his liability cannot exceed £50 (or the limit of credit if lower) in regard to the *whole* of the period he is not in possession. The section does not apply to misuse by a user who obtained possession with the debtor's consent.

The section further provides that the debtor is not liable for any misuse after he has given notice to the creditor, e.g. Barclaycard. Notice may be oral, e.g. by telephone, but the agreement may provide for confirmation in writing. At least seven days must be allowed. If no confirmation is received in those circumstances the oral notice is invalid and the debtor becomes liable for all misuse. A debtor cannot be made liable for misuse unless the name, address, and telephone number of the person to whom notice of loss or theft is to be given, is shown clearly and legibly in the agreement. The creditor is required under s.171 to prove that any misuse occurred before notice was given.

LIABILITY FOR DEFECTIVE GOODS

As we have seen, s.75 of the 1974 Act gives the debtor rights against a creditor where the purchase of goods or services is financed, either by a loan arranged through the supplier or by the use of a credit card, and there has been a misrepresentation or breach of contract by the supplier. We have also noted that where a consumer has a claim against a creditor under s.75 the creditor has a claim to be indemnified by the supplier for any resulting loss. It should be noted that an action under s.75 is only available where the credit card agreement is a 'regulated agreement' (see above), so that while those issuing bank credit cards are liable for the defaults of their franchise holders, cards such as American Express or Diners Club are not.

OTHER IMPORTANT PROVISIONS OF THE 1974 ACT

Licensing. Those who grant credit, or arrange credit, or who offer goods to consumers on hire, must have a licence from the Office of Fair Trading or be covered by a group licence. For example, the Law Society has a group licence covering solicitors with a practising certificate. Licences are granted for periods of 10 years but can be withdrawn at any time. (Ss. 31 and 32.) Details of licence applications are kept in a public register maintained by the Director of Fair Trading. (S.35.) Under s.39 unlicensed trading is a criminal offence. In addition, agreements made with unlicensed traders may be unenforceable against the debtor or hirer, In recent times prosecutions for unlicensed trading have averaged 20 to 25 a year.

Canvassing. Under ss.48 and 49 it is an offence to canvas debtor–creditor agreements other than on trade premises. Thus traders are restricted from offering credit in a person's home. However, if a previous request has come from the potential debtor, which must be in writing and signed, no offence is committed. Convictions under these sections have, in the main, been for canvassing in response to an oral request.

Fees of credit brokers. A consumer may go through a credit broker for an introduction to a person who will give him credit. This is very often the trader who supplies the goods or services to the consumer. Under s.155 the credit broker cannot charge more than £1 for his services if no credit agreement is made by the consumer within six months of the introduction.

Credit reference agencies. Before a supplier of goods or services gives credit he may consult a credit reference agency. This is an organization which collects information relating to the financial standing of people, e.g. how quickly they pay their debts. The trader can obtain the facts on a particular person's file. Section 158 gives a consumer the right to know what information is held by the agency in regard to him and ask that it be corrected if it is wrong.

The Act also helps the consumer to find the agency. There are national credit agencies and also local ones. If the consumer knows the name of the agency he can write at any time asking for a copy of any file relating to him. He does not have to be seeking credit at the time. A fee of 25p is payable. (S.158.) If a trader is asked for credit the consumer has a right under s.157 to be given the name and address of any agency which the trader intends to contact. The consumer's request must be in writing and made within 28 days after the consumer last dealt with the trader on the matter. The trader has seven working days to supply the information.

A consumer who thinks an entry on the file of a credit agency is wrong and may prejudice him may, under s.159, require the agency to remove or correct it. The agency then has 28 days to say whether or not it has done this. If it has not the consumer can require the agency to put on his file a notice of correction of not more than 200 words which the consumer has drawn up. If the agency will not do this, then either the consumer or the agency may apply to the Director of Fair Trading who may make such order as he thinks fit. Failure to obey the Director's order is a criminal offence.

There have been few convictions under this head, but they have occurred in the case of an agency which refused to disclose a file and in the case of a trader who refused to say which agency he was consulting.

Advertising. Section 56 of the 1974 Act forbids advertisements for credit or hire which are misleading. Regulations made under the Act set out the form which advertisements must take. There are three kinds of advertisements about credit as follows—

(*a*) *Simple advertisements.* These give the trader's name, information about his business and state that he gives credit. They must not include an address or telephone number, nor prices, or interest rates. An example would be: 'Joe Soap Ltd, Videos bought and sold. Loans available'.

(*b*) *Intermediate advertisements.* Once again, the trader's name and address is given but this time a telephone number may be included. The advertisement may also say that a quotation is available on request. Provided no specific goods or services are offered at a particular price, the APR (annual percentage rate—see below) need not be given. An example would be: 'Banger Motors Ltd. Cars bought and sold. Open 9–6 Monday to Saturday. Credit terms available. Call and see us at 123 High Street, Barchester, or ring 987 6543'.

(*c*) *Full advertisements.* These must give the APR (see below) and details of the total cost of credit, the number and amount of payments to be made and the frequency of them, e.g. weekly or monthly. Where APR varies a typical APR must be shown and more prominently than the other credit details, but not so prominently as the cash price. An example would be: 'Sparks Electric Ltd have a wide variety of videos and music centres at their shop in High Street, Barchester. We give a list of prices. We have a wide variety of credit arrangements with deposits from 10 per cent. Details and written quotations for credit are obtainable from our High Street shop. Typical APR is 30.8 per cent'.

Annual percentage rate (APR). APR includes the interest on the loan itself *plus* any charges which have had to be paid as a condition of getting the loan, e.g. maintenance charges for a TV set on hire purchase. The reason why we must have APR is to make it possible to compare the cost of one type of credit with another. The concept removes problems of comparison which arise from, e.g. different periods of payment and different levels of deposit. Credit traders must calculate APR according to standard formulae which are laid down in regulations made under the 1974 Act. It should be noted that simply because APR is expressed as a percentage, it should not be confused with rates of interest. For example, APR 30 per cent does not mean that the consumer will be paying a flat rate of 30 per cent, i.e. £30 on £100 over 12 months.

Calculating APR. In, say, a purchase of goods, the total charge for credit is divided by the price of the goods, and the resulting figure is looked up on the Consumer Credit Tables. This gives the APR. Thus in the purchase of a music centre for a cash price of £375 one would calculate as follows—

(1) *Hire purchase from Barchester Stores:* Repayment by 24 monthly instalments of £21.39.

(2) *Borrowing from the Barchester Bank:* Loan of £375 repayment by 24 monthly instalments of £19.17

APR for hire purchase—Cost of credit $= 24 \times £21.39 = £513.36$

less cash price	£375.00
cost of credit	£138.36

$$\text{APR} = \frac{\text{cost of credit}}{\text{cash price}}\ \frac{£138.36}{£375.00} = 0.3690$$

0.3690 in the Consumer Credit Tables gives an APR of 37.3 per cent

APR for bank loan—Cost of credit $= 24 \times £19.17 = £460.08$

less value of loan	£375.00
cost of credit	£ 85.08

$$\text{APR} = \frac{\text{cost of credit}}{\text{loan}}\ \frac{£\ 85.08}{£375.00} = 0.2269$$

0.2269 in the Consumer Credit Tables gives an APR of 22.4 per cent

Clearly, the bank loan is the best bet. This is obvious enough from the instalments but the *precise* measure of the difference is given by the APR. APR is of greater assistance in comparing, e.g. different repayment periods and different sizes of loan, and cash prices. Suppose we are trying to compare the following credit with the two above.

A loan of £500 from a finance house repayable at £34.10 per month over 18 months.

Cost of credit $= 18 \times £34.10 = £613.80$

less value of loan	£500.00
cost of credit	£113.80

$$\text{APR} = \frac{\text{cost of credit}}{\text{loan}}\ \frac{£113.80}{£500.00} = 0.2276$$

0.2276 in the Consumer Credit Tables gives an APR of 30.7 per cent. Thus the loan from the bank is the best, the loan from the finance house is second, and the hire purchase from Barchester Stores is the worst.

Quotations. Under s.52 those offering credit must give a quotation if the consumer asks for one. The quotation need not be given if the terms of credit are set out full, e.g. in an advertisement. A quotation can be requested by telephone, or in writing, or of course, in person at the trader's shop or office. A request by telephone need not be answered unless the trader has put out an advertisement inviting the consumer to telephone for further details.

6 Partnerships

The Partnership Act 1890 provides the basic rules which govern the relationship between the partners, unless varied by the partnership agreement. Other provisions of the Act govern the relationship between the firm and third parties and these cannot be varied. The Act gives only a brief outline of the more important aspects of partnership law. This is confirmed by s.46 which provides that the rules (in effect case law) of equity and common law, which apply to partnership shall continue in force unless they are inconsistent with the provisions of the Act. All section references are to the Act of 1890 unless otherwise stated.

Nature of Partnership

A partnership is the relationship which subsists between persons carrying on a business in common with a view of profit. (S.1(1).)

An explanation of the definition and its practical consequences is set out below.

(1) *The relationship is one of contract and agency.* On entering into a contract of partnership 'every partner is both an agent of his fellow partners and also their principal'. (*Per* James, L.J., in *Baird's* case, *Re Agriculturalist Cattle Insurance Co.* (1870) L.R. 5 Ch. 725.)

However, the agreement must be accompanied by a business which has commenced. If A and B agree to become partners in a launderette they will not, in general, be partners until the business is in operation. Conversely, if the launderette is in operation A and B may be partners even though there is no formal contract of partnership.

Nevertheless, the existence of a partnership is largely a matter of fact and the ingredients of the definition, whilst helpful, are not slavishly followed. The court is concerned to find the *intention* of the parties which is to be ascertained from their writings, words, or conduct. Thus, although there is usually a formal agreement of partnership, it can arise without a formal expression of intent. (*Reid* v *Hollinshead* 1825.)[341] Also in *Keith Spicer Ltd* v *Mansell* 1970[342] two persons did in fact agree to engage in business activities by opening a bank account and ordering goods, but in the circumstances the Court did not regard them as partners since their intention appeared to be to promote a company.

(2) *Since the relation is between 'persons' there cannot be a 'sole partner'.*

However, the expression is used of a person engaged in a professional practice, e.g. accountancy, on his own. A better expression would be 'a sole practitioner'. Nevertheless, a corporation may be a partner with a human person and two or more companies may form a consortium by means of a partnership for a particular project or, in a more long-term way, as an alternative to merger. An example of the merger alternative is provided by *Stevenson & Sons Ltd* v *A.G. für Cartonnagen Industrie* 1918.[257]

(3) *The expression 'business' includes, under s.45 every trade, occupation, or profession.* Although it may not seem so at first sight 'business' includes a single venture or project. (*Reid* v *Hollinshead* 1825.)[341] However, there must be an element of commerciality. Thus members of a non-profit making club are not partners. (*Wise* v *Perpetual Trustee Co.* [1903] A.C. 139.) This means that the members of the club are not personally liable for debts incurred by, e.g. a management committee without their authority. Partners are personally liable for the debts of the firm arising from contracts made by fellow partners even, in appropriate circumstances, for debts incurred without authority. (See further p. 224.)

(4) *The business must be carried on 'in common'.* Therefore each general partner has, in the absence of a contrary agreement, a statutory right to participate in management. (S.24(5).) It is not enough for a partnership that the persons concerned have a financial interest in the association or a mere charge upon its profits. (*Cox* v *Hickman* 1860.)[343]

(5) *There must be a view of profit.* A partnership is an undertaking for gain. Thus the members of, e.g. an unincorporated railway preservation society are unlikely to be regarded as partners.

There is no partnership where the association is a company incorporated under the Companies Acts, or by statute or letters patent or Royal Charter. (S.1(2).) Such associations are governed by separate rules. However, as we have seen, a company may be a partner.

Division of profits does not appear to be a requirement of the Act but must be implied. As Tindal, C.J., said in *Green* v *Beesley* (1835) 2 Bing. N.C. 108: 'I have always understood the definition of partnership to be a mutual participation in profit and loss.'

PARTNERSHIPS AND OTHER RELATIONSHIPS

An important test of the existence of a partnership is the sharing of profits, but while a person in receipt of such a share is *prima facie* a partner, the test is not conclusive. Nor is a payment contingent on or varying with such profits.

The following relationships do not of themselves create a partnership or give rise to the obligations of partners—

(1) Ownership of property under a joint tenancy or tenancy in common, whether the owners do or do not share any profits made by the use of the property. (S.2(1).) The making of mutual profits is not enough

unless those profits arise from a business. Thus if the joint owners of land lease it for their mutual profit, arising from the rent, they are not partners. However, if they use the land in a business, e.g. market gardening, then they are partners as regards the profits from the business. However, it does not follow that the land becomes partnership property merely because it is used in the business. (See further p. 239.)

Our law refuses to recognize landowning as in itself a business and capable of being the subject-matter of a partnership. This attitude is not followed in countries whose law is based on the Code Napoléon, e.g. France, where landowning as such may be the subject of partnership arrangements.

(2) The sharing of gross returns of a business, whether the persons sharing such returns are co-owners of the property from which or from the use of which the returns are derived, does not *of itself* create a partnership. (S.2(2).) (*Cox* v *Coulson* 1916.)[344]

(3) The payment by a person of a debt or other liquidated amount by instalments or otherwise out of the accruing profits of the business. (S.2(3)(*a*).) (*Cox* v *Hickman* 1860.)[343]

(4) The payment of a servant or agent by a share of the profits of a business. (S.2(3)(*b*).) (*Walker* v *Hirsch* 1884.)[345]

(5) The payment to a widow or a child of a deceased partner of an annuity by way of a portion of the profits made in the business in which the deceased was a partner. (S.2(3)(*c*).)

Provision for these annuities is often found in partnership agreements. If that is not so the surviving partners may agree with the widow to an annuity arrangement rather than a withdrawal of capital, even *after* the death of the partner concerned. The subsection protects these annuitants from creditors who might wish to sue them as liable for the debts of the firm. It is important, as in all s.2 cases, that the annuitant does not take part in management. Annuities payable to a *widower* are covered. (See Interpretation Act 1978, s.6(b): 'words importing feminine gender include masculine modes unless a contrary intention appears'.)

It is worth noting while on the subject that if such an annuity is provided for in the partnership agreement but is not paid by the surviving partners, the widow or child could have difficulty in enforcing it because they would not be parties to the partnership agreement. The executors of a deceased partner could sue but they may not do so if, as is not uncommon, they are the partners of the deceased who will not pay the annuity. There are, as we have seen, also problems regarding the measure of damages paid to executors in this situation. Presumably it would be better to ask for specific performance (see *Beswick* v *Beswick*, 1967[30] and *Woodar, etc* v *Wimpey* 1980, p. 368).

The partnership agreement should be drafted in a form which will make the surviving partners trustees of the annuity. Problems of privity do not then arise and the widow and/or child could sue the partners directly if they were not paid the agreed annuity.

(6) The advance of money by way of loan to a person engaged, or

about to engage, in any business, the contract of loan providing that the lender shall receive a rate of interest varying with the profits, or shall receive a share of the profits arising from carrying on the business, provided that the contract is in writing and signed by or on behalf of all the parties hereto. (S.2(3)(*d*).)

A written contract of loan while useful in rebutting a partnership is not conclusive. Nor can it be assumed that if there is no written contract there is a partnership. The terms of the contract, whether written or otherwise, must persuade the court that there is no partnership. Thus in *Pooley* v *Driver* (1876) 5 Ch. 458 the contract provided that the lender should have a share in the capital; a share in the profits, and a right to require the partners to manage the firm properly. The court of Appeal held that the lender was a partner in spite of the agreement.

Thus a loan agreement should not give any management powers to the lender. Nor is it wise to pay a profit share which is directly related to the capital of the firm, e.g. if the contributed capital is £18,000 and the loan £2000, it would not be wise to pay the lender a 10 per cent share of profits per annum.

Of course, if the lender is paid a fixed sum, say 12 per cent per annum by way of interest and not 12 per cent of annual profits, he is obviously a creditor and s.2(3)(*d*) has no relevance.

If the assets of the business are charged with repayment of the loan, the lender would appear to be a partner, though a security taken, e.g. by a charge on the private house of a partner would not have this effect. The lender will also be a partner if he can claim a share in the surplus assets of the business should it be dissolved.

(7) The receipt by a person by way of annuity or otherwise of a portion of the profits of a business in consideration of the sale by him of the goodwill of the business. (S.2(3)(*e*).) (*Pratt* v *Strick* 1932.)[346]

The recipients of money under the headings (6) and (7) above are deferred creditors where the proprietor of the business is adjudged bankrupt, or enters into an agreement to compound with his creditors, or dies insolvent. In such circumstances the lender of the loan will not be entitled to recover anything in respect of his loan and the seller of the goodwill cannot recover anything in respect of the share of profit until the claims of the other creditors of the borrower or buyer, as the case may be have been satisfied.(S.3.)

All creditors have priority: those existing when the transaction was made and those acquiring rights later. The personal (or non-business) creditors of the partners also have priority. (*Taylor ex parte, Re Grason* (1879) 12 Ch. D. 366.)

Section 3 applies to loan agreements made orally and so not protected by s.2(3)(*d*) (*Re Fort, ex parte Schofield* [1897] 2 Q.B. 495) and obviously also to written agreements which are within the section. (*Re Young, ex parte Jones* [1896] 2 Q.B. 484.)

A contract that a person shall receive a fixed sum 'out of the profits' of a business is equivalent to a contract that he shall receive 'a share of the profits' within the meaning of s.3. (*Re Young, ex parte Jones* [1896] 2 Q.B. 484.) However, where there is a contract to pay, e.g. an annuity whether profits are made or not, s.3 does not apply. (*Re Gieve* 1899.)[347]

As regards a lender, it is not certain whether he can avoid the section by taking a security for the loan. Certainly, prior to the enactment of the 1890 Act there were cases which said that a lender might take a security over partnership assets and sell it in order to recoup his loan if it were not repaid. (See *Badeley* v *Consolidated Bank* (1888) 38 Ch. D. 238.) Additionally, in *Re Lonergan, ex parte Sheil* (1877) 4 Ch. D. 789 Jessel, M.R., accepted that a lender deferred by s.3 could enforce, i.e. sell, any security he had to recoup his loan because the right to sue for the loan and the right to enforce the security were *independent*.

However, s.3 says that the lender 'shall not be entitled to recover anything in respect of his loan . . . until the claims of the other creditors of the borrower have been satisfied'. It may be that by the use of the word 'anything' the Act has ruled out evasion by a person taking a security, though the matter is not certain. However, it may be that following the reasoning in *Re Lonergan, ex parte Sheil* (above) only the right to sue is deferred by the section.

An important modern application of the above rules is found in franchising. It is usual for a franchisor to insist that there be a provision in the franchising agreement stating that the parties are not partners. This should weigh heavily with the court if the matter were raised since partnership is as we have seen, a matter of intention of the parties.

If a partnership were construed between, say the franchisor and the franchisee of a photocopying franchise, then the franchisor might find himself saddled with the liabilities of a failed franchisee. Any property belonging to the franchisor might become partnership property and be available for the franchisee's creditors. Finally, it may be alleged that the franchisee could pledge the credit of the franchisor on the basis of the agency of partners.

SALARIED PARTNERS

The act does not deal with a person who does not receive a share of the profits or a payment contingent on or varying with such profits but a salary in any event. However, a salaried partner may be liable for the debts and other liabilities of the business by reason of 'holding out' under s.14 of the Act. (See p. 235.) He should, therefore, agree with the full partners that they will indemnify him if, for example, he has to pay the firm's debts.

However, it is unlikely that the court will dissolve a partnership on the request of a salaried partner because he will not normally have contributed capital to the business. Therefore he can have no interest in a dissolution in the sense that there is no capital coming to him. (*Stekel* v *Ellice* 1973.)[348]

NUMBER OF PARTNERS

It has always been the policy of company legislation to compel registration of all but the smaller associations of persons. The purpose is to achieve better control since company legislation is much more restrictive than partnership legislation.

In general partnerships, including those in a banking business, are restricted to a maximum of 20 partners. The rule that a banking partnership was restricted to 10 partners was abolished by s.46 of the Banking Act 1979. However, under the provisions of the Companies Act 1967, s.120(1), partnerships of more than 20 persons may be constituted in the case of solicitors and accountants (provided all are qualified) and stock jobbers/brokers (provided all are members of the Stock Exchange).

Furthermore, by reason of Department of Trade regulations made under the Companies Act 1967, s.120, partnerships of more than 20 persons may be constituted, e.g. in the case of patent agents, actuaries, surveyors, auctioneers, valuers, estate agents, estate managers, building designers, and consulting engineers.

If an organization does not comply with the above rules it is illegal. The main sanction is that the organization is disabled in the field of contract because the contracts which it makes are not enforceable by the association or by the members individually. However, third parties who contract with the firm without notice of the excess of members have an action against the partners individually.

As between the partners themselves, the most important consequence of the illegality is that the members of the firm have no action against each other for a contribution, so that if one partner has paid the debts of the firm from his own funds he has no claim against the others for their share.

The above rules apply only to an organization which is running a 'business' which has for its object the acquisition of 'gain'. This covers most forms of commercial undertaking but it should be noted, for example, that a unit trust may have more than 20 members without the need for registration because the members are not in 'business' with the managers of the trust. The managers of the trust invest as they see fit and are not agents for the members or in any way under their instruction. (*Smith* v *Anderson* (1880) 15 Ch. D. 247.)

DISCRIMINATION

Sexual and racial discrimination provisions are extended to partnerships, as regards failure to offer a partnership or the terms on which it is offered, including benefits, facilities and services, such as cheap mortgages. (See s.11, Sex Discrimination Act 1975 and s.10, Race Relations Act 1976.) However, the provisions apply only to firms of six or more partners and this would allow discrimination in the smaller practices, but not, e.g. in major accounting or law firms.

The partnership agreement

FORM

There are no legal requirements regarding form, and a partnership agreement may be made by deed, in writing or orally.

ILLEGALITY

The partnership agreement is void if the partners intend—

(1) To carry on an illegal business. (Thus in *Foster* v *Driscoll* [1929] 1 K.B. 470, where a partnership was formed to equip a ship and load it with whisky to be smuggled into the US during the period of prohibition in that country. The partnership was held to be illegal. However, a partnership between bookmakers is not illegal in spite of the fact that wagering contracts are void under the public policy rules of contract. (*Dungate* v *Lee* [1967] 1 All E.R. 241.)

(2) To carry on a lawful business but in an unlawful way. If X and Y are in partnership as doctors, and one of them is not qualified, the partnership agreement will be void. (See also *Hudgell Yeates & Co.* v *Watson* 1978, p. 251.)

Where, as in (1) and (2) above it is unlawful to carry on the business of the firm, or for the members of it to carry on in partnership, s.34 brings about an automatic dissolution. (See further p. 251.)

CAPACITY

Some brief treatment is needed of certain cases in which a person may become a partner but with special attributes.

Minors

As regards the relationship with other partners, a minor, i.e. a person under 18 years of age, can repudiate the contract—

(*a*) at any time during minority; or
(*b*) within a reasonable time thereafter.

The problems of minors in partnerships are generally of no concern in practice. However, the following short account of their position is included. A minor/partner will not normally be liable for the debts of the firm since they are not for 'necessaries'. (See p. 23) The other partners are liable. Contracts made by a minor/partner on behalf of the firm under actual or usual authority (see p. 224) are binding on the other partners but not on him. The minor is liable for debts incurred on behalf of the firm if he remains a partner after reaching 18, but not for those debts incurred before reaching 18. (See *Lovell* v *Beauchamp* [1894] A.C. 607.)

Married women

There are no disabilities preventing married women from entering into partnership and being liable thereafter for its debts and liabilities along with the other partners. In addition, it is clear that husband and wife may enter into a valid partnership agreement but in this case the terms of the partnership should be set out clearly in a partnership agreement since the courts are reluctant to assume that spouses living together in amity intend to create legal relations. A partnership contract is, of course, not a domestic one and so should be regarded as binding. Nevertheless a written agreement provides good evidence of intention to create legal relations.

Persons of unsound mind

At common law a person of unsound mind may avoid by rescission (see further p. 26) a contract of partnership if he can prove—

(1) that he did not understand the nature of the contract; and
(2) that the other partners knew this.

In addition, under s.96 of the Mental Health Act 1983, unsoundness of mind, either when the partnership was entered into or subsequently, is a ground for dissolution of the firm by the court. The Master of the Court of Protection may make such order as he thinks fit regarding the terms of the dissolution, including the appointment of a receiver to deal with the property and accounts.

Mental disability of a partner does not dissolve the firm automatically as death or bankruptcy does. It is necessary to petition the court. This may be done by the other partners or on behalf of the partner who is mentally disabled.

Partners are agents one of the other (see p. 224). In the law of agency the mental disorder of a principal revokes the authority of his agent so that he cannot legally contract on behalf of the principal, whether or not the third party is aware of the principal's disability. (*Yonge* v *Toynbee* 1910.)[258] The partnership agency would not seem to be the same. Mental disability does not automatically dissolve the firm. There must be an application to the court for an order of dissolution or rescission. Thus it would seem that while a person of unsound mind remains in a partnership he is fully liable for its debts and liabilities. A partner who is of unsound mind is presumably capable of binding his co-partner by contact if he knows what he is doing unless the other party is aware of his unsoundness of mind.

THE FIRM

Persons who have entered into a partnership with one another are called collectively a firm and the name under which their business is carried on is called the firm name. (S.4.)

The firm is not a *persona at law*, i.e. the firm is not a legal entity separate and distinct from the partners. In Scotland the firm is an entity. (S.4(2).) In England the firm name is merely a convenient shorthand form for a collective designation of all the partners as joint creditors or debtors. Thus, when a contract is made in the firm name it will be construed and take effect, as if the individual names of all the members of the firm were substituted for the firm name.

However, the Rules of the Supreme Court, Order 81, Rule 1 contain an element of personification in that they allow—

(1) actions by and against outsiders in the firm name;
(2) actions by a partner against his firm and *vice versa*.

Order 81, Rule 2 provides that those partners who are known and are joined in the action in the firm name can be required to disclose the names and addresses of all the members who make up the firm.

In addition, a judgment against the firm may be executed by taking the property of the firm. (S.23(1).) Order 81, Rule 5 provides that execution to enforce the judgment can also issue against the private property of those joined in the action as partners or persons acknowledged to be partners although not named.

Thus a plaintiff by suing in the firm name is able to enforce the judgment by a sale of the firm's property and also, if necessary, against the private property of all the partners.

Even so, there is nothing to prevent an outsider from suing some or all of the partners in their personal capacity, though in that case the outsider could not levy execution against the firm's assets but only the private assets of the partners concerned.

Thus, although in theory a partnership firm is not a *persona at law*, yet for practical purposes, e.g. contracting, suing and being sued, the firm is regarded as a kind of independent entity. Certain accounting practices also suggest this, e.g. partnership accounts are drafted in such a way as to suggest that the firm owes to the partners the capital they have contributed.

THE FIRM NAME

Generally speaking, the partners may choose any name they wish as the firm name. There are, however, certain restrictions which are set out below.

BUSINESS NAMES (See Preface)

(1) *Generally.* The use of the words 'company', or 'and Company', or '& Company' is allowed even though this suggests corporate status. However, s.439 of the Companies Act 1948 makes it an offence for persons to use a trade name ending in the word 'Limited' for an unincorporated association. This includes partnerships, whether ordinary or limited. An association which contravenes the section is liable on summary conviction before magistrates to a fine. (See Companies Act 1980, Sch. 2.)

(2) *Business names.* The Companies Act 1981 controls the use of a business name. This is, e.g. the name of a firm which does not consist *only* of the surnames of all the partners who are human persons and the corporate names of all corporate partners. (S.28(1)(*a*).) Forenames or initials are permitted additions. (S.28(3)(*b*).)

Therefore, if William Jones and Charles Brown are in business as 'Jones & Brown', or 'W. Jones & C. Brown, or 'William Jones & Charles Brown', they are not affected by the Act. These names are not business names. They may also use recognized abbreviations, e.g. 'Wm. Jones & Chas. Brown' without being affected.

However, if they are in business as 'High Road Car Repairs', or 'Wm. Jones & Co. Chartered Accountants', or 'Wm. Jones & Chas. Brown & Co.', then they are using business names as defined in s.28(1)(*a*) above. They must then comply with the disclosure requirements of the Act. The purpose of these requirements is to enable persons dealing with a business to know who the actual owners are where this is not made clear by the name used for the business.

The disclosure rules do not apply where the only addition to the names of the partners is an indication that the business is being carried on in succession to a former owner. (S.28(3)(*c*).) This might be done in order to make use of the goodwill attached to the former owner's name. (See further p. 254). For example, if William Jones and Charles Brown bought a business called 'Village Stores' from Harry Lime, the new business could be called 'Jones & Brown (formerly Harry Lime's)' and would not be affected by the Act. 'Jones & Brown, Village Stores, formerly Harry Lime's' would have to comply with the Act, as would the use of the phrase 'Village Stores' on its own.

What must be disclosed?

Users of business names must disclose the names of the partners together with a business or other address in Great Britain for each partner. This is to enable documents, e.g. writs to be served there if necessary. (S.29(1)(*a*).)

Where must the information be disclosed?

(1) Legibly on all business letters; written orders for the supply of goods or services; invoices and receipts issued in the course of the business, and written demands for payment of debts arising in the course of the business. (S.29(1)(*a*).)

(2) Prominently, so that it is easy to read, in any premises where the business is carried on, *but only if customers or suppliers have access.* (S.29(1)(*b*).)

(3) Disclosure must also be made *immediately and in writing* to anyone with whom anything is done or discussed in the course of business if the person concerned asks for disclosures as, e.g. in business negotiations.

Exemptions

In a partnership of more than 20 partners (s.29(3))—(i) the names of *all* partners may be included in the documents discussed above, or (ii) the names of *all* of them may be omitted. In the latter case the documents concerned must give the address of the principal place of business and state that a full list of *all* the partners' names and relevant addresses may be inspected there during normal business hours. (S.29(4).) If (ii) above is chosen, none of the partners' names may appear in the documents except when mentioned, e.g. in the text of the letter, or as a signatory.

What if the firm does not comply? The partners commit a criminal offence and are liable to a fine. (S.28.) Also, failure to disclose, display, or make available the required details of ownership may mean that the firm cannot enforce its contracts, e.g. successfully sue for a debt. (S.30.) This will be so where the other party to the contract can show that he has been unable to pursue a claim against the business or has suffered financial loss as a result of the breach. The judge may, however, allow the firm's claim to be enforced even in the above situation if he thinks it is just and equitable to do so.

Other restrictions

Under s.28(2)(*a*) of the Companies Act 1981 a partnership business must not be carried on in Great Britain (i) under a name which gives the impression that it is connected with central or local government unless the Department of Trade and Industry agrees. This is to prevent a possibly false impression of security because these authorities levy income through taxes and rates. (ii) Under a sensitive name in terms of regulations issued by the Department of Trade and Industry under s.31, e.g.

'Bank', 'Royal', unless the 'relevant body' agrees, e.g. for 'Bank' the Bank of England, for 'Royal', the Home Office.

PASSING OFF

The firm name must not be one which is so like that of an existing concern that the public will confuse the two businesses. Similarity of name is not enough; normally the two concerns must also carry on similar business. However, it is not absolutely necessary for two concerns to carry on similar businesses. Thus in *Annabel's (Berkeley Square)* v *G. Schock (trading as Annabel's Escort Agency)* [1972] R.P.C. 838, the proprietors of Annabel's Club successfully prevented the defendant from carrying on a so-called 'escort agency' under the name of 'Annabel's Escort Agency'. The essence of the decision was the probability of public confusion in thinking that there was some association between the Club and the Agency. This combined with the risk that the public would regard the Club as having the same low general reputation as enjoyed by escort agencies, could lead to injury to the Club's goodwill.

Where the name chosen raises the possibility of confusion, the rival concern may ask the court for an injunction to restrain the use of the name and, if there is evidence that the name was used knowingly to cause confusion, there may be an action for damages.

Nevertheless a firm may use a name consisting of the proper names of one or more of the partners even though there is the possibility of confusion, provided it does not advertise or mark its goods with the firm name in such a way as to confuse its products with those of an existing concern.

However, a person may not use his own name where this is part of a scheme to deceive the public deliberately by making them believe they are dealing with someone else. Thus in *Croft* v *Day* (1843) 7 Beav. 84, a firm called Day and Martin were well-known makers of boot polish, having premises in Holborn. The original Mr Day and Mr Martin had been dead for some time but Mr Croft carried on the business in the 'Day and Martin' name. Mr Croft was held to be entitled to restrain by injunction a real 'Mr Day' and a real 'Mr Martin' who were trading as 'Day and Martin' in the manufacture of boot polish because they had adopted the name in connection with their business for the fraudulent purpose of representing to the public that they were the old and widely known firm of that name.

Where one or more of the partners has previously traded in an assumed name, the firm may use that name also. (*Jay's Ltd* v *Jacobi* 1933.)[349]

OBJECTS

In the absence of special agreement no change may be made in the nature of the partnership business without the consent of all existing partners. (S.24(8).) Even a dormant partner should be consulted.

If some of the partners carry on a new business without the consent of the others, the non-consenting partners may rescind the partnership agreement for breach of a condition, or dissolve the firm. They may be able to obtain an injunction to stop the carrying on of the offending business on the grounds that the partners who are continuing with it are in breach of a fiduciary duty to their fellow partners. There seems to be no infringement of s.24(8) where the *same* business is carried on in a different way. (See *Mann* v *D'Arcy*, 1968.)[351]

The partnership agreement usually states the objects or business which the firm will carry on, but if the firm contracts outside the stated objects, there is no question of the contract being *ultra vires* and void, as would be the case with a company. (See further p. 27.)

Relations of partners to persons dealing with them

PARTNER'S POWERS

Under s.5 every partner is an agent of the firm and his other partners for the purpose of the business of the partnership; and the acts of every partner done for carrying on the business in the usual way will bind the firm and his partners.

The first part of the section sets up the agency situation. As James, L.J., said in *Baird's* case, *Re Agriculturalist Insurance Co.* (1870) L.R. 5 Ch. 725: '. . . every partner is both an agent of his fellow partners and also their principal.' The second part gives partners *usual authority* to carry out acts which are within the ordinary course of business. Such acts will bind fellow partners because of the agency situation. This form of usual authority appears also in contracts made by directors and other executives on behalf of their companies. (See *Freeman & Lockyer* v *Buckhurst Park Properties* 1964 and *Panorama Developments (Guildford)* v *Fidelis Furnishing Fabrics* 1971, p. 92.) A limited partner does not have this authority (see p. 261). For illustrations of the operation of s.5 see *Mercantile Credit Co. Ltd* v *Garrod* 1962[350] and *Mann* v *D'Arcy* 1968.[351]

However, the firm and co-partners will not be bound where the partner who acts has in fact no authority to bind the firm in the particular matter and the person who deals with him knows that he has no authority (s.8) or does not know or believe him to be a partner (s.5).

Section 8, by providing that internal restrictions in the articles on the authority of partners to enter into transactions on behalf of the firm, are effective only if the outsider dealing with a partner has *actual notice* of them, means that there is no major problem of *ultra vires* in partnerships. Partnership agreements are not filed and there is no constructive notice of their contents. (Compare companies at p. 394.)

The act in question must not only be within the scope of the business carried out by the firm but must also be executed 'in the usual way' of such business. Thus in *Goldberg* v *Jenkins* (1889) 15 V.L.R. 36 a partner borrowed money on behalf of the firm at 60 per cent per annum interest when money could be had at between 6 per cent and 10 per cent per annum. He had no actual authority to enter into the transaction and the firm was held by Hodges, J., in the Victorian Supreme Court not to be bound because although the firm borrowed money it was not 'usual' to borrow at that high rate.

As regards dormant partners, if the dormant partner has actual authority to enter into the transaction (which may be a contradiction in terms since he is supposed to be inactive) then the firm is bound. But if the dormant partner has no actual authority so that the outsider relies on apparent authority under s.5, then the position is that if the outsider knew that the dormant partner was a member of the firm then the dormant partner and the firm will be bound.

The provisions of the Companies Act 1981 (see p. 221) should ensure that even dormant partners' names are known to outsiders. They should, therefore, be able to bind the firm and be bound by a transaction entered into by them or an active partner under the usual authority provisions of s.5. However, if the Companies Act 1981 is not being complied with, so that the existence of the dormant partner is not known to the outsider in that way, then the following common-law rules will apply—

(1) If, as likely, the outsider did not know that the dormant partner was a member of the firm, then the firm (in the sense of the other partners) is not bound and it seems that the dormant partner is not bound in a personal capacity either, provided he made the contract in his character of partner, not intending to contract for himself but on behalf of the firm.

(2) The knowledge or belief that the dormant partner is a partner must come from a source other than the dormant partner himself. A person cannot hold himself out to be a partner without the knowledge or consent of the other partners.

(3) Furthermore, if the Companies Act 1981 provisions regarding names have not been complied with a dormant partner may not be bound by a transaction entered into by a general partner beyond his actual authority because the outsider may not know of the existence of the dormant partner and may therefore believe that the general partner is a sole principal.

However, if there are *two or more active partners*, a dormant partner may be liable because the outsider may then know or believe the active partner he deals with to be a partner. That is, a partner of the other active partners of whose existence he may be aware if they attend at and are active in the business.

It should be noted that s.5 imposes no liability on a firm for acts done by a partner who is acting and is dealt with as acting on his own behalf and not on behalf of the firm, nor does s.5 have any application to those who merely own property jointly either as tenants in common or joint tenants. (See p. 213.)

Situations of usual authority as laid down by case law

Section 5 does not itemize what acts are within the usual course of business. However, the courts have over the years, sometimes in cases before the Act codified the law, laid down a number of areas in which a partner has usual authority. These are as follows—

All partners, regardless of the nature of the business

(1) To sell goods or personal chattels of the firm. Thus in *Dore* v *Wilkinson* (1817) 2 Stark. 287 the firm was held bound when a partner without authority sold the partnership books to a person who wanted the names of its customers.

(2) To purchase on account of the firm goods necessary for, or usually employed in, the business. Thus in *Bond* v *Gibson* (1808) 1 Camp. 185, A and B were in partnership as harness makers and B bought bits to be made into bridles on the firm's account. B later pawned them and kept the money and it was held that the firm was liable to pay the person from whom B bought the bits.

(3) To receive payment of debts due to the firm and give valid receipts. (*Stead* v *Salt* (1825) 3 Bing. 101.) It should be noted that there is no converse rule so that payment to the firm will not discharge a seperate debt due to a partner unless the firm has authority to receive it. (*Powell* v *Brodhurst* [1910] 2 Ch. 160.)

A partner has usual authority to assign the book debts of the firm, e.g. he can factor the debts for money to, say, a bank, which will then collect them. (*Marchant* v *Morton* [1901] 2 K.B. 829.) There is no such authority to accept payment of a debt to the firm at a discount, nor in kind, e.g. shares in a company. (*Niemann* v *Niemann* (1889) 43 Ch. D. 198.) However, there is authority to pay debts owed by the firm and the other partners cannot recover sums so paid. (*Goodwin* v *Parton* (1880) 42 L.T. 568.)

(4) To engage employees for the business (*Beckham* v *Drake* (1841) 9 M.&W. 79) and also to discharge them unless, in the case of discharge, the other partners object. (*Donaldson* v *Williams* (1833) 1 Cr.&M. 345.) This is because an employee is a servant of *all* the partners. (*R.* v *Leech* (1821) 3 Stark. 70.) The partnership agreement may give the power of appointment and dismissal to some only of the partners.

(5) To employ a solicitor to *defend* the firm should an action be brought against it. (*Tomlinson* v *Broadsmith* [1896] 1 Q.B. 386.) Authority to engage a solicitor to bring an action on behalf of the firm would seem to be confined to the recovery of debts due to the firm. (*Court* v *Berlin* [1897] 2 Q.B. 396.)

A partner cannot commence criminal proceedings. All partners must agree because the bringing of such proceedings will not be within the ordinary scope of a trading business or professional practice. (*Arbuckle* v *Taylor* 1815.)[354]

(6) A partner has an insurable interest in the property of the firm and may insure it. (*Mann* v *D'Arcy* 1968.)[351]

(7) By s.15 an admission or representation made by a partner in the ordinary course of business regarding the affairs of the firm, e.g. as to the fact that the firm owes money, is evidence against it. (*Stead* v *Salt* (1825) 3 Bing. 101.)

(8) Section 16 confers upon a partner authority to receive notice on behalf of the firm, e.g. that a contract is *ultra vires* a company, thus ruling out the use of s.9 of the European Communities Act 1972 (see p. 28) by the firm.

It should be noted that where the business is not of a commercial nature, as where it is a professional business (e.g. the practice of law or accountancy), then the partners cannot make, accept, or issue negotiable instruments other than ordinary cheques, nor borrow or pledge the partnership property as security unless they have authority.

Additional powers where there is trading partnership. Partners in trading firms have wider powers than those in non-trading firms. There appears to be no good reason for this but the distinction has by now occurred in many cases and cannot be ignored. Although he was not purporting to give an exhaustive definition of what constitutes a trader, Ridley, J., in *Wheatley* v *Smithers* [1906] 2 K.B. 321 said: 'One important element in any definition of the term would be that trading implies buying or selling.' On this basis he held that an auctioneer was not a trader because he does not buy goods and, although he sells, he sells goods belonging to other people rather than to himself. This distinction as regards trading firms was approved in *Higgins* v *Beauchamp* [1914] 3 K.B. 1192 in which it was held that a partner in a firm of cinematographic theatre proprietors had no power to borrow on the credit of the firm. The partnership agreement did not give a power to borrow and the non-trading character of the firm prevented an implied power to borrow from arising. In the course of his judgement Lush, J., said: 'In my opinion it would be wrong to say that every business which involves spending money is a trading business. To my mind a trading business is one which carries on the buying and selling of goods.'

If, therefore, the firm is engaged in trade the additional implied powers of the partners by way of usual authority, are as follows—

(1) To draw, issue, accept, transfer, and endorse bills of exchange, either by signing the firm's name or the partner's own name 'for and on behalf of' the firm, provided the transaction is connected with the business and is performed in the usual way. (*Harrison* v *Jackson* (1797) 7 T.R. 207.) In a non-trading firm this authority will not exist unless

there has been a course of dealing as where the firm has in the past honoured instruments signed by one partner. Thus in *Hedley* v *Bainbridge* (1842) 3 Q.B. 316, where there was no such course of dealing, a solicitor was held to have no apparent authority to bind his firm by promissory note, even in respect of a debt which was due from the firm.

However, a partner in a non-trading practice, e.g. a solicitor or accountant, does have usual authority to draw cheques in the firm's name on the firm's bankers. (*Laws* v *Rand* (1857) 3 C.B. (N.S.) 442.) If the name of the firm is printed on the cheque the other partners are liable on it. (*Ringham* v *Hackett* 1980.)[352]

(2) To borrow money on the credit of the firm regardless of any limitation of authority agreed between the partners unless such limitation is known to the third party. (*Bank of Australasia* v *Breillat* (1847) 6 Moo. P.C.C. 152.) Borrowing includes the overdrawing of a bank account. Even if the partner concerned misappropriates the money for his own purposes, his fellow partners are liable to repay it. (*Okell* v *Eaton* (1874) 31 L.T. 330.)

(3) To secure the loan—

(*a*) by pledging personal property of the firm (*Gordon* v *Ellis* (1844) 2 C.B. 821);

(*b*) by depositing title deeds of land, whether freehold or leasehold, so as to create an equitable mortgage even after dissolution. (See *Re Bourne* 1906 at p. 546.) A legal mortgage requires a deed and the consent of all the partners (*Harrison* v *Jackson* (1799) 7 T.R. 207);

(*c*) a partner can accept a security from an outsider where it is the firm which makes the loan to the outsider. (*Re Land Credit Co of Ireland* (1873) L.R.8 Ch. App. 831.)

Cases in which there is no implied power regardless of the nature of the firm. No partner, whether in a trading firm or not, has apparent authority in the following areas. However, his co-partners may ratify the act so that it becomes binding on the firm. Subject to this, a partner cannot—

(1) Bind the firm by deed unless the other partners have given him express authority under seal. The fact that the partnership agreement is under seal does not suffice for this purpose. (*Harrison* v *Jackson* 1797 (above).)

(2) Give a guarantee so as to bind the firm even in relation to the firm's business. The subject was considered in *Brettel* v *Williams* (1849) 4 Ex. 623. There the defendants, who were railway contractors, made a subcontract for the performance of part of certain work which they had undertaken. The subcontractor required a quantity of coal to enable him to get on with the job and one of the defendants, in the name of the firm, guaranteed to the plaintiffs, who were coal merchants, payment for coals to be supplied by them to the subcontractors. It was held that this guarantee did not bind the partners of the contractor signing it on

the grounds that it is not usual for persons in business to make themselves answerable for the conduct of other people.

(3) Compromise a debt by taking something else instead of money, e.g. shares in a company. (*Niemann* v *Niemann* (1899) 43 Ch. D. 198.) However, he may take a cheque which is not regarded as a compromise of the debt. (*Tomlins* v *Lawrence* (1830) 3 M.&P. 555.)

(4) Bind the firm by submitting a dispute to arbitration. (*Adams* v *Bankhart* (1835) 4 L.J. Ex. 69.) This is because he cannot compromise the basic legal right of the partners to have disputes settled by the courts. (But see *Mann* v *D'Arcy* 1968.)[351]

(5) Convey or enter into a contract for the sale or purchase of land. (*Brettel* v *Williams* (above).)

Form

Section 5 (above) is concerned with the binding nature of unauthorized acts of partners. Section 6 makes it clear that the firm is liable for authorized acts, not only of partners but also of employees of the firm. It provides that an act or instrument relating to the business of the firm and done or executed in the firm's name, or in any other way showing an intention to bind the firm, by an authorized agent, whether a partner or not, is binding on the firm and all partners, but this does not affect the law relating to the execution of deeds and negotiable instruments.

Thus the firm will not be bound by deed unless—

(1) all the partners sign it; or

(2) if one partner or other agent signs it, he must be appointed by and act within the scope of a power of attorney, i.e. an authority under seal, given by all the partners.

But if a deed has been used in circumstances where the law does not require one, the firm will be bound if the deed is signed by one partner.

As regards bills of exchange, cheques, and promissory notes, s.23(2) of the Bills of Exchange Act 1882 provides as we have seen that the signing of the name of a firm is equivalent to the signature by the person so signing of the names of all the persons liable as partners in that firm. Instead of putting the name of the firm on the instrument the partner who subscribed to it can put the names of the partners on it. (S.91(1) *ibid.*) (*Ringham* v *Hackett* 1980.)[352]

Partner using credit of firm for private purposes

Where one partner pledges the credit of the firm for a purpose apparently not connected with the firm's ordinary course of business, the firm is not bound unless he is in fact specially authorized by the other partners. (S.7.)

This section supports s.5 in making it quite clear that a firm is not bound where a partner pledges the firm's credit for purposes apparently not connected with its business.

PARTNERS' LIABILITIES

The Partnership Act 1890 (as amended) lays down the liabilities of the partners in several important respects—

Debt and breaches of contract by firm

If, as a result of actual or apparent authority, a partner (or other agent) makes the firm liable in debt or in contract and the firm does not pay the debt or perform the contract, as where a partner orders goods and the firm refuses to take delivery, the liability of partners was *joint*, not *several* (s.9, which was based on the decision of the House of Lords in *Kendall* v *Hamilton* [1879] 4 A.C.504). So, if A, B and C were in partnership, and X, a creditor, sued A alone and the judgment was not paid, B and C were discharged and X could not sue them even if he did not know until later that they were partners.

The matter is now controlled—

(1) by s.3 of the Civil Liability (Contribution) Act 1978 which provides as follows—

> 'Judgment recovered against any person liable in respect of any debt or damage shall not be a bar to an action, or to the continuance of an action, against any other person who is jointly liable with him in respect of the same debt or damage.'

(2) By Order 81, Rule 1, of the Rules of the Supreme Court, which provides that if a creditor sues in the firm name and obtains a judgment in the firm name, this operates as a judgment against the firm and each individual partner and all are liable on it, and this is without the aid of the 1978 Act.

The present position is, then, that the liability of partners for contract debt or damages is joint and several with rights of contribution. The liability remains joint under s.9, but s.3 of the 1978 Act states in effect, that if one partner has been sued to judgment and nothing obtained, this is not a bar to proceedings against other partners.

Joint liability for all debts and obligations of the firm means that a partner can be pursued to the full extent of his personal assets by the firm's creditors. Since a creditor may proceed against any partner for a partnership debt it follows that only if the partners are unable to pay that debt is the firm itself insolvent. In such a case the major problems to be solved will be the competing claims of the joint (firm) and separate (individual partners) creditors against the firm's assets and those of individual partners. (See further, p. 258.)

As regards contribution, s.1 of the 1978 Act provides that any partner who is held liable or reaches a compromise of a claim may recover contribution from his co-partners. Under s.2 the amount is such as the court thinks just and equitable, although a person may be exempted from contribution or be compelled to make a complete indemnity if the court thinks fit. Very often, however, the contribution will be equal. Thus if partner A has paid a judgment of £300 he would be entitled to £100 each from his fellow-partners B and C. Under s.7 of the 1978 Act the right to contribution can only be excluded by means of an express contractual provision to that effect. The right to contribution is lost two years from the date when the right to claim it accrued. (S.10(1), Limitation Act 1980.)

Torts

The firm may become liable for torts as follows—

(1) Under s.10 the partners are liable for the torts of partners committed in the ordinary course of partnership business, but not where the partner acts outside the scope of the firm's usual activities. (*Hamlyn* v *Houston* 1903[353] and *Arbuckle* v *Taylor* 1815.)[354]

(2) At common law the firm is liable for the torts of employees acting within the scope of their employment so that if the firm's van driver injures a pedestrian by negligent driving both he and the firm would be liable under the doctrine of vicarious liability.

As to the nature of the liability, this is *joint* and *several*. (S.12.) Thus, a judgment against one partner is no bar to an action against the others. Thus if the one first sued becomes bankrupt, the fact that he has been sued alone does not bar an action against the other partners. As regards a deceased partner, his estate is liable for the firm's torts committed during his lifetime subject, as in the case of debt and contract, to the prior payment of his private debts, though if the action is for defamation of character, the deceased partner's liability ends on his death and his estate cannot be sued. (Law Reform (Miscellaneous Provisions) Act 1934, s.1.)

Once again, if one partner pays the damages in respect of a tort he can ask for a contribution from his other partners, the rules being the same as those for debt or contract, which are set out above.

It would appear that a partner injured by another partner in the course of business cannot claim against the firm under s.10. Section 10 provides for injuries to a person 'not being a partner in the firm'.

Misapplication of money of property

Section 11 provides that the firm is liable to make good the loss incurred if a partner has tortiously misapplied the money or property of a third person—

(1) where the partner in question was acting within the scope of his apparent authority when he received the money or property; or

(2) where the firm in the course of its business received the money or property, and it was misapplied by one or more of the partners while it was in the custody of the firm.

(1) above seems to envisage a case where the firm never received the money because the partner misappropriated it.

(2) above deals with misappropriation by a partner *after* the money or property had been received by the firm and whilst it was in its custody.

However, there may be in practice little difference between (1) and (2) above since receipt by a partner within the scope of his apparent authority will normally amount to a receipt into custody by the firm in the course of its business. In situations (1) and (2) above the partners of the dishonest members of the firm are liable even though they are innocent of the misappropriation. (See *Rhodes* v *Moules* 1895 (below).)

There are very many cases illustrating the application of s.11 of which three only have been selected as examples of the three most likely sorts of situation leading to the invoking of s.11.

(1) Where one partner acting within the scope of his authority, as evidenced by the business of the firm, obtains money and misapplies it, then the firm is answerable for it. Thus in *Rhodes* v *Moules* [1895] 1 Ch. 236 Rhodes, a member of a firm of solicitors, was employed by one of the firm's clients to obtain him a loan on a mortgage of his property. Rhodes obtained the loan but told the client falsely that the lenders required some security. The client handed to Rhodes some share warrants which were payable to bearer, intending that these should be used as security. Rhodes misappropriated the share warrants and absconded. His partners had no knowledge of the deposit of the warrants and were innocent of any fraud. However, the firm had on previous occasions received through Rhodes the same share warrants from the same client in order to obtain loans for him and the firm was in the habit of receiving from, and holding for, clients bearer bonds. In this sitution it was held that the transaction was clearly a partnership transaction and that Rhodes' partners were liable for the value of shares misappropriated.

(2) Where the firm in the course of its business has received money belonging to other people and one of the partners misapplies that money whilst it is in the custody of the firm, then the firm must make it good. Thus in *Devaynes* v *Noble, Clayton's Case* (1816) 1 Mer. 572 certain exchequer bills were deposited by their owners with a firm of bankers and were sold by one of the partners of the firm without the owner's knowledge. The money which resulted from the sale was applied by the firm in its business. It was held to be clear that the money, having been received by the firm, the amount became a partnership debt whether all the individual partners were or were not parties to the sale.

(3) If a partner in the course of some transaction which is not connected with the business of the firm and is not within the scope of such

business, obtains money and misapplies it, then the firm is not generally liable to make good the loss. Thus in *Cleather* v *Twisden* (1884) 28 Ch. D. 340 bonds made payable to bearer were placed for safe custody by trustees in the hands of one partner in a firm of solicitors and he misappropriated them. It was held that the other partners were not liable since it was no part of the business of the firm to accept such securities for safe custody. In addition, the other partners did not know that the defaulting partner had the bonds. If they had known, then they would have been held to have had the bonds in their own custody and would have been liable for the misappropriation.

Misapplication by employees

This is covered by the common law and the firm is liable only if the servant was *entrusted* with the money or property. The fact that the employee's job helps him to misapply the property is not enough. Thus, if a firm's managing clerk is entrusted with funds as part of his job and he misapplies them, then the firm is liable, but if a junior employee misapplies the funds and is assisted in doing this merely because he knows where the safe key is, then the firm is not liable. Of course, by stealing the money both the clerk and the junior went beyond the scope of their employment. Obviously they are not employed to steal. In earlier times the employer would not have been liable. However, modern decisions, e.g. *Morris* v *C.W. Martin and Sons Ltd* [1965] 2 All E.R. 725, show that the employer will be liable even though the employee was acting beyond the scope of his employment, *provided* he was entrusted with the task of looking after or dealing with the money or property concerned. In *Morris* a cleaner of furs was liable for the theft of a fur by a person employed in its cleaning.

As regards employees who are not entrusted, the employer may be liable for misappropriation by these if he employs persons whom he knows to be dishonest, or where he is negligent as by not having a reasonable system of control of clients' money or property.

Under s.11, however, the rule is different for partners. A partner who misapplies property need not have been entrusted with it. Thus if A and B are in partnership as dry-cleaners, A working at the London branch and B working at the Birmingham branch, then if B comes down to London and steals a fur from the London branch, the firm and A are nevertheless liable.

Under s.12 liability for misappropriation by partners and employees (if this arises) is joint and several.

Improper employment of trust money

Under s.13, if a trustee/partner improperly employs trust property, then the other partners are joint and severally liable to make good the deficiency only if they knew of the breach, as where they all agreed to use the money in the business. If the co-partners were not involved in the breach and had no knowledge of it, then the firm is not liable. Thus in *Re Bell's Indenture* [1980] 3 All E.R. 425 a son and his mother became the sole trustees of a will trust by the husband. The mother was not a beneficiary; the son had a life interest only. Others were entitled on the death of the son. In seven years the son and his mother dissipated the whole trust fund. They did this with the knowledge and assistance of the solicitor who acted for them, who by intermeddling in this way became a constructive trustee. In fact, part of the money had been paid in breach of trust into the firm's client account. There were two partners, the other partner having had no knowledge of the breach of trust. Vinelott, J., held that the innocent partner was not liable under s.13 as a constructive trustee, nor was he liable under s.11. As regards liability under s.11, it was decided that a partner might have the implied authority of his fellow partner to receive client's money in the course of business as a solicitor. However, s.11 did not apply if when he received the property it was as a trustee, not as a solicitor in the course of business. According to the judge, a solicitor in the ordinary course of his practice does not have the implied authority of his co-partners to accept office as a trustee, and so make his co-partners liable for a misapplication of the trust property. The partners of a solicitor who receives money as a trustee which is lost are not liable for his default because the monies have been received by him as a trustee and not as a solicitor.

However, the beneficiaries under the trust are not without a remedy and may trace their property into the assets of the firm. This is based upon the notion that the true owner of property traced to the possession of another has a right to have it restored, not because it is a debt, but because it is his property. His right is incidental to his ownership.

Thus, if the trust property is other than money and the beneficiary can identify it in the firm's assets, he can recover it. Thus, if a trustee/partner was using in his office a gold carriage clock which was part of the trust property, the beneficiaries could recover it. As regards money, if this has been placed in a separate account, then the beneficiaries may take all of it. If, on the other hand, it is in a mixed account which contains trust money and partnership money, then *Hallett's Case* applies if the other partners knew that it was trust money. If the other partners did not know then *Hallett* applies if the partner concerned is a trustee as part of his work for the firm. If the partner concerned is a trustee in a purely personal capacity the beneficiaries can only trace *pari passu*, under *Re Diplock* if the money is mixed in an account other than a bank current account. If it is mixed in the firm's bank current account, tracing is under the rule in *Clayton's Case* (see below.)

The effect of this is that if all the partners knew that the money was trust money, or if the partner concerned was a trustee as part of his work for the firm, then under the rule in *Re Hallett's Estate* (1880) 13 Ch. D. 696 the partners draw out the firm's money first and the trust money last and the rule in *Clayton's Case* (1816) 1 Mer. 572, which states that money first paid in is first drawn out, does not apply.

Thus, if there was a balance of £1000 on the firm's account when £1000 of trust money was paid in and later £500 of the firm's money was paid in, then drawings from the account in excess of £1500 would be required before any trust money was spent and any balance on the account after that would belong to the beneficiaries.

On the other hand if the partner concerned is a trustee in a purely personal capacity then, because the other partners are not regarded as trustees, the rule in *Hallett*, which applies only where tracing is into the account of a trustee, is not available. The rule in *Re Diplock* [1948] 2 All E.R. 318 applies if the money is mixed in, e.g. a bank deposit account, and that case states that persons making claims on a mixed fund of that type which is not the account of a trustee do so on the basis of the amounts they have each put into it. Thus, if there is a balance of £1000 in the firm's deposit account and then £1000 of trust money is paid in and then £1000 of the firm's money, then the partners do not spend the firm's money first. Any balance on the account at *any time* is shared as to one-third to the trust and two-thirds to the firm. Thus, if the account had been drawn down to £300 the beneficiaries under the trust would get £100 and the firm would be left with £200.

If the money is mixed in the firm's bank current account, then *Clayton's Case* (first in, first out) applies. In the example given above the firm's £1000 would be drawn first, then the £1000 of trust money, then the firm's £1000 paid in last. This is a less helpful rule than *Diplock* but nevertheless is the one applied to current accounts.

PARTNERSHIP BY ESTOPPEL

Everyone who 'by words spoken or written' or 'by conduct' represents himself, or knowingly allows himself to be represented, as a partner in a particular firm, is liable as a partner to anyone who has on the faith of any such representation given credit to the firm. (S.14(1).)

He may be sued by the third party as if he were a partner. It is not enough that a person knows he is being held out as a partner; there must also be evidence of consent. Carelessness or negligence is not enough. (*Tower Cabinet Co. Ltd* v *Ingram* 1949.)[355]

The most usual way of being held out in practice is where a partner who has retired fails to remove his name from the headed notepaper of the firm. He will then be liable for debts if he knew the paper was in use. He would not seem to be liable if he has arranged for the stock of notepaper to be destroyed but it is in fact used in breach of that arrangement. The agreement of the continuing partners to destroy the stock of notepaper should be enough to avoid s.14, since it shows that the retiring partner did not consent to its continued use. A salaried partner can, of course, become liable for the debts of the firm under s.14 as an ostensible partner.

Section 14(2) provides that where after a partner's death the business is continued in the old firm name, the continued use of that name, or of the deceased partner's name as part of it, shall not of itself render his personal representatives or his estate liable for partnership debts contracted after his death. Under English law the authority of an agent is terminated by the death of his principal, whether the fact of death is known or not.

As regards internal relations between the partners, the fact that A holds out B as his partner will not necessarily by itself create the rights, duties and liabilities of partners between them. Section 14 describes a relationship between the person held out and those who give credit on the faith of that situation. In other words, it is an external rather than an internal doctrine. (*Floydd* v *Cheney* 1970.)[356]

LIABILITIES OF INCOMING AND OUTGOING PARTNERS

A person who is admitted as a partner into an existing firm does not thereby become liable to the firm's creditors for debts incurred before he became a partner (s.17(1)), and a partner who retires from a firm does not thereby cease to be liable for partnership debts or obligations incurred before his retirement (s.17(2)).

The date when the contract was made decides the question of liability. Thus in a contract for the sale of goods a partner is liable if he was a partner when the contract was made, even though the goods were delivered after he ceased to be a partner.

Where goods are delivered by instalments the position is as follows:

(1) Where the contract is not severable, the retiring partner will be liable for each instalment delivered, whether before or after his retirement, provided the contract ordering *all* of the goods was made while he was a member of the firm, delivery to be by instalments.

(2) However, where the contract is severable the retiring partner would normally be liable for deliveries made under orders while he was still with the firm, but not deliveries made afterwards: for these, the new firm and its partners will be liable.

The way in which the contractual arrangement is expressed decides the issue of severability. For example, if a person receives an order to supply 'gravel as required at £10 per tonne' the contractual arrangement is severable, since the parties appear to be prepared to deal piecemeal at a price per tonne.

On the other hand, a person who receives an order for '1000 tonnes of gravel for £10,000 delivery to be by weekly instalments of 100 tonnes' has a non-severable contract because the parties have not dealt on a 'per tonne' basis.

Thus in *Dyke* v *Brewer* (1849) 2 Car. and K. 828 D agreed with A to supply him with bricks at a price per 1000 and began to supply them accordingly. B then entered into partneship with A, and the plaintiff continued to supply bricks as ordered as before. It was held that both

A and B were liable to pay at the rate agreed upon for the bricks supplied to them both after the partnership began.

The basis of this decision was that as A had not ordered any definite number of bricks, each order and acceptance of the order and delivery raised a new tacit agreement to pay on the old terms. However, if *all* the bricks delivered had been ordered by A in the first instance, he alone would have been liable to pay for them.

Section 17(3) provides that a retiring partner may be discharged from any existing liabilities by an agreement to that effect between himself, the members of the firm as newly constituted, and the creditors. This agreement, which is called a *novation*, may be either express or inferred from the course of dealing between the creditors and the firm as newly constituted. (*Thompson* v *Percival* 1834.)[357]

The creditors cannot be made to accept a novation, and if a particular creditor refuses to enter into such an arrangement, he may still hold the retired partner liable for liabilities existing at his retirement. However, the new or continuing partners may agree to indemnify him.

A partnership may take part in a continuing guarantee either as guarantor, creditor or principal debtor. If the firm which is the creditor or principal debtor changes its composition, the guarantee is, in the absence of contrary agreement revoked, but a change in the composition of the guarantor firm has no such effect (*Bradford Old Bank* v *Sutcliffe* [1918] 2 K.B. 833) and a retiring partner remains liable and an incoming partner does not become liable. (S.18.)

As an example of the operation of s.18, suppose A.B. & Co. enter into a fidelity bond guaranteeing that C.D. & Co. will faithfully discharge their duties as debt collectors for E.F. & Co. for a period of 12 months so that A.B. & Co. would be liable to make good losses arising from C.D. & Co.'s failure to account.

Under s.18, if there is a change in the membership of C.D. & Co. or E.F. & Co. the bond is discharged unless there is a contrary agreement between the parties. However, a person who is a partner in A.B. & Co. remains liable for 12 months and cannot get rid of that liability by retiring from A.B. & Co., nor even by assignment or novation from A.B. & Co. to a new firm. He can, however, take an indemnity from the continuing partners.

EFFECT OF CHANGES IN CONSTITUTION

When a person retires from a partnership he may remain liable for debts of the firm incurred after his retirement. (S.36(1).) The reason for this requirement is that a person who deals with a firm is entitled, in fairness, to regard all apparent members of the old firm as being still members, until he has notice of a change or until any partner dies.

To avoid this liability the retiring partner must—

(1) Ensure that individual notices are sent to all those who were cus-

tomers of the firm while he was a partner. Interestingly enough, those who have read the section will have noticed that it does not say this. However, there is case law (e.g. *Graham* v *Hope* (1792) Peake 208) which tells us that unless this is done the apparent partner concept will apply.

Notice can be given by circular. However, no particular form of notice is required so no doubt, if the next communication received from the partnership was on new notepaper showing only the continuing partners, actual notice would have been given. In addition, the change of names printed on cheques should constitute notice of change of partners to a recipient of the cheque.

(2) Advertise the fact of his retirement in the *London Gazette*. This operates as notice to all who have not dealt with the firm before while he was a partner but knew or believed him to be one. It is not necessary that these persons actually read the advertisement which binds them anyway.

There is no need to advertise or send a notice in respect of those who had no previous dealings with the firm and did not know or believe that the retiring partner was a partner before he retired. (*Tower Cabinet Co. Ltd* v *Ingram* 1949.)[355]

The estate of a deceased or bankrupt partner is not liable for debts incurred after death or bankruptcy, even if no notice of any sort is given. (S.36(3).)

Relations of partners to one another

GENERALLY

Sections 19–31 of the Act cover the relations of partners to one another, which is based upon two main principles as follows—

(1) freedom to construct and vary the partnership agreement, and
(2) a duty of honest disclosure as between the partners as regards the business.

The broad general principle of utmost good faith set out in (2) above is an implied term of the contract of partnership and is not set out as such in the Act of 1890. The Act deals with the matter somewhat inadequately by reference to particular circumstances. These are to be found in s.28 (duty to account); s.29 (accounting for private profits) and s.30 (duty not to compete with the firm).

VARIATION OF THE PARTNERSHIP AGREEMENT

The mutual rights and duties of the partners, whether expressed in the partnership agreement or implied under the Act of 1890, may be varied by the consent of all the partners, and such consent may be either express or inferred from the course of dealing. (S.19.) Thus, to give Lord Eldon's example in *Const* v *Harris* (1824) T.&R. 496, partners may agree that no single partner may draw or accept bills of exchange in his own name without the concurrence of all, yet 'slide into' the practice, which the courts will condone, of allowing this to be done as a matter of course. (And see *Pilling* v *Pilling* 1865[358] where the books were kept otherwise than in accordance with the partnership agreement.) The partnership agreement, even if under seal, can be varied by an informal agreement of the partners. This follows from the fact that the initial partnership agreement needs no writing.

Section 19 in effect gives partners a general right to contract out of the Act and vary the otherwise implied provisions of the Act as regards *their relationship between each other*. Such variations will not affect outsiders unless they have actual notice of the restriction. Section 8 of the Act provides that if it has been agreed between the partners that any restriction shall be placed on the power of one or more of them to bind the firm, no act done in contravention of the agreement is binding on the firm with respect to persons having notice of the agreement. Thus, by implication, it is binding on the firm in respect of those who do not have notice of it.

Another advantage of s.19 is that partnership can change its objects freely provided all the partners agree to such a change. (S.24(8).) In addition, partnership agreements are not registered and for that reason there is no constructive notice of the objects of a partnership. Because of this and the ease with which the partners may change the objects, the *ultra vires* rule, which is somewhat of a problem in companies, is not a problem in a partnership, particularly when one takes into account s.5 which gives partners a wide usual authority to bind the firm.

PARTNERSHIP PROPERTY

Difficult questions may arise in regard to whether property is property of the firm or the property of individual partners, since property may be used in the business for the purposes of the business and yet may not be part of the property of the firm but may remain property of one partner only. This matter is of some importance—

(1) *To the partners themselves*, since an increase in value of partnership property belongs to the firm, but if the property belongs to one partner only the increased value belongs to him alone. The same issues are raised by a decrease in value.

(2) *As between the creditors of the firm and creditors of the partners individually*, since this governs their entitlement to the property as a means of paying what is owed to them. Judgment creditors of an individual partner cannot levy execution against the firm's property. (S.23.) Furthermore, on dissolution if *all* partners are insolvent, then under s.33 of the Bankruptcy Act 1914 the firm's creditors prove first against the firm's assets and not against the individual assets of the

partners. Private creditors prove first against the individual assets of the partners and not against the firm's assets.

(3) *As between the persons who take the estate of a deceased partner* since if a deceased partner has left by will all his realty to R and all his personalty to P, then P will get the value of the partnership land because such land is personal property and not real property. Under s.22 the equitable doctrine of conversion applies to partnership realty and it becomes personalty.

Under s.20(1), property originally brought into the partnership or subsequently acquired by it is *jointly owned*, as tenants in common, by the partners. However, it can be stolen by one partner, on the grounds that under the Theft Act 1968 he dishonestly appropriates his co-owner's share (*R* v *Bonner* 1970.)[359]

The presumption in s.20(1) is rebuttable. In fact, the subsection is not much help because it begs the question when property is brought into or acquired by the firm. In practice most professionally drawn partnership agreements state or define carefully what is to be treated as partnership property. Property brought in will normally be as part of a partnership's capital contribution.

As regards *land*, under s.20(2) this is held on trust for *sale* by the partners for—

(1) Each partner, whose interest in the land therefore becomes personalty and goes on death to the person who is to receive personalty and not to the person who is to receive the real property.

(2) Others interested, e.g. retired partners who have annuties.

The conversion to personal property is not part of partnership law but is merely an aspect of the general equitable rule of conversion which is expressed in s.22 of the Act of 1890.

The equitable rule of conversion relates to a change in the nature of property by which, for certain purposes, real estate is considered as personal, and personal estate as real, and transmissible and descendible as such. Thus money directed to be employed in the purchase of land, and land directed to be sold and turned into money, are considered as that species of property in which they are directed to be converted before the conversion takes place.

The basis of the rule is that on dissolution the land will be sold and converted into money which is personal estate in order to repay the capital contributed by the partners. Thus in equity it is so converted when it comes into the firm in accordance with the maxim 'equity regards that as done which will be done'. If a partner leaves all his personalty to P and all his realty to R, then, as we have seen, P will get the value of partnership land. The point behind the equitable maxim is that if one has put one's money into land it should be regarded as land, even though the land is not yet purchased. Equally, if one has agreed to sell land the land should be regarded as money, even though the sale has not yet gone through.

The nature of the trust under s.20(2) is uncertain so that when land is conveyed into a partnership it should be conveyed 'on trust for sale' to ensure that there is a power of sale and that when it is sold the purchaser takes the land free of the interest of the partners or other interested parties in it. These trusts attach, of course, to the purchase money which is received. The trust property then becomes the purchase money.

Property may be originally brought into a partnership in the following ways—

(1) by transferring the property on trust for sale to all the partners including the partner whose property it was. By reason of the Law of Property Act 1925, land cannot be vested in more than four partners. This helps sale because only a maximum of four signatures are required on the conveyance. If there are more than four partners, four must be chosen to hold the land on trust for themselves and the others; or

(2) by transferring the property to trustees, e.g. some only of the partners to hold for the firm; or

(3) by the partner whose property it was retaining the ownership of it but declaring himself to be a trustee on behalf of the firm; or

(4) by a partner who owns a freehold granting a lease to himself and the other partners. If there are more than four partners, once again four must be chosen to hold on trust for themselves and others.

If there is no such transfer then what is said in the partnership agreement decides the issue, or failing that the Court must look at the intentions of the partners as revealed by the evidence of their conduct.

Property bought with partnership money, e.g. by a cheque drawn on the firm's account, is presumed to be partnership property, but again this is a rebuttable presumption (s.21), as will property brought into common stock and credited in the books as the capital of one or more of the partners. (*Robinson* v *Ashton* (1875) L.R. 20 Eq. 25.)

However, mere use of the property in the business is not enough to transfer the property to the firm, certainly as regards important assets such as leases and valuable equipment. Thus in *Eardley* v *Broad* (1970) 120 N.L.J. 432, a partnership deed between father and son did not specifically refer to a farm lease held by the father so that the lease did not become partnership property, although it had been used in the business. (See also *Miles* v *Clark* 1953[360] and *Waterer* v *Waterer* 1873,[361] the latter being, perhaps, an exceptional case due to the nature of the business.)

In addition, if there is an agreement about what is to be brought in, it will be construed stictly. The mere fact that the agreement mentioned the bringing in of 'assets' was held in *Singh* v *Nahar* [1965] 1 All E.R. 768 to be insufficient to bring in a lease of premises. The lease should have been mentioned specifically.

As regards property subsequently acquired, under s.21 property bought with money belonging to the firm, as where it is bought with a cheque drawn on the firm's account, is deemed to be the firm's *unless a contrary intention appears.* Again, it is a rebuttable presumption. Thus the ultimate test is the agreement and intention of the partners. If other funds are used there is no such presumption and other evidence, if any, must be sought. (*Davis* v *Davis* 1894.)[362]

Section 21 applies if the asset is acquired from profits as well as capital. This does not apply to land if the profits arise from mere co-ownership. (See s.20(3) and *Davis* v *Davis* 1894.)[362]

The presumption in s.21 applies even if the property is conveyed into the name of only one partner. Thus in *Forster* v *Hale* (1800) 5 Ves. 308 land was bought from partnership funds but was taken in the name of the partner who made the purchase. Nevertheless, it was regarded as partnership property. The same principle applied in *Ex parte Connel* (1838) 3 Deac. 201 where company shares were bought with the firm's funds and were regarded as partnership property even though they were transferred into the name of one of the partners only whose name appeared on the company's register.

This is really an example of the doctrine of the resulting trust which arises where property is purchased in the name of another. That other holds the property on a resulting trust for the person who provided the funds, in this case the firm, unless a contrary intention is expressed.

Withdrawal of assets

If the partners agree, one partner may withdraw an asset from the firm either by buying it or taking a reduction in his capital. If the property is withdrawn at a time when the firm is insolvent, the withdrawal is void as against the creditors, who may require the return of the property to the firm.

Partner's separate judgment debt

Section 23 of the Partnership Act provides that, where the creditor of a partner has obtained a judgment against that partner in respect of a private debt, the creditor cannot execute judgment against the partnership property. Only judgment against the firm in the firm name allows execution of it by writ of *fi. fa.* (or warrant) against the firms property. (S.23(1).) The separate creditor may apply to the court for an order charging the partner's share of capital and profits with payment of the debt. The court has power to appoint a receiver of the partner's share of the profits and, should the firm be dissolved, of the assets.

The receiver has a limited function which is to collect the sums which would otherwise have been paid to the debtor partner. The receiver has no right to manage or participate in management. In this connection genuine salary payments could reduce the amount of profit available to pay the debtor partner's debts. If the salary payments were fraudulent, of course, the receiver could have them set aside.

The other partners may redeem the charge at any time by paying off the judgment creditor, in which case the charge becomes vested in them. They can enforce the charge if necessary *gradually* against the partner in default. The court may order a sale of the partner's share and, if it does, the other partners may purchase the share.

A separate creditor who obtains a charging order becomes a secured creditor and can demand payment out of the property charged before the separate creditors of the partner concerned but ranks after those of the firm. This is because a partner has no share in the partnership assets except subject to the payment of the debts of the firm. The separate creditors of a partner are entitled to be paid first out of his separate estate but the creditors of the firm are entitled to be paid first out of its assets and consequently to be paid in full before the share of the partner in those assets becomes available for the payment of his separate creditors. (*Re Ritson* [1899] 1 Ch. 128.) If a partner's share is charged under s.23 his co-partners are entitled *at their option* to have the partnership dissolved. (S.33(2).)

The dissolution is not automatic and indeed there is no authority as to the manner or time in which the option is to be exercised, nor whether it is exercisable by any partner, or a majority of partners, or by all unanimously. Since it is similar in a way to expulsion, it may require unanimous consent.

Because of the problems created by charging orders it is usual to insert a clause in a partnership agreement which requires prompt discharge of partners' private debts and makes breach of the clause a ground for expulsion.

CAPITAL

Section 24(1) provides that all the partners are entitled to share equally in the capital and profits of the business and must contribute equally towards the losses, whether of capital and otherwise, sustained by the firm. The section applies, in the absence of agreement to the contrary, regardless of the value of assets brought in by each partner. This means that on a repayment of capital, e.g. on dissolution, capitals which the partners have contributed unequally will be treated as one aggregate fund to be divided between the partners in equal shares. However, as we have seen, the partners may have an agreement to the contrary, providing for repayment on the basis of contribution. Section 24(1) also provides that losses of capital like other losses must be shared equally and not in accordance to capital contributed.

The office of 'salaried partner' should rebut the presumption regarding the sharing of profits and losses. The provision of a salary may well be regarded as inconsistent, certainly with a liability to contribute to losses, and probably also in terms of a participation in profits.

Losses resulting from acts in breach of duty are borne by the partner who is in breach alone, unless the other partners agree expressly or impliedly to take them over.

Any agreement to sharing losses is binding only as between the partners. The partners remain fully liable towards outsiders for all the firm's debts. (*Robinson (Executors') Case*, (1856) 6 De G.M.&G. 572.)

Finally, it should be noted that if there is an agreement to share profits unequally this applies also to losses, so that the profit-sharing ratio is also the loss-sharing ratio.

Loans

A partner may advance money to the firm over and above the amount of his capital, by lending money to the firm or by paying certain of its debts from his own funds. Such advances of payments are not deemed to have increased his capital unless the partners have so agreed, and he is entitled to interest at 5 per cent per annum from the date of the payment or advance if the partners do not come to some other arrangment. (S.24(3).) The interest is payable whether profits are made or not. Interest on advances is payable before interest on capital.

Interest on capital

This is only payable if the partnership agreement expressly provides for it and sufficient profits are earned to pay it. (S.24(4).) Thus there can be no payment of money to the partners as interest on capital if no profit is made, nor can there be a payment out of money as interest on capital which represents more than the profit made where this is not sufficient to cover all interest on capital. However, as a matter of accounting practice there is no reason why interest on capital should not be charged in order to show the true position in accounting terms of the business, though a loss produced solely by charging interest on capital against a profit not sufficient to cover it is not a loss for revenue purposes.

Reduction of capital

A reduction of capital may be effected, if the partners agree—

(1) By the repayment of money to the partner concerned (though if the firm is insolvent such a payment may be set aside as a fraud on creditors); or

(2) Where the firm has incurred losses, by writing down the capital accounts of the partners to correspond with the reduced value of the assets.

PROFITS

The partnership agreement will usually provide for the sharing of profits in certain proportions. In the absence of such agreement the Act provides that all partners are entitled to share equally in the profits of the business and must contribute equally towards the losses. (S.24(1).) The Act does not require partners to keep books or to draw up a profit and loss account and balance sheet, but the partnership agreement usually does so, and under s.28 partners are bound to render true accounts and full information of all things affecting the partnership to any partner or his legal representatives.

INDEMNITY

The firm must indemnify each partner in respect of payments made and personal liabilities incurred by him in the ordinary and proper conduct of its business, or in doing anything necessary to preserve the business or property of the firm. (S.24(2).)

Thus if a partner pays the firm's debts or pays a premium to insure the firm's property, he can look to the firm for reimbursement or, if the firm is insolvent, to his fellow partners for a contribution.

MANAGEMENT

The partnership agreement usually outlines the powers of the partners in the matter of management; otherwise every partner may take part in the management of the partnership business. (S.24(5).) The partnership books are to be kept at the place of business of the partnership (or the principal place if there is more than one) and every partner may, when he thinks fit, have access to and inspect and copy any of them. (S.24(9).) He can, however, be restrained from doing this if he intends to take the names of the firm's customers in order to solicit them for his own business, and in any case his power to inspect is subject to any contrary agreement between the partners, as is the whole of s.24.

The Act provides that no partner shall be entitled to remuneration for acting in the partnership business (S.24(6)), but where a firm consists of active and non-active partners, the partnership agreement often provides that the active or managing partners shall have a salary in addition to their share of profit.

Even where the amount of the services rendered by the partners is very unequal, still, if there is no agreement that their services shall be remunerated, no charge in respect of them can be allowed in taking the partnership accounts. In such a case remuneration for personal services exceeding those contributed by the other partners is considered as left to the honour of the others to pay for it. If they do not do so the court will not, in general, award remuneration.

However, where, as is normally the case, it is the duty of each partner to attend the partnership business and one partner in breach of his duty *wilfully* leaves the others to carry on the partnership unaided, they are probably entitled to compensation for their services on a dissolution. The Act does not specifically provide, but the law implies, that each partner shall attend to and work in the business, and if he fails to do so it is a ground for dissolution, and the court may order him to make compensation to the industrious partner for the extra trouble thrown upon him by the other's idleness.

Thus, in *Airey* v *Borham* (1861) 29 Beav. 620, two partners had agreed to devote their whole time to the partnership business but they quarrelled and one of them only afterwards attended to it. The partnership was dissolved and the court directed an inquiry for the purpose of ascertaining what allowance ought to be made to the partner who had carried on the business alone.

No person may be introduced as a partner, nor may any change be made in the nature of the partnership business, without the consent of *all* existing partners. It makes no difference that the new business is very profitable. (*Attorney General* v *Great Northern Railway* (1860) 1 Dr. and Sm. 154.) However, as we have seen in *Mann* v *D'Arcy* 1968,[351] the section does not apply to a different way of running the same business. However differences between the partners in other matters connected with the ordinary business of the firm may be settled by a majority in number of the partners, regardless of the capital introduced by each. (S.24(7),(8).) Such majority decisions must be made after consultation with the other partners—even a dormant partner should be consulted—and in good faith, and no majority of the partners can dissolve the firm by expulsion of any partner unless a power to do so has been conferred by express agreement between the partners. (S.25.) If the partners are equally divided those who forbid the change must have their way and things stay as they are.

Even where the partnership agreement provides that a majority can expel a partner, the power of expulsion must be exercised in good faith. Thus in *Carmichael* v *Evans* [1904] 1 Ch. 486 it was held that the expulsion of a partner in a firm of drapers who had been convicted of travelling on a train without a ticket was a proper exercise of the power conferred by the articles to expel for 'scandalous conduct detrimental to the partnership business' or for 'flagrant breach of the duties of a partner'. And, again in *Greenaway* v *Greenaway* (1939) 84 S. J. 43 it was held that an assault on fellow partners was a good ground for expulsion under a majority power.

The court cannot control the exercise of a power to expel a partner if it is exercised in good faith, which involves the right to give an explanation, or if the power is exercisable under the partnership agreement at the mere will and pleasure of one partner. (*Russell* v *Russell* (1880) 14 Ch. D. 471.) An invalid notice of expulsion is inoperative and the partner whom the others purport to expel cannot recover damages for wrongful expulsion because he has not been expelled in law. (*Wood* v *Woad* (1874)

L.R. 9 Ex. 190.)

The expulsion must be for the benefit of the firm and not for the personal gain of those partners who remain. If the expulsion is for the personal gain of the remaining partners, then the court will set aside the expulsion. (*Blisset* v *Daniel* (1853) 10 Hare 493.)

An expulsion clause should provide how the partner who is expelled is to be notified of this, e.g. in writing, and whether the expulsion is to take immediate effect. There should also be provisions as to how the expelled partner is to take his share of the firm, e.g. over a period of time, or at once. If the expulsion is unjustified the court can offer relief by way of an injunction or the appointment of a receiver and manager. (*Const* v *Harris* (1824) T.&R. 496.)

DUTIES OF PARTNERS

The partners have the following duties—

(1) *Duty to render accounts and disclose information.* Partners are bound to render true accounts and full information of all things, e.g. dealings and transactions affecting the partnership to any partner or his legal representative. (S.28.)

The duty arises out of the *fiduciary relationship* of partners and a partner must disclose full information regarding the firm whether it is asked for or not. (*Law* v *Law* 1905.)[363] No such duty is owed to incoming partners, but an incoming partner can rescind the contract if the existing partners have been guilty of misrepresenting by statements made the prospects and worth of the firm.

(2) *Duty to account for private profits.* Every partner must account to the firm for any benefit derived by him without the consent of the other partners from any transaction concerning the partnership, or from any use by him of the partnership property, name or business connection. (S.29(1).) (*Bentley* v *Craven* 1853;[364] *Pathirana* v *Pathirana* 1966.)[365] There is no need to account if the transaction could not possibly have affected the partnership business, as where it is outside its scope. (*Aas* v *Benham* 1891.)[366]

This duty to account applies also to transactions undertaken after the partnership has been dissolved by the death of a partner and before the affairs of the partnership have been completely wound up. (S.29(2).) A potential partner is accountable to the other potential partners of the firm when it comes into being for profits made during the negotiations leading up to the formation of the firm, if the transaction out of which he made the profit would have affected the firm had it been in existence. (*Fawcett* v *Whitehouse* 1829.)[367]

(3) *Duty of partners not to compete with the firm.* If a partner, without the consent of the other partners, carries on any business of the same nature as and competing with that of the firm, he must account for

and pay over to the firm all profits made by him in that business. (S.30.) The business must be a competing business. Thus, if X and Y were partners in a firm of Savile Row tailors, Y would not have to account to the Savile Row firm if he set up a cheap clothing store in another area. (See also *Aas* v *Benham* 1891.)[366] Where a partner carries on a business not connected with or competing with that of the firm, his partners cannot claim the profits that he makes, and this is so even if he has agreed not to carry on any separate business. (*Dean* v *Macdowell* (1878) 8 Ch. D. 345.)

Section 30 merely provides for an account of profits and does not prohibit the carrying on of a competing business. However, the partnership agreement may do so, in which case the competing partner could be restrained by injunction from carrying on with competing business. Even where there is no specific prohibition in the agreement, the court may be prepared to dissolve the partnership where one partner persists in competition.

ASSIGNMENT OF A SHARE IN A PARTNERSHIP

An assignment by any partner of his share in the partnership, either absolutely or by way of mortgage or redeemable charge, as where the share is used as security for a loan, does not not make the assignee a partner. The assignee is not entitled to interfere in the management or administration of the firm or to require accounts or to inspect the firm's books. He is entitled only to receive the share of profits to which the assigning partner would otherwise be entitled and he must accept the account of profits agreed to by the partners. (S.31(1).) However the partners cannot alter their shares of profit and/or capital so as to reduce the share to which the assignee is entitled, unless this is done in good faith and for reasons acceptable to the court. (*Garwood's Trusts, Garwood* v *Paynter* 1903.)[368]

In the case of a dissolution of a partnership, whether as respects all the partners or as respects the assigning partner, the assignee is entitled to receive the share of the partnership assets to which the assigning partner is entitled as between himself and the other partners, and for the purpose of ascertaining that share to an account as from the date of the dissolution. (S.31(2).)

The assignee is not personally liable for the debts of the firm, though where the assignment is absolute and not by way of mortgage he must indemnify the assigning partner against the latter's liability to pay the firm's debt whether incurred before or after the assignment.

The assignee may become a partner if the other partners agree, but as a mere assignee he has no control over the way in which the partners manage the firm. (*Re Garwood's Trusts, Garwood* v *Paynter* 1903.)[368]

The Partnership Act 1890 does not state that the assignment of a share in a partnership is a ground for dissolution. This does not matter very much when the partnership is at will because it can be dissolved by notice, but in a partnership for a fixed term it may be of importance. It is possible that it is a ground under the general heading of just and equitable in s.35. However, the Act does not give the assignee a right to apply for dissolution.

TRANSMISSION OF A SHARE IN THE PARTNERSHIP

When a partner dies or becomes bankrupt, his property vests by operation of law in his personal representatives or trustee in bankruptcy as the case may be. A partner's property includes his interest in the assets of the firm. The personal representatives or trustee do not become partners in the firm and the firm will under s.33 have been dissolved as regards *all* the partners by the death or bankruptcy unless, as is usual, the partnership agreement provides that the business shall continue under the remaining partner(s). The personal representatives or trustee are entitled to receive the deceased's or bankrupt's share of the assets, unless the partnership agreement gives the other partners an option, which they exercise, to buy a deceased or bankrupt partner's share. In the latter case, the personal representatives or the trustee are only entitled to the price payable under the option which may be less valuable than a share of the assets.

REMEDIES FOR BREACH OF THE PARTNERSHIP AGREEMENT

Since a partnership in terms particularly of the relationship between the partners is governed by the regime of equity, one partner cannot bring an action for damages against another partner who is in breach of his duties under the partnership agreement, but may ask for an injunction to enforce a negative stipulation in it. Thus, where a partner agrees not to compete with the firm, he may be restrained by injunction from doing so provided the restraint is in negative form. (See p. 88.)

Specific performance will rarely be available to enforce the partnership agreement, since a partnership is a contract for personal services and such contracts are not enforceable by specific performance. (But see *England* v *Curling* 1844.)[369]

The only real remedy in such a case is to dissolve the firm. (See further p. 251.)

An action for damages would seem to be possible if it is brought for a reason other than a breach of duty. Thus if A and B went into partnership and A agreed to acquire premises which he later refused to do, causing loss, B would seem to have a claim in damages, but not if A spent all day on the golf course, not getting business but leaving B to do all the work.

Dissolution of partnership

A partnership may be terminated in a number of ways.

DISSOLUTION WITHOUT A COURT ORDER

By expiration or notice

The partnership agreement often stipulates the duration of the partnership, e.g.—

(1) it shall last for a certain number of years and continue thereafter until one partner gives a certain length of notice to the other or others;

(2) it shall last for the life or lives of one or more partners;

(3) it shall be terminated by mutual agreement, in which case all must agree, although the death or bankruptcy of one also terminates it.

Such partnerships are not determinable by notice but only in accordance with the terms of the agreement. Section 32 of the Act (see below) does not apply.

Subject to such agreement, the 1890 Act provides that a partnership is dissolved—

(1) if entered into for a fixed term, by the expiration of the term;

(2) if entered into for a single adventure or undertaking by its completion;

(3) if entered into for an undefined time, by any partner giving notice to the other or others of his intention to dissolve the partnership, such notice operating from the date (if any) mentioned in the notice, or, if no date is mentioned, from the date of communication of the notice. (S.32.)

Where no fixed period has been agreed for the duration of the partnership, or where the partners carry on the business after the expiration of a fixed term of partnership without any express new agreement, the partnership is a *partnership at will*. In both cases it can be terminated by any partner at any time. (*Firth* v *Armslake* 1964.)[370] In the second case, while it continues, it is governed by the provisions of the former partnership agreement, except insofar as that agreement is inconsistent with a partnership at will. (S.27). A notice of dissolution in such circumstances cannot be withdrawn by the partner giving it.

By s.26(2) the notice must be in writing if the partnership articles are in the form of a deed, otherwise the Act does not require writing. There is no need to invoke the aid of the court unless some dispute or difficulty arises in the administration of the winding up.

Dissolution by bankruptcy, death or charge

Subject to any agreement between the partners, every partnership is dissolved as regards all the partners by the death or bankruptcy of any partner. (S.33(1).) Dissolution operates from the date of death or the commencement of bankruptcy. A partnership may, if the other partners wish it, be dissolved if any partner's share is charged to secure a separate judgment debt. (S.33(2).) Assignment does not effect an automatic dissolution, though it is probably a ground on which the court might be petitioned under s.35, i.e. just and equitable.

Dissolution by illegality

A partnership is in every case dissolved by the happening of any event which makes it unlawful for the business of the firm to be carried on, or for the members of the firm to carry it on in partnership. (S.34.) (*Stevenson* v *A.G. für Cartonnagen Industrie* 1918.)[257]

A modern example is to be found in the case of *Hudgell & Yeats & Co* v *Watson* [1978] 2 All E.R. 363. A firm of solicitors conducted litigation on behalf of a client and later sued for fees. One of the partners in the firm had failed to renew his practising certificate. The court held that this dissolved the firm under s.34 but the remaining partners must be regarded as a new firm arising by conduct. Since the partner who had not renewed his certificate had not taken part in the litigation work, the defendant owed the fees to the new firm which could successfully sue for them.

DISSOLUTION BY THE COURT

On application by a partner the court may decree a dissolution of the partnership in any of the following cases—

(1) Under the Mental Health Act 1983, s.96, where a partner is suffering from mental disorder;

(2) Under s.35 of the Partnership Act 1890, where a partner, *other than the partner suing,*—

(*a*) becomes permanently incapable, other than by mental disorder, of performing his part of the partnership contract; or

(*b*) has been guilty of misconduct in his business or private life likely to be harmful to the carrying on of the business. Thus in *Essell* v *Hayward* (1860) 30 Beav. 130, where one partner had become liable to a criminal prosecution for fraudulent breach of trust, it was held that his co-partner had a right to have the partnership dissolved although it was not a partnership at will. However, where the act has no direct connection with the firm's business, it is necessary to show that there has been some injury to the firm. Thus in *Snow* v *Milford* (1868) 16 W.R. 654 an action was brought under the articles of a banking partnership alleging that a banker partner's adultery with various persons in Exeter amounted to 'discredit or injury' of the firm. However, in the absence of evidence of injury to the firm the court held that there was no ground for dissolution, either under the articles of the general law, or

(*c*) wilfully or persistently commits a breach of the partnership agreement or makes it impracticable for the others to carry on the business in partnership with him. Examples of this are to be seen in *Cheeseman* v *Price* (1865) 35 Beav. 142 (keeping erroneous accounts), *De Berenger* v *Hamel* (1829) 7 Jar. & Blyth 25 ed. 2 (refusing to meet on business), *Baxter* v *West* (1858) 1 Dr. & Sm. 173 (continued quarrelling), *Anderson* v *Anderson* (1857) 25 Beav. 190 (father and son in partnership, father opening all son's letters). Ill temper or rudeness is not enough unless it interferes with the business.

(3) Under s.35, *ibid.*, where the business of the partnership can only be carried on at a loss. The court must be satisfied that the business losses are not merely temporary because if so a dissolution may not be ordered. (*Handyside* v *Campbell* (1901) 17 T.L.R. 623.);

(4) Under s.35, *ibid.*, where circumstances have arisen which, in the opinion of the court, render it just and equitable that the partnership be dissolved, e.g. where there is hostility between the partners. (*Re Yenidje Tobacco Co. Ltd* 1916.)[371]

(5) Under s.18 of the Banking Act 1979 the Bank of England may petition the court for the winding up of a recognized bank or licensed institution. On presentation of the petition the court may wind up such an institution if it is 'unable to pay sums due and payable to its depositors or is able to pay such sums only by defaulting on its obligations to its other creditors' or if 'the value of the institution's assets is less than the amount of its liabilities'. By reason of s.18(2) and (4) the court's jurisdiction extends to partnerships having fewer than eight members and also to limited partnerships.

Dissolution generally takes effect from the date of the court order.

Creditors cannot petition the court to dissolve the firm but can only proceed against the individual partners under the bankruptcy laws if the firm is not paying its debts. However, if the partnership has eight or more partners it can be wound up under the Companies Act 1948 and creditors can seek the winding up on the same general terms as they could if the partnership was a company. Section 398 of the Companies Act 1948 applies. By reason of s.399 of the 1948 Act the grounds for winding up include the situation where the partnership is unable to pay its debts and also where the court is of the opinion that it is just and equitable to be wound up. The winding-up proceedings are conducted in the same way as in the case of a company registered under the Companies Acts; even though this results in the assets being distributed in a manner different from the usual distribution under the 1890 Act and the Bankruptcy Act 1914.

Powers on dissolution

The partners possess certain rights and may exercise authority in certain respects for the purpose of winding up the firm.

NOTIFICATION

On the dissolution of a partnership or the retirement of a partner, any partner may publicly notify the same, and may require the other partner or partners to concur in all necessary or proper acts to achieve that purpose. (S.37.) (*Troughton* v *Hunter* 1854.)[372]

AUTHORITY OF PARTNERS AFTER WINDING UP

After the dissolution of the partnership the authority of each partner to bind the firm continues so far as may be necessary to wind up the affairs of the partnership and to complete transactions begun but unfinished at the date of dissolution. Partners will not bind the firm if they enter into new transactions after dissolution. (S.38.) (*Re Bourne* 1906.)[373] However, the firm is in no case bound by the acts of a partner who has become bankrupt unless the partners (1) have represented themselves, or (2) have knowingly allowed themselves to be represented, as still the partners of the bankrupt. (S.38.)

PARTNER'S LIEN FOR PROPER ADMINISTRATION

On the dissolution of a partnership every partner is entitled, as against his co-partners and all persons claiming through them (e.g. personal representatives or trustees in bankruptcy), to have the property of the partnership applied in payment of the debts and liabilities of the firm, and to have the surplus assets, after such payment, applied in payment of what may be due to the partners, after deducting any sums which the partners may owe the firm. In order to achieve this purpose, any partner or his representative may on the termination of the partnership apply to the court to wind up the business and affairs of the firm. (S.39.)

The section creates a lien which is in the nature of a personal right against co-partners and their representatives. The lien assists a partner in getting proper administration of the winding up, and prevents the assets from being used to pay the separate debts of the partners before the firm's debts. The lien created by s.39 does not allow a partner to sell the assets to third parties in the course of the winding up; it is merely a personal right against co-partners and their representatives to assist in obtaining proper administration.

APPORTIONMENT OF PREMIUMS

Where one partner has paid a premium to another on entering into a partnership for a fixed term, and the partnership is dissolved before the expiration of that term, the court may order the repayment of the premium or such part of it as it thinks just, having regard to the partnership agreement, the length of time the partnership has lasted and how long it had to run.

However, the court cannot order the return of any part of the premium if—

(1) the dissolution is, in the judgment of the court, wholly or chiefly due to the misconduct of the partner who paid the premium; or
(2) the partnership has been dissolved by an agreement containing no provision for the return of any part of the premium; or
(3) the dissolution is due to the death of a partner. (S.40.)

Treatment of assets on dissolution

In addition to the physical assets of the firm most partnerships have an asset called goodwill, i.e. a number of customers or clients who will probably continue to resort to the firm even if it changes hands. On dissolution these assets may be disposed of in the following ways—

THE FIRM MAY BE SOLD AS A GOING CONCERN

The firm may be sold as a going concern, either to outsiders or to the other partners who may have a right under the agreement to acquire it. Where the firm is sold as a going concern, goodwill is an asset and the purchaser of the firm may use the firm name and restrain outgoing partners from using it or from soliciting their former customers. The value of goodwill is allocated among the partners according to the terms of the dissolution agreement, e.g. ratio of capitals, and, in the absence of agreement, must be sold. (*Pawsey* v *Armstrong* (1881) 18 Ch. D. 698.)

Goodwill is a word which is difficult to define. In *Cruttwell* v *Lye* (1810) 17 Ves. 335, Lord Eldon said that it was no more than the probability that old customers would resort to the old place. However, it can exist independently of location or place. Sir Arthur Underhill said that it was 'the public approbation which has been won by the business, and that, considered as a marketable thing, it is the probability of the customers of the firm resorting to the persons (or person) who succeed to the business as a going concern'. Sometimes it will depend on a particular *situation*, e.g. an hotel overlooking Windermere, or the *quality* of goods as with a Savile Row tailor or their *cheapness*, as in the case of a supermarket, or *reputation* for a certain class of article, e.g. a Dunhill pipe.

Furthermore, Sir George Jessel said in *Ginesi* v *Cooper* (1880) 14 Ch. D. 596: 'it is a connection formed by years of work', or, in the words or Lord Lindley, it is 'a benefit arising from connection and reputation'.

In *Trego* v *Hunt* [1896] A.C. 7 the House of Lords decided that the rule of goodwill does not prevent the partners from carrying on a competing business with the purchaser. They can be prevented by injunction from actually soliciting old customers and from representing to the world that they are carrying on the actual business sold. However, the fact that they can compete does affect the value of a firm's goodwill.

The partnership agreement may provide that *on retirement of a partner* the goodwill shall accrue to the continuing partners, though there may be no restriction on the retiring partner setting up practice or going into business again. Where this is so the customers or clients of the firm cannot be circularized in a way which could be regarded as soliciting. In *Fulwell* v *Bragg, The Times*, 6 January 1983 it was held, in the case of a firm of solicitors, that on retirement of a partner only three types of client could be circularized with notice of his retirement, i.e. (1) those for whom he was currently acting; (2) those who normally consulted him; and (3) those for whom he was executor in regard to wills deposited with the firm.

It may also be necessary in professional practices to have regard to any advertising guidelines which a particular professional body may have produced.

THE ASSETS MAY BE DIVIDED AMONG THE PARTNERS *IN SPECIE*

In this case the goodwill of the business disappears and the partners take the assets forming their own particular share in accordance with their agreement, subject to cash adjustments if the values of the assets taken do not correspond precisely with the shares due to each partner. Where the assets are divided in this way there is no goodwill left, and any partner may use the firm name so long as he does not involve his former partners in liability for the debts of the new business.

If the partners agree on a division *in specie* in general terms but ultimately cannot agree on the price disposition of the physical assets, the court will order the business to be sold and if it is sold as an entity, goodwill will once again form one of the assets.

APPLICATION OF ASSETS ON DISSOLUTION

Unless there is a contrary agreement between the partners, the assets are applied as follows—

(1) in paying the debts and liabilities of the firm to persons who are not partners therein, i.e. secured and unsecured creditors;

(2) in paying to each partner rateably what is due from the firm to him for advances as distinct from capital;

(3) The costs of winding up. (*Potter* v *Jackson* (1880) 13 Ch. D. 845.);

(4) in paying each partner what is due to him in respect of capital;

(5) the ultimate residue, if any, to be divided among the partners in the proportion in which profits were divisible. (S.44(*b*).) This is protected by a lien for proper distribution under s.39.

If the assets are not sufficient to satisfy the creditors, partners advances and repayment of capital, the deficiency is to be made up—

(*a*) out of profits (if any) brought forward from previous years, though such reserves would not often exist today;

(*b*) out of partners' capital;

(*c*) by the partners individually in the proportion in which they were entitled to share profits. (S.44(*a*).) The profit-sharing ratio applies even though one partner has put more capital in than another. (*Nowell* v *Nowell* (1869) L.R. 7 Eq. 538.)

PARTNER'S INSOLVENCY ON DISSOLUTION

Where a partner is insolvent and the firm's assets are not sufficent to repay the creditors and partners' advances, this deficiency must be borne by the solvent co-partners in the ratio in which they were entitled to share profits.

Where the assets of the firm are more than sufficient to pay the firm's creditors and partners' advances, but are not sufficient to repay the partners' capitals, then each partner must contribute to this deficiency in the proporation in which he shares profits and losses. However, where a partner is insolvent and cannot pay in his share of the deficiency, the other partners need only pay in their own share. (*Garner* v *Murray* 1904.)[374] The effect of the Rule in *Garner* v *Murray* is that the solvent partners pay in their share of the loss in the profit-sharing ratio and receive whatever capital there is after this in proportion to their last agreed capital ratios.

Suppose A, B and C are partners whose last agreed capitals were £6000, £4000 and £700 respectively and who agreed to share profits and losses equally. After the creditors had been paid off there was a fund left of £8000, leaving a deficiency of £2700 on capital. Each partner must, therefore, contribute £900. However, if C is insolvent and can pay nothing, he will lose his right to a repayment of his capital of £700. A and B will each notionally pay in £900, i.e. one-third of £2700. This will make up a capital fund of £8000 plus £1800 equals £9800. A and B share this in capital ratio, i.e. 6/10ths (A) and 4/10th (B) equals A: £5880; B: £3920. Having reached these figures it would be pointless for A and B to pay in £900 each and then draw it out, so of the £8000 remaining, A gets £5880 less £900 equals £4980, and B £3920 less £900 equals £3020. C receives nothing.

It should be noted that if the assets only realize sufficient money to repay or partly repay partners' advances, then the loss will fall upon the solvent partners in the proportion of their advances because the money obtained from the assets does not go far enough to pay off capital.

PROFITS MADE AFTER DISSOLUTION BUT BEFORE WINDING UP

Sometimes, after the dissolution of the firm or the retirement of one of the partners, the surviving or continuing partners carry on the business of the firm with its capital or assets without any final settlement of accounts as between the firm and the outgoing partner or his estate. In the absence of any agreement to the contrary, the outgoing partner or his estate is entitled at the option of himself or his representatives—

(1) to such share of the profits made since the dissolution as the court may find to be attributable to the use of his share of the partnership assets (*Pathirana* v *Pathirana* 1966),[365] or

(2) to interest at 5 per cent per annum on the amount of his share of the partnership assets. (S.42(1).) (*Barclays Bank Trust Co Ltd* v *Bluff* 1981.)[315]

Thus the outgoing partner is not entitled to the same proportion of the profits as he was when the firm existed, and the court has discretion as to the amount to be awarded. If the post-dissolution profits have, in the opinion of the court, been earned mainly by the skilful management of the continuing partners and not from the use of the outgoing partner's capital, the court will exclude such profits when ascertaining what is due to the outgoing partner. (*Manley* v *Sartori* 1927.)[376]

However, where by the partnership agreement an option is given to surviving or continuing partners to purchase the interest of a deceased or outgoing partner, and that option is duly exercised, the estate of the deceased partner, or the outgoing partner or his estate, as the case may be, is not entitled to any further share of the profits. But if the person exercising the option does not comply with its material terms, or does not exercise it within the time allowed, he is liable to account for a proporation of the post-dissolution profits. (S.42(2).)

RESCISSION OF PARTNERSHIP AGREEMENT

Where a partnership agreement is rescinded on the grounds of the fraud or misrepresentation of one of the parties to it, the person entitled to rescind is entitled under s.41—

(1) to a lien on the surplus assets of the firm after the firm's liabilities have been paid for any sum of money paid by him for the purchase of a share in the partnership and for any surplus capital contributed by him;

(2) to be subrogated to the rights of the creditors of the firm for any payment made by him in respect of the firm's liabilities;

(3) to be indemnified by the person guilty of the fraud or making the misrepresentation against all the debts and liabilities of the firm. The right to contribution is excluded by fraud or misrepresentation, as where a person induces another by a false or fraudulent representation to join him in partnership. In such a situation the person defrauded has, as we have seen, a right to rescind the contract of partnership and as between himself and the co-partner to throw all the partnership losses on to the co-partner alone.

The object of this section is to give the partner rescinding as much assistance as possible to get his capital back. An order of rescission, unlike a judgment for debt, does not allow the person who is given the order a right to levy execution on the property of the person subject to the order. The latter is merely bound in equity to hand the money over or face a fine or imprisonment for contempt of court if he does not. Section 41 gives various rights to an ex-partner to get a writ of execution (as where he sues under subrogation) and to use his lien to prevent distribution of assets until he has had his capital.

Bankruptcy of partners

The following effects flow from a partner's bankruptcy.

BANKRUPTCY OF ONE PARTNER

This will, in the absence of any agreement to the contrary, dissolve the partnership leaving the administration of the dissolution in the hands of the other partners. (S.38.)

BANKRUPTCY OF ALL PARTNERS

A receiving order may be made against the firm but it acts as a receiving order against each partner. The firm must present a statement of affairs and each partner must also submit a statement regarding his separate estate. The adjudication order is made against the partners individually and not against the firm. The first meeting of creditors consists of the joint creditors and of each partner's private creditors. Each estate is entitled to appoint a committee of inspection but the joint creditors appoint the trustee.

APPLICATION OF THE PARTNERSHIP ESTATE

The firm's property is called the *joint estate* and the separate property of each partner is called the *separate estate*. The principle applied is that the joint estate is used to pay the debts of the firm and each partner's separate estate is applied in payment of his private debts. If there is a surplus on a separate estate, it is transferred to the joint estate should that estate be insufficient. Suppose P and Q are partners and the firm has debts of £1000 and assets totalling £800. P has private means of £300 and debts of £600; Q has £500 and has debts of £400. P's creditors will get 50p in the £ and there will be no surplus for the creditors of the firm. Q can pay of his debts in full, and the surplus of £100 will be available for the firm's creditors.

If there is a surplus on the joint estate, it is transferred to the separate estates of the partners in a ratio based on each partner's capital in the firm.

The following special cases are worthy of note—

(1) If a partner has fraudulently used partnership property for private

purposes, the joint estate may prove against the fraudulent partner's separate estate in *equal competition* with the separate creditors.

(2) A firm creditor whose debt was the result of a fraud by a partner or partners has an *election*. He may prove *either* against the firm *or* against the separate estates of the partner or partners guilty of the fraud.

(3) It is also possible for one estate to prove against another where a partner also carries on an independent business and debts have been incurred in the course of trading between that business and the partnership.

(4) If there is no joint estate and no solvent partner, the firm creditors can prove against the separate estates equally with the separate creditors, but partners cannot compete with the firm's creditors against either the joint or separate estates.

A partner can, however, prove in the separate estate of another partner—

(*a*) where the firm's creditors have been paid off; or

(*b*) where the separate estate of a partner is not enough to pay his separate debts in full. Here the firm's creditors are not prejudiced because there would have been no surplus to come to them in any event.

X and Y are partners and Y is insolvent having creditors amounting to £900 as well as owing £100 to X on a private matter. If Y's assets are £500 there is no reason why X should not prove for the £100, since if he abstains the creditors of the partnership will get nothing, X would merely lose £50 and Y's separate creditors would get a slightly larger dividend.

SECURED CREDITORS

The position is as follows—

(1) A creditor of the firm with a security on the separate property of a partner may prove against the joint estate and need not give up the security against the separate estate.

(2) A partner's separate creditor who has a security on the partnership property may prove against the separate estate and need not give up the security on the joint estate.

In neither case may the creditor, by the exercise of both rights, receive more than the full amount of his debt.

Limited partnerships

The Limited Partnerships Act 1907 provides for the formation of limited partnerships in which one or more of the partners has only limited liability for the firm's debts. Such partnerships are not common because in most cases the objective desired may be better achieved by incorporation as a private company, though the ever-growing restrictions on directors of companies in terms of loans and property dealings with their companies may make the partnership more popular.

A limited partnership is not a persona at law or legal entity and must not have more than 20 members, though this provision does not apply to limited partnerships of solicitors, accountants or stockbrokers among others. (Companies Act 1967, s.120(1), see p. 217.) There must also be one general partner whose liability for the debts of the firm is unlimited. A body corporate may nevertheless be a limited partner.

REGISTRATION

Every limited partnership must be registered with the Registrar of Joint Stock Companies. The following particulars must be registered by means of a statement signed by the partners—

(1) the firm name;
(2) the general nature of the business;
(3) the principal place of business;
(4) the full name of each partner;
(5) the date of commencement and the term of the partnership, if any;
(6) a statement that it is a limited partnership;
(7) particulars of each limited partner and the amount contributed by him whether in cash or otherwise.

Any change in the above particulars, or the fact that a general partner becomes a limited partner, must be notified to the Registrar within seven days. Failure to register means that a limited partner is fully liable as a general partner. When a general partner becomes a limited partner, or an assignment of a limited partner's share is made to another person, the fact must be advertised in the *London Gazette* if the transactions are to be effective in law.

The Register of Limited Partnerships is open to inspection by the public who may also obtain certified copies of, or extracts from, any registered statement.

RIGHTS AND DUTIES OF LIMITED PARTNERS

(1) *In relation to the unlimited partners.* A limited partner has no right to take part in the management of the firm and is in effect a dormant partner. Indeed, if he does manage the firm he becomes liable for all debts and liabilities incurred by the firm during that period. Nevertheless, he may give advice on management to the other partners and he may also inspect the books. As in the case of salaried partner, the death, bankruptcy, or mental disorder of the limited partner does not dissolve the firm, nor is his consent required for the admission of a new partner, nor can he dissolve the firm by notice. However, changes in the nature

of the partnership business require the agreement of all general or limited partners.

In addition, while a limited partner is entitled to an equal share of profit, unless there is an agreement to the contrary, he is not liable for losses including deficiences of capital beyond the amount of capital which he has agreed to contribute.

(2) In relation to customers of the firm. A limited partner cannot bind the firm by reason of s.6(1) of the Limited Partnerships Act 1907. For this reason, customers of the firm cannot safely deal with a limited partner in terms of business transactions in which, in any case, a limited partner would not normally engage.

Even these days, when the names of all partners must be displayed in various ways so that the public knows of them, s.6(1) would presumably override s.5 of the 1890 Act and rule out the apparent authority principles in terms of limited partners.

(3) *In relation to creditors.* A limited partner is not liable for the debts of the firm beyond the capital he has agreed to contribute, provided he takes no part in managament and provided the firm is registered under the Limited Partnerships Act of 1907. If he withdraws his capital he would still be liable to the firm's creditors up to the mount of capital he originally agreed to subscribe.

7 Cheques and banking law

Negotiability

MEANING OF NEGOTIABILITY

Items of property are transferable physically from one person to another but ownership cannot pass unless a good title accompanies the physical transfer.

A good title will not pass if the person who owns the property did not consent in any way to its transfer. Thus, if B's car is stolen by T so that there is no consent of any kind by B to the transfer of the property and T sells the car to C then C does not get a good title, even though he takes in good faith and for value without knowledge of the theft. B can recover the car from C or sue T or C for damages in conversion. If, on the other hand, T obtains B's car by fraud as where he offers a cheque for the car and the cheque is not met, then if T subsequently sells the car to C, C obtains a good title because B did consent to the transfer, though no doubt he afterwards regretted it.

Certain items of property referred to as negotiable instruments are capable of transfer with a good title even where the true owner does not consent in any way to the transfer. These items of property were created by the custom of merchants in years past but are now recognized by statute, i.e. the Bills of Exchange Act 1882 and the Cheques Act 1957.

TYPES OF NEGOTIABLE INSTRUMENTS

There are a number of different types of negotiable instruments. For example, bank notes, bankers drafts, dividend warrants and treasury bills are negotiable. However, we are concerned mainly with cheques and not with other bills of exchange or promissory notes. Cheques are to a large extent governed by the Bills of Exchange Act 1882, and all section references are, unless otherwise stated, to sections of that Act.

NEGOTIABILITY FOLLOWING THEFT—A RESTRICTED CONCEPT

While it is true to say that the attribute of negotiability allows a person to obtain a good title to a negotiable instrument from a thief, the concept of negotiability after a theft is very restricted and applies in practice only to bearer bills. Before an instrument can be negotiated in such a way as to give the transferee a better title than the transferor it must be in a negotiable state. A bearer bill is in a negotiable state without endorsement. However, since most cheques are order cheques payable to the order of a particular person, they are not in a negotiable state unless they are endorsed. If, therefore, they are stolen, they can only be passed on without endorsement or by means of a forged endorsement and in both these instances the transferee will not get a good title even if he takes for value with no notice of defects in the title of the transferor.

For example, if T steals a bearer cheque from A and transfers it to B for value, B having no notice of the theft, then B's title will be good. If, however, the cheque was made payable to A, B's title will be incomplete because he will either take the cheque without an endorsement or as a result of T forging A's endorsement and in either event B's title will be affected adversely. A forged endorsement does not pass on the drawer's promise to pay 'to order' under s.55 of the 1882 Act.

Examples of use of bills and cheques

BILLS OF EXCHANGE

Bills of exchange are not frequently used now except in foreign trade. However, their two main uses are as follows—

(1) *A tripartite transaction with credit.* C. Jones Ltd in London has sold goods worth £1000 to A. Ziegler in Amsterdam, payment to be in sterling. C. Jones Ltd owes £1000 to C. Poutier in Paris. Jones draws a bill on Ziegler payable to Poutier.

£1000 London, 1 July 1985

Three months after date pay to C. Poutier or order the sum of One Thousand Pounds, value received.

To A. Ziegler,
Polskistraat, Amsterdam. C. Jones Ltd

If Ziegler accepts, Poutier may keep the bill for three months and ask Ziegler to pay or he may discount it at a bank or endorse it over to pay a debt or, more likely, part of a debt which he owes to one of his creditors.

(2) *Solely to obtain credit.* A. Adams Ltd has sold goods to B. Brown Ltd. Adams Ltd wants prompt payment; Brown Ltd wants four months' credit. Adams draws a bill on Brown payable at four months which Brown accepts.

£300.00 London, 7 July 1985

Four months after date pay to our order the sum of Three Hundred Pounds, value received.

To B. Brown Ltd
3 High Street, Barchester. A. Adams Ltd

Adams may discount the bill at a bank for, say, £285. The bank will wait four months and then obtain payment from Brown.

CHEQUES

A cheque is a bill of exchange, but the following differences should be noted—

(1) the drawee is always a bank, and there is no need for a cheque to be accepted;

(2) a cheque is payable on demand (s.73);

(3) there is no indication on the face of a cheque as to the date on which it is payable, but s.10(1) of the Bills of Exchange Act 1882 says that a bill is payable on demand if no time is stated, and for this reason a cheque is payable on demand, unless post-dated. The treatment of such cheques is further considered on p. 279.

Barchester Bank Ltd, High Street Branch. 2 July 1985

Pay John Smith or order Two Hundred Pounds. £200.00

William Brown

In the example given above John Smith may cash the cheque at the Barchester Bank, High Street Branch, or pay it into his own bank for collection or endorse it over to someone else.

As we have seen, bills of exchange proper are used mainly in export transactions and as such have little relevance, except in that rather specialized field. In addition, many practitioners in the field of business will conclude their careers without ever having seen a promissory note, other than a bank note. For these reasons the rest of this chapter interprets legislation relating to negotiable instruments in terms of the cheque, referring to bills of exchange proper only where it is necessary in order to understand the law relating to cheques.

THE USEFULNESS OF AN ACTION ON A CHEQUE

It should be borne in mind throughout this chapter that if a cheque is dishonoured then, unless it was a gift, e.g. a birthday present, the holder may at his option sue upon the cheque or upon the consideration, i.e. the underlying contract. Thus in a sale of goods, if the buyer gives the seller a cheque and that cheque is not met, the seller can sue either on the cheque or upon the contract of sale under which he is entitled to cash (legal tender).

It is advisable to sue upon the cheque (1) because it makes the debt certain—it is a promise to pay a sum certain in money; (2) the cheque provides good evidence of the promise to pay; and (3) the defendant to an action on a cheque may not normally set up a counterclaim. He must pay the cheque in full and bring a separate action if he has any complaint, e.g. about the quality of goods supplied in exchange for which he gave the cheque. (See *Jade International Steel* v *Robert Nicholas (Steels)* 1978, p. 553.)

Statutory definition

A cheque is a bill of exhange drawn on a banker and payable on demand. As such it must comply with certain aspects of the definition of a bill of exchange.

The definition given in the Bills of Exchange Act 1882, s.3(1), is as follows—

> 'A bill of exchange is an unconditional order in writing, addressed by one person to another, signed by the person giving it, requiring the person to whom it is addressed to pay on demand or at a fixed or determinable future time a sum certain in money to or to the order of a specified person, or to bearer.'

This definition must be analysed in some detail because any instrument which does not comply with the relevant aspects of it cannot be a cheque. If it is not, the concept of negotiability does not apply to it and certain protections given to bankers who pay out or collect instruments to or on behalf of persons who have no title would not apply.

UNCONDITIONAL ORDER

An order to pay is not a cheque if it is conditional on a certain event happening or a certain thing being done. Problems have arisen in the following areas—

(1) *Receipts on cheques.* Some cheques contain a form of receipt together with a form of words indicating that it must be signed by the payee. If it appears that the instruction that the receipt must be signed is *directed to the banker*, the instrument is conditionalal and cannot be a cheque. If the instruction to sign the receipt is *addressed to the payee* and not the bank the cheque is an unconditional instrument. (*Bavins* v *London and South Western Bank* 1900[377] and *Nathan* v *Ogdens* 1906.)[378]

However, bankers usually obtain an indemnity from customers having receipt forms on their cheques. This indemnity protects the bank if it incorrectly treats an instrument requiring a receipt as a cheque, although the bank should be protected by the Cheques Act 1957. (See below.)

It should be noted that receipts on the backs of cheques are not common now because of s.3 of the Cheques Act 1957, which provides than an unendorsed cheque which appears to have been paid by the banker on whom it is drawn is evidence of receipt by the payee of the sum payable by the cheque. In addition, where receipts are used they must, by reason of banking practice, carry a large 'R' on the face because bankers are not required to look for endorsements on cheques under the Cheques Act 1957. Furthermore, if an unconditional instrument was not regarded as a cheque a banker should still be protected by ss.1, 4 and 5 of the Cheques Act 1957, since these sections protect a banker who collects an instrument which is not a cheque or pays an instrument which is not.

(2) *Special accounts.* An order to pay out of a particular fund and that fund only is not unconditional. However, an unqualified order to pay coupled with an indication of a particular fund out of which the money is to come is unconditional. (S.3(3) of the 1882 Act.) Thus a cheque is perfectly good although there is an indication on it that one particular account rather than another should be debited with the amount. Thus the cheque may, for example, be overstamped 'client account' or 'No. 2 account' but this will not render the cheque a conditional order provided it is clear that the payee is to be paid anyway, even if the particular account is not large enough.

WRITING

The Act provides that 'writing' includes print. (S.2.)

ONE PERSON TO ANOTHER

The drawer and drawee are usually different persons, e.g. the customer (drawer) and a bank (drawee) but they may be the same person. The commonest example is a *banker's draft.* This is an order by the bank addressed to itself in favour, for example, of the vendor of property, the purchaser being the bank's customer whose account the bank has already debited. This kind of draft is a safer method of payment from the vendor's point of view than a cheque signed only by the purchaser which may not be honoured. Under s.5(2) such a draft is negotiable as a bill of exchange or promissory note.

SIGNATURE

A 'signature' is not defined in the Act but it would seem to permit a mechanically produced signature, and certainly a mark may be used if there is evidence that the person signing by mark habitually so signs. A bank will take an indemnity from a customer using cheques which bear a printed facsimile reproduction of an official signature.

Under s.23(2) no person is liable as drawer, indorser, or acceptor of a bill who has not signed it as such: provided that the signature of the name of a firm is equivalent to the signature by the person so signing of the names of all persons liable as partners in that firm. It is quite usual for a partner to sign on behalf of all the partners by writing the name of the partnership, e.g. 'Bloggs & Co.'. (And see *Ringham* v *Hackett* 1980.)[352]

ON DEMAND

This is dealt with by s.10(1) which provides, amongst other things, that a bill is payable on demand if no time for payment is stated. It has already been noted that a cheque contains no specific indication that it is payable on demand but is so payable by reason of this sub-section, unless post-dated.

SUM CERTAIN IN MONEY

This is dealt with by s.9 and its main relevance in practice is where the words and figures on a cheque are different. In such a case the words prevail and are taken to be the sum payable. in practice, however, bankers usually return such cheques with the comment 'words and figures differ'.

TO OR TO THE ORDER OF A SPECIFIED PERSON

Sections 7 and 8 of the Act apply here and the main points arising are as follows—

(1) Joint payees. Payment may be to A and B (as joint payees) as where A and B are partners.

(2) A cheque may be payable in the alternative to one of two or more payees, e.g. 'Pay A or B'. This form is not usual in the UK, but in some jurisdictions, e.g. the USA where married persons have had separate bank accounts for much longer than perhaps is the case in the UK, the alternative form is more common, e.g. a US public utility, such as a gas company, may in making a refund for an overpayment, send a cheque in the alternative form, payment being to the husband or wife. Either party can then pay that cheque into their own account as they decide.

(3) Holders of offices. A bill may also be payable to the holder of an office for the time being, e.g. 'The Treasurer of Barchester Football Club'.

(4) Payments to wages or cash. Instruments made out in a form 'pay wages' or 'pay cash' are not payable to a specified person and cannot be regarded as cheques. Such an instrument is not therefore negotiable but it is, under the Cheques Act 1957 a mandate to the bank concerned to pay unless countermanded. Thus, unless the instrument is countermanded by the drawer the bank may properly pay out on it and debit the drawer's account. (*Orbit Mining & Trading Co. Ltd* v *Westminster Bank* 1962.)[379]

'OR ORDER' ASSUMED

By s.8 such directions on a bill as 'Pay C' or 'Pay C or order' all have the same meaning and amount to a direction to pay C or the person to whom the instrument is subsequently transferred. Therefore merely crossing out the words 'or order' does not render a cheque not-transferable or not-negotiable.

INSTRUMENTS MARKED 'NOT TRANSFERABLE'

By s.8 these are valid as between the parties only. The same is true of an instrument which is drawn in favour of 'C only'. If such a cheque is endorsed by C to D then D cannot sue upon it. However, D will normally have an action on the underlying contract, e.g. a sale of goods, which gave rise to the transfer of the cheque.

INSTRUMENTS MARKED 'NOT NEGOTIABLE'

Where this appears on a cheque the results is that the *cheque is transferable* but subject to equities, i.e. to defects in title of previous holders. Thus a person who takes a cheque crossed 'not negotiable' does not acquire and cannot give a better title to it than that of the person from whom he received it.

'TO BEARER'

By the provisions of s.8(3) a bearer cheque is a cheque payable to bearer or one on which the only or last endorsement is in blank. The following points should be noted—

(1) *Bearer cheques generally.* These do not require endorsement and are transferred by delivery. Bearer cheques can be converted into order cheques by an appropriate endorsement, e.g. 'Pay C or order', and converted back to bearer cheques again by an appropriate endorsement, e.g. the signature of the endorsee without more.

(2) *Non-existing payees.* Section 7(3) provides that where the payee is a non-existing person the cheque is to be treated as payable to bearer. Thus forged or unauthorized endorsements are irrelevant and a good title can pass under a forged or unauthorized endorsement to a *bona fide* third party who takes the instrument for value. The judicial interpretation of this section is as follows—

(*a*) The payee is *existing* when the drawer knows of him an intends that he should receive payment. (See *Vinden* v *Hughes* 1950.)[380]

(*b*) The payee is *non-existing* when the drawer does not know of him through a person with that name may exist. (*Clutton* v *Attenborough* 1879.)[381]

The basis of the above provision is that the drawer is negligent when he signs a cheque in the non-existing payee situation, and a *bona fide* third party for value is protected against that negligence because the Act converts the cheque into a bearer bill to which a good title can pass, forged or unauthorized endorsements being irrelevant.

Negotiation

Negotiation takes place where there is a transfer of a cheque from A to B in such a way as to make B the holder. (S.31.)

In the case of a bearer cheque this is achieved by simple delivery and in the case of an order cheque by means of endorsement plus delivery. Thus the holder of a bearer cheque is the person in possession of it, even a thief, while the holder of an order cheque must be in possession of it either as payee or endorsee.

RESTRICTIVE ENDORSEMENTS

A restrictive endorsement makes the endorsee a holder, but for certain limited or restricted purposes only.

There are two types of restrictive endorsements as follows—

(1) Where further negotiation is prohibited, i.e. 'pay D only'. Cheques are seldom endorsed like this.

(2) Where negotiation is permitted but with mere authority to deal as directed, e.g. 'pay D for the account of Y' or 'Pay D or order for collection'. Examples of the use of the above restrictive endorsements are as follows—

(*a*) X, the payee of a cheque, owes a debt to an overseas supplier B, and wants to endorse the cheque to B's agent, A, who is in England but wishes to make it clear that A is not the beneficial owner of the cheque. X can endorse 'Pay A for the account of B'. A can now obtain payment but must then account to B, though A cannot transfer the bill.

(*b*) Suppose X is the payee of a cheque drawn on a German bank and wishes A, his German agent, to collect payment for him. X can endorse 'Pay A for collection' or 'Pay A or order for collection'. A can obtain payment but must then account to X who authorized him to collect. Where the words 'or order' are used, A can transfer the cheque to another person but such person cannot obtain a better title than A because A's ownership is restricted and these restrictions pass with the cheque. It is therefore unlikely that a cheque so endorsed would ever be taken, say, for goods supplied. The use of the words 'or order' might, however, be useful where A was known to have sub-agents and make collection through them. In these circumstances

A may be given the power to endorse over a particular sub-agent for collection.

HOLDER OF A BILL

It should be noted that a holder of a bill is *not necessarily the person who is legally entitled to it*. Thus a thief who steals a bearer cheque is a person in possession and therefore a holder, though obviously he has no title to the cheque and cannot sue upon it.

However, if he delivers it to D who takes in good faith and for value, then D will get a good title. (S.38(3)(*a*).) But if D knows of the theft and is not in good faith or does not give value or both, then his title is no better than the thief's.

This arises because where there is a 'defect' on the cheque as where it has been stolen or obtained by fraud or undue influence, then no one can sue upon it and obtain its face value unless he has taken it in good faith for value and without knowledge of previous defects. (See further p. 271.)

HOLDER FOR VALUE: CONSIDERATION

Section 27 deals with the matter of consideration sufficient to support a bill as follows—

(1) Section 27(1)(*a*) provides that any consideration sufficient to support a simple contract will support a bill of exchange. (*Pollway Ltd* v *Abdullah* 1974.)[382]

(2) Section 27(1)(*b*) provides that a form of *past considerations*, i.e. an antecedent debt or liability is enough. This is essential, particularly in the case of cheques, many of which are based on this form of past consideration. Thus if S sells goods to B a debt comes into being when the contract is made so that when B decides to pay S by cheque the cheque is based on a previous or antecedent debt or liability and is for past consideration. However, if in *Re McArdle* 1951[27] Mrs McArdle had received a cheque from the estate she would not have succeeded in an action on the cheque because there was no antecedent debt or liability.

(3) Section 27(2) provides that *consideration need not have moved from the holder* so that the doctrine of privity of contract does not apply. Therefore, if P signs a cheque in favour of Q for the price of goods sold by Q to P and Q endorses the cheques to R as a gift, R may not sue Q on the cheque, but he may sue P, since R is a holder for value to that extent under s.27(2). As between immediate parties absence of consideration prevents an action on the bill.

Consideration must exist, but it is not essential that consideration has passed from one party to a cheque to another party on the *same* cheque. (See *Diamond* v *Graham* 1968.)[383] But it must if the holder relies on past consideration. (See *Oliver* v *Davis* 1949.)[384]

HOLDER IN DUE COURSE

If there is no 'defect' on a cheque the holder can claim its full face value merely by being a holder for value within s.27.

If there is a 'defect' on a cheque it is not enough to be a holder for value, and in order to claim its full face value the holder must show that he is either—

(1) a holder in due course under s.29(1), or

(2) a person who has taken the bill through a holder in due course under s.29(3).

Thus, if a cheque drawn in favour of C has been negotiated by C to D as a result of fraud or misrepresentation or duress or undue influence on D's part or for an illegal consideration, there is a 'defect' on the bill. Let us then suppose that D negotiates it for value to E. E will undoubtedly be a holder for value, but because there is a 'defect' on the cheque E can only take it free from the defect in the title of D and successfully sue on it if he is a holder in due course, which means amongst other things that he took it without notice of any defect in the title of D.

If it is established that E is a holder in due course then the defect is said to 'cured' and E can sue the various parties to the cheque for its full face value. Further, if E subsequently negotiated the cheque to F, then even though F himself may not be a holder indue course because, say, he gave no value and/or had notice of the defect in the title of D, then provided F was not a party to any fraud or illegality affecting the cheque, he has all the rights of a holder in due course as regards the drawer and all endorsers prior to the holder in due course from whom he took the cheque. (S.29(3).) A person taking from F will not be a holder in due course unless he can satisfy the definition in s.29(1) himself.

Section 29(3) is the most cogent illustration of the favoured position which the holder in due course occupies. If the subsection did not exist the holder in due course might be prejudiced, for in order to dispose of a cheque with a defect upon it, he would have to find a transferee who knew nothing of the irregularity. The subsection makes this unnecessary.

A modern example of the use of s.29(3) is to be seen in *Jade International Steel* v *Robert Nicholas (Steels)* 1978.[385]

HOLDER IN DUE COURSE: DEFINITION

Section 29(1) provides that a holder in due course is a holder who has taken a cheque, complete and regular on the face of it, under the following conditions; namely—

> that he became the holder of it before it was overdue and without notice that it had been previously dishonoured if such was the fact; that he took the cheque in good faith and for value; and that at the

time that the cheque was negotiated to him he had no notice of any defect in the title of the person who negotiated it to him.

This important definition is analysed as follows—

(1) *Complete and regular on the face of it.* If someone takes a cheque which is lacking or defective in any material particular, e.g. as where the amount or the payee's name is omitted or appears to have been materially altered, or the endorsement and the payee's name do not match he cannot be a holder in due course. (*Arab Bank* v *Ross* 1952.)[386]

(2) *Before it was overdue.* A bill payable on demand is deemed to be overdue when it appears on the face of it to have been in circulation for an unreasonable length of time. What is an unreasonable length of time for this purpose is a question of fact. (S.36(3).) In the case of a cheque and in the absence of special circumstances. 10 days or so would normally be held to be the limit. (Paget's *Law of Banking*.)

If a cheque is overdue it is still valid and can be transferred but the transferee obtains no better title than the transferor since no one can be a holder in due course after a bill is overdue.

The rules relating to overdue cheques should be distinguished from those which relate to out-of-date cheques which a bank will not pay. (See p. 276.)

(3) *Without notice that it had previously been dishonoured if such was the fact.* If a cheque is dishonoured by non-payment a subsequent holder can only be a holder in due course if he had no notice of the dishonour. Subsequent holders with notice of dishonour take the bill subject to defects in title at the time of dishonour. (S.36(5).)

It would be difficult for an endorsee to suggest that he had taken a dishonoured cheque without notice. Cheques are dishonoured for two main reasons as follows—

(*a*) that the drawer has no funds in the sense of cash in his account or an agreed overdraft; or

(*b*) that the drawer has stopped payment.

In each case the bank will return the cheque to the holder marked 'refer to drawer'. If the cheque was then put back into circulation by the holder and endorsed over to another person, the endorsee could hardly claim that he had no notice of dishonour and therefore would not be a holder in due course.

(4) *For value.* A holder in due course must give value *himself*, but as we have seen past consideration in the form of an antecedent debt or liability is enough.

(5) *In good faith and without notice of any defect in the title of the person who negotiated it.* Notice means actual knowledge or wilful disregard of the means of knowledge. (*Sheffield (Earl)* v *London Joint Stock Bank* 1888.)[387]

The original payee of an order cheque cannot be a holder in due course because the cheque is *issued* to him and not *negotiated* to him, and the concept of holder in due course arises only when the cheque is negotiated by the payee to the first endorsee who may be a holder in due course.

Thus if the fraud of X causes A to draw a cheque in favour of C, A has a good defence to a claim by C, though C is innocent of X's fraud. (*Jones* v *Waring and Gillow* 1926.)[388] A would not, however, have a good defence to claim on the cheque made by any subsequent holder of it provided he had no knowledge of the fraud and was in all other respects a holder in due course.

THE EFFECT OF A FORGED OR UNAUTHORIZED ENDORSEMENT

By s.24 a *forged endorsement* is wholly inoperative and no title passes even to a person who would in other circumstances be a holder in due course. However, there may be rights against those taking after the forgery by reason of s.55(2).

Suppose a cheque is drawn by X in favour of C and endorsed by C to D. It is then stolen from D by a thief who forges D's endorsement and negotiates the cheque to E who endorses it to F, who endorses it to G. G has no knowledge of the forgery and in all respects complies with the definition of a holder in due course in s.29. G has no title to the cheque because it rests on a forgery. He cannot, therefore, sue D or C, but he has rights against E or F by virtue of s.55(2). When E endorsed the cheque to F he impliedly guaranteed that it was a valid cheque and that the signatures of the drawer and previous endorsers were valid signatures; F made a guarantee to the same effect when he endorsed the cheque to G. In the result, because one of the earlier endorsements (D's) was forged, E is liable for the amount of the cheque to G or if G chooses to claim it from F, E is then liable to indemnify F. A forged endorsement does not pass on the guarantees.

If X stops the cheque then he must give D another cheque or settle with him otherwise X is unjustly enriched. He has had goods and has not paid. G and F may sue E and get payment. E must sue the thief on the underlying contract.

If the cheque is not stopped and G obtains payment then there is no need for G to sue F or E. D has sold goods to C and has not been paid, but the the risk of the loss of the cheque is his. X has received goods from C but has paid and is not unjustly enriched, so that the only claim is by D against the thief for conversion of the cheque.

The only proviso to the above rule is if the party against whom it is sought to enforce payment of the bill is precluded (i.e. estopped)j from setting up the forgery or want of authority. (*Greenwood* v *Martins Bank* 1933.)[221]

The position is the same where the *endorsement is unauthorized* as where an agent endorses a cheque made payable to his principal for and on behalf of that principal although he has no authority to do so.

It should be noted, however, that an unauthorized signature may be ratified. Thus, if a cheque is made payable to a company and a clerk in the company's employ without authority endorses the cheque on behalf of the company to creditors of the company, and, where, say, the principal disputes the debt or the debt is not yet due, then the creditors have no title to the cheque, but the company can ratify the unauthorized endorsement and the creditors (the endorsees) could then sue the company on the cheque. If the clerk had endorsed the cheque over to his private creditors to clear his own debts, the company would not normally wish to ratify his acts but could not do so in any case because the law does not allow ratification of a forgery or fraud.

NEGOTIATION OF A BEARER CHEQUE

Since a bearer cheque can be transferred without endorsement, the person who transfers it does not give the 'guarantees' of an endorser under s.55(2) in regard to the validity of the cheque. Instead s.58 of the Act applies to the transferor of a bearer cheque who is called a transferor by delivery and under s.58 warrants to his immediate transferee bring a holder for value, *and him alone*—

(1) that the cheque is valid,
(2) that he has the right to transfer it, and
(3) that he is not aware at the time of the transfer that it has become valueless, e.g. as where payment has been stopped.

Thus if a bearer cheque apparently drawn by A is negotiated to B who negotiates it to C, who negotiates it to D, then if A's signature is forged D cannot sue A on it, nor can he sue B or C on the cheque. He can only sue C for breach of warranty. C has an action against B and could join him as defendant in any action which D brought against him.

ORDER CHEQUES TRANSFERRED WITHOUT ENDORSEMENT

If an order cheque is transferred without endorsement the transferee for value is merely an equitable assignee. (S.31(4).) Thus, if D transfers an order cheque without endorsement to E, E would have to join D in any action on the cheque and could not sue in his own name. Under s.39 of the Supreme Court Act 1981, D could be required to endorse by the court and if he will not do so the court can appoint someone else to do it in his stead. Often the court order directs that the transferee, E, may sign the endorsement.

DELIVERY

Section 21(1) provides that every contract on a cheque, whether it be the drawer's or an endorser's, is incomplete and revocable until delivery of the instrument. Thus, where an endorsement or other signature is required the mere fact that a signature is placed upon the instrument is not enough; there must also be delivery, which would not be the case where an order instrument was stolen after endorsement. The endorser must deliver it. However, there are certain presumptions of delivery as follows—

(1) Under s.21(2) valid delivery by all prior parties is *conclusively* presumed in favour of a holder in due course but not if the bill is inchoate or incomplete. (See below.)

(2) Under s.21(3) valid delivery is presumed *until the contrary is proved* in the case of other holders.

Thus presumption of valid delivery cannot be disproved against a holder in due course but it may be as regards other holders.

INCHOATE CHEQUES

These are cheques lacking in some material particular(s) such as the names of the parties other than the drawer and the amount of the cheque. Problems arise from completion of the cheque in excess of authority given by the drawer. Section 20 applies and requires 'delivery by the signer in order that it may be converted into a bill'. The law does not presume delivery under s.21 because two elements are required—

(1) delivery, and
(2) the intention in the signer that the order be converted into a bill.

Thus, if A signs a cheque form and does not complete it and it is stolen from his desk and filled in, A is under no liability to anyone on his signature, not even to a holder in due course, because he did not deliver it *in order that it might be converted into a bill.*

However, if A signs a blank cheque and gives it to his gardener to buy a lawn mower and the gardener fills it in and pays a private debt, then A would be liable to a holder in due course because he did deliver it with the intention that it should be converted into a bill. The gardener's lack of authority is a 'defect' so far as a holder for value is concerned and A would not be liable to him.

It has already been noted that a payee cannot be a holder in due course (*Jones* v *Waring & Gillow* 1926),[388] so that the private creditor of the gardener would not be able to sue A because, being the payee, he would only be a holder for a value. However, an endorsee from the private creditor could sue A if the cheque had been passed on in that way. However, an original payee may rely on the doctrine of estoppel. Thus in *Lloyds Bank* v *Cooke* [1907] 1 K.B. 794, Cooke signed his name on a blank promissory note and gave it to another person with authority to complete it for £250 payable to the plaintiffs as security for an advance made by them. The other person completed it for £1000 and took the balance for himself. It was held that although the bank were payees and not holders in due course, Cooke was liable to them by estoppel. He had held out the other party as having authority.

Duties of a holder

Cheques must be presented within a reasonable time—

(1) of *issue* in order to make the *drawer* liable:
(2) of *endorsement* to make the *endorser* liable. (S.45(2).)

Bankers usually return a cheque marked 'out of date' or 'stale' if it bears a date more than six months prior to presentation.

NOTICE OF DISHONOUR

Where a cheque is dishonoured by non-payment, the holder must give notice to prior endorsers (but not the drawer) otherwise they will be discharged. However, it is likely that if the holder only gives notice to his immediate endorser that endorser will give notice to prior parties and it will be passed back in this way.

Furthermore, it should be noted that under s.49(3) 'notice of dishonour operates for the benefit of all subsequent holders and all prior endorsers who have a right of recourse against the party to whom notice was given', Thus, let us assume that on a cheque B is the drawer and C is the payee. Let us now assume that C has negotiated the cheque to D, D to E, and E to F. Suppose that F is the holder at the time of dishonour and that he gives notice to E and to C but not to D. The result would be that F could claim on E and C because he gave notice. E could claim on C by reason of s.49(3), being a prior endorsor who had a right of recourse against C. Finally, endorsers subsequent to F can also claim on E and C by reason of F's notice to them being subsequent holders. Furthermore, D can sue C because he is a prior endorser who has a right of recourse against C.

FORM

Notice may be given in writing or orally and the return of a dishonoured cheque to an endorser is deemed sufficient notice.

TIME FOR GIVING NOTICE

Notice may be given as soon as the cheque is dishonoured (but not before) or within a reasonable time thereafter. (*Eaglehill Ltd* v *J. Needham (Builders)* 1972.)[389] As regards what is reasonable time, s.49(12) provides that notice will not have been deemed given within a reasonable time unless—

(1) where the parties live in the *same place* notice must have been

given or sent off so that it arrives on the day after the dishonour of the cheque;

(2) where the parties live in *different places* notice was sent off on the day after the dishonour or if there is no post on that day then by the next post thereafter.

There is no definition of the word 'place' in the Act but it is suggested by Chalmers on Bills of Exchange that it means postal district.

It should be noted that the endorsers receiving notice have the same time in which to pass it on to other endorsers whose names appear on the cheque. If the notice of dishonour is properly addressed and posted it is deemed to have been given although it miscarried in the post and arrived late. (S.49(15).)

EXCUSES FOR NON-NOTICE AND DELAY

The relevant rules are as follows—

(1) *Delay.* This is excused by circumstances beyond the control of the person giving notice so long as the delay was not caused by his misconduct or negligence. Thus the existence of a a postal strike or civil disturbance could provide circumstances beyond the control of the sender excusing him for delay. When the reason for delay is over notice must be given with reasonable diligence. (S.50(1).)

(2) *Non-notice—endorsers.* If after the exercise of due diligence the holder cannot give notice then notice is excused. Once again this assumes the situation of a civil disturbance or postal strike. In addition notice may be waived either expressly *where* the particular party to whom notice is being given has said that he does not require it, or has in the past waived notice, thus setting up a course of dealing. (S.50(2)(*a*) and (*b*).)

(3) *Non-notice—drawer.* Notice to the drawer of a cheque need not be given because dishonour normally results from his lack of funds or countermand and the 1882 Act excuses notice being given if dishonour is for these reasons. (S.50(2)(*c*).)

Discharge of a cheque

A cheque or one or more of the parties thereto may be discharged as follows—

PAYMENT

In most cases a cheque is discharged when it is paid by a bank on which it is drawn to a holder who is entitled to the cheque.

Where payment is made to a thief the bank will be protected (see later) if it acts in good faith without negligence and in the ordinary course of business. The drawer or endorser will not be liable provided the cheque reached the party from whom it was stolen.

CANCELLATION

Cancellation takes place where a holder crosses out the signature of a party and writes 'cancelled' on the cheque or burns it. The cancellation must be apparent, intentional, and not by mistake or by an agent without authority. (S.63(1).) Any party may discharged by cancellation. If an endorser's signature is cancelled, subsequent endorsers are also discharged. (S.63(2).)

An unintentional or mistaken cancellation or one made without authority is inoperative, but if it is apparent on the bill then the burden of proving that the cancellation was unintentional, mistaken or without authority is on the party who alleges that it was so made. (S.63(3).)

MATERIAL ALTERATION

The results of this depends upon whether the alteration is apparent or not, as follows—

(1) *Apparent alteration.* If the material alteration is apparent then the cheque may be totally avoided except against the person who made the alteration and subsequent endorsers. (S.64.) For example, suppose that A draws a cheque for £100 in favour of C and C endorses it to D who alters it to £1000 before endorsing it to E, who in turn endorses it to F. If the alteration is apparent the cheque is avoided except as against D and E. Only these two can be sued for £1000 by F.

Such a cheque would not be paid by a bank but actions between the parties to the cheque would be affected by the above rules.

(2) *Non-apparent alteration.* If the alteration cannot be ascertained by reasonable scrutiny all the parties can retain some liability, at least to a holder in due course, C and A would be liable up to £100 to F or to E if F had sued for E £1000. Such a cheque would be paid by the bank and the bank would normally be able to debit the customer's account, since such an alteration could only arise from the customer's negligence in drawing the cheque. (See further p. 281.)

The following alterations to a cheque are regarded as material—

(*a*) to the date;
(*b*) to the sum payable.

LIMITATION ACT 1980

Actions on a cheque are barred after six years from the time when the action accrued.

As regards the accrual of an action, this is six years from dishonour as regards the drawer and notice of dishonour as regards endorsers.

Capacity

The general law of contract applies and capacity to incur liability as a party to a cheque is co-extensive with a capacity to contract. (S.22.)

If a limited company, therefore, acts *ultra vires* in drawing a particular cheque, it is not bound, but a company incorporated for the purposes of trade does have implied authority to make itself liable as a party to a cheque because such a power is clearly incidental to the performance of its objects.

A minor will never be liable on a cheque even though he might have been liable on the transaction giving rise to it. Thus a minor cannot be made liable on a cheque drawn by him in payment for necessaries. However, the seller could sue the minor in quasi-contract for a reasonable price.

If a cheque is drawn or endorsed by a minor or by a corporation having no capacity to incur liability on the cheque, the drawing or the endorsement is effective for all purposes except to make the minor or corporation liable.

In consequence the holder can proceed against any other party. Suppose, for example, a cheque is drawn by A on his bank in favour of C who is a minor. C endorses the cheque to D in return for goods sold by D to C. A stops payment of the cheque. D has no right to sue C but C's endorsement was effective to transfer the title in the cheque to D so D has a right of action on the cheque against A. If a minor draws a cheque his bank has the same right to debit his account on paying the holder as if the drawer were an adult.

Cheques, and relationship of banker and customer

DEFINITION

Section 73 of the 1882 Act defines a cheque as 'a bill of exchange drawn on a banker payable on demand'.

Thus a postdated cheque, i.e. a cheque dated later than the date of its issue, is not in the strict sense a cheque at all but operates as a bill of exchange. However, under s.13(2) the cheque is not invalid merely because it is postdated. However, if the banker pays before the date given on the cheque he cannot debit the drawer's account until the date arrives and not then if the drawer has countermanded payment.

In practice even though a banker may pay a postdated cheque in law, if a postdated cheque is presented for payment it will be returned 'postdated'. The banker will not pay it or hold it until the due date or hold funds for it and he is under no duty to do so.

DIFFERENCES BETWEEN CHEQUES AND OTHER BILLS

The provisions of the 1882 Act applicable to bills of exchange payable on demand apply to cheques. However, there are certain important differences between cheques and other bills. These are as follows—

(1) The drawee of a cheque is always a banker and therefore a cheque is never accepted.

(2) The holder of a cheque has no rights against the banker himself if the cheque is not paid. Instead he must pursue his remedies against the drawer or any endorser.

(3) Notice of dishonour is not required in order to render the drawer of a cheque liable on it. This is because non-payment usually results from the fact that the drawer has no funds or has countermanded the cheque and s.50(2)(*c*) excuses notice of dishonour being given in those cases. However, notice to an endorser is necessary to make him liable.

(4) Crossings are instructions to a banker and do not apply to bills of exchange, though they are of course used on cheques. A 'not negotiable' crossing affects endorsees and is not addressed to the banker.

(5) Considerable protection is given to a banker in respect of payment out on a forged or unauthorized endorsement. Such protection is not given to the acceptor of a bill who is liable if he pays out on forged or unauthorized endorsements. (See further p. 288.)

Mutual duties of banker and customer

The relationship is basically that of debtor and creditor and demand for repayment is necessary before there is an enforceable debt. However, time under the Limitation Act 1980 does not begin to run against a customer until he has made the demand for repayment and it has been rejected. Thus, if A deposited £500 with his bank in a current account in 1978 and up to the present has not written any cheques on that account, the banker is not excused from paying the money on the grounds that the deposit was made more than six years ago. However, if a cheque is drawn on the account and the banker refuses to pay it, then the customer must take action against the bank within six years, otherwise the debt will be statute barred. The relationship of banker and customer is not that of principal and agent, so that the banker can do what he likes with the customer's money, subject to his willingness to repay a like sum.

However, the relationship goes in some respects beyond the ordinary creditor–debtor situation as follows—

THE BANKER MUST OBEY HIS CUSTOMER'S MANDATE

Thus, a bank has no right to debit a customer's account for the amount of a cheque on which the customer's signature has been forged because the bank has then no mandate from the customer to pay. However, the customer may be estopped in some cases from denying the validity of his signature and in these circumstances the bank may debit his account even on the basis of a cheque on which the customer's signature was forged. (See *Greenwood* v *Martins Bank Ltd* 1933.)[221]

Generally, *knowledge* by the customer of the forgery is required if an estoppel is to be successfully raised by the bank. In the USA an estoppel can be raised where the customer fails to examine and draw inferences from his bank statements on which the forged cheques are recorded. However, McNeill, J., refused to bring UK law into line on this in *Wealden Woodlands (Kent) Ltd* v *National Westminster Bank Ltd, The Times*, 12 March 1983. In that case cheques drawn on the plaintiffs' account required the signatures of two directors. One director got money from the company's account by forging the signature of another director. The Court held that the plaintiffs were not estopped from making a claim against the bank even though they might have discovered the fraud by diligent examination of the company's bank statements. They had not discovered the fraud in this way and the Court held they could not be regarded as negligent because they had not done so.

It should also be noted that if a bank pays a cheque on which the signature of its customer as drawer has been forged the bank can sue the person to whom payment was made for restitution of the amount paid out, for the money with which payment was made was the property of the bank. A paying bank merely by paying a cheque on which its customer's signature has been forged does not thereby represent that the signature is genuine so as to estop itself from recovering the money paid to the recipient in quasi-contract. (*National Westminster Bank Ltd* v *Barclays Bank International Ltd* [1974] 3 All E.R. 834.)

Furthermore, the bank has no right to debit a customer's account where the mandate requires two signatures and only signature in fact has been used. (See *Ligget (Liverpool) Ltd* v *Barclays Bank* 1928.)[390]

It should also be noted that if the bank's failure to pay in accordance with its customer's mandate is caused by the customer's negligence, the bank is entitled to debit the customer's account with the cheque. (See *London Joint Stock Bank Ltd* v *Macmillan and Arthur* 1918.[391] Compare, however, *Slingsby* v *District Bank* 1931.)[392]

As regards joint accounts, in *Brewer* v *Westminster Bank* [1952] 2 All E.R. 650 McNair, J., decided that in the case of a joint account, the bank's duties were owed to the account holders *jointly* and not *severally*. The result of this decision was that where one account holder forged the other's signature on cheques drawn on the account and then added his own signature, the innocent account holder had no action against the bank.

However, in *Jackson* v *White and Midland Bank Ltd* [1967] 2 Lloyd's Rep. 68, where one joint account-holder forged the signature of the other, Park, J., declined to follow *Brewer's case*, holding that where there was a joint account with, say, A and B, the bank in effect agreed with A and B *jointly* that it would honour cheques signed by them both and with A *separately* that it would not honour cheques unless signed by him, and with B *separately* that it would not honour cheques unless signed by him. Thus where the bank honours a cheque on which B has forged A's signature, A should be able to sue the bank because it is in breach of the separate agreement with him. The reasoning in *Jackson's case* seems to be more satisfactory and makes better commercial sense. It was applied in *Catlin* v *Cyprus Finance Corporation (London) Ltd, The Times*, 27 October 1982. Mr & Mrs Catlin had a joint deposit account with the defendants. Withdrawals required the written instructions of them both. They separated in 1972. At that time there was £21,642 in the account. In 1975 the bank let Mr Catlin take various sums from the account on his signature alone. Mrs Catlin eventually discovered this. The account then stood at £897. Mrs Catlin claimed against the bank for the money withdrawn on the grounds that they had failed to observe the mandate. Mr Catlin was not joined in the action, either as co-plaintiff or co-defendant. Could Mrs Catlin succeed on her own? Bingham, J., preferred the type of reasoning in *Jackson*. Therefore Mrs Catlin succeeded in her claim. The judge said, among other things: 'The duty could, in theory, have been owed jointly, but in my mind, to make sense has to be owed severally. The only possible purpose of requiring two signatures is to obviate the possibility of independent action by one account holder to the detriment of the other. A duty on the bank which could only be performed jointly with Mr Catlin would be worthless to Mrs Catlin in practical terms and would deprive her of any remedy.' Thus joint account-holders also have separate actions against the bank.

A BANKER MUST HONOUR HIS CUSTOMER'S CHEQUES

A bank is bound to honour its customer's cheques to the extent that the customer is in credit or to the extent of any agreed overdraft.

If a cheque is 'referred to drawer' although the customer is in funds or has an agreed overdraft the matter is treated as follows—

(1) If the customer is in business or practice as a profession it is assumed that his credit-worthiness has been affected and damages will be awarded without proof of actual loss. Thus in *Davidson* v *Barclays Bank Ltd* [1940] 1 All E.R. 316, the plaintiff, who was a bookmaker, drew a cheque for £2.78 and the bank erroneously returned it to the payee marked 'not sufficient' on its face. It was held that the plaintiff was entitled to substantial damages of £250 for libel.

(2) Where the customer is not in trade or practising a profession damage to credit is not assumed and nominal damages (i.e. £2) will be awarded unless a particular loss is proved as where, for example, the customer can show that a particular creditor has refused to do busi-

ness with him again. Thus in *Gibbons* v *Westminster Bank Ltd* [1939] 3 All E.R. 577, the plaintiff, who was not in trade, paid into her bank account a sum of money which, because of the bank's error, was credited to another customer's account. The plaintiff then issued a cheque to pay her rent and this cheque was dishonoured by the bank because there were insufficient funds to meet it. The plaintiff brought a claim for libel but it was held that she was entitled to nominal damages only; she was not in trade and was not able to prove any special damage.

The bank's duty to honour cheques ceases on the customer countermanding payment. In this connection it should be noted that notice to the bank must be actual, not constructive. (See *Curtice* v *London, City & Midland Bank Ltd* 1908.)[393] It should also be noted that for the purposes of countermand of payment the branches of a bank are treated as separate parties. Thus a countermand must be sent to the branch on which the cheque is drawn. (But see *Burnett* v *Westminster Bank* 1965.)[394]

A bank which overlooks its customer's instructions to stop payment of a cheque and consequently pays the cheque when it has been presented, can recover the money from the payee because it has been paid under a mistake of fact. (See *Barclays Bank* v *W.J. Simms Son and Cooke (Southern)* [1979] 3 All E.R. 522.)

The bank's duty to honour cheques ceases also on receiving notice of the customer's death, i.e. probate of a will or letters of administration. This is because the death of a customer revokes his mandate to the bank and where this happens the payee of the cheque must settle the matter with the deceased customer's personal representatives. Cheques are returned stamped 'deceased'. However, death does not revoke the mandate of a living person who is party to a joint account with the deceased.

The duty of a bank to honour cheques also ceases on receiving notice of the customer's mental incapacity, usually notice of the appointment of a receiver. This again revokes the mandate and the payee of the cheque must deal with the drawer's representatives. These representatives are normally appointed by the court on application and may be, for example, a relative, or a solicitor who has been put in charge of the estate, or in some cases there may be a committee of several persons concerned to deal with the estate.

Other situations in which a banker's duty to honour his customer's cheques ceases are as follows—

(1) If the customer is a company and the banker has notice that it has commenced winding up. Winding up commences in the case of a compulsory liquidation on presentation of a petition and in the case of a voluntary liquidation on the passing of a resolution for voluntary winding up.

(2) The service of a garnishee order. Such an order can be used where, for example, A owes B £200 and will not pay but B knows that A has

an account with the Barchester Bank in which he has £500. B may ask the court for a garnishee order *nisi* freezing A's account with the bank in the hope that this inconvenience will cause A to pay. If not B may ask the court for an order absolute and if he obtains it the bank will be required to pay B £200 plus his costs out of A's account.

Service of an order *nisi* with no sum mentioned prevents any use of the account until the order is discharged, even though there is more money in the account than the order requires. However, if a sum is mentioned and the account is more than that sum then it can be operated by the customer as to the balance.

A garnishee order issues only on a judgment debt. The order *nisi* is addressed to the customer against whom a judgment has been obtained asking if there is any good reason why the judgment debt has not been paid. A copy of this order is sent to the bank. An order absolute will be made if the customer cannot show good cause as to why he has not paid and then, as we have seen, the bank is ordered to pay the plaintiff.

(3) After a receiving order in bankruptcy. Before the receiving order the bank is protected if—

(*a*) it has no notice of an act of bankruptcy; or

(*b*) no notice of the presentation of a petition.

(4) Where the bank knows, or ought to know, that the cheque is a misapplication of funds. For example, the use of a company's money to buy its own shares would be a misapplication of the funds in its account since it is forbidden, subject to certain exceptions, by ss.42–44, Companies Act 1981. If the bank was therefore aware or put on enquiry that the company's money was being used for this purpose it would be liable for honouring cheques in those circumstances. Thus a takeover bidder may obtain a bridging loan from the bank in order to purchase a controlling interest in the shares of a company and then use the company's funds by means of a cheque immediately to repay the loan. In such circumstances the bank should not honour the company's cheque. (*Karak Rubber Co.* v *Burden* [1971] 3 All E.R. 1118.) The same rule applies to money paid by the bank in breach of trust. These cases make life difficult for bankers, particularly where the money of companies is misapplied in breach of trust by the directors, the relevant cheque(s) having been drawn within the mandate on which the account is operated. An example of payment in breach of trust is to be found in *International Sales & Agencies* v *Marcus* (1982).[89] In that case money was owed to a moneylender by a Mr Fancy who died intestate. One of the directors of a company in which Mr Fancy was a substantial shareholder had promised the moneylender that he would do all he could to see that the debts were paid. In fact the director concerned paid the debts from money standing to the credit of the accounts of the company. This was, of course, a breach of trust. There could be no question that the debt was an obligation of the company. In an action brought on behalf of the company it succeeded in recovering the money paid by the bank.

BANKER'S DUTY TO OBSERVE SECRECY

A bank must not disclose the financial affairs of a customer. This is based on an implied term in the contract between the banker and his customer (see *Tournier* v *National Provincial and Union Bank of England* 1924)[395] and continues even after the account is closed.

However, Bankes, L.J., said in *Tournier's case* that there were four exceptions as follows—

(1) Where disclosure is required by law. Thus, under s.7 of the Banker's Books Evidence Act 1879 the court may by order authorize a party to an action to inspect and copy entries in a banker's books although the power is exercised with cautiion. Section 9 of the 1879 Act provides that 'expressions in this Act relating to "bankers" books include legers, day books, cash books, account books, and all other books used in the ordinary business of the bank'. Under Sch. 6 of the Banking Act, 1979 'books' include microfilm records.

Letters contained in a bank correspondence file are not within the terms of s.9 and are inadmissable in evidence. Thus in *R.* v *Dadson, The Times*, 11 March 1983, a main plank of the prosecution's case against the accused who was allegedly guilty of dishonestly borrowing by way of overdraft by *knowingly* drawing cheques in excess of his bank balance, were two letters written to him by the bank giving information about the state of his account. The defendant was convicted of the offence but his appeal was allowed by the Court of Appeal on the basis that the letters had been exhibited in the Court at the trial but should not have been admitted in evidence.

Furthermore, under the Taxes Management Act 1970, s.17, a bank must report to the Revenue authorities any case where interest of £25 or more is paid per year. In practice, only accounts showing £150 per annum interest or more are sent automatically, though the Revenue may request a statement to be made in respect of interest in excess of £25 per annum or more.

In addition to the above, there is power to require disclosure of a bank account under the Companies Act 1948 on a prosecution of a company's officers or on an inspection by the Department of Trade or in a winding up. In addition, the Taxes Management Act 1970, s.20, as extended by Sch.6 of the Finance Act 1976 allows the Inspector of Taxes to call for documents of a taxpayer if relevant to tax liability. This could include the taxpayer's bank account.

(2) Where there is a public duty to disclose as where a banker can see that a customer is trading with the enemy in time of war, or more importantly where information is given to the police to protect the public against crime. Such information is not, however, given in evidence unless the bank is ordered to give it under the 1879 Act.

(3) Where disclosure is required in the interest of the bank, as where the bank is suing to recover an overdraft, since the amount of the over-

draft is stated on the face of the writ, or where the bank is claiming against a person who has guaranteed an overdraft.

(4) Where the customer gives permission. Permission may be given *expressly* as when a customer gives the banker's name as reference. An additional example of this is where a corporate customer of the bank gives the bank permission to disclose the state of its account to the company's auditors. Permission may also be regarded as having been given by implication from conduct. (See *Sunderland* v *Barclays Bank* 1938.)[396]

Disclosure without authority is an open question; there are those who believe that the state of an account can be disclosed on the basis of the implied consent of the customer when he joins the bank. However, the Younger Committee, which reported on new laws of privacy but has not yet received legislation, said that banks should tell customers of a reference system in use and get a standing consent or ask them every time the reference system was used.

BANKER'S DUTY TO COLLECT CHEQUES PAID IN BY A CUSTOMER

A bank is under a duty to collect for its customer's account cheques paid in by the customer. The bank then acts as a collecting bank and has certain protections if its customer has a defective title to the cheque.

FIDUCIARY RELATIONSHIP OF BANKER AND CUSTOMER

There is a special relationship between a banker and his customer which can give rise to a contract, to give a security between the bank and the customer being set aside for undue influence. (*Lloyds Bank* v *Bundy* 1974.)[129] The best way for a bank to avoid this situation is to recommend that the customer take independent legal advice.

Crossed cheques (Ss.76–82 Bills of Exchange Act 1882.)

Where a cheque bears across its face an addition of the words 'and Co.' or any abbreviation thereof between two parallel transverse lines, or simply two parallel transverse lines, in either case with or without the words 'not negotiable', the cheque is said to be crossed generally. Such a cheque will only be paid by the bank on which it is drawn through another bank, and not over the counter. It is therefore a hindrance for someone who obtains the cheque wrongly because he could only obtain payment through a bank and the loss may be discovered meanwhile and the cheque stopped. In addition, collection through a bank may help trace a thief.

If the cheque bears across its face the addition of the name of a banker it will only be paid by the paying bank to the bank which is so named. The cheque is then said to be specially crossed whether there are

Examples of crossings on cheques:

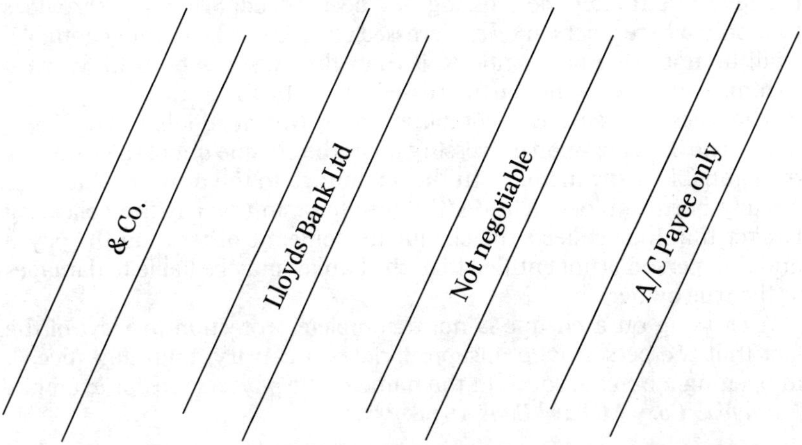

transverse parallel lines on the cheque as well or not. If the drawer does not know where the payee banks he can only write '& Co.'. In early banking days the words '& Co.' were essential to ensure collection through a bank. They are absolutely unnecessary today.

If the words 'Not negotiable' appear on or near the crossing of a cheque no one can claim to have a better title than the previous holder, i.e. no one can claim to be a holder in due course taking the cheque free from defects (if any). A person may satisfy the definition of a holder in due course but because of the 'Not negotiable' crossing will not take the cheque free from defects. So if a person is giving a cheque for goods which may be defective, he should cross his cheque 'Not negotiable' so that no one, not even a holder in due course, can sue him for the full price if the cheque is stopped and the goods turn out to be defective.

The crossing 'A/C Payee' is not provided for in the 1882 or other Act. It is an instruction to the collecting banker, addressed to him by a person who has no contract with him, and it would be negligence in a banker if he collected the money for some other account, for a person with no title. The crossing has no effect on a paying banker since it merely states what is to happen to money after receipt. The crossing does not prevent the cheque from being transferred or indeed from being negotiable. (*National Bank* v *Silke* [1891] 1 Q.B. 435.) Obviously, no banker would normally collect the money for an endorsee but the drawer would remain liable on the instrument and would have to pay the amount of the cheque to an endorsee.

Bankers will sometimes collect a cheque crossed 'A/C Payee' for someone other than the payee, particularly if the cheque is for a small amount and the customer is one of long standing.

If a cheque is issued uncrossed a holder can cross it generally or specially, and if it is issued crossed generally a holder may turn the crossing into a special crossing. In addition, a holder may also add the words

'Not negotiable' to a crossing. This would only affect those who took the instrument after the crossing had been added. Section 81 provides that only where a person *takes* a crossed cheque marked 'Not negotiable' shall he not get a better title to it than the person who transferred it to him. A cheque cannot be uncrossed except by the drawer.

The safest crossing is a combination of 'Not negotiable. A/C Payee only'. The 'Not negotiable' crossing takes the cheque out of the category of negotiable instruments with the advantage to the drawer which has already been outlined. The 'A/C Payee' crossing warns the collecting banker that if he collects the cheque for someone other than the payee and that person is not entitled to it, the banker may be liable to damages to the true owner.

A crossing on a cheque is not a complete protection in view of the fact that the person who misappropriates it can try, and may suceed, in opening a bank account in the name of the payee. (See, for example, *Marfani & Co.* v *Midland Bank* 1968.)[400]

Statutory protection of paying banker

Section 60 of the Bills of Exchange Act 1882 and s.1 of the Cheques Act 1957 provide some protection to a paying banker who pays a cheque to a person who is not the owner of it. In the absence of this statutory protection the banker would be liable in conversion to the true owner. It should be noted that these statutory protections do not apply where the banker pays out a cheque on which his customer's signature as a drawer is forged. The banker will not be allowed to debit the cheque to the customer's account unless the customer is estopped from denying that the forged signature is his, as in *Greenwood* v *Martins Bank* 1933.[221]

It should be noted that a banker who honours a cheque upon which the drawer's signature has been forged does not thereby impliedly represent the signature to be genuine and can recover the money paid thereunder from the recipient. Thus, in *National Westminster Bank* v *Barclays Bank International* [1974] 3 All E.R. 834, A stole a cheque from B and forged B's signature in order that C (the payee) could obtain money from B's account as part of a fraudulent scheme to acquire sterling. It was held that although the bank could not debit B's account with the amount of the cheque which it had paid, it could recover the money from C on the grounds that it was paid under circumstances of mistake of fact.

The main purpose of the Cheques Act 1957 was to make it unnecessary for the payee of a cheque or a subsequent endorsee to endorse the cheque before paying it in to his own bank account. Endorsement of a cheque is still necessary to effect the negotiation of an order cheque and it is the practice of banks to require an endorsement when cashing uncrossed cheques across the counter.

The Cheques Act merely amended the law in certain respects and in the absence of consolidating legislation there is at the present some overlapping between the statutory provisions that give the paying banker his protection when paying someone who has no title.

A paying banker may pay a cheque to a person who is not the owner of it (and thus convert it) in four situations as follows—

(1) Where the cheque has been negotiated under a forged or unauthorized endorsement before being paid into the collecting bank. Here the banker is protected in respect of a crossed cheque by s.80 and s.60 of the Bills of Exchange Act 1882. Under s.80 the banker must make the payment in good faith and without negligence in order to be protected. However, under s.60 the banker has merely to act in good faith and in the ordinary course of business so that he could be protected even if negligent. If the cheque is uncrossed then s.60 applies but s.80 does not.

(2) Where a crossed cheque has not been negotiated but was paid in to the collecting bank without endorsement. Here s.1 of the Cheques Act 1957 protects a banker who pays in good faith and in the ordinary course of business.

(3) Where an uncrossed cheque has been paid over the counter on a forged endorsement. Here a banker who pays in good faith and in the ordinary course of business would be protected by s.60 of the Bills of Exchange Act 1882.

(4) Where an uncrossed cheque has been paid over the counter on an irregular endorsement, as where the payee's name and the endorsement do not match. Here the banker would be protected by s.1 of the Cheques Act 1957 provided he paid in good faith and in the ordinary course of business.

Where these protections apply the banker is entitled to debit his customer's account with the amount of the cheque.

It should also be noted that a banker can plead the contributory negligence of his customer under s.47 of the Banking Act 1979 in order to reduce damages payable by the banker, as where one director signs cheques in blank before going on a business trip and leaves the cheque book in an unlocked drawer so that the signature of another director is forged by a clerk and the cheques paid. Although the banker would have paid out contrary to the mandate, the amount of compensation he was liable to pay to the company whose funds are converted could be reduced in such a case by the contributory negligence of the director concerned.

Statutory protection on the collecting banker

At common law a banker who collects a cheque for his customer in circumstances where that customer has no title to it is liable in convervsion to the true owner. Statutory protection is, however, given to the collecting banker by s.4(1) of the Cheques Act 1957, provided—

(1) He collects for a customer. It is clear from the cases that a person who has handed in a cheque for an account to be opened is immediately 'a customer' within the meaning of s.4. It should also be noted that s.4 applies to protect a banker even where he has allowed his customer to draw against the cheque before it was cleared so that in effect when he collects the cheque he is collecting it for himself and not for a customer. Nevertheless, s.4 applies.

(2) He acts without negligence. Broadly, whenever the terms of a cheque would raise a doubt in the mind of a bank cashier of ordinary intelligence and care as to whether the customer has a good title to it, the bank owes a duty to make inquiries as to the customer's title. The application of this principle can be seen in *Lloyds Bank* v *Savory & Co.* 1933,[397] *Bute (Marquess)* v *Barclays Bank Ltd* 1954,[398] and *Underwood* v *Bank of Liverpool* 1924[399] in which the bank was found negligent and *Orbit Mining and Trading Co.* v *Westminster Bank Ltd* 1962[379] and *Marfani* v *Midland Bank Ltd* 1968[400] where the bank was found not negligent.

The main areas of a collecting bankers negligence are as follows—

(1) Failure to obtain references or follow them up on opening an account. (*Lumsden & Co.* v *London Trustee Savings Bank* [1971] 1 Lloyd's Rep. 114.)

(2) Failure to obtain the name of the customer's employers. (*Lloyds Bank Ltd* v *E.B. Savory & Co* 1933.)[397] It would appear, however, from the case of *Orbit Mining & Trading Co. Ltd* v *Westminster Bank* 1962[379] that the bank need not update this information.

(3) Failure to obtain the name of the husband's employers when an account is opened for a married woman. (*Lloyds Bank Ltd* v *E.B. Savory & Co.* 1933.)[397]

(4) Collecting for the private account of a partner or a director cheques payable to the firm or to the company. (*Underwood* v *Bank of Liverpool* 1924.)[399]

(5) Collecting for an employee cheques payable to his employer or drawn by his employer. (*Lloyds Bank Ltd* v *E.B. Savory & Co.* 1933.)[397]

(6) Collecting for the private account of an agent cheques which he receives only as an agent. (*Bute (Marquess)* v *Barclays Bank Ltd* 1954.)[398]

(7) Collecting cheques payable to a limited company for an account other than that of the company. (*London & Montrose Shipbuilding and Repairing Co. Ltd* v *Barclays Bank Ltd* (1925) 31 Com. Cas. 182.) However, the matter is not beyond doubt because in *Penmount Estates Ltd* v *National Provincial Bank* (1945) 173 L.T. 344 a bank in a similar situation successfully defended itself in an action in conversion. However, it can be said that a bank would not collect a cheque payable to a limited company for an account other than that of the company without very strict inquiry.

(8) Collecting account payee cheques for someone else.

Bank as a holder for value or holder in due course

Section 2 of the Cheques Act provides that a banker who gives value for a cheque payable to order which the holder delivers to him for collection without endorsing it has such (if any) rights as he would have had if upon delivery the holder of what is in effect under the statute a bearer bill.

This concept is useful to a banker where, for example he has allowed a customer to have an overdraft and the customer pays in a cheque which the banker uses to reduce that overdraft because, should the cheque which the banker uses to reduce that overdraft not be met and the customer be unable or unwilling to sue upon it, the bank can itself take action against the drawer in the hope of reducing the overdraft by bringing an action under s.2 of the Cheques Act 1957 instead of the customer.

However, before an action can be brought the bank must show that it is at least a holder for value and under s.2 value must be given by the bank itself. Value could be given, for example, where the bank could prove that it had reduced the customer's overdraft and had charged interest for a period of time only on the overdraft as reduced by the cheque. It is much more likely, however, that the bank will show that it has given value by allowing a customer to draw against a cheque before it is cleared because the customer is using the bank's money and not his own at that stage. It would be necessary for the bank to show that it was a holder for value in order that a successful action could be maintained on a cheque which had no defects. However, if there is a defect on the cheque the bank would have to prove that it was a holder in due course and could only do this—

(1) if it had no knowledge of the defect and took the instrument in good faith;
(2) the bank's title did not depend upon a forged endorsement; and
(3) there were no irregularities on the face of the cheque.

A good illustration of the use of s.2 of the Cheques Act 1957 by a bank can be seen in *Westminster Bank Ltd* v *Zang* 1965,[401] and *Barclays Bank Ltd* v *The Astley Industrial Trust Ltd* 1970.[402]

Consumer Credit Act and banking practice

Some of the more important ways in which banking law and practice has been affected by the Act appear below.

OVERDRAFTS

Section 82 of the Consumer Credit Act 1974 takes in all commercial lending including overdrafts to an amount not exceeding £15,000. Section 82 deals with variation of agreements and provides that if a regulated agreement for goods up to, say, a repayable balance of £14,000, is modified by the addition of further goods so that the repayable balance is, say, £17,000, the agreement is still a regulated one and the provisions of Part V of the Act, e.g. rights of cancellation and the supply of copies of documents in connection with the new credit, apply. In addition, regulations provide for formalities to be used in the variation. This could present difficulties in terms of overdrafts. Suppose a bank has agreed to an overdraft for the person A of up to £15,000 and A, having drawn up to that amount issues a cheque for, say, £5. This would take the amount to £15,005 thus varying the agreement which could carry with it the need to follow the formalities prescribed by regulations in regard to this variation. However, this does not occur because s.10(2) in defining 'credit limit' states that one may disregard any term of an agreement allowing the maximum to be exceeded on a temporary basis only. In the event, therefore, the overdraft agreement remains one for £15,000 but allowing a temporary excess. Thus the variation formalities are not required and the agreement remains a regulated one.

CANVASSING

By s.48 oral canvassing off trade premises in regard to entering into a regulated agreement is an offence unless it is in response to a request made in writing by the debtor and signed on a previous occasion, e.g. before the canvasser comes to the debtor's home. However, this applies only where the canvasser has gone to the premises for the purpose of soliciting a loan agreement. Thus a bank manager who suggests an overdraft during a social occasion, e.g. a golf match or on a visit to the customer's home, will not be canvassing because he will not have gone there for the purpose of soliciting a agreement.

However, the Director of Fair Trading may excempt overdrawing on a current account already kept from the provisions of s.48. Thus, for example, a bank manager could visit a sick customer in hospital or go to the golf club of a customer in response to a telephone call and agree to allow him to overdraw. Such exemption would not, however, apply if the bank manager used the occasion to suggest alternative forms of lending such as loan account.

CHEQUE GUARANTEE CARDS

Credit cards should be distinguished from cheque guarantee cards which merely constitute an undertaking by the issuing bank to persons generally that a cheque backed by the card will be honoured if it does not exceed the limit on the card, which at the present time is £50.

Section 187(3) of the 1974 Act makes it clear that cheque guarantee cards issued by banks do not generate a debtor-supplier agreement merely because the bank undertakes to persons who supply goods that it will honour cheques drawn by the card holder up to the limit currently in force. Neither is a cheque card a credit-token since the bank in paying the supplier is not paying for goods or services but is merely honouring its guarantee of payment of the cheque.

Thus the bank is not liable with the supplier of goods under a cheque guarantee card for any breach of contract or misrepresentation perpetrated by the supplier.

CASH CARDS

Cards which can be used at a bank cash dispensing machine do not constitute a debtor-supplier agreement either. The liability of the customer and the banker if there is misuse depends upon the agreement between them. Generally speaking, the agreement will be regarded as broken if the cash dispenser card and the official note of the customer's personal identification number to use at the machine are kept together and have been lost together.

In these circumstances the customer is liable for all losses, even where money is abstracted from a cash dispensing machine *after* the loss is reported to the bank.

This is very different from the situation which we have already considered in relation to bank and credit cards. However, fortunately for the customer, it is only possible in most cases to draw £100 in one day, by which time the bank would normally have taken the number out of the computer once it had been reported that a cash dispenser card had been stolen.

CHEQUES

Formerly, suppliers of goods and services have taken from consumers negotiable instruments such as promissory notes which they discounted with a finance institution. The institution then became a holder in due course entitled to enforce the negotiable instrument free from any defects arising out of the supplier's breach of the original contract. In order to prevent circumvention of the Act in this way the taking by creditors or owners of goods of negotiable instruments other than cheques or bank notes is prohibited. In addition, cheques lawfully taken may be negotiated only through banks. Furthermore, although a cheque may be taken as discharge for the sums payable, no negotiable instrument of *any kind* may be taken as security for those sums. Thus a post-dated cheque could not be taken to guarantee prompt payment of instalments as they fall due. If a negotiable instrument is taken contrary to the Act or a cheque is negotiated other than through a bank, the creditor or owner can only enforce the agreement if the court so orders. If, however, an unlawfully negotiated instrument comes into the hands of a holder in due course, who in addition to satisfying the definition set out on p. 271 must also show that he had no knowledge of infringement of the 1974 Act, his rights are not diminished and he will be able to claim on the cheque free from any defects in terms of the creditor or owner's breach of contract. However, the problem is solved by making the creditor or owner liable to indemnify the debtor who has had to meet the cheque.

8 General principles of insurance law

The first form of insurance concerned marine risks, i.e. the insurance of ships and their cargoes, but other forms of insurance have since developed, notably at first fire insurance and life assurance. More recently the range of insurance has been enormously extended and now includes Motor vehicle insurance, personal accident insurance, fidelity insurance under which, e.g. an insurance company agrees to reimburse an organisation for the losses caused by a dishonest employee, such as a cashier, professional indemnity insurance, and many other types; indeed there is hardly any limit to the scope of insurance contracts.

Obviously each branch of insurance is a specialist subject and this chapter can only deal with the general principles of the law involved. Perhaps the most specialized of all is marine insurance and this is not covered by the chapter except where an Act or case on the subject has relevance to insurance generally, nor is the chapter concerned with Acts of Parliament which control the insurance industry in terms, e.g., of its solvency, since these have no relation to the general principles of insurance law.

THE NATURE OF INSURANCE

A contract of insurance is one in which one party (called the insurer) agrees in consideration of a single or periodical payment (called the premium) to accept a risk to which the assured is subject, and to compensate or indemnify the assured for or against any loss which may occur if the risk insured against happens.

There is a practical difference between the terms *insurance* and *assurance,* although there is an increasing tendency to treat them as synonymous.

Insurance implies that the contract is designed to indemnify the insured against unforeseeable loss or damage which may or may not occur, e.g. damage to property by fire. A contract of assurance is one in which the assured or his representatives are to receive a sum of money on the occurrence of an event which is bound to happen at some time, although the time of happening is uncertain, e.g. the death of the assured.

It is a requirement in a contract of insurance that the insured has an insurable interest, which means that the happening against which he insures must be one adverse to him, and likely to cause him loss or to saddle him with a liability.

Furthermore, the contract of insurance is governed by general principles of contract law and thus it is contrary to public policy for a court to enforce a contract of insurance in respect of goods imported into the United Kingdom in breach of the law. Thus in *Geismar* v *Sun Alliance and London Insurance* [1977] 3 All E.R. 570 the plaintiff had insured various goods against loss and they were stolen. When he claimed on his insurance policy it appeared that he had imported the goods into the UK without paying customs duty on them and, furthermore, he did not intend to pay that duty. It was held by Talbot, J., that in these circumstances the plaintiff was not entitled to an indemnity in respect of the articles stolen, since to give him one would assist him in deriving a profit from a breach of the law.

The contract of insurance

A contract of insurance comes into being when one party makes an offer and the other party makes a valid acceptance. Sometimes, as where baggage is insured, it is the insurer who makes the offer, and the insured, by signing a standardized form or even by merely paying a premium, acquires the rights of insurance set out in the form. In most cases, however, the would-be insured fills in a proposal form inviting the insurer to cover him for certain risks, and when the insurer accepts this proposal, the contract of insurance comes into being. Although acceptance may have taken place earlier, it is normally conclusive once a policy has been issued in accordance with the proposal.

While writing is essential in the case of marine insurance (s.22, Marine Insurance Act 1906) since oral evidence of its existence is not admissible in case of dispute, and Fidelity Guarantees (s.4, Statute of Frauds 1677), there is no legal necessity in other cases, and if the insurer accepted the proposal and a premium without qualification, he would probably be held bound after a reasonable time had elapsed. However, in view of the practical difficulties which would arise in ascertaining the precise terms of the contract if it was wholly oral, insurance contracts are in fact made in writing.

THE PROPOSAL

A standard form called a proposal form, is usually handed by the insurer to the proposed insured and contains details of the risk the insured wishes to be covered. It asks him to answer a number of questions on the basis of which the insurer will decide whether to accept the risk and complete the contract.

When an insurer issues a blank proposal form he is not making an offer of insurance even if premium rates are quoted on the form. The blank proposal form is an invitation to treat. If, however, an insurer, on receipt of a completed proposal form, indicates that he will accept the insurance on the basis of, say, an increased premium, this would operate as an offer which could be accepted by the proposer.

The proposal asks for the name, address and occupation of the insured, and where a person has several occupations it might be relevant to declare them all. The form then goes on to describe the scope of the risk to be covered and to elicit the former experience of the proposer in connection with such a risk. For instance, if it is insurance against fire, has he had previous fires, or if it is against motor accidents, has he had previous accidents? Clearly this information is of value to the insurer in estimating the degree of risk, and may in fact induce him to charge a higher premium. It is also usual to ask the insured whether he has previously been refused insurance by other insurers, or whether they have refused to renew insurances formerly held.

The duty of the proposer to make full disclosure of all material facts means that he must scrutinize the proposal form with great care. Where the specific questions to be answered appear to be exhaustive, the matter is comparatively simple, but in other cases the proposer may be in doubt as to what additional information he ought to supply, and the line between what is material and what is immaterial is not always easy to draw. He should, therefore, in his own interests, amplify the information specifically requested if he feels that there are other material facts which he ought to disclose. (*London Assurance* v *Mansel* 1879.)[403] Neglect to do this may mean that, if the insurer accepts the proposal and the loss actually occurs, the insured may find that the insurer can avoid the contract and have no liability beyond the return of the premiums paid. (*Roselodge Ltd* v *Castle* 1966.)[404]

Proposal forms seldom if ever ask for disclosures relating to the integrity or morality of the insured, and yet these matters can affect the risk and lead to avoidance of the insurance by the insurer. For example, a history of heavy drinking or drug dependence is likely to be material to most risks and yet would seldom be disclosed voluntarily. It would seem more satisfactory, therefore, to ask a question dealing broadly with integrity in order to minimize the risk that a particular policy which the insured is relying on is not in fact voidable.

The matter came before the court in *Woolcott* v *Sun Alliance and London Insurance* [1978] 1 All E.R. 1253. In that case the plaintiff was granted a mortgage by a building society and the application form which the plaintiff completed said that the society would insure the property. No information was required to be supplied by the plaintiff for the purposes of the insurance which was arranged under a block policy held by the society with the defendants. Later the property was destroyed by fire and the insurance company managed to avoid the policy on the basis that the plaintiff had not disclosed the fact that he had been convicted of the offence of robbery some years previously for which he had been sentenced to 12 years' imprisonment. It was held in the High Court that the non-disclosure was a material non-disclosure of facts which a reasonable or prudent insurer might have treated as material and, accordingly, that the policy was avoided. The case is a particularly hard one since the plaintiff was never asked to fill in any forms in relation to the insurance. In addition, it should be noted that the conviction which the plaintiff failed to disclose would never have become a 'spent' conviction under the Rehabilitation of Offenders Act 1974 because it was too long a prison sentence.

Most proposals require the proposer to sign a declaration in which he warrants that the statements he has made are true, and agrees that they be incorporated into the contract. (*Dawsons Ltd* v *Bonnin* 1922.)[123] Thus the proposal and the policy of insurance issued by the insurer must be read together.

As we have seen, the Unfair Contract Terms Act 1977 does not apply to contracts of insurance following a deal between the insurance companies and the Government under which the insurance companies agreed to abide by voluntary statements of practice. In this connection there is a statement of long-term insurance practice issued by the Life Offices' Association. The statement relates to long-term insurance effected by individuals resident in the UK in a private capacity and will apply, for example, to life assurance. The statement is not mandatory but is recognized as an indication of insurance practice. As regards proposal forms, the statement says that proposal forms should draw the attention of those completing them to the consequences of failure to disclose all materials facts and a warning that if the signatory is in any doubt about whether certain facts are material, these facts should be disclosed. Furthermore, those matters which insurers have commonly found to be material should be the subject of clear questions in proposal forms. Insurers should avoid asking questions which would require knowledge beyond that which the signatory could reasonably be expected to possess.

It is quite common for the insurance to be effected by an employee of the insurer, who often fills in, or assists in filling in, the proposal form. In doing this the agent is not regarded as the agent of the insurer but of the insured, and when the latter signs the form, he should read it carefully, since he will be bound by the answers as if he had filled them in himself. (*Newsholme Brother* v *Road Transport and General Insurance Co.* 1929[405] and *O'Connor* v *Kirby* 1971[406]; but see *Stone* v *Reliance Mutual Insurance Society Ltd* 1972[407] and *Woolcott* v *Excess Insurance Co.* 1979.[408])

This is not so in the case of industrial assurance, i.e. life policies for small amounts, where the agent has authority to fill in the form on behalf of his employers.

COVER NOTES

It is not unusual for some time to elapse between the completion of the proposal form and the acceptance of the contract by the insurer and the issue of a policy. In these circumstances it is common for the agent to hand over to the person who has made the proposal a *cover note* which stipulates a number of days during which the insurers will accept the risk of the insurance. This cover note gives the assured the benefit of cover while the insurers are deciding whether to accept the proposal or not, and expires at the end of the number of days specified, although it may be terminated earlier by the insurers giving notice to the assured that they do not propose to issue a policy. Whenever we refer to insurers we mean either an insurance company or Lloyd's underwriters and in the case of insurances effected at Lloyd's, a *slip* is issued and not a cover note, the difference being that a slip, once initialled, constitutes an acceptance of the proposal and is binding on the insurers.

UBERRIMAE FIDEI

We have already seen that the insured must disclose all material facts and a contract of insurance is *uberrimae fidei*, i.e. a contract based on the utmost good faith. Thus either party may avoid a contract of insurance if he can establish that the other party failed to disclose a material fact or made a misrepresentation, even if innocent, of such a fact. Although the duty lies heaviest on the insured, there is nevertheless a similar duty on the insurer. Thus if an insurer misrepresents in a prospectus the effects of an insurance, the insured can obtain rectification of his policy, and claim on the basis of the actual representations. The Marine Insurance Act 1906 has general relevance in this area and section numbers are quoted below.

The insured must disclose every material circumstance which is known to him, and he is deemed to know every circumstance which, in the ordinary course of business, ought to be known to him. (S.18(1).) A circumstance is material which would influence the judgment of a prudent insurer in fixing the premium, or determining whether he will take the risk. (S.18(2).) (*March Cabaret Club and Casino* v *London Assurance* 1975[409]; but see *Mutual Life Insurance Company of New York* v *Ontario Metal Products Co. Ltd* 1925.[410]) However, in the absence of inquiry by the insurer, the insured need not disclose any circumstance—

(1) which diminishes the risk, e.g. the existence of a sprinkler system in premises proposed for fire insurance;

(2) which is known or presumed to be known to the insurer, e.g. the existence of a state of war;

(3) regarding matters of law, e.g. the contents of factory legislation which are particularly relevant to employer's liability insurance;

(4) which it is superfluous to disclose because it is already covered by an express or implied warranty (s.18(3)); e.g. a particular policy for burglary insurance may be subject to a warranty that a certain form

of lock be fitted, but it is superfluous to disclose whether they are or are not fitted since the policy operates only if they are;

(5) which the insurer's representative fails to notice on a survey, e.g. hazardous features in premises proposed for fire insurance, provided there is no concealment by the proposer. (*Re Universal Non-Tariff Fire Insurance Co., Forbes & Co.'s Claim* 1875[411])

It is a question of fact whether a circumstance which is not disclosed is material or not. (*Ionides* v *Pender* 1874.)[412]

The duty of disclosure continues throughout the negotiations, and where circumstances alter, previous statements should be corrected. (*Looker* v *Law Union and Rock Insurance Co. Ltd* 1928.)[413] Thus, if between submitting a proposal for life assurance and receiving the actual acceptance the insured learns that he has a serious disease, he must disclose this fact to the insurer, and even the fact that the insurer has compelled him to undergo a medical examination does not relieve him of this duty. Nevertheless the duty of disclosure ceases when the contract is completed.

Even if a misstatement is honest, and not in the ordinary sense material, it may still invalidate the contract. Thus, in contracting for life assurance, proposers have to make statements concerning their state of health and, while they are here expressing their opinions, which is all they can express, they may find that, if the proposal is made the basis of the assurance by a basis clause, they will be held to have warranted the truth of the statements made. If the statements turn out to be false, the insurer can avoid the contract without having to prove that the facts were or were not material. (*Dawson's Ltd* v *Bonnin* 1922.)[123] In special cases the court may prevent the operation of a basis clause by regarding a statement as a mere description of the risk. (*Farr* v *Motor Traders' Mutual Insurance Society* 1920.)[414] The insurer cannot take advantage of a misstatement if he is really aware or ought to be aware of the true facts of the case. (*Re Universal Non-Tariff Fire Insurance Co., Forbes & Co.'s Claim* 1875.)[411]

The duties of disclosure cannot be avoided by appointing an agent, and the insured is bound to disclose to his agent every material circumstance unless it has come to his knowledge too late to communicate it. The agent must disclose to the insurer every material circumstance which is known to himself (*Woolcott* v *Excess Insurance Co.* 1979[408]), and he is deemed to know every circumstance which, in the ordinary course of business, ought to be known by, or to have been communicated to, him. (S.19.)

However, there are certain cases, e.g. in fire insurance, where an agent of the company makes inspection of premises on behalf of his employers, and any such knowledge he ought to have acquired is imputed to the insurer, and non-disclosure of such facts by the insured would not invalidate the policy. (*Re Universal Non-Tariff Fire Insurance Co., Forbes & Co's. Claim* 1875.)[411] In addition to his duty of full disclosure the insured has a duty to see that material representations made while the contract is beng negotiated are true. The insurer may avoid the contract if any material representation is untrue. (S.20).

THE POLICY

Normally, before the expiry of the cover note, the insurer delivers to the insured a contractual document called the policy, which contains the undertaking of the insurer to pay to the policy holder the sum assured on the happening of the specified event. The policy is not the contract but merely written evidence of it. Nevertheless a court will regard it as containing the expressed intentions of the parties in the absence of proof to the contrary. It contains all the terms necessary for the contract, including the name, address and occupation of the insured, the subject matter of the insurance and the scope of the risk, the period of the insurance, the premium, and the amount for which the risk is insured. The policy contains the general conditions governing the insurance, commonly endorsed on the back, and, where a policy continues from year to year, variations may be incorporated by means of endorsement slips which are stuck on the back of the policy.

The general conditions include such matters as the giving of notice of an event leading to a claim, the information which must be given in support of a claim, and many others. Most policies also contain a clause which incorporates the relevant parts of the proposal, and makes the truth of its contents a condition precedent to the liability of the insurer to pay claims under the policy.

Types of policy

LIFE ASSURANCE

The characteristics of life assurance are that the person insured pays specified premiums at regular intervals and the amount for which he is covered is payable on his death. There may, however, be modifications of such insurance, the commonest being that of endowment insurance. In this case the insured pays regular premiums for a specified term of years, and an agreed sum is payable either at the end of the period to the insured himself, or on his earlier death to his personal representatives.

PERSONAL ACCIDENT INSURANCE

An insured sometimes insures himself against the possibility of accidental injury which may result in disablement or death, and the loss of income occasioned thereby. Such an insurance may be a continuing contract like life assurance, or may be for a year or for a shorter period, and it is not a contract of indemnity since the loss suffered may not be capable of accurate estimation.

FIRE INSURANCE

This is a very common form of insurance and is intended to indemnify the insured against loss of property by fire, including lightning and explosion. In the ordinary way it does not matter what caused the fire, and a claim can be made even where the fire is due to the negligence of the insured or the wilful act of a third party. (*Harris* v *Poland* 1941.)[415]

But the insured is not entitled to recover for loss which is due to his wilful misconduct, (*Slattery* v *Mance* 1962)[425] and he cannot recover if he intentionally sets fire to his own property. This may happen where a company is insolvent and its directors decide to set fire to its premises in order to recover the insurance money. A claim in such circumstances is fraudulent and will fail. However, it was held in *Watkins & Davis Ltd* v *Legal & General Assurance Co.*, [1981] 1 Lloyd's Rep. 674 that the burden of proof upon the insurance company to prove that the claim is fraudulent is a heavy one. In addition, scientific evidence is required to prove fraud in these cases. In order to constitute a loss by fire there must be actual ignition. Loss by heating or fermentaiton is not enough.

Most policies contain expected perils and these include fires caused by riot, civil commotion and war. The connection between an explosion and a fire is of interest, since an explosion may cause damage by blast or by fire. Where the property is consumed by fire then a claim can clearly be made, but where the damage is due to the blast of the explosion only, there will be no claim under a fire policy unless the explosion was actually caused by a fire and not by some other means. Actually, explosions are usually dealt with by specific clauses in the policy, and the wording of these clauses covers the situation. In general, the policy provides that, where there is an explosion, any damage due to fire is covered and any damage due to blast or concussion is excluded.

GENERAL LIABILITY INSURANCE

Everyone runs the risk of becoming liable to pay damages to some other person as a result of committing a tort or in some other way. Cover for such liability is a frequent part of other types of insurance, e.g. the insurance of houses, or of motor vehicles, but the scope of third-party liability is much wider and can be separately insured against. The object of such an insurance is to be indemnified against legal liabilities, and the legal liability must come within the categories of the policy.

A policy covering liability for negligence is valid but an insured person cannot recover for an intentional criminal act, nor presumably for a tort intentionally committed such as defamation. However, acts of criminal negligence, such as reckless driving, or the committing of statutory offences, such as speeding, do not prevent the insured recovering under a liability insurance.

Employers must insure themselves against claims which may be made upon them by their employees for personal injury. (Employers' Liability

(Compulsory Insurance) Act 1969.) Clearly in such cases the risk run by insurers depends on such factors as the number of persons employed or, in the case of equipment, the extent and range of its use. It is, therefore, customary to charge at the outset of the insurance a provisional premium which is adjusted at the end of the year when the degree of risk borne can be calculated from the figures of the number of persons employed or the amount of wages paid or the extent to which equipment was used. Insurers usually reserve to themselves the power to take over and defend any proceedings which may be taken against the assured.

PROFESSIONAL NEGLIGENCE

Professional indemnity policies are available for a whole range of professional persons and experts, e.g. accountants, solicitors, company directors, and insurance brokers. These policies carry an excess clause under which the insured bears the first, say, £500 of the claim. The risk covered is variously described but there is now a tendency to cover 'full civil liability' followed by exclusions from cover of things such as libel. The policies usually cover loss caused to a client (i.e. by breach of contract), and to a non-client (i.e. in tort) such as might have arisen in *JEB Fasteners* v *Marks Bloom*. (See p. 416.)

THE EXTENT OF THE INDEMNITY MAY BE LIMITED IN VARIOUS WAYS

The policy may provide for a full indemnity, or it may fix a maximum indemnity which will be exhausted when a sufficient number of smaller claims reach such an aggregate. A policy may provide for a maximum sum in respect of any one incident, or it may provide that the insured bears the first proportion of each claim up to a specified amount so that he only makes claims of a substantial character. The policy normally provides for an indemnity to the insured for costs of any proceedings against him in connection with any claims made under the policy.

The insurer is not liable to pay unless the insured is legally liable in respect of the damage and in this connection the Law Reform (Husband and Wife) Act 1962 enables a husband and wife to sue each other in tort. Thus, if a husband negligently injures his wife he will be legally liable and could claim an indemnity under a liability policy.

MOTOR VEHICLE INSURANCE

Although a motorist will often take out a comprehensive policy covering a variety of risks, the Road Traffic Act 1972, s.143, places a legal duty on the motorist to insure in respect of damages for death and personal injury to third parties. Third parties include other road users, pedestrians, or the insured's passengers. There is no need for compulsory insurance in respect of injuries to the *property* of third parties. Failure to take out this compulsory insurance is a criminal offence and both owner and driver, where these are different persons, are liable to prosecution.

Under s.148 of the 1972 Act certain provisions designed to limit the insurer's liability are void in respect of *compulsory risks.* These include any provisions which relate to the physical or mental condition of the driver, the condition or loading of the vehicle, and also the policy-holder's failure to notify the insurer of an accident within a set time. Thus, if the insured was using the vehicle for an authorized purpose but was driving while ill and/or failed to report an accident, the insurer could refuse to pay for repairs to the vehicle of the insured and to any others involved, but would still have to pay damages for the victim's physical injuries or, of course, death.

A voidable policy does not operate as an infringement of the Act (*Adams* v *Dunn* 1978),[416] though compulsory insurance is still required even when the car cannot be driven but can be moved. (*Elliot* v *Grey* 1959.)[417] This section also imposes a statutory duty for the purposes of a civil action in negligence and this is useful to a plaintiff in circumstances where it would be difficult to establish a duty in the defendant on general principles. (*Monk* v *Warbey* 1904.)[418]

In order to comply with the provisions of the Act the assured must receive a *certificate of insurance* from the insurer, or, under s.144(1) of the 1972 Act, if the vehicle is driven under his own control, he must have deposited the lamentably low sum of £15,000 with the Accountant-General of the Supreme Court, in which case the Act will not apply. Some very large organizations with a large fleet of vehicles do take advantage of this provision. By s.144(2) local authorities and police authorities and certain other public bodies are excluded from the compulsory provisions of s.143.

It is possible to insure a motor vehicle to cover both driving by the owner and by other persons who may from time to time use the vehicle, and s.148(4) of the Road Traffic Act 1972 provides that the insurers must indemnify any person driving the vehicle with the owner's consent, thus providing a statutory exception to the doctrine of privity of contract.

It is interesting to note that the House of Lords held, in *Kelly* v *Cornhill Insurance Co.* [1964] 1 All E.R. 321, that permission given by the insured before his death can continue afterwards, thus rendering the policy effective even though the insured is dead. The subsection applies to all risks covered by the policy and is not restricted to cases of compulsory insurance. (*Digby* v *General Accident Fire and Life Assurance Corporation* 1943.)[419]

In the case of compulsory insurance, s.149 of the Road Traffic Act 1972 requires the insurer to pay a third party who has obtained judgment against the insured. However, the judgment must be in respect of a compulsory risk; the liability must be covered by the policy, so that the section would not apply if, when the accident happened, the car was being used for business purposes when it was insured for private purposes only, a certificate of insurance must have been issued to the insured; notice of the action in which the judgment was obtained must have been given to the insurer not later than seven days after it began. The insurer need not meet the judgment if—

(1) an appeal is pending; or

(2) the policy was cancelled before the accident, though the certificate of insurance must have been surrendered, or the insured must have made a statutory declaration that it was lost or destroyed, or the insurer must commence proceedings to recover it not later than 14 days after cancelling; or

(3) the insurer obtains a declaration from the court that the policy is void for non-disclosure or misrepresentation, provided that the action for the declaration was commenced within three months from the commencement of the proceedings in which the third party obtained his judgment.

Section 149 will not assist a third party whose injury or damage is non-compulsory though if the insured is bankrupt or has compounded with his creditors or, in the case of a company, goes into liquidation the Third Party (Rights against Insurers) Act 1930 may apply. (See p. 324.) Policies of motor insurance may, in addition to covering a specified vehicle, extend cover to the insured while driving some other vehicle not owned by him. However, the policy becomes ineffective if the insured ceases to have an interest in the specified vehicle. This principle applies to comprehensive policities (*Tattershall* v *Drysdale* 1935),[420] and to third party policies. (*Boss* v *Kingston* 1963.)[421] The seller of a vehicle cannot transfer the policy of insurance to the buyer unless the insurer consents.

The policy must cover the persons insured against liability as a result of the death of, or bodily injury to, any person arising out of the vehicle's use of the road. The policy need not cover (1) liability to an employee of the person insured in respect of death or bodily injury arising out of and in the course of employment; (2) liability arising under a contract.

The Road Traffic Act 1972 has the effect of requiring users of motor vehicles to be covered against any liability which they might incur in respect of the death or personal injuries to their passengers arising out of the use of their motor vehicles on the roads. The Act also renders ineffective 'own risk' agreements under which a passenger agrees to accept the risk of injury without compensation from the owner of the vehicle.

A person injured is not prejudiced in his claim by restrictive conditions in the policy, and if a judgment is obtained against the assured, the insurers must pay, although they may have a claim on the assured for violating the conditions. Nor shall third parties be prejudiced by the fact that the assured does some act, or fails to do some act, required by the policy after the accident, e.g. if the assured fails to give proper notice of the accident within the time specified by the policy.

Where, however, a policy covering compulsory risks provides that it shall only apply when the vehicle is being used 'for social, domestic and pleasure purposes', then the insurers are under no liability if the insured incurs liability for the death or injury of a third party while driving the vehicle for business purposess. (*Seddon* v *Binions* 1978.)[422] The third party is also prejudiced by such a restriction and cannot recover.

Most motorists take out insurance policies of a much more comprehensive character than the law requires, of which the following are examples—

(1) *Third party only.* This gives cover for all third party claims, both in regard to compulsory risks and damage to property, but gives nothing in respect of the insured's own vehicle and other property damage.

(2) *Third party, fire and theft.* Such a policy gives the same third party cover as third party only but it also requires the insurer to pay the value of the insured's car should it be stolen or destroyed by fire, or the cost of repairing damage caused in this way.

(3) *Comprehensive.* A policy of this kind will not only provide cover against liability to third parties for both compulsory and non-compulsory risks, but will also require the insurer to pay the value of the insured's vehicle should it be stolen or destroyed, or for repairs or replacement in the event of damage, no matter how that damage is caused, including damage sustained in an accident which is caused by the insured's own negligence.

There are many modifications to these policies, e.g. where a policy applies to one named driver only, where the assured agrees to bear the first £X of any claim, where the policy provides for some personal accident insurance, or for compensation for loss of use if the vehicle is out of action.

A motor insurance policy will almost invariably specify the user in respect of which the insurer takes risk, e.g. a vehicle may only be covered for 'social, domestic and pleasure purposes.' (*D. H. R. Moody (Chemists)* v *Iron Trades Mutual Insurance Co.* 1970.)[423] Policies often exclude liability where the vehicle is used for hiring or reward and where the vehicle is in an unroadworthy state.

With regard to the use of seatbelts, insurers have often been pressed to offer a discount off motor premiums for policy holders who wear a seatbelt but at the present time this has not been taken up. Failure to wear a seatbelt is relevant to an insurer in the sense that it can reduce damages payable by the insurance company on the ground that it is contributory negligence not to wear a belt in certain cases. In *Froom* v *Butcher* [1975] 3 All E.R. 520, Lord Denning, M.R., decided that where injuries would have been altogether prevented by the wearing of a seat-belt, the damages should be reduced by 25 per cent; where injuries would have been 'a good deal less severe', the reduction should be 15 per cent. He did say, however, that exceptions would be made in the case of people who were overweight or in the case of women who were pregnant. The response of insurance companies since the wearing of seatbelts has become compulsory would be to reduce the indemnity payable but not to give discounts to those who do not wear them since the criminal law provides the necessary sanctions by way of fine. Presumably the indemnity would not be reduced to a person in an exempt category.

On the issue of disclosure in motor insurance, the Rehabilitation of Offenders Act 1974 should be mentioned. The Act removes the need to disclose convictions, *resulting in a fine*, recorded more than five years before the date of the application for insurance. Thus, since 1 July 1975, when the Act came into force, an answer which, at common law, would breach the duty of utmost good faith, must now be deemed to be accurate although it is in fact untrue. The Act may not make a great deal of difference to the practice of motor insurance. Many insurers restrict the duty of disclosure to a period of five years in any event and the Act will probably affect them only marginally. Other insurers who seek to go back further into the proposed insured's past may, of course, be more concerned.

All sentences are subject to rehabilitation, except imprisonment for life and imprisonment for a term exceeding 30 months. The rehabilitation period for a sentence of imprisonment for a term exceeding six months, but not exceeding 30 months, is 10 years; and for a term not exceeding six months it is seven years, or, as we have seen, if the sentence was a fine it is five years.

Duration of policy

The policy should stipulate the period for which the insurance is to continue and, although a common term is 12 months, any period may be fixed by mutual agreement. In some cases, e.g. fire insurance, the duration of the policy is specified to the precise day and hour, but where no such specification occurs, the policy runs from the first moment of the day next after issue to the last moment of the day specified for the termination of the policy. However, since an insurance policy is not effective until it is issued, the person insured will have no claim for losses occurring between the proposal and the issue of the policy unless the policy so provides, as it may do if it replaces a cover note previously issued. In other cases it is stipulated that the policy does not operate until the premium has been paid.

TERMINATION OF POLICY

A policy may expire with the effluxion of time. It may also come to an end when the risk which is covered occurs and the insurer pays out an indemnity on the basis of total loss. Thus, where a house is insured for a period of 12 months and it is totally destroyed after a month, the insurance company ends its liability on payment of the value of the loss. Nevertheless, if there are in the same house a number of fires during the course of one year's insurance and not one of them causes total loss, the insurer is liable successively for each fire as it occurs, but only if in the aggregate the losses do not exceed the sum insured.

A policy may also be ended by either the insured or the insurer under the provisions contained in it. For instance, many life insurance policies provide for the insured to surrender his rights under the policy at any time instead of paying renewal premiums and, on such surrender, he usually receives a sum calculated in relation to the premiums paid and the amount of cover he has enjoyed. Similarly policies often stipulate the terms upon which the insurer may bring them to an end.

(1) *Policies of a continuing character.* It is clear that certain types of insurance, such as life assurance, are of a continuing character, and it is expected that the insurance will remain valid until the death of the insured. It would be inequitable for the insurers to continue to take premiums while a man was young and, as he grew older, refuse to renew the insurance when the risk of death became greater. Such contracts, therefore, are treated as continuing contracts for the life of the insured, and the insurers are bound to accept the periodic premiums if they are offered on the due date, or within the period of grace allowed for each successive payment. (*Stuart* v *Freeman* 1903.)[424] Only if the premium is not paid when due may the insurers terminate the policy.

(2) *Policies not of a continuing character.* Other forms of insurance, e.g. fire insurance, are not of a continuing character and the policy is renewable with the consent of the parties at the expiration of each specific period. The renewal depends on mutual consent but, since it is expected that the policy may be renewed time after time, provision is often made for renewal. In practice, the insurers normally send out a renewal notice specifying the renewal premium, and a period of grace is allowed for payment. The payment of the premium so requested renews the insurance for a further period.

(3) *Renewal.* It should be noted that each renewal is a fresh contract. In the case of indemnity insurance the same duty of disclosure attaches on renewal as on making the original proposal, so that any changes of circumstances which would affect the insurers must be brought to their notice. This is not the case, however, with life assurance because the insurance policy being continuous, is governed by the proposal originally made. It is obvious that the risk to the insurers will increase as the insured grows older, but this must have been within the contemplation of the parties when the contract was originally made.

(4) *Period of grace.* It is common in insurance policies to make provision for a period of grace during which a renewal premium may be paid, and this is often 30 days in the case of life assurance, and 15 days in other forms. This period is in the nature of an option to renew on pay-

ment of a specific premium, and the insured can accept the offer by making such a payment. If the insured avails himself of the days of grace and a loss occurs after the renewal date but before the expiration of the period of grace, the question arises as to whether the insurers must indemnify him for the loss so suffered. This situation will normally be covered by the terms of the policy which lay down the conditions under which grace for payment is allowed. However, in the case of life assurance, where the premium is paid during the period of grace it is regarded as having been paid on the due date and, if a person so insured dies after the due date of the premium but before the expiry of the days of grace, his representatives can pay the premium and claim the benefit of the policy. (*Stuart* v *Freeman* 1903.)[424]

The risk

The policy should clearly set out the nature and precise extent of the peril which the insured wishes to be protected against. The subject matter of the policy must be adequately identified and this may be done either by limiting the insurance to objects specifically described, or by taking out an insurance to cover all objects which fall within a particular class. A policy frequently includes details of the circumstances which affect the risk, e.g. details of the construction and use of buildings insured against fire, or of the nature of the insured's business, or the uses to which he proposes to put an insured motor vehicle. When an insurer has undertaken to insure against a specific risk, he will not be able to escape liability by virtue of the fact that the insured's conduct, e.g. his increased use of the property insured, has increased the likelihood of loss, unless specific clauses are inserted in the policy to achieve this. Insurance companies, however, do commonly include such clauses so as to restrict or remove their liability if the circumstances of the contemplated insurance are changed.

Even in an 'all risks' policy there are certain types of loss which cannot be covered in the absence of an express provision. Thus, the insured cannot recover for losses resulting from his wilful acts, e.g. a deliberate destruction of property. An accident policy would not cover death from natural causes nor would such a policy cover depreciation of the goods insured. Further, it is not lawful to cover certain risks, e.g. a criminal cannot insure against imprisonment. The insured is required to prove that the loss comes within the risk covered, though where the insurers wish to repudiate the contract for fraud or arson the burden of proof is on them. (*Slattery* v *Mance* 1962.)[425]

Before leaving the subject of risk, it would be as well to consider the Congenital Disabilities (Civil Liability) Act 1976. This Act establishes civil liability giving rise to an action for damages by a child who is born disabled in consequence of the intentional act or the negligence or the breach of statutory duty of some person before the child's birth. The

Act distinguishes between matters arising *before* conception (where the injury can be to either parent) and matters arising when the child's mother is pregnant or during the actual process of childbirth (where the injury can only be to the mother). Thus the injury could result, for example, from irradiation which damages the progenitive capacity of the father. Thus all occupiers of factories, shops or offices now have to face the prospect of claims from unborn children of employees of whose existence they can generally have known nothing and for whose safety, health and welfare they are now legally liable. As regards insurance aspects, the Act, in providing help to, e.g. victims of drug damage such as the thalidomide children, has extended the boundaries of employers' liabilities by a considerable amount. Any claim under this Act can be transferred to the employers' liability insurers, however. So far as employers are concerned, every duty owed to an employee is transferred to that employer's unborn children in appropriate circumstances.

Other forms of non-marine insurance

Set out below are the main legal principles governing certain other types of non-marine insurance, other than road traffic policies which have already been considered.

LIFE ASSURANCE

In the normal case the sum insured is payable on death however caused, but the payment of money due under an insurance policy may in certain circumstances be illegal as being contrary to public policy. So neither a person guilty of murder or manslaughter, nor persons claiming through him, e.g. assignees, can obtain a benefit under a policy on the life of the victim. (*Cleaver* v *Mutual Reserve Fund Life Association* 1892,[426] and *Gray* v *Barr* 1971.)[427]

Section 2 of the Forfeiture Act 1982 now gives power to the court to make an order to alleviate the public policy rule referred to above. The court is required to bear in mind the conduct of the offender who has unlawfully killed the deceased and of the deceased himself. Thus the adulterous conduct of the deceased in *Gray* v *Barr* 1971[427] would be relevant. The Act was prompted in large measure by cases where widows who had killed their husbands in circumstances of little moral blame had forfeited social welfare benefits, but it also applies in the area of insurance as well. It should be noted that under s.5 no order can be made by the court in respect of an offenders who have been convicted of the crime of murder. Application must be made to the court within three months of the conviction of the offender. In the context of life assurance, the court order could allow the offender to benefit under a relevant insurance policy.

Furthermore, a person who dies while committing the offences of dangerous driving and/or drunken driving may not be able to claim on a life insurance policy. (*Marcel Beller* v *Hayden* [1978] 3 All E.R. 111.)

The same was formerly true of sane suicide (*Beresford* v *Royal Insurance Co. Ltd* 1938)[428] but, since the Suicide Act 1961, suicide is no longer a crime and the question of public policy may not arise. However, the concept of risk does not include loss due to the wilful act of the insured, unless there is an express provision to this effect. Thus, insurers may still be able to reject a claim in the absence of an express provision to the contrary, and it is perhaps unlikely that a policy would be issued specifically covering suicide. If the insured commits suicide while insane his act will not be regarded as wilful and the insurers will be liable unless the policy provides to the contrary.

Some policies specifically state that the insurance shall be void on a sane suicide unless the policy has been assigned for value in which case the assignee can claim. In many policies restrictive clauses prohibit the assured from engaging in hazardous enterprises.

A proposal for life assurance requires the insured to give detailed information on his health, habits and medical history, and, of course, his age is of great importance, since different premiums are quoted to people of different ages. The questions on the form indicate the scope of the information the company requires, but if there is a clause that the insured warrants the truth of the information given, and if he has made general statements that he is in good health, he may find, if this proves not to be the case, that the insurance is invalidated. In the case of people who are getting on in years, or who wish to insure themselves for substantial amounts, it is common for insurance companies to insist on a medical examination.

It should be noted that under s.75 of the Insurance Companies Act 1982 life companies are required to send policy holders a statutory notice setting out the main features of the policy and the right of policy holders to a cooling off period. In particular s.76 provides that where a person has received a statutory notice he may before the expiry of (1) the tenth day after that on which he received the notice, or (2) the earliest day on which he knows that both the contract has been entered into and that the first or only premium has been paid, whichever is the later, serve a notice of cancellation on the insurer.

If the insurer fails to send a statutory notice, the proposer may serve a notice of cancellation on the insurer at any time. However, if the insurer sends a statutory notice before the proposer serves a notice of cancellation, then the right of cancellation is limited as set out in (1) above. The statutory notice must have annexed to it a form of notice of cancellation but the notice of cancellation need not be in that form. The major requirement is that it effectively indicates the proposer's intention to withdraw from the transaction. The result of service of the notice of cancellation is to rescind the contract of it has at that time been entered into; otherwise the service of the notice operates as a withdrawal of the proposer's offer to enter into the contract. On any such rescission or withdrawal any sum paid by either party under the contract is recoverable. Policies where there is no cooling off period are single premium policies, policies bought as a condition of obtaining a loan, e.g. endowment mortgage and mortgage protection, and term policies which run for no more than seven years. Home service policies, i.e. where an agent calls at the purchaser's home, are also excluded from the cooling-off rules.

PERSONAL ACCIDENT INSURANCE

An accident has been defined as an unlooked for mishap or an untoward event which was not expected or designed, though even the murder of a person may be regarded as accidental so far as he is concerned. (*Trim Joint District School Board of Management* v *Kelly* 1914.)[429] An injury, even if caused by another's negligence, is still accidental, as indeed may be hernias or injuries to the spine resulting from lifting or carrying heavy loads. In the case of diseases, where an occupational disease develops over a long period of time, this will probably not be regarded as accidental, but where a disease has a definite and specific cause, e.g. anthrax, then the disease may well come within the meaning of the word accident.

Types of benefit are (1) lump sum benefits in the case of death, or of specific injuries such as the loss of a limb or an eye; or (2) periodical payments made during disablement through accident, either for its duration or for a specified period named in the policy, e.g. 16 weeks.

A policy will often exclude cover for certain risks, such as war risks, and may forbid the assured to expose himself to certain specified perils.

Most policies exclude disablement through disease, although, if the disease is not the proximate but only the remote cause of disablement or death, then the event may still be regarded as an accident. Thus death would be accidental (1) if a person walking along the pavement had a fit, and falling into the street, was killed by a passing bus; or (2) if the disease followed and resulted from the accident, as where a person bitten by a dog died of hydrophobia.

FIRE INSURANCE

In estimating the loss caused by fire, consequential damage may be included. Thus where is a wall is burnt it may cause the rest of the building to collapse without being consumed, and other property may be destroyed by those who are attempting to extinguish the fire or to stop it from spreading. However, the insured may not be able to claim for all the consequential loss he has suffered and if, as a result of premises being destroyed by fire, he has to take over others to carry on his business, he will not be able to claim for any loss of profits or additional expenses so incurred.

The sum insured is specified in the policy and this represents the maximum liability of the insurer. The insured, therefore, cannot recover more than the amount for which he has insured, even though the property insured and lost was worth more.

The premium

In return for the acceptance by the insurer of the risk, the insured person pays a premium which may be either a single lump sum, or a series of payments made at appropriate intervals. The premium is calculated by the insurers, having regard to the frequency with which claims will have to be met and the amount of loss they will entail. These premiums are calculated on a statistical basis and it would normally be expected that the premiums collected from insured persons covered for a particular type of risk would be sufficient to pay all claims, and leave a margin for the costs of administration and residue of profit.

A contract of insurance cannot be completed until a premium is agreed but, where the precise degree of risk cannot be calculated in advance, it is possible to pay a provisional premium, and this can be adjusted in either direction at the expiry of the term of insurance when the precise cover has been ascertained. The premium may be paid either direct to the insurers or, if an agent, i.e. a broker has authority to receive payment, it may be paid to him and the insurers will then be bound. The person insured is liable for the premium immediately on completion of the contract, and the insurance company may make payment of the premium a condition precedent to the assumption of liability. If payment is made by cheque it is conditional only. Thus, if a policy provided for forfeiture on non-payment of premium by 1 March the giving of a cheque on that date would not prevent forfeiture if it was dishonoured. In most types of insurance, except life, the policy requires renewal and the insurers are not bound to accept a renewal premium. (See p. 308.) It is also common for policies to make provision for a period of grace during which a renewal premium may be paid. (See p. 308.)

The person insured may claim a return of premiums if there has been total failure of consideration, e.g. where a person whose life was insured had in fact died before the insurance contract was made.

We have seen that, where a proposal form contains misrepresentations, however innocent, the insurers may be able to refuse to indemnify the insured, but if they avoid the policy they will have to return any premiums paid.

If the insured obtained the policy by fraud he cannot claim return of premium, though if the insurer brings an action to rescind the contract the court may ask him to return the premium on the maxim 'he who seeks equity must do equity'.

Where there is no insurable interest the policy will be illegal and premiums cannot generally be recovered, though there are exceptions. (*Hughes* v *Liverpool Victoria Friendly Society* 1916.)[430]

Actually an insurance policy frequently lays down conditions governing the return of premiums, e.g. in the case of motor insurance it is often provided that a premature termination of the insurance by either party may give rights to some repayment premium.

Claims

When the insured suffers the loss insured, he is normally required to make a formal claim and to give the insurer speedy notice of the loss. The question of notice is governed by the terms of the policy which may be very strict, but normally notice must be given 'within a reasonable time or as soon as possible.' (*Verelst's Administratix* v *Motor Union Insurance Co. Ltd* 1925.)[431] It need not be in writing and may be given either by the insured in person or by someone acting on his behalf, and may be given either to the insurers themselves or to any of their authorized agents. If a clause regarding notice makes it a condition precedent of liability of the insurers, they are entitled to notice as soon as an accident or mishap occurs, even if there is no immediate damage. (*Cassel* v *Lancashire and Yorkshire Accident Insurance Co. Ltd* 1885.)[432]

If the insured does not give notice in accordance with the policy the insurer may repudiate liability. However, many insurance companies would compensate the injured party even in the absence of a claim by their customer. There is more difficulty where the insured tells his insurance company that he intends to settle with the injured party himself, e.g. to save his no-claims bonus. In this event the insurance company will not normally pay but hope that the insured will do what he says. Lapse of time in repudiating liability will not operate against the insurer unless there is prejudice to other parties or implied acceptance of liability. (*Allen* v *Robles* 1969.)[433]

An insurer sued directly by an employee under the Third Parties (Rights against Insurers) Act 1930 can set up any defence available against the employer including failure to notify a claim on time. (*Farrell* v *Federated Employers Insurance Association* [1970] 3 All E.R. 632.)

Where a specific procedure is laid down, the claimant should adhere to it. The normal procedure is for the insured to fill in a claim form supplied to him by the insurance company or its agent, the object of the form being to supply the insurers with all the information they require in order to deal with the claim. Where there is a dispute arising as a result of a claim, it is common for the policy to contain an arbitration clause which may require various matters to be submitted to an arbitrator, e.g. the amount payable under the claim or even the question of liability under the policy. An arbitration clause does not necessarily stop the insured from bringing an action but it may restrict the scope of the action to the amount of the award, and require the question of liability to be settled by an arbitrator before an action can be brought.

Where it is possible to give more than one meaning to a clause in a policy or proposal form, the court will generally adopt the meaning most favourable to the insured, because the policy and proposal form are documents drafted by the insurers whose position is, therefore, stronger than that of the assured. This is called the *contra proferentem* rule, but it only applies where there is real ambiguity. (*Provincial Insurance Co* v *Morgan and Foxon* 1933[434] and *Harris* v *Poland* 1941.)[415]

Claims are usually paid in cash, though the policy may provide for reinstatement. Payments must be made to the proper person but, where on the death of the insured there are conflicting claims to the money payable under the policy, the insurers may pay the money into court. In other cases they must interplead. This is a process under which the parties making the conflicting claims on a policy may be brought into court at the initiative of the insurance company so that the dispute as to entitlement is settled.

LIFE ASSURANCE CLAIMS

The sum payable under the policy is often augmented by the addition of annual bonuses which are a share of the profits made by the insurance company. Moreover, even if the insured does not continue to pay premiums for the full period of the insurance, or until death as the case may be he will not necessarily be without any claim on the company. He will usually have the choice of two alternatives—

(1) to surrender the policy and accept a sum of money called its surrender value;

(2) to accept a fully paid policy which will provide that, on his death, a reduced amount may be payable based on the number of premiums already paid and his probable expectation of life.

FIRE INSURANCE CLAIMS

In valuing the property in the case of total loss, the value is the intrinsic value of the property destroyed with no allowance for loss of possible profits or for sentimental value. It is the value at the place of the fire and at the time of the fire, irrespective of whether the property has increased or decreased in value since the taking out of the insurance, and subject only to the fact that no more can be recovered than the sum for which the property was insured.

Where the property is marketable, the value is its market value, but where the property is not strictly marketable, as for instance business premises which the assured would wish to have reinstated, the assured can recover the cost of reinstatement even if this would be in excess of the market value. Clearly, in the case of specialized buildings, such as a church or an art gallery, the notion of market value has no particular significance. Where the loss is partial, the indemnity is the cost of repairing the damage caused by the fire.

The Fires Prevention (Metropolis) Act 1774, which in spite of its name applies also outside London, creates a statutory obligation on insurance companies to reinstate a house or building damaged by fire if the insured requests this, but the cost of reinstatement must not exceed the sum insured. In addition to the insured owners, mortgagors, morgagees, lessors and lessees, tenants for life and remaindermen may request reinstatement, since they have an interest in the continued existence of the property.

In other circumstances the insurers have an obligation to pay money compensation only and cannot insist on reinstatement without the consent of the assured, unless they have reserved the right in the policy. Most insurers find it in their interest to reserve the option of either paying the claim or reinstating the property. Where the policy is a valued policy the agreed value is paid on total loss, or a proportion of that value on partial loss, and nothing in excess of this is recoverable. (*Elcock* v *Thomson* 1949.)[435]

MOTOR VEHICLE INSURANCE—CLAIMS AGAINST MOTOR INSURERS' BUREAU

A person may be injured by a motorist who does not carry the compulsory insurance required by the current Road Traffic legislation, or in circumstances where a vehicle insured is used outside the scope of its cover. In such a case, although the injured person may obtain a judgment against the motorist, he may not be able to enforce it because of the motorist's lack of funds.

He may, however, have a claim against the Motor Insurers' Bureau. By an agreement made in 1946 with the Ministry of Transport, and the Motor Insurers' Bureau, an incorporated body kept in funds by the motor vehicle insurers under what is called the 'Domestic Agreement' which was revised in 1972 and entitled Motor Insurers' Bureau (Compensation of Victims of Uninsured Drivers) and (Compensation of Victims of Untraced Drivers), will satisfy any judgment in respect of a compulsory insurable risk which is not satisfied within seven days against a motorist who is not covered by a policy as required by law. The risk involved must be one against which the motorist must insure (*Lees* v *Motor Insurers' Bureau* 1952)[436], as regards the traced but uninsured driver, the agreement can only be enforced if the Bureau receives notice of the proceedings either before or within seven days of their commencement. If the driver cannot be traced, as in a 'hit and run' case, the MIB will pay compensation if in all probability the untraced driver would have been liable to pay damages, if an application is made within three years of the accident. The claimant must take all reasonable steps, subject to full indemnity by the Bureau as to costs, to enforce his legal rights if the Bureau requires him to do so, and any judgment so obtained must be assigned to the Bureau or its nominee.

Under the Untraced Drivers Agreement the Bureau will accept applications for compensation where (1) the applicant cannot trace the person responsible for death or injury; (2) the death or injury was caused in circumstances that on the balance of probabilities the untraced person would be liable to pay damages; and (3) the untraced person's liability is one required to be covered by insurance under the Road Traffic Act 1972. There is a right of appeal against any decision of the Bureau to an arbitrator who is a Queen's Counsel selected by the Minister of Transport from a panel appointed by the Lord Chancellor.

In practice, the MIB nominates a member insurance company to deal with claims on its behalf.

Under the agreement the plaintiff must not 'know or have reason to believe' that the driver concerned did not have a contract of insurance. The issue was raised in *Porter* v *Addo*; *Porter* v *Motor Insurers' Bureau, The Times* 18 May 1978, where the plaintiff told the defendant that she was not insured to drive her car and that she needed an insured driver to drive it. The defendant, who was insured to drive another car, agreed to drive the plaintiff's car and in the course of the journey she was injured by his negligence. It later emerged that the defendant's insurance did not cover his driving of the plaintiff's car. It was held by Forbes, J., that the plaintiff did not 'know or have reason to believe' that there was no contract within the MIB agreement and accordingly the Bureau were bound to indemnify her under the agreement.

The liability of the insured to a permitted driver is not a compulsory risk and in consequence not a liability which the MIB has agreed to meet. (*Cooper* v *MIB* 1983.)[437]

POLICYHOLDERS' PROTECTION ACT 1975

This Act provides for the protection of non-business policyholders who may be affected by the inability of authorized insurance companies carrying on business in the United Kingdom to meet their liabilities. The protection scheme is administered by the Policyholder's Protection Board. The Board's duties arise when an insurance company goes into liquidation. Where insurance is compulsory, e.g. under the Employers' Liability (Compulsory Insurance) Act 1969 and the Road Traffic Act 1972, the Act requires the Board to secure that the liabilities of an insurance company in liquidation are met in full. In the case of insurance required by the Road Traffic Acts, however, the Motor Insurers' Bureau will in practice continue to ensure that liabilities are met. The Board's expediture is financed principally by levies on authorized insurance companies.

In the case of non-compulsory policies other than marine, aviation, and transport, the board must secure 90 per cent of the liability to each policyholder.

The Act also gives the board power to protect policyholders of companies which are not yet in liquidation but have financial problems. Interim payments can be made to policyholders and the board may facilitate the transfer of all or any part of the insurance business of the concern that is in difficulties to another authorized company if this costs less than the protection of the policyholders if the company were to go into liquidation.

INSURANCE OMBUDSMAN BUREAU AND THE PERSONAL INSURANCE ARBITRATION SERVICE

Before leaving the subject of claims, some mention should be made of the Ombudsman and PIAS services which deal with disputes between insurance companies and their customers. The service provided by both of these organizations is free, though disputes relating to commercial and industrial insurance are not dealt with by them. The PIAS will deal with life policies but the Ombudsman will not in general do so. Both services provide arbitration schemes and the Ombudsman can currently award up to £100,000 on arbitration but PIAS has a maximum range from £25,000 to £100,000, depending on the company providing the insurance.

Insurable interest

LIFE ASSURANCE

An insured person must have an insurable interest and the Life Assurance Act 1774, s.1, states that 'No insurance is to be made on the life or lives of any person or persons, or on any other event or events whatsoever, wherein the person for whose use or benefit, or on whose account the policy is made, has no interest, or by way of gaming or wagering; every insurance made contrary to this provision is void.' The names of the person or persons for whose benefit the policy is made must be stated in the policy, and the amount recoverable from the assurance is limited to the value of the insurable interest.

The Life Assurance Act 1774 applies also to personal accident insurance, but does not apply to insurance on ships or goods (*Prudential Staff Union* v *Hall* 1947)[438] or to motor vehicle insurance. The Act does not apply to insurances taken out by the insured on his own life and for his own benefit, or to insurances by husband and wife of each other's lives.

Insurable interest for the purposes of life assurance is the financial loss which will be suffered by the insured on the death of the person insured. An insurable interest is not presumed in the case of parents and children, or brothers and sisters, or more distant relatives, unless there may be a legal, not merely a moral obligation, to pay funeral expenses. However, creditors may insure the lives of their debtors, and employers and employees may insure each other's lives. Where the insured contracts for the benefit of another person, that person must be named in the policy.

While no more can be recovered under the policy than the value of the insurable interest, this value is determined at the commencement of the policy. It may well be, therefore, that, when death occurs, the loss may be less than the sum assured, but this sum will nevertheless be payable since a life assurance is not strictly one of indemnity. For example, a creditor who insures the life of his debtor may continue to maintain the insurance after the debt has been repaid. There is no need for the insurable interest to exist at the time of death, so long as there was such an interest at the time the contract was made.

FIRE INSURANCE

In the case of an insurance of buildings, e.g. against fire, an interest must exist (1) when the contract is made (by virtue of the Life Assurance Act 1774); and (2) when the loss occurs, because such a contract is in the nature of an indemnity. Whereas in life assurance the sum assured will normally be paid out in full on the death of the insured, in fire insurance the amount payable will be such sum as does not exceed the sum assured and is just sufficient to indemnify the assured against the loss which has occurred. (*Castellain* v *Preston* 1883[439] and *Leppard* v *Excess Insurance Co. Ltd* 1979.)[440]

INSURANCE OF GOODS

Contracts of insurance of goods are not within the Life Assurance Act 1774, but are covered by the Gaming Act 1845. Thus they require an insurable interest at the time of making the contract, or an expectation of such interest. Therefore a buyer may insure goods before purchase, and a warehouseman may take out a policy to cover all the goods in his warehouse at the time of loss up to a fixed amount. Nevertheless the goods must be ascertainable in some way or other.

It is not necessary to be the owner of the thing in question, and an insurable interest may be based on possession. A bailee has an insurable interest to cover his liability to the owner in the event of loss, or to cover any lien he may have on the goods for his charges. In some cases the court may take the view that on a proper interpretation of the policy the bailee has also assumed the interest of the bailor who is the owner of the goods. Where this is so the bailee is entitled to keep what is owing to him out of the insurance money and holds the rest in trust for the bailor regardless of the doctrine of privity of contract. (*A. Tomlinson (Hauliers) Ltd* v *Hepburn* 1966.)[441] However, possession must be coupled with liability, and if the person in possession has no liability in respect of the goods, he has no insurable interest. (*Macaura* v *Northern Assurance Co. Ltd* 1925.)[442]

Insurance on behalf of a person with an insurable interest may be effected by an agent, or by a person entrusted with the goods, even though the agent or person entrusted has no insurable interest in the property. There is no general requirement of ratification by the party with an interest, or that the person having the interest be mentioned in the policy. An agent can make a valid contract of insurance in respect of the principal's goods, and either the agent or the principal can sue on the contract.

The word 'trustee' is often used of a person entrusted with goods, but the word is not used in its strict technical sense, for a trustee under a trust is the legal owner and has an insurable interest arising from that fact. Nevertheless a person without an insurable interest may insure so long as he does so as a *quasi-trustee* for those with an interest. (*Prudential Staff Union* v *Hall* 1947.)[438] In such cases of trusteeship the intention to protect the intests of others must be clear from the terms of the policy or the circumstances.

Double insurance

It sometimes happens that a person takes out more than one policy in respect of the same risk of loss and, if each of the insurers were required to pay the full extent of the loss, the insured person would gain by this procedure. Provided a particular policy does not forbid it, the insured person may insure the same risk as often as he chooses but, in the case of indemnity insurance, he cannot recover more than the amount of his loss. He may either claim a rateable proporation from each insurer or, if there is no contribution clause in one of the policies, he may claim the full amount under that policy, leaving the various insurers to claim contribution among themselves.

Double insurance occurs when the policies cover the same adventure, the same risk and the same interest in the same subject-matter. Where the interests covered by the policies are different, there is no double insurance. (*North British and Mercantile Insurance Co.* v *London, Liverpool and Globe Insurance Co.* 1877.)[443] Such insurance if often effected unintentionally, as where both the consignor and the consignee insure to protect the consignee's interests. It may, however, be done intentionally as where the insured doubts the security of one of the insurers.

Fire policies commonly contain a contribution clause and in this case the insured cannot claim the whole of the loss from any one insurer, but must claim from each the proportion each is liable for. Thus if a property worth £20,000 is totally destroyed and is insured for £16,000 with Company A and for £24,000 with Company B, and the policies contain contribution clauses, the insured must claim £8000 from A and £12,000 from B. If, however, the policy with B did not contain a contribution clause, the insured could claim £20,000 from B, leaving B to assert his right of contribution against A in order to recover the contribution of £8000.

The right to a contribution is worked out in practice by complex calculations which are based on formulae agree between insurers, and if the matter comes to litigation the amount payable by each is largely a matter of construction of the formulae by the court.

In many cases where there has been double insurance and the claim is met in part by several insurers, they will make a proportionate return of premium for the risk they have escaped, but where a policy has for any length of time borne the whole of the risk, no return of premium will be made in respect of that policy. Where the insured claims and receives more than the indemnity to which he is entitled, the balance is held in trust and will be shared by the insurers in proportion to their liability to contribute.

Average

It may occur to the insured that the risk of total loss is very slight, and he may, therefore, under-insure, e.g. insure for £24,000 a house worth £32,000. This is quite permissible and, unless there is an average clause in the policy, he will be able to recover the total loss suffered subject to a maximum of £24,000. Thus, if the house suffers damage to the tune of £8000, he will be able to recover £8000.

Nevertheless, there is a principle called *average* under which the insured is regarded as being *his own insurer* for any difference between the amount for which he has insured his property and the actual value. In the case we have mentioned, therefore, if the policy had an average clause in it and £8000 damage were done to the property, the insured would only be able to claim £6000 namely three-quarters of the loss, since he would be regarded as his own insurer for one-quarter of the property.

Re-insurance

An insurer who has undertaken a risk on a marine or non-marine policy of insurance may wish to be relieved of his commitment and the Marine Insurance Act 1906 specifically gives him an insurable interest in his risk and the right to re-insure. There may be many reasons why an underwriter might wish to re-insure. He may not wish to run a large risk on a single hazard. He may have accepted a comprehensive risk and wish to be rid of certain elements of it. He may even be able to re-insure at a cheaper premium, thus ridding himself of a liability and gaining the difference between the premium received and the premium paid. When a ship is missing or when news is heard that a loss is imminent, he may still find a market for re-insurance, and exchange a doubtful and possibly large contingent liability for a stiff but definite re-insurance premium.

Normally a policy of re-insurance contains a re-insurance clause which stipulates that the re-insurance is subject to the same clauses and conditions as the original policy and will be paid on the same terms. Unless the policy otherwise provides, the original insured has no right or interest in respect of the re-insurance. (S.9(2).) The two policies are quite distinct; the person who re-insures is solely liable to the original insured and has the sole right of claim against the re-insurer.

Subrogation

Where the loss under a contract is total and the insurer pays the full amount, the insurer is entitled to all the interest of the insured in what is left of the subject-matter of the contract. He is thereby subrogated to all the relevant rights and remedies of the insured and in effect in a legal sense is substituted for him. Where the insurer pays for a partial loss, he acquires no title to the subject-matter insured, or what remains of it, but he is subrogated to all the rights and remedies of the insured in, and in respect of, the subject-matter insured as from the time of the casualty causing the loss, in so far as the insured has been indemnified in respect of it.

Thus, if X's motor car collides with that of Y, and the collision is due to Y's negligence, X may sue Y and recover damages, in which case X's insurers will not need to indemnify him. Alternatively X may claim from his insurers who, when they have indemnified him, will be able to take over X's claim and recover from Y the amount so paid. X cannot claim both from the insurers and also from Y by means of an action. Indeed, as we have seen, it is a general principle of indemnity insurance that a person suffering loss under an insurance policy cannot claim to be idemnified by a sum of money greater than his actual loss. (*Darrell* v *Tibbitts* 1880.)[444]

The insurers, therefore, acquire a right as againt third parties to all the rights which the insured person had, and this is particularly important in cases of tortious damage. (*Goole and Hull Steam Towing Co.* v *Ocean Marine Insurance Co.* 1928.)[445] However, it is not confined to tort, and where the insured has a remedy under a contract, the insurers can take over his rights and remedies. If the insurers recover more than the amount they have paid to the insured, they must hand over the excess to him. It follows from the right of subrogation that insured persons must not settle or compromise claims with third parties without the consent of the insurers. (*Phoenix Assurance Co.* v *Spooner* 1905.)[446]

The right of subrogation does not apply to life assurance, and if the insured were killed in a road accident, the full sum assured under the policy would be payable, and any rights of action in respect of the accident would remain with the legal representatives of the insured.

In the majority of cases of loss the insured will naturally claim against the insurance company, leaving them to their rights of subrogation. In the case of collisions between motor vehicles insured by different companies, the companies could sue each other under their rights of subrogation. However, most insurers have a *knock for knock* agreement in regard to comprehensive policyholders, each insurer compensating his own assured for the damage, without regard to which of the drivers was legally reponsible. This saves much costly litigation and probably does rough justice in the long run as between insurers, although it may lead to both drivers losing their *no-claims bonus*, which is a reduction in premium for careful drivers. However, this is not necesarrily the result, for each insurance company, having compensated its own policyholder, will decide whether or not any no-claims bonus earned is to be lost by the policyholder. Most insurance companies will not forfeit the no-claims bonus of the insured where a claim subject to 'knock for knock' was not has fault. The matter is not entirely satisfactory because it leads to insurance companies apportioning blame for accidents when conflicting accounts of how they happened have never been tested in a court of law. Nevertheless, it is still open to one of the drivers who thinks he has an action to refrain from claiming against his insurer and to pursue his legal remedy if he so chooses, and the fact that he has rights against his insurers is no bar to such an an action. (*Morley* v *Moore* 1936.)[447]

Assignment

The right to receive the proceeds of an insurance policy is a proprietary right known as a *chose in action* and may be assigned in the same way as other choses in action. Clearly this is a great convenience and is often essential where the property which is at risk passes through the hands of various owners, e.g. when cargoes are transported from buyer to seller and when goods and houses are bought and sold.

LIFE ASSURANCE

The insured benefit under a life policy may be assigned like any other chose in action, but may also be assigned under the rules of assignment set out in the Policies of Assurance Act 1867. Under the Act assignment is effected by writing, either in the form of an endorsement on the policy or by a separate instrument. The assignment must be attested and stamped. The assignee must give the insurers written notice of the assignment and they must acknowledge it if requested to do so. If the proceeds of the policy are assigned more than once, the date of receipt of the notice governs the priority of the various assignees. The Act enables the assignee to sue the insurers in his own name, but his right is still subject to equities. Even where a policy forbids assignment, though this will prevent a legal assignment, it will not affect the equitable rights of an assignee.

FIRE INSURANCE

In the case of fire insurance when the insured dies or becomes bankrupt, his insurable interest is assigned by operation of law to his personal representatives or his trustee, respectively, and they can enforce the policy. Where the insured parts with his interest in the subject-matter he must, if he wishes the insurance to remain effective, assign the policy. This requires the consent of the insurers whose consent must take the form prescribed by the policy, and the assignment of both policy and interest must take place at the same time.

In the case of real property, once a contract of sale is signed, the purchaser acquires an equitable interest therein but does not acquire the legal estate until conveyance. He can insure his interest in the property and it is advisable for him to do so. If he does not do so, and the house is destroyed or damaged by fire between the time of the contract and the time of the conveyance, s.47 of the Law of Property Act 1925 obliges the vendor to hold any moneys received under a policy for the benefit of the purchaser to be paid to him on completion provided, of course, the vendor has a valid policy. The purchaser may be able to require reinstatement under s.83 of the Fires Prevention (Metropolis) Act 1774. This procedure requires the consent of the insurers, and the purchaser must pay the proportionate part of the premium from the date of the contract.

For assignment to be effective there must be continuity of insurable interest and where the insured has parted with or lost his interest in the subject-matter insured, and has not, before or at the time of so doing, expressly or impliedly agreed to assign the policy, any subsequent assignment of the policy is inoperative; but this does not affect the assignment of a policy after loss. (S.51.)

What has been said above on the matter of assignment refers to the assignment of the policy moneys, and not to the transfer of the policy itself. A life policy cannot be transferred from the life of one person to another. In the case of indemnity policies a transfer is possible only with the consent of the insurer.

Bankruptcy or liquidation of insured

The insured may either before or after incurring liability to a third party become bankrupt, or in the case of a company go into liquidation. In such a case the injured party would have to obtain judgment and prove in the insolvency for the judgment debt but for the Third Party (Rights against Insurers) Act 1930, which provides that on bankruptcy or liquidation of the insured, the right of the insured under any liability insurance vests in the injured third party for the full amount of the judgment. Moreover, he is not to be defeated by any provision in the policy purporting to exclude the Act, although he may be affected by the provisions of the policy short of exclusion, e.g. he may be required to submit to arbitration if the policy so provides. The insurance company cannot set-off any premium due but must prove for this in the bankruptcy or liquidation. (*Murray* v *Legal and General Assurance Society* [1969] 3 All E.R. 794.) However, an insurer sued directly by an employee under the Act of 1930 can set up any defence, as distinct from a counter-claim, available against the employer, e.g. the employer's failure to notify a claim on time. (*Farrell* v *Federated Employers' Insurance Association* [1970] 3 All E.R. 632.)

9 Law of employment protection

An ever-increasing feature of contract law is the way in which particular contracts are controlled by legislation to which the general principles of contract law yield; nowhere is this more obvious than in the contract of employment. Accordingly, the main features of this legislation, which are so important in all walks of business life, are given below. The statutes concerned are abbreviated for convenience so that the Employment Protection (Consolidation) Act, 1978 becomes the EPCA; the Sex Discrimination Act, 1975 the SDA; the Race Relations Act, 1976 the RRA; the Trade Union and Labour Relations Act, 1974 the TULRA; the Health and Safety at Work Act, 1974 the HASAWA; the Employment Act, 1980, the EA, 80 and the Employment Act, 1982, the EA, 82.

Recruitment and selection of employees

Here the employer must take account of race relations and sex discrimination legislation. The RRA establishes a Commission for Racial Equality with a duty to work towards the elimination of discrimination on the grounds of race. Its powers are much the same as those of the Equal Opportunities Commission set up under the SDA. It is unlawful for an employer to discriminate between applicants for jobs on the grounds of colour, race, nationality, or ethnic or national origins. It is also unlawful to publish an advertisement which could be interpreted as discriminatory.

Under the SDA it is unlawful for a person to discriminate against another on grounds of sex or marital status when determining who will be offered a job and in regard to the terms and conditions of the job. There are exceptions where the sex or marital status of the person required is a genuine occupational qualification (GOQ), e.g. for reasons of physiology (as in the employment of a model) or for reasons of decency or privacy (as in the case of single-sex establishments such as schools and prisons) (and see *Sisley* v *Britannia Security Systems* 1983)[448] or where the job is one of two held by a married couple.

It should be noted that it is unlawful for a firm of six or more partners to discriminate in regard to the selection of new partners and benefits, facilities, or services given to partners, unless a GOQ applies.

As regards enforcement, those who believe they have been discriminated against may complain to an industrial tribunal within three months of the date of the act complained of. A conciliation officer of the Advisory Conciliation and Arbitration Service will try to settle the complaint without the need for a tribunal hearing. If this is not possible and the matter goes to a tribunal the tribunal may make an order declaring the rights of the parties in relation to the complaint. In addition, it may make an order for compensation which could cover loss of prospective earnings and injured feelings. It may also recommend that the employer take, within a specified period, action which appears to the tribunal to be practicable for the purpose of obviating or reducing the adverse effect of any act of discrimination on which the complaint is based. Proceedings (relating for example to discriminatory advertisements and instructions to discriminate) may only be instituted by the Commission for Racial Equality or the Equal Opportunities Commission, as the case may be.

Protection during employment

THE CONTRACT OF EMPLOYMENT

The EPCA provides that an employee is entitled to one week's notice after four weeks' service. After two years' service, the minimum notice is increased to two weeks, and for each year of service afterwards it is increased by one week, to a maximum of 12 weeks after 12 years' service. The statutory minimum period of notice which an employee must give is one week, irrespective of the period of employment, provided he has been employed for at least four weeks.

In addition, an employer must give his employee written information about the terms of employment not later than 13 weeks after the employment has commenced. This statement must contain the names of the employer and the employee; the date when the employment began; whether employment with a previous employer is to be counted as part of the employee's 'continuous period of employment' and, where this is so, the date on which it began (this is important to the employee, for example, in terms of redundancy payments); the title of the job; the scale or rate of remuneration or the method of calculating remuneration; the intervals at which remuneration is paid; any terms and conditions relating to the hours worked, entitlement to holidays and holiday pay, sickness or injury and sick pay, pensions and length of notice; there must also be a note specifying any disciplinary rules, the name of a person to whom the employee can apply in case of any disciplinary decision or grievance; and the disciplinary and grievance procedures, where these are laid down. The rules for calculating continuous employment, normal hours and a week's pay are in the EPCA.

An employee who does not receive written particulars or who wants to dispute their accuracy or sufficiency may refer the matter to an industrial tribunal. The tribunal may then make a declaration that the employee has a right to a statement and what particulars should be included in it or amended within it. The statement approved by the tribunal is then deemed to have been given by the employer to the employee and will form the basis of his rights.

PAY

Under the EPCA, an employee is entitled to an itemized pay statement, containing the gross amount for wages or salary; the amounts of any variable and fixed deductions and the reasons for them; and the net amount of wages or salary payable. As only gross and net amounts and deductions are required, it is apparently unnecessary for workers to be informed as to details of their basic rates, overtime payments or shift premiums. The fixed deductions can be aggregated so long as the employee is issued with a statement of fixed deductions which is re-issued every 12 months, and he is notified of any alterations when they are made. If an employee does not receive a pay statement or if he receives one that is inadequate, he may refer the matter to an industrial tribunal. The industrial tribunal will make a declaration which will include answers to questions relating to the employer's failure to give particulars or his failure to give accurate amounts. The declaration then determines these matters. Where there have been unnotified deducations from pay during the previous 13 weeks, the tribunal may order the employer to pay to the employeee a sum not exceeding the total unnotified deductions.

EQUAL TREATMENT IN TERMS AND CONDITIONS OF EMPLOYMENT AS BETWEEN MEN AND WOMEN IN THE SAME EMPLOYMENT

The Equal Pay Act, 1970, as amended by the SDA, implies a term into womens' contracts of employment which requires equal treatment in terms of pay, holidays, sick pay, and hours of work.

The Equal Pay Act 1970 provides that the contracts of employment of all women are regarded as containing an equality clause which operates on pay when a women is employed on 'like work' or on work 'rated as equivalent' to that of a man, e.g. by a job evaluation study. (*Capper Pass* v *Lawton* 1976[449] and *Navy, Army and Air Force Institutes* v *Varley* 1977[450]).

Under the Equal Pay (Amendment) Regulations 1983, there is a further instance when equality is to have effect, i.e. where a women is employed on work which is, in terms of the demands made on her, for instance under such headings as effort, skill, and 'decision', of equal value to that of a man in the same employment. In addition, under the Regulations a complaint may go before an industrial tribunal, even if the two jobs under comparison have already been shown to be unequal in a job evaluation study. However, there will have to be reasonable grounds for saying that the evaluation study discriminated on the grounds of sex.

A women who believes she is not being treated equally may complain to an industrial tribunal, which may award arrears of remuneration or damages.

DISCRIMINATION IN THE TREATMENT OF EMPLOYEES

Under the SDA and RRA, it is unlawful to discriminate against a person on grounds of race, sex or marital status as regards opportunities for promotion, training or transfer, or in the provision of benefits, facilities or services or by dismissal or any other disadvantages (*Price* v *The Civil Service Commission* 1979)[451]. However, the EPCA allows women to receive special treatment when they are pregnant, and employers may provide different retiring ages based on sex. There is no discrimination where the sex or marital status of the employee is a genuine occupational qualification.

If an unlawful act of discrimination is committed by an employee, such as a personnel officer, the employer is held responsible for the act along with the employee unless the employer can show that he took all reasonable steps to prevent the employee from discriminating. If he can do this, only the employee is responsible. As regards enforcement by employees, those who believe that they have been discriminated against may make a complaint to an industrial tribunal within three months of the date of the act complained of. It is then the duty of a conciliation officer to see whether the complaint can be settled without going to a tribunal. If, however, a tribunal hears the complaint, it may make an order declaring the rights of the employee and employer in regard to the complaint, the intention being that both parties will abide by the order for the future. The tribunal may also give the employee money compensation, and may additionally recommend that the employer take, within a specified period, action appearing to the tribunal to be practicable for the purpose of obviating or reducing discrimination.

DISCLOSURE OF INFORMATION

The Employment Act, 1975 requires employers to disclose information necessary for the purpose of collective bargaining and for purposes of good industrial relations to representatives of trade unions. The Advisory Conciliation and Arbitration Service has published a code of practice indicating the sort of information that should be disclosed.

If a union representative asks for information for collective bargaining purposes and the employer fails to disclose it, a complaint may be made to the Central Arbitration Committee. Conciliation may be attempted at this stage. If it fails, or is not attempted, the Committee will hear the complaint and may make a declaration upholding it and pass on the necessary information obtained from the employer to the union representative. If the employer continues to fail to disclose information, a further complaint may be lodged, and if this is upheld after another hearing, it allows the Committee to force arbitration on an employer if the union presents a claim.

GUARANTEE PAYMENTS

Employees with not less than four weeks' continuous service are entitled to a guarantee payment, currently £10.00 per day, if they are not provided with work on a normal working day (EPCA). This guarantee is, under the EA, 80, limited to five days in any three-month period. The provisions do not apply if the failure to provide work is due to a trade dispute, or if the employee has been offered suitable alternative work but has refused it.

An employee may present a complaint to an industrial tribunal that his employer has failed to pay the whole or any part of a guarantee payment to which the employee is entitled. The industrial tribunal may make an order to pay the employee the amount of guarantee payment which it finds is due to him.

SUSPENSION FROM WORK ON MEDICAL GROUNDS

An employee with not less than four weeks' continuous service who is suspended from work under the provisions of an Act of Parliament (e.g. the HASAWA) or a code of practice, not because he is ill but because he is exposed to a health hazard at his work and may become ill if he continues at work, is entitled to be paid normal wages while suspended for up to 26 weeks (EPCA).

An employee may present a complaint to an industrial tribunal that his employer has failed to pay the whole or any part of remuneration to which he is entitled on suspension, and the tribunal may order the employer to pay the employee the renumeration due to him.

MATERNITY

There are five areas to consider under the EPCA (as amended by the EA, 80); these are:

(1) Dismissal of pregnant employee. A woman who is dismissed because she is pregnant will be treated as having been unfairly dismissed unless certain circumstances apply, e.g. she is unable to do her job and cannot be offered or has refused suitable alternative work. It should be noted that the qualifying period for dismissal is as for other cases of unfair dismissal—52 weeks' continuous employment with the employer or any associated employer—and in the case of an employee whose employ-

ment began on or after 1 October, 1980, the employee must have been employed for a period exceeding two years.

(2) *Ante-natal care.* A pregnant employee who has, on doctor's advice, made an appointment to obtain ante-natal care must have time off to keep it. She must also be paid. An employer can ask for documentary proof, e.g. an appointment card. An employer who acts in breach of these provisions may be taken before a tribunal by the employee within three months of the breach. Compensation may be awarded to the employee.

(3) *Maternity pay.* Women who are absent because of pregnancy are, if they have completed two years' service and been at work up to the eleventh week before the expected week of confinement, entitled to maternity pay from their employers. The maternity pay is paid for the first six weeks of absence starting on or falling after the beginning of the eleventh week before the expected week of confinement, and is in each week nine-tenths of a week's pay, less the amount of the standard rate of maternity allowance even if the particular employee is not in receipt of this. The employee must, at least three weeks beforehand tell her employer in writing if the employer requires it, that she will be absent, and he may require her to produce a medical certificate showing the expected week of confinement. Employers may claim a rebate for the full amount of maternity pay from a Maternity Pay Fund.

(4) *Return to work.* If a woman returns to her job within 29 weeks after her baby is born, she must be given back her old job or a suitable alternative. However, she must have informed her employer in writing, of her intention to return at the time she notified him that she was going to be absent to have a baby. She must notify her employer at least 21 days before she intends to return, and the employer may postpone her return by up to four weeks, as may the employee if she provides a medical certificate giving reasons. Temporary replacements must be told at the start that the job is temporary, and there is no unfair dismissal of the temporary on the return of the original employee if the method of dismissal is reasonable.

The EA, 80 provides an employer with two additional grounds of defence where the employee began her absence from work on or after 1 October, 1980. The first ground is that it is not reasonably practical to reinstate the employee and that she has been offered a suitable alternative job which she has either accepted or unreasonably refused. The second ground is that immediately before her absence began the employer, together with associated employers, if any, employed five or fewer employees and that it is not reasonably practical either to reinstate the employee or even to offer her other suitable employment.

In addition, an employer may write to an employee not earlier than 49 days after the beginning of the expected week of confinement asking her to confirm that she intends to return to work. The employer's letter must explain that unless she replies within 14 days she will not be entitled to return to work. If the employer avails himself of this right the employee must reply to his request within 14 days or as soon after that as is reasonably practicable, or she will lose her right to return to work.

(5) *Failure to pay maternity pay.* An employee may within three months of the last day of the payment period present a complaint to an industrial tribunal that her employer has failed to pay the whole or any part of maternity pay due, and may question its amount. The tribunal may order the employer to pay the employee the amount of maternity pay which the tribunal finds is due to her. If she cannot recover payment, as where the employer will not pay or is insolvent, the employee may apply to the Secretary of State, who will pay her what is due out of the Maternity Fund. The Secretary of State may then recover such sums as he thinks reasonable not exceeding the amount the employer has failed to pay from the employer. Where an employer will not take back a woman after absence for maternity leave, she will be treated as dismissed from the notified date of return. Then she may be treated as redundant or unfairly dismissed, and may pursue remedies on that basis.

TIME OFF

Time off with pay must be granted by employers to trade union officials to carry out their trade union duties and to receive training both on and off the premises (EPCA). Employees are also entitled to unpaid time off to take part in union activities (other than industrial action). The Advisory Conciliation and Arbitration Service has issued a Code of Practice as to what is reasonable. Reasonable unpaid time off must also be given to employees who hold certain public offices, e.g. as JPs or local councillors. Redundant employees must be given reasonable paid time off to look for work or arrange training for a job.

In addition the Health and Safety Commission has approved a Code of Practice to govern the exercise of the right of safety representatives appointed by recognized trade unions to have time off with pay to undergo training in health and safety matters. Furthermore, as we have seen, under the EA, 80, there is a right for pregnant employees to take time off to attend ante-natal clinics. Unreasonable refusal to allow time off or to pay for time taken off gives the employee grounds to complain to an industrial tribunal.

INSOLVENCY OF EMPLOYER

An employee whose employer becomes insolvent is entitled to obtain payment of certain debts which are owed to him through the Redundancy Fund (EPCA). The legal rights and remedies in respect of the debts covered are transferred to the Secretary of State for Employment so that he can try and recover from the assets of the insolvent employer the cost of any payments made. Employees must apply for payment to the employer's representative, e.g. receiver or liquidator, who, if unable to pay the claim in the near future, will submit the application to the Secretary of State for payment from the Redundancy Fund. Debts included are arrears of pay up to £145 per week for a period not exceeding eight weeks, holiday pay up to £145 per week with a limit of six weeks in the last 12 months of employment; payment in lieu of notice for the minimum statutory period, up to £145 per week; any outstanding payment in regard to an award by an industrial tribunal of compensation for unfair dismissal; reimbursement of the fees of an apprentice or articled clerk.

The administrators of an occupational pension scheme can apply to the Secretary of State for financial assistance where the insolvent employer has not been able to pay the contributions.

HEALTH AND SAFETY AT WORK

The HASAWA lays down certain general duties of employers to their employees in the field of health and safety. There is a general duty on employers to ensure as far as is reasonbly practicable the health, safety and welfare of all employees while at work. However, in particular, the employer must provide and maintain plant and equipment and safe systems of work; avoid risks to safety and health in handling, storing and transporting articles and substances; provide and maintain safe premises and safe means of entering and leaving them, provide and maintain adequate welfare facilities and arrangements; provide information, training and supervision as required in order to ensure the safety and health of employees; prepare and/or revise policy statements on the safety and health of employees and give proper publicity to these; consult in these matters with safety representatives appointed by trade unions; establish safety committees where union representatives ask for this.

An employer must also conduct his undertaking in such a way that so far as is reasonably practicable those who are not his employees are not exposed to risk. Additionally, an employer must ensure so far as is reasonably practicable that premises which are open to others not employed by him are safe. There is also a duty to use the best practical methods to prevent noxious or offensive substances going into the atmosphere.

Directors are required to set out in their annual reports what their companies are doing in safety and health matters, and regulations will be issued specifying the classes of company that will have to comply with this provision and the kind of information which should be included.

Employees must take reasonable care of their own and other people's health and safety and co-operate with the employer in the carrying out of his duties. The Act also states that no person shall intentionally or recklessly interfere with or misuse anything which is provided in the interests of health, safety and welfare, e.g. safety equipment, and no employer may charge any employee for anything done or provided to comply with the employer's statutory duties.

Finally, those who design, manufacture, import, or supply equipment, machinery and plant must ensure that the design and construction is safe.

Enforcement is in the hands of the inspectorate of the Health and Safety Executive set up by the Act. Inspectors may issue a prohibition notice if there is a risk of serious personal injury. This operates to stop the activity concerned until remedial action specified in the notice has been taken. They may also issue an improvement notice if there is a contravention of any of the relevant statutory provisions, under which the employer must remedy the fault within a specified time. They may prosecute any person contravening the relevant statutory provision instead of or in addition to serving a notice. Failure to comply with a prohibition notice could lead to imprisonment, though there is an appeal to an industrial tribunal.

TRADE UNIONS

An employee must not be penalised (i.e. action taken against him short of dismissal) by his employer for joining or trying to join a trade union or for playing a part in its activities at appropriate times. An employer must not penalise an employee in order to compel him to join a trade union. (EA, 82.)

Unfair dismissal

Under the EPCA, as amended by the EA, 80 employees with 52 weeks or more of continuous service have a right not to be unfairly dismissed. For employees whose employment began on or after 1 October, 1980, the period of continuous employment must exceed two years where the employer, together with any associated employer, employed 20 employees or less throughout the period. This does not apply where the dismissal is automatically unfair. There is no qualifying period where the dismissal is alleged to have been for an inadmissable reason, e.g. membership of a trade union or sex or race discrimination, and the period continues to be four weeks where the dismissal is on medical grounds in compliance with a health and safety requirement. The following matters should be noted;

(1) WHAT IS DISMISSAL?

A dismissal means the termination of an employee's contract of service by the employer. Constructive dismissal is included, as where the employee is forced to terminate the contract because the employer breaks, or proposes to break, the contract, e.g. by changing, or proposing to change, the nature of the employment, the place of employment, or important terms of the contract, such as pay. (*Western Excavating Ltd* v *Sharp* 1978)[452].

In fixed-term contracts, as where a person is employed for, say, five years, there is a dismissal if the contract is not renewed when the fixed term ends, though this is not so where the fixed term is one year or more and the employee has agreed not to complain of unfair dismissal.

(2) REASONS JUSTIFYING DISMISSAL

Dismissal may be justified if an employee is dismissed because of—

(*a*) *Lack of capability.* An example would be where a brick-layer cannot lay a level or straight line of bricks. This would usually arise at the beginning of employment, where it becomes clear at an early stage that the employee cannot do the job in terms of lack of skill or mental or physical health. The longer a person is in employment, the more difficult it is to establish lack of capability.

(*b*) *Conduct.* This is always a difficult matter to deal with, and much will depend upon the circumstances of the case. However, incompetance and neglect are relevant, as are disobedience and misconduct, e.g. by assaulting fellow employees. Immorality and habitual drunkenness could also be brought under this head, as could the falsification of claims for expenses (and see *Boychuk* v *H. J. Symons (Holdings) Ltd* 1977)[453].

(*c*) *Redundancy.* Where a person is redundant, his employer cannot be expected to continue the employment, although there are safeguards in the matter of unfair selection for redundancy (see below).

(*d*) *Dismissal for failure to join a trade union.* This will be fair if it is the practice in accordance with a union membership agreement for employees of the same class to belong to one (or more) independent trade unions, and the only or principal reason for the dismissal was that the employee ceased to be a member of, or refused to join, or proposed to refuse to join or remain a member of the union in accordance with the union agreement, provided the union membership agreement has been approved by ballot and that a ballot has been held within five years of the notice of dismissal.

Under the EA, 82, if a union membership agreement is to be effective for the purposes of a fair dismissal, there must have been a ballot within the five years before dismissal. In this connection it should be noted—

(i) that if the first ballot on the union membership agreement took place *after* 14 August 1980, it was approved by not less than 80% of those entitled to vote, or

(ii) where the original union membership agreement came into effect *before* 15 August 1980, a review ballot has been held within five years of that agreement and not less than 85% of those who voted were in favour of a closed shop. This provision came into force on 1 November 1984 and applies to dismissals after that date.

Those entitled to vote must have cast their votes on one day, being then obviously in the employment of the employer on that day, or if the voting was done over a period of days, then a qualifying day must have been specified and only those in employment on that day must have been allowed to vote.

Dismissal for failure to belong to a trade union will, however, become *unfair* even though there has been a requisite ballot if—

(i) the employee has an objection to being a member of the union on grounds of conscience or other deeply held personal conviction.

(ii) The employee holds the qualifications necessary for the job which are subject to a code of practice which precludes him from taking part in industrial action, including strikes, and he is expelled, or refused membership of the union because of that code. This is particularly important in the Health Service, or

(iii) he has been unreasonably expelled or excluded from the union and a tribunal has so declared under the provisions of the EA, 80.

(*e*) *Statutory restriction placed on employer or employee.* If, for example, the employer's business is found to be dangerous and was closed down under an Act of Parliament or ministerial order, the employees would not be unfairly dismissed. Furthermore, a lorry driver who was banned from driving for 12 months could be dismissed fairly.

(*f*) *Other grounds.* Apart from the specific grounds mentioned above, whether the dismissal is fair depends in the last analysis on whether an industrial tribunal is satisfied that it was reasonable to dismiss the employee in all the circumstances of the case. It is difficult to generalize from the cases, most of which depend upon their own facts. For example, the dismissal of an employee absent through sickness may be regarded as unfair in most situations, but has been held to be fair where the employee concerned was the sole driver of a business operating deliveries with only one van.

(3) UNACCEPTABLE REASONS FOR DISMISSAL

These are as follows—

(*a*) *Trade union membership.* Under the EA, 82 if the only (or principal) reason for the dismissal is as set out below, the dismissal will be automatically unfair.

(i) Because the employee was, or proposed to become a member of an independent trade union; or

(ii) because he had taken part, or proposed to take part in the activities of an independent trade union at an appropriate time; or

(iii) because he was not a member of a trade union, or had refused or had proposed to refuse to join or remain a member, unless (in which case the dismissal will be fair) there is a properly balloted closed shop, or unless (in which case dismissal will become unfair) the employee has an objection to being a member of the union on the grounds of conscience or other deeply held personal conviction, or he holds qualifications necessary for his job which make him subject to a code of practice precluding him from taking part in industrial action, including strikes, and he has been expelled from or refused membership of the union because of that code. The dismissal is also unfair if he has been unreasonably expelled or excluded from the union and a tribunal has so declared under the EA, 80.

(*b*) *Unfair selection for redundancy.* Even an employee dismissed for redundancy may complain that he has been unfairly dismissed if he is of the opinion that he has been unfairly selected for redundancy, as where the employer has disregarded redundancy selection arrangements, e.g. 'last in, first out'. Ideally, all employers should have proper redundancy agreements on the lines set out in the Department of Employment booklet. 'Dealing With Redundancies'.

However, even though there is in existence an agreed redundancy procedure, the employer may defend himself by showing a 'special reason' for departing from that procedure, e.g. because the person selected for redundancy lacks the skill and versatility of a junior employee who is retained.

(*c*) *Transfer of business.* The Transfer of Undertakings (Protection of Employment) Regulations 1981, SI 1981/1974, apply to transfers of business which take place on or after 1 May 1982. Under the Regulations if a business or part of it is transferred and an employee is dismissed because of this, the dismissal will be treated as automatically unfair. However, the person concerned is not entitled to the extra compensation given to other cases of automatically unfair dismissals. (See *Meikle* v *McPhail* 1983)[454].

If the old employer dismissed before transfer or the new employer dismissed after the transfer, either will have a defence if he can prove that the dismissal was for 'economic, technical, or organisational' reasons requiring a change in the workforce and that the dismissal was reasonable in all the circumstances of the case.

(*d*) *Lock-outs and strikes.* If an employee is dismissed during a lock-out or a strike, that dismissal will not be regarded as unfair unless other employees involved were not dismissed or, if dismissed, were afterwards offered re-engagement.

(*e*) *Pressure on employer to dismiss unfairly.* It is no defence for an employer to say that pressure was put upon him to dismiss an employee unfairly. Thus, if other workers put pressure on an enployer to dismiss a non-union member so as, for example, to achieve a closed shop, the employer will have no defence to a claim for compensation for the dismissal if he yields to that pressure. However, the EA, 82 now gives the right to an employer to join a union or person as a third party to proceedings for unfair dismissal in a situation where he was pressurized to dismiss by the calling, organizing, procuring, or financing of a strike, or a threat to do so. This applies where the pressure was exercised because the employee was not a member of any trade union or of a particular trade union. If the industrial tribunal finds the employer's complaint well-founded the union or person concerned may be ordered to contribute towards the employee's compensation. If necessary this can be 100% indemnity.

(4) COMPLAINTS OF UNFAIR DISMISSAL

Employees may make a complaint of unfair dismissal to an industrial tribunal at any time from the date on which they receive notice until three months after the date of dismissal.

(*a*) *Conciliation.* An industrial tribunal will usually not hear a complaint until a conciliation officer has had a chance to see whether he can help. A copy of the complaint made to the industrial tribunal is sent to the conciliation officer, and if he is unable to settle the complaint, nothing said by employer or employee during the process of conciliation will be admissible in evidence before the tribunal.

(*b*) *Hearing by tribunal.* Where an industrial tribunal hears the case, the procedure is as follows—

(i) it must be established that the employee has been dismissed and is eligible to complain, e.g. on the grounds of continuous service;

(ii) the employer must then attempt to justify the reason for dismissal, i.e. that the circumstances were reasonable, and the way in which it was done was reasonable.

(*c*) *Remedies.* If a complaint of unfair dismissal is upheld, there are the following possibilities—

(i) *Reinstatement or re-engagement.* The employee must be told of his right to reinstatement or re-engagement, and asked whether he wishes such an order to be made. If he does, the tribunal must consider whether it would be practicable and reasonable in all the circumstances to make such an order. If such an order is made, the employer who does not comply with it when it is practical for him to do so, may find that the tribunal will increase the amount of compensation payable by an amount equal to between 13 and 26 weeks of the employee's pay; or where the dismissal involved racial or sexual discrimination, or was because of trade union activities, to between 26 and 52 weeks' pay.

(ii) *Compensation.* If the tribunal does not make an order of reinstatement or re-engagement, or makes one which the employer does not comply with, although it would have been practicable and reasonable for him to do so, the tribunal must make a basic award of compensation and may make, in addition, a compensatory award. The basic award is calculated according to the formula for redundancy payments, i.e. for each year of service up to a maximum of 20 years a number of weeks' pay up to a maximum of £145 per week as follows—

18 but under 22, ½ week's pay.

22 but under 41, 1 week's pay.
41 to 60 (women), 65 (men), $1\frac{1}{2}$ weeks' pay

There is no minimum age limit for unfair dismissal claims as there is for redundancy, so a person of, say, 17 who was unfairly dismissed, could use a '17 but under 22' formula and get half a week's pay.

There is a maximum payment of £4200 and a minimum of two weeks' pay, though if the dismissal is automatically unfair it is £2000. There may also be a compensatory award based on financial loss as a result of dismissal, the maximum compensatory award being £7500. Furthermore, if the dismissal is for trade union activities or on grounds of sex or race discrimination, there may be an additional award, the maximum amount of which is £7280. Thus a person who is dismissed for such activities or on such grounds may now be awarded a maximum of £18,980. Any contributory fault of the employee, e.g. a history of lateness for work, is taken into account and will reduce the money he obtains.

(iii) *Dismissal for union membership or activities.* An employee who is of the opinion that he has been unfairly dismissed for a reason connected with his trade union membership or activities may apply to an industrial tribunal for an order for reinstatement or re-engagement, or if this is not possible, for an order that he be suspended on full pay until his complaint is settled. The application must be made within seven days of dismissal, and has to be supported by a signed certificate from an official of the relevant trade union, stating that there are reasonable grounds for believing that the dismissal was for trade union reasons.

Redundancy

The EPCA gives an employee a right to compensation by way of a redundancy payment if he is dismissed because of redundancy.

(1) MEANING OF REDUNDANCY

Redundancy occurs where the services of employees are dispensed with because the employer ceases, or intends to cease, carrying on business, or does not require so many employees to do work of a certain kind (see *Murphy* v *Epsom College* 1983[455] and *Robinson* v *British Island Airways* 1979)[456]. Employees who have been laid off or kept on short time without pay for four consecutive weeks (or for a broken series of at least six weeks in a period of 13 weeks) are entitled to terminate the employment and apply for a redundancy payment if there is no reasonable prospect that normal working will be resumed.

(2) ELIGIBILITY

Employees who have completed two years' continuous service since reaching the age of 18 are eligible for a redundancy payment. Additionally, they must work 16 hours or more per week (or eight hours or more where the employment has been for five years or more).

An employee who accepts an offer of suitable alternative employment with his employer is not entitled to a redundancy payment. Neither is an employee who is offered new employment on the same terms by the same employer, or an associated employer, e.g. a subsidiary company, and unreasonably refuses; or on different terms in a different place, and after a reasonable trial period of not less than four weeks, also unreasonably refuses.

(3) AMOUNT OF REDUNDANCY PAYMENT

As we have seen, those aged 41 to 65 (60, women) receive $1\frac{1}{2}$ weeks' pay (up to a maximum of £145 per week) for each year of service up to a maximum of 20 years. In other age groups, the above provisions apply except that the week's pay changes, i.e. for those aged 22 to 40, it is one week's pay, and for those aged 18 to 21, it is a half-week's pay.

Employees over 64 (59, women) have their redundancy payment reduced progressively, so that for each complete month by which the age exceeds 64 (or 59) on the Saturday of the week in which the contract ends, the normal entitlement is reduced by one-twelfth. Thus, a man aged 64 years and three months would have three-twelfths of the award deducted. Complaints by employees in respect of the right to a redundancy payment, or questions as to its amount, may be made to an industrial tribunal which will make a declaration as to the employee's right which forms the basis on which payment can be recovered from the employer.

(4) REBATES FOR EMPLOYERS

Employers who have made a redundancy payment may claim a rebate of 41% from the Redundancy Fund. To obtain the rebate, the employer must notify the local office of the Department of Employment that he intends to make a claim, three weeks or more before the expected date of dismissal if 10 or more employees are involved, or two weeks or more in the case of redundancies involving less than 10 employees. If the employer fails to give adequate prior notice of his intention to claim a rebate, the Secretary of State may reduce that rebate by up to 10%. The notice requirements for claiming rebate are separate and distinct from those involved in the handling of redundancies. (See below.)

(5) PROCEDURE FOR HANDLING REDUNDANCIES

This is as follows:

(*a*) *Notification.* Employers must notify the Department of Employment of redundancies being planned which would involve the dismissal of more than 10 employees in a period of 30 days or less. The minimum notification period is 30 days, before the first dismissals take effect. This notification is different from the one referred in (4) above. If the employer fails to notify the Secretary of State of proposed redundancies, the Secretary of State may reduce the redundancy payments rebate to 10% or a magistrates' court may impose a fine not exceeding £800.

(*b*) *Consultation.* Employers are required to consult with trade union representatives as soon as possible which (in line with EEC requirements) if 100 or more employees are to be dismissed within a period of 90 days or less is not less than 90 days before the first redundancies take effect, or 30 days if 10 or more employees are to be dismissed in a period of 30 days or less. Consultation involves the employer in telling the unions the reason for the proposals, together with number and type of employees to be dismissed, the total number of employees of that type at the establishment involved, the proposed method of selection and of carrying out the dismissals.

Representations made by the unions must be received and replied to. If this is not done, an industrial tribunal may, on the complaint of a trade union (or in a multi-union situation, by any one of them) make a declaration of the tribunal's findings, and the tribunal may make a 'protective award' under which the employees will be kept in employment and paid for not more than a period corresponding to the minimum time required for prior consultation, i.e. 90 or 30 days as the case may be. If an employee is not paid during all or part of the period for which the protective award applies, he may apply to an industrial tribunal, which will issue an order to the employer to pay the amount of remuneration due to the employee.

(*c*) *Collective agreements on redundancy.* The Secretary of State may, on the application of the employer and unions involved make an order modifying the requirements of redundancy pay legislation if he is satisfied that there is a collective agreement which makes satisfactory alternative arrangements for dealing with redundancies. The provisions of the agreement must be 'on the whole at least as favourable' as the statutory provisions, and must include, in particular, arrangements allowing an employee to go to independent arbitration or to make a complaint to an industrial tribunal.

Minimum period of notice

Under the EPCA, an employee is entitled to one week's notice after four weeks' service; after two years' service the minimum entitlements is increased to two weeks, and for each years of service after that it is increased by one week up to a maximum of 12 weeks' notice after 12 years' service. An employee who is engaged for a specific job on a 12-

week or shorter contract is not entitled to any notice unless in the event the contract is extended or he is retained for a period longer than 12 weeks.

Three matters should be noted. Firstly, the legislation does not affect the common law right of an employer to dismiss an employee summarily without notice for misconduct, e.g. disobedience, neglect or drunkenness. Secondly, the legislation does not prevent employer and employee from agreeing to longer periods of notice to be given by the employer. Thirdly, such longer periods of notice may be implied by law or custom, and an industrial tribunal will not necessarily consider the minimum period of notice laid down by legislation as sufficient. Consideration will be given to the employee's length of service, his age, and the possibility of his finding alternative employment.

Breach of the provisions relating to minimum period of notice do not involve an employer in any penalty, but the rights conferred by the Act will be taken into account in assessing the employer's liability for breach of contract. Thus an employer who has dismissed his employee without due notice is generally liable for the wages due to the employee for the appropriate period of notice at the contract rate.

Offences by corporations

The EPCA provides that where an offence under that Act is committed by a body corporate, and it is proved that the offence was committed with the consent or connivance of, or neglect by, any director, manager, secretary or similar officer of the body corporate, or any person who was purporting to act in such capacity, that person as well as the body corporate shall be equally guilty of the offence and may be punished accordingly.

Appendices
A: Cases and materials
B: Graded questions and tutorial problems

Appendix A
Cases and materials

The law of contract

Formation. Where an offer is in the form of a promise for an act, performance of the act is the acceptance. Offers of this type may be made either to a particular person or to the world at large.

(1) *Carlill* v *Carbolic Smoke Ball Co.* [1893] 1 Q.B. 256

The defendants were proprietors of a medical preparation called 'The Carbolic Smoke Ball.' They inserted advertisements in various newspapers in which they offered to pay £100 to any person who contracted influenza after using the ball three times a day for two weeks. They added that they had deposited £1000 at the Alliance Bank, Regent Street 'to show our sincerity in the matter.'

The plaintiff, a lady, used the ball as advertised, and was attacked by influenza during the course of treatment, which in her case extended from 20 November 1891 to 17 January 1892. She now sued for £100 and the following matters arose out of the various defences raised by the company—(1) It was suggested that the offer was too vague since no time limit was stipulated in which the user was to contract influenza. The Court said that it must surely have been the intention that the ball would protect its user during the period of its use, and since this covered the present case it was not necessary to go further. (2) The suggestion was made that the matter was an advertising 'puff' and that there was no intention to create legal relations. Here the Court took the view that the deposit of £1000 at the bank was clear evidence of an intention to pay claims. (3) It was further suggested that this was an attempt to contract with the whole world and that this was impossible in English law. The Court took the view that the advertisement was an *offer* to the whole world, not an attempt to *contract* with the whole world but only with that limited portion of the public who came forward and performed the condition on the faith of the advertisement, and that, by analogy with the reward cases, it was possible to make an *offer* of this kind. (4) The company also claimed that the plaintiff had not supplied any consideration, but the Court took the view that using this inhalant three times a day for two weeks or more was sufficient consideration.

It was not necessary to consider its adequacy. (5) Finally the defendants suggested that there had been no communication of acceptance but here the Court, looking at the reward cases, stated that in contracts of this kind acceptance may be by conduct.

Comment. (i) Motive was also irrelevant in this case because Mrs Carlill presumably did not use the ball with the motive of obtaining the reward, but with the motive of protection against influenza.

(ii) Most business contracts are bilateral. They are made by an exchange of promises and not, as here, by the exchange of a promise for an act. Nevertheless, *Carlill's case* has occasionally provided a useful legal principle in the field of business law. (See, e.g. *The New Zealand Shipping Co. Ltd* v *A.M. Satterthwaite and Co. Ltd* [1974] 1 All E.R. 1015, p. 13.)

An invitation to treat is not an offer. It is part of the process of negotiation which may lead to an offer.

(2) *Harris* v *Nickerson* (1873) L.R. 8 Q.B. 286

The defendant, an auctioneer, advertised in London newspapers that a sale of office furniture would be held at Bury St. Edmunds. A broker with a commission to buy furniture came from London to attend the sale. Several conditions were set out in the advertisement, one being: 'The highest bidder to be the buyer.' The lots described as office furniture were not put up for sale but were withdrawn, though the auction itself was held. The broker sued for loss of time in attending the sale. *Held*—He could not recover from the auctioneer. There was no offer since the lots were never put up for sale, and the advertisement was simply an invitation to treat.

(3) *Partridge* v *Crittenden* [1968] 2 All E.R. 421

Mr Partridge inserted an advertisement in a publication called *Cage and Aviary Birds* containing the words 'Bramblefinch cocks, bramblefinch hens, £1.25p each.' The advertisement appeared under the general heading 'Classified Advertisements' and in no place was there any direct use of the words 'offer for sale'. A Mr Thompson answered the advertisement enclosing a cheque for £1.25 and asking that a 'bramblefinch hen' be sent to him. Mr Partridge sent one in a box, the bird wearing a closed ring.

Mr Thompson opened the box in the presence of an RSPCA inspector, Mr Crittenden, and removed the ring without injury to the bird. Mr. Crittenden brought a prosecution against Mr Partridge before the Chester magistrates alleging that Mr Partridge had offered for sale a brambling contrary to s.6(1) of the Protection of Birds Act 1954 (see now, s.6(1), Wildlife and Countryside Act 1981), the bird being other than a close-ringed specimen bred in captivity and being of a species which was resident in or visited the British Isles in a wild state.

The justices were satisfied that the bird had not been bred in captivity but had been caught and ringed. A close-ring meant a ring that was completed closed and incapable of being forced or broken except with the intention of damaging it; such a ring was forced over the claws of a bird when it was between three and ten days old, and at that time it was not possible to determine what the eventual girth of the leg would be so that the close-ring soon became difficult to remove. The ease with which the ring was removed in this case indicated that it had been put on at a much later stage and this, together with the fact that the bird had no perching sense, led the justices to convict Mr Partridge.

He appealed to the Divisional Court of the Queen's Bench Division where the conviction was squashed. The Court accepted that the bird was a wild bird, but since Mr Partridge had been charged with 'offering for sale,' the conviction could not stand. The advertisement constituted in law an invitation to treat, not an offer for sale, and the offence was not, therefore, established. There was of course a completed sale for which Mr Partridge could have been successfully prosecuted but the prosecution in this case had relied on the offence of 'offering for sale' and failed to establish such an offer.

Comment. The case shows how concepts of the civil law are sometimes at the root of criminal cases.

(4) *Pharmaceutical Society of Great Britain* v *Boots Cash Chemists (Southern) Ltd* [1953] 1 All E.R. 482

The defendants' branch at Edgware was adapted to the 'self-service' system. Customers selected their purchases from shelves on which the goods were displayed and put them into a wire basket supplied by the defendants. They then took them to the cash desk where they paid the price. One section of shelves was set out with drugs which were included in the Poisons List referred to in s.17 of the Pharmacy and Poisons Act 1933, though they were not dangerous drugs and did not require a doctor's prescription.

Section 18 of the Act requires that the sale of such drugs shall take place in the presence of a qualified pharmacist. Every sale of the drugs on the Poison List was supervised at the cash desk by a qualified pharmacist, who had authority to prevent customers from taking goods out of the shop if he thought fit. One of the duties of the society was to enforce the provisions of the Act, and the action was brought because the plaintiffs claimed that the defendants were infringing s.18. *Held*—The display of goods in this way did not constitute an offer. The contract of sale was not made when a customer selected goods from the shelves, but when the company's servant at the cash desk accepted the customer's offer to buy what had been chosen. There was, therefore, supervision in the sense required by the Act at the appropriate moment in time.

Comment. (i) It was held in *Esso Petroleum Ltd* v *Customs and Excise Commissioners* [1976] 1 All E.R. 117 by the House of Lords that an indication of the price at which petrol is to be sold at a filling station is also only an invitation to treat.

(ii) The relevant provisions of the Pharmacy and Poisons Act 1933 are now enacted in ss.2 and 3 of the Poisons Act 1972.

Invitation to treat. Negotiations for the sale of land.

(5) *Harvey* v *Facey* [1893] A.C. 552

The plaintiffs sent the following telegram to the defendant: 'Will you sell us Bumper Hall Pen? Telegraph lowest cash price.' The defendant telegraphed in reply: 'Lowest price for Bumper Hall Pen £900.' The plaintiffs then telegraphed: 'We agree to buy Bumper Hall Pen for £900 asked by you. Please send us your title deeds in order that we may get early possession.' The defendant made no reply. The Supreme Court of Jamaica granted the plaintiffs a decree of specific performance of the contract. On appeal the Judicial Committee of the Privy Council held that there was no contract. The second telegram was not an offer, but was in the nature of an invitation to treat at a minimum price of £900. The third telegram could not therefore be an acceptance resulting in a contract.

Comment. The matter of invitation to treat and offer in the context of the sale of land produced the most interesting case of *Gibson* v *Manchester City Council* [1979] 1 All E.R. 972. The City Treasurer wrote to Mr Gibson saying that the Council 'may be prepared' to sell the freehold of his council house to him at £2725 less 20 per cent, i.e. £2180. The letter said that Mr G should make a formal application which he did. Following local government elections three months later the policy of selling council houses was reversed. The Council did not proceed with the sale to Mr Gibson. He claimed a binding contract existed. The House of Lords said that it did not. The Treasurer's letter was only an invitation to treat. Mr G's application was the offer, but the Council had not accepted it. In the Court of Appeal Lord Denning had said that there was an 'agreement in fact' which was enforceable. It was not always necessary to stick to the strict rules of offer and acceptance in order to produce a binding agreement. The House of Lords would not accept this and Lord Denning's view has not as yet found a place in the law.

Acceptance. If the acceptor knows the offer exists his reason for accepting it is of no importance in deciding whether a contract has come into being.

(6) *Williams* v *Carwardine* (1833) 5 C. & P. 566

The defendant published a handbill by the terms of which he promised to pay the sum of £20 to any person who should give information, leading to the discovery of the murderer of Walter Carwardine. Two persons were tried for the murder at Hereford Assizes and were acquitted. Shortly afterwards the plaintiff, who was living with one Williams, was severely beaten by him and, believing that she was going to die and to ease her conscience, she gave information leading to the conviction of the man Williams for the murder. In an action to recover the reward the jury found that the plaintiff was not induced to give the information by the reward offered, but by motives of spite and revenge. *Held*—She was nevertheless entitled to the reward, for she had seen the handbill and had given information. Patteson, J., said: 'We cannot go into the plaintiff's motives.'

Acceptance 'subject to contract'. This phrase, which is used in sales of land and agreements for leases, indicates that the contract is merely in the stage of negotiation.

(7) *Winn* v *Bull* (1877) 7 Ch. D. 29

The defendant had entered into a written agreement with the plaintiff for the lease of a house, the term of the lease and the rent being agreed. However, the written agreement was expressly made 'subject to the preparation and approval of a formal contract.' It appeared that no other contract was made between the parties. The plaintiff now sued for specific performance of the agreement. *Held*—The written agreement provided a memorandum sufficient to satisfy s.4 of the Statute of Frauds 1677 (now s.40 of the Law of Property Act 1925), but there was no binding contract between the parties because, although certain covenants are normally implied into leases, it is also true that many and varied express covenants are often agreed between the parties. The words 'subject to contract' indicated that the parties were still in a state of negotiation, and until they entered into a formal contract there was no agreement which the court could enforce.

A counter-offer is not an acceptance. It rejects the original offer which then lapses.

(8) *Hyde* v *Wrench* (1840) 3 Beav. 334

The defendant offered to sell his farm for £1000. The plaintiff's agent made an offer of £950 and the defendant asked for a few days for consideration, after which the defendant wrote saying he could not accept it, whereupon the plaintiff wrote purporting to accept the offer of £1000. The defendant did not consider himself bound, and the plaintiff sued for specific performance. *Held*—The plaintiff could not enforce this 'acceptance' because his counter offer of £950 was an implied rejection of the original offer to sell at £1000.

As regards rejection of an offer, a distinction must be made between a counter-offer and a request for information.

(9) *Stevenson* v *McLean* (1880) 5 Q.B.D. 346

The defendant offered to sell to the plaintiffs a quantity of iron 'at £2.00

nett cash per ton till Monday.' On Monday the plaintiffs telegraphed asking whether the defendant would accept £2.00 for delivery over two months, or if not what was the longest limit the defendant would give. The defendant received the telegram at 10.1 a.m. but did not reply, so the plaintiffs, by telegram sent at 1.34 p.m., accepted the defendant's original offer. The defendant had already sold the iron to a third party, and informed the plaintiffs of this by a telegram despatched at 1.25 p.m. arriving at 1.46 p.m. The plaintiffs had therefore accepted the offer before the defendant's revocation had been communicated to them. If, however, the plaintiffs' first telegram constituted a counter-offer, then it would amount to a rejection of the defendant's original offer. *Held*—The plaintiffs' first telegram was not a counter-offer, but a mere inquiry for information as to the availability of credit which did not amount to a rejection of the defendant's original offer, so that the offer was still open when the plaintiffs accepted it.

A process involving exchange of terms may continue for some time until an act by one of the parties can be regarded as an acceptance of the other's terms.

(10) *Butler Machine Tool Co. Ltd* v *Ex-Cell-O Corporation (England) Ltd* [1979] 1 All E.R. 965

In this case it appeared that on 23 May 1969 Butler quoted a price for a machine tool of £75,535, delivery to be within 10 months of order. The quotation gave terms and conditions which were stated expressly to prevail over any terms and conditions contained in the buyer's order.

One of the terms was a price variation clause which operated if costs increased before delivery. Ex-Cell-O ordered the machine on 27 May 1969, their order stating that the contract was to be on the basis of Ex-Cell-O's terms and conditions as set out in the order. These terms and conditions did not include a price variation clause but did contain additional items to the Butler quotation, including the fact that Ex-Cell-O wanted installation of the machine for £3100 and the date of delivery of 10 months was changed to 10/11 months.

Ex-Cell-O's order form contained a tear-off slip which said: 'Acknowledgement: please sign and return to Ex-Cell-O. We accept your order on the terms and conditions stated therein—and undertake to deliver by—date—signed.' This slip was completed and signed on behalf of Butler and returned with a covering letter to Ex-Cell-O on 5 June 1969.

The machine was ready by September 1970, but Ex-Cell-O could not take delivery until November 1970 because they had to rearrange their production schedule. By the time Ex-Cell-O took delivery, costs had increased and Butler claimed £2892 as due under the price variation clause. Ex-Cell-O refused to regard the variation clause as a term of the contract.

The Court of Appeal, following a traditional analysis, decided that Butler's quotation of 23 May 1969 was an offer and that Ex-Cell-O's order of 27 May 1969 was a counter-offer introducing new terms and that Butler's communication of 5 June 1969 returning the slip was an acceptance of the counter-offer; so that the contract was on Ex-Cell-O's terms and not Butler's, in spite of the statement in Butler's original quotation.

Thus there was no price variation clause in the contract and Ex-Cell-O need not pay the £2892.

Comment. Most commonly the parties will exchange terms relating to delivery dates, rights of cancellation, the liability of the supplier for defects, fluctuations in price (as here), and arbitration clauses to settle differences.

The 'acceptance' of a tender may not produce a binding contract.

(11) *Great Northern Railway* v *Witham* (1873) L.R. 9 C.P. 16

The company advertised for tenders for the supply for one year of such stores as they might think fit to order. The defendant submitted a tender in these words: 'I undertake to supply the company for twelve months with such quantities of (certain specified goods) as the company may order from time to time.' The company accepted the tender, and gave orders under it which the defendant carried out. Eventually the defendant refused to carry out an order made by the company under the tender, and this action was brought. *Held*—The defendant was in breach of contract. A tender of this type was a standing offer which was converted into a series of contracts as the company made an order. The defendant might revoke his offer for the remainder of the period covered by the tender, but must supply the goods already ordered by the company.

An agreement may be vague or incomplete. If the vague provision cannot be resolved and concerns a matter which is vital to the agreement there is no contract.

(12) *Scammell (G.) and Nephew Ltd* v *Ouston* [1941] A.C. 251

Ouston wished to acquire a new motor van for use in his furniture business. Discussions took place with the company's sales manager as a result of which the company sent a quotation for the supply of a suitable van. Eventually Ouston sent an official order making the following stipulation, 'This order is given on the understanding that the balance of the purchase price can be had on hire-purchase terms over a period of two years.' This was in accordance with the discussions between the sales manager and Ouston, which had taken place on the understanding that hire purchase would be available. The company seemed to be content with the arrangement and completed the van. Arrangements were made with the finance company to give hire-purchase facilities, but the actual terms were not agreed at that stage. The appellants also agreed to take Ouston's present van in part exchange, but later stated that they were not satisfied with its condition and asked him to sell it locally. He refused and after much correspondence he issued a writ against the appellants for damages for non-delivery of the van. The appellants' defence was that there was no contract until the hire-purchase terms had been ascertained. *Held*—The defence succeeded; it was not possible to construe a contract from the vague language used by the parties.

Comment. If there is a trade custom, business procedure or previous dealings between the parties, which assist the court in construing the vague parts of an agreement, then the agreement may be enforced. Here there was no such evidence.

If a contract contains meaningless provisions on matters which are not of great importance they may be ignored and the rest of the contract enforced.

(13) *Nicolene Ltd* v *Simmonds* [1953] 1 All E.R. 822

The plaintiffs alleged that there was a contract for the sale by them of 3000 tons of steel reinforcing bars and that the defendant seller had broken his contract. When the plaintiffs claimed damages the seller set up the defence that, owing to one of the sentences in the letters which constituted the contract, there was no contract at all. The material words were 'We are in agreement that the usual conditions of acceptance apply.' In fact there were no usual conditions of acceptance so that the words were meaningless but the seller nevertheless suggested that the contract was unenforceable since it was not complete. *Held*—by the Court of Appeal—that the contract was enforceable and that the meaningless clause could be ignored. 'In my opinion a distinction must be drawn between a clause which is meaningless and a clause which is yet to be agreed. A clause which is meaningless can often be ignored, whilst still leaving the contract good; whereas a clause which has yet to be agreed may mean that there is no contract at all, because the parties have not agreed on all the essential terms. . . . In the present case there was nothing yet to be agreed. There was nothing left to further negotiation. All that happened was that the parties agreed that 'the usual conditions of acceptance apply'. That clause was so vague and uncertain as to be incapable of any precise meaning. It is clearly severable from the rest of the contract. It can be rejected without impairing the sense or reasonableness of the contract as a whole, and it should be so rejected. The contract should be held good and the clause ignored. The parties themselves treated the contract as subsisting. They regarded it as creating binding obligations between them; and it would be most unfortunate if the law should say otherwise. You would find defaulters all scanning their contracts to find some meaningless clause on which to ride free.' (Per Denning, L.J.)

If the price of goods or services is to be fixed in the future by the further agreement of the parties, there is no enforceable contract if they do not

agree. If, however, they have agreed upon a price-fixing formula, e.g. by arbitration, the agreement is enforceable.

(14) *Foley* v *Classique Coaches Ltd* [1934] 2 K.B. 1

F owned certain land, part of which he used for the business of supplying petrol. He also owned the adjoining land. The company wished to purchase the adjoining land for use as the headquarters of their carabanc business. F agreed to sell the land to the company on condition that the company would buy all their petrol from him. An agreement was made under which the company agreed to buy its petrol from F 'at a price to be agreed by the parties in writing and from time to time'. It was further agreed that any dispute arising under the agreement should be submitted 'to arbitration in the usual way'. The agreement was acted upon for three years. At this time the company felt it could get petrol at a better price, and the company's solicitor wrote to F repudiating the contract. *Held*—Although the parties had not agreed upon a price, there was a contract to supply petrol at a reasonable price and of reasonable quality, and although the agreement did not stipulate the future price, but left this to the further agreement of the parties, a method was provided by which the price could be ascertained without such agreement, i.e. by arbitration. An injunction was therefore granted requiring the company to take petrol from F as agreed.

Comment. If the contract is completely silent on a term the court may fill in a gap by implying a reasonable term. Thus in a contract for the sale of goods where no price at all is agreed, a reasonable price must be paid. (S.8(2), Sale of Goods Act 1979.) However, where, as in *Foley*, there is an agreement for the sale of goods 'at a price to be agreed', the contract is not silent on the matter of price and the court cannot use s.8(2) of the 1979 Act.

Previous dealings between the parties may make a subsequent agreement sufficiently certain to be binding.

(15) *Hillas & Co Ltd* v *Arcos Ltd* [1932] All E.R. Rep 494

The plaintiffs had entered into a contract with the defendants under which the defendants were to supply the plaintiffs with '22,000 standards of soft wood (Russian) of fair specification over the season 1930.' The contract also contained an option allowing the plaintiffs to take up 100,000 standards as above during the season 1931. The parties managed to perform the contract throughout the 1930 season without any argument or serious difficulty in spite of the vague words used in connection with the specification of the wood. However, when the plaintiffs exercised their option for 100,000 standards during the season 1931, the defendants refused to supply the wood, saying that the specification was too vague to bind the parties, and the agreement was therefore inchoate as requiring a further agreement as to the precise specification. *Held*—by the House of Lords—that the option to supply 100,000 standards during the 1931 season was valid. There was a certain vagueness about the specification, but there was also a course of dealing between the parties which operated as a guide to the Court regarding the difficulties which this vagueness might produce. Since the parties had not experienced serious difficulty in carrying out the 1930 agreement, there was no reason to suppose that the option could not have been carried out without difficulty had the defendants been prepared to go on with it. Judgment was given for the plaintiffs.

The communication of acceptance. There is a rule that silence cannot amount to acceptance. It is to ensure that the offeror cannot impose a contract on an offeree who simply ignores his offer.

(16) *Felthouse* v *Bindley* (1862) 11 C.B. (N.S.) 869

The plaintiff had been engaged in negotiations with his nephew John regarding the purchase of John's horse, and there had been some misunderstanding as to the price. Eventually the plaintiff wrote to his nephew as follows: 'If I hear no more about him I consider the horse is mine at £30.75p.' The nephew did not reply but, wishing to sell the horse to his uncle, he told the defendant, an auctioneer who was selling farm stock for him, not to sell the horse as it had already been sold. The auctioneer inadvertently put the horse up with the rest of the stock and sold it. The plaintiff now sued the auctioneer in conversion, the basis of the claim being that he had made a contract with his nephew and the property in the animal was vested in him (the uncle) at the time of the sale. *Held*—The plaintiff's action failed. Although the nephew intended to sell the horse to his uncle, he had not communicated that intention. There was, therefore, no contract between the parties, and the property in the horse was not vested in the plaintiff at the time of the auction sale.

Comment. (i) The general principle laid down in this case, i.e. that an offeree who does not wish to accept an offer should not be put to the trouble of refusing it is quite acceptable. However, it is difficult to support the decision on its own facts. John wanted to accept the offer and intended to accept it and since the uncle by his letter waived any right to receive an acceptance, there appears on the facts to be no reason why there should not have been a contract.

(ii) It should also be noted that the communication of acceptance must be authorized. In *Powell* v *Lee* (1908) 99 L.T. 284 Powell offered his services to the managers of a school as headmaster. The secretary to the managers told P that he had been selected, which was true. The secretary had no authority, actual or otherwise, to do this. The managers later selected another candidate as headmaster. P's action for breach of contract failed.

The mode of communication of acceptance may be prescribed by the offeror, but very clear words are required to make the court treat the mode of communication as mandatory.

(17) *Yates Building Co* v *R.J. Pulleyn & Sons (York)* (1975) 119 SJ 370

An option to purchase a certain plot of land was expressed to be exercisable by notice in writing by or on behalf of the intending purchaser to the intending vendor 'such notice to be sent by registered or recorded delivery post'. *Held*—by the Court of Appeal—that the form of posting described was directory rather than mandatory, or, alternatively, permissive rather than obligatory, and in consequence the option was validly exercised by a letter from the intending purchaser's solicitors to the intending vendor's solicitors sent by ordinary post and arriving well within the option period.

Where instantaneous methods of communication over long distances are used actual communication is necessary.

(18) *Entores Ltd* v *Miles Far Eastern Corporation* [1955] 2 Q.B. 327

The plaintiffs, who conducted a business in London, made an offer to the defendants' agent in Amsterdam by means of a teleprinter service. The offer was accepted by a message received on the plaintiffs' teleprinter in London. Later the defendants were in breach of contract and the plaintiffs wished to sue them. The defendants had their place of business in New York and in order to commence an action the plaintiffs had to serve notice of writ on the defendants in New York. The Rules of Supreme Court allow service out of the jurisdiction when the contract was made within the jurisdiction. On this point the defendants argued that the contract was made in Holland when it was typed into the teleprinter there, stressing the rule relating to posting. *Held*—Where communication is instantaneous, as where the parties are face to face or speaking on the telephone, acceptance must be received by the offeror. The same rule applied to communications of this kind. Therefore the contract was made in London where the acceptance was received.

Comment. (i) The suggestion was made that the doctrine of estoppel may operate in this sort of case so as to bind the offeror, e.g. suppose X telephones his acceptance to Y, and Y does not hear X's voice at the moment of acceptance, then Y should ask X to repeat the message, otherwise Y may be estopped from denying that he heard X's acceptance and will be bound in contract, presumably because the failure of communication is to some extent the fault of X, the offeror.

If this is so, the estoppel provides another example of a situation in which acceptance need not actually be communicated.

(ii) The House of Lords approved the *Entores* decision in *Brinkibon* v *Stahag Stahl* [1982] 1 All E.R. 293. The plaintiff wanted leave to serve a writ out of the jurisdiction, as in *Entores*. The message accepting an offer had been sent by telex from London and Vienna. The House of Lords held that the writ could not be served because the contract was made in Vienna and not London.

Where a post is the proper or recognized method of communication, acceptance takes place when the letter of acceptance is properly posted.

(19) *Household Fire Insurance Company* v *Grant* (1879) 4 Ex. D. 216

The defendant handed a written application for shares in the company to the company's agent in Glamorgan. The application stated that the defendant had paid to the company's bankers the sum of £5, being a deposit of 5p per share on an application for one hundred shares, and also agreed to pay 95p per share within 12 months of the allotment. The agent sent the application to the company in London. The company secretary made out a letter of allotment in favour of the defendant and posted it to him in Swansea. The letter never arrived. Nevertheless the company entered the defendant's name on the share register and credited him with dividends amounting to 25p. The company then went into liquidation and the liquidator sued for £94.75, the balance due on the shares allotted. *Held*—by the Court of Appeal—that he defendant was liable. Acceptance was complete when the letter of allotment was posted.

Comment. (i) The rule is clearly one based on convenience rather than principle and, indeed, Bramwell, L.J., in a dissenting judgment, regarded actual communication as essential. If the letter of acceptance does not arrive, he said, an unknown liability is imposed on the offeror. If actual communication is required the status quo is preserved, i.e. the parties have not made a contract.

(ii) If the statements of the parties appear to exclude the rule then the court will not apply it and there will be no contract unless the letter is received. Thus in *Holwell Securities Ltd* v *Hughes* [1974] 1 All E.R. 161, Dr Hughes gave the plaintiffs an option to purchase his premises, the agreement providing that the option was to be exercised 'by notice in writing'. The plaintiffs exercised the option by a letter which was not received by Dr Hughes and it was held that there was no contract because 'notice' meant that the letter must be received.

The offeror's right to revoke his offer is limited by a rule of law which insists that the revocation be communicated to the offeree.

(20) *Byrne* v *Van Tienhoven* (1880) 5 C.P.D. 344

On 1 October the defendants in Cardiff posted a letter to the plaintiffs in New York offering to sell them tin plate. On 8 October the defendants wrote revoking their offer. On 11 October the plaintiffs received the defendants' offer and immediately telegraphed their acceptance. On 15 October the plaintiffs confirmed their acceptance by letter. On 20 October the defendants' letter of revocation reached the plaintiffs who had by this time entered into a contract to resell the tin plate. *Held*—(1) that revocation of an offer is not effective until it is communicated to the offeree; (2) the mere posting of a letter of revocation is not communication to the person to whom it is sent. The rule is not, therefore, the same as that for acceptance of an offer. Therefore the defendants were bound by a contract which came into being on 11 October.

Revocation need not be communicated by the offeror. It is enough that the offeree gets to know from a reliable source that the offeror no longer wishes to deal with him.

(21) *Dickinson* v *Dodds* (1876) 2 Ch. D. 463

The defendant offered to sell certain houses by letter stating, 'This offer to be left over until Friday, 9 a.m.' On Thursday afternoon the plaintiff was informed by a Mr Berry that the defendant had been negotiating a sale of the property with one Allan. On Thursday evening the plaintiff left a letter of acceptance at the house where the defendant was staying. This letter was never delivered to the defendant. On Friday morning at 7 a.m. Berry, acting as the plaintiff's agent, handed the defendant a duplicate letter of acceptance explaining it to him. However, on the Thursday the defendant had entered into a contract to sell the property to Allan. *Held*—Since there was no consideration for the promise to keep the offer open, the defendant was free to revoke his offer at any time. Further, Berry's communication of the dealings with Allan indicated that Dodds was no longer minded to sell the property to the plaintiff and was in effect a communication of Dodds' revocation. There was therefore no binding contract between the parties.

An offer may lapse by the passage of time. If no time is stated lapse takes place after a reasonable time which is a matter of fact according to the circumstances of the case.

(22) *Ramsgate Victoria Hotel Co.* v *Montefiore* (1866) L.R. 1 Exch. 109

The defendant offered by letter dated 8 June 1864 to take shares in the company. No reply was made to the company, but on 23 November 1864 they allotted shares to the defendant. The defendant refused to take up the shares. *Held*—His refusal was justified because his offer had lapsed by reason of the company's delay in notifying their acceptance.

In an offer to buy goods there is an implied term under which it cannot be accepted after the goods are damaged in a serious way.

(23) *Financings Ltd* v *Stimson* [1962] 3 All E.R. 386

On 16 March 1961, the defendant saw a motor car on the premises of a dealer and signed a hire-purchase form provided by the plaintiffs (a finance company), this form being supplied by the dealer. The form was to the effect that the agreement was to become binding only when the finance company signed the form. It also carried a statement to the effect that the hirer (the defendant) acknowledged that before he signed the agreement he had examined the goods and had satisfied himself that they were in good order and condition, and that the goods were at the risk of the hirer from the time of purchase by the owner. On 18 March the defendant paid the first instalment and took possession of the car. However, on 20 March the defendant, being dissatisfied with the car, returned it to the dealer though the finance company were not informed of this. On the night of 24–25 March the car was stolen from the dealer's premises and was recovered badly damaged. On 25 March the finance company signed the agreement accepting the defendant's offer to hire the car. The defendant did not regard himself as bound and refused to pay the instalments. The finance company sold the car, and now sued for damages for the defendant's breach of the hire-purchase agreement. *Held*—The hire-purchase agreement was not binding on the defendant because—

(1) he had revoked his offer by returning the car, and the dealer was the agent of the finance company to receive notice;

(2) there was an implied condition in the offer that the goods were in substantially the same condition when the offer was accepted as when it was made.

Death of offeror before acceptance.

(24) *Bradbury* v *Morgan* (1862) 1 H. & C. 249

The defendants were the executors of J.M. Leigh who had entered into a guarantee of his brother's account with the plaintiffs for credit up to £100. The plaintiffs, not knowing of the death of J.M. Leigh, continued to supply goods on credit to the brother, H.J. Leigh. The defendants now refused to pay the plaintiffs in respect of such credit after the death of J.M. Leigh. *Held*—The plaintiffs succeeded, the offer remaining open until the plaintiffs had knowledge of the death of J.M. Leigh.

Comment. This was a continuing guarantee which is in the nature of a standing offer accepted piecemeal whenever further goods are advanced on credit. Where the guarantee is not of this nature, it may be irrevocable. Thus in *Lloyds* v *Harper* (1880) 16 Ch. D. 290, the defendant, while living, guaranteed his son's dealings as a Lloyds underwriter in consideration of Lloyds admitting the son. It was held that, as Lloyds had admitted the son on the strength of the guarantee, the defendant's executors were still liable under it, because it was irrevocable and was not affected by the defendant's death. It continued to apply to defaults committed by the son after the father's death.

Death of offeree before acceptance.

(25) *Re Cheshire Banking Co., Duff's Executors' Case* (1886) 32 Ch. D. 301

In 1882 the Cheshire and Staffordshire Union Banking Companies amalgamated, and Duff received a circular asking whether he would exchange his shares in the S Bank for shares in the C Bank which took the S Bank over. Duff held 100 £20 shares on which £5 had been paid, but he did not reply to the circular and died shortly afterwards. The option was exercised on behalf of his executors, Muttlebury, Bridges and Watts, and a certificate was made out in their names and an entry made in the register in which they were entered as shareholders, described as 'executors of William Duff, deceased'. The executors objected to having the share certificate in their names, so the directors of the Cheshire Banking Co. cancelled the certificate and issued a fresh one in the name of William Duff. On 23 October 1884, the company went into voluntary liquidation, and on 26 October it was ordered that the winding up should be under supervision. *Held*—The liquidator acted rightly when he restored the executors' names to the register. The executors wished to enter into a new contract which had not previously existed. They could not make a dead man liable and so could only make themselves personally liable. Their names were improperly removed and must be restored. Insofar as the executors alleged that they were accepting on behalf of Duff deceased, they could not do so.

Comment. This case probably has more to do with the liability of personal representatives in the law of succession than with the law of contract. Personal representatives, like receivers, can be personally liable on contracts which they make, subject to a right of indemnity from the estate. The benefit of the contract is held on trust for the estate. This personal liability rule is essential in order to ensure that personal representatives cannot subject the estate to further debt without risk to themselves. There seems to be no direct contract law authority as to the effect of the death of the offeree. In *Reynolds* v *Atherton* (1922) 127 I.T. 189 Warrington, L.J., said: 'The offer having been made to a living person who ceases to be a living person before the offer is accepted, there is no longer an offer at all. The offer is not intended to be made to a dead person, nor to his executors, and the offer ceases to be an offer capable of acceptance.' There is, however, some Canadian authority. In *Re Irvine* [1928] 3 D.L.R. 268 an offeree gave his son a letter of acceptance to post. The son did not post it until after the offeree's death. The Supreme Court of Ontario held that the acceptance was invalid.

Sometimes a contract comes into being without the usual stages of offer and acceptance being identifiable.

(26) *Rayfield* v *Hands* [1958] 2 All E.R. 194

The articles of a private company provided by Art. 11 that 'Every member who intends to transfer his shares shall inform the directors who will take the said shares . . . at a fair price.' The plaintiff held 725 fully-paid shares of £1 each, and he asked the directors to buy them but they refused. *Held*—The directors were bound to take the shares. Having regard to s.20(1) of the Companies Act 1948, the provisions of Art. 11 constituted a binding contract between the directors, as members, and the plaintiff, as a member, in respect of his rights as a member. The word 'will' in the article did not import an option in the directors. Vaisey, J., did say that the conclusion he had reached in this case may not apply to all companies, but it did apply to a private company, because such a company was an intimate concern closely analogous with a partnership.

Comment. (i) Although the articles placed the obligation to take shares of members on the directors, Vaisey, J., construed this as an obligation falling upon the directors in their capacity as members. Otherwise the contractual aspect of the provision in the articles would not have applied.

(ii) The leading case is *Clarke* v *Dunraven* [1896] A.C. 59, where it was *held* that competitors in a regatta had made a contract not only with the club which organized the race but also with each other, so that one competitor was able to sue another for damages when his boat was fouled and sank under a rule which said that each competitor was liable 'to pay all damages' that he might cause.

If an unrequested service is given without promise of payment, a subsequent promise to pay is supported only by past consideration and is not binding.

(27) *Re McArdle* [1951] 1 All E.R. 905

Certain children were entitled under their father's will to a house. However, their mother had a life interest in the property and during her lifetime one of the children and his wife came to live in the house with the mother. The wife carried out certain improvements to the property and, after she had done so, the children signed a document addressed to her saying: 'In consideration of your carrying out certain alterations and improvements to the property . . . at present occupied by you, the beneficiaries under the Will of William Edward McArdle hereby agree that the executors, the National Provincial Bank Ltd, . . . shall repay to you from the said estate when so distributed the sum of £488 in settlement of the amount spent on such improvements. . . .' On the death of the testator's widow the children refused to authorize payment of the sum of £488, and this action was brought to decide the validity of the claim. *Held*—Since the improvements had been carried out before the document was executed, the consideration was past and the promise could not be enforced.

A subsequent promise to pay is binding if the act to be rewarded was done on a commercial basis at the request of the person making the promise. Consideration is then said to be 'executed' and not 'past'.

(28) *Re Casey's Patents, Stewart* v *Casey* [1892] 1 Ch. 104

Patents were granted to Stewart and another in respect of an invention concerning appliances and vessels for transporting and storing inflammable liquids. Stewart entered into an arrangement with Casey whereby Casey was to introduce the patents. Casey spent two years 'pushing' the invention and then the joint owners of the patent rights wrote to him as follows: 'In consideration of your service as the practical manager in working both patents we hereby agree to give you one-third share of the patents.' Casey also received the letters patent. Some time later Stewart died and his executors claimed the letters patent from Casey, suggesting that he had no interest in them because the consideration for the promise to give him a one-third share was past. *Held*—The previous request to render the services raised an implied promise to pay. The subsequent promise could be regarded as fixing the value of the services so that Casey was entitled to one-third share of the patent rights.

A person who is not a party to a contract may not sue upon it even if it is made for his benefit. A person who is a party is still unable to sue unless he has supplied consideration or the contract is under seal.

(29) *Dunlop* v *Selfridge* [1915] A.C. 847

The appellants were motor tyre manufacturers and sold tyres to Messrs Dew & Co. who were motor accessory dealers. Under the terms of the contract Dew & Co. agreed not to sell the tyres below Dunlop's list price, and as Dunlop's agents, to obtain from other traders a similar undertaking. In return for this undertaking Dew & Co. were to receive discounts, some of which they could pass on to retailers who bought tyres. Selfridge & Co. accepted two orders from customers for Dunlop covers at a lower price. They obtained the covers through Dew & Co. and signed an agreement not to sell or offer the tyres below list price. It was further agreed that £5 per tyre so sold should be paid to Dunlop by way of liquidated damages. Selfridge's supplied one of the two tyres ordered below list price. They did not actually supply the other, but informed the customer that they could only supply it at list price. The appellants claimed an injunction and damages against the respondents for breach of the agreement made with Dew & Co., claiming that Dew & Co. were their agents in the matter. *Held*—There was no contract between the parties. Dunlop could not enforce the contract made between the respondents and Dew & Co. because they had not supplied consideration. Even if Dunlop were undisclosed principals, there was no consideration moving between them and the respondents. The discount received by Selfridge was part of that given by Dunlop to Dew & Co. Since Dew & Co. were not bound to give any part of their discount to retailers the discount received by Selfridge operated only as consideration between themselves and Dew & Co. and could not be claimed by Dunlop as consideration to support a promise not to sell below list price. (See now Resale Prices Act 1976, s.26 (See pp. 67 and 68).)

A contract between A and B for the benefit of C, cannot be enforced

by C. It is binding between A and B and remedies for breach are available between A and B including specific performance.

(30) *Beswick* v *Beswick* [1967] 2 All E.R. 1197

A coal merchant agreed to sell the business to his nephew in return for a weekly consultancy fee of £6.50 payable during his lifetime, and after his death an annuity of £5 per week was to be payable to his widow for her lifetime. After the agreement was signed the nephew took over the business and paid his uncle the sum of £6.50 as agreed. The uncle died on 3 November 1963, and the nephew paid the widow one sum of £5 and then refused to pay her any more. On 30 June 1964, the widow became the administratrix of her husband's estate, and on 15 July 1964 she brought an action against the nephew for arrears of the weekly sums and for specific performance of the agreement for the future. She sued in her capacity as administratrix of the estate and also in her personal capacity. Her action failed at first instance and on appeal to the Court of Appeal [1966] 3 All E.R. 1, it was decided amongst other things that—

(1) Specific performance could in a proper case be ordered of a contract to pay money.

(2) 'Property' in s.56(1) of the Law of Property Act 1925 included a contractual claim not concerned with realty and that therefore a third party could sue on a contract to which he was a stranger. The widow's claim in her personal capacity was therefore good. (Per Denning, M.R. and Danckwerts, L.J.)

(3) The widow's claim as administratrix was good because she was not suing in her personal capacity but on behalf of her deceased husband who had been a party to the agreement.

(4) No trust in her favour could be inferred.

There was further appeal to the House of Lords, though not on the creation of a trust, and there it was held that the widow's claim as administratrix succeeded, and that specific performance of a contract to pay money could be granted in a proper case. However, having decided the appeal on these grounds their Lordships went to to say that the widow's personal claim would have failed because s.56 of the Law of Property Act 1925 was limited to cases involving realty. The 1925 Act was a consolidating not a codifying measure, so that if it contained words which were capable of more than one construction, effect should be given to the construction which did not alter the law. It was accepted that when the present provision was contained in the Real Property Act 1845, it had applied only to realty. Although s.205(1) of the 1925 Act appeared to have extended the provision to personal property, including things in action, it was expressly qualified by the words: 'unless the context otherwise requires,' and it was felt that Parliament had not intended to sweep away the rule of privity by what was in effect a sidewind.

Comment. Here the problem of whether or not to award nominal damages referred to in *Jackson's case*[31] (below) was overcome because the Court awarded specific performance. However, four Law Lords said that if damages had been awarded they would have been nominal only, though Lord Pearce would have awarded substantial damages. Furthermore, it is unlikely that s.56 does have a very wide application. The subsection says that a person may take the benefit of an agreement although he is not 'named as a party'. The legislation does not say that he need not *be a party*. There are those who take the view, therefore, that s.56(1) is designed to cover the situation where there is a covenant over land in favour of, say, 'the owner of Whiteacre', so that the owner of Whiteacre could benefit from the covenant, provided he could be ascertained, even though he was not named in the instrument creating the covenant. If this interpretation is correct then s.56(1) of the 1925 Act has little effect on the law of contract generally.

If a party to a contract does recover damages in respect of a third party's failure to receive an agreed benefit under the contract, he holds the money recovered either as a constructive trustee or in quasi-contract for the third party. He does not own it himself.

(31) *Jackson* v *Horizon Holidays* [1975] 3 All E.R. 92

Mr Jackson sued successfully on a contract *he made* with the defendants to provide a holiday which, in the event, was not of the high standard described in the brochure. He received damages for his own loss and disappointment and also for that of his family since the contract *was also made for their benefit.*

Comment. This judgment by Lord Denning has been much criticized since it infringes a very old rule of English contract law which states that if A contracts with B in return for B's promise to do something for C, then if B repudiates the contract, C has no enforceable claim, and A is restricted to an action for nominal damages by reason of his having suffered no loss. The judgment was criticized by the House of Lords in *Beswick* (see above) and again in *Woodar Investment Development* v *Wimpey Construction UK* [1980] 1 All E.R. 571 and must therefore be regarded with caution.

The doctrine of privity of contract is not applied when a person seeks to enforce a covenant over land.

(32) *Smith and Snipes Hall Farm Ltd* v *River Douglas Catchment Board* [1949] 2 All E.R. 179

In 1938 the defendants entered into an agreement with 11 persons owning land adjoining a certain stream, that, on the landowners paying some part of the cost, the defendants would improve the banks of the stream and maintain the said banks for all time. In 1940 one landowner sold her land to Smith, and in 1944 Smith leased the land to Snipes Hall Farm Ltd. In 1946, because of the defendants' negligence, the banks burst and the adjoining land was flooded. *Held*—The plaintiffs could enforce the covenant in the agreement of 1938 even though they were strangers to it. The covenants were for the benefit of the land and affected its use and value and could therefore be transferred with it.

(33) *Tulk* v *Moxhay* (1848) 2 Ph. 774

The plaintiff was the owner of several plots of land in Leicester Square and in 1808 he sold one of them to a person called Elms. Elms agreed, for himself, his heirs and assigns, 'to keep the Square Garden open as a pleasure ground and uncovered with buildings'. After a number of conveyances, the land was sold to the defendant who claimed a right to build on it. The plaintiff sued for an injunction preventing the development of the land. The defendant, whilst admitting that he purchased the land with notice of the covenant, claimed that he was not bound by it because he had not himself entered into it. *Held*—An injunction to restrain building would be granted because there was a jurisdiction in equity to prevent, by way of injunction, acts inconsistent with a restrictive covenant on land, so long as the land was acquired with notice of that covenant, and the defendant retains land which can benefit from the covenant.

Comment. Such notice may now be constructive where the covenant is registered under s.2(5) of the Land Charges Act 1972.

Consideration need not be adequate but must be real which means capable of estimation in terms of value.

(34) *White* v *Bluett* (1853) 23 L.J. Ex. 36

This action was brought by White who was the executor of Bluett's father's estate. The plaintiff, White, alleged that Bluett had not paid a promissory note given to his father during his lifetime. Bluett admitted that he had given the note to his father, but said that his father had released him from it in return for a promise not to keep on complaining about the fact that he had been disinherited. *Held*—The defence failed and the defendant was liable on the note. The promise not to complain was not real consideration to support his release from the note.

Comment. This case is the only major illustration of the principle and, although included in formation of contract, actually related to the discharge of one contract by another.

Acts or omissions of trivial value can amount to consideration. This is so even where what is received is of no use to the person receiving it so long as it has some value.

(35) *Chappell & Co. Ltd* v *Nestlé Co. Ltd* [1959] 2 All E.R. 701

The plaintiffs owned the copyright in a dance tune called 'Rockin' Shoes', and the defendants were using records of this tune as part of an advertising scheme. A record company made the records for Nestlé who advertised them to the the public for $7\frac{1}{2}$p each but required in addition three wrappers from their $7\frac{1}{2}$p bars of chocolate. When they received the wrappers they threw them away. The plaintiffs sued the defendants for infringement of copyright. It appeared that under the Copyright Act of 1956 a person recording musical works for retail sale need not get the permission of the holder of the copyright, but had merely to serve him with notice and pay $6\frac{1}{4}$ per cent of the retail selling price as royalty. The plaintiffs asserted that the defendants were not retailing the goods in the sense of the Act and must therefore get permission to use the musical work. The basis of the plaintiffs' case was that retailing meant selling entirely for money, and that as the defendants were selling for money plus wrappers, they needed the plaintiffs' consent. The defence was that the sale was for cash because the wrappers were not part of the consideration. *Held*—The plaintiffs succeeded because the wrappers were part of the consideration and the question of their adequacy did not arise.

Comment. Presumably the wrappers could have formed the whole consideration.

Forbearance to sue provides consideration. The person who forbears to sue may actually promise not to do so or merely forbear in fact. A promise is not essential.

(36) *Horton* v *Horton* [1960] 3 All E.R. 649

The parties were husband and wife. In March 1954, by a separation agreement under seal, the husband agreed to pay the wife £30 a month. On the true construction of the deed the husband should have deducted income tax before payment but for nine months he paid the money without deductions. In January 1955 he signed a document, not under seal, agreeing that instead of 'the monthly sum of £30' he would pay such a monthly sum as 'after deduction of income tax should amount to the clear sum of £30'. For over three years he paid this clear sum but then stopped payment. To an action by his wife he pleaded that the later agreement was unsupported by consideration and that the wife could sue only on the earlier deed. *Held*—by the Court of Appeal—that there was consideration to support the later agreement. It was clear that the original deed did not implement the intention of the parties. The wife therefore might have sued to rectify the deed and the later agreement represented a compromise of this possible action. Whether such an action would have succeeded was irrelevant; it sufficed that it had some prospect of success and that the wife believed in it.

A promise to perform a pre-existing public duty does not provide consideration.

(37) *Collins* v *Godefroy* (1831) 1B. & Ad. 950

The plaintiff was subpoenaed to give evidence for the defendant in an action to which the defendant was a party. The plaintiff now sued for the sum of six guineas which he said the defendant had promised him for his attendance. *Held*—The plaintiff's action failed because there was no consideration for the promise. Lord Tenterden said: 'if it be a duty imposed by law upon a party regularly subpoenaed to attend from time to time to give his evidence, then a promise to give him any remuneration for loss of time incurred in such attendance is a promise without consideration.'

Where a promise induces a person to do more than the pre-existing public duty, the promise is enforceable.

(38) *Glasbrook Bros* v *Glamorgan County Council* [1925] A.C. 270

The question had arisen as to how best to protect a coal mine during a strike. The police authorities thought it enough to prove a mobile force but the colliery manager wanted a stationary guard. It was ultimately agreed to provide the latter at a rate of payment which involved the sum of £2200. The company refused to pay and when sued pleaded the absence of consideration. The House of Lords gave judgment for the plaintiffs. The police were bound to afford protection but they had a discretion as to the form it should take, and an undertaking to provide more protection than in their discretion they deemed necessary was consideration for the promise of reward.

(39) *Ward* v *Byham* [1956] 2 All E.R. 318

An unmarried mother sued to recover a maintenance allowance by the father of the child. The defence was that, under s.42 of the National Assistance Act 1948, the mother of an illegitimate child was bound to maintain it. However, it appeared that in return for the promise of an allowance the mother had promised—

(1) to look after the child well and ensure that it was happy; and
(2) to allow it to decide whether it should livc with her or the father.

Held—There was sufficient consideration to support the promise of an allowance because the promises given in (1) and (2) above were in excess of the statutory duty, which was merely to care for the child.

Comment. 'Is a promise to make a child happy adequate consideration?' This point is not taken in the above case and shows the considerable power which judges have to find or not to find contractual obligations.

Pre-existing contractual duties between the parties. There is no consideration for the variation of a contract which does not involve the plaintiff in any additional obligation.

(40) *Stilk* v *Myrick* (1809) 2 Camp. 317

A sea-captain, being unable to find any substitutes for two sailors who had deserted, promised to divide the wages of the deserters among the rest of the crew if they would work the ship home shorthanded. *Held*—The promise was not enforceable because of absence of consideration. In sailing the ship home the crew had done no more than they were already bound to do. Their original contract obliged them to meet the normal emergencies of the voyage of which minor desertions were one.

A variation involving an extra obligation is enforceable.

(41) *Hartley* v *Ponsonby* (1857) 7 E. & B. 872

A greater remuneration was promised to a seaman to work the ship home when the number of deserters was so great as to render the ship unseaworthy. *Held*—This was a binding promise because the sailor had gone beyond his duty in agreeing to sail an unseaworthy ship. In fact the number of desertions was so great as to discharge the remaining seamen from their original contract, leaving them free to enter into a new bargain.

The performance of a contractual duty owed to a third party can be good consideration.

(42) *Shadwell* v *Shadwell* (1860) 9 C.B. (N.S.) 159

The plaintiff was engaged to marry a girl named Ellen Nicholl. In 1838 he received a letter from his uncle, Charles Shadwell, in the following terms: 'I am glad to hear of your intended marriage with Ellen Nicholl and, as I promised to assist you at starting, I am happy to tell you that I will pay you one hundred and fifty pounds yearly during my life and until your income derived from your profession of Chancery barrister shall amount to six hundred guineas, of which your own admission will be the only evidence that I shall receive or require.' The plaintiff duly married Ellen Nicholl and his income never exceeded 600 guineas during the 18 years his uncle lived after the marriage. The uncle paid 12 annual sums and part of the thirteenth but no more. On his death the plaintiff sued his uncle's executors for the balance of the 18 instalments to which he suggested he was entitled. *Held*—The plaintiff succeeded even though he was already engaged to Ellen Nicholl when the promise was made. His marriage was sufficient consideration to support his uncle's promise, for, by marrying, the plaintiff had incurred responsibilities and changed his position in life. Further the uncle probably derived some benefit in that his desire to see his nephew settled had been satisfied.

Comment. An engagement to marry is no longer binding as a contract—Law Reform (Miscellaneous Provisions) Act 1970, s.1.

At common law a promise by a creditor to take a part-payment in full settlement of his debt is not enforceable unless there is consideration for his promise.

(43) *Foakes* v *Beer* (1884) 9 App. Cas 605

Mrs Beer had obtained a judgment against Dr Foakes for debt and costs.

Dr Foakes agreed to settle the judgment debt by paying £500 down and £150 per half-year until the whole was paid, and Mrs Beer agreed not to take further action on the judgment. Foakes duly paid the amount of the judgment plus costs. However, judgment debts carry interest by statute, and while Dr Foakes had been paying off the debt, interest amounting to £360 had been accruing on the diminishing balance. In this action Mrs Beer claimed the £360. *Held*—She could do so. Her promise not to take further action on the judgment was not supported by any consideration moving from Dr Foakes.

Comment. Since the development of equitable estoppel in the *High Trees case* (see p. 368), there is no reason why a part-payment should not be enough discharge the contract. Perhaps *Foakes* will in future be confined to cases where the acceptance of the part-payment results from threats as in *D. & C. Builders* v *Rees* 1965. (See below.)

(44) *D. & C. Builders Ltd* v *Rees* [1965] 3 All E.R. 837

D. & C. Builders, a small company, did work for Rees for which he owed £482 13s 1d. There was at first no dispute as to the work done but Rees did not pay. In August and October 1964, the plaintiffs wrote for the money and received no reply. On 13 November 1964, the wife of Rees (who was then ill) telephoned the plaintiffs, complained about the work, and said, 'My husband will offer you £300 in settlement. That is all you will get. It is to be in satisfaction.' D. & C. Builders, being in desperate straits and faced with bankruptcy without the money, offered to take the £300 and allow a year to Rees to find the balance. Mrs Rees replied: 'No, we will never have enough money to pay the balance. £300 is better than nothing.' The plaintiffs then said: 'We have no choice but to accept.' Mrs Rees gave the defendants a cheque and insisted on a receipt 'in completion of the account.' The plaintiffs, being worried, brought an action for the balance. The defence was bad workmanship and also that there was a binding settlement. The question of settlement was tried as a preliminary issue and the judge, following *Goddard* v *O'Brien* (1882) 9 Q.B.D. 37, decided that a cheque for a smaller amount was a good discharge of the debt, this being the generally accepted view of the law since that date. On appeal it was *held* (per The Master of the Rolls, Lord Denning) that *Goddard* v *O'Brien* was wrongly decided. A smaller sum in cash could be no settlement of a larger sum and 'no sensible distinction could be drawn between the payment of a lesser sum by cash and the payment of it by cheque.'

In the course of his judgment Lord Denning said of *High Trees*: 'It is worth noting that the principle may be applied, not only so as to suspend strict legal rights but also so as to preclude the enforcement of them.

'This principle has been applied to cases where a creditor agrees to accept a lesser sum in discharge of a greater. So much so that we can now say that, when a creditor and debtor enter on a course of negotiation, which leads the debtor to suppose that on payment of the lesser sum, the creditor will not enforce payment of the balance, and on the faith thereof the debtor pays the lesser sum and the creditor accepts it as satisfaction: then the creditor will not be allowed to enforce payment of the balance when it would be inequitable to do so. . . . But he is not bound unless there has been truly an accord between them.'

In the present case there was no true accord. The debtor's wife had held the creditors to ransom, and there was no reason in law or equity why the plaintiffs should not enforce the full amount of the debt.

A debtor may make a composition agreement with his creditors. The creditors agree with each other and the debtor to take a part-payment in full settlement. The creditors cannot then sue the debtor for the balance.

(45) *Good* v *Cheesman* (1831) 2 B. & Ad. 328

The defendant had accepted two bills of exchange of which the plaintiff was the drawer. After the bills became due and before this action was brought, the plaintiff suggested that the defendant meet his creditors with a view perhaps to an agreement. The meeting was duly held and the defendant entered into an agreement with his creditors whereby the defendant was to pay one-third of his income to a trustee to be named by the creditors, and that this was to be the method by which the defendant's debts were to be paid. It was not clear from the evidence whether the plaintiff attended the meeting, though he certainly did not sign the agreement. There was, however, evidence that the agreement had been in his possession for some time and it was duly stamped before the trial. No trustee was in fact appointed, though the defendant was willing to go on with the agreement. *Held*—The agreement bound the plaintiff and the action on the bills could not be sustained. The consideration, though not supplied to the plaintiff direct, existed in the forbearance of the other creditors. Each was bound in consequence of the agreement of the rest.

Comment. The basis of this decision may be found in both the law of contract and in tort. In tort because once an agreement of this kind has been made it would be a fraud on the other creditors for one of their number to sue the debtor separately. In contract because an action by a creditor would be a breach of his contract with the other creditors.

A creditor who has accepted a part-payment from a third party cannot sue the debtor for the balance.

(46) *Welby* v *Drake* (1825) 1 C. & P. 557

The plaintiff sued the defendant for the sum of £9 on a debt which had originally been £18. The defendant's father had paid the plaintiff £9 and the plaintiff had agreed to take that sum in full discharge of the debt. *Held*—The payment of £9 by the defendant's father operated to discharge the debt of £18.

Comment. Here again the basis of the decision may be that it would be a fraud on the third party to sue the original debtor. 'If the father did pay the smaller sum in satisfaction of this debt, it is a bar to the plaintiff's now recovering against the son; because by suing the son, he commits fraud on the father, whom he induced to advance his money on the faith of such advance being a discharge of his son from further liability.' (Per Lord Tenterden, C.J.). Also, of course, the creditor breaks his contract with the third party.

The doctrine of promissory estoppel. This does not effect a binding variation of the contract but merely suspends the rights of the creditor.

(47) *Central London Property Trust Ltd* v *High Trees House Ltd* [1947] K.B. 130

In 1937 the plaintiffs granted to the defendants a lease of 99 years of a new block of flats at a rent of £2500 per annum. The lease was under seal. During the period of the war the flats were by no means fully let owing to the absence of people from the London area. The defendant company, which was a subsidiary of the plaintiff company, realized that it could not meet the rent out of the profits then being made on the flats, and in 1940 the parties entered into an agreement which reduced the rent to £1250 per annum, this agreement being put into writing but not sealed. The defendants continued to pay the reduced rent from 1941 to the beginning of 1945, by which time the flats were fully let, and they continued to pay the reduced rents thereafter. In September 1945, the receiver of the plaintiff company investigated the matter and asked for arrears of £7916, suggesting that the liability created by the lease still existed, and that the agreement of 1940 was not supported by any consideration. The receiver then brought this friendly action to establish the legal position. He claimed £625, being the difference in rent for the two quarters ending 29 September and 29 December 1945. *Held*—(1) A simple contract can in equity vary a deed (i.e. the lease), though it had not done so here because the simple contract was not supported by consideration. (2) As the agreement for the reduction of rent had been acted upon by the defendants, the plaintiffs were estopped in equity from claiming the full rent from 1941 until early 1945 when the flats were fully let. After that time they were entitled to do so because the second agreement was only operative during the continuance of the conditions which gave rise to it. To this extent the limited claim of the receiver succeeded.

Comment. The rule established by the case, in its developed state, seems that to be that where a person has indicated by a promise that he is not going to insist upon his strict rights, as a result of which the other party acts on the belief induced by the other's promise which may mean no more than making the reduced payments, as in this case, then the law, although it does not give a cause of action in damages if the promise is broken, will require it to be honoured to the extent of refusing to allow the promissor the right to act inconsistently with it, even though the promise is not supported by consideration. The doctrine has been called 'equitable estoppel', 'quasi-estoppel', and 'promissory estoppel', in order to distinguish it from estoppel at common law. At common law estoppel arises when the defendant by his conduct suggests that certain existing facts are true. Here the estoppel was based on a promise not conduct, and the promise related to future conduct not to existing facts.

(48) *Tool Metal Manufacturing Co. Ltd* v *Tungsten Electric Co. Ltd* [1955] 2 All E.R. 657

The appellants were the registered proprietors of British letters patent. In April 1938 they made a contract with the respondents whereby they gave the latter a license to manufacture 'hard metal alloys' in accordance with the inventions which were the subject of patent. By the contract the respondents agreed to pay 'compensation' to the appellants if in any one month they sold more than a stated quantity of metal alloys.

Compensation was duly paid by the respondents until the outbreak of war in 1939, but thereafter none was paid. It was found as a fact that in 1942 the appellants agreed to suspend the enforcement of compensation payments pending the making of a new contract. In 1944 negotiations for such new contracts were begun but broke down. In 1945 the respondents sued the appellants for breach of contract and the appellants counter-claimed for payment of compensation as from 1 June 1945. As regards the arguments on the counter-claim, it was eventually *held* by the Court of Appeal that the agreement of 1942 operated in equity to prevent the appellants demanding compensation until they had given reasonable notice to the respondents of their intention to resume their strict legal rights and that such notice had not been given.

In September 1950 the appellants themselves issued a writ against the respondents claiming compensation as from 1 January 1947. The respondents pleaded the equity raised by the agreement of 1942 and argued that reasonable notice of its termination had not been given. When this action reached the House of Lords it was *held*—affirming *Hughes* v *Metropolitan Railway Co.* and the *High Trees* case, that the agreement of 1942 operated in equity to suspend the appellants' legal rights to compensation until reasonable notice to resume them had been given. However, the counter-claim in the first action in 1945 amounted to such notice, and since the appellants were not now claiming any compensation as due to them before 1 January 1947, the appellants succeeded in this second action and were awarded £84,000 under the compensation clause.

It is not an essential requirement of the operation of equitable estoppel that the defendant should have acted to his detriment on the strength of the promise.

(49) *W.J. Alan & Co.* v *El Nasr Export and Import Co.* [1972] 2 All E.R. 127

A contract for the sale of coffee provided for the price expressed in Kenyan shillings to be paid by irrevocable letter of credit. The buyers procured a confirmed letter expressed in sterling and the sellers obtained part payment thereunder. While shipment was in progress sterling was devalued and the sellers claimed such additional sum as would bring the price up to the sterling equivalent of Kenyan shillings at the current rate. Orr, J., held that the buyers were liable to pay the additional sum as the currency of account was Kenyan shillings. On appeal by the buyers it was *held*—allowing the appeal—that the sellers by accepting payment in sterling had irrevocably waived their right to be paid in Kenyan currency or had accepted a variation of the sale contract, and that a party who has waived his rights cannot afterwards insist on them if the other party has acted on that belief differently from the way in which he would otherwise have acted; and the other party need not show that he has acted to his detriment. In the course of his judgment Lord Denning, M.R., said . . . 'if one party, by his conduct, leads another to believe that the strict rights arising under the contract will not be insisted on, intending that the other should act on that belief, and he does act on it, then the first party will not afterwards be allowed to insist on the strict legal rights when it would be inequitable for him to do so. . . . There may be no consideration moving from him who benefits by the waiver. There may be no detriment to him acting on it. There may be nothing in writing. Nevertheless, the one who waives his strict rights cannot afterwards insist on them. His strict rights are at any rate suspended so long as the waiver lasts. He may on occasion be able to revert to his strict legal rights for the future by giving reasonable notice in that behalf, or otherwise making it plain by his conduct that he will thereafter insist on them. . . . I know that it has been suggested in some quarters that there must be a detriment. But I can find no support for it in the authorities cited by the judge. The nearest approach to it is the statement by Viscount Simonds in the *Tool Metal* case that the other must have been led "to alter his position" which was adopted by Lord Hodson in *Emmanuel Ayodeji Ajayi* v *R.T. Briscoe (Nigeria) Ltd* [1964] 3 All E.R. 556. But that only means that he must have been led to act differently from what he otherwise would have done. And, if you study the cases in which the doctrine has been applied, you will see that all that is required is that one should have "acted on the belief induced by the other party". That is how Lord Cohen put it in the *Tool Metal* case and it is how I would put it myself.'

Comment. Since, as in *High Trees*, a tenant who only pays one-half of his rent can hardly be said to have 'acted to his detriment', the better view is that acting to one's detriment is not a requirement of equitable estoppel. It is a requirement of common law estoppel.

Promissory estoppel is essentially defensive in its nature.

(50) *Combe* v *Combe* [1951] 1 All E.R. 767

The parties were married in 1915 and separated in 1939. In February 1943, the wife obtained a decree nisi of divorce, and a few days later the husband entered into an agreement under which he was to pay his wife £100 per annum, free of income tax. The decree was made absolute in August 1943. The husband did not make the agreed payments and the wife did not apply to the court for maintenance but chose to rely on the alleged contract. She brought this action for arrears under that contract. Evidence showed that her income was between £700 and £800 per annum and the defendant's was £650 per annum. Byrne, J., at first instance, held that, although the wife had not supplied consideration, the agreement was nevertheless enforceable, following the decision in the *High Trees* case,[47] as a promise made to be acted upon and in fact acted upon. *Held*—(1) That the *High Trees* decision was not intended to create new actions where none existed before, and that it had not abolished the requirement of consideration to support simple contracts. In such cases consideration was a cardinal necessity. (2) In the words of Birkett, L.J., the doctrine was 'a shield not a sword', i.e. a defence to an action, not a cause of action. (3) The doctrine applied to the modification of existing agreements by subsequent promises and had no relevance to the formation of a contract. (4) It was not possible to find consideration in the fact that the wife forbore to claim maintenance from the court, since no such contractual undertaking by her could have been binding even if she had given it. Therefore this action by the wife must fail because the agreement was not supported by consideration.

Comment. Promissory estoppel usually protects a promisee from being sued upon his original promise. Thus in a case such as *Stilk* v *Myrick* 1809[40] the sailors could not presumably sue successfully under the equitable doctrine for the extra pay they were promised.

An agreement is not binding as a contract if it was made without an intention to create legal relations. The court takes the view that many domestic agreements between husband and wife are not intended to be legally binding.

(51) *Balfour* v *Balfour* [1919] 2 K.B. 571

The defendant was a civil servant stationed in Ceylon. In November 1915, he came to England on leave with his wife, the plaintiff in the present action. In August 1916, the defendant returned alone to Ceylon because his wife's doctor had advised her that her health would not stand up to a further period of service abroad. Later the husband wrote to his wife suggesting that they should remain apart, and in 1918 the plaintiff obtained a decree nisi. In this case the plaintiff alleged that before her husband sailed for Ceylon he had agreed, in consultation with her, that he would give her £30 per month as maintenance, and she now sued because of his failure to abide by the said agreement. The Court of Appeal *held* that there was no enforceable contract because the parties did not intend to create legal relations. The provision for a flat payment of £30 per month for an indefinite period with no attempt to take into account changes in the circumstances of the parties did not suggest a binding agreement. Duke, L.J., seems to have based his decision on the fact that the wife had not supplied any consideration.

It is possible for a husband and wife to make a binding contract regarding their domestic affairs. For example, separation agreements may be binding where the parties agree to live apart.

(52) *Merritt* v *Merritt* [1970] 2 All E.R. 760

After a husband had formed an attachment for another woman and had left his wife a meeting was held between the parties on 25 May 1966, in the husband's car. The husband agreed to pay the wife £40 per month maintenance and also wrote out and signed a document stating that in consideration of the wife paying all charges in connection with the matrimonial home until the mortgage repayments had been completed, he would agree to transfer the property to her sole ownership. The wife took the document away with her and in the following months paid off the mortgage. The husband did not subsequently transfer the property to his wife and she claimed a declaration that she was the sole beneficial owner and asked for an order that her husband should transfer the property to her forthwith. The husband's defence was that the agreement was a family arrangement not intended to create legal relations. *Held*—by the Court of Appeal—

(1) that the agreement, having been made when the parties were not living together in amity, was enforceable (*Balfour* v *Balfour* 1919,[51] distinguished); and

(2) that the contention that there was no consideration to support the husband's promise could not be sustained. The payment of the balance of the mortgage was a detriment to the wife and the husband had received the benefit of being relieved of liability to the building society.

Accordingly the wife was entitled to the relief she claimed.

An agreement between persons sharing a common household raises the issue of intention to create legal relations. However, such an agreement may be binding if it is not concerned with the routine management of the household.

(53) *Simpkins* v *Pays* [1955] 3 All E.R. 10

The defendant and the defendant's grand-daughter made an agreement with the plaintiff, who was a paying boarder, that they should submit in the defendant's name a weekly coupon, containing a forecast by each of them, to a Sunday newspaper fashion competition. On one occasion a forecast by the grand-daughter was correct and the defendant received a prize of £750. The plaintiff sued for her share of that sum. The defence was that there was no intention to create legal relations but that the transaction was a friendly arrangement binding in honour only. *Held*—There was an intention to create legal relations. Far from being a friendly domestic arrangement, the evidence showed that it was a joint enterprise and that the parties expected to share any prize that was won.

(54) *Parker* v *Clark* [1960] 1 All E.R. 93

The plaintiffs, Mr & Mrs Parker, were a middle-aged couple and lived in their own cottage in Sussex. The defendants, Mr & Mrs Clark, who were aged 77 and 78, respectively, lived in a large house in Torquay. Mrs Parker was the niece of Mrs Clark. In 1955 the plaintiffs visited the defendants and, as a result of certain conversations held at that time, Mrs Clark wrote to Mrs Parker suggesting that the plaintiffs should come to live in the defendants' house in Torquay, setting out detailed financial terms as to the sharing of expenses. Mrs Clark also suggested that the plaintiffs' cottage might be sold and the proceeds invested, and that the defendants would leave the house in Torquay, and its major contents, to Mrs Parker, her sister and her daughter. Mrs Parker wrote accepting this offer and the cottage was sold. After the mortgage was paid off, £2000 of the remaining money was lent to their daughter to enable her to buy a flat. The plaintiffs then moved into the defendants' house in Torquay. For a time all went well and Mr Clark executed a will leaving the property as agreed. In 1957 differences between the parties arose, and after much unpleasantness Mr Clark told the plaintiffs to go, and they left in December 1957. The plaintiffs claimed damages for breach of contract. *Held*—There was an intention to create legal relations arising from the circumstances. In view of the fact that the plaintiffs had sold their home and lent £2000 to their daughter, it was obvious that, having 'burned their boats,' they must have relied on the agreement. The letter from Mrs Clark was an offer sufficiently precise and detailed; it was not merely a statement of terms for a future agreement. Further it was a sufficient memorandum to satisfy s.40 of the Law of Property Act 1925. Finally, the fact that Mr Clark had altered his will indicated that he regarded the agreement as binding.

The damages awarded were divided as follows—

(1) Damages of £1200 plus costs, in favour of the parties jointly, based on the value per annum of living rent-free in the house. (£300 multiplied by four because of the expectation of life of the defendants.)

(2) Damages of £3400 in favour of Mrs Parker separately, in respect

of the value of her of inheriting a share in the defendants' house on their death.

Contractual intention may be negatived by the vague terms of the agreement.

(55) *Jones* v *Padavatton* [1969] 2 All E.R. 616

In 1962 the plaintiff, Mrs Jones, who lived in Trinidad, made an offer to the defendant Mrs Padavatton, her daughter, to provide maintenance for her at the rate of £42 a month if she would leave her job in Washington in the United States and go to England and read for the Bar. Mrs Padavatton was at that time divorced from her husband, having the custody of the child of that marriage. The agreement was an informal one and there was uncertainty as to its exact terms. Nevertheless the daughter came to England in November 1962, bringing the child with her, and began to read for the Bar, her fees and maintenance being paid for by Mrs Jones. In 1964 it appeared that the daughter was experiencing some discomfort in England, occupying one room in Acton for which she had to pay £6 17s 6d per week. At this stage Mrs Jones offered to buy a large house in London to be occupied by the daughter and partly by tenants, the income from rents to go to the daughter in lieu of maintenance. Again there was no written agreement but the house was purchased for £6000 and conveyed to Mrs Jones. The daughter moved into the house in January 1965, and tenants arrived, it still being uncertain what precisely was to happen to the surplus rent income (if any) and what rooms the daughter was to occupy. No money from the rents was received by Mrs Jones and no accounts were submitted to her. In 1967 Mrs Jones claimed possession of the house from her daughter, who had by that time married again, and the daughter counter-claimed for £1655 18s 9d, said to have been paid in connection with running the house. At the hearing the daughter still had one subject to pass in Part I of the Bar examinations and also the whole of Part II remained to be taken. *Held*—by the Court of Appeal—

(1) That the arrangements were throughout family agreements depending upon the good faith of the parties in keeping promises made and not intended to be rigid binding agreements. Furthermore, the arrangements were far too vague and uncertain to be enforceable as contracts. (Per Danckwerts and Fenton Atkinson, L.J.J.)

(2) That although the agreement to maintain while reading for the Bar might have been regarded as creating a legal obligation in the mother to pay (the terms being sufficiently stated and duration for a reasonable time being implied), the daughter could not claim anything in respect of that agreement which must be regarded as having terminated in 1967, five years being a reasonable time in which to complete studies for the Bar. The arrangements in relation to the home were very

vague and must be regarded as made without contractual intent. (Per Salmon, L.J.)

The mother was therefore entitled to possession of the house and had no liability under the maintenance agreement. The counter-claim by the daughter was left to be settled by the parties.

Contractual intention may be expressly ruled out by a term of the agreement.

(56) *Jones* v *Vernon's Pools Ltd* [1938] 2 All E.R. 626

The plaintiff said that he had sent to the defendants a football coupon on which the penny points pool was all correct. Defendants denied having received it and relied on a clause printed on every coupon. The said clause provided that the transaction should not 'give rise to any legal relationship . . . or be legally enforceable . . . but . . . binding in honour only'. *Held*—that this clause was a bar to any action in a court of law.

Comment. This case was followed by the Court of Appeal in *Appleson* v *Littlewood Ltd* [1939] 1 All E.R. 464, where the contract contained a similar clause.

(57) *Rose and Frank Co* v *Crompton (J.R.) & Brothers Ltd* [1925] A.C. 445

In 1913 the plaintiffs, an American firm, entered into an agreement with the defendants, an English company, whereby the plaintiffs were appointed sole agents for the sale in the USA of paper tissues supplied by the defendants. The contract was for a period of three years with an option to extend that time. The agreement was extended to March 1920, but in 1919 the defendants terminated it without notice. The defendants had received a number of orders for tissues before the termination of the contract, and they refused to execute them. The plaintiffs sued for breach of contract and for non-delivery of the goods actually ordered. The agreement of 1913 contained an 'Honourable Pledge Cause' drafted as follows: 'This arrangement is not entered into nor is this memorandum written as a formal or legal agreement and shall not be subject to legal jurisdiction in the courts of the United States of America or England. . . .' *Held*—by the House of Lords—that the 1913 agreement was not binding on the parties, but that in so far as the agreement had been acted upon by the defendants' acceptance of orders, the said orders were binding contracts of sale. Nevertheless the agreement was not binding for the future.

A contract of indemnity is not within the Statute of Frauds and need not be evidenced in writing.

(58) *Mountstephen* v *Lakeman* (1871) L.R. 7 Q.B. 196

The defendant was chairman of the Brixham Local Board of Health. The plaintiff, who was a builder and contractor, was employed in 1866 by the board to construct certain main sewage works in the town. On 19 March 1866, notice was given by the board to owners of certain homes to connect their house drains with the main sewer within 21 days. Before the expiration of the 21 days Robert Adams, the surveyor of the board, suggested to the plaintiff that he should make the connection. The plaintiff said he was willing to do work if he would see him paid. On the 5 April 1866, i.e. before the expiration of the 21 days, the plaintiff commenced work on the connections. However, before work commenced it appeared that the plaintiff had had an interview with the defendant at which the following conversation took place—

Defendant—'What objection have you to making the connections?'
Plaintiff—'I have none, if you or the board will order the work or become responsible for the payment.'
Defendant—'Go on Mountstephen and do the work and I will see you paid.'

The plaintiff completed the connections in April and May 1866, and sent an account to the Board on 5 December 1866. The board disclaimed responsibility on the ground that they never entered into any agreement with the plaintiff nor authorized any officer of the board to agree with him for the performance of the work in question. *Held*—that Lakeman had undertaken a personal liability to pay the plaintiff and had not given a guarantee of the liability to pay the plaintiff and had not given a guarantee of the liability of a third party, i.e. the board. In consequence Lakeman had given an indemnity which did not need to be in writing under s.4 of the Statute of Frauds 1677. The plaintiff was therefore entitled to enforce the oral undertaking given by the defendant.

Comment. Section 4 of the Statute of Frauds 1677 provides that 'No action shall be brought . . . whereby to charge the defendant upon any special promise to answer for the debt default or miscarriage of another person . . . unless the agreement upon which such action shall be brought or some memorandum or note thereof shall be in writing and signed by the party to be charged therewith or some other person thereunto by him lawfully authorised.' It was held in *Birkmyr* v *Darnell* (1805) 1 Salk. 27 that the words 'debt default of miscarriage of *another person*' meant that the section applied only where there was some other person other than the surety who was primarily liable.

The memorandum required by s.40 of the Law of Property Act 1925 must contain a statement of the material terms of the contract, e.g. that the purchase price of property is to be paid in instalments.

(59) *Tweddell* v *Henderson* [1975] 2 All E.R. 1096

Mr Henderson, a builder, agreed with Miss Tweddell, a potential purchaser, that she should buy a house when built on a plot of land at Tintagel for £8700. There was an oral agreement that Miss Tweddell should pay the purchase price in four instalments, the first when the footings of the house were built. Mr Henderson wrote to Miss Tweddell at a later stage saying that he had asked his solicitor to get a contract drawn up, but this letter did not mention the system of payment. After a draft contract had been drawn up Mr Henderson said he could not go ahead with the sale unless Miss Tweddell could pay £9500, which she refused to do, and Mr Henderson sold the house to somebody else. Miss Tweddell now claimed damages for breach of contract. *Held*—by Plowman, V.C.,—that the contract was not enforceable because there was not a sufficient memorandum in writing. In the course of his judgment Plowman, V.C., said: 'It seems to me that the provision that the purchase money was to be paid, not at the end of the day, when the bungalow had been completed and was ready for handing over, but by the four stages to which I have referred, is a material term in every relevant sense, and there is no reference to it anywhere in the alleged memorandum. Accordingly, with some regret, because I think the plaintiff has been hardly treated, I have come to the conclusion that the defence of s.40 must succeed.'

If no single document sets out the material terms of the transaction it may be possible to produce an adequate memorandum by joining together two or more documents by oral evidence.

(60) *Pearce* v *Gardner* [1897] 1 Q.B. 688

The plaintiff brought this action to recover damages for breach of a contract by the defendant under the terms of which the defendant had agreed to sell the plaintiff certain gravel which was *in situ* on the land. At the trial the plaintiff put in evidence a letter signed by the defendant and commencing 'Dear Sir'. The letter did not contain the plaintiff's name. The plaintiff then put in evidence an envelope which had been used to post the letter, which showed the plaintiff's name and address. *Held*—The letter and the envelope together provided a memorandum sufficient to satisfy the Statute of Frauds.

Comment. (i) These documents did not refer to each other but could be joined by oral evidence because they were connected by human experience.

(ii) In *Williams* v *Lake* (1860) 2 E. & E. 349 the plaintiff put in evidence as a memorandum a letter similar to the one put forward in the above case. He was not able to produce an envelope, however, and the court held that the letter was not a memorandum sufficient to satisfy the Statute of Frauds.

Documents can be joined if one refers to the other or at least refers to the transaction concerned.

(61) *Timmins* v *Moreland Street Property Ltd* [1957] 3 All E.R. 265

The defendants agreed to buy certain property belonging to the plaintiff for £39,000 and gave him a cheque for £3900 as a deposit, the cheque being made payable to his solicitors. The plaintiff made out a signed deposit receipt which stated that the sum of £3900 was a deposit for the purchase of the property which was adequately described, and that the plaintiff agreed to sell for £39,000. Subsequently the defendants stopped the cheque and repudiated the contract. The plaintiff sued for breach of contract and the defendants pleaded absence of a memorandum under s.40 of the Law of Property Act 1925. The plaintiff claimed that a sufficient memorandum existed if the deposit receipt were read together with the cheque containing the defendants' signature. *Held*—The two documents could not be connected, because the cheque was made payable to the plaintiff's solicitors and there was no necessary connection between it and the deposit receipt.

Comment. (i) In addition the cheque contained no reference to the deposit receipt. It is unlikely that a cheque will ever refer to another document or transaction.

(ii) It is not necessary for one document to refer to the other. As Jenkins, L.J., said in *Timmins*: '. . . it is still indispensably necessary, in order to justify the reading of documents together . . . that there should be a document signed by the party to be charged which, while not containing in itself all the necessary ingredients of the required memorandum, does contain some reference express or implied, to some other document or transaction.'

This passage was taken to be a correct statement of the modern law by the Privy Council in *Elias* v *George Sahely & Co.* [1982] 3 All E.R. 801. The case concerned the purchase of a property in Swan Street, Bridgetown, Barbados. There was a letter containing all the material terms but this was not signed by the party to be charged, i.e. the defendant. However, a deposit receipt was signed by his agent. If the letter and receipt could be connected there was an adequate memorandum. The Privy Council held that they could be connected. The deposit receipt did not refer specifically to the letter but it did refer to the transaction, being worded as follows: 'Received from Fawzi Elias the sum of $39,000 being deposit on property at Swan Street, B'town agreed to be sold by George Sahely & Co B'dos Ltd to Fawzi Elias and/or his nominees'.

A contract which does not comply with the statutory requirements as to writing is not void but only unenforceable.

(62) *Monnickendam* v *Leanse* (1923) 39 T.L.R. 445

The plaintiff orally agreed to buy a house from the defendant and paid a deposit of £200. Later the plaintiff refused to go on with the contract and pleaded lack of memorandum in writing, though the defendant was always willing to complete. The plaintiff now sued to recover the deposit. *Held*—He could not recover the deposit.

Comment. The case illustrates that the difficulties arising out of the absence of a memorandum in writing are procedural rather than substantive. The contract, though unenforceable, is not wholly without effect, for in the above case the contract was raised as a defence to an action for the deposit. It is essential of course that the vendor be prepared to complete the bargain; he cannot deny the enforceability of the contract and yet claim its existence as a defence to the action for recovery of the deposit.

The court may order the equitable remedy of specific performance of an oral contract which statute requires to be evidenced in writing if the plaintiff has partly performed it. The acts of part performance must point to the existence of a contract.

(63) *Wakeham* v *MacKenzie* [1968] 2 All E.R. 783

Some two years after his wife's death a widower aged 72 orally agreed with the plaintiff, a widow of 67, that if she would move into his house and look after him for the rest of his life she should have the house (of which he was the owner) together with the contents on his death. It was also agreed that the plaintiff should pay her own board and buy her own coal.

The plaintiff gave up her council flat and moved into the widower's house and looked after him as agreed, paying for her board and coal. He died in February 1966, but did not leave the house or contents to her. The executor of the widower's estate contended that if there was a contract no action could be brought upon it at common law because there was no memorandum in writing as required by s.40 of the Law of Property Act 1925, which was accepted. However, in respect of the plaintiff's claimn for the equitable remedy of specific performance the adequancy of her acts of part performance was in question. On this matter Stamp, J., *held*—

> 'I conclude from *Kingswood Estate Co. Ltd* v *Anderson*, first that it is not the law that the acts of part performance relied on must be not only referable to a contract such as that alleged, but referable to no other title, the doctrine to that effect laid down by Warrington, L.J., in *Chaproniere* v *Lambert* having been exploded; and secondly that the true rule is that the operation of acts of part performance requires only that the acts in question be such as must be referred to some contract and may be referred to the alleged one; that they prove the existence of some contract and one consistent with the contract alleged.'

His Lordship accordingly made an order for specific performance of the oral agreement on which the plaintiff relied.

(64) *Re Gonin (deceased)* [1977] 2 All E.R. 720

In this case a daughter tried to claim a contract under which she was to have her mother's house. There was no memorandum in writing and she pleaded acts of part performance. These were that she had left her lodgings in Stroud to come and live with her mother in her mother's house at Bromley and to look after her on the basis (she said) of a contract for the property. Her mother died intestate and did not leave her the property by will, so that the daughter's only method of getting the property was to establish a contract. *Held*—by Walton, J.,—that her acts of part performance did not necessarily suggest the existence of a contract. In the course of his judgment he said: 'Applying the law as I see it, therefore, to the present case, are the acts done by Miss Gonin such as in themselves must be referable to some contract concerning The Gables? I regret that in my opinion they are not. Here. . . . Miss Gonin had no home of her own to give up, she was simply billetted out at Stroud, and she did not move into the house of strangers. She went back to the house which had, down to 1940, been and doubtlessly still was in her mind's eye, home, back to her parents, back to the same kind of position and standing which she had had before she had left home because of the call of the war. This does not seem to me to indicate the likelihood of any contract at all, let alone one concerning land.'

Section 3 of the Sale of Goods Act 1979 provides that where necessaries have been sold and delivered to a minor he must pay a reasonable price for them. The section defines necessaries as goods suitable to the condition in life of the minor and to his actual requirements at the time of the sale and delivery.

(65) *Nash* v *Inman* [1908] 2 K.B. 1

The plaintiff was a Savile Row tailor and the defendant was an infant undergraduate at Trinity College, Cambridge. The plaintiff sent his agent to Cambridge because he had heard that the defendant was spending money freely, and might be the sort of person who would be interested in high-class clothing. As a result of the agent's visit, the plaintiff supplied the defendant with various articles of clothing to the value of £145 0s 3d during the period October 1902 to June 1903. The clothes included 11 fancy waistcoats. The plaintiff now sued the infant for the price of the clothes. Evidence showed that the plaintiff's father was in a good position, being an architect with a town and country house, and it could be said that the clothes supplied were suitable to the defendant's position in life. However, his father proved that the defendant was amply supplied with such clothes when the plaintiff delivered the clothing now in question. *Held*—The plaintiff's claim failed because he had not established that the goods supplied were necessaries.

A minor can make a binding contract in regard to his education or instruction if it is in general terms beneficial.

(66) *Roberts* v *Gray* [1913] 1 K.B. 520

The defendant wished to become a professional billiards player and entered into an agreement with the plaintiff, a leading professional, to go on a joint tour. The plaintiff went to some trouble in order to organize the tour, but a dispute arose between the parties and the defendant refused to go. The plaintiff now sued for damages of £6000. *Held*—The contract was for the infant's benefit, being in effect for his instruction as a billiards player. Therefore the plaintiff could sustain an action for damages for breach of contract, and damages of £1500 were awarded.

(67) *Chaplin* v *Leslie Frewin (Publishers* [1965] 3 All E.R. 764

The plaintiff, the infant son of a famous father, made a contract with the defendants under which they were to publish a book written for him and telling his life story. The plaintiff sought to avoid the contract on the ground that the book gave an inaccurate picture of his approach to life. *Held*—amongst other things—that the contract was binding if it was for the infant's benefit. The time to determine that question was when the contract was made, and at that time it was for the infant's benefit and could not be avoided.

Comment. In *Denmark Productions* v *Boscobel Productions* (1967) 111 S.J. 715, Widgery, J., held that a contract by which an infant appoints managers and agents to look after his business affairs is, in modern conditions, necessary if he is to earn his living and rise to fame, and if it is for his benefit it will be upheld by analogy with a contract of service.

There is no general rule that any contract which is beneficial is binding. Trading contracts made by minors are not binding on them even if beneficial in the sense of being profitable.

(68) *Mercantile Union Guarantee Corporation* v *Ball* [1937] 2 K.B. 498

The purchase on hire-purchase terms of a motor lorry by an infant carrying on business as a haulage contractor was held not to be a contract for necessaries, but a trading contract by which the infant could not be bound.

Comment. It would be possible for the owner to recover the lorry because a hire-purchase contract is a contract of bailment not a sale. Thus ownership does not pass when the goods are delivered.

A minor may enter into a binding contract of service or apprenticeship. However, the validity of the contract will depend upon whether it is as a whole beneficial to the minor. If not it is unenforceable.

(69) *De Francesco* v *Barnum* (1890) 45 Ch. D. 430

Two infants bound themselves in contract to the plaintiff for seven years to be taught stage dancing. The infants agreed that they would not accept any engagements without his consent. They later accepted an engagement with Barnum and the plaintiff sued Barnum for interfering with the contractual relationshp between himself and the infants, and also to enforce the apprenticeship deed against the infants and to obtain damages for its breach. The contract was, of course, for the infants' benefit and was *prime facie* binding on them. However, when the court considered the deed in greater detail, it emerged that there were certain onerous terms in it. For example, the infants bound themselves not to marry during the apprenticeship; the payment was hardly generous, the plaintiff agreeing to pay them 9d per night and 6d for matinee appearances for the first three years, and 1s per night and 6d for matinee performances during the remainder of the apprenticeship. The plaintiff did not undertake to maintain them whilst they were unemployed and did not undertake to find them engagements. The infants could also be engaged in performances abroad at a fee of 5s per week. Further the plaintiff could terminate the contract if he felt that the infants were not suitable for the career of a dancer. It appeared from the contract that the infants were at the absolute disposal of the plaintiff. *Held*—The deed was an unreasonable one and therefore unenforceable against the infants. Barnum could not, therefore, be held liable, since the tort of interference with a contractual relationship presupposes the existence of an enforceable contract.

Some terms of a contract of service or apprenticeship may be beneficial and others not. However, if the contract taken as a whole is to the minor's advantage he is bound.

(70) *Clements* v *L. & N. W. Railway* [1894] 2 Q.B. 482

Clements became a porter with the railway company and agreed to join the company's insurance scheme and to forgo his rights under the Employers Liability Act 1880. He sustained an injury at work and claimed under the company's scheme. He now made a claim under the Act on the grounds that the contract was not for his benefit since it deprived him of an action under the Act. The company's scheme was on the whole a favourable one because it covered more injuries than the statute, but the scale of compensation was lower. *Held*—The contract as a whole was for the infant's benefit and was binding on him. He had no claim under the Act.

In some cases the expression 'absolutely void' in s.1 of the Infants Relief Act 1874 is applied in its true literal sense.

(71) *Coutts & Co.* v *Browne-Lecky* [1946] 2 All E.R. 207

The first defendant, an infant, had been permitted to overdraw his account with the plaintiffs, who were bankers. The overdraft was guaranteed by the second and third defendants, who were adults. The overdraft was not repaid and the plaintiffs now sued the adult guarantors. *Held*—Since the loan to the infant was void under the Infants Relief Act 1874, the infant could not be in default because he was not liable to repay the loan. Since the essence of a guarantee is that the guarantor is liable for the default or miscarriage of the principal debtor, it followed that the adult guarantors could not be liable. The action therefore failed.

Comment. Had the contract been one of indemnity the adult defendants would have been liable, because, under a contract of indemnity, the person giving the indemnity is in effect the principal debtor and his liability does not depend on the default of any other person. (*Yeoman Credit Ltd* v *Latter* [1961] 2 All E.R. 294.)

In other cases the expression 'absolutely void' has not been given its literal meaning. Ownership of goods does not normally pass under a void contract but the following case suggests that it does.

(72) *Stocks* v *Wilson* [1913] 2 K.B. 235

An infant obtained non-necessary furniture from the plaintiff by falsely stating that he was of full age. *Held*—The property in the furniture passed to the infant, under the Infants Relief Act 1874. Even if he sold the property the infant could not be sued in conversion. The infant had sold part of the furniture to a third party for £30, and Lush, J., *held* that the plaintiff could recover this sum by applying the equitable principle of restitution.

Comment. *Pearce* v *Brain* 1929[76] supports *Stocks* v *Wilson* because, if the property in the car had not passed to the infant, there would have been total failure of consideration, thus enabling him to recover his motorcycle.

If a minor makes a contract involving the acquisition of an interest in property of a permanent nature, e.g. shares, a lease, or a partnership, the contract is voidable. The minor may avoid it either during minority or within a reasonable time thereafter. However, nothing which has been paid under the contract can be recovered unless there has been total failure of consideration. The same principle is applied to void contracts, e.g. contracts for non-necessary goods. Once again, there can be no recovery of money paid or property transferred unless there has been total failure of consideration.

(73) *Steinberg* v *Scala (Leeds) Ltd* [1923] 2 Ch. 452

The plaintiff, Miss Steinberg, purchased shares in the defendant company and paid certain sums of money on application, on allotment and on one call. Being unable to meet future calls, she repudiated the contract whilst still an infant and claimed—

(1) Rectification of the Register of Members to remove her name therefrom, thus relieving her from liability on future calls; and
(2) The recovery of the money already paid.

The company agreed to rectify the register and issue was joined on the claim to recover the money paid.

Held—The claim under (2) above failed because there had not been total failure of consideration. The shares had some value and gave some rights, even though the plaintiff had not received any dividends and the shares had always stood at a discount on the market.

(74) *Davies* v *Beynon-Harris* (1931) 47 T.L.R. 424

An infant took a lease of a flat a fortnight before attaining his majority. Three years later he was sued for arrears of rent and claimed that he could avoid the contract. *Held*—He was liable to pay the rent because the lease was voidable not void, and was now binding on him because he had not repudiated it during minority or within a reasonable time thereafter.

Comment. An infant cannot take a legal estate in land (s.1(6), Law of Property Act 1925). This prevents him from taking a lease at law. However, he does obtain an equitable interest and must observe the covenants in the lease so long as he retains a beneficial interest in the property.

(75) *Goode* v *Harrison* (1821) 5 B. & Ald. 147

An infant partner, who took no steps to avoid a partnership contract upon attaining his majority, was held liable for the debts of the firm incurred after he came of age.

(76) *Pearce* v *Brain* [1929] 2 K.B. 310

Pearce, an infant, exchanged his motor cycle for a motor car belonging to Brain. The infant had little use out of the car, and had in fact driven it only a short distance when it broke down because of serious defects in the back axle. Pearce now sued to recover his motor cycle, claiming that the consideration had wholly failed. *Held*—(1) That a contract for the exchange of goods, whilst not a sale of goods, is a contract for the supply of goods, and that if the goods are not necessaries, the contract is void if with an infant. (2) The car was not a necessary good and therefore the contract was void. (3) Even so the infant could only recover the motor cycle in the same circumstances as he could recover money paid under a void contract, i.e. if the consideration had wholly failed. The Court considered that the infant had received a benefit under the contract, albeit small, and that he could not recover the motor cycle.

(77) *Corpe* v *Overton* (1833) 10 Bing 252

An infant agreed to enter into a partnership and deposited £100 with the defendant as security for the due performance of the contract. The infant rescinded the contract before the partnership came into being. *Held*—He could recover the £100 because he had received no benefit, having never been a partner. There had been total failure of consideration.

A minor is liable in tort. However, if the claim is a contractual one and

the minor is not liable on the contract, the plaintiff cannot succeed by framing an action in tort. In addition, a minor who has obtained money or non-necessary goods by fraud can be compelled to refund the money or restore the goods, but if he has spent the money or sold the goods he cannot be required to pay an equivalent amount from his general resources since this would, in effect enforce a void contract.

(78) *Leslie* v *Sheill* [1914] 3 K.B. 607

Sheill, an infant, borrowed £400 from R. Leslie Ltd, moneylenders, by fraudulently representing that he was of full age. The contract was void under s.1 of the Infants Relief Act 1874, and the plaintiffs sued for the return of the money, either as damages for the tort of deceit, or as money had and received to the plaintiff's use. *Held*—Neither claim could succeed because they were attempts to circumvent the Act and the infant was entitled to retain the money advanced. With regard to the equitable doctrine of restitution, it was suggested that, since the money had been spent and could not be precisely traced, restitution was not possible; for to order restitution would mean that the infant would have to pay an equivalent sum out of his present or future resources, and this would be closer to enforcing a void contract than to granting equitable restitution. It was also suggested that *Stocks* v *Wilson*[72] was wrongly decided (though not overruled) in so far as Lush, J., granted restitution of the £30 which the infant had received by selling the property to a third party. The Court in this case suggested that 'Restitution ends where repayment begins'. Unless the actual property passing under the contract can be recovered, the remedy of restitution does not lie to recover money or property received in its stead.

A mentally disordered or drunken person is bound by his contracts unless he can show that because of his condition he did not understand what he was doing and that the other party was aware of this. A person suffering from mental disorder may be bound if the contract is made during a lucid interval. In the case of both categories of persons they will be bound if they ratify the contract after recovery.

(79) *Imperial Loan Co.* v *Stone* [1892] Q.B. 599

This was an action on a promissory note. The defendant pleaded that at the time of making the note he was insane and that the plaintiff knew he was. The jury found that he was in fact insane but could not agree on the question of whether the plaintiff knew it. The judge entered judgment for the defendant. *Held*—that he was wrong. The defendant in order to succeed must convince the jury on both issues.

(80) *Matthews* v *Baxter* (1873) L.R. 8 Exch. 132

Matthews agreed to buy houses from Baxter. He was so drunk as not to know what he was doing. Afterwards, when sober he ratified and confirmed the contract. It was held that both parties were bound by it.

Comment. A contract with a drunken person must in effect always be voidable by him because presumably the fact that he is drunk will be known to the other party. This is not so in regard to unsoundness of mind which might not be known to the other party.

From the date of incorporation a company is a separate legal entity distinct from its members. It can act only through agents and its contractual and other activities and those of its agents are regulated by its memorandum and articles of association.

(81) *Salomon* v *Salomon & Co.* [1897] A.C. 22

Salomon carried on business as a leather merchant and boot manufacturer. In 1892 he formed a limited company to take over the business. The Memorandum of Association was signed by Salomon, his wife, daughter and four sons. Each subscribed for one share. The company paid £30,000 to Salomon for the business and mode of payment was to give Salomon £10,000 in debentures, secured by a floating charge, and 20,000 shares of £1 each. The company fell on hard times and a liquidator was appointed. The debts of the unsecured creditors amounted to nearly £8000, and the company's assets were approximately £6000. The unsecured creditors claimed all the remaining assets on the ground that the company was a mere alias or agent for Salomon. *Held*—The company was a separate and distinct person. The debentures were perfectly valid and therefore Salomon was entitled to the remaining assets in part payment of the secured debentures held by him.

A member may obtain an injunction to restrain a company from acting beyond its powers.

(82) *Jenkin* v *Pharmaceutical Society* [1921] 1 Ch. 392

The defendant society was incorporated by Royal Charter in 1843 for the purpose of advancing chemistry and pharmacy and promoting a uniform system of education of those who should practise the same, and also for the protection of those who carried on the business of chemists and druggists. *Held*—The expenditure of the funds of the society in the formation of an industrial committee, to attempt to regulate hours of work and wages and conditions of work between masters and employee members of the society, was *ultra vires* the charter, because it was a trade union activity which was not contemplated by the Charter of 1843. Further, the expenditure of money on an insurance scheme for members was also not within the powers given in the charter, for it amounted to converting the defendant society into an insurance company. The plaintiff, a member of the society, was entitled to an injunction to restrain the society from implementing the above schemes.

If a company enters into a contract the subject-matter of which is outside the scope of its constitution the contract is *ultra vires* and void.

(83) *Ashbury Railway Carriage & Iron Co.* v *Riche* (1875) L.R. 7 H.L. 653

The company was formed for the purposes (stated in the memorandum of association) of making and selling railway wagons and other railway plant and carrying on the business of mechanical engineers and general contractors. The company bought a concession for the construction of a railway system in Belgium and entered into an agreement whereby Messrs Riche were to construct the railway line. Messrs Riche commenced the work and the company paid over certain sums of money in connection with the contract. The Ashbury Company later ran into difficulties, and the shareholders wished the directors to take over the contract in a personal capacity and indemnify the shareholders. The directors thereupon repudiated the contract on behalf of the company and Messrs Riche sued for breach of contract. *Held*—The directors were able to repudiate because the contract to construct a railway system was *ultra vires* and void. On a proper construction of the objects, the company had power to supply materials for the construction of railways but had no power to engage in the actual construction of them. Further, the subsequent assent of all the shareholders could not make the contract binding, for a principal cannot ratify the *ultra vires* contracts of his agent.

At common law persons dealing with a company have constructive notice of the contents of its memorandum and articles.

(84) *Re Jon Beauforte* [1953] 1 All E.R. 634

The company was authorized by its memorandum to carry on the business of costumiers, tailors, drapers, haberdashers, milliners and the like. It decided to manufacture veneered wall panels, and for this purpose had a factory erected, and ordered and was supplied with veneers. It was clear that the contracts for the erection of the factory and supply of veneers were *ultra vires* and void, but one of the questions before the court was whether the liquidator of the company had been correct in disallowing a claim made by a supplier of coke. The supplier argued that the coke might have been used in the good side of the business, and that he did not know that the coke was to be used for an *ultra vires* purpose. The Court decided against him because the order for the coke was on headed paper describing the company as 'veneered panel manufacturers.' From this the coke supplier was deemed to know that the contract was *ultra vires*, because everyone is deemed to know the contents of the memorandum of association of a registered company, which is registered at the Companies' Registry, Cardiff, and can be inspected.

Comment. (i) This common-law doctrine of constructive notice of a company's objects is now well established and yet it is based on the assumption that, because inspection is possible, it should always be made before contracts are entered into. However, business would grind to a halt if this sort of inquiry were made every time a contract was made; it does not accord, therefore, with normal business practice.

(ii) This transaction was decided on by the directors. Therefore the coke supplier (or persons in a similar position) would be protected these days by s.9 of the European Communities Act 1972. The coke supplier had only constructive notice of the company's memorandum and would not now be deemed to have such notice by reason of s.9.

Clauses in an objects clause which contains a multiplicity of activities will not be construed restrictively, i.e. as containing mere powers to further the main object, where it is expressly provided that all clauses are to be read separately and are not to be limited by reference to any of the others.

(85) *Cotman* v *Brougham* [1918] A.C. 514

The parties to this action were liquidators. Cotman was liquidator of the Essequibo Rubber Estates Ltd, and Brougham was liquidator of Anglo-Cuban Oil Co. It appeared that E underwrote the shares in A–C although the main clause of E's objects clause was to develop rubber estates abroad. However, a sub-clause allowed E to promote companies and deal in the shares of other companies and gave numerous other powers. The final clause of E's objects clause said in effect that each sub-clause should be considered as an independent main object. The E Company, not having paid for the shares which it had agreed to underwrite, was put on the list of contributories of A–C, and E's liquidator asked that his company be removed from that list because the contract to underwrite was *ultra vires* and void. *Held*—by the House of Lords, that it was not, and that the E Company was liable to pay for the shares underwritten. The final clause of E's objects clause meant that each object could be pursued alone, because the Registrar had accepted the memorandum in this form and had registered the company. All the judges of the House of Lords deplored the idea of companies being registered with an objects clause in this wide form, and thought that the matter ought to have been raised by *mandamus* by the Registrar refusing to register the company. However, since the certificate of incorporation had been issued, it was conclusive: and matters concerning the company's registration could not be gone into.

A power to borrow cannot be converted into an object by a *Cotman* clause. Borrowing is a means to an end and not an end in itself.

(86) *Introductions Ltd* v *National Provincial Bank Ltd* [1969] 1 All E.R. 887

Introductions Ltd was incorporated in 1951 and the objects of the company were to promote and provide entertainment and accommodation for overseas visitors. This business was not successful, and in November 1960 the company embarked on a new business, pig farming. The company ran short of cash and arranged to borrow money from the defendants. The company executed certain debentures in favour of the bank for its indebtedness, which at the time of the winding-up order in November 1965 was £29,571.

The bank now wished to enforce its security under the debentures and recover the loan. The liquidators of the company claimed that the loan was *ultra vires* and void, and the bank did not dispute that it was aware that the company's business was that of pig breeding and had notice of the company's objects. However, one of the sub-clauses of the memorandum related to borrowing and the bank said it was entitled to lend money on the strength of the sub-clause alone as it formed one of the objects of the company. There was a proviso to the memorandum which clearly stated that all sub-clauses of the memorandum were to be treated as separate and independent objects. *Held*—by the Court of Appeal, that the loan was *ultra vires* and void. The bare power to borrow contained in the sub-clause could not legitimately stand alone. The company must have had in view purposes to which the money was to be applied, i.e. for the purposes of the objects of the company. This being so the sub-clause did not authorize the raising or borrowing of money for something which was not an object of the company. However if the bank had not known the purpose for which the money was required the loan would have been valid because the bank was not bound to inquire as to its purpose.

Comment. Section 9 of the European Communties Act 1972 would not have assisted the bank in this case. They had seen the company's memorandum and were aware that this did not authorize the carrying on of the business in pig breeding. They also knew that this was the purpose for which the loan was required.

Any contract made by a company which may be regarded as fairly incidental to or consequential upon those things which the memorandum authorizes will be regarded as *intra vires*.

(87) *Deuchar* v *The Gas Light and Coke Co.* [1925] A.C. 691

The plaintiff was a shareholder in the defendant company and was also the secretary of a company which supplied the defendants with caustic soda. The plaintiff sought a declaration from the court that the manufacture of caustic soda and chlorine by the defendants, and the erection of a factory for the purpose, was *ultra vires* the company. He also asked for an injunction to restrain the defendants from manufacturing caustic soda and chlorine. Astbury, J., at first instance, had found that the activities were fairly incidental to the powers given in the objects clause, and the Court of Appeal affirmed this decision. On appeal to the House of

Lords it appeared that the defendants derived their powers from a special Act of Parliament, the Gas Light and Coke Companies Act 1868, which gave them power to make and supply gas and deal with and sell by-products. The Act authorized the conversion of the by-products into a marketable state. One of the residuals of gas-making was naphthalene which could be converted into beta-naphthol and profitably sold, conversion being by the use of caustic soda. The company had formerly purchased this from the company of which the plaintiff was secretary, but later erected a factory on their land and began to make it themselves, though they only made what they required for their own use and did not make caustic soda for resale. Chlorine was a by-product of the manufacture of caustic soda, and the chlorine, it was admitted, was converted into bleaching powder and sold. The House of Lords *held* that the manufacture of caustic soda was fairly incidental to the company's powers, and although the sale of the bleaching powder was not incidental, the matter was trivial and on the basis of the maxim *de minimis non curat lex* (the law does not concern itself with trifles) the court would not interfere.

If the memorandum gives the directors a discretion as to the type of business which the company can pursue this will allow them to extend the company's activities without infringing the *ultra vires* rule.

(88) *Bell Houses Ltd* v *City Wall Properties Ltd* [1966] 2 All E.R. 674

The plaintiff company claimed £20,000 as commission under an alleged contract with the defendant company for the introduction of the latter to a financier who would lend the defendant company £1,000,000 for property development. As a preliminary issue the defendant company alleged that the contract was *ultra vires* and could not be enforced against them.

The principal business of the plaintiff company was the development of housing estates, and therefore the occasional raising of finance formed a necessary part of its activities. In consequence the company had obtained valuable knowledge of various sources of finance and because of this the company was able to arrange finance for the defendants. The defendants contended that the plaintiff company, in arranging finance for an outside organization, was, in effect, embarking on a new type of business, i.e. 'mortgage broking,' and since this was not expressly included in the objects, nor reasonably incidental thereto, it was *ultra vires*. One of the sub-clauses in the objects clause of the plaintiff company was as follows: 'To carry on any other trade or business whatsoever which can in the opinion of the board of directors be advantageously carried on by (the company) in connection with, or as ancillary to, any of the above businesses or the general business of the (company).' *Held*—by the Court of Appeal, that the alleged contract was *intra vires* in particular because of the clause set out above. In the Court's view the *bona fide* opinion of the board, in this case represented by the managing director who arranged the finance, that the contract could be advantageously carried on with the company's principal business, was enough no matter how unreasonable in the objective sense that opinion might seem to be.

An *ultra vires* transaction is binding on the company where it is made on behalf of the company by a director to whom all actual authority to act for the board has effectively been delegated.

(89) *International Sales and Agencies Ltd* v *Marcus* [1982] 3 All E.R. 551

The second defendant in this case, Bentinck Securities Ltd which was owned by Mr Marcus, made a loan of £30,000 to a Mr Fancy. Mr Fancy was a major shareholder in International Sales and Agencies and also in the second plaintiff Janthorpe Properties Ltd. He was also the dominant director in both companies. Mr Munsey, who was also a shareholder in and a director of ISA and Janthorpe was a friend of Mr Marcus. Mr Fancy died insolvent. The loan of £30,000 was not repaid. However, Mr Fancy had told Mr Marcus prior to his death that Mr Munsey would see that the loan was repaid if anything happened to Mr Fancy. Shortly after Mr Fancy's death his widow and their son Ismat were made directors. However, Mr Munsey assumed control of the companies and became the dominant director. He arranged for cheques to be drawn on ISA and Janthorpe to the value of £30,000 to repay Bentinck. Mrs Fancy and Ismat, together with other shareholders, on discovering that had been done, brought the two companies into court to recover the money.

Mr Justice Lawson had no difficulty in deciding that the payments were *ultra vires*. The company had a standard form objects clause allowing it to draw cheques but the payment of money is not an independent transaction. It is always related to something else and here the payment was a mere handout. The company's money had not been used for its business but had been given away to a person who was in no way connected with it. This was *ultra vires*. The transaction was void and the money recoverable.

Furthermore, Mr Munsey was in breach of his fiduciary duty to the company as a director. He was in effect a constructive trustee of its funds and he broke that trust in making the payments. Mr Marcus was aware, and Bentinck was also aware through him, of this breach and therefore both Mr Marcus and Bentinck were also liable to replace the company's funds as constructive trustees having intermeddled with what was in effect trust property. In Mr Justice Lawson's view this decided the matter and allowed the company to recover its money. However, an amended defence had been entered on the basis that the defendants were protected by s.9 of the European Communities Act 1972. The judge held that s.9 did not apply to situations of constructive trust but since the section had been raised he made a number of observations on it as set out below.

(1) Since the defendants were not 'dealing' with ISA and Janthorpe the section could not apply. They were dealing with Mr Munsey. The company's cheques were a mere vehicle of his personal generosity to Mr Marcus.

(2) The defendants were not acting in good faith. The burden of proof in this matter was upon the plaintiffs and not upon the defendant. However, a lack of good faith can be found, said the judge, in proof of a person's actual knowledge that the transaction is *ultra vires* or where it can be shown that in all the circumstances the person concerned could not have been unaware that he was party to an *ultra vires* transaction. There was ample evidence in this case of a lack of good faith which, again, would prevent the section from applying.

(3) However, and most importantly, the judge did decide that in the circumstances of the case the transaction had been decided on by the directors within the meaning of s.9, although, of course, only one director had made the decision. Nevertheless, as the dominant director who was the sole effective director to whom all actual authority to act for the companies had been effectively delegated, the judge felt that this aspect of the section had been satisfied. This is an important ruling and one which should help outsiders when dealing with a dominant director in a company's management.

A mistake as to the existence or meaning of a statute is a mistake of law.

(90) *Sharp Bros and Knight* v *Chant* [1917] 1 K.B. 771

Landlord and tenant agreed that the rent of a certain small house should be increased by the sum of 6d per week. The tenant paid this increased rent for some time and it was then discovered that Rent Restriction legislation prevented the landlord from recovering any increase in rent he might make on certain properties of which the small house in question was one. *Held*—The tenant had paid the extra rent under a mistake of law, and could not sue for its return or deduct it from future payments of rent.

Comment. For an interesting contrast where the Court of Appeal felt that a mistake as to the provisions of the Rent Acts was a mistake of fact and not law, see *Solle* v *Butcher*, p. 407.

The defence of *non est factum* is available where the mistake is as to the kind of transaction entered into.

(91) *Foster* v *Mackinnon* (1869) L.R. 4 C.P. 704

The plaintiff was a person entitled to receive payment on a bill of exchange for £3000; the defendant was an endorser of the bill and was *prima facie* liable on it. The evidence showed that the defendant was an old man of feeble sight, and that he had signed the bill under the mistaken impression that it was a guarantee having been induced to do so by a fraudulent person called Callow. *Held*—The defendant was not negligent under the circumstances in signing the bill and his plea of mistake was successful so that he was not liable on it.

Comment. The mistake need not be induced by fraud as it was here. Byles, J., said in this case that the defence of *non est factum* would be available where it could be shown '. . . that the mind of the signor did not accompany the signature; in other words that he never intended to sign, and therefore in contemplation of law never did sign, the contract to which his name is appended.'

The defence of *non est factum* is available to a person who has made a fundamental error in signing a document whether the error be as to the kind of document it is or as to its contents. However, negligence on the part of the signor will exclude the defence.

(92) *Saunders* v *Anglia Building Society* [1970] 3 All E.R. 961

Mrs Gallie, a widow aged 78 years, signed a document which Lee, her nephew's friend, told her was a deed of gift of her house to her nephew. She did not read the document but believed what Lee had told her. In fact the document was an assignment of her leasehold interest in the house to Lee, and Lee later mortgaged that interest to a building society. In an action by Mrs Gallie against Lee and the building society it was *held* at first instance—(1) that the assignment was void and did not confer a title on Lee, (2) although Mrs Gallie had been negligent she was not estopped fron denying the validity of the deed against the building society for she owed it no duty. The Court of Appeal, in allowing an appeal by the building society, held that the plea of *non est factum* was not available to Mrs Gallie. The transaction intended and carried out was the same, i.e. an assignment.

The appeal to the House of Lords was brought by Saunders, the executrix of Mrs Gallie's estate. The House of Lords affirmed the decision of the Court of Appeal but took the opportunity to restate the law relating to the avoidance of documents on the ground of mistake as follows—

(1) The plea of *none est factum* will rarely be available to a person of full capacity who signs a document apparently having legal effect without troubling to read it i.e. negligently.

(2) A mistake as to the identity of the person in whose favour the document is executed will not normally support a plea of *non est factum* though it may do if the court regards the mistake as fundamental (Lord Reid and Lord Hodson). Neither judge felt that the personality error made by Mrs Gallie was sufficient to support the plea.

(3) The distinction taken in *Howatson* v *Webb* [1908] 1 Ch. 1, that the mistake must be as to the class or character of the document and not merely as to its contents was regarded as illogical. Under the *Howatson* test, if X signed a guarantee for £1000 believing it to be an insurance policy he escaped all liability on the guarantee, but if he signed a guaran-

tee for £10,000 believing it to be a guarantee for £100 he was fully liable for £10,000. Under *Saunders* the document which was in fact signed must be 'fundamentally different', 'radically different', or 'totally different'. This test is more flexible than the character/contents one and yet it still restricts the operation of the plea of *non est factum.*

Unilateral mistake occurs when one of the parties to a contract is mistaken and the other party knows or ought, as a reasonable person, to know that this is so. Where this is not the case the contract is enforceable.

(93) *Legal and General Assurance Society* v *General Metal Agencies* (1969) 113 S.J. 876

Legal and General, who were the landlords of General Metal Agencies, served a statutory notice of termination of the tenancy. General Metal applied to the County Court for a new tenancy but Legal and General opposed the application on the grounds of persistent late payment of rent and it was dismissed. However, Legal and General subsequently sent by mistake a computerized demand for the next quarter's rent in advance over the signature of their general manager. General Metal sent a cheque for the rent and this was presented to the bank and was paid. In this action Legal and General claimed possession of the premises and General Metal contended that Legal and General by demanding and accepting the next quarter's rent in advance had by implication created a new tenancy. It was *held*, by Fisher, J., that—

(1) Legal and General were entitled to show that the demand was sent and the rent received by mistake. There was no intention to create a new tenancy, the use of a computer making no difference to the established common law principle;

(2) in consequence, Legal and General were entitled to possession of the premises.

(94) *Higgins (W.) Ltd* v *Northampton Corporation* [1927] 1 Ch. 128

The plaintiff entered into a contract with the corporation for the erection of dwelling houses. The plaintiff made an arithmetical error in arriving at his price, having deducted a certain sum twice over. The corporation sealed the contract, assuming that the price arrived at by the plaintiff was correct. *Held*—The contract was binding on the parties. Rectification of such a contract was not possible because the power of the Court to rectify agreements made under mistake is confined to common not unilateral mistake. Here, rectification would only have been granted if fraud or misrepresentation had been present.

Comment. Since this case was decided the courts have moved away from the idea that rectification of a contract for unilateral mistake is permissable only if there is some form of sharp practice. (See *Thomas Bates & Son Ltd* v *Wyndham's (Lingerie) Ltd* 1981.)[108] Even so, rectification would not have been granted in this case because Northampton Corporation were not aware of the plaintiff's error which is still a requirement for rectification.

For a mistake as to identity to be operative it must be a mistake as to the person with whom the contract is being made. Mistakes as to attributes such as solvency are not enough.

(95) *Cundy* v *Lindsay* (1878) 3 App. Cas. 459

The respondents were linen manufacturers with a business in Belfast. A fraudulent person named Blenkarn wrote to the respondents from 37 Wood Street, Cheapside, ordering a quantity of handkerchiefs but signed his letter in such a way that it appeared to come from Messrs Blenkiron, who were a well-known and solvent house doing business at 123 Wood Street. The respondents knew of the existence of Blenkiron but did not know the address. Accordingly the handkerchiefs were sent to 37 Wood Street. Blenkarn then sold them to the appellants, and was later convicted and sentenced for the fraud. The respondents sued the appellants in conversion claiming that the contract they had made with Blenkarn was void for mistake, and that the property had not passed to Blenkarn or to the appellants. *Held*—The respondents succeeded; there was an operative mistake as to the party with whom they were contracting.

(96) *King's Norton Metal Co. Ltd* v *Edridge Merrett & Co. Ltd* (1897) 14 T.L.R. 98

The plaintiffs were metal manufacturers in Worcestershire, the defendants being metal manufacturers at Birmingham. In 1896 the plaintiffs received a letter from a firm called Hallam & Co., Soho Wire Works, Sheffield. The letter was written on headed paper, the heading depicting a large factory, and in one corner was a statement that the company had depots and agencies at Belfast, Lille and Ghent. The letter requested a quotation for the supply of brass rivet wire, and a quotation was sent and later an order was received and the goods dispatched. These goods were never paid for. It later emerged that a person named Wallis had set up in business as Hallam & Co. and had fraudulently obtained the goods by the above methods. Wallis sold the goods to the defendants who bought *bona fide* and for value. The plaintiffs had previously done business with Wallis's firm, Hallam & Co., and had been paid by cheque signed Hallam & Co. The plaintiffs sued the defendants in conversion, regarding this as a better action than the one for fraud against Wallis. In order to sustain the action in conversion, the plaintiffs had to establish that the contract with Hallam & Co. was void for mistake, and that because of this the defendants had no title to the wire. *Held*—The plaintiffs' claim failed because the contract with Hallam & Co. was voidable for fraud but not void for mistake. The firm Hallam & Co. was a mere alias for Wallis, and since there was no other firm of Hallam & Co. with whom the plaintiffs had previously done business, they were really dealing with one person who from time to time used different names, i.e. Wallis or Hallam & Co. Although the contract was voidable for fraud, it had not been avoided when the goods were sold to the defendants; their title was good and they were not liable in conversion. 'There was only one entity trading, it might be under an alias, and there was a contract by which the property passed to him.' (Per A.L. Smith, L.J.)

Comment. The Court of Appeal held, in effect, that the plaintiffs had intended to contract with the writer of the letter. They had no personal knowledge of any other Wallis or any other Hallam & Co.

(97) *Ingram and others* v *Little* [1961] 1 Q.B. 31

The plaintiffs, three ladies, were the joint owners of a car. They wished to sell the car and advertised it for sale. A fraudulent person, introducing himself as Hutchinson, offered to buy it. He was taken for a drive in it and during conversation said that his home was at Caterham. Later the rogue offered £700 for the car but this was refused, though a subsequent offer of £717 was one which the plaintiffs were prepared to accept. At this point the rogue produced a cheque book and one of the plaintiffs, who was conducting the negotiations, said that the deal was off and that they would not accept a cheque. The rogue then said that he was P.G.M. Hutchinson, that he had business interests in Guildford, and that he lived at Stanstead House, Stanstead Road, Caterham. One of the plaintiffs checked this information in a telephone directory and, on finding it to be accurate, allowed him to take the car in return for a cheque. The cheque was dishonoured, and in the meantime the rogue had sold the car to the defendants and had disappeared without trace. The plaintiffs sued for the return of the car, or for its value as damages in conversion, claiming that the contract between themselves and the rogue was void for mistake, and that the property had not passed. At the trial judgment was given for the plaintiffs, Slade, J., finding the contract void. His judgment was *affirmed* by the Court of Appeal, though Devlin, L.J., dissented, saying that the mistake made was as to the creditworthiness of the rogue, not as to his identity, since he was before the plaintiffs when the contract was made. A mistake as to the substance of the rogue would be a mistake as to quality and would not avoid the contract. Devlin, L.J., also suggested that legislation should provide for an apportionment of the loss incurred by two innocent parties who suffer as a result of the fraud of a third.

Comment. The distinctions drawn in some of these cases are fine ones. It is difficult to distinguish *Ingram* from *Lewis*. (See below.) The question for the court to answer in these cases is whether or not the offeror at the time of making the offer regarded the identity of the offeree as a matter of vital importance. The general rule seems to be that where the parties are face to face when the contract is made identity will not be vital and the contract voidable only. Ingram would appear to be the exceptional case.

Though each case must be decided upon its own facts, there is a strong presumption against holding a contract void for mistake where the parties are face to face.

(98) *Lewis* v *Averay* [1971] 3 All E.R. 907

Mr Lewis agreed to sell his car to a rogue who called on him after seeing an advertisement. Before the sale took place the rogue talked knowledgeably about the film world giving the impression that he was the actor Richard Green in the 'Robin Hood' serial. He signed a dud cheque for £450 in the name of 'R.A. Green' and was allowed to have the log book and drive the car away late the same night when he produced a film studio pass in the name of 'Green'. *Held*—by the Court of Appeal, that Mr Lewis had effectively contracted to sell the car to the rogue and could not recover it or damages from Mr Averay, a student, who had bought it from the rogue for £200. The contract between Mr Lewis and the rogue was voidable for fraud but not void for unilateral mistake.

Comment. It is thought that the contract would be void for mistake in a case such as this if the dishonest person assumed a disguise so that he appeared physically to be the person he said he was.

Specific performance is a discretionary remedy. A court may refuse to grant it against a defendant who has contracted under circumstances of unilateral mistake.

(99) *Webster* v *Cecil* (1861) 30 Beav. 62

The parties had been negotiating for the sale of certain property. Later Cecil offered by letter to sell the property for £1250. Webster was aware that his offer was probably a slip because he knew that Cecil had already refused an offer of £2000, and in fact Cecil wished to offer the property at £2250. Webster accepted the offer and sued for specific performance of the contract. The court refused to grant the decree.

A common mistake as to the quality of the subject-matter of a contract does not make the contract void.

(100) *Bell* v *Lever Bros Ltd* [1932] A.C. 161

Lever Bros had a controlling interest in the Niger Company. Bell was the chairman, and a person called Snelling was the vice-chairman, of the Niger Company's Board. Both directors had service contracts which had some time to run. They became redundant as a result of amalgamations and Lever Bros contracted to pay Bell £30,000 and Snelling £20,000 as compensation. These sums were paid over and then it was discovered that Bell and Snelling had committed breaches of duty against the Niger Company during their term of office by making secret profits of £1360 on a cocoa pooling scheme. As directors of the Niger Company, Bell and Snelling attended meetings at which the selling price of cocoa was fixed in advance. Both of them bought and sold on their own account before the said prices were made public. They could therefore, have been dismissed without compensation. Lever Bros sought to set aside the payments on the ground of mistake. *Held*—The contract was not void because Lever Bros had got what they bargained for, i.e. the cancellation of two service contracts which, though they might have been terminated, were actually in existence when the cancellation agreement was made. The mistake was as to the quality of the two directors and such mistakes do not avoid the contracts. The case is one of common mistake because although Bell and Snelling admitted that they were liable to account to the company for the profit made from office, they convinced the court that they had forgotten their misdemeanour of insider dealing when they made the contract for compensation. They thought they were good directors who were entitled to that compensation.

Comment. The case also decided that an employee was not under a duty to disclose to his employer his *own misconduct* or breaches of duty towards his employer. However, employee/directors do have a duty to disclose their *own* breaches of contract to their companies. This is because their fiduciary position as directors overrides the ordinary employer/employee relationship. However, in the *Bell* case the directors concerned kept the compensation and were not required to disclose their wrongdoing to Lever Bros because they were not directors of Lever Bros but only of Niger. However, a director of, say, company A, is under a duty to disclose his wrongdoing, if any, towards company A where he receives his compensation from company A itself. Failure to so disclose will allow the company to claim back a golden handshake of the kind given to Bell and Snelling.

It is worth mentioning that an employee is under a duty to disclose breaches of duty/misconduct of subordinate employees, even though he is not under a duty to disclose to his employer his own misconduct or breaches of duty. This follows from the decision of the Court of Appeal in *Sybron Corporation* v *Rochem Ltd* [1983] 2 All E.R. 707.

(101) *Leaf* v *International Galleries* [1950] 1 All E.R. 693

In 1944 the plaintiff bought from the defendants a drawing of Salisbury Cathedral for £85. The defendants said that the drawing was by Constable. Five years later the plaintiff tried to sell the drawing and was told that this was not so. He now sued for rescission of the contract, no claim for damages being made. The following points of interest emerged from the decision of the Court of Appeal: (1) It was possible to restore the status quo by the mere exchange of the drawing and the purchase money so that rescission was not affected by inability to restore the previous position. (2) The mistake made by the parties in assuming the drawing to be a Constable was a mistake as to quality and did not avoid the contract. (3) The statement that the drawing was by Constable could have been treated as a warranty giving rise to a claim for damages, but it was not possible to award damages because the appeal was based on the plaintiff's right to rescind. (4) The Court, therefore, treated the statement as a representation and, finding it to be innocent, refused to rescind the contract because of the passage of time since the purchase.

Comment. Although this case was decided after *Solle* v *Butcher* (see below), there was presumably no need for the equitable relief of rescission in regard to the common mistake. After all, Leaf had paid only £85 for the drawing and the court may have regarded the contract as a speculation, each party taking a risk as to the authenticity of the drawing.

At common law where the subject-matter of the contract is not in existence when the contract is made, money paid under it can be recovered, and money which has not been paid cannot be demanded. The same is true when one party purchases something he already owns.

(102) *Couturier* v *Hastie* (1856) 5 H.L.C. 673

Messrs Hastie dispatched a cargo of corn from Salonica and sent the charter-party and bill of lading to their London agents so that the corn might be sold. The London agents employed Couturier to sell the corn and a person named Callander bought it. Unknown to the parties the cargo had become overheated, and had been landed at the nearest port and sold, so that when the contract was made the corn was not really in existence. Callander repudiated the contract and Couturier was sued because he was a *del credere* agent, i.e. an agent who, for an extra commission, undertakes to indemnify his principal against losses arising out of the repudiation of the contract by any third party introduced by him. *Held*—The claim against Couturier failed because the contract presupposed that the goods were in existence when they were sold to Callander.

(103) *Cochrane* v *Willis* (1865) L.R. 1 Ch. App. 58

Cochrane was the trustee in bankruptcy of Joseph Willis who was the tenant for life of certain estates in Lancaster. Joseph Willis had been adjudicated bankrupt in Calcutta where he resided. The remainder of the estate was to go to Daniel Willis, the brother of Joseph, on the latter's death, with eventual remainder to Henry Willis, the son of Daniel. Joseph Willis had the right to cut the timber on the estates during his life interest, and the representative of Cochrane in England threatened to cut and sell it for the benefit of Joseph's creditors. Daniel and Henry wished to preserve the timber and so they agreed with Cochrane through his representatives to pay the value of the timber to Cochrane if he would refrain from cutting it. News then reached England that when the above agreement was made Joseph was dead, and therefore the life interest had vested in (i.e. become owned by) Daniel. In this action by the trustee to enforce the agreement it was *held* that Daniel was making a contract to preserve something which was already his and the Court found, applying the doctrine of *res sua*, that the agreement was void for an identical or common mistake.

A person who buys his own property is entitled in equity to rescind the contract.

(104) *Cooper* v *Phibbs* (1867) L.R. 2 H.L. 149

Cooper agreed to take a lease of a fishery from Phibbs, his uncle's daughter who became apparent owner of it on her uncle's death. Unknown to either party the fishery already belonged to Cooper. This arose from a mistake by Cooper's uncle as to how the family land was held. The uncle innocently thought he owned the fishery and before he died had told Cooper so, but in fact it was owned by Cooper himself. Cooper now brought this action to set aside the lease and for delivery up of the lease. *Held*—The lease must be set aside on the grounds of common or identical bilateral mistake. however, since Equity has the power to give ancillary relief, Phibbs was given a lien on the fishery for the improvements he had made to it during the time he believed it to be his. This lien could be discharged by Cooper giving Phibbs' daughter the value of the improvements.

In equity there is a discretionary power to grant rescission where a contract is affected by common mistake if in the circumstances this is required to do justice.

(105) *Solle* v *Butcher* [1950] 1 K.B. 671

Butcher had agreed to lease a flat in Beckenham to Solle at a yearly rental of £250, the lease to run for seven years. Both parties had acted on the assumption that the flat, which had been substantially reconstructed so as to be virtually a new flat, was no longer controlled by the Rent Restriction legislation then in force. If it were so controlled, the maximum rent payable would be £140 per annum. Nevertheless Butcher would have been entitled to increase that rent by charging 8 per cent of the cost of repairs and improvements which would bring the figure up to about £250 per annum, the rent actually charged, if he had served a statutory notice on Solle before the new lease was executed. No such notice was in fact served. Actually they both for a time mistakenly thought that the flat was decontrolled when this was not the case. Solle realized the mistake after some two years, and sought to recover the rent he had over-paid and to continue as tenant for the balance of the seven years as a statutory tenant at £140 per annum. Butcher counter-claimed for rescission of the lease in Equity. It was *held* by a majority of the Court of Appeal that the mistake was one of fact and not of law, i.e. the fact that the flat was not within the provisions of the Rent Acts, and this was a bilateral mistake as to quality which would not invalidate the contract at common law. However, on the counter-claim for rescission, it was held that the lease could be rescinded. In order not to dispossess Solle, the court offered him the following alternatives—

(1) to surrender the lease entirely; or

(2) to remain in possession as a mere licensee until a new lease could be drawn up after Butcher had had time to serve the statutory notice which would allow him to add a sum for repairs to the £140 which would bring the lawful rent up to £250 per annum.

Comment. It is impossible to say at the present time what are the limits of this case. Equitable remedies are discretionary and it is not certain whether it applies to a contract for the sale of goods, nor whether it requires some form of sharp practice before it is implemented.

When asking for rectification the plaintiff need not show that there was a concluded contract prior to the execution of the written contract. There must however be some outward expression of agreement.

(106) *Joscelyne* v *Nissen* [1970] 1 All E.R. 1213

The plaintiff, Mr Joscelyne, sought rectification of a written contract made on 18 June 1964, under which he had made over his car hire business to his daughter, Mrs Margaret Nissen. It had been expressly agreed during negotiations, that in return for the car hire business Mrs Nissen would pay certain expenses including gas, electricity and coal bills but the agreement on these matters was not expressly incorporated in the written contract. Furthermore, the parties had agreed that no concluded contract was to be regarded as having been made until the signing of a formal written document.

Mrs Nissen failed to pay the bills and the plaintiff brought an action in the Edmonton County Court claiming amongst other things a declaration that Mrs Nissen should pay the gas, electricity and coal bills and alternatively that the written agreement of 18 June 1964, should be rectified to include a provision to that effect. The county court judge allowed the claim for rectification although there was no binding antecedent contract between the parties on the issue of payment of the expenses. The Court of Appeal, after considering different expressions of judicial views upon what was required before a contractual instrument might be rectified by the court, *held* that the law did not require a binding antecedent contract, provided there was some outward expression of agreement between the contracting parties. Rectification could be made even though there was no binding contract until the written agreement which was to be rectified was entered into.

Rectification is not available unless there is a literal difference in the terms of the prior agreement and the written contract.

(107) *Frederick Rose (London) Ltd* v *William Pim & Co. Ltd* [1953] 2 All E.R. 739

The plaintiffs received an order from an Egyptian firm for feveroles (a type of horse bean). The plaintiffs did not know what was meant by feveroles and asked the defendants what they were and whether they could supply them. The defendants said that feveroles were horse beans and that they could supply them, so the plaintiffs entered into a written agreement to buy horse beans from the defendants which were then supplied to the Egyptian firm under the order. In fact there were three types of horse beans: feves, feveroles and fevettes, and the plaintiffs had been supplied with feves, which were less valuable than feveroles. The plaintiffs were sued by the Egyptian firm and now wished to recover the damages they had had to pay from the defendants. In order to do so they had to obtain rectification of the written contract with the defendants in which the goods were described as 'horsebeans'. The word 'horsebeans' had to be rectified to 'feveroles', otherwise the defendants were not in breach. *Held*—

(1) Rectification was not possible because the contract expressed what the parties had agreed to, i.e. to buy and sell horsebeans. Thus the supply of any of the three varieties would have amounted to fulfilment of the contract.

(2) The plaintiffs might have rescinded for misrepresentation but they could not restore the status quo, having sold the beans.

(3) The plaintiffs might have recovered damages for breach of warranty, but the statement that 'feveroles are horsebeans and we can supply them' was oral, and warranties in a contract for the sale of goods of £10 and upwards had in 1953 to be evidenced in writing. This is not the case today.

(4) The defence of mistake was also raised, i.e. both buyer and seller thought that all horsebeans were feveroles. This was an identical bilateral or common mistake, but since it was not a case of *res extincta* or *res sua* it had no effect on the contract.

Rectification is available in cases of unilateral mistake.

(108) *Thomas Bates & Son Ltd* v *Wyndham's (Lingerie) Ltd* [1981] 1 All E.R. 1077

The plaintiff granted in 1956 a lease to the defendants with an option for renewal. This lease had a clause under which the rent on renewal was to be agreed by the parties or by arbitration. The option was exercised in 1963 for a seven-year lease, and again in 1970 for a 14-year lease at a rent of £2350 per annum for the first five years and thereafter subject to rent review every five years. This lease, which was drafted by the plaintiffs' managing director, did not contain an arbitration clause. The defendants knew that it did not. At the end of the first five-year period the plaintiffs suggested that a new rent should be agreed. The defendants would not agree and took the view that the rent of £2350 should continue for the whole 14 years unless there was an agreement between the parties to the contrary. Deputy Judge Michael Wheeler, Q.C., sitting in the High Court, ordered rectification and the Court of Appeal affirmed that decision. The clause inserted by the Court allowed the rent to be settled by arbitration if the parties did not agree.

Comment. At one time it was thought that rectification was available only for a common mistake by both parties. However, as appears from this case, rectification can be given for unilateral mistake. The principles on which it is granted appear in the judgment of Buckley, L.J., who said: 'First, that one party, A, erroneously believed that the documents sought to be rectified contained a particular term or provision, or possibly did not contain a particular term or provision, which, mistakenly, it did contain; second that the other party, B, was aware of the omission or the inclusion and that it was due to a mistake on the part of A; third that B has omitted to draw the mistake to the notice of A. And I think there must be a fourth element involved, namely that the mistake must be calculated to benefit B.' The general principle upon which the judgment is based would appear to be one of equitable estoppel.

By applying an objective test, i.e. what sort of contract would a reasonable person think had been made, the court may hold the parties bound despite a mistake.

(109) *Wood* v *Scarth* (1858) 1 F. & F. 293

The plaintiff was suing for damages for breach of contract alleging that the defendant had entered into an agreement to grant the plaintiff a lease of a public house, but had refused to convey the property. It was shown in evidence that the defendant intended to offer the lease at a rent, and also to include a premium on taking up the lease of £500. The defendant had told his agent to make this clear to the plaintiff, but the agent had not mentioned it. After discussions with the agent the plaintiff wrote to the defendant proposing to take the lease 'on the terms already agreed upon' to which the defendant replied accepting the proposal. There was a mutual or non-identical bilateral mistake. The defendant thought that he was agreeing to lease the premises for a rent plus a premium, and the plaintiff thought he was taking a lease for rental only because he did know of the premium. The plaintiff had sued for specific performance in 1855, and the court in the exercise of its equitable jurisdiction had decided that specific performance could not be granted in view of the mistake, as to grant it would be unduly hard on the defendant. However, in this action the plaintiff sued at common law for damages, and damages were granted to him on the ground that in mutual or non-identical mistake the court may find the sense of the promise and regard a contract as having been made on these terms. Here it was quite reasonable for the plaintiff to suppose that there was no premium to be paid. Thus a contract came into being on the terms as understood by the plaintiff, and he was entitled to damages for breach of it.

If the parties are at cross purposes as regards the subject-matter of the contract and the objective test does not point to one view or another being more probable, the contract is necessarily void.

(110) *Raffles* v *Wichelaus* (1864) 2 H. & C. 906

The defendants agreed to buy from the plaintiffs 125 bales of cotton to arrive 'ex Peerless from Bombay'. There were two ships called Peerless sailing from Bombay, one in October and one in December. The defendants thought they were buying the cotton on the ship sailing in October, and the plaintiffs meant to sell the cotton on the ship sailing in December. In fact the plaintiffs had no cotton on the ship sailing in October. The defendants refused to take delivery of the cotton when the second ship arrived and were now sued for breach of contract. *Held*—Since there was a mistake as to the subject matter of the contract there was in effect no contract between the parties.

When the plaintiff asks for an equitable remedy, e.g. specific performance, the court will also enforce the contract according to the sense of the promise unless to do so would inflict considerable hardship on the defendant.

(111) *Tamplin* v *James* (1880) 15 Ch. D. 215

James purchased a public house at an auction sale. The property was adequately described in the particulars of sale and by reference to a plan. James thought he knew the property and did not bother to refer to the particulars. In fact a field which had been occupied by the publican, and which James thought to be included in the sale, was held under a separate lease and was not part of the lot offered. Tamplin sued for specific performance and James raised this mistake as a defence. *Held*—Specific performance would be granted. Although the parties were not at one on the question of the subject-matter, James had by his conduct raised an implication that he was prepared to buy the property offered, and the price, although for the public house alone, was a fair one.

Although silence cannot amount to misrepresentation, partial non-disclosure may do so.

(112) *With* v *O'Flanagan* [1936] 1 All E.R. 727

The defendant was a medical practitioner who wished to sell his practice. The plaintiff was interested and in January 1934, the defendant represented to the plaintiff that the income from the practice was £2000 a year. The contract was not signed until May 1934, and in the meantime the defendant had been ill and the practice had been run by various other doctors as *locum tenentes*. In consequence the receipts fell to £5 per week, and no mention of this fact was made when the contract was entered into. The plaintiff now claimed rescission of the contract. *Held*—

He could do so. The representation made in January was of a continuing nature and induced the contract made in May. The plaintiff had a right to be informed of a change of circumstances, and the defendant's silence amounted to a misrepresentation.

A statement of intention can be regarded as a misrepresentation of existing fact if when it was made there was neither the will nor the ability to carry out the intention.

(113) *Edgington* v *Fitzmaurice* (1855) 29 Ch.D. 459

The plaintiff was induced to lend money to a company by a representation made by its directors that the money would be used to improve the company's buildings and generally expand the business. In fact the directors intended to use the money to pay off the company's existing debts as the creditors were pressing hard for payment. When the plaintiff discovered that he had been misled, he sued the directors for damages for fraud. The defence was that the statement that they had made was not a statement of a past or present fact but a mere statement of intention which could not be the basis of an action of fraud. *Held*—The directors were liable in deceit. Bowen, L.J., said: 'There must be a mistatement of an existing fact; but the state of man's mind is as much a fact as the state of his digestion. It is true that it is very difficult to prove what the state of a man's mind at a particular time is, but if it can be ascertained, it is as much a fact as anything else. A misrepresentation as to the state of a man's mind is, therefore, a misstatement of fact.'

A statement of opinion may be regarded as a misstatement of fact if the person who gave the opinion did not hold it or could not, as a reasonable man having his knowledge of the circumstances, have held it.

(114) *Smith* v *Land and House Property Corporation* (1884) 28 Ch.D. 7

The plaintiffs put up for sale on 4 August 1882, the Marine Hotel, Walton-on-the-Naze, stating in the particulars that it was let to 'Mr Frederick Fleck (a most desirable tenant) at a rental of £400 for an unexpired term of 27½ years'. The directors of thc defendant company sent the Secretary, Mr Lewin, to inspect the property and he reported that Fleck was not doing much business and that the town seemed to be in the last stages of decay. The directors, on receiving this report, directed Mr Lewin to bid up to £5000, and in fact he bought the hotel for £4700. Before completion Fleck became bankrupt and the defendant company refused to complete the purchase, whereupon the plaintiffs sued for specific performance. It was proved that on 1 May 1882, the March quarter's rent was wholly unpaid; that a distress was then threatened, and that Fleck paid £30 on 6 May, £40 on 13 June, and the remaining £30 shortly before the sale. No part of the June's quarter's rent had been paid. The chairman of the defendant company said that the hotel would not have been purchased but for the statement in the particulars that Fleck was a most desirable tenant. *Held*—Specific performance would not be granted. The description of Fleck as a most desirable tenant was not a mere expression of opinion, but contained an implied assertion that the vendors knew of no facts leading to the conclusion that he was not. The circumstances relating to the unpaid rent showed that Fleck was not a desirable tenant and there was a misrepresentation. Bowen, L.J., said—

> 'It is material to observe that it is often fallaciously assumed that a statement of opinion cannot involve the statement of a fact. In a case where the facts are equally well known to both parties, what one of them says to the other is frequently nothing but an expression of opinion. The statement of such opinion is in a sense a statement of a fact about the condition of the man's own mind, but only of an irrelevant fact, for it is of no consequence what the opinion is. But if the facts are not equally known to both sides, then a statement of opinion by the one who knows the facts best involves very often a statement of a material fact, for he impliedly states that he knows facts which justify his opinion.'

A person seeking relief in regard to misrepresentation must show that he was a representee, i.e. that he is a person (or within a class of persons) to whom the misrepresentation was addressed.

(115) *Peek* v *Gurney* (1873) L.R. 6 H.L. 377

Peek purchased shares in a company on the faith of statements appearing in a prospectus issued by the respondents who were directors of the company. Certain statements were false and Peek sued the directors. It appeared that Peek was not an original allottee, but had purchased the shares on the market, though he had relied on the prospectus. *Held*—Peek's action failed because the statements in the prospectus were only intended to mislead the original allottees. Once the statements had induced the public to be original subscribers, their force was spent.

It is not an acceptable defence to an action of misrepresentation that the representee was given the means of discovering that the statement was untrue.

(116) *Redgrave* v *Hurd* (1881) 20 Ch. D. 1

The plaintiff was a solicitor who wished to take a partner into the business. During negotiations between the plaintiff and Hurd the plaintiff stated that the income of the business was £300 a year. The papers which the plaintiff produced showed that the income was not quite £200 a year, and Hurd asked about the balance. Redgrave then produced further papers which he said showed how the balance was made up, but which only showed a very small amount of income making the total income up to about £200. Hurd did not examine these papers in any detail, but agreed to become a partner. Later Hurd discovered the true position and refused to complete the contract. The plaintiff sued for breach and Hurd raised the misrepresentation as a defence, and also counter-claimed for rescission of the contract. *Held*—Hurd had relied on Redgrave's statements regarding the income and the contracts could be rescinded. It did not matter that Hurd had the means of discovering their untruth; he was entitled to rely on Redgrave's statement.

Comment. Relief is not barred simply because there is an unsuccessful attempt by the person misled to discover the truth where the misrepresentation is fraudulent. (*S. Pearson & Son Ltd* v *Dublin Corporation* [1907] A.C. 351.)

A misrepresentation must have operated on the mind of the representee. If it has not, as where the representee could not have been influenced by it, there is no claim.

(117) *Smith* v *Chadwick* (1884) 9 App. Cas. 187

This action was brought by the plaintiff, who was a steel manufacturer, against Messrs Chadwick, Adamson and Collier, who were accountants and promoters of a company called the Blochairn Iron Co. Ltd. The plaintiff claimed £5750 as damages sustained through taking shares in the company which were not worth the price he had paid for them because of certain misrepresentations in the prospectus issued by the defendants. The action was for fraud. Among the misrepresentations alleged by Smith was that the prospectus stated that a Mr J.J. Grieves, M.P., was a director of the company, whereas he had withdrawn his consent the day before the prospectus was issued. *Held*—that the statement regarding Mr Grieves was untrue but was not material to the plaintiff, because the evidence showed that he had never heard of Mr Grieves. His action for damages failed.

(118) *Gosling* v *Anderson, The Times* 8 February 1972

Miss Gosling, a retired schoolmistress, entered into negotiations for the purchase of one of three flats in a house at Minehead owned by Mrs Anderson. Mr Tidbury, who was Mrs Anderson's agent in the negotiations, represented to Miss Gosling by letter that planning permission for a garage to go with the flat had been given. Mrs Anderson knew that this was not so. The purchase of the flat went through on the basis of a contract and a conveyance showing a parking area but not referring to planning permission which was later refused. Miss Gosling now sought damages for misrepresentation under s.2(1) of the Misrepresentation Act 1967. *Held*—The facts revealed an innocent misrepresentation by Mr Tidbury made without reasonable grounds for believing it to be true. Mrs Anderson was liable for the acts of her agent and must pay damages under the Act of 1967. The Court ordered an inquiry as to damages before the local County Court judge.

Comment. This action was against Mrs Anderson who was the other party to the contract. It was decided in *Resolute Maritime Inc and Another* v *Nippon Kaiji Kyokai and Others* [1983] 2 All E.R. 1 that no action is available against an agent such as Mr Tidbury under s.2(1) of the Misrepresentation Act 1967. Section 2(1) of the 1967 Act begins: 'Where a person has entered into a contract after a misrepresentation has been made to him by another party thereto . . .'. Thus the subsection only applies where the representee has entered into a contract after a misrepresentation has been made to him by another party to the contract. Where an agent acting within the scope of his authority makes a misrepresentation under s.2(1), the principal is liable to the third party misled, but not the agent. The agent will be liable to the third party only if he is guilty of fraud, or, under the rule in *Hedley Byrne* v *Heller* (1963)[120] for negligence at common law. Here, too, the principal will be liable vicariously along with the agent for the latter's fraud or negligence if the agent is acting within the scope of his authority.

In order to establish fraud it must be shown that the defendant did not have an honest belief in his statement.

(119) *Derry* v *Peek* (1889) 14 App. Cas 337

The Plymouth, Devonport and District Tramways Company had power under a special Act of Parliament to run trams by animal power, and with the consent of the Board of Trade by mechanical or steam power. Derry and the other appellants were directors of the company and issued a prospectus, inviting the public to apply for shares in it, stating that they had power to run trams by steam power, and claiming that considerable economies would result. The directors had assumed that the permission of the Board of Trade would be granted as a matter of course, but in the event the Board of Trade refused permission except for certain parts of the tramway. As a result the company was wound up and the directors were sued for fraud. The court decided that the directors were not fraudulent but honestly believed the statement in the prospectus to be true. As Lord Herschell said: 'Fraud is proved when it is shown that a false representation has been made (1) knowingly, or (2) without belief in its truth, or (3) recklessly, careless whether it be true or false.'

Comment. This case gave rise to the Directors' Liability Act 1890, now s.43 of the Companies Act 1948, which makes directors liable to pay compensation for misrepresentation in a prospectus, subject to a number of defences. (See p. 38.)

Where a person is induced to make a contract as the result of a misrepresentation by a third party, the Misrepresentation Act 1967 does not apply. However, a remedy may be sought in the tort of negligence.

(120) *Hedley Byrne & Co. Ltd* v *Heller & Partners Ltd* [1963] 2 All E.R. 575

The appellants were advertising agents and the respondents were merchant bankers. The appellants had a client called Easipower Ltd who were customers of the respondents. The appellants had contracted to place orders for advertising Easipower's products on television and in newspapers, and since this involved giving Easipower credit, they asked the respondents, who were Easipower's bankers, for a reference as to the creditworthiness of Easipower. The respondents said that Easipower Ltd was respectfully constituted and considered good, though they said in regard to the credit: 'These are bigger figures than we have seen' and also that the reference was given 'in confidence and without responsibility on our part'. Relying on this reply, the appellants placed orders for advertising time and space for Easipower Ltd, and the appellants assumed personal responsibility for payment to the television and newspaper companies concerned. Easipower Ltd went into liquidation, and the appellants lost over £17,000 on the advertising contracts. The appellants sued the respondents for the amount of the loss, alleging that the respondents had not informed themselves sufficiently about Easipower Ltd before writing the statement, and were therefore liable in negligence. *Held*—In the present case the respondents' disclaimer was adequate to exclude the assumption by them of the legal duty of care, but, in the absence of the disclaimer, the circumstances would have given rise to a duty of care in spite of the absence of a contract or fiduciary relationship.

Comment. The need for a special relationship cut down the number of claims for negligent misstatements. The courts required that the person making the statement should *know* the person or persons who would rely on it, as Hellers knew that Hedley Byrne would. However, in *JEB Fasteners* v *Marks Bloom* [1981] 3 All E.R. 289 it was decided that the test of knowledge should give way to a test of *foresight* and that in a contract to take over a company the purchasers could sue the accountants who had prepared allegedly negligently the annual accounts of the company. These accounts were alleged to have influenced the purchasers and although the accountants did not know that they would be used by those considering a take-over, the Court held that it was within their foresight. The accounts suggested that the company would require finance before its next annual accounts were completed and it was held to be within the accountants' foresight that the accounts might be used by a lender to or an investor in or a purchaser of the company. This is a much wider test for duty of care in negligence than was contemplated in *Hedley Byrne* or *Esso Petroleum* v *Mardon* (see p. 38) where the representee had to be *known* to the maker of the statement.

If the person misled by a misrepresentation discovers it but declares his intention to carry on with the contract expressly, or, alternatively does some act which is inconsistent with a desire to rescind, he will be bound by the contract on the grounds of affirmation.

(121) *Long* v *Lloyd* [1958] 2 All E.R. 402

The plaintiff and the defendant were haulage contractors. The plaintiff was induced to buy the defendant's lorry by the defendant's misrepresentation as to condition and peformance. The defendant advertised a lorry for sale at £850, the advertisement describing the vehicle as being in 'exceptional condition'. The plaintiff saw the lorry at the defendant's premises at Hampton Court on a Saturday. During a trial run on the following Monday the plaintiff found that the speedometer was not working, a spring was missing from the accelerator pedal, and it was difficult to engage top gear. The defendant said there was nothing wrong with the vehicle except what the plaintiff had found. He also said at this stage that the lorry would do 11 miles to the gallon.

The plaintiff purchased the lorry for £750, paying £375 down and agreeing to pay the balance at a later date. He then drove the lorry from Hampton Court to his place of business at Sevenoaks. On the following Wednesday, the plaintiff drove from Sevenoaks to Rochester to pick up a load, and during that journey the dynamo ceased to function, an oil seal was leaking badly, there was crack in one of the road wheels, and he used 8 gallons of petrol on a journey of 40 miles. That evening the plaintiff told the defendant of the defects, and the defendant offered to pay half the cost of a reconstructed dynamo, but denied any knowledge of the other defects. The plaintiff accepted the offer and the dynamo was fitted straight away. On Thursday the lorry was driven by the plaintiff's brother to Middlesbrough, and it broke down on the Friday night. The plaintiff, on learning of this, asked the defendant for his money back, but the defendant would not give it to him. The lorry was subsequently examined and an expert said that it was not roadworthy. The plaintiff sued for rescission. *Held*—at first instance, by Glyn-Jones, J.,—that the defendant's statements about the lorry were innocent and not fraudulent because the evidence showed that the lorry had been laid up for a month and it might have deteriorated without the defendant's precise knowledge. The Court of Appeal affirmed this finding of fact and made the following additional points—

(1) The journey to Rochester was not affirmation because the plaintiff was merely testing the vehicle in a working capacity.

(2) However, the acceptance by the plaintiff of the defendant's offer to pay half the cost of the reconstructed dynamo, and the subsequent journey to Middlesbrough, did amount to affirmation, and rescission could not be granted to the plaintiff.

Comment. (i) Damages could now be obtained for negligent misrepresentation under the Misrepresentation Act 1967, s.2(1), for how could the seller say he had reasonable grounds for believing that the lorry was in exceptional condition?

(ii) It seems remarkable that Glyn-Jones, J., did not find fraud. However, fraud must be proved according to the criminal standard, i.e. beyond a reasonable doubt and not according to the civil standard which is on balance of probabilities. Fraud is therefore difficult to prove and in this case there was presumably a reasonable doubt in the mind of the judge on the issue of fraud.

The aim of rescission is to put the parties in the position they were in before the contract was made. Therefore, the remedy is not available if the parties are not able to restore themselves to their original state before the contract.

(122) *Clarke* v *Dickson* (1858) 27 L.J. Q.B. 223

In 1853 the plaintiff was induced by the misrepresentation of the three defendants, Dickson, Williams and Gibbs, to invest money in what was in effect a partnership to work lead mines in Wales. In 1857 the partnership was in financial difficulty and with the plaintiff's assent it was converted into a limited company and the partnership capital was converted into shares. Shortly afterwards the company commenced winding-up proceedings and the plaintiff, on discovery of the falsity of the representations, asked for rescission of the contract. *Held*—Rescission could not be granted because capital in a partnership is not the same as shares in a company. The firm was no longer in existence, having been replaced by the company, and it was not possible to restore the parties to their original positions.

Comment. It should be noted that in addition to the problem of restoration, third-party rights, i.e. creditors, had accrued on the winding-up of the company and this is a further bar to rescission.

The duty of disclosure in insurance contracts may be widened by the terms of the contract itself.

(123) *Dawsons Ltd* v *Bonnin* [1922] 2 A.C. 413

Dawsons Ltd insured their motor lorry against loss by fire with Bonnin and others, and signed a proposal form which contained the following as Condition 4: 'Material misstatement or concealment of any circumstances by the insured material to assessing the premium herein, or in connection with any claim, shall render the policy void.' The policy also contained a clause saying that the 'proposal shall be the basis of the contract and shall be held as incorporated therein'. Actually the proposal form was filled up by an insurance agent, and although he stated the proposer's address correctly as 46 Cadogan Street, Glasgow, he also stated that the vehicle would usually be garaged there, although there was no garage accommodation at the Cadogan Street address and the lorry was garaged elsewhere. Dawsons' secretary, who signed the proposal, overlooked this slip made by the agent. The lorry was destroyed by fire and Dawsons claimed under the policy. *Held*—on appeal, by the House of Lords—The statement was not material within the meaning of Condition 4. However, the basis clause was an independent provision, and since the statement, though not material, was untrue, the policy was void. Viscount Cave said: 'The meaning and effect of the basis clause, taken by itself, is that any untrue statement in the proposal, or any breach of its promissory clauses, shall avoid the policy, and if that be the contract of the parties, the question of materiality has not to be considered.'

Comment. The Unfair Contract Terms Act 1977 does not apply to contracts of insurance. This resulted from a deal between the insurance companies and the Government under which the insurance companies agreed to abide by voluntary statements of practice. These have no legal effect but some moral force. If the insurance company follows these statements of practice then certainly in consumer, i.e. non-business insurance the worst effects of the basis clause should be eliminated.

In family arrangements there is a duty to disclose all material facts known to those involved in the arrangement.

(124) *Gordon* v *Gordon* (1819) 3 Swan. 400

Two brothers made an agreement for division of the family estates. The elder supposed he was born before the marriage of his parents and was therefore illegitimate. The younger knew that their parents had been married before the birth of the elder brother and the elder brother was therefore legitimate and his father's heir. He did not communicate this information to his elder brother. Nineteen years afterwards the elder brother discovered that he was legitimate and the agreement was set aside following this action brought by him. He would have had no case if at the time of the agreement both brothers had been in honest error as to the date of their parents' marriage.

By reason of the concept of duress the law allows a person to avoid a contract made under threats of violence.

(125) *Welch* v *Cheesman* (1973) 229 E.G. 99

Mrs Welch lived with the defendant, C, for many years in a house which she owned. C was a man given to violence, and after he threatened her Mrs Welch sold the house to him for £300. C died and his widow claimed the house which was worth about £3000. Mrs Welch brought this action to set aside the sale of the house to C on the grounds of duress and she succeeded.

Transactions between parent and child are presumed to have been made as a result of undue influence, even though the child has attained majority.

(126) *Lancashire Loan Ltd* v *Black* [1934] 1 K.B. 380

A daughter married at 18 and went to live with her husband. Her mother was an extravagant woman and was in debt to a firm of moneylenders. When the daughter became of age, her mother persuaded her to raise £2000 on property in which the daughter had an interest, and this was used to pay off the mother's debts. Twelve months later the mother and daughter signed a joint and several promissory note of £775 at 85 per cent interest in favour of the moneylenders, and the daughter created a further charge on her property in order that the mother might borrow more money. The daughter did not understand the nature of the transaction, and the only advice she received was from a solicitor acting for the mother and the moneylenders. The moneylenders brought this action against the mother and daughter on the note. *Held*—The daughter's defence that she was under undue influence of her mother succeeded, in spite of the fact that she was of full age and married with her own home.

The ability of the court to presume undue influence is not restricted to any particular type of relationship. The presumption can be applied whenever one person is in a position to take unfair advantage of another because of the trust and confidence which exists between them.

(127) *Hodgson* v *Marks* [1970] 3 All E.R. 513

Mrs Hodgson, who was a widow of 83, owned a freehold house in which she lived. In 1959 she took in a Mr Evans as a lodger. She soon came to trust Evans and allowed him to manage her financial affairs. In June 1960, she transferred the house to Evans, her sole reason for so doing being to prevent her nephew from turning Evans out of the house. It was orally agreed between Mrs Hodgson and Evans that the house was to remain hers although held in the name of Evans. Evans later made arrangements to sell the house without the knowledge or consent of Mrs Hodgson. The house was bought by Mr Marks and Mrs Hodgson now asked for a declaration that he was bound to transfer the property back to her. The following questions arose—

(1) whether Evans held the house in trust for Mrs Hodgson. It was *held*—by Ungoed-Thomas, J.,—that he did. The absence of written evidence of trust as required by s.53 of the Law of Property Act 1925 was not a bar to Mrs Hodgson's claim. The section does not apply to implied trusts of this kind.;

(2) whether Evans had exercised undue influence. It was held that he had and that a presumption of undue influence was raised. Although the parties were not in the established categories, Evans had a relationship of trust and confidence with Mrs Hodgson of a kind which raised a presumption of undue influence.

However, Mrs Hodgson lost the case because Mr Marks was protected by s.70 of the Land Registration Act 1925, which gives rights to a purchaser of property for value in respect of interests in that property of which the purchaser is not aware. In this case Mr Marks bought the house from Mr Evans, the house being in the name of Evans and he had no reason to suppose that Mrs Hodgson had any interest in it.

Comment. Mrs Hodgson's appeal to the Court of Appeal [1971] 2 All E.R. 684 succeeded and she got her house back, the court holding that in spite of s.70 a purchaser must pay heed to the possibility of rights in all *occupiers*. Mrs Hodgson was obviously in occupation with Mr Evans and inquiries should have been made by the purchaser as to her rights in the property.

If the parties to a contract were at the time it was made in a particular relationship of confidence then undue influence is presumed.

(128) *Allcard* v *Skinner* (1887) 36 Ch. D. 145

In 1868 the plaintiff joined a Protestant institution called the sisterhood of St Mary at the Cross, promising to devote her property to the service of the poor. The defendant Miss Skinner was the Lady Superior of the Sisterhood. In 1871 the plaintiff ceased to be novice and became a sister in the order, taking her vows of poverty, chastity and obedience. By this time she had left her home and was residing with the sisterhood. The plaintiff remained a sister until 1878 and, in compliance with the vow of poverty, she had by then given property to the value of £7000 to the defendant. The plaintiff left the order in 1879 and became a Roman Catholic. Of the property she had transferred, £1671 remained in 1885 and the plaintiff sought to recover this sum, claiming that it had been transferred in circumstances of undue influence. *Held*—The gifts had been made under pressure of an unusually persuasive nature, particularly since the plaintiff was prevented from seeking outside advice under a rule of the sisterhood which said, 'Let no sister seek the advice of any extern without the superior's leave.' However, the plaintiff's claim was barred by her delay because, although the influence was removed in 1879, she did not bring her action until 1885.

The court will intervene to protect a person from situations of improper pressure and inequality of bargaining power.

(129) *Lloyds Bank* v *Bundy* [1974] 3 All E.R. 757

The defendant and his son's company both banked with the plaintiffs, the defendant having been a customer for many years. The company's affairs deteriorated over a period of years and at the son's suggestion the bank's assistant manager visited the defendant and said that the bank could not continue to support an overdraft for the company unless the defendant entered into a guarantee of the account. The defendant received no independent advice, nor did the bank's assistant manager suggest that he should do so. The defendant charged his house as security for the overdraft and shortly afterwards the company went into receivership. The bank obtained possession of the house from the defendant in the county court, where the assistant branch manager in evidence said that he thought that the defendant had relied upon him implicitly to advise him about the charge.

The defendant appealed to the Court of Appeal in an attempt to set aside the guarantee of the security and it was *held*—allowing the defendant's appeal—that in the particular circumstances a special relationship existed between the defendant and the bank's assistant manager, as agent for the bank, and the bank was in breach of its duty of fiduciary care in procuring the charge which would be set aside for undue influence. The defendant, without any benefit to himself, had signed away his sole remaining asset without taking independent advice.

Comment. (i) While the majority of the Court of Appeal (Cairns, L.J., and Sir Eric Sachs) were content to decide the appeal on the conventional ground that a fiduciary relationship existed between the bank and its customer, which is to suggest that a new fiduciary relationship has come into being, Lord Denning took the opportunity to break new ground by deciding that in addition to avoiding the contract on the grounds of fiduciary relationship, Mr Bundy could also have done so on the basis of 'inequality of bargaining power'. Although inequality of bargaining power obviously includes undue influence. Lord Denning made it clear that the principle does not depend on the will of one party being dominated or overcome by the other. This is clear from that part of the judgment where he says: 'One who is in extreme need may knowingly consent to a most improvident bargain, solely to relieve the straits in which he finds himself'. This approach is, of course, at variance with the traditional view of undue influence which was that it was based on dominance resulting in an inferior party being unable to exercise independent judgment.

(ii) It should be noted that cases such as this which introduce into the law a requirement that a contract must be fair may eventually develop to the point where adequacy of consideration is required in contract. This is not the case at the present time.

In reaching a conclusion as to whether a statement is a representation or term of the contract the court will take into account the importance to be attached to the truth of the statement.

(130) *Bannerman* v *White* (1861) 10 C.B. (N.S.) 844

The defendant was intending to buy hops from the plaintiff and he asked the plaintiff whether sulphur had been used in the cultivation of the hops, adding that if it had he would not even bother to ask the price. The plaintiff said that no sulphur had been used, though in fact it had. It was *held* that the plaintiff's assurance that sulphur had not been used was a term of the contract and the defendant was justified in raising the matter as a successful defence to an action for the price.

In deciding whether the statements of the parties are terms of the con-

tract the court will have regard to any special skill or knowledge which the parties may have.

(131) *Oscar Chess Ltd* v *Williams* [1957] All E.R. 325

In May 1955, Williams bought a car from the plaintiffs on hire-purchase terms. The plaintiffs took Williams' Morris car in part exchange. Williams described the car as a 1948 model and produced the registration book, which showed that the car was first registered in April 1948, and that there had been several owners since that time. Williams was allowed £290 on the Morris. Eight months later the plaintiffs discovered that the Morris car was a 1939 Model there being no change in appearance in the model betweeen 1939 and 1948. The allowance for a 1939 model was £175 and the plaintiffs sued for £115 damages for breach of warranty that the car was a 1948 model. Evidence showed that some fraudulent person had altered the registration book but he could not be traced, and that Williams honestly believed that the car was a 1948 model. *Held*—The contract might have been set aside in equity for misrepresentation but the delay of eight months defeated this remedy. This mistake was a mistake of quality which did not avoid the contract at common law and in order to obtain damages the plaintiffs must prove a breach of warranty. The Court was unable to find that Williams was in a position to give such a warranty, and suggested that the plaintiffs should have taken the engine and chassis number and written to the manufacturers, so using their superior knowledge to protect themselves in the matter. The plaintiffs were not entitled to any redress. Morris, L.J., dissented, holding that the statement that the car was a 1948 model was a fundamental condition.

Comment. No doubt Mr Williams would have been liable for innocent and not negligent misrepresentation under the Misrepresentation Act 1967 for he had reasonable grounds to believe that the car was a 1948 Morris.

In deciding whether a term is a condition or warranty the court will form an impression from the facts of the case and the effect of the breach.

(132) *Poussard* v *Spiers and Pond* (1876) 1 Q.B.D. 410

Madame Poussard had entered into an agreement to play a part in an opera, the first performance to take place on 28 November 1874. On 23 November Madame Poussard was taken ill and was unable to appear until 4 December. The defendants had hired a substitute, and discovered that the only way in which they could secure a substitute to take Madame Poussard's place was to offer that person the complete engagement. This they had done, and they refused the services of Madame Poussard when she presented herself on 4 December. The plaintiff now sued for breach of contract. *Held*—The failure of Madame Poussard to perform the contract as from the first night was a breach of condition, and the defendants were within their rights in regarding the contract as discharged.

Comment. This case merely illustrates the availability of repudiation for serious breach of contract. Madame Poussard was not liable to pay damages for breach because she could not help the breach, the contract being also frustrated. (See p. 82.)

(133) *Bettini* v *Gye* (1876) 1 Q.B.D. 183

The plaintiff was an opera singer. The defendant was the director of the Royal Italian Opera in London. The plaintiff had agreed to sing in Great Britain in theatres, halls and drawing rooms for a period of time commencing on 30 March 1875, and to be in London for rehearsals six days before the engagement began. The plaintiff was taken ill and arrived on 28 March 1875, but the defendant would not accept the plaintiff's services, treating the contract as discharged. *Held*—The rehearsal clause was subsidiary to the main purposes of the contract, and its breach constituted a breach of warranty only. The defendant had no right to treat the contract as discharged and must compensate the plaintiff, but he had a counter-claim for any damage he had suffered by the plaintiff's late arrival.

Comment. The Court suggested that Bettini was liable in damages, whereas Madame Poussard was not. Presumably, therefore, unless the illness causes frustration, as it often will if the condition cannot be complied with, then the person concerned is liable in damages for a breach he could not help but commit.

In some cases the court will imply terms to an express contract by reference to customs prevailing in a trade, profession, or locality.

(134) *Hutton* v *Warren* (1836) 150 E.R. 517

The plaintiff was the tenant of a farm and the defendant the landlord. At Michaelmas, 1833, the defendant gave the plaintiff notice to quit on the Lady Day following. The defendant insisted that the plaintiff should cultivate the land during the period of notice which he did. The plaintiff now asked for a fair allowance for seeds and labour of which he had no benefit having left the farm before harvest. It was proved that by custom a tenant was bound to farm for the whole of his tenancy and on quitting was entitled to a fair allowance for seeds and labour. *Held*—The plaintiff succeeded. 'We are of opinion that this custom was, by implication, imported into the lease. It has long been settled, that, in commercial transactions, extrinsic evidence of custom and usage is admissable to annex incidents to written contracts in matters with respect to which they are silent. The same rule has also been applied to contracts in other transactions of life, in which known usages have been established and prevailed; and this has been done upon the principle of presumption that, in such transactions, the parties did not mean to express in writing the whole of the contract by which they intended to be bound, but a contract with reference to those known usages.' (Per Parke, B.)

A term will be implied in a contract if it is necessary in order to give business efficacy to it.

(135) *The Moorcock* (1889) 14 P.D. 64

The appellants in this case where in possession of a wharf and a jetty extending into the River Thames, and the respondent was the owner of the steamship Moorcock. In November 1887, the appellants and the respondent agreed that the ship should be discharged and loaded at the wharf and for that purpose should be moored alongside the jetty. Both parties realized that when the tide was out the ship would rest on the river bed. In the event the Moorcock sustained damage when she ceased to be waterborne owing to the centre of the vessel settling on a ridge of hard ground beneath the mud. There was no evidence that the appellants had given any warranty that the place was safe for the ship to lie in, but it was *held*—by the Court of Appeal—that there was an implied warranty by the appellants to this effect, for breach of which they were liable in damages.

> 'Now, an implied warranty, or as it is called, a covenant in law, as distinguished from an express contract or express warranty, really is in all cases founded on the presumed intention of the parties, and upon reason. The implication which the law draws from what must obviously have been the intention of the parties, the law draws with the object of giving efficacy to the transaction and preventing such a failure of consideration as cannot have been within the contemplation of either side; and I believe if one were to take all cases, and they are many, of implied warranties or covenants in law, it will be found that in all of them the law is raising an implication from the presumed intention of the parties with the object of giving to the transaction such efficacy as both parties must have intended that at all events it should have. In business transactions such as this, what the law desires to effect by the implication is to give such business efficacy to the transaction as must have been intended at all events by both parties who are business men; not to impose on one side all the perils of the transaction, or to emancipate one side from all chances of failure, but to make each party promise in law as much, at all events, as it must have been in the contemplation of both parties that he should be responsible for in respect of those perils or chances.' (Per Bowen, L.J.)

Comment. This statement of the law is to the effect that the court cannot imply a term because it is reasonable to do so but only when it is commercially necessary to do so. Lord Denning, particularly, in *Liverpool City Council* v *Irwin* 1977 (see p. 50) put forward the view that the court could imply a term whenever it was reasonable to do so even if it was not necessary to do so to make the contract work in a commercial sense. This view is still is not entirely accepted by the judiciary in general.

Where the document containing an agreement has been signed by one or both of the parties, the party signing will be bound by the terms of that agreement whether he has read them or not or understood their legal effect or not.

(136) *L'Estrange* v *Graucob (F.)* [1934] 2 K.B. 394

The defendant sold to the plaintiff a slot machine, inserting in the order form the following clause: 'Any express or implied condition, statement or warranty, statutory or otherwise, is hereby excluded.' The plaintiff signed the order form but did not read the relevant clause, and she now sued in respect of the unsatisfactory nature of the machine supplied. *Held*—The clause was binding on her, although the defendants made no attempt to read the document to her nor call her attention to the clause. 'Where a document containing contractual terms is signed, then in the absence of fraud, or I will add, misrepresentation, the party signing it is bound, and it is wholly immaterial whether he has read the document or not.' (Per Scrutton, L.J.).

Comment. It will, of course, be realised that s.6(3) of the Unfair Contract Terms Act 1977 would now apply so that the clause could only be effective if reasonable.

A person who misrepresents innocently or fraudulently the terms or effect of an exclusion clause which he has put into a contract will not be allowed to rely on it even if it would otherwise have been reasonable under the Unfair Contract Terms Act of 1977 to allow him to do so.

(137) *Curtis* v *Chemical Cleaning and Dyeing Co.* [1951] 1 All E.R. 631

The plaintiff took a wedding dress, with beads and sequins, to the defendant's shop for cleaning. She was asked to sign a receipt which contained the following clause: 'This article is accepted on condition that the company is not liable for any damage howsoever arising.' The plaintiff said in evidence: 'When I was asked to sign the document I asked why? The assistant said I was to accept any responsibility for damage to beads and sequins. I did not read it all before I signed it'. The dress was returned stained, and the plaintiff sued for damages. The company relied on the clause. *Held*—The company could not rely on the clause because the assistant had misrepresented the effect of the document so that the plaintiff was merely running the risk of damage to the beads and sequins.

The document which contains the exclusion clause must be of a type which a reasonable person would expect to contain contractual conditions.

(138) *Chapelton* v *Barry Urban District Council* [1940] 1 All E.R. 356

The plaintiff Chapelton wished to hire deck chairs and went to a pile owned by the defendants, behind which was a notice stating: 'Hire of chairs 2d per session of three hours.' The plaintiff took two chairs, paid for them, and received two tickets which he put into his pocket after merely glancing at them. One of the chairs collapsed and he was injured. A notice on the back of the ticket provided that 'The council will not be liable for any accident or damage arising from hire of chairs'. The plaintiffs sued for damages and the council sought to rely on the clause in the ticket. *Held*—The clause was not binding on Chapelton. The board by the chairs made no attempt to limit the liability, and it was unreasonable to communicate conditions by means of a mere receipt.

Comment. The defendants would now have had to face an additional problem, i.e. was the clause reasonable?

Provided the document containing the exclusion clause is suitable as a means of communication for the class of persons at which it is aimed it is irrelevant that a party actually receiving it is under a disability, such as illiteracy, blindness, or lacking knowledge of the English language. He will, nevertheless, be bound by the clause, subject to the Unfair Contract Terms Act 1977.

(139) *Thompson* v *L.M.S. Railway* [1930] 1 K.B. 41

Thompson, who could not read, asked her niece to buy her an excursion ticket, on the front of which were printed the words, 'Excursion. For conditions see back'. On the back was a notice that the ticket was issued subject to the conditions in the company's timetables, which excluded liability for injury however caused. Thompson was injured and claimed damages. *Held*—Her action failed. She had constructive notice of the conditions which had, in the court's view, been properly communicated to the ordinary passenger.

Comment. (i) The railway ticket was regarded as a contractual document. (Contrast *Chapelton.*)[138]

(ii) The injuries, which were caused when the train did not draw all the way into the station so that the plaintiff fell down a ramp, would have been the subject of an action at law today because the Unfair Contract Terms Act 1977 outlaws exclusion clauses relating to death and personal injury. Thus, on its own facts, this case is of historical interest only, though still relevant on the question of constructive notice.

The exclusion clause must be communicated, either expressly or constructively, at or before the time when the contract is made, otherwise it will not apply.

(140) *Olley* v *Marlborough Court Ltd* [1949] 1 All E.R. 127

Husband and wife arrived at an hotel as guests and paid for a room in advance. They went up to the room allotted to them; on one of the walls was the following notice: 'The proprietors will not hold themselves responsible for articles lost or stolen unless handed to the manageress for safe custody.' The wife closed the self-locking door of the bedroom and took the key downstairs to the reception desk. There was inadequate staff supervision of the keyboard. A third party took the key and stole certain of the wife's furs. In the ensuing action the defendants sought to rely on the notice as a term of the contract. *Held*—The contract was completed at the reception desk and no subsequent notice could affect the plaintiff's rights.

A party to a contract will not be able to rely on an exclusion clause if he gives an express undertaking which is repugnant, or runs contrary to the clause.

(141) *J. Evans & Son (Portsmouth) Ltd* v *Andrea Merzario Ltd* [1976] 2 All E.R. 930

The plaintiffs imported machines from Italy. They had contracted with the defendants since about 1959 for the transport of these machines. Before the defendants went over to the use of containers the plaintiffs' machines had always been crated and carried under deck. When the defendants went over to containers they orally agreed with the plaintiffs that the plaintiffs' goods would still be carried under deck. However, on a particular occasion a machine being transported for the plaintiffs was carried in a container on deck. At the start of the voyage the ship met a swell which caused the container to fall off the deck and the machine was lost. The contract was expressed to be subject to the printed standard conditions of the forwarding trade which contained an exemption clause excusing the defendants from liability for loss or damage to the goods unless the damage occurred whilst the goods were in their actual custody and by reason of their wilful neglect or default, and even in those circumstances, the clause limited the defendants' liability for loss or damage to a fixed amount. The plaintiffs claimed damages against the defendants for loss of the machine alleging that the exemption clause did not apply. It was *held* by the Court of Appeal that it did not apply. The printed conditions were repugnant to the oral promise for, if they were applicable, they would render that promise illusory. Accordingly, the oral promise was to be treated as overriding the printed conditions and the plaintiffs' claim succeeded, the exemption clause being inapplicable.

In a contract for the carriage of goods an unnecessary deviation from the route is a breach of contract. Once there has been an unnecessary deviation the carrier cannot rely on exclusion clauses in the contract of carriage.

(142) *Thomas National Transport (Melbourne) Pty Ltd and Pay* v *May and Baker (Australia) Pty Ltd* [1966] 2 Lloyd's Rep. 347

The owners of certain packages containing drugs and chemicals made a contract with carriers under which the packages were to be carried from Melbourne to various places in Australia. The carriers employed a subcontractor to collect the parcels and take them to the carriers' depot in Melbourne. When the subcontractor arrived late at the Melbourne depot it was locked and so he drove the lorry full of packages to his own house and left it in a garage there. This was in accordance with the carriers' instructions to their subcontractors in the event of late arrival at the depot. There was a fire and some of the packages were destroyed. The cause of the fire was unknown. However, the alleged negligence of the carriers consisted in their instruction to their subcontractors to take the goods home. The Court said it was unthinkable that valuable goods worth many thousands of pounds should be kept overnight at a driver's house, regardless of any provision for their safety. The owners sued the carriers who pleaded an exemption clause in the contract of carriage. *Held*—by the High Court of Australia—that the plaintiffs succeeded. There had been a fundamental breach of contract. The intention of the parties was that goods would be taken to the carriers' depot and not to the subcontractors' house, in which case the carriers could not rely on the clause. The decision in the *Suisse Case* was applied. (See p. 424.)

A party faced by a serious breach of contract where the breach was apparently excused by the exclusion clause, could plead the doctrine of fundamental breach. It is no longer necessary to raise this doctrine. The same result can often be obtained by applying rules of construction and/or the Unfair Contract Terms Act 1977.

(143) *Karsales (Harrow) Ltd* v *Wallis* [1956] 2 All E.R. 866

The defendant inspected a Buick car which a Mr Stanton wished to sell him. The defendant found it to be in excellent condition and agreed to pay £600 for it, effecting the purchase through a finance company. The car was badly damaged before it was delivered to Wallis; the new tyres which were on the car when Wallis saw it had been replaced by old ones; the radio had been removed; the cylinder head was off; all the valves were burnt; and the engine had two broken pistons. Wallis would not agree to take delivery of the car but it was towed to his place of business and left there. The finance company originally involved assigned its rights under the agreement with Wallis to Karsales, and in this action Karsales were trying to recover the instalments due under the agreement. In so doing they relied on the following clause in the agreement assigned to them: 'No condition or warranty that the vehicle is roadworthy, or as to its age condition or fitness for any purpose, is given by the owner or implied herein.' The County Court judge decided that the exemption clause was effective and ordered Wallis to pay. Wallis now appealed. The Court of Appeal *held* that Wallis was not liable because exemption clauses, no matter how widely expressed, only avail the party who includes them when he is carrying out his contract in its essential respects. Here there was a breach of a fundamental term amounting to non-performance. As Birkett, L.J., said: 'A car that will not go is not a car at all.' Thus Wallis could repudiate the contract and the finance company was not entitled to rely on the exclusion clause in the agreement.

Comment. Note the point of repugnance. The contract was for a car in reasonable running order and what was delivered was a car that would not go. The clause purporting to excuse that sort of performance must be repugnant in a contract for a car in running order.

(144) *Alexander* v *Railway Executive* [1951] 2 All E.R. 442

Alexander was a magician who had been on a tour together with an assistant. He left three trunks at the parcels office at Launceston station, the trunks containing various properties which were used in an 'escape illusion'. The plaintiff paid 5d for each trunk deposited and received a ticket for each one. He then left saying that he would send instructions for their dispatch. Some weeks after the deposit and before the plaintiff had sent instructions for the dispatch of the trunks, the plaintiff's assistant persuaded the clerk in the parcels office to give him access to the trunks, though he was not in possession of the ticket. The assistant took away several of the properties and was later convicted of larceny. The plaintiff sued the defendants for damages for breach of contract, and the defendants pleaded the following term which was contained in the ticket and which stated that the Railway Executive was 'not liable for loss mis-delivery or damage to any articles where the value was in excess of £5 unless at the time of the deposit the true value and nature of the goods was declared by the depositor and an extra charge paid'. No such declaration or payment had been made. *Held*—The plaintiff succeeded because, although sufficient notice had been given constructively to the plaintiff of the term, the term did not protect the defendants because they were guilty of a breach of a fundamental obligation in allowing the trunks to be opened and things to be removed from them by an unauthorized person.

Comment. (i) Devlin, J., said that a deliberate delivery to the wrong person did not fall within the meaning of 'mis-delivery', and this may be regarded as the real reason for the decision, as it involved the application of the *contra proferentum* rule.

(ii) Note also that the receipt or ticket for the goods deposited was held to be a contractual document. (Contrast *Chapelton.*)[138]

For some years certain members of the judiciary asserted and applied the principle that as a matter of law no agreement of the parties by way

of exclusion clause could overcome a fundamental breach. In the *Suisse* case the House of Lords stated that the matter was one of construction of the contract.

(145) *Suisse Atlantique Societe D'Armement Maritime S.A.* v *N.V. Rotterdamsche Kolen Centrale* [1966] 2 All E.R. 61

The plaintiffs were shipowners and the defendants chartered a ship from them for 'two years' continuous voyages'. Under the contract, demurrage of $1000 per day had to be paid by the charterers to the owners if the ship was detained in port longer than the loading time permitted and specified by the contract. There were substantial delays and the demurrage was paid, but the shipowner's loss of freight was greater than the demurrage they had received and they claimed general damages over and above the demurrage. It was suggested for the owners that the delay was deliberate and enabled them to regard the contract as repudiated so that the demurrage provisions did not apply and they could recover their full loss. The owners further argued that because of the cases relating to fundamental breach and exemption clauses the demurrage clause could not cover a breach as serious as this. The House of Lords, after consideration of the fundamental breach cases, *held* that—

(1) a fundamental breach no longer as a matter of law automatically nullifies an exemption clause. The matter is one of construction of the contract.

(2) The demurrage clause was not so much an exemption clause as a provision for liquidated damages, but was wide enough to cover the breaches complained of.

(3) Even if the charterer's conduct had given the owners the right to treat the contract as repudiated, they had not done so and the contract including the demurrage clause remained in force.

(146) *Photo Production Ltd* v *Securicor Transport Ltd* [1980] 1 All E.R. 556

The plaintiff company had contracted with the defendant security company for the defendant to provide security services at the plaintiff's factory. A person employed by the defendant lit a fire in the plaintiff's premises while he was carrying out a night patrol. The fire got out of control and burned down the factory. The trial judge was unable to establish from the evidence precisely what the motive was for lighting the fire—it may have been deliberate or merely careless. The defendant relied on an exclusion clause in the contract which read—

> 'Under no circumstances shall the company (Securicor) be responsible for any injurious act or default by any employee of the company unless such act or default could have been foreseen and avoided by the exercise of due diligence on the part of the company as his employer. . . .'

It was accepted that Securicor were not negligent in employing the person who lit the fire. He came to them with good references and there was no reason for them to suppose that he would act as he did. It was *held* by the House of Lords that the exclusion clause applied so that Securior were not liable. All the judges in the House of Lords were unanimous in the view that there was no rule of law by which exclusion clauses became inapplicable to fundamental breach of contract, which this admittedly was. Although the Unfair Contract Terms Act of 1977 was not in force at the time this action was brought and therefore could not be applied to the facts of this case, the existence of the Act and its relevance was referred to by Lord Wilberforce who said that the doctrine of fundamental breach had been useful in its time as a device for avoiding injustice. He then went on to say: 'But . . . Parliament has taken a hand: it has passed the Unfair Contract Terms Act 1977. This Act applies to consumer contracts and those based on standard terms and enables exception clauses to be applied with regard to what is just and reasonable. It is significant that Parliament refrained from legislating over the whole field of contract. After this Act, in commercial matters generally, when the parties are not of unequal bargaining power, and when risks are normally borne by insurance . . . there is everything to be said . . . for leaving the parties free to apportion the risks as they think fit. . . .'

Comment. (i) In *Harbutt's 'Plasticine' Ltd* v *Wayne Tank & Pump Co. Ltd* [1970] 1 All E.R. 225 Lord Denning accepted that the principle which said that no exclusion clause could excuse a fundamental breach was not a rule of law when the injured party carried on with (or affirmed) the contract. Where this was so rules of construction must be used and the exclusion clause might have to be applied. However, if the injured party elected to repudiate the contract for fundamental breach and, as it were, pushed the contract away, the exclusion clause went with it and could never apply to prevent the injured party from suing for the breach. The same, he said, was true where the consequences were so disastrous (as they were in *Photo Production*) that one could assume that the injured party had elected to repudiate. The *Photo Production* case overrules *Harbutt*, as does s.9(1) of the Unfair Contract Terms Act 1977. This provides that if a clause, as a matter of construction, is found to cover the breach and if it satisfies the reasonableness test, it can apply and be relied on by the party in breach, even though the contract has been terminated by express election or assumed election following the disastrous results of the breach.

(ii) The House of Lords also allowed a Securicor exemption clause to apply in circumstances of fundamental breach in *Ailsa Craig Fishing Co. Ltd* v *Malvern Fishing Co. Ltd* [1983] 1 All E.R. 101. In that case the appellants' ship sank while berthed in Aberdeen harbour. It fouled the vessel next to it which was owned by Malvern. The appellants sued Malvern. Securicor were the second defendants. Securicor had a contract with the appellants to protect the ship. The accident happened as a result of a rising tide. At the time the Securicor patrolman had left his post to become involved in New Year celebrations. Although there were arguments by counsel to the contrary, the House of Lords held that the exclusion clause covered the circumstances of the case provided the words were given their natural and plain meaning. It therefore applied to limit the liability of Securicor and the appellants failed to recover all their loss.

(147) *Mitchell (George) (Chesterhall) Ltd* v *Finney Lock Seeds Ltd* [1983] 1 All E.R. 108

This case is a landmark. It was the last case heard by Lord Denning in the Court of Appeal. In it he gave a review of the development of the law relating to exclusion clauses in his usual clear and concise way. The report is well worth reading in full. Only a summary of the main points can be given here.

George Mitchell ordered 30lbs of cabbage seed and Finney supplied it. The seed was defective. The cabbages had no heart; their leaves turned in. The seed cost £192 but Mitchell's loss was some £61,000, i.e. a year's production from the 63 acres planted. Mitchell carried no insurance. When sued Finney defended the claim on the basis of an exclusion clause limiting their liability to the cost of the seed or its replacement. In the High Court Parker, J., found for Mitchell. Finney appealed to the Court of Appeal. The major steps in Lord Denning's judgment appear below.

(1) *The issue of communication—was the clause part of the contract?* Lord Denning said that it was. The conditions were usual in the trade. They were in the back of Finney's catalogue. They were on the back of the invoice. 'The inference from the course of dealing would be that the farmers had accepted the conditions as printed—even though they had never read them and did not realise that they contained a limitation on liability . . .'.

(2) *The wording of the clause.* The relevant part of the clause read as follows: 'In the event of any seeds or plants sold or agreed to be sold by us not complying with the express terms of the contract of sale or with any representation made by us or by any duly authorised agent or representative on our behalf prior to, at the time of, or in any such contract, or any seeds or plants proving defective in varietal purity we will, at our option, replace the defective seeds or plants, free of charge to the buyer or will refund all payments made to us by the buyer in respect of the defective seeds or plants and this shall be the limit of our obligation. We hereby exclude all liability for any loss or damage arising from the use of any seeds or plants supplied by us and for any consequential loss or damage arising out of such use or any failure in the performance of or any defect in any seeds or plants supplied by us or for any other loss or damage whatsoever save for, at our option, liability for any such replacement or refund as aforesaid.'

Lord Denning said that the words of the clause did effectively limit Finney's liability. Since the Securicor cases (see *Photo Production* and

Ailsa Craig above) words were to be given their natural meaning and not strained. A judge must not proceed in a hostile way towards the wording of exclusion clauses as was, for example, the case with the word 'misdelivery' in *Alexander* v *Railway Executive* 1951.[144]

(3) *The test of reasonableness.* Lord Denning then turned to the new test of reasonableness which could be used to strike down an exclusion clause, even though it had been communicated, and in spite of the fact that its wording was appropriate to cover the circumstances. On this he said: 'What is the result of all this? To my mind it heralds a revolution in our approach to exemption clauses; not only where they exclude liability altogether and also where they limit liability; not only in the specific categories in the Unfair Contract Terms Act 1977, but in other contracts too. . . . We should do away with the multitude of cases on exemption clauses. We should no longer have to go through all kinds of gymnastic contortions to get round them. We should no longer have to harrass our students with the study of them. We should set about meeting a new challenge. It is presented by the test of reasonableness.'

(4) *Was the particular clause fair and reasonable?* On this Lord Denning said: 'Our present case is very much on the borderline. There is this to be said in favour of the seed merchant. The price of this cabbage seed was small: £192. The damages claimed are high: £61,000. But there is this to be said on the other side. The clause was not negotiated between persons of equal bargaining power. It was inserted by the seed merchants in their invoices without any negotiation with the farmers. To this I would add that the seed merchants rarely, if ever, invoked the clause. . . . Next, I would point out that the buyers had no opportunity at all of knowing or discovering that the seed was not cabbage seed: whereas the sellers could and should have known that it was the wrong seed altogether. The buyers were not covered by insurance against the risk. Nor could they insure. But as to the seed merchants the judge said (Lord Denning here refers to Parker, J., at first instance): "I am entirely satisfied that it is possible for seedsmen to insure against this risk . . ." To that I would add this further point. Such a mistake as this could not have happened without serious negligence on the part of the seed merchants themselves or their Dutch suppliers. So serious that it would not be fair to enable them to escape responsibility for it. In all the circumstances I am of the opinion that it would not be fair or reasonable to allow the seed merchants to rely on the clause to limit their liability'.

Oliver and Kerr, L. J.J., also dismissed the appeal.

The suppliers asked for leave to appeal to the House of Lords but the Court of Appeal refused. However, the House of Lords granted leave and affirmed the decision of the Court of Appeal. (See [1983] 2 All E.R. 737.)

Comment. This is in effect an application of s.6(3) of the Unfair Contract Terms Act 1977. It was actually brought under the Sale of Goods Act 1979 which contained transitional provisions and s.55(3) of the 1979 Act plus para. 11 of Sch.1 applied to this contract. For contracts made after 31 January 1978 the Unfair Contract Terms Act 1977, s.6(3) would apply.

(148) *Walker* v *Boyle* [1982] 1 All E.R. 634

The vendor of a house was asked in a pre-contract enquiry whether the boundaries of the land were the subject of any dispute. The vendor asked her husband to deal with the enquiries. He said that there were no disputes. There were, in fact, disputes but the husband did not regard them as valid because he believed that he was in the right and his view could not be contradicted. His answers were nevertheless wrong and misleading. Contracts were later exchanged. These contracts were on the National Conditions of Sale (19th Edition) produced under the aegis of the Law Society. Condition 17(1) excluded liability for misleading replies to preliminary enquiries. The purchaser later heard of the boundary disputes and claimed in the High Court for rescission of the contract and the return of his deposit. Dillon, J., held that condition 17(1) did not satisfy the requirements of reasonableness as set out in s.3 of the Misrepresentation Act 1967 (As substituted by s.8(1) of the Unfair Contract Terms Act 1977). The plaintiff therefore succeeded.

Comment. The National Conditions of Sale (20th Edition) have been revised and as regards misrepresentation, the contract now only attempts a total exclusion of the purchaser's remedies if the misrepresentation is not material or substantial in terms of its effect and is not made recklessly or fraudulently.

A contract which tends to abuse the course of justice, e.g. a contract to commit a crime, is void as against public policy.

(149) *Dann* v *Curzon* (1911) 104 L.T. 66

An agreement was made for advertising a play by means of collusive criminal proceedings brought as a result of a pre-arranged disturbance at the theatre. The plaintiffs, who agreed to create the disturbance and did in fact do so, sued for the remuneration due to them under the agreement. *Held*—The action failed because it was an agreement to commit a criminal offence and was therefore against public policy.

A contract, the objects of which are to further immorality, are contrary to public policy and unenforceable. However, the party who is not in equal wrong, as where he has no knowledge of the illegal purpose, can enforce the contract.

(150) *Pearce* v *Brooks* (1866) L.R. 1 Exch. 213

The plaintiffs hired a carriage to the defendant for a period of 12 months during which time the defendant was to pay the purchase price by instalments. The defendant was a prostitute and the carriage, which was of attractive design, was intended to assist her in obtaining clients. One of the plaintiffs knew that the defendant was a prostitute but he said that he did not know that she intended to use the carriage for purposes of prostitution. The evidence showed to the contrary. The jury found that the plaintiffs knew the purpose for which the carriage was to be used and thereupon the court *held* that the plaintiffs' claim for the sum due under the contract failed for illegality.

Comment. The contract would, of course, have been valid if the person hiring the carriage had intended to put it to some innocent use.

Where the object of the contract is to perpetrate a fraud, e.g. upon the bankruptcy laws or upon the Revenue, the contract is illegal as it is if made with objects likely to injure proper government, e.g. the procuring of honours.

(151) *John* v *Mendoza* [1939] 1 K.B. 141

The defendant owed the plaintiff £852 15s 6d. The defendant was made bankrupt and the plaintiff was intending to prove for his debt in the bankruptcy. The defendant asked him not to do so, but to say that the £852 15s 6d was a gift whereupon the defendant would pay the plaintiff in full regardless of the sum received by other creditors. In view of the defendant's promise the plaintiff withdrew his proof, but in the event all the other creditors were paid in full and the bankruptcy was annulled. The plaintiff now sued for the debt. *Held*—There was no claim, for the plaintiff abandoned all right to recover on failure to prove in the bankruptcy, and the defendant's promise to pay in full was unenforceable, being an agreement designed to defeat the bankruptcy laws.

(152) *Parkinson* v *The College of Ambulance Ltd and Harrison* [1925] 2 K.B. 1

The first defendants were a charitable institution and the second defendant was the secretary. Harrison fraudulently represented to the plaintiff, Colonel Parkinson, that the charity was in a position to obtain some honour (probably a knighthood) for him if he would make a suitable donation to the funds of the charity. The plaintiff paid over the sum of £3000 and said he would pay more if the honour was granted. No honour of any kind was received by the plaintiff and he brought this action to recover the money he had donated to the College. *Held*—The agreement was contrary to public policy and illegal. No relief could be granted to the plaintiff.

(153) *Napier* v *National Business Agency Ltd* [1951] 2 All E.R. 264

The defendants engaged the plaintiff to act as their secretary and accountant at a salary of £13 per week plus £6 per week for expenses. Both parties were aware that the plaintiff's expenses could never amount to £6 a week and in fact they never exceeded £1 per week. Income tax was deducted on £13 per week, and £6 per week was paid without deduction of tax as reimbursement of expenses. The plaintiff, having been summarily dismissed, claimed payment of £13 as wages in lieu of notice. *Held*—The agreement was contrary to public policy and illegal. The plaintiff's action failed.

A plaintiff who has transferred property under an illegal contract can recover it provided he can base his action upon a right which is independent of the contract.

(154) *Bowmakers Ltd* v *Barnet Instruments Ltd* [1944] 2 All E.R. 579

Bowmakers bought machine tools from a person named Smith. This contract was illegal because it contravened an Order made by the Minister of Supply under the Defence Regulations, Smith having no licence to sell machine tools. Bowmakers hired the machine tools to Barnet Instruments under hire-purchase agreements which were also illegal because Bowmakers did not have a licence to sell machine tools on hire purchase or otherwise. Barnet Instruments failed to keep up the instalments, sold some of the machine tools and refused to give up the others. Bowmakers sued, not on the illegal hire-purchase contracts, but in conversion, and judgment was given for Bowmakers. The Court of Appeal declared the contracts illegal but, since Bowmakers were not suing under the contracts but as owners, the action succeeded. The wrongful sales by Barnet Instruments terminated the hire-purchase contracts.

Money paid under an illegal contract cannot normally be recovered. However, the presence of some form of duress may enable the person threatened to plead that he was not in equal wrong and thereby recover his money.

(155) *Atkinson* v *Denby* (1862) 7 H. & N. 934

The plaintiff was in financial difficulties and offered to pay his creditors the sum of 5s in the £ as a full settlement. All the creditors except the defendant agreed to this. The defendant said that he would only agree if the plaintiff paid him £50. Afraid that the scheme would not go through without the defendant's co-operation, the plaintiff made the payment. *Held*—He could recover it because he had been coerced into defrauding his creditors.

Comment. The judgment was, of course, a desirable one because the £50 became available for distribution among all creditors.

Where the illegal purpose has not been substantially carried out, a party may repent, repudiate the contract and recover his money or property. He cannot do this where the non-performance is merely due to the fact that the other party will not carry out the contract.

(156) *Bigos* v *Bousted* [1951] 1 All E.R. 92

The defendant was anxious to send his wife and daughter abroad for the sake of the daughter's health, but restrictions on currency were in force so that a long stay abroad was impossible. In August 1947, the defendant, in contravention of the Exchange Control Act 1947, made an agreement under which the plaintiff B was to supply £150 of Italian money to be made available at Rapallo, the defendant undertaking to repay the plaintiff with English money in England. As security, the defendant deposited with the plaintiff a share certificate for 140 shares in a company. The wife and daughter went to Italy but were not supplied with currency, and had to return sooner than they would have done. The defendant, thereupon. asked for the return of his share certificate but the plaintiff refused to give it up. This action was brought by the plaintiff to recover the sum of £150 which she insisted she had lent to the defendant. He denied the loan, and counter-claimed for the return of his certificate. In the course of the action the plaintiff abandoned her claim, but the defendant proceeded with his counter-claim saying that, although the contract was illegal, it was still executory so that he might repent and ask the court's assistance. *Held*—The Court would not assist him because the fact that the contract had not been carried out was due to frustration by the plaintiff and not the repentance of the defendant. In fact his repentance was really want of power to sin and he could not recover his securities.

(157) *Taylor* v *Bowers* (1876) 1 Q.B.D. 291

The plaintiff was under pressure from his creditors and in order to place some of his property out of their reach he assigned certain machinery to a person named Adcock. The plaintiff then called a meeting of his creditors and tried to get them to settle for less than the amount of their debts, representing his assets as not including the machinery. The creditors would not and did not agree to a settlement. The plaintiff now sued to recover his machinery from the defendants who had obtained it from Adcock. *Held*—The plaintiff succeeded because the illegal fraud on the creditors had not been carried out.

There can be no recovery of money or property passing under an illegal contract if the illegal purpose has been substantially carried out.

(158) *Kearley* v *Thomson* (1908) 24 Q.B.D. 742

The plaintiff had a friend who was bankrupt and wished to obtain his discharge. The defendant was likely to oppose the discharge and accordingly the plaintiff paid the defendant £40 in return for which the defendant promised to stay away from the public examination and not to oppose the discharge. The defendant did stay away from the public examination but before an application for discharge had been made the plaintiff brought this action claiming the £40. *Held*—The claim failed because the illegal scheme had been substantially effected.

Where the parties try by what they regard as a contract enforceable at law to take any dispute in regard to it to an arbitration tribunal or

to an individual without further recourse to the courts, the contract is to that extent contrary to public policy.

(159) *Re Davstone Estates Ltd* [1969] 2 All E.R. 849

The plaintiffs were landlords of a block of flats in St Albans. The plaintiffs agreed with the tenants to keep the common parts of the block in good repair and the tenants agreed to pay £15 per year to the plaintiffs for this service. The tenants were also required to agree to a clause which provided that if the tenants' proportionate share of the actual cost of repairs incurred by the plaintiffs should exceed £15 in any year the tenants would pay the excess. A certificate by the plaintiffs' surveyor was to be conclusive as to the tenants liability to pay any excess. The plaintiffs had to make good any structural defects as distinct from repairs and maintenance and the Court was required as a matter of construction of the tenancy agreement to say whether any of these costs were recoverable from the tenants. In the course of his judgment, Ungoed-Thomas, J., said that the provision as to the finality of the plaintiffs' surveyor certificate ousted the jurisdiction of the court and was void as contrary to public policy.

The rules relating to restraint of trade are applied to clauses in employment agreements which limit the rights of the employee to work once his employment has ended.

(160) *Wyatt* v *Kreglinger and Fernau* [1933] 1 K.B. 793

In June 1923, the defendants wrote to the plaintiff, who had been in their service for many years, intimating that upon his retirement they proposed to give him an annual pension of £200, subject to the condition that he did not compete against them in the wool trade. The plaintiff's reply was lost and he did not appear ever to have agreed for his part not to engage in the wool trade, but he retired in the following September and received the pension until June 1932 when the defendants refused to make any further payments. The plaintiff sued them for breach of contract. The defendants denied any contract existed and also pleaded that if a contract did exist, it was void as being in restraint of trade. The Court of Appeal gave judgment for the defendants and although there was no unanimity with regard to the *ratio decidendi*, it appeared to two judges that the contract was injurious to the interests of the public, since to restrain the plaintiff from engaging in the wool trade was to deprive the community of services from which it might derive advantage.

Comment. The basis of this decision seems to be that if a contract did exist it was supported only by an illegal consideration moving from Wyatt, i.e. an agreement not to engage in the wool trade. If he had been entitled to a pension as part of his original contract of service then no doubt the pension arrangements would have been severed and enforced.

An agreement restraining competition is enforceable if it is to prevent the exploitation of trade secrets by an employee.

(161) *Forster & Sons Ltd* v *Suggett* (1918) 35 T.L.R. 87

The works manager of the plaintiffs who were mainly engaged in making glass and glass bottles was instructed in certain confidential methods concerning, amongst other things, the correct mixture of gas and air in the furnaces. He agreed that during the five years following the termination of his employment he would not carry on in the United Kingdom, or be interested in, glass bottle manufacture or any other business connected with glass-making as conducted by the plaintiffs. It was *held* that the plaintiffs were entitled to protection in this respect and that the restraint was reasonable.

Even a restraint of trade which is unlimited in time will be upheld if reasonable. However, the fact that there is no limit is an unusual matter which requires special justification.

(162) *Fitch* v *Dewes* [1921] 2 A.C. 158

A solicitor at Tamworth employed a person who was successively his articled clerk and managing clerk. In his contract of service, the clerk agreed, if he left the solicitor's employment, never to practice as a solicitor within seven miles of Tamworth Town Hall. *Held*—The agreement was good because during his service the clerk had become acquainted with the details of his employer's clients, and could be restrained even for life from using that knowledge to the detriment of his employer.

Comment. Although the restraint was for life, it did cover a comparatively small area in which at the time there were comparatively few people. It is unlikely that such a restraint would be regarded as valid today, particularly in a more densely populated area.

An employer can restrain an ex-employee from soliciting the former employer's customers provided the clause is reasonable in regard to time, space or area being of less importance.

(163) *Home Counties Dairies* v *Skilton* [1970] 1 All E.R. 1227

Skilton, a milk roundsman employed by the plaintiffs, agreed, amongst other things, not 'to serve or sell milk or dairy produce' to persons who within six months before leaving his employment were customers of his employers. Skilton left his employment with the plaintiffs in order to work as a roundsman for Westcott Dairies. He then took the same milk round as he had worked when he was with the plaintiffs. *Held*—by the Court of Appeal—that this was a flagrant breach of agreement. The words 'dairy produce' were not too wide. On a proper construction they must be restricted to things normally dealt in by a milkman on his round. 'A further point was taken that the customer restriction would apply to anyone who had been a customer within the last six months of the employment and had during that period ceased so to be, and it was said that the employer could have no legitimate interest in such persons. I think this point is met in the judgment in *G.W. Plowman & Sons Ltd* v *Ash* 1964, where it was said that a customer might have left temporarily and that his return was not beyond hope and was therefore a matter of legitimate interest to the employer.' (Per Harman, L.J.)

In restraints between vendor and purchaser of a business, the only thing which can be protected is the business sold. The purchaser cannot protect other businesses which he controls.

(164) *British Reinforced Concrete Co* v *Schelff* [1921] 2 Ch. 563

The plaintiffs carried on a large business for the manufacture and sale of 'B.R.C.' Road Reinforcements. The defendant carried on a small business for the sale of 'Loop Road Reinforcements'. The defendant sold his business to the plaintiffs and agreed not to compete with them in the manufacture or sale of road reinforcements. It was *held* that the covenant was void. All that the defendant transferred was the business of selling the reinforcements called 'Loop'. It was therefore only with regard to that particular variety that it was justifiable to curb his future activities.

A world-wide restraint may be upheld but only if the restraint must be world-wide in order to be effective.

(165) *Nordenfelt* v *Maxim Nordenfelt Guns and Ammunition Co.* [1894] A.C. 535

Nordenfelt was a manufacturer of machine guns and other military weapons. He sold the business to a company, giving certain undertakings which restricted his business activities. This company was amalgamated with another company and Nordenfelt was employed by the new concern as managing director. In his contract Nordenfelt agreed that for 25 years he would not manufacture guns or ammunition in any part of the world, and would not compete with the company in any way. *Held*—The covenant regarding the business sold was valid and enforceable, even though it was world-wide, because the business connection was world-wide and it was possible in the circumstances to sever this undertaking from the rest of the agreement. However, the further undertaking not to compete in any way with the company was unreasonable and void.

The courts are concerned to prevent an employer from obtaining by an indirect method of restraint protection which he could not have obtained in an express contract with the employee.

(166) *Kores Manufacturing Co. Ltd* v *Kolok Manufacturing Co. Ltd* [1958] 2 All E.R. 65

The two companies occupied adjoining premises in Tottenham and both manufactured carbon papers, typewriter ribbons and the like. They made an agreement in which each company agreed that it would not, without the written consent of the other, 'at any time employ any person who during the past five years shall have been a servant of yours'. The plaintiffs' chief chemist sought employment with the defendants, and the plaintiffs were not prepared to consent to this and asked for an injunction to enforce the agreement. *Held*—by the Court of Appeal—

(1) A contract in restraint of trade cannot be enforced unless—

(*a*) it is reasonable as between the parties, and

(*b*) it is consistent with the interests of the public.

(2) The mere fact that the parties are dealing on equal terms does not prevent the Court from holding that the restraint is unreasonable in the interests of those parties.

(3) The restraint in this case was grossly in excess of what was required to protect the parties and accordingly was unreasonable in the interests of the parties.

(4) The agreement therefore failed to satisfy the first of the two conditions set out in (1) above and was void and unenforceable.

An important application of the doctrine of unreasonable restraint of trade has been in regard to exclusive purchasing agreements. Where the restraints are in a contract it is likely that five years will be the maximum term acceptable to the court.

(167) *Esso Petroleum Co. Ltd* v *Harper's Garage* (*Stourport*) *Ltd* [1967] 1 All E.R. 699

The defendant company owned two garages with attached filling stations, the Mustow Green Garage, Mustow Green, near Kidderminster, and the Corner Garage at Stourport-on-Severn. Each garage was tied to the plaintiff oil company, the one at Mustow Green by a solus supply agreement only with a tie clause binding the dealer to take the products of the plaintiff company at its scheduled prices from time to time. There was also a price-maintenance clause which was no longer enforceable and a 'continuity clause' under which the defendants, if they sold the garage, had to persuade the buyer to enter into another solus agreement with Esso. The defendants also agreed to keep the garage open at all reasonable hours and to give preference to the plaintiff company's oils. The agreement was to remain in force for four years and five months from 1 July 1963, being the unexpired residue of the 10-year tie of a previous owner. At the corner Garage there was a similar solus agreement for 21 years and a mortgage under which the plaintiffs lent Harpers £7000 to assist them in buying the garage and improving it. The mortgage contained a tie covenant and forbade redemption for 21 years. In August 1964, Harpers offered to pay off the loan but Esso refused to accept it. Harpers then turned over all four pumps at the Corner Garage to V.I.P. and later sold V.I.P. at Mustow Green. The plaintiff company now asked for an injunction to restrain the defendants from buying or selling fuels other than Esso at the two garages during the subsistence of the agreements. *Held*—by the House of Lords—that the rule of public policy against unreasonable restraints of trade applied to the solus agreements and the mortgage. The shorter period of four years and five months was reasonable so that the tie was valid but the other tie for 21 years in the solus agreement and the mortgage was invalid, so that the injunction asked for by the plaintiffs could not be granted.

Comment. The House of Lords appears to have been influenced by the report of the Monopolies Commission on the Supply of Petrol to Retailers in the United Kingdom (Cmnd 1965 No 264) which recommended the period of five years.

Where the restraint on the use of land is contained in a conveyance or lease, the common law doctrine of restraint of trade does not apply. The person entering under the conveyance or lease has given nothing up. In fact he has acquired a limited right which he did not have before.

(168) *Cleveland Petroleum Co. Ltd* v *Dartstone Ltd* [1968] 1 All E.R. 201

The owner of a garage and filling station at Crawley in Sussex leased the property to Cleveland and they in turn granted an underlease to the County Oak Service Station Ltd. The underlease contained a covenant under which all motor fuels sold were to be those of Cleveland. There was power to assign in the underlease and a number of assignments took place so that eventually Dartstone Ltd became the lessees, having agreed to observe the covenants in the underlease. They then challenged the covenant regarding motor fuels and Cleveland asked for an injunction to enforce it. The injunction was granted. Dealing in the court of Appeal with *Harper's Case*[167] Lord Denning M.R., said—

> '. . . it seems plain to me that in three at least of the speeches of their Lordships a distinction is taken between a man who is already in possession of the land before he ties himself to an oil company and a man who is out of possession and is let into it by an oil company. If an owner in possession ties himself for more than five years to take all his supplies from one company, that is an unreasonable restraint of trade and is invalid. But if a man, who is out of possession, is let into possession by the oil company on the terms that he is to tie himself to that company, such a tie is good.'

The regulation of professional services is governed also by the common-law rules relating to restraint of trade.

(169) *Pharmaceutical Society of Great Britain* v *Dickson* [1968] 2 All E.R. 686

The Society passed a resolution to the effect that the opening of new pharmacies should be restricted and be limited to certain specified services, and that the range of services in existing pharmacies should not be extended except as approved by the Society's council. The purpose of the resolution was clearly to stop the development of new fields of trading in conjunction with pharmacy. Mr Dickson, who was a member of the Society and retail director of Boots Pure Drug Company Ltd, brought this action on the grounds that the proposed new rule was *ultra vires* as an unreasonable restraint of trade. A declaration that the resolution was *ultra vires* was made and the Society appealed to the House of Lords where the appeal was dismissed, the following points emerging from the judgment—

(1) Where a professional association passes a resolution regulating the conduct of its members the validity of the resolution is a matter for the courts even if binding in honour only, since failure to observe it is likely to be construed as misconduct and thus become a ground for disciplinary action.

(2) A resolution by a professional association regulating the conduct of its members is *ultra vires* if not sufficiently related to the main objects of the association. The objects of the society in this case did not cover the resolution, being 'to maintain the honour and safeguard and promote the interests of the members in the exercise of the profession of pharmacy'.

(3) A resolution by a professional association regulating the conduct of its members will be void if it is an unreasonable restraint of trade.

A marriage brokage contract under which a person undertakes for reward to arrange a marriage between two parties is contrary to public policy.

(170) *Hermann* v *Charlesworth* [1905] 2 K.B. 123

C agreed that he would introduce gentlemen to Miss Hermann with a view to marriage. She agreed to make an immediate payment of £52 and a payment of £250 on the day of marriage. He introduced her to several gentlemen and corresponded with others on her behalf but no marriage took place. Miss Hermann now sued for the return of the £52 and succeeded. Although the claim succeeded at common law on the ground of total failure of consideration, Sir Richard Henn-Collins said in the course of his judgement that he could have granted the return of the money even after a marriage had taken place. Thus money paid under a marriage brokeage contract is recoverable whether a marriage takes place or not.

Only those parts of the contract which are against public policy are frowned on by the law. The court may sever other parts where this is possible and enforce them.

(171) *Wallis* v *Day* (1837) 2 M. & W. 273

The plaintiff was in business as a carrier and he sold that business to the defendant. The plaintiff agreed in return for a weekly salary of £2

3s 10d to serve the defendant as assistant for life and further agreed that except as assistant he would not for the rest of his life exercise the trade of carrier. This action was brought by the plaintiff to recover 18 weeks' arrears of salary. The defence was that the contract was void as being an unlawful restraint of trade and that no part of it was enforceable. It was unnecessary to decide this point because the court held that the restraint was reasonable but Lord Abinger, dealing with the defence, said: 'The defendants demurred on the ground that the covenant being in restraint of trade was illegal and therefore the whole contract was void. I cannot however accede to that conclusion. If a party enters into several covenants one of which cannot be enforced against him he is not therefore released from performing the others, and in the present case the defendants might have maintained an action against the plaintiff for not rendering them the services he covenanted to perform, there being nothing illegal in that part of the contract.'

If a seller delivers the goods ordered mixed with goods of a different description, the buyer may reject the whole consignment.

(172) *Moore & Co.* v *Landauer & Co.* [1921] 2 K.B. 519

The plaintiffs entered into a contract to sell the defendants a certain quantity of Australian canned fruit, the goods to be packed in cases containing 30 tins each. The goods were to be shipped 'per S.S. Toromeo'. The ship was delayed by strikes at Melbourne and in South Africa, and was very late in arriving at London. When the goods were discharged about one half of the consignment was packed in cases containing 24 tins only, instead of 30, and the buyers refused to accept them. *Held*—Although the method of packing made no difference to the market value of the goods, the sale was by description under s.13 of the Sale of Goods Act, and the description had not been complied with. Consequently the buyers were entitled to reject the whole consignment by virtue of the provisions of what is now s.30(4) of the Sale of Goods Act.

A major exception to the principle that a person who partly performs an entire contract cannot recover any part of the price is the rule relating to substantial performance.

(173) *Hoenig* v *Isaacs* [1952] 2 All E.R. 176

The defendant employed the plaintiff who was an interior decorator and furniture designer to decorate a one-room flat owned by the defendant. The plaintiff was also to provide furniture, including a fitted bookcase, a wardrobe and a bedstead, for the total sum of £750. The terms of the contract regarding payment were as follows—'Net cash as the work proceeds and the balance on completion'. The defendant made two payments to the plaintiff of £150 each, one payment on the 12 April and the other on the 19 April. The plaintiff claimed that he had completed the work on 28 August, and asked for the balance, i.e. £450. The defendant asserted that the work done was bad and faulty, but sent the plaintiff a sum of £100 and moved into the flat and used the furniture. The plaintiff now sued for the balance of £350, the defence being that the plaintiff had not performed his contract, or in the alternative that he had done so negligently, unskilfully and in an unworkmanlike manner.

The Official Referee assessed the work that had been done, and found that generally it was properly done except that the wardrobe door required replacing and that a bookshelf was too short and this meant that the bookcase would have to be remade. The defendant claimed that the contract was entire and that it must be completely performed before the plaintiff could recover. The Official Referee was of opinion that there had been substantial performance, and that the defendant was liable for £750 less the cost of putting right the above mentioned defects, the cost of this being assessed at £55 18s 2d. The Court accordingly gave the plaintiff judgment for the sum of £294 1s 10d.

If it appears that the parties have made a new contract under which it is agreed to accept a partial performance, the person making the partial performance is entitled to *quantum meruit.* However, the party receiving the benefit of the part-performance must have accepted it. This implies that he must have had an opportunity to accept or reject it.

(174) *Sumpter* v *Hedges* [1898] 1 Q.B. 673

The plaintiff entered into a contract with the defendant under the terms of which the plaintiff was to erect some buildings for the defendant on the defendant's land for a price of £565. The plaintiff did partially erect the buildings up to the value of £333, and the defendant paid him for that figure. The plaintiff then told the defendant that he could not finish the job because he had run out of funds. The defendant them completed the work by using material belonging to the plaintiff which had been left on the site. The plaintiff now sued for work done and materials supplied, and the court gave him judgment for materials supplied, but would not grant him a sum of money by way of *quantum meruit* for the value of the work done prior to his abandonment of the job. The reason given was that, before the plaintiff could sue successfully on a *quantum meruit*, he would have to show that the defendant had voluntarily accepted the work done, and this implied that the defendants must be in a position to refuse the benefit of the work as where a buyer of goods refuses to take delivery. This was not the case here; the defendant had no option but to accept the work done, so his acceptance could not be presumed from conduct. There being no other evidence of the defendant's acceptance of the work, the plaintiff's claim for the work done failed.

Comment. In practice this form of injustice to the builder is avoided because a building contract normally provides for progress payments, thus making it a divisible agreement.

A *quantum meruit* is available for work done under a contract which is terminated by the defendant's breach.

(175) *De Barnardy* v *Harding* (1853) 8 Exch. 822

The plaintiff agreed to act as the defendant's agent for the purpose of preparing and issuing certain advertisements and notices designed to encourage the sale of tickets to see the funeral procession of the Duke of Wellington. The plaintiff was to be paid a commission of 10 per cent upon the proceeds of the tickets actually sold. The plaintiff duly issued the advertisements and notices, but before he began to sell the tickets, the defendant withdrew the plaintiff's authority to sell them and in consequence the plaintiff did not sell any tickets and was prevented from earning his commission. The plaintiff now sued upon a *quantum meruit* and his action succeeded.

Time will be regarded as of the essence of the contract where the circumstances indicate this is so. Thus in a mercantile contract, such as a sale of goods, the time fixed for delivery of the goods is of the essence.

(176) *Bowes* Shand (1877) 2 App. Cas. 455

The action was brought for damages for non-acceptance of 600 tons (or 8200 bags) of Madras rice. The sold note stated that the rice was to be shippped during 'the months of March and/or April 1874'. 8150 bags were put on board ship on or before 28 February 1874, and the remaining 50 bags on 2 March 1874. The defendants refused to take delivery because the rice was not shipped in accordance with the terms of the contract. *Held*—The bulk of the cargo was shipped in February and therefore the rice did not answer the description in the contract and the defendants were not bound to accept it.

Comment. A buyer can reject in these circumstances even though he is not prejudiced and merely wants to reject because the market price has fallen.

A person who has waived his right to performance is entitled on reasonable notice to impose a new time limit.

(177) *Chas. Rickards Ltd* v *Oppenhaim* [1950] 1 K.B. 616

The defendant ordered a Rolls-Royce chassis from the plaintiffs, the chassis being delivered in July 1947. The plaintiffs found a coach builder prepared to make a body within six or at the most seven months. The specification for the body was agreed in August 1947, so that the work should have been completed in March 1948. The work was not completed by then but the defendant still pressed for delivery. On 29 June 1948, the defendant wrote to the coach-builders saying that he would not accept delivery after 25 July 1948. The body was not ready by then and the defendant bought another car. The body was completed in October 1948, but the defendant refused to accept delivery and counter-claimed for the value of the chassis which he had purchased. *Held*—Time was of the essence of the original contract, but the defendant had waived the question of time by continuing to press for delivery after the due date. However, by his letter of 29 June he had again made time of the essence, and had given reasonable notice in the matter. Judgment was given for the defendant on the claim and counterclaim.

Where there is a current account there is a presumption that the creditor has not appropriated his payments to any particular item. Appropriation is then on a chronological basis, i.e. the first item on the debit side of the account is reduced by the first item on the credit side. This follows the rule in *Clayton's Case.*

(178) *Deeley* v *Lloyds Bank Ltd* [1912] A.C. 756

A customer of the bank had mortgaged his property to the bank to secure an overdraft limited to £2500. He then mortgaged the same property to the appellant for £3500, subject to the bank's mortgage. It is the normal practice of bankers, on receiving notice of a second mortgage, to rule off the customer's account, and not to allow any further withdrawals since these will rank after the second mortgage. In this case the bank did not open a new account but continued the old current account. The customer thereafter paid in sums of money which at a particular date, if they had been appropriated in accordance with the rule in *Clayton's Case*, would have extinguished the bank's mortgage. Even so the customer still owed the bank money, and they sold the property for a price which was enough to satisfy the bank's debt but not that of the appellant. *Held*—The evidence did not exclude the rule in *Clayton's Case*, which applied, so that the bank's mortgage had been paid off and the appellant, as second mortgagee, was entitled to the proceeds of the sale.

If before the time for performance arrives one party states that he will not perform the contract or acts in such a way as to make this clear, the other party may sue for damages at once or wait for the time of performance and then sue.,

(179 *Hochster* v *De la Tour* (1835) 2 E. & B. 678

The defendant agreed in April 1852 to engage the plaintiff as a courier for European travel, his duties to commence on 1 June 1852. On 11 May 1852, the defendant wrote to the plaintiff saying that he no longer required his services. The plaintiff commenced an action for breach of contract on 22 May 1852, and the defence was that there was no cause of action until the date due for performance, i.e. 1 June 1852. *Held*—The defendant's express repudiation constituted an actionable breach of contract.

(180) *Omnium D'Enterprises and Others* v *Sutherland* [1919] 1 K.B. 618

The defendant was the owner of a steamship and agreed to let her under a charter to the plaintiff for a period of time and to pay the second plaintiffs a commission on the hire payable under the agreement. The defendant later sold the ship to a purchaser, free of all liability under his agreement with the plaintiffs. *Held*—The sale by the defendant was a repudiation of the agreement and the plaintiffs were entitled to damages for breach of the contract.

Comment. The charterer would have no claim against the purchaser of the vessel because restrictive covenants do not pass with chattels (which a ship is) but only with land. Compare *Dunlop* v *Selfridge* 1915[29] and *Tulk* v *Moxhay* 1848.[33]

Where there is an antipatory breach the innocent party is not bound to treat the contract as discharged. He may, in appropriate circumstances, elect to continue with it.

(181) *Whiter and Carter (Councils) Ltd* v *McGregor* [1961] 3 All E.R. 1178

The respondent was a garage proprietor on Clydebank and on 26 June 1957, his sales manager, without specific authority, entered into a contract with the appellants whereby the appellants agreed to advertise the respondent's business on litter bins which they supplied to local authorities. The contract was to last for three years from the date of the first advertisement display. Payment was to be by instalments annually in advance, the first instalment being due seven days after the first display. The contract contained a clause that, on failure to pay an instalment or other breach of contract, the whole sum of £196 4s became due. The respondent was quick to repudiate the contract for on 26 June 1957, he wrote to the appellants asking them to cancel the agreement, and at this stage the appellants had not taken any steps towards carrying it out. The appellants refused to cancel the agreement and prepared the advertisement plates which they exhibited on litter bins in November 1957, and continued to display them during the following three years. Eventually the appellants demanded payment, the respondent refused to pay, and the appellants brought an action against him for the sum due under the contract. *Held*—The appellants were entitled to recover the contract price since, although the respondents had repudiated the contract, the appellants were not obliged to accept the repudiation. The contract survived and the appellants had now completed it.

Comment. Although the respondent's agent had no actual authority, he had made a similar contract with the appellants in 1954, and it was not disputed that he had apparent authority to bind his principal.

It is worth pointing out that there was in this case no evidence that the appellants could have mitigated their loss. No evidence was produced to show that the demand for advertising space exceeded the supply so it may be that the appellants could not have obtained a new customer for the space on the litter bins intended for the respondent. Thus White & Carter may have had a 'legitimate interest' in continuing with the contract. Perhaps if evidence that mitigation was possible had been produced the House of Lords would have applied the principles of mitigation to the case, or held that White & Carter had a 'legitimate interest' in continuing the agreement. This view is supported by a decision of the Court of Appeal in *Attica Sea Carriers Corporation* v *Ferrostaal Poseidon Bulk Reederei GmbH* [1976] 1 Lloyd's Rep 250 where the charterer of a ship agreed to execute certain repairs before he redelivered it to the owner and to pay the agreed hire until that time. He did not carry out the repairs but the owner would not take redelivery of the ship until they had been done and later sued for the agreed hire. It was *held* that the owner was not entitled to refuse to accept redelivery and to sue for the agreed hire. The cost of the repairs far exceeded the value which the ship would have if they were done and the owner had therefore no legal interest in insisting on their execution and the payment of the hire. The Court held that he should have mitigated his loss by accepting redelivery of the unrepaired ship so that his only remedy was damages and not for the agreed hire.

This line was followed also in the case of *Clea Shipping Corporation* v *Bulk Oil International, The Times* 6 August 1983. A vessel had been chartered by the plaintiff owners to the defendants, the hire charge having been paid in advance. However, the ship broke down and required extensive repairs. The charterers thereupon gave notice that they intended to end the contract. However, the plaintiffs decided to keep the agreement open and undertook the repairs and then informed the defendants that the vessel was at their disposal. The plaintiffs said they were exercising their right of election conferred upon the innocent party in such circumstances to keep the contract open, thus entitling them to keep the hire money instead of suing for damages. Lloyd, J., denied the existence of an unfettered right of election for an innocent party to keep a contract running in such circumstances. He found that, in the absence of a 'legitimate interest' in the contract's perpetuation by the party faced with repudiation, the party concerned could, though innocent, be forced to accept damages in lieu of sums falling due under the contract subsequent to the actionable event. This restraint is founded on general equitable principles, to be based on what is reasonable on the facts of each case.

A party who chooses not to accept an anticipatory breach but to wait until the time for performance arrives, takes the risk that the contract may become discharged, e.g. by frustration or illegality thus excusing the other party from performance.

(182) *Avery* v *Bowden* (1855) 5 E. & B. 714

The defendant chartered the plaintiff's ship and agreed to load her with a cargo at Odessa within 45 days. The ship went to Odessa and remained there for most of the 45 day period. The defendant told the captain of the ship that he did not propose to load a cargo and that he would do well to leave, but the captain stayed on at Odessa, hoping that the defendant would change his mind. Before the end of the 45 day period the Crimean War broke out so that performance of contract would have been illegal. *Held*—The plaintiff might have treated the defendant's refusal to load a cargo as an anticipatory breach of contract but his agent, the captain, had waived that right by staying on at Odessa, and now the contract had been discharged by something which was beyond the control of either party.

Whether a contract of employment is frustrated by the illness or incapacity of an employee depends upon the duration of that illness or incapacity in the sense that if the contractual duties cannot be performed in the way envisaged by the contract, then it will be frustrated but not otherwise.

(183) *Storey* v *Fulham Steel Works* (1907) 24 T.L.R. 89

The plaintiff was employed by the defendant as manager for a period of five years. After he had been working for two years he became ill, and had to have special treatment and a period of convalescence. Six months later he was recovered, but in the meantime the defendant had terminated his employment. The plaintiff now sued for breach of contract, and the defendants pleaded that the plaintiff's period of ill-health operated to discharge the contract. *Held*—The plaintiff's illness and absence from duty did not go to the root of the contract, and was not so serious as to allow the termination of the agreement.

Where an employee by his own fault makes the performance of the contract of employment impossible, the contract is not frustrated. The employee is in breach of contract and the employer may repudiate the contract and dismiss him.

(184) *Norris* v *Southampton City Council, The Times*, 27 January 1982

Mr Norris was employed as a cleaner. He was convicted of assault and reckless driving and was sentenced to a term of imprisonment. His employers wrote dismissing him and Mr Norris complained to an industrial tribunal that his dismissal was unfair. The Tribunal held that the contract of employment was frustrated and that the employee was not dismissed and therefore not entitled to compensation. The Employment Appeal Tribunal, to which Mr Norris appealed, laid down that frustration could only arise where there was no fault by either party. Where there was fault, such as deliberate conduct leading to an inability to perform the contract, there was no frustration but a repudiatory breach of contract. The employer had the option of whether or not to treat the contract as repudiated and if he chose to dismiss the employee he could do so, regarding the breach as repudiatory. The question then to be decided was whether the dismissal was fair. The case was remitted to the Industrial Tribunal for further consideration of whether there was unfair dismissal on the facts of the case.

Supervening illegality operates to frustrate a contract.

(185) *Re Shipton, Anderson & Co. and Harrison Bros' Arbitration* [1915] 3 K.B. 676

A contract was made for the sale of wheat lying in a warehouse in Liverpool. Before the seller could deliver the wheat, and before the property in it had passed to the buyer, the Government requisitioned the wheat under certain emergency powers available in time of war. *Held*—Delivery being impossible by reason of lawful requisition by the Government, the seller was excused from performance of the contract.

Physical destruction of the subject-matter of the contract operates to frustrate it.

(186) *Taylor* v *Caldwell* (1863) 3 B & S. 826

The defendant agreed to let the plaintiff have the use of a music hall for the purpose of holding four concerts. Before the first concert was due to be held the hall was destroyed by fire without negligence by any party, and the plaintiff now sued for damages for wasted advertising expenses. *Held*—The contract was impossible of performance and the defendant was not liable.

Where the taking place of an event is at the root of the contract its cancellation or postponement will in the absence of a contrary provision, frustrate it.

(187) *Krell* v *Henry* [1903] 2 K.B. 740

The plaintiff owned a room overlooking the proposed route of the Coronation procession of Edward VII, and had let it to the defendant for the purpose of viewing the procession. The procession did not take place because of the King's illness and the plaintiff now sued for the agreed fee. *Held*—The fact that the procession had been cancelled discharged the parties from their obligations, since it was no longer possible to achieve the real purpose of the agreement.

If the substantial purpose of the contract can still be achieved it will not be frustrated.

(188) *Herne Bay Steamboat Co.* v *Hutton* [1903] 2 K.B. 683

The plaintiffs agreed to hire a steamboat to the defendant for two days, in order that the defendant might take paying passengers to see the naval review at Spithead on the occasion of Edward VII's Coronation. An official announcement was made cancelling the review, but the fleet was assembled and the boat might have been used for the intended cruise. The defendant did not use the boat, and the plaintiffs employed her on ordinary business. The action was brought to recover the fee of £200 which the defendant had promised to pay for the hire of the boat. *Held*—The contract was not discharged, as the review of the fleet by the sovereign was not the foundation of the contract. The plaintiffs were awarded the difference between £200 and the profits derived from the use of the ship for ordinary business on the two days in question.

Comment. It may be thought that it is difficult to reconcile this case with *Krell.* However, whatever the legal niceties may or may not be, there is clearly a difference in fact. To cruise round the fleet assembled at Spithead, even though the figure of the Sovereign (miniscule to the viewer, anyway) would not be present, is clearly more satisfying as the subject-matter of a contract than looking through the window at ordinary London traffic.

Physical destruction of the subject matter is not essential to frustration. It extends to cases where although there is no physical destruction the essential commercial purpose of the contract cannot be achieved; a doctrine referred to as 'frustration of the common venture'.

(189) *Jackson* v *Union Marine Insurance Co.* (1874) L.R. 10 C.P. 125

The plaintiff was the owner of a ship which had been chartered to go with all possible dispatch from Liverpool to Newport, and there load a cargo of iron rails for San Francisco. The plaintiff had entered into a contract of insurance with the defendants, in order that he might protect himself against the failure of the ship to carry out the charter. The vessel was stranded in Caernarfon Bay whilst on its way to Newport. It was not refloated for over a month, and could not be fully repaired for some time. The charterers hired another ship and the plaintiff now claimed on the policy of insurance. The insurance company suggested that since the plaintiff might claim against the charterer for breach of contract there was no loss, and the court had to decide whether such a claim was possible. *Held*—The delay consequent upon the stranding of the vessel put an end, in the commercial sense, to the venture, so that the charterer was released from his obligations and was free to hire another ship. Therefore, the plaintiff had no claim against the charterer and could claim the loss of the charter from the defendants.

The operation of the doctrine of frustration is based upon the assumption that the frustrating event was not the fault of either party.

(190) *Maritime National Fish Ltd* v *Ocean Trawlers Ltd* [1935] A.C. 524

The respondents were the owners and the appellants the charterers of a steam trawler, the *St Cuthbert.* The *St Cuthbert* was fitted with, and could only operate with, an otter trawl. When the charter party was renewed on 25 October 1932, both parties knew that it was illegal to operate with an otter trawl without a licence from the Minister. The appellants operated five trawlers and applied for five licences. The Minister granted only three and said that the appellants could choose the names of three trawlers for the licences. The appellants chose three but deliberately excluded the *St Cuthbert* though they could have included it. They were now sued by the owners for the charter fee, and their defence was that the charter party was frustrated because it would have been illegal to fish with the *St Cuthbert*. It was *held* that the contract was not frustrated, in the sense that the frustrating event was self-induced by the appellants and that therefore they were liable for the hire.

Comment. An otter trawl is a type of net which can, because of its narrow mesh, pick up small immature fish. Its use is restricted for environmental reasons.

Judicial opinion has been divided upon the issue of whether leases and contracts for the sale of land can be frustrated.

(191) *Cricklewood Property and Investment Trust Ltd* v *Leighton's Investment Trust Ltd* [1945] A.C. 221

In May 1936, a building lease was granted between the parties for 99 years, but before any building had been erected war broke out in 1939 and government restrictions on building materials and labour meant that the lessees could not erect the buildings as they intended, these buildings being in fact shops. Leighton's sued originally for rent due under the lease and Cricklewood, the builders, said the lease was frustrated. The House of Lords *held* that the doctrine of frustration did no apply because the interruption from 1939 to 1945 was not sufficient in duration to frustrate the lease, and so they did not deal specifically with the general position regarding frustration of leases, basing their judgment on the question of the degree of interruption. In so far as they did deal with the general position this was *obiter*, but Lord Simon thought that there could be cases in which a lease would be frustrated, and the example that he quoted was a building lease where the land was declared a permanent open space before building took place; here he thought that the fundamental purpose of the transaction would be defeated. Lord Wright took much the same view on the same example. Lord Russell thought frustration could not apply to a lease of real property, and Lord Goddard, C.J., took the same view. Lord Porter expressed no opinion with regard to leases generally and so this case does not finally solve the problem.

Comment. (i) Even if the courts were prepared to apply the doctrine of frustration, it would not often apply to leases, particularly long leases. In a lease for 99 years a tenant temporarily deprived of possession as by requisition of the property would hardly ever be out of possession long enough to satisfy the test of frustration (See below.)

(ii) In *National Carriers* v *Panalpina (Northern)* [1981] 1 All E.R. 161 the House of Lords were of the opinion that a lease could be frustrated. The plaintiffs leased a warehouse to the defendants for 10 years. The Hull City Council closed the only access to it because a listed building nearby was in a dangerous condition. The access road was closed for 20 months. The defendants refused to pay the rent for this period. The House of Lords said that they must. A lease could be frustrated, they said, but 20 months out of 10 years was not enough to frustrate it in the particular circumstances of this case. Once again, therefore, the decision of the House of Lords on the matter of frustration of leases was *obiter*.

(192) *Hillingdon Estates Co.* v *Stonefield Estates Ltd* [1952] Ch. 627

By a contract dated 13 January 1938, the vendors, Stonefield, and the plaintiffs, Hillingdon, who were the purchasers, agreed to buy and sell a freehold. The purchasers were to take a conveyance on 31 January 1939, and the use of the land was to be for building an estate only. The completion was delayed by the outbreak of war and on 11 October 1948, the contract was still not completed by a conveyance, and at that time the Middlesex County Council compulsorily purchased the land, leaving the owners with the compensation which would, of course, be less than the market value in 1948. The plaintiffs said that the contract was discharged. They did not ask for rescission but for a declaratory judgment to this effect and the defendants claimed specific performance. It was *held* that the plaintiffs failed and the defendants succeeded and specific performance was granted, the plaintiffs' claim being refused. It would appear from this case therefore that the doctrine of frustration does not apply to a contract for the sale of land once a legal or equitable estate has passed.

Comment. In *Amalgamated Investment and Property Co Ltd* v *John Walker & Sons Ltd* [1976] 3 All E.R. 509, Buckley, L.J., was prepared to presume that the doctrine of frustration could be applied to contracts for the sale of land, though once again this decision was *obiter* because he did not have to apply the doctrine in this case. Walker sold a warehouse to Amalgamated, both parties believing that the property was suitable and capable of being redeveloped. After the contract was made the Department of the Environment included it in a list of buildings of architectural and historic interest so that development became more difficult. The Court of Appeal held that the contract was not frustrated. The listing merely affected the value of the property and the purchaser always took the risk of this in terms of a listing order or, indeed, compulsory purchase. The contract could be completed according to its terms and specific performance was granted to Walkers. Nor was the contract voidable under *Solle* v *Butcher* 1950[105] because the mistake did not exist at the date of the contract.

Before the Law Reform (Frustrated Contracts) Act 1943 the position at common law was that frustration did not rescind the contract *ab initio* (from the beginning), it only released the parties from further performance, leaving intact any legal rights already accrued.

(193) *Chandler* v *Webster* [1904] 1 K.B. 493

The defendant agreed to let the plaintiff have a room for the purpose of viewing the Coronation procession on 26 June 1902, for £141 15s. The contract provided that the money be payable immediately. The procession did not take place because of the illness of the King and the plaintiff, who had paid £100 on account, left the balance unpaid. The plaintiff sued to recover the £100 and the defendant counter-claimed for £41 15s. It was *held* by the Court of Appeal that the plaintiff's action failed and the defendant's counter-claim succeeded because the obligation to pay the rent had fallen due before the frustrating event.

The fact that the plaintiff does not know that he can sue is, with the exception of claims for personal injuries, irrelevant to the claim being statute-barred. There is, however, an exception where the plaintiff's lack of knowledge results from the defendant's fraud or from an operative mistake.

(194) *Lynn* v *Bamber* [1930] 2 K.B. 72

In 1921 the plaintiff purchased some plum trees from the defendant, and was given a warranty that the trees were 'Purple Pershores'. In 1928 the plaintiff discovered that the trees were not 'Purple Pershores' and sued for damages. The defendant pleaded that the claim was barred by the Statutes of Limitation. *Held*—The defendant's fraudulent misrepresentation and fraudulent concealment of the breach of warranty provided a good answer to this plea, so that the plaintiff could recover.

Comment. The present jurisdiction is s.32 of the Limitation Act 1980.

Income tax must be taken into account in assessing damages. This is but one aspect of the rule that damages are compensatory. The plaintiff must not be made better off.

(195) *Beach* v *Reed Corrugated Cases Ltd* [1956] 2 All E.R. 652

This was an action brought by the plaintiff for wrongful dismissal by the defendants. The plaintiff was the managing director of the company and he had a 15-year contract from 21 December 1950 at a salary of £5000 per annum. His contract was terminated in August 1954 when he was 54 years old and the sum of money that he might have earned would have been £55,000, but the general damages awarded to him were £18,000 after the Court had taken into account income tax, including tax on his private investments.

Comment. In *C. & P. Haulage* v *Middleton* [1983] 3 All E.R. 94, C. & P. let Mr Middleton have a licence for six months, renewable, of premises from which he conducted a business as a self-employed engineer. He lived in a council house and would have used his own garage there, but the council objected. There was a quarrel between the parties and M was evicted from the premises before the licence term expired. This was a breach of contract by C. & P. M stopped a cheque which was payable to C. & P. because of his grievance. They sued him on it. He counter-claimed for damages because of his eviction. In fact the council had let him use his own garage for the remainder of the six months' term. *Held*—by the Court of Appeal—that since he had paid no rent for the premises in which he had worked following his eviction, he was not worse off than if the contract had been properly carried out. It was not the function of the Court to put a plaintiff in a better position than he would have been if the contract had not been broken. Only nominal damages were awarded.

The principles regarding remoteness of damage laid down in the following case have been restated on a number of occasions, latterly by the House of Lords in the *Heron II.* Damage will be recoverable if it is in the contemplation of the reasonable man or where there is knowledge of special circumstances involving risk which the evidence indicates that the defendant has accepted.

(196) *Hadley* v *Baxendale* (1854) 9 Exch. 341

The plaintiff was a miller at Gloucester. The driving shaft of the mill being broken, the plaintiff engaged the defendant, a carrier, to take it to the makers at Greenwich so that they might use it in making a new one. The defendant delayed delivery of the shaft beyond a reasonable time, so that the mill was idle for much longer than should have been necessary. The plaintiff now sued in respect of loss of profits during the period of additional delay. The Court decided that there were only two possible grounds on which the plaintiff could succeed—(1) That in the usual course of things the work of the mill would cease altogether for want of the shaft. This the Court rejected because, to take only one reasonable possibility, the plaintiff might have had a spare. (2) That the special circumstances were fully explained, so that the defendant was made aware of the possible loss. The evidence showed that there had been no such explanation. In fact the only information given to the defendant was that the article to be carried was the broken shaft of a mill, and that the plaintiff was the miller of that mill. *Held*—The plaintiff's claim failed, the damage being too remote.

(197) *Horne* v *Midland Railway Co.* (1873) L.R. 8 C.P. 131

The plaintiff had entered into a contract to sell 4595 pairs of boots to the French Army at a price above the market price. The defendants were responsible for a delay in the delivery of boots, and the purchasers refused to accept delivery, regarding time as the essence of the contract. The plaintiff's claim for damages was based on the contract price, namely 4s per pair, but it was held that he could only recover the market price of 2s 9d per pair unless he could show the defendants were aware of the exceptional profit involved, and that they had undertaken to be liable for its loss.

(198) *Victoria Laundry Ltd* v *Newman Industries Ltd* [1949] 2 K.B. 528

The defendants agreed to deliver a new boiler to the plaintiffs by a certain date but failed to do so, being 22 weeks late, with the result that the plaintiff lost (1) normal business profits during the period of delay, and (2) profits from dyeing contracts which were offered to them during the period. It was *held* that (1) but not (2) were recoverable as damages.

(199) *The Heron II* (*Koufos* v *Czarnikow*) [1967] 3 All E.R. 686

Shipowners carrying sugar from Constanza to Basrah delayed delivery at Basrah for nine days during which time the market in sugar there fell and the charterers lost more than £4000. It was *held* that they could recover that sum from the shipowners because the very existence of a 'market' for goods implied that prices might fluctuate and fall in sugar prices was likely or in contemplation.

Comment. It is not enough that the defendant knows that there are special circumstances; there must also be evidence that he accepts the risk. In this case the House of Lords held that the carrier must be regarded as having accepted the risk. The carriers knew that there was a market in Basrah and that delay would cause loss which is why the contract provided for carriage 'with all convenient speed'.

The law imposes a duty upon the plaintiff to take all reasonable steps to mitigate (or minimize) the loss following from a breach of contract. Failure to do so prevents a claim by the plaintiff for any part of the damage which is due to his failure to mitigate.

(200) *Brace* v *Calder* [1895] 2 Q.B. 253

The defendants, a partnership consisting of four members, agreed to employ the plaintiff as manager of a branch of the business for two years. Five months later the partnership was dissolved by the retirement of two of the members and the business was transferred to the other two who offered to employ the plaintiff on the same terms as before but he refused the offer. The dissolution of the partnership constituted a wrongful dismissal of the plaintiff and he brought an action for breach of contract seeking to recover the salary that he would have received had he served the whole period of two years. It was *held* that he was entitled only to nominal damages since it was unreasonable to have rejected the offer of continued employment.

There is a presumption of penalty where a single sum is payable by way of compensation on the occurrence of a number of events, some of which might cause serious loss, but not others.

(201) *Ford Motor Co. (England) Ltd* v *Armstrong* (1915) 31 T.L.R. 267

The defendant was a retailer who received supplies from the plaintiffs. As part of his agreement with the plaintiffs the defendant had undertaken—

(1) not to sell any of the plaintiffs' cars or spares below list price;
(2) not to sell Ford cars to other dealers in the motor trade;
(3) not to exhibit any car supplied by the company without their permission.

The defendant also agreed to pay £250 for every breach of the agreement as being the agreed damage which the manufacturer will 'sustain'. The defendant was in breach of the agreement and the plaintiffs sued. It was *held* by the Court of Appeal that the sum of £250 was in the nature of a penalty and not liquidated damages. The same sum was payable for different kinds of breach which were not likely to produce the same loss. Furthermore its size suggested that it was not a genuine pre-estimate of loss.

If the compensation agreed between the parties is in the nature of liquidated damages, the Court cannot give more or less than the sum agreed.

(202) *Cellulose Acetate Silk Co. Ltd* v *Widnes Foundry Ltd* [1933] A.C. 20

The Widnes Foundry entered into a contract to erect a plant for the Silk Co. by a certain date. It was also agreed that the Widnes Foundry would pay the Silk Co. £20 per week for every week they took in erecting the plant beyond the agreed date. In the event the erection was completed 30 weeks late, and the Silk Co. claimed for their actual loss which was £5850. *Held*—The Widness Foundry were only liable to pay £20 per week as agreed.

A claim on a *quantum meruit* may be brought where work is done under a void contract.

(203) *Craven-Ellis* v *Canons Ltd* [1936] 2 All E.R. 1066

The plaintiff was employed as managing director by the company under a deed which provided for remuneration. The Articles provided that directors must have qualification shares, and must obtain these within two months of appointment. The plaintiff and other directors who appointed him never obtained the required number of shares so that the deed was invalid. However the plaintiff had rendered services, and he now sued on a *quantum meruit* for a reasonable sum by way of remuneration. *Held*—He succeeded on a *quantum meruit*, there being no valid contract.

Where a contract contains an express negative stipulation breach of that stipulation may be restrained by injunction. A negative stipulation will not be implied for this purpose.

(204) *Warner Brothers Pictures Incorporated* v *Nelson* [1937] 1 K.B. 209

The defendant, the film actress Bette Davis, had entered into a contract in which she agreed to act exclusively for the plaintiffs for 12 months. She was anxious to obtain more money and so she left America, and entered into a contract with a person in England. The plaintiffs now asked for an injunction restraining the defendant from carrying out the English contract. *Held*—An injunction would be granted. The contract contained a negative stipulation not to work for anyone else, and this could be enforced. However, since the contract was an American one, the Court limited the operation of the injunction to the area of the Court's jurisdiction, and although the contract stipulated that the defendant would not work in any other occupation, the injunction was confined to work on stage or screen.

Comment. Even where, as here, there is a negative stipulation, the court will not grant an injunction if the pressure to work for the plaintiffs is so severe as to be for all practical purposes irresistable. In this case it was said that Bette Davis could still earn her living by doing other work.

(205) *Whitwood Chemical Co.* v *Hardman* [1891] 2 Ch. 416

The defendant entered into a contract of service with the plaintiffs and agreed to give the whole of his time to them. In fact he occasionally worked for others, and the plaintiffs tried to enforce the undertaking in the service contract by injunction. *Held*—An injunction could be granted because there was no express negative stipulation. The defendant had merely stated what he would do, and not what he would not do. and to read into the undertaking an agreement not to work for anyone else required the court to imply a negative stipulation from a positive one. No such implication could be made.

Comment. It is because of the fact that the granting of an injunction of a negative stipulation is so close to specific performance that it is restricted to cases where the negative stipulation is express.

Where money has been paid under a contract of which there is total failure of consideration, e.g. on a sale of goods failure to obtain a title, the payer may recover the money paid in quasi-contract.

(206) *Rowland* v *Divall* [1923] 2 K.B. 500

In April 1922, the defendant brought an 'Albert' motor car from a man who had stolen it from the true owner. One month later the plaintiff, a dealer, purchased the car from the defendant for £334, repainted it, and sold it for £400 to Colonel Railsdon. In September 1922, the police seized the car from Colonel Railsdon and the plaintiff repaid him the £400. The plaintiff now sued the defendant for £344 on the grounds that there had been a total failure of consideration since the plaintiff had not obtained a title to the car. *Held*—The defendant was in breach of s.12 of the Sale of Goods Act, which implies conditions and warranties into a sale of goods relating to the seller's right to sell, and there had been a total failure of consideration in spite of the fact that the car had been used by the plaintiff and his purchaser. The plaintiff contracted for the property in the car and not the mere right to possess it. Since he had not obtained the property, he was entitled to recover the sum of £334 and no deductions should be made for the period of use.

Comment. Although the court purported to deal with this case as a breach of s.12(1) of the Act, it would appear that in fact they operated on common-law principles and gave complete restitution of the purchase price because of total failure of consideration arising out of the seller's lack of title. The condition under s.12(1) had by reason of the plaintiff's use of the car and the passage of time become a warranty when the action was brought, and if the Court had been awarding damages for breach of warranty it would have had to reduce the sum of £334 by a sum representing the value to the plaintiff of the use of the vehicle which he had had.

The drawback to making an allowance to the seller for use is that he gets an allowance for a car which is not his and the owner might sue the buyer in damages for conversion so that he would have to pay an allowance and damages to the true owner in conversion. In other words pay for use twice.

Agency

A court may be prepared to add to an agent's actual authority by implying powers not expressly contained in the contract of agency.

(207) *Comber* v *Anderson* (1808) 1 Camp. 523

A merchant instructed his agent, an insurance broker, to insure a cargo of corn, but gave no specific instructions as to the type of policy or with whom it was to be effected. The broker effected a policy with a company which used an exception clause excluding liability for the loss of cargo by the stranding of the ship. There were private underwriters who did not insist on such a clause. The ship carrying the cargo was stranded and there was a loss for which the merchant could not recover under the insurance. The question arose as to whether the agent was liable as having no authority to make such a policy. *Held*—Since the agent was given a discretion, authority to make the sort of policy he had made was implied. There was no suggestion of fraud and the agent was free to elect as between insurers.

(208) *Australia and New Zealand Bank* v *Ateliers de Constructions Electriques de Charleroi* [1966] 2 W.L.R. 1216

The Belgian company sued the Australian bank for conversion of cheques drawn payable to the company and indorsed and paid by the company's Australian agent into his own account at the bank. The agent had no express authority to pay the company's cheques into his own account though if he had been paid cash he would have had authority to receive the money. The company had no bank account in Australia and they knew that their agent there had previously paid large sums into his own account, at the bank under other contracts. The company had given no instructions and had made no enquiry as to their agent's methods of receiving money and making remittances and had no complaint about the method on discovering what it was, until the Australian agent could not, because of liquidation, pay over £55,540 18s 7d of the company's money. *Held*—by the Privy Council—that in all the circumstances authority could be implied in the agent and the company's action failed.

A principal is bound by acts falling within the usual authority of his agent. Secret instructions limiting the authority of the agent are of no effect.

(209) *Watteau* v *Fenwick* [1893] 1 Q.B. 346

For some time prior to 1888 the Victoria Hotel, Stockton-on-Tees, had been owned by a Mr Humble. In 1888 he sold the hotel to the defendants but remained in the hotel as manager, his name remaining on the door and the licence continuing in his name. The defendants had forbidden Humble to buy cigars on credit, but he bought a supply from the plaintiff who gave credit to Humble personally since he did not know of the existence of the defendants. When the plaintiff discovered what the true situation was, he brought this action against the defendants for the price of the cigars. *Held*—The cigars were articles which would usually be supplied to and dealt in at such an establishment, and Humble was acting within the scope of his *usual authority* as the manager of such a house. The defendants were bound by the contract made by Humble and could not set up secret instructions to him as a defence to the plaintiff's action.

Comment. If the third party knows of the agent's lack of authority he does not obtain a contract with the principal.

By reason of the rule of apparent authority (or agency by estoppel), a third party may be able to rely on the appearance of consent by the principal to a contract made through a person held out as an agent.

(210) *Spiro* v *Lintern* [1973] 3 All E.R. 319

The defendant owned a house which he was considering selling. He agreed with his wife that she would find a purchaser for the property. However, he did not authorize her to enter into any contract. Nevertheless, she made a contract to sell the house to the plaintiff, and the defendant, knowing of this, allowed the plaintiff to have repairs carried out to the house and also to have work done in the garden. In this action for specific performance by the plaintiff it was *held* that as the defendant knew that the plaintiff was acting on the assumption that the defendant's wife had authority, he, the defendant was under a duty to tell him she had no authority, and as he had not done so he was estopped from denying her authority to enter into the contract. Thus the plaintiff's action succeeded.

(211) *Dodsley* v *Varley* (1840) 12 A. & E. 632

The defendant's agent W occasionally employed B to purchase wool on behalf of the defendant. B's previous puchases from the plaintiff had always been ratified by the defendant. In June 1839, the defendant wrote to B saying that he did not wish B to make any further purchases for him. In July 1839 B bought wool from the plaintiff which the defendant refused to pay for and the plaintiff now sued for the price. *Held*—The plaintiff succeeded. B was the defendant's agent by *apparent authority*, and although there was some doubt as to whether the revocation of authority was notified to the plaintiff, the jury found as a fact that the plaintiff did not have such notice when he sold the wool.

(212) *Povey* v *Taylor* (1966) 116 New L.J. 1656

The defendants ran an agency for pop artists and from time to time they had leaflets printed by the plaintiffs. The defendants let a room on their premises to X who also ran an entertainment agency. X placed orders with the plaintiffs for leaflets and the defendants were aware that he had done so and, in fact, advertised their own agency in one of X's leaflets. The plaintiffs sent a number of invoices on behalf of X's leaflets to the defendants who did not challenge them. X disappeared owing the plaintiff £75 for work done to his order and in this action the plaintiffs sought to recover that sum from the defendants. The defendants denied liability, saying that X was not their agent and had no authority to order leaflets on their behalf. *Held*—by the Court of Appeal—the defendants were aware that the plaintiffs were printing leaflets to X's order and had not challenged invoices sent by the plaintiffs. In the circumstances it was reasonable for the plaintiffs to assume that X was ordering the leaflets with the authority of the defendants and the defendants were therefore estopped from denying that X had such authority.

In an emergency a person may have an implied authority to bind

another by an act done in good faith on his behalf in circumstances of commercial necessity where there is no opportunity of communicating with him.

(213) *Great Northern Railway Co* v *Swaffield* (1874) L.R. 9 Ex. 132

The defendant sent an unattended horse by the plaintiffs' trains from King's Cross to Sandy, Bedfordshire. The horse arrived at Sandy at 10.8 p.m. but there was no one to meet it. The officials at Sandy station did not know the defendant or his address and accordingly the station master directed that the horse be put into a livery stable near to the station. Shortly afterwards the defendant's servant arrived to collect the horse and was told that it was in the livery stable and that he could have it for a charge of 6d. He refused to pay, as did the defendant when informed of the situation. The dispute over the charges went on and the horse was eventually delivered to the defendant four months later, the plaintiffs having paid £17 for stable charges. They now sued to recover this sum of money. *Held*—They could recover it. The plaintiffs were agents of necessity to incur expense in looking after the horse which they could not deliver.

(214) *Springer* v *Great Western Railway Co.* [1921] 1 K.B. 257

The defendants agreed to carry tomatoes for the plaintiff from Jersey to Covent Garden market. The ship was late in arriving at Weymouth, and when it did arrive the defendant's employees were on strike. When the cargo was unloaded by casual labour some of the tomatoes were good and some were bad. However, the defendants' traffic agent decided to sell the whole consignment locally because he felt that they could not be taken to Covent Garden in time to arrive in saleable condition. He did not communicate with any of the consignees, the plaintiff being one. The plaintiff claimed damages in conversion based on the market price of the goods at Covent Garden, and since the strike had caused shortages, this price was high. The defendants claimed that in the circumstances they must be considered as having a right to sell. The plaintiff said that if he had been informed of the position he could have got lorries to transport the goods to London. *Held*—The plaintiff was entitled to damages because the defendants were not in the position of agents of necessity so long as they could communicate with the owner and get his instructions.

(215) *Prager* v *Blatspiel, Stamp and Heacock Ltd* [1924] 1 K.B. 566

The plaintiff was a fur dealer in Bucharest and the defendants were fur dealers in London. Between 1915 and 1916 the plaintiff asked the defendants to buy certain skins for him and to have them dressed and delivered to Bucharest as soon as possible. Skins to the value of £1900 were bought by the defendants, but they were unable to deliver them to the plaintiff because of the occupation of Rumania by the Germans at the end of 1916. During 1917 and 1918, when the market in skins was rising rapidly, the defendants sold the skins. When hostilities ceased the plaintiff wrote to the defendants asking for delivery of the skins, but was informed that they had been sold. He now sued in conversion. The defendants contended that they were agents of necessity. *Held*—They were not, and were liable for conversion. The furs being dressed, could have been stored until the end of hostilities and the plaintiff was entitled to damages.

(216) *Sachs* v *Miklos* [1948] 1 All E.R. 67

In 1940 the plaintiff made an arrangement with the defendant under which she was to store the plaintiff's dining room furniture in a room in her boarding house. In 1944 the boarding house was damaged by enemy action and the plaintiff found it necessary to use the storage room for her boarders. The plaintiff had ceased to visit the defendant in 1941 but she obtained an address from his bank and wrote to him asking him to remove the furniture. She received no reply and wrote again saying that unless she was instructed to the contrary she would sell the furniture. No reply was received to this letter and, after further attempts to get in touch with the plaintiff by telephone, the defendant sold the furniture in July 1944, by auction. The furniture realized £13. The plaintiff later heard of the sale and now sued Mrs Miklos and the auctioneer in detinue and for conversion, claiming £115, the current value of the furniture. *Held*—The defendants were not agents of necessity and were liable. In this sort of action damages are usually awarded on the value of goods at the date of judgment, but in this case a new trial was ordered in the county court to decide whether the plaintiff ever received the letters, because, if he did, damages would be assessed as at the date of receipt.

Comment. A somewhat similar case is *Munro* v *Willmott* [1949] 1 K.B. 295, where the owner of a motor car parked it in the yard of an inn with the landlord's consent. She left the district and the car was then causing an obstruction to other garage users. The landlord, being unable to communicate with the owner, sold the car but was held liable in conversion.

Not everyone who preserves or confers a benefit on the property of another will be regarded as entitled to deal with it as an agent of necessity. However, the Court can, under the Rules of Supreme Court, order a sale in an appropriate case.

(217) *Larner* v *Fawcett* [1950] 2 All E.R. 727

The defendant owned a racehorse and made an agreement with a Mr Davis under which it was agreed that Davis would train and race the filly and receive half of any prize money she might win. Davis, unknown to the defendant, agreed to let Larner have the animal to train. Larner did so, and when his charges had reached £125, he discovered that Fawcett was the true owner. Larner, being unable to recover the cost of training and feeding the filly from Davis, who had no funds, now applied to the Court for an order of sale. Fawcett was brought in as defendant. *Held*—by the Court of Appeal—that Larner had a common-law lien for his charges, and although such a lien does not carry with it a power of sale, the power given in the Rules of the Supreme Court to make an order for sale was appropriate here, particularly since the filly 'was eating her head off'. Fawcett had not made any attempt to get his property back but had made Davis look like the owner. An order for sale would therefore be made unless Fawcett paid into Court the amount of Larner's charges by a given date.

(218) *Binstead* v *Buck* (1777) 2 Wm. Bl. 1117

The plaintiff lost his pointer dog and one year later found it on the defendant's property. The defendant said that it had strayed there and refused to give up the dog unless the plaintiff paid him £1 per week for the 20 weeks it had been in the defendant's possession. *Held*—The plaintiff was entitled to recover the animal and, although the point was not fully considered by the Court, it appears that the defendant was not entitled to any compensation for the cost of keeping the dog.

Comment. A finder of livestock which has done damage to his property may detain it, subject to the notice to the owner and police, for compensation supported by a right of sale. (Animals Act 1971.)

(219) *Nicholson* v *Chapman* (1793) 2 Hy. Bl. 254

Certain timber which was stacked on the bank of a river accidentally slipped into the water and was carried downstream where the defendant took it into his care. The owner, having discovered its whereabouts, now claimed it back, but the defendant would not release it until he was paid £6 10s 4d for looking after it. *Held*—The defendant was liable in conversion and had no right to compensation for the cost of looking after the timber.

An undisclosed principal is unable to ratify a contract made on his behalf by an agent.

(220) *Keighley, Maxsted & Co.* v *Durant* [1901] A.C. 240

The appellants were corn merchants at Hull and the respondent was a corn merchant in London. On 11 May, Durant offered wheat by telegram to a corn merchant in Wakefield by the name of Roberts. The offer was to sell 500 tons of White Wheat of 46s per quarter and 500 tons of Red Wheat at 45s per quarter. Roberts discussed the offer with the appellants' manager, a Mr Wright, and Wright told Roberts that if Roberts could get White Wheat for 45s 3d and the Red for 44s 3d,

Roberts and Keighley, Maxsted and Co. would buy it on joint account. Roberts could not get the price but later on, after apparently abandoning the joint account purchase, Roberts bought the wheat for 45s 6d white, and 44s 6d red. Roberts informed Wright of this and Wright said that it was too dear but to go ahead. It was a question whether this statement could be treated by the court as a ratification. Roberts refused to take delivery of the wheat and Durant resold it at a loss and now sued Roberts and the appellants as joint purchasers. *Held*—The appellants were not liable. Where a person makes a contract purporting to act on his own behalf, but having an undisclosed intention to give the benefit of the contract to a third party, the contract cannot be ratified by that third party so as to make him able to sue or liable to be sued on the contract.

A forgery cannot be *ratified.* However a person may be *estopped* from denying the genuineness of his signature.

(221) *Greenwood* v *Martins Bank Ltd* [1933] A.C. 51

The appellant, who was a dairyman in Blackpool, opened with the respondents a joint account in the name of himself and his wife. Cheques drawn on this account were to bear the signatures of them both. Later on the appellant opened a further account with the respondents in his own name, though the wife kept the pass books and cheque books in respect of both accounts. In October 1929, Greenwood asked his wife to give him a cheque, saying he wanted to draw £20 from his own account. His wife then told him that there was no money in the bank, and that she had used it to help her sister who was involved in legal proceedings over property. He asked her who had forged his signature but she would not say. However, she did ask him not to inform the respondents of the forgeries until her sister's case was over. Greenwood complied with this request until 5 June 1930, when he discovered that there were no legal proceedings instituted by his wife's sister and that his wife had been deceiving him. He told his wife that he intended to go to the bank and reveal her forgeries, but before he actually made the visit she shot herself. Greenwood now claimed £410 6s 0d from the Bank on the grounds that this sum had been paid out of his own account and the joint account by means of forged cheques. The Bank pleaded ratification, adoption or estoppel. *Held*—There could be no ratification or adoption in this sort of case, but the essential elements of estoppel were present. The appellant's failure to inform the Bank was a representation that the cheques were good. The Bank has suffered a detriment because, if Greenwood had told the Bank when his wife first confessed to forgery, they might have brought an action against her. Under the law *existing at that time* they could not bring such an action after her death. The Bank had, therefore, a legal right to debit Greenwood's account with the amount of the forged cheques.

Comment. The facts of this case occurred before the passing of the Law Reform (Miscellaneous Provisions) Act 1934. At common law a personal action died with the person. Under the 1934 Act causes of action existing at the time of a person's death survive for or against his estate.

Ratification dates back to the time when the agent did the act being ratified. The agent is thus put in the same position as if he had had authority to do the act at the time when he did it.

(222) *Bolton Partners* v *Lambert* (1889) 41 Ch.D. 295

The plaintiffs claimed specific performance of an agreement under which the defendant was to take a lease of the plaintiffs' premises. Preliminary negotiations had taken place between Lambert and a Mr Scratchley, who was a director of the plaintiff company. As a result of these negotiations, the defendant wrote to the plaintiffs on 8 December 1887, offering to take the lease. On 9 December, Scratchley wrote to Lambert to say that the offer would be placed before the Board, and on 13 December 1887 Scratchley wrote to the defendant stating erroneously that the directors had accepted his offer. On 13 January 1888, the defendant wrote to the plaintiffs alleging that he had been misled as to the value of certain plant and machinery on the premises, and stated that he withdrew all offers made to the plaintiffs in any way. Evidence showed that Scratchley had no authority to bind the company when he wrote the letters of 9 and 13 December. The matter had not been put before the Board but merely a works committee which had no authority to bind the company. The Board did ratify Scratchley's acts but not until after 13 January 1888. *Held*—The acceptance by Scratchley would have constituted a contract in all respects except for his lack of authority. However, once that authority was given, it was thrown back to the time when the act was done by Scratchley and prevented the defendant from withdrawing his offer because it was then no longer an offer but a binding contract.

A principal cannot ratify an insurance policy made by his agent without authority if the loss insured against has occurred. There is an exception in the case of marine insurance.

(223) *Grover and Grover Ltd* v *Mathews* [1910] 2 K.B. 401

The plaintiffs claimed to be entitled to recover for total loss under a policy of fire insurance on their pianoforte factory at New Southgate effected with the defendant and other underwriters at Lloyds. The plaintiffs took out a Lloyd's policy in March 1908, for 12 months from 26 March 1908. This policy was effected through a Mr Brows who was the manager of the London and Provincial Bank at New Southgate. Brows had dealt with a broker named Dott. In March 1909, Brows wrote to Dott asking him whether a renewal notice would be sent for the plaintiffs' policy. At the time he wrote the letter Brows had moved to another bank and had no instructions from the plaintiffs to insure. Nevertheless Dott prepared a slip to insure the plaintiffs' factory for a further 12 months from 26 March 1909. The slip was initialled by the defendants' representative, but Brows did not tell the plaintiffs at the time that he had effected the insurance. When he did inform them there was an argument about the amount of the premium which lasted from 19 March until 26 March, when Brows wrote the plaintiffs saying he could not get the rate reduced. On the afternoon of 27 March, the factory was destroyed by fire, and later the same day the directors of the plaintiff company tendered a cheque for the premium and reported the fire. The underwriters would not accept liability. *Held*—There could be no retrospective ratification in this case. The rule that a principal could ratify an insurance even after the loss was anomalous. Such a right existed only in connection with marine insurance (see Marine Insurance Act 1906, s.86) and it was not desirable to extend it.

Comment. Whether the principal knew or not that the property was lost would seem irrelevant. A contract cannot be ratified at a time when the principal could not have made it. Thus, if the principal's property was in fact lost he could not have validly insured it himself.

The rule of retrospective ratification does not apply if it would cause excessive hardship to the third party.

(224) *Walter* v *James* (1871) L.R. 6 Exch. 124

One Southall, who was acting for the defendant, induced the plaintiff to accept £60 in full discharge of a liability the defendant had to the plaintiff on a bill. Before the money was handed over, James withdrew Southall's authority, but Southall nevertheless paid Walter. When Walter discovered that the payment had been made without authority, he agreed to return the money to Southall. Walter then sued James for the money, and at that stage James purported to ratify Southall's act of payment, hoping to prevent Walter from succeeding on the grounds that the money had already been paid by his agent and that Walter had handed it back voluntarily. *Held*—Ratification was not possible here because, if it was allowed, the plaintiff would lose his action and would suffer undue hardship.

An acceptance by an agent subject to ratification by his principal is legally a nullity until ratification. If, by the time ratification takes place the offer concerned has been withdrawn, there is no contract.

(225) *Watson* v *Davies* [1931] 1 Ch. 455

The plaintiff sued on behalf of the Board of Management of an Institution for the Blind and asked for specific performance of a contract to sell premises called Colet House situated at Rhyl and owned by the defendant. The following facts emerged from the evidence. Preliminary negotiations had taken place between the plaintiff and a Mr Bannister, one of the directors of the Institution, regarding the purchase of Colet House but nothing was settled at that stage. On 7 January 1930, the defendant wrote to Bannister stating a price of £6500 for Colet House, plus fittings, and adding that a Miners' Welfare Committee was also interested. The Board of the Institution for the Blind met on 9 January 1930, and authorized certain members of the Board to accept the defendant's offer if they thought Colet House suitable for a home for the blind. On 11 January 1930, 12 members of the Board went with the plaintiff and Mr Bannister to inspect the premises. They agreed to buy 'subject to the ratification of the full Board'. A meeting of the full Board was called for 14 January to ratify the agreement. On the morning of 14 January, the defendant, having received a better offer from the Miner's Welfare Committee, sent a telegram to Mr Bannister saying: 'Colet House, Rhyl. Please treat all negotiations between us as cancelled. Property not for sale. R.L. Davies,' This telegram was before the Board of the Institution for the Blind when it met on the afternoon of the 14 January. The Board nevertheless ratified the acts of the deputation of 11 January, and purported to accept the offer made at that time by Davies. *Held*—The ratification was ineffective. An acceptance by an agent subject to ratification by his principal is legally a nullity until ratification, and, being a conditional acceptance, is not binding on the other party. Since the defendant had revoked the offer before ratification took place, he was not bound to the plaintiffs.

(226) *Warehousing and Forwarding Company of East Africa Ltd* v *Jafferali and Sons Ltd* [1963] 3 All E.R. 571

The respondents were trying to lease a warehouse to the appellants. The appellants' branch manager seemed to have entered into an agreement for a lease but his acts were subject to the ratification of the appellants' general manager. Whether the respondents knew this or not, they certainly knew that the branch manager did not have a general authority to bind the appellants. Before ratification the offer to lease the warehouse was withdrawn. *Held*—Following *Watson* v *Davies*[225] the branch manager's acceptance was conditional and no contract came into being before ratification. Until then the offer could be revoked. The Privy Council also suggested (*obiter*) that, even when the agent's acceptance is not made expressly 'subject to ratification' but the third party is on notice that the agent's authority is limited, neither the agent's principal nor the third party is bound until ratification. The decision throws doubt on the case of *Bolton Partners* v *Lambert*[222]

A sub-agent who merely assists the agent in his work and is not in privity of contract with the principal cannot normally be sued by the principal. There is an exception in the case of sub-bailees of goods.

(227) *Learoyd Bros & Co.* v *Pope & Sons* [1966] 2 Lloyd's Rep. 142

The plaintiffs entered into an agreement with a carrier for the transport of their goods. The carrier subcontracted the work to the defendants, who were also a firm of carriers, though the plaintiffs had no notice of this arrangement. The lorry was stolen while the defendant's driver was in the wharf office upon arrival at London Docks, and the carrier with whom the plaintiffs had contracted paid some of the plaintiffs' loss and the plaintiffs now sued the defendants for the balance. *Held*—The defendants were bailees to the plaintiffs, notwithstanding the absence of any contract between them, and the defendants' driver was negligent in leaving the lorry unattended, and therefore the defendants were liable for the plaintiffs' loss.

An agent has a duty to show proper skill and care in carrying out his agency.

(228) *Keppel* v *Wheeler* [1927] 1 K.B. 577

The plaintiff sued the defendants, who were estate agents at Walham Green, for damages for breach of duty whilst acting as his agents. The plaintiff had instructed the defendants to sell a block of flats of which he was the owner. The flats were valued at £7000 but the plaintiff was desirous of a quick sale, and when the defendants introduced a purchaser, E, who was prepared to offer £6150, the plaintiff instructed the defendants to go ahead, and an agreement to sell 'subject to contract' was made. This agreement was not, of course, binding on the parties. Before contracts were exchanged, another purchaser, D, offered to pay £6750 but the defendants told him that the flats were sold, and instead of communicating with the plaintiff they put D in touch with E. Contracts were exchanged between the plaintiff and E at a price of £6150, and later between E and D for £6950 which was the price eventually agreed between E and D. The plaintiff heard of the transaction between E and D and sued the defendants. *Held*—The defendants were under a duty to tell the plaintiff of D's offer because at the time he was not bound to E. The defendants were therefore liable in damages. The measure of damages was the difference between the two offers, i.e. £600, but the defendants were entitled to commision on the offer of £6150 and also on the damages, and since the agreement provided for $1\frac{1}{2}$ per cent commission which had already been paid on the £6150, the plaintiff recovered £591.

(229) *Kenney* v *Hall, Paine and Foster* (1976) 239 E.G. 355

In an action for negligence in the valuation of his property, the plaintiff asked for damages from estate agents who had overvalued his house. Having, on the estate agents' advice, put the property on the market at £150,000, the plaintiff bought another house, obtaining a bridging loan from a bank and having building work carried out on the new property. The original house remained unsold. It was *held*, by Goff, J., that to all intents and purposes the plaintiff was bankrupt, owing the bank £85,000 and having no capital of his own apart from the house.

The figure quoted by the estate agents as the price likely to be realized was a valuation and a negligent one. Damages of £40,225 were awarded to the plaintiff.

An agent for one party to a transaction is not forbidden to act for the other party but the court may set the transaction aside if there is evidence of conflict of interest.

(230) *Anglo-African Merchants Ltd* v *Bayley* [1969] 2 All E.R. 421

The plaintiff instructed a broker to effect the insurance of a quantity of government-surplus army leather jerkins. The broker negotiated insurance with the defendant who was an underwriter at Lloyds. Some of the insured property was stolen and the plaintiffs claimed under the policy. It appeared that the broker had, without telling the plaintiffs, taken instructions from the underwriter to obtain a report from an assessor as to the value of the property stolen. The broker gave the report to the underwriter but would not give the plaintiffs a copy. *Held* (on this point)—by Megaw, J.—that the broker was in breach of his duty as an agent. Even if what he had done was a customary practice, it would not be upheld since it contradicted the rule that an agent should not serve two principals in the same transaction unless he has obtained the informed consent of both.

The fiduciary duty which exists between principal and agent may continue to rest upon an ex-agent.

(231) *Reiger* v *Campbell-Stuart* [1939] 3 All E.R. 235

The plaintiff was anxious to buy property suitable for conversion into flats and she asked the defendant to look for suitable properties. During his search and whilst the plaintiff's agent, the defendant found a leasehold house selling at £2000, but instead of informing the plaintiff, he arranged that his brother-in-law should buy it for £2000, after which the defendant then purported to buy it from his brother-in-law for £4500. This transaction was a sham. The defendant then offered to sell the house, which was by now his own property, to the plaintiff for £5000, having told her that he had paid £4000 for it. When the defendant told the plaintiff that the property was his own and began to sell it as a principal, the agency relationship between plaintiff and defendant was brought to an end; and when the plaintiff eventually bought the house from the defendant for £5000 the defendant was not her agent. The plaintiff later discovered what had really happened and claimed the profit made by the defendant. *Held*—She could do so. Although the agency had been terminated before the sale, the defendant was, even as an ex-agent, bound to act honestly and faithfully and must therefore account for the profits he had made on the deal.

An agent may recover his commission even if in breach of duty, provided the breach was merely incidental to the transaction concerned.

(232) *Hippisley* v *Knee Bros* [1905] 1 K.B. 1

The plaintiff employed Knee Bros, who were auctioneers, to sell certain pictures on commission. Knee Bros arranged for printing and advertising and debited the principal with the full cost although they had received from the printer a discount of 10 per cent in accordance with normal trade practice. Hippisley claimed the discount and would not pay the defendants their commission. *Held*—by the Court of Appeal—that the discount could be recovered but the commission was payable. Although the defendants had acted honestly they were in breach of their obligations as agents in respect of the extra profit. Since they had not perpetrated any fraud on the principal they were entitled to commission. 'In this case the discounts were allowed in respect of matters incidental to the work which the defendants had to do on behalf of the plaintiff in relation to the sale of his goods. It cannot be suggested that the plaintiff has suffered in any way in the sale of his goods by reason of the defendants' conduct in the matter of the discounts. . . . In this case the neglect to account had no effect whatever on the performance of his duty by the agent. It was purely incidental and had nothing to do with the duty.' (*Per* Lord Alverstone, C.J.)

An agent has an obligation of obedience and must carry out the express instructions of his principal but not if they are unlawful.

(233) *Bertram, Armstrong & Co.* v *Godfray* (1830) 1 Knapp 381

Godfray was a broker and Bertram gave him instructions to sell certain stock when the market price reached £85 per unit of stock. Godfray did not sell when the price reached £85, but held on to the stock, and later sold it at less than £85. Bertram now sued to recover the difference. There was no agreement or usage in the profession of broker which allowed Godfray to use his discretion and wait for the price to rise further, and it was *held* that by doing so he had in effect bought the stock himself when the price reached £85, and must now account to Bertram for the price plus interest. However, Bertram must also account to Godfray for the dividends he had received when he did not know that the price had reached £85 and still thought the stock was his.

(234) *Bexwell* v *Christie* (1776) 1 Cowp. 395

An auctioneer at a sale expressed to be 'without reserve' was given secret instructions by the owner not to sell articles below a certain price. The auctioneer did in fact sell the goods and was now sued for breach of the agency agreement. *Held*—Since the instructions were unlawful, as a fraud on those attending the sale, the auctioneer was not bound to follow them so that he was not liable for breach of the agreement.

An agent who takes a bribe loses his right to his remuneration or commission. The principal may also recover the bribe and sue the person who bribed the agent for damages without deduction of any bribe recovered from the agent. The principal may also repudiate the contract with the third party and it is not necessary to show that the bribe had any effect upon the agent.

(235) *Andrews* v *Ramsay & Co.* [1903] 2 K.B. 635

The plaintiff was a builder and the defendants were auctioneers and estate agents. The plaintiff instructed the defendants to find a purchaser for certain property belonging to the plaintiff, the price to be £2500 and the agreed commission £50. A month later the defendants wrote to the plaintiff saying that a person named Clutterbuck had made an offer of £1900 for the property, but the plaintiff would not sell. Later Clutterbuck offered £2100 and as the defendants said they could not get more, the plaintiff agreed to sell. Clutterbuck paid the defendants a deposit of £100 and the defendants paid £50 to the plaintiff and retained £50 as commission. After the sale had been completed the plaintiff discovered that the defendents had received a commission of £20 from Clutterbuck. The plaintiff recovered the £20 in the county court and now sought to recover the £50 commission because of the defendants' breach of duty whilst acting as agents. *Held*—He could do so. Where an agent takes a secret commission, the principal can recover that commission and also any commission which he himself has paid to the agent.

(236) *Salford Corporation* v *Lever* [1891] 1 Q.B. 168

The defendant was a coal supplier and had at various times supplied coal to the corporation. The negotiations regarding these sales were conducted by the corporation's gas manager, a Mr Hunter. Evidence showed that Hunter induced Lever to put up the price of his coal by 1s per ton and to pay this over to Hunter by saying that unless Lever agreed to do this, he would buy coal for the corporation elsewhere. At the time of the action the excess paid by the corporation to Lever was £2329 and they sought to recover that sum from Lever. Lever's defence was that the corporation had already recovered the money from Hunter. *Held*—Lever was guilty of fraud, and his fraud was wholly independent of that of Hunter and therefore both were liable to pay to the corporation the sums obtained by their separate frauds.

(237) *Shipway* v *Broadwood* [1899] 1 Q.B. 369

The defendant wished to buy a pair of horses and asked a veterinary named Pinkett to find him a pair. Pinkett suggested that the defendant should buy a pair of horses which was being sold by a Worcester horse dealer. The defendant agreed to buy them if Pinkett passed them as sound. Pinkett gave the defendant a certificate of soundness and the horses were delivered to the defendant who sent a cheque to the dealer. On delivery the horses were found to be unsound, and the defendant returned them and stopped the cheque. The dealer now sued on the cheque, and the defence was that there had been total failure of consideration and that the plaintiff had warranted the horses sound. The plaintiff succeeded at first instance, the judge finding that no warranty had been given and that the defendant had simply agreed to buy if Pinkett certified the horses sound, as he had done. Evidence showed that Pinkett had received a commission from Shipway, but the judge gave no ruling as to the effect of this on Pinkett's judgment. It was *held*, by the Court of Appeal, that no such ruling was necessary. It was possible to find for the defendant merely on the evidence that a commission had been paid. It was not necessary to inquire whether Pinkett had been biased by receiving it.

The rules relating to the taking of secret profits and bribes apply also to an agent who is not receiving payment.

(238) *Turnbull* v *Garden* (1896) 20 L.T. 218

An agent who was employed without payment to buy clothing for the principal's son received certain discounts from the seller. The agent tried to charge his principal the full price. *Held*—the principal was only required to pay the agent the sum charged by the seller of his son's outfit. The agent could not make a secret profit out of the transaction.

Under a particular lien the agent has the right to sue a purchaser in his own name for the whole purchase price, even though he has been paid his agent's commission, by reason of the contract between him and the purchaser which gives a lien on the goods for the whole purchase price.

(239) *Chelmsford Auctions Ltd* v *Poole* [1973] 1 All E.R. 810

The plaintiffs, who were auctioneers, sold a car to Poole for £57. Poole paid £7 deposit, which was adequate to cover the plaintiffs' commission and charges, but he failed to pay the balance or take delivery of the vehicle. The plaintiffs paid the vendor the price of the vehicle and claimed the unpaid balance from Poole. It was *held* by the Court of Appeal, that an auctioneer's lien did not come to an end on payment of his commission and charges and, accordingly, the plaintiffs' right to sue for the whole purchase price remained.

If the agent wishes to sue for remuneration under the contract then it must comply with the general law of contract, and must not, for example, be illegal.

(240) *Crouch & Lees* v *Haridas* [1971] 3 All E.R. 172

The plaintiffs, who were estate agents though not retained by the landlords, gave the defendant particulars of a flat provided he agreed to pay them 10 per cent of a year's rent if he took a lease of it. *Held*—by the Court of Appeal—that the plaintiffs had demanded payment of a sum of money in consideration of supplying particulars of a flat within s.1(1)(*b*) of the Accommodation Agents Act 1953, which forbade such conduct. The agreement was illegal and unenforceable and it did not matter that no part of the commission had been demanded or paid.

An agent who promises to bring about a certain transaction is not entitled to remuneration unless he substantially achieved that transaction.

(241) *Rimmer* v *Knowles* (1874) 30 L.T. 496

The plaintiff was a surveyor and the defendant asked him to sell an estate for an agreed commission of £50 if the plaintiff obtained a price of £2000. The defendant then raised the price to £3000 and, although the plaintiff could not get an outright purchaser, he did make a contract with a builder who was prepared to take a lease for 999 years for £150 per annum, with an option to purchase during the first 20 years of the lease. The plaintiff now sued for his commission, but the County Court judge refused this on the grounds that he had not substantially performed the contract. On appeal it was *held* that there had been substantial performance and the plaintiff was able to recover his commission.

(242) *Coles* v *Enoch* [1939] 3 All E.R. 327

The defendant was the owner of a shop in Victoria Street, London. The plaintiff was the proprietor of certain pin-table arcades in the North of England and was desirous of finding a site in London. In December 1937, the plaintiff had a conversation with the defendant regarding the purchase of the Victoria Street premises. The plaintiff said that if he could not raise the money to buy the premises, he would turn agent and find a purchaser for the defendant on commission terms. The defendant agreed and the plaintiff later spoke to a Mr Adickes regarding the purchase of the premises by his firm. This conversation was overheard by a person named Wilkie who was in the offices of the firm at the time. Wilkie asked Adickes about the premises but was merely told that they were in the neighbourhood of Victoria. Wilkie then found the premises himself and, having read the notice on the empty shop window, got in touch with the defendant and took a lease at £1000 per annum. The plaintiff now sued for his commission. *Held*—He failed. His action was not the direct cause of Wilkie taking the shop. Adickes was the plaintiff's sub-agent for the purposes of the conversation with Wilkie and the fact that he deliberately withheld the actual address meant that Wilkie really found the premises for himself.

(243) *Rolfe & Co.* v *George* (1969) 113 S.J. 244

The plaintiffs undertook to sell a grocery business for the defendant. In the event a third party introduced a potential purchaser to the defendant but the plaintiffs were asked to be present at the negotiations, which they were. *Held*—The plaintiffs must by reason of their presence at, and involvement in, the negotiations have been the efficient cause of the sale or produced the sale and were entitled to commission.

The liability of a principal to pay an estate agent's commission is a matter of construction of the express terms of the contract in each case. There is a presumption against implying terms relating to liability to pay unless the property is sold.

(244) *Luxor (Eastbourne) Ltd* v *Cooper* [1941] A.C. 108

The appellants wished to raise money and decided to dispose of certain cinemas which they owned. The respondent was appointed agent for the purpose of sale, and commission was to be payable on its completion. The respondent did introduce a company, the London and Southern Super Cinemas Ltd, who were at all times ready, willing and able to buy for the figure of £185,000 asked by the appellants, *but no contract was made.* The appellants then decided to raise the money they required by a sale of shares and would not proceed with the sale of the cinemas. The respondent sued for his commission claiming that, although his agreement stated that commission was payable on completion of the sale, the Court should imply a term to the effect that the vendor would not refuse to go on with the sale. *Held*—No such term could be implied. The appellants were not liable for breach of contract and the respondent's claim failed.

Comment. A term will normally be implied where the principal and third party make a contract after they have been introduced by the agent, but the principal refuses to perform it. Thus in *Alpha Trading* v *Dunnshaw-Patten* [1981] 1 All E.R. 482, the parties entered into a contract to buy cement after the plaintiff agents had introduced them. The defendants, who were the principals, refused to go on with the contract. The Court of Appeal implied a term that commission was payable. And see *Christie Owen & Davies* v *Rapacioli* 1974 (p. 478) where the third party had signed the contract but the principal refused to sign. Again the Court implied a term that commission was payable.

(245) *Christie, Owen & Davies Ltd* v *Stockton* [1953] 2 All E.R. 1149

The defendant instructed the plaintiffs to sell a London restaurant business for him and agreed to pay them commission on any completed transaction. The agreement also provided that 'should the owner withdraw after having accepted an offer to purchase by a person able and willing to enter into a formal contract' the plaintiffs should be entitled to commission. The plaintiffs introduced a Mr Hannay as a possible purchaser and the defendant met him and they agreed orally on a sale 'subject to contract'. The defendant's solicitors sent a draft contract to Mr Hanney's solicitors and, both firms of solicitors having agreed it, Mr Hannay signed his part and paid a deposit to his solicitors. The defendant then refused to sign his part and would not go on with the transaction. The plaintiffs claimed commission in accordance with the agreement. *Held*—They failed. The word *offer* meant an offer capable of being turned into a contract by mere acceptance. An offer 'subject to contract' was not such an offer. Further, it was not possible to say that at the time of the oral agreement Mr Hannay was in the legal sense willing to buy, because the words 'subject to contract' indicated that the matter was still in negotiation.

(246) *Christie, Owen and Davies* v *Rapacioli* [1974] 2 All E.R. 311

The defendant agreed that the plaintiffs, who were estate agents, would sell his house, commission being payable on the agents effecting an introduction of a person ready, able and willing to purchase. The plaintiffs introduced X whose offer was accepted by the defendant, and a contract was signed by X. However, the defendant refused to sign and go on with the sale. It was held by the Court of Appeal that the plaintiffs were entitled to commission under the terms of their contract.

(247) *Drewery and Drewery* v *Ware Lane* [1960] 3 All E.R 529

The defendant owned a leasehold house and there were 78 years of the lease to run. He instructed the plaintiffs to sell it at £2250 and they got an offer from S of £2160 which the defendant agreed to accept. The defendant then signed a *letter of authority* in which he agreed to the plaintiffs' commission 'if and when (*a*) a prospective purchaser signs your "purchaser's agreement"; and (*b*) I sign your "vendor's agreement"'. The defendant also signed the vendor's agreement. On the same day S signed the purchaser's agreement. Both agreements were expressed to be 'subject to contract'. S delayed in completion, being anxious to buy the freehold property but prepared to buy the lease. The defendant sold the house to another purchaser and the agents sued for their commission on the deal with S. *Held*—They were entitled to commission. S was at all times a prospective purchaser and the conditions as to signing the agreement had been fulfilled.

(248) *Peter Long and Partners* v *Burns* [1956] 3 All E.R. 207

The defendant instructed the plaintiffs to sell her garage business. She agreed that she would not sell except to a person introduced by the plaintiffs. She also agreed to pay commission upon the plaintiffs introducing 'a person ready, willing and able to enter into a binding contract to purchase' the business. The plaintiffs found a possible purchaser who signed a contract of sale, but afterwards avoided the contract because of the plaintiffs' innocent misrepresentation as to a road widening scheme. It appeared that the purchaser had seen work going on down the road from the garage, and had asked the plaintiffs about its effect on the garage. The plaintiffs, acting on the defendant's statement but without checking it, told the purchaser that the scheme would take two or three feet off the frontage, whereas in fact it took in the whole site. The defendant and the purchaser having mutually agreed to call the contract off, the plaintiffs now sued for their commission. *Held*—The contract which the purchaser signed was not a 'binding contract' but a voidable one, and the plaintiffs were not entitled to their commission.

(249) *Blake & Co.* v *Sohn* [1969] 3 All E.R. 123

The plaintiffs, who were estate agents, introduced to the defendants a potential purchaser of an hotel and adjoining land. A written agreement was made and signed but the defendants were not able to give a good title to the adjoining land. They had an easement over it and felt they could establish squatters' rights. This was not good enough for the defendant who obtained rescission of the contract. *Held*—by Nield, J.,—that neither the commission agreement nor the failure of the defendants to make out a title gave the plaintiffs any cause of action for commission. There was no implied promise by a vendor that the title to land could be made out and the contract being voidable, no binding agreement had been achieved by the plaintiffs.

(250) *Scheggia* v *Gradwell* [1963] 3 All E.R. 114

The appellant Scheggia was the proprietor of a leasehold café and snack bar off Finchley Road, and the respondent Gradwell was in business as an estate agent. Scheggia was anxious to sell the business and he signed an agreement with Gradwell, the form used providing by clause 5(*a*) that the vendor would pay the agency commission 'if within three months any person introduced by the agents enters into a legally binding contract to purchase the business and the property'. The agents introduced a purchaser, a Mr Yik Ping Chung, and he signed an agreement to buy the business. The contract required the purchaser to submit suitable references for the landlord's approval. The references produced by Chung were not thought satisfactory by the landlord and the sale went off. The County Court judge held that the agents were entitled to their commission of £172 in accordance with the agreement. The appellant appealed. *Held*—by the Court of Appeal—that the agents were entitled to their commission because the event in clause 5(*a*) of the agreement had happened. Lord Denning dissented and thought that the agents were not entitled to their commission since the purchaser they introduced ought to be able to purchase, this being implicit in an agreement such as this.

Comment. This case illustrates the point made in *Luxor*[244] that the court will construe the contract according to its *express* terms. In this case the events had occurred on which the commission was payable and there was no room for the implied term which Lord Denning wanted.

(251) *Wilkinson* v *Brown* [1966] 1 All E.R. 509

Mrs Brown engaged the plaintiffs, who were estate agents, to sell her fruit and vegetable business. She agreed to make them agents for two months and to pay them commission in the event of their introducing 'a person prepared to enter into a contract to purchase'. The plaintiffs introduced a Mr Norton and it was agreed that the right price for this leasehold property and business was £2500 with stock at valuation. Negotiations proceeded with Mr Norton for the period of two months and although he was interested in buying the property there were always one or two matters unsettled during the period of the agency. In the first place Mr Norton had to sell his present property, and secondly, there were financial arrangements to make with moneylenders. There were also difficulties in obtaining the landlord's consent to the assignment of the leasehold business premises because Mr Norton's references were not, at first, satisfactory to the landlord. The period of the agency expired without Mr Norton entering into a contract, and shortly afterwards the defendant sold the property to someone else; the plaintiffs now sued for their commission of £250. *Held*—by the Court of Appeal—that their action failed. Mr Norton could not be said to have been 'prepared' to enter into a contract to purchase at any time during the period of the agency, his willingness to buy was always conditional on matters never resolved. Commenting on the decision in *Scheggia* v *Gradwell* 1963,[250] Salmon, L.J., said, 'in my judgment, however, the scope of that decision ought not to be extended'. In his view the decision in *Scheggia's Case* turned on the use of the words 'any person' in the contract. The Court of Appeal in *Scheggia's Case* would not imply into a contract that the words 'any person' meant a person ready, willing and able, to buy. Having reached that position the prospective vendor in *Scheggia's Case* was making himself liable to pay commission to the estate agent in consideration of his obtaining anyone's signature on a contract even though that person was not in a position to complete. Although *Scheggia's Case* may have to be applied in a case in which the contract is couched in the same language as the language used in *Scheggia's Case*, or language indistinguishable from it, the method of construction applied in *Scheggia's Case* ought not to be extended. The contract in that case was, according to Salmon, L.J., 'a ridiculous bargain'.

A potential purchaser can generally recover any deposit paid if he does not continue with a 'subject to contract' purchase.

(252) *Chillingworth and another* v *Esche* [1923] All E.R. Rep. 97

By a document dated 10 July 1922, Chillingworth and Cummings agreed to purchase the defendant's nursery gardens at Cheshunt, Herts., for £4800 'subject to a proper contract to be prepared by the vendor's solicitors'. The plaintiffs paid a deposit of £240. After the solicitors on both sides had agreed on the terms of a contract the plaintiffs refused, without reason, to go on and claimed a declaration that the document of 20 July 1922 was not binding and that the deposit must be repaid. *Held*—by the Court of Appeal—that the document was nothing more than a conditional offer and a conditional acceptance and would only ripen into a binding agreement when a formal document was signed. Further, on the construction of the documents and in the circumstances, the plaintiffs were entitled to the repayment of the deposit. The plaintiffs' solicitors were not agents of their clients, so as to bind them, when they agreed with the defendant's solicitors on the terms of the contract.

An agent employed to sell a property has no implied authority to receive a deposit.

(253) *Sorrell* v *Finch* [1976] 2 All E.R. 371

A Mr Levy, an undischarged bankrupt, was an estate agent. The appellant asked him to find a purchaser for his house. There was no agreement between the appellant and Mr Levy about deposits or commission. Mr Levy took deposits from five people, then disappeared. Mr Finch, one of those who had paid a deposit, sued the appellant for its return. It was *held*—by the House of Lords—that in the absence of express or implied agreement that he do so, an estate agent has no authority to receive a pre-contract deposit on behalf of the vendor, and the fact that the vendor knows a deposit has been received does not impose upon him an obligation to repay it.

The agent may in the course of his duty incur liabilities or make payments of money for the principal, and he has a right to be indemnified against such liabilities and to recover any money paid.

(254) *Christoforides* v *Terry* [1924] A.C. 566

The appellant employed a Mr Thomson who was a broker on the Cotton Exchanges of Liverpool and New York. Thomson was to make transactions on these exchanges for the appellant. The terms of the agreement were that if at any time the indebtedness of either party to the other should exceed £1000, the party in credit should be entitled to call upon the other party for the payment of that sum. In November 1920, the market in cotton fell and the appellant owed Thomson a large sum of money, which Thomson called for under the terms of the agreement but which was not paid. Thomson closed the account, as he was entitled to do, and sold the appellant's cotton, which he held at the time, at a loss of £6385 13s 1d. Thomson called for an indemnity for this loss but the appellant did not pay it. Thomson got into financial difficulties and assigned his property for the benefit of his creditors, Terry being the trustee of the assignment. In this action Terry tried to recover the indemnity for the benefit of Thomson's creditors. *Held*—Terry succeeded. Thomson, as agent, was entitled to the indemnity now claimed on his behalf.

An agent has no right to an indemnity if he acts without or against authority, nor can he recover if, although obeying instructions, he commits a breach of a fiduciary duty or does not use skill and care.

(255) *Davison* v *Fernandes* (1889) 6 T.L.R. 73

The plaintiff was a stockbroker and the defendant was the holder of stock which he wished to sell. He asked the plaintiff for a price *ex* (or without) *dividend* but the plaintiff negligently quoted a price which was *cum* (or with) *dividend*. The defendant, thinking that the price was *ex dividend*, authorized the plaintiff to sell, because if the price had really been *ex dividend* it would have been a good one. The broker sold the shares and when the plaintiff discovered the error he repudiated the contract. In accordance with the custom of the Stock Exchange, the plaintiff had to pay certain sums of money to the purchaser of the shares by way of compensation for losses incurred by the defendant's repudiation and the plaintiff now sought to recover those sums by way of an indemnity. *Held*—He could not do so as his negligence in giving the wrong price barred any claim to an indemnity.

The period for which the relationship of principal and agent is to last may be fixed expressly by the parties in the contract or implied by trade or other usage or custom.

(256) *Dickinson* v *Lilwal* (1815) 4 Camp. 279

An agent was given authority to sell the goods of a principal who was in the Irish provision trade. By a custom of the trade the authority of an agent expired with the day on which it was given. *Held*—A contract made by the agent some days after he had been appointed was not binding on the principal.

An agent's authority ends when the happening of an event makes the continuance of the agency unlawful.

(257) *Stevenson & Sons* v *Aktiengesellschaft für Cartonnagen Industrie* [1918] A.C. 239

The plaintiffs were an English company and the defendants were a Germany company carrying on business at Dresden. By an agreement in writing dated 22 November 1906, the plaintiffs became (1) sole agents of the defendants for Great Britain and the Colonies for the sale of the defendants' machines which were used for fixing metal edges and studs to cardboard boxes, and (2) partners in the business of manufacturing in England and selling here and in the Colonies the metal edges and studs. The plaintiffs asked for a declaratory judgment confirming that the agency and partnership were terminated by the outbreak of war on 4 August 1914, and what the financial position of the partners was in consequence. *Held*—(1) That a contract of agency between a foreign principal and a British agent resident in their respective countries, under which the agent is to sell the principal's goods in Britain and the colonies, is terminated by the outbreak of war between the two countries. (2) A partnership between a British partner and a foreign partner which involves the carrying on of a business in this country is dissolved by the outbreak of war between the respective countries of the partners.

Insanity of the principal terminates the agency. An agent can be sued for breach of warranty of authority even though he did not know that his authority to act had come to an end.

(258) *Yonge* v *Toynbee* [1910] 1 K.B. 215

The plaintiff alleged that the defendant had written and published a letter which was a libel on her and proceeded to bring an action against him. The defendant instructed a firm of solicitors, W and Sons, to act for him in the matter. Before the action commenced the defendant was certified as being of unsound mind. However, W and Sons, not knowing of this, entered an appearance in the action for the defendant after his insanity and also delivered a defence. Various other interlocutory proceedings took place but the action was not in fact tried, and the plaintiff's solicitors asked that all proceedings be struck out, and that W and Sons, who had acted for the defendant after his insanity, should be personally liable to pay the plaintiff's cost because they had acted without authority. *Held*—by the Court of Appeal—that W and Sons had impliedly warranted that they had authority to act when they had not, and that they were personally liable for the plaintiff's costs.

Where a principal has held out an agent as having authority the principal will be bound by the acts of that agent, even though the principal is insane, so long as the third party does not know of the insanity.

(259) *Drew* v *Nunn* (1879) 4 Q.B.D. 661

The plaintiff was a tradesman and brought this action to recover from the defendant the price of boots and shoes supplied to the defendant's wife between April 1876 and June 1877. Evidence showed that the plaintiff began to supply goods on credit to the defendant's wife in 1872 and the defendant was present when some of the goods were ordered and had paid for certain of them by cheque. In 1873 the defendant fell ill and made arrangements for his income to be paid to his wife, directing his bankers to honour cheques drawn by her and to allow her to deal with his securities. In December 1873, the defendant became insane and was placed in an asylum until April 1877, when he recovered his reason. Whilst the defendant was in the asylum the plaintiff sold the above mentioned goods to the defendant's wife on credit without knowing of the defendant's insanity. When sued for the price the defendant claimed that his insanity revoked his wife's authority so that he was not liable. The Court of Appeal *held* that he was liable for the price of the goods supplied.

Comment *Drew* v *Nunn* was approved and followed in a later Canadian case—*Re Parks, Canada Permanent Trust Co.* v *Parks* [1957] 8 D.L.R. (2d) 155. There is some difficulty in reconciling this case with *Yonge* (above). (See further p. 109.)

The principal cannot successfully revoke the agent's authority once the agent has acted upon it.

(260) *Chappell* v *Bray* (1860) 30 L.J. (Ex.) 24

The defendant was part owner of a ship, and on 23 January 1860 he authorized the plaintiff along with the other part owner to make a contract with the shipbuilder to cut the ship in two and lengthen her. On 24 January 1860, the plaintiff made the contract with a shipbuilder and work commenced almost immediately on the job. On 26 January 1860, the defendant wrote to the plaintiff saying he would not be answerable for the cost of the work on the ship. The work was completed and the plaintiff paid for it. The plaintiff then claimed an indemnity from the defendant for a proportion of the cost. *Held*—The defendant could not revoke the agency after it had been acted upon by both agent and shipbuilder. The plaintiff was entitled to his indemnity.

Where the principal is undisclosed the third party may elect to sue either the agent or the principal. In order to constitute an election against one of them which will bar proceedings against the other the election must be unequivocal or beyond doubt.

(261) *Clarkson, Booker Ltd* v *Andjel* [1964] 3 All E.R. 260

The plaintiff company carried on the business of travel agents and supplied the defendant with airline tickets from Athens to London to the value of £728 7s 6d. The defendant contracted as if he were a principal. Later the plaintiffs received a letter from a company called Peters & Milner Ltd, which said that the debt was due by Peters & Milner Ltd, and was not a personal debt of the defendant. The plaintiffs replied that when the defendant had booked the flights in question he had not made it clear that anyone else was responsible for payment. In the same letter the plaintiffs requested a settlement. There was further correspondence between the plaintiffs and the defendant and the plaintiffs and Peter & Milner Ltd, in which the plaintiffs made it clear that they regarded both the defendant and Peters & Milner Ltd as liable, but eventually the plaintiffs issued a writ against Peters & Milner Ltd. Two months later the plaintiffs were informed that Peters & Milner Ltd was insolvent and they discontinued their action against that company and commenced the present proceedings against the defendant. His defence was, that since the plaintiffs had made a claim against the undisclosed principal, they had lost their right to sue him. *Held*—by the Court of Appeal—that in order to constitute an election the decision to commence proceedings must be taken with full knowledge of all relevant facts and must be a truly unequivocal act. In this case the plaintiffs had never withdrawn their claim against the defendant and there had, therefore, been no unequivocal election.

An undisclosed principal is not allowed to enforce a contract made by his agent where his personality is a material matter.

(262) *Said* v *Butt* [1920] 3 K.B. 497

The plaintiff was a wealthy Russian gentleman and the defendant was the managing director of a theatre. The plaintiff had put on a light opera at the theatre but takings had been poor, mainly because of a railway strike. After much argument the defendant gave the plaintiff notice to take the light opera off, and it was taken off on 18 October 1919. On 23 December 1919, a new play was to begin at the theatre and the plaintiff wanted tickets but had been refused. He asked a friend, Mr Pollock, to get the tickets for him but not to reveal whom they for. The tickets were obtained but by the defendant's orders the plaintiff was refused admission. He now sued the defendant for maliciously procuring the theatre company to break its contract with him. *Held*—There was no such contract. The tickets had been bought for the plaintiff as an undisclosed principal, and since the identity of the principal was of importance to the proprietors of the theatre company, the plaintiff could not intervene and claim the contract as his. The defendant was not therefore liable in tort for procuring a breach of contract.

An agent may be sued for damages for breach of warranty of authority by a third party who has relied to his detriment on the representation of the agent that he had the authority of his principal. The agent's liability is strict and does not depend on his being guilty of misrepresentation or fraud.

(263) *Starkey* v *Bank of England* [1903] A.C. 114

Starkey was a member of a firm of stockbrokers in London. In December 1897, two trustees, Frederick and Edgar Oliver, held stock in trust for others and were registered as holders of the stock in the respondents' books. Starkey received authority to sell the stock under a power of attorney purporting to be signed by both trustees, but in fact the signature of Edgar Oliver was forged. Starkey's firm sold the stock and send the proceeds to Frederick Oliver who paid them into his private account. Frederick Oliver died 18 months later. On discovering what had happened. Edgar Oliver brought an action against the Bank for replacement of the stock, and the Bank brought in Starkey as liable to indemnify them. *Held*—by the House of Lords—that Edgar Oliver succeeded against the Bank, and they in turn succeeded against Starkey for an indemnity, because Starkey had impliedly warranted his authority to the Bank.

A special or particular agent has authority only to do a specific act. He does not have implied power to act in all matters concerning a particular trade or business, e.g. to give warranties. In this connection an estate agent has no implied authority to warrant that the premises he is employed to sell can be used for a particular purpose.

(264) *Brady* v *Todd* (1861) 9 C.B.N.S. 59

Todd was a tradesman living in London who also had a farm in Essex. The farm was managed by his bailiff, Grieg. Todd gave Grieg authority to sell a horse, and in the course of selling it to the plaintiff, Grieg warranted it quiet to ride and quiet in harness. The plaintiff sued for breach of warranty when he discovered that the horse was not quiet. It appeared that Todd had not given Grieg any authority to give warranties of any kind. *Held*—The servant of a private owner instructed to sell, as in this case, has no authority to give warranties unless he has his master's permission to give them. However, the servant of a *horse dealer* would be able to give such warranties.

(265) *Hill* v *Harris* [1956] 2 All E.R. 358

The defendant's estate agent told the plaintiff that certain premises which he was interested in subleasing could be used for a confectionery and tobacco business when in fact the use of the premises was limited in the head lease to the trade of boot and shoe making. The plaintiff took a sublease and the freeholder prevented his use of the premises for his confectionery and tobacco business. The plaintiff sought to recover damages from the defendant for breach of what was described as a 'warranty' given by the estate agent. *Held*—by the Court of Appeal—that the estate agent had no express authority to give the warranty and no authority could be implied.

The fact that the agent acts with his own interest in mind and in fraud of his principal will not protect the principal from liability if the agent was acting within the scope of his actual or apparent authority.

(266) *Lloyd* v *Grace, Smith & Co.* [1912] A.C. 716

The respondent, Smith, was a Liverpool solicitor and the appellant, Lloyd, was a widow who owned two properties at Ellesmere Port and had also lent money on mortgage. She was dissatisfied with the income from these investments and so she went to see the respondent's managing clerk, Sandles, for advice. He advised her to sell the properties and call in the mortgages and re-invest the proceeds. He got her to sign two deeds which, unknown to her, transferred the properties and the mortgages to him. Sandles then mortgaged the properties, and transferred the other mortgages for value and paid a private debt with the proceeds. *Held*—The firm was responsible, because a principal is liable for his agent's frauds if the agent is acting within the scope of his authority, whether the fraud is for the benefit of the principal or, as here, for the sole benefit of the agent.

A principal cannot be held liable for fraud when there has been no element of fraud, either on the part of himself or on the part of anyone for whose acts he is responsible.

(267) *Armstrong* v *Strain* [1952] 1 All E.R. 139

The plaintiffs purchased a bungalow from Strain and during the negotiations Strain's agent made certain statements about the property and in particular that it was in nice condition. The property was subject to subsidence of the clay foundations, and had been underpinned several times, but the agent was aware of one underpinning only. After the plaintiffs had purchased the bungalow, large cracks appeared in the walls and the plaintiffs sued Strain and the agent for fraudulent misrepresentation. *Held*—They were unable to prove fraud because the ingredients of deceit were split, Strain having knowledge of the defects but not having made the statement, and the agent having made the statement without full knowledge of the defects. Devlin, J., at first instance suggested that Strain might have been liable if the evidence had shown that he had deliberately kept his agents in ignorance of the defects in the expectation and hope that they would mislead the plaintiff, but the evidence did not establish this. Regarding an action for breach of warranty, Devlin, J., held that no warranty could arise out of the rather casual conversations which preceded the sale. Regarding liability of the agent in negligence, there was no duty of care in respect of careless misstatements of this sort, following *Candler* v *Crane, Christmas* [1951] 2 K.B. 164.

Comment. In *Hedley Byrne* v *Heller and Partners*[120] in 1963, the House of Lords decided that there was a duty of care in respect of careless misstatements of this kind, and this decision may provide a remedy in negligence in a situation like that in *Armstrong* v *Strain* although there is no remedy in the tort of deceit. (See also Misrepresentation Act 1967 under which the principal but not the agent is liable for the agent's negligent misrepresentation under s.2(1), see p. 408.)

Notice will not be imputed where the agent acts contrary to the principal's interests and the third party knows this.

(268) *Wells* v *Smith* [1914] 3 K.B. 722

The plaintiff was the owner of a furnished house and put it into the hands of agents, B and Co., for the purpose of letting. A Mrs Pridgeon wished to take it, and she gave the defendant's name as a referee. The agents wrote to the defendant and he gave her a favourable reference. Mrs Pridgeon took the house but was an immoral woman and was visited at the house by men for immoral purposes. She did not regularly pay the rent or keep the place in good order. It appeared that B and Co. knew that Mrs Pridgeon was not a respectable woman and so did the defendant. The plaintiff now sued for damages for loss of rent and damage to her furniture. The defence was that the agent's knowledge of Mrs Pridgeon's character must be imputed to the plaintiff so that when she let the house to Mrs Pridgeon, the plaintiff knew in effect of her character and the defendant's reference could not have misled her. *Held*—The fact that the plaintiff's agent knew of the untruth of the defendant's statement could not be imputed to the plaintiff and she could therefore recover damages from the defendant because she had relied on his statement which was fraudulent.

In regard to imputed notice, the agent must normally receive the information in the course of his agency for the principal. However, the principal may sometimes be affected by the knowledge of the agent gained in another capacity.

(269) *Dresser* v *Norwood* (1864) 17 C.B. (N.S.) 466

The plaintiff placed timber into the possession of his agent, Holderness, so that Holderness could sell it in his own name. The defendants bought the timber from Holderness through their agent, Chaplin, believing Holderness to be the owner of the timber. When the plaintiff sued for the price of the timber the defendants sought to set-off against the plaintiff's claim the sum of £600 due to them from Holderness. This set-off would have been possible if the plaintiff had been an undisclosed principal, i.e. if the defendants could show they did not know they were dealing with an agent. However, it appeared that Chaplin knew that the timber did not belong to Holderness and knew he was a *del credere* agent acting for various principals. *Held*—The knowledge of Chaplin must be imputed to his employers, the defendants, so they were not entitled to set-off the money Holderness owed them.

A person who acts for one principal only can nevertheless be a mercantile agent.

(270) *Lowther* v *Harris* [1927] 1 K.B. 393

The plaintiff wished to sell certain antiques and he arranged with a Mr Prior that Prior should find purchasers. Prior was an antique dealer in a small way of business. Among the articles to be sold were certain tapestries called the Aubusson and the Leopard tapestries. To facilitate the sale of the articles, the plaintiff took a house near to Prior's shop and stored the antiques in the house. Prior lived in a flat on the top floor of the house, and used a sitting room on the floor below. People who were taken to view the antiques were not in general told that Prior was an agent. Prior claimed that he could sell the Aubusson tapestry for £525 to a purchaser who did not in fact exist, and the plaintiff allowed him to take it away and Prior later sold it to the defendant for £250. Prior also sold the Leopard tapestry to the defendant but was never given authority to sell or remove that tapestry. The plaintiff now sued the defendant for damages for detinue or conversion. *Held*—Prior's authority was limited and he was not acting for other principals; yet he could still be a mercantile agent and was one in this case. He was in possession of the Aubusson tapestry with the consent of the plaintiff and gave a good title to the defendant under the Factors Act 1889. Regarding the Leopard tapestry Prior was never in possession of it with the plaintiff's consent; this did not give a good title and the plaintiff could recover its value.

A person who buys goods from a mercantile agent will not get a good title to them if the agent is not in possession of them in his capacity as mercantile agent for sale or where he is a mere bailee to do work on the goods.

(271) *Staffordshire Motor Guarantee Ltd* v *British Wagon Co. Ltd* [1934] 2 K.B. 305

A Mr Heap, who was a dealer in motor cars at Stoke-on-Trent, made an agreement with the defendants under which he sold to them a motor lorry, of which he was the owner, and they let it out to him on hire. Later Heap, representing himself as still the owner, sold the lorry to a Mr Pettit, the lorry being taken on hire purchase and sold to the plaintiffs who hired it out to Pettit. Heap allowed his payments to fall in arrear and the defendants repossessed the lorry and now refused to deliver it up to the plaintiffs. The plaintiffs sued for damages for detention of the lorry and for its return. *Held*—Heap was not in possession as a mercantile agent for the purpose of the Factors Act 1889, s.2(1). He was merely a bailee and the sale by him to the plaintiffs was not rendered valid by the Act.

(272) *Kendrick* v *Sotheby & Co.* (1967) 117 New L.J. 408

The plaintiff bought a statuette which he later left with X to arrange for a photograph of the statuette to be taken and signed by the sculptor's widow. X handed the statuette to the defendants, who were auctioneers, with instructions to sell it. The defendants gave him an advance. *Held*—The plaintiff was the true owner. The defendants had been unable to establish a defence under the Factors Act 1889, that X was a mercantile agent and were ordered to deliver the statuette to the plaintiff. X was ordered to repay the advance paid by the defendants and also to pay all the costs.

A mercantile agent may be regarded as in possession of the goods with

the consent of the owner even where he has obtained possession of them and/or the documents of title to them by some form of deception.

(273) *Pearson* v *Rose and Young Ltd* [1951] 1 K.B. 275

The plaintiff was the owner of a motor car and entrusted it for the purpose of sale to a Mr Hunt who was the managing director of a firm of car dealers. It was admitted that Mr Hunt was a mercantile agent. There was at the time a system whereby purchasers of new cars agreed not to sell them for a certain period of time and, in order to convince Hunt that this car could be sold without being in breach of a covenant not to sell, the plaintiff showed Hunt the registration book as proof of the date of its first registration. Hunt, who had formed the intention to defraud the plaintiff, then asked him to give Mrs Hunt a lift to a local hospital, thus diverting the plaintiff's attention from the registration book. The plaintiff left without it and forgot it, but later the same day Hunt sold the car to a person named Little, who then sold to one Marshall, who then sold to the defendants. The plaintiff now sued the three purchasers in conversion and they claimed a good title under s.2(1) of the Factors Act 1889. *Held*—The plaintiff consented to Hunt's possession of the car as a mercantile agent, but did not consent to his possession of the registration book as a mercantile agent. The sale of a car without its registration book was not a sale 'in the ordinary course of business' for the purposes of s.2(1). Further, the consent required to pass a good title here was consent to possession of the car and the registration book. The plaintiff succeeded, as the defendants had not obtained a good title.

Comment. The point was made in the case that if the mercantile agent had obtained the car by deception (see s.15, Theft Act 1968), e.g. by giving a worthless cheque, or by coming to view the car and representing himself to be another reputable dealer (as in *Cundy* v *Lindsay* 1878),[95] he would nevertheless be in possession of the car 'with the consent of the owner' for the purposes of s.2(1) of the Factors Act 1889.

It is not in the ordinary course of business for a mercantile agent to sell a car without its registration document.

(274) *Stadium Finance Ltd* v *Robbins* [1962] 2 All E.R. 633

The defendant, wishing to sell his Jaguar car, left it with a car dealer, Palmer, with a view to sale. Palmer was to inform him if inquiries were made. The defendant did not leave the ignition key but by accident left the registration book in the glove compartment which was locked. Palmer obtained a key, opened the glove compartment and took possession of the registration book. Palmer sold the car to one of his salesmen, Grossman who bought it on hire purchase, the deal being financed by the plaintiffs. Grossman defaulted on his payments and the plaintiffs sought to take possession of the car. However, the defendant, having discovered what had happened, had already retaken possession of the car. The question of title now arose. *Held*—The car was 'goods' for the purposes of s.2(1) even without the ignition key. However, the sale of the car by a mercantile agent who had not been put into possession of the registration book or key was not a sale in the 'ordinary course of business' for the purposes of s.2(1). Further, since Palmer was not given the registration book or key by the defendant, he was not in possession of the vehicle with the 'consent' of the owner for the purposes of s.2(1).

(275) *George* v *Revis* (1966) 116 New L.J. 1544

The plaintiff offered his car for sale and X, a fraudulent person, agreed to buy it subject to a satisfactory engineer's report. The plaintiff allowed X to drive the car away in order to obtain an engineer's report but he did not allow X to take the registration book. However, X managed to steal the registration book before leaving with the car. Later X sold the car to the defendant, who was an innocent purchaser. The plaintiff now claimed damages for conversion of the car and it was *held*—by Megaw, J.,—that since X did not obtain possession of the registration book with the plaintiff's consent, and since the book was of great importance in the sale of a car, the defendant did not acquire a title under the Factors Act 1889 and was liable in damages.

Sale of Goods

(Section references are to the Sale of Goods Act (now 1979) unless otherwise indicated.)

The common-law doctrine of frustration of contract will apply to a contract for the sale of future goods which do not materialise. Section 7 of the Sale of Goods Act will also apply to frustrate the contract if the goods are future and specific. It is possible to take the view that s.7 applies to goods which are specifically described whether they exist at the time the contract was made or not.

(276) *Howell* v *Coupland* (1876) 1 Q.B.D. 258

In March 1892, the defendant agreed to sell to the plaintiff 200 tons of potatoes to be grown on the defendant's land at Whaplode. The potatoes were to be delivered in the following September and October. The defendant accordingly sowed enough seed potatoes on his land at Whaplode to meet the requirements of the contract in the ordinary course of events. Before the time for the performance of the contract arrived, a large portion of the crop was destroyed by disease without any fault on the defendant's part. The plaintiff now sued for damages for non-delivery. *Held*—The contract was for the sale of a specific crop. There was no warranty that the crop would exist at the time of performance and the defendant was excused from performance, the contract being frustrated at common law. The decision in *Taylor* v *Caldwell* 1863[186] was applied.

Comment. (i) A transaction of the type set out above may, according to the circumstances, be treated in four ways, *viz.* (1) as a sale of specific goods, the destruction of which frustrates the contract under s.7 and at common law; (2) as a contingent sale under s.5(2) so that if the crop does not come into existence the contract does not operate and neither party is bound; (3) as a sale where the seller is regarded as warranting the eventual existence of the crop and is liable for non-delivery if it fails; (4) as a sale of a mere chance so that the buyer risks the failure of the crop and must still pay the price.

(ii) If the contract had been for '200 tons of potatoes' the failure of the crop at Whaplode would not have frustrated the contract either under s.7 or at common law. The defendant would have been bound to deliver the quantity contracted for or been liable in damages, since in that event the goods would not have been specific.

Section 6 applies if some only of the goods are perished. The contract is then void.

(277) *Barrow Lane and Ballard Ltd* v *Phillip Phillips & Co. Ltd* [1929] 1 K.B. 574

The plaintiffs bought 700 bags of Chinese ground nuts, marked E.C.P. and known as 'Lot 7 of Chinese Ground Nuts in shell now lying at National Wharves in London'. The plaintiffs later resold the ground nuts to the defendants. Because of fraudulent abstraction by the wharfingers, there were only 591 bags left when the contract with the defendants was made, but the defendants obtained 150 bags from the warehouse before the discrepancy was discovered. The wharfingers subsequently went into liquidation, and the defendants were unable to obtain any further consignments. The defendants had made payment by means of two bills of exchange, which they now dishonoured, and the plaintiffs sued on the bills, or alternatively for the price of goods sold and delivered. The defendants denied liability, saying that there was an express or implied condition that there were 700 bags lying at the wharf and available for the defendants. The defendants had also tendered £180 for the 150 bags they had received and the plaintiffs had rejected it. The money had been paid into court. *Held*—Where there is a contract for the sale of specific goods and at the date of the contract some but not all of the goods have ceased to exist without the knowledge of either seller or buyer, the case falls within s.6 of what is now the Sale of Goods Act 1979, and the contract if not severable is void. The plaintiffs therefore failed in their claim, but were entitled to the money tendered for the 150 bags received by the defendants.

Comment. (i) This case leaves open the question of when stolen goods can be regarded as perished. The groundnuts were likely to have been sold after the theft and consumed. If the subject-matter is a durable product, e.g. a car, it is likely to be in existence for some time after theft and the position of the parties left uncertain.

(ii) If the contract had been severable, as where it had been a sale of separate bags of nuts to be paid for separately, the contract would have been void only as to those bags destroyed. The seller would have had to deliver, and the buyer take and pay for, the remainder or be liable in breach of contract. The same might, of course, be true even if the contract was not severable, as was the position in the *Barrow* case. This would seem to follow from the decision in *Sainsbury* v *Street* 1972.[278] (See below.)

The rule that a contract of sale, e.g. of a crop, is subject to an implied condition that the parties are to be excused if before breach performance becomes impossible because the subject-matter of the contract perishes without any fault in the seller, only operates to release the seller from his obligation to deliver that part of the crop which has failed.

(278) *H.R. & S. Sainsbury* v *Street* [1972] 3 All E.R. 1127

The defendant agreed to sell to the plaintiffs a crop of some 275 tons of barley which was to be grown by him on his farm. There was a crop failure and only about 124 tons were produced but the defendant sold and delivered these to a third party at a substantially higher price than the original contract price. It was *held*, by McKenna, J., that this was not a sale of specific goods so that ss.6 and 7 did not apply. The matter therefore had to be decided at common law and the decision was that although the contract was frustrated as to that part of the crop which had actually failed, this did not excuse the defendant from offering the crop actually produced to the plaintiffs, and he was liable in damages for failing to do so. Oddly enough, the judge did not seem to regard the plaintiffs as being under an obligation to take the 140 tons. This would suggest that the seller must tender delivery of the balance to the buyer who is not bound to take it.

Comment. Presumably, if the goods had been specific goods the same conclusion would have been arrived at. Therefore it would seem that the buyers in *Barrow Lane* would have been entitled to insist on delivery of the bags of nuts which remained, regardless of the provisions of ss. 6 and 7.

Section 6 applies only in the absence of a contrary agreement by the parties. Where the court feels as a mattter of construction of the contract that the seller has undertaken to accept the risk that the goods may not exist, he may be liable in damages to the buyer if they do not.

(279) *McRae* v *The Commonwealth Disposals Commission* (1951) 84 C.L.R. 377

The defendants had invited tenders for the purchase of a tanker, said to be lying on the Journand Reef off Papua, together with the oil it was said to contain. The plaintiff submitted a tender of £285 which the defendants accepted. The plaintiff went to considerable trouble and expense to modify a ship which he owned for salvage work, and also bought equipment and engaged a crew. In fact there was no tanker anywhere near the latitude and longitude given by the defendants, and there was no such place as the Jourmand Reef. The plaintiff sued for damages for breach of contract. The High Court of Australia *held* that the plaintiff succeeded because the defendants had impliedly warranted that the goods existed. The Court distinguished *Couturier* v *Hastie* (1856)[102] on the ground that in that case the goods had existed but had perished, whereas in the present case the goods had never existed at all.

Comment. The implied term solution is not too sound because when the court implies a term it generally does so on the ground that the parties would have included it had they addressed themselves to the matter. (But see Lord Denning in *Liverpool City Council* v *Irwin* 1977, p. 50.) It is by no means certain in this case that the defendants would have agreed to such a term. However, there would now be a possible solution in tort if the plaintiff chose to sue in negligence because since the decision of the House of Lords in *Hedley Byrne* v *Heller and Partners* (1963),[120] there is a liability for careless mistatements resulting in monetary loss.

Before the Supply of Goods and Services Act 1982 contracts for work and materials were governed only by the common law. The court would normally imply into those contracts terms which were similar to those implied into contracts of sale by the Sale of Goods Act. The matter is now covered by the Act of 1982.

(280) *Myers (G. H.) & Co.* v *Brent Cross Service Co.* [1934] 1 K.B. 46

The plaintiffs gave instructions to the defendants, who were motor engineers, to repair a car belonging to the plaintiffs. The defendants were authorized to replace such parts as in their opinion needed replacement. In order to repair the car it was necessary for the defendants to supply and fit six remetalled connecting rods, five of which were obtained from the manufacturers of the car, and one from the manufacturers' authorized agent. The car had run for 1500 miles after the repair when one of the connecting rods supplied and fitted by the defendants broke whilst the car was in motion, causing extensive damage to the engine. The plaintiffs now sued for damages. Evidence showed that there was no faulty workmanship by the defendants and that they had used reasonable skill and care throughout; neither could they have discovered the flaw in the connecting rods. *Held*—Although the contract was not one of sale of goods, but was a contract for work and materials, the liability of a contractor supplying goods in the ordinary course of doing work of this nature was not less than the liability of a seller of goods. There was an implied warranty as to fitness and merchantable quality similar to that in the Sale of Goods Act for breach of which the plaintiffs could claim damages.

Where a seller delivers goods to a person on sale or return, then if that person pledges the goods he adopts the sale and the pawnbroker obtains a good title.

(281) *London Jewellers Ltd* v *Attenborough* [1934] 2 K.B. 206

A fraudulent person named Waller told the plaintiffs that he could sell jewellery to a well-known actress and the plaintiffs gave him certain items of jewellery for that purpose. Waller signed a note in respect of each article and the note described the goods as being 'on appro' or on approval. Waller was also entitled to the difference between the selling price and the price marked on the note. Waller pledged the goods, using women agents, and the defendants, who were pawnbrokers, received the goods *bona fide*. Waller was later arrested and charged with larceny while a bailee, and the plaintiffs sued the defendants in detinue and conversion. *Held*—The defendants had a good title and were not liable. When Waller pledged the goods he signified that he adopted the transaction and had approved them. The property therefore passed to him at that moment and he was able to give the defendants a good title.

In granting the remedy of rescission of contract equity will give a money indemnity but only in regard to the performance of obligations created by the contract and not all loss.

(282) *Whittington* v *Seale-Hayne* (1900) 82 L.T. 49

The plaintiffs were breeders of prize poultry and they took a lease of the defendant's premises. The defendant misrepresented, though not fraudulently, that the premises were in a sanitary condition, but in fact the water supply was poisoned, and this caused the illness of the plaintiff's manager. In addition, certain of their poultry died or became valueless for breeding purposes. The local authority required the plaintiffs to carry out certain work in order to render the premises sanitary, the plaintiffs having agreed in the lease to do such work if it became necessary. The plaintiffs now asked for rescission of the contract and for an indemnity against the following losses: stock lost, £750; loss of profit on sales, £100; loss of breeding season, £500; removal of stores and rent, £75; medical expenses, £100. *Held*—The lease could be rescinded, but the plaintiffs' indemnity was restricted to the losses necessarily incurred by taking a lease of the premises i.e. rent, rates and the cost of the repairs ordered by the local authority.

Comment. The reason for restricting the indemnity in this sort of case seems to be based on the fact that although equity is prepared to rescind contracts for innocent misrepresentation, thus providing a remedy where the common law does not, equity will not circumvent the law by making an indemnity (the object of which is to help restore the *status* *quo*) the equivalent of damages for fraud. (See now s.2(1) of the Misrepresentation Act 1967, and *Hedley Byrne* v *Heller & Partners* 1963[120] which potentially provide a remedy of damages for negligent misrepresentation.

The court may decide that a term of a contract is an intermediate obligation. Whether it is then a condition or a warranty may be decided upon the EFFECT of the breach of it.

(283) *Cehave NV* v *Bremer Handelsgesellschaft mbH* [1975] 3 All E.R. 739

The defendants sold citrus pulp pellets to the plaintiffs. A term of the contract was 'shipment to be made in good condition'. The goods were not delivered all at once but in consignments, and when a particular consignment arrived at Rotterdam the market price of the goods had fallen and it was found that 1260 tons of the goods out of a total consignment of 3293 tons was damaged. The plaintiffs rejected the whole cargo on the grounds that the shipment was not made in good condition. They then claimed the recovery of the price which amounted to £100,000. In the event, a middle man bought the goods at the price of £33,720 and resold them to the plaintiffs at the same price. The plaintiffs then used the pellets for making cattle food as was the original intention. The total result of the transaction, if it had been left that way, was that the plaintiffs had received goods which they had bought for £100,000 for the reduced price of £33,720. The Court of Appeal decided in favour of the sellers. The Court *held* that the contractual term 'shipment to be made in good condition' was not a condition within the meaning of the Sale of Goods Act, but was an intermediate term. As Lord Denning, M.R., said: 'If a small portion of the whole cargo was not in good condition and arrived a little unsound, it should be met by a price allowance. The buyers should not have the right to reject the whole cargo unless it was serious or substantial'.

Lord Denning also rejected the view that the goods were not of merchantable quality simply because they were not perfect in every way. He said that the definition now contained in s.14(2) of the Sale of Goods Act 1979 was to be preferred because it was more flexible than some of the earlier judicial decisions on previous legislation. In fact the definition delegates to the court the task of deciding what is merchantable in the circumstances of each particular case.

Comment. This intermediate term approach was endorsed by the House of Lords in *Reardon Smith Line* v *Hansen-Tangen* [1976] 3 All E.R. 570.

The condition in s.12 is broken if the seller is not the owner and also if for any other reason he does not have the right to sell the goods.

(284) *Niblett Ltd* v *Confectioners' Materials Co. Ltd* [1921] 3 K.B. 387

The defendants agreed to sell to the plaintiffs 3000 cases of condensed milk to be shipped from New York to London. 1000 cases bore labels with the word 'Nissly' on them. This came to the notice of the Nestlé Company and they suggested that this was an infringement of their registered trade mark. The plaintiffs admitted this and gave an undertaking not to sell the milk under the title of 'Nissly'. They tried to dispose of the goods in various ways but eventually discovered that the only way to deal with the goods was to take off the labels and sell the milk without mark or label, thus incurring loss. *Held*—by the Court of Appeal—that the sellers were in breach of the implied condition set out in s.12(1) of the Sale of Goods Act. A person who can sell goods only by infringing a trade mark has no right to sell, even though he may be the owner of the goods. Atkin, L.J., also found the sellers to be in breach of the warranty under s.12(2) because the buyer had not enjoyed quiet possession of the goods.

Section 13 applies where the purchaser has not seen the goods but relies on the description. However, to take advantage of s.13 the buyer need not rely exclusively upon the description. He may, for example, have inspected the goods.

(285) *Beale* v *Taylor* [1967] 3 All E.R. 253

The defendant advertised a car for sale as being a 1961 Triumph Herald 1200 and he believed this description to be correct. The plaintiff answered the advertisement and later visited the defendant to inspect the car. During his inspection he noticed, on the rear of the car, a metal disc with the figure 1200 on it. The plaintiff purchased the car, paying the agreed price. However, he later discovered that the car was made up of the rear of a 1961 Triumph Herald 1200 welded to the front of an earlier Triumph Herald 948. The welding was unsatisfactory and the car was unroadworthy. *Held*—by the Court of Appeal—that the plaintiff's claim for damages for breach of the condition implied in the contract by s.13 of the Sale of Goods Act succeeded. The plaintiff had relied on the advertisement and on the metal disc on the rear and the sale was one by description even though the plaintiff had seen and inspected the vehicle.

(286) *Varley* v *Whipp* [1900] 1 Q.B. 513

The plaintiff, who was not a dealer, told the defendant that he had a piece of farming equipment called a self-binder for sale. The plaintiff also said that the machine had been used for one season only and had cut 50 to 60 acres. The defendant agreed to buy the machine although he had not seen it. When the machine was delivered, the defendant discovered that it was rather old and had been mended. He wrote to the plaintiff repudiating the contract and returned the machine. The plaintiff now sued to recover £21, the price of the machine. *Held*—The plaintiff's action failed, for in a contract of sale of specific goods or ascertained goods where the buyer has not seen the goods but relies on a description, the contract is a sale by description under s.13 of the Sale of Goods Act, and there is an implied condition that the goods shall correspond with the description.

Comment. It will be noted from this case that s.13 applies to sales where the seller is not a dealer.

If the defect is a matter of quality and condition rather than description, s.14 but not s.13 applies.

(287) *Ashington Piggeries Ltd* v *Christopher Hill Ltd* [1971] 1 All E.R. 847

Ashington Piggeries, who were breeders of animals, contracted with Hill for the supply of food for mink. The food was a form of herring meal to be made up according to a formula supplied by the breeders and agreed by the suppliers. Hill obtained the food from a firm named Norsildmel who were also involved in this action. Unknown to the parties the food supplied contained a poison harmful to most animals and seriously dangerous to mink, and many of the mink who ate it died. The presence of the poison (D.M.N.A.) was the result of treating the herring with a preservative, sodium nitrate, which was poisonous to mink.

Hill sued Ashington for the price of the feed and Ashington counterclaimed for the loss of the mink. Hill also claimed an indemnity against Norsildmel. The case eventually reached the House of Lords where it was *held*—

(1) The suppliers were not liable for breach of s.13 of the 1979 Act. The substance had been described as 'herring meal' and this was not a misdescription even though what was supplied was herring meal plus D.M.N.A. (*Pinnock Bros* v *Lewis and Peat* 1923 (see p. 516 distinguished on the grounds that the adulteration in that case was much greater.)

(2) The suppliers were liable under s.14(3) since the goods were not fit for the purpose. Although the breeders had supplied the formula they had relied on the supplier's skill and judgment to exercise discretion and obtain at least non-poisonous food. Furthermore, the suppliers were, in general terms, in business to supply animal foods and it did not matter that they had not sold this particular brand of food before (this decision was unanimous).

(3) The suppliers were also liable under s.14(2). The section was capable of application even in a situation in which the seller was selling a particular article for the first time.

(4) The suppliers were entitled to be indemnified by Norsildmel, the defence of remoteness of damage being unacceptable in view of the fact that feeding to mink was a possibility contemplated by both Norsildmel and Hill.

Comment. The Court treated the contract as a contract of sale even though it had an element of labour and materials, being a contract to make up animal foodstuffs according to a formula.

The condition of fitness for the purpose operates when the buyer makes known to the seller the purpose for which the goods are being bought. However, there is no need to reveal a usual purpose.

(288) *Priest* v *Last* [1903] 2 K.B. 148

The plaintiff, a draper who had no special knowledge of hot-water bottles, bought such a bottle from the defendant who was a chemist. It was in the ordinary course of the defendant's business to sell hot-water bottles and the plaintiff asked him whether the indiarubber bottle he was shown would stand boiling water. He was told that it would not, but that it would stand hot water. The plaintiff did not state the purpose for which the bottle was required. In the event the bottle was filled with hot water and used by the plaintiff's wife for bodily application to relieve cramp. On the fifth time of using, the bottle burst and the wife was severely scalded. Evidence showed that the bottle was not fit for use as a hot-water bottle. *Held*—The plaintiff was entitled to recover for the defendant's breach of s.14(3) of the Sale of Goods Act. The circumstances showed that the plaintiff had relied on the defendant's skill and judgment, and although he had not mentioned the purpose for which he required the bottle, he had in fact used it for the usual and obvious purpose.

In actions relating to fitness for the purpose the courts seem quite prepared to infer the necessary reliance except sometimes in cases where the seller is known to sell only one brand of goods.

(289) *Grant* v *Australian Knitting Mills Ltd* [1936] A.C. 85

This was an appeal from the High Court of Australia to the Privy Council in England by a Dr Grant of Adelaide, South Australia. Dr Grant bought a pair of long woollen underpants from a retailer, the respondents being the manufacturers. The underpants contained an excess of sulphite which was a chemical used in their manufacture. This chemical should have been eliminated before the product was finished, but a quantity was left in the underpants purchased by Dr Grant. After wearing the pants for a day or two, a rash, which turned out to be dermatitis, appeared on the appellant's ankles and soon became generalized, compelling the appellant to spend many months in hospital. He sued the retailers and the manufacturers for damages. *Held*—(1) The retailers were in breach of the South Australian Sale of Goods Act 1895 (which is in the same terms as the English Act of 1979). They were liable under s.14(3) because the article was not fit for the purpose. They were liable under s.14(2) because the article was not of merchantable quality. (2) The manufacturers were liable in negligence, following *Donoghue* v *Stevenson.*[304] This was a latent defect which could not have been discovered by a reasonable examination. It should also be noted that the appellant had a perfectly normal skin. (Compare *Griffiths* v *Peter Conway Ltd* 1939.)[295]

Comment. Section 13 (sale by description) also applied even though this was a sale of a specific object which was seen by the purchaser. On the issue of reliance Lord Wright said: '. . . the reliance will be in general inferred from the fact that a buyer goes to the shop in confidence that the tradesman has selected his stock with skill and judgement'.

(290) *Wren* v *Holt* [1903] 1 K.B. 610

The plaintiff was a builder's labourer at Blackburn, and the defendant was the tenant of a beerhouse in the same town. The beerhouse was a tied house so that the defendant was obliged to sell beer brewed by a firm called Richard Holden Limited. The plaintiff was a regular customer and knew that the beerhouse was a tied house, and that only one type of beer was supplied. The plaintiff became ill and it was established that his illness was caused by arsenical poisoning due to the beer supplied to him. He now sued the tenant. *Held*—There was no claim under s.14(3) because the plaintiff could not have relied on the defendant's skill and judgment in selecting his stock, because he was bound to supply Holden's beer. However, s.14(2) applied, and since the beer was not of merchantable quality, the plaintiff was entitled to recover damages.

(291) *Manchester Liners Ltd* v *Rea* [1922] 2 A.C. 74

The defendants supplied coal to the owners of a ship called the *Manchester Importer*. The coal was not suitable for that particular vessel and the sellers were *held*—by the House of Lords—to be in breach of s.14(3), even though the buyers suspected that the sellers might not have suitable coal owing to a rail strike. Thus a mere suspicion (as distinct from certainty) that only goods of a certain kind can be sold is not enough.

Comment. *Griffiths* v *Peter Conway Ltd* 1939[295] was distinguished. The defendants had undertaken to supply coal for a particular class of ship and knew ships differed as to type and fuel requirements. There were no normal or standard ships. There are normal human beings who would not have been affected by the coal supplied in *Griffiths'* case. See also *Ashington Piggeries*[287] where it was regarded as essential to show that the herring meal was toxic to most animals and not just to mink.

Under s.14(3), which applies to manufactured and non-manufactured goods, liability is strict. A seller who has taken all possible care will still be liable.

(292) *Frost* v *Aylesbury Dairy Co. Ltd* [1905] 1 K.B. 608

The defendants, whose business was the selling of milk, supplied milk to the plaintiff's household. The account book supplied to him contained several statements regarding the precautions taken by the defendants to keep their milk free from germs. This action was brought by the plaintiff for damage sustained by him on the death of his wife by typhoid fever contracted from the milk supplied by the defendants. *Held*—The plaintiff succeeded because the circumstances showed that he had relied on the defendants' skill and judgment to select and supply milk free from germs. He was, therefore, entitled to the benefit of s.14(3) of the Sale of Goods Act because the milk was not fit for human consumption. It was not a defence that no skill or judgment would have enabled the sellers to find out the defect.

The implied terms relating to fitness and merchantable quality extend also to goods supplied under the contract, e.g. returnable bottles and foreign matter.

(293) *Geddling* v *Marsh* [1920] 1 K.B. 668

The defendants were manufacturers of mineral waters and they supplied the same to the plaintiff who kept a small general store. The bottles were returnable when empty. One of the bottles was defective, and whilst the plaintiff was putting it back into a crate, it burst and injured her. *Held*—Even though the bottles were returnable, they were supplied under a contract of sale within s.14 of the Sale of Goods Act. The fact that the bottles were only bailed to the plaintiff was immaterial. There was an implied warranty of fitness for the purpose for which they were supplied, and the defendant was liable in damages.

Comment. Bray, J., was careful to point out that his decision was an interpretation of s.14 of the Sale of Goods Act only. It does not decide that the liability of a bailor is the same as that of a vendor.

(294) *Wilson* v *Rickett, Cockerell & Co. Ltd* [1954] 1 Q.B. 598

The plaintiff, a housewife, ordered from the defendants, who were coal merchants, a ton of 'Coalite'. The Coalite was delivered and when part of it was put on a fire in an open grate, it exploded causing damage to the plaintiff's house. In this action the plaintiff claimed damages for breach of s.14 of the Sale of Goods Act. The County Court judge found that the explosion was not due to the Coalite but to something else, possibly a piece of coal with explosive embedded in it, which had got mixed with the Coalite in transit and had not come from the manufacturers of the Coalite. Therefore, he held that s.14(3) applied only to the Coalite and dismissed the action since the Coalite itself was fit for the purpose. The Court of Appeal, however, in allowing the appeal, pointed out that fuel of this kind is not sold by the lump but by the bag, and a bag containing explosive materials is, as a unit, not fit for burning. The explosive matter was 'goods supplied under the contract' for the purposes of s.14, and clearly s.14(2) applied, because the goods supplied were not of merchantable quality. Damages were awarded to the plaintiff. Regarding the applicability of s.14(3), the Court of Appeal did not think this applied since the sale was under a trade name, and the plaintiff had not relied on the defendants' skill and judgment in selecting a fuel.

If ordinary goods in everyday use are required for a special purpose then this must be made known to the seller and will not be implied.

(295) *Griffiths* v *Peter Conway Ltd* [1939] 1 All E.R. 685

The defendants, who were retail tailors, supplied the plaintiff with a Harris tweed coat which was made to order for her. The plaintiff wore the coat for a short time and then developed dermatitis. She brought this action for damages alleging that the defendants were in breach of s.14(3) of the Sale of Goods Act because the coat was not fit for the purpose for which it was bought. Evidence showed that the plaintiff had an abnormally sensitive skin and that the coat would not have affected the skin of a normal person. *Held*—The plaintiff failed because s.14(3) did not apply. The defendants did not know of the plaintiff's abnormality and could not be expected to assume that it existed.

Often goods which are not fit for the purpose under s.14(3) are also unmerchantable under s.14(2), but s.14(3) can operate independently.

(296) *Baldry* v *Marshall* [1925] 1 K.B. 260

The plaintiff was the owner of a Talbot racing car and was anxious to change it for a touring car because his wife refused to ride in the Talbot. The plaintiff wrote to the defendants asking for details of the Bugatti car for which they were agents. The plaintiff knew nothing of the Bugatti range, but asked for a car that would be comfortable and suitable for touring purposes. The defendants' manager said that a Bugatti would be suitable. The plaintiff later inspected a Bugatti chassis and agreed to buy it when a body had been put on it. When the car was delivered it was to all intents and purposes a racing car and not suitable for touring. The plaintiff returned the car, but he had paid £1000 under the contract and now sued for its return on the grounds that the defendants were in breach of s.14(3) of the Sale of Goods Act, the car not being fit for the purpose. *Held*—The plaintiff had relied on the skill and judgment of the defendants and it was in the course of their business to supply cars. Therefore, there was a breach of s.14(3) even though the car was sold under a trade name.

In deciding the matter of fitness for the purpose in the case of secondhand goods, the buyer must expect that defects are likely to emerge sooner or later. However, if defects occur fairly quickly after sale this is strong evidence that the goods were not reasonably fit at the time of sale.

(297) *Crowther* v *Shannon Motor Company* [1975] 1 All E.R. 139

The plaintiff, relying on the skill and judgment of the defendants, bought a secondhand car from them. After being driven for over 2000 miles in the three weeks after the sale the engine seized and had to be replaced. In his evidence the previous owner said that the engine was not fit for use on the road when he sold it to the defendants and on that basis the Court of Appeal *held* that there was a breach of s.14(3) at the time of resale. The fact that a car does not go for a reasonable time after sale is evidence that the car was not fit for the purpose at the time of sale.

A retailer does not warrant the safety of goods when they are used by the purchaser after that purchaser knows of the defects.

(298) *Lambert* v *Lewis* [1981] 1 All E.R. 1185

Mr Lewis owned a Land Rover and a trailer. His employee, Mr Larkin, was driving it when the trailer broke away. It collided with a car coming from the opposite direction. Mr Lambert, who was driving that car, was killed and so was his son. His wife and daughter, who were also passengers, survived and then sued Mr Lewis for damages in negligence. He joined the retailer who sold him the towing hitch which had become detached from the trailer and was basically the cause of the collision. The retailer was sued under s.14 (goods not fit for the purpose nor of merchantable quality). The Court found that the towing hitch was badly designed and a securing brass spindle and handle had come off it so that only dirt was keeping the towing pin in position. It had been like that for some months and Mr Lewis had coupled and uncoupled the trailer once or twice a week during that time and knew of the problem.

The plaintiffs succeeded in their action against Mr Lewis. He failed in his claim against the retailer. The House of Lords decided that when a person first buys goods he can rely on s.14. However, once he discovers that they are defective but continues to use them and so causes injury, he is personally liable for the loss caused. He cannot claim an indemnity under s.14 from the retailer. The chain of causation is broken by the buyer's continued use of the goods while knowing that they are faulty and may cause injury.

Comment. The above summary does not concern itself with the possible liability of the manufacturers in terms of the design problem. However, a point of interest arises in connection with it. The issue of the manufacturer's liability was taken by an action in negligence. The Court refused to construe a collateral contract between Mr Lewis and the manufacturers although he bought the hitch on the strength of the manufacturers' advertising. (Compare *Carlill*[1] where such a contract was rather exceptionally construed.)

As regards goods of unmerchantable quality, a buyer is in a better position if he fails to examine the goods than if he does make an examination but fails to find the defect.

(299) *Thornett and Fehr* v *Beers and Son* [1919] 1 K.B. 486

The plaintiffs were dealers in glue and the defendants, being interested in purchasing glue, sent a representative to the plaintiffs to discuss the matter. The representative was given a sample of the glue but the defendants said that it was not large enough to ascertain the quality. It was therefore arranged that the defendants should send a representative to the plaintiffs' factory at Nottingham to inspect the glue. The plaintiffs gave instructions that every facility was to be given to the defendants' representative to carry out the examination. In the event, the representative who went to the factory discussed the quality of the glue but did not have the casks opened, although the plaintiffs would have allowed this. If the casks had been opened, the defects which the defendants later complained of would have been revealed. The defendants bought some of the glue at an agreed price, and on finding it not of suitable quality, refused to pay for it. The plaintiffs now sued for the agreed price and the defendants counter-claimed that there was a breach of s.14(2) because the goods were not of merchantable quality. *Held*—There was no implied condition of merchantable quality under s.14(2) because the provision in the section relating to examination applied.

Comment. This was not a sale by sample because, since the sample was too small, the defendants did not rely on it but relied instead on the inspection carried out by their representative.

The resale price of goods has some bearing on their original merchantability.

(300) *B. S. Brown & Son Ltd* v *Craiks Ltd* [1970] 1 All E.R. 823

Brown and Son ordered a quantity of cloth from Craiks who were manufacturers. Brown's wanted it for making dresses but did not make this purpose known to Craiks who thought the cloth was wanted for industrial use. The price paid by Brown's was 36·25p per yard which was higher than the normal price for industrial cloth but not substantially so. The cloth was not suitable for making dresses and Brown's cancelled the contract and claimed damages. Both parties were left with substantial quantities of cloth but Craiks had managed to sell some of their stock for 30p per yard. Having failed in the lower court to establish a claim under s.14(3) since they had not made the purpose known to Craiks, Brown's now sued for damages under s.14(2). *Held*—by the House of Lords—that the claim failed. The cloth was still commercially saleable for industrial purposes though at a slightly lower price. It was not a necessary requirement of merchantability that there should be no difference between purchase and resale price. If the difference was substantial, however, it might indicate that the goods were not of merchantable quality. The difference in this case was not so material as to justify any such inference.

A reasonable examination for the purpose of a sale by sample is such an examination as is usually carried out in the trade concerned.

(301) *Godley* v *Perry* [1960] 1 All E.R. 36

The first defendant, Perry, was a newsagent who also sold toys, and in particular displayed plastic toy catapults in his window. The plaintiff, who was a boy aged six, bought one for 6d. While using it to fire a stone, the catapult broke, and the plaintiff was struck in the eye, either by a piece of the catapult or the stone, and as a result he lost his left eye. The chemist's report given in evidence was that the catapults were made from cheap material unsuitable for the purpose and likely to fracture, and that the moulding of the plastic was poor, the catapults containing internal voids. Perry had purchased the catapults from a wholesaler with whom he had dealt for some time, and this sale was by sample, the defendant's wife examining the sample catapult by pulling the elastic. The wholesaler's supplier was another wholesaler who had imported the catapults from Hong Kong. This sale was also by sample and the sample catapult was again tested by pulling the elastic. In this action the plaintiff alleged that the first defendant was in breach of the conditions implied by s.14(2) and (3) of the Sale of Goods Act. The first defendant brought in his supplier as third party, alleging against him a breach of the conditions implied by s.15(2)(*c*), and the third party brought in his supplier as fourth party, alleging breach of s.15(2)(*c*) against him. *Held*—

(1) The first defendant was in breach of s.14(2) and (3) because—
(*a*) The catapult was not reasonably fit for the purpose for which it was required. The plaintiff relied on the seller's skill or judgment, this being readily inferred where the customer was of tender years. (S.14(3).)
(*b*) The catapult was not merchantable. (S.14(2).)

(2) The third and fourth parties were both in breach of s.15(2)(*c*) because the catapult had a defect which rendered it unmerchantable, and this defect was not apparent on reasonable examination of the sample. The test applied, i.e. the pulling of the elastic, was all that could be expected of a potential purchaser. The third and fourth parties had done business before, and the third party was entitled to regard without suspicion any sample shown to him and to rely on the fourth party's skill in selecting his goods.

The Sale of Goods Act deals only with contractual rights and duties. However, a seller of goods may be liable in the tort of negligence to the buyer or to third parties because the goods sold are dangerous. There is also a duty of care in regard to chattels which are not dangerous in themselves. The duty of care in respect of chattels dangerous in themselves is, however, much higher.

(302) *Clarke* v *Army and Navy Co-operative Society Ltd* [1903] 1 K.B. 155

The defendants sold to the plaintiff a tin of chlorinated lime for use as disinfectant. The defendants knew that other tins from the consignment had caused injury to persons opening them because the tins were badly constructed. No warning was given to the plaintiff when the goods were purchased and she was injured when in the course of opening the tin, lime flew into her eyes. In this action by the plaintiff for damages, it was *held* that a seller of goods, which have a dangerous quality which the seller knows and the buyer does not, has a duty to warn the buyer of that dangerous quality. Therefore, the defendants were liable for their negligent act in not warning the plaintiff that the tins were dangerous.

(303) *Fisher* v *Harrods* (1966) 110 S.J. 133

The defendants bought a jewellery cleaner from a manufacturer without making enquiries as to its safety in use. It contained substances which were injurous to the eyes but no indication or warning of this was given either on the bottle or in any other way. A bottle of the cleaner sold by the defendants injured the plaintiff when the contents exploded, damaging her eyes. She now claimed damages from the defendants and it was *held* that they had been negligent in the circumstances of the case by failing to make enquiries of the manufacturer; failing to have the cleaner analysed; and selling it without a warning.

(304) *Donoghue (or M'Alister)* v *Stevenson* [1932] A.C. 562

The appellant's friend purchased a bottle of ginger beer from a retailer in Paisley and gave it to her. The respondents were the manufacturers of the ginger beer. The appellant consumed some of the ginger beer and her friend was replenishing the glass, when, according to the appellant, the decomposed remains of a snail came out of the bottle. The bottle was made of dark glass so that the snail could not be seen until most of the contents had been consumed. The appellant became ill and served a writ on the manufacturers claiming damages. The question before the House of Lords was whether the facts outlined above constituted a cause of action in negligence. The House of Lords *held* by a majority of three to two that they did. It was stated that a manufacturer of products, which are sold in such a form that they are likely to reach the ultimate consumer in the form in which they left the manufacturer with no possibility of intermediate examination, owes a duty to the consumer to take reasonable care to prevent injury. This rule has been broadened in subsequent cases so that the manufacturer is liable more often where defective chattels cause injury. The following important points also arise out of the case.

(1) It was in this case that the House of Lords formulated the test

that the duty of care in negligence is based on the foresight of the reasonable man.

(2) Lord Macmillan's remark that the categories of negligence are never closed suggests that the tort of negligence is capable of further expansion. (See, for example, *Junior Books.*)[306]

(3) The duty of care with regard to chattels as laid down in the case relates to chattels not dangerous in themselves. The duty of care in respect of chattels dangerous in themselves, e.g. explosives, is much higher.

(4) The appellant had no cause of action against the retailer in contract because her friend bought the bottle, so that there was no privity of contract between the retailer and the appellant. Therefore terms relating to fitness for purpose and merchantable quality, implied into such contracts by the Sale of Goods Act, did not apply here.

While the action in the tort of negligence was used successfully in the preceding cases, it has one major disadvantage, and that is the plaintiff must prove negligence in the process of manufacturer. However, assistance is given by the plea of *res ipsa loquitur* (the think speaks for itself).

(305) *Daniels* v *R. White and Sons Ltd* [1938] 4 All E.R. 258

The plaintiffs, who were husband and wife, sued the first defendants, who were manufacturers of mineral waters, in negligence. The plaintiffs had been injured because a bottle of the first defendants' lemonade, which they had purchased from a public house in Battersea, contained carbolic acid. The plaintiffs pleaded *res ipsa loquitur*. This plea was accepted by the Court and the defendant was therefore required to produce evidence of a safe system and proper supervision. Evidence showed that the manufacturer took all possible care to see that no injurious matter got into the lemonade, and that the husband when he bought the lemonade from the public house asked for it by mentioning the manufacturers' name. it was *held* that the manufacturers were not liable in negligence because the duty was not one to ensure that the goods were in perfect condition but only to take reasonable care to see that no injury was caused to the eventual consumer. This duty had been fulfilled. The second defendant, who was the landlady of the Battersea public house from which the goods were purchased, was held liable under s.14(2) of the Sale of Goods Act, because the goods were not of merchantable quality.

Comment. The Court in this case does not seem to have taken the point that if the system was a good one then the alien matter must have got into the lemonade because of the negligence of an employee, and since an employer is liable for the negligence of his employees, White's ought to have been liable in this case. The decision has been much criticized and MacKenna, J., in *Hill* v *James Crowe (Cases)* [1978] 1 All E.R. 812 refused to follow it saying that a manufacturer can be vicariously liable for the negligence of his workman, notwithstanding the fact that he has a good system of work and adequate supervision.

Product liability in negligence may now extend to complaints relating to defects in the goods which have caused economic loss rather than physical injury.

(306) *Junior Books Ltd* v *Veitchi Co. Ltd* [1982] 3 All E.R. 201

Junior Books (J) owned a building. Veitchi (V) were flooring contractors working under a contract for the main contractor who was doing work on the building. There was no privity of contract between J and V. It was alleged by J that faulty work by V left J with an unserviceable building and high maintenance costs so that J's business became unprofitable. The House of Lords decided in favour of J on the basis that there was duty of care. V were in breach of a duty owed to J to take reasonable care to avoid acts or omissions including laying an allegedly defective floor which they ought to have known would be likely to cause the owners economic loss, including loss of profits caused by the high cost of maintaining the allegedly defective floor, and insofar as J were required to mitigate the loss by replacing the floor itself, the cost of replacement was the appropriate measure of V's liability. The standard of care required is apparently the contractual duty and so long as the work is up to contract standard, then the defendant in a case such as this will not be in breach of his duty. Lord Fraser of Tullybelton said: 'Where a building is erected under a contract with a purchaser, then provided the building, or part of it, is not dangerous to persons or to other property and subject to the law against misrepresentation, I can see no reason why the builder should not be free to make with the purchaser whatever contractual arrangements about the quality of the product the purchaser wishes. However jerry-built the product, the purchaser would not be entitled to damages from the builder if it came up to the contractual standards'.

Comment. This case concerns damage to real property by alleged defective workmanship. Whether the same principle would apply to defective chattels which are unsatisfactory in their use is not absolutely certain. There would seem to be no insuperable difficulty in extending this case to chattels, but it may be some time before all the implications are known.

Under s.18, Rule 1, where there is an unconditional contract for the sale of specific goods, the property passes when the contract is made, but only if the goods are in a deliverable state.

(307) *Underwood Ltd* v *Burgh Castle Brick & Cement Syndicate* [1922] 1 K.B. 343

The plaintiffs agreed to sell a condensing engine to the defendants. At the time the contract was made the engine was at the plaintiffs' premises in Millwall and was fixed to a bed of concrete by bolts. It was necessary to detach the engine before it could be delivered. The engine was damaged in the course of preparing it for dispatch, and when it was delivered the defendants refused to accept it. The plaintiffs argued that the property had passed when the contract was made, so that the defendants must accept their own goods. *Held*—The property had not passed to the defendants because the goods were not in a deliverable state when the contract was made. The engine was at that time a fixture and not in the true sense of the word a movable chattel.

Comment. If the goods are identified and agreed upon and ready for delivery, the buyer becomes owner immediately the contract is made unless there is a contrary intention under s.17. Thus in *Dennant* v *Skinner and Collom* [1948] 2 All E.R. 29 a van in a deliverable state was knocked down at auction to a purchaser. He paid by cheque and when he paid he signed a statement that the ownership was not to pass him until the cheque had cleared. The Court held that the ownership had passed to him on the fall of the hammer. The condition in the statement was made too late and after the purchaser became owner. Section 18, Rule 1 applied.

What is a reasonable time for the purposes of s.18, Rule 4(*b*) is a matter of fact depending on the circumstances of each case.

(308) *Poole* v *Smith's Car Sales (Balham) Ltd* [1962] 2 All E.R. 482

In August 1960, the plaintiff, a car dealer, supplied two secondhand cars to the defendants who were also car dealers. The cars were supplied on 'sale or return' terms whilst the plaintiff went on holiday, the agreement being that the defendants would return the cars if they were not sold in that time. One car was sold and paid for on 21 September 1960, but the other car, a 1956 Vauxhall Wyvern, had not been sold or returned by the end of October 1960. The plaintiff tried to get it returned to making telephone calls but finally he wrote a letter to the defendants, dated 7 November, in which he said that, if the car was not returned by 10 November 1960, it would be deemed sold to the defendants. The car was not returned until about 24 November and was then in a bad condition, having been used by the defendants' employees for their own purposes. The plaintiff rejected the car and sued for its price, i.e. £325, which was the sale or return value agreed in August 1960. *Held*—The contract was one of delivery 'on a sale or return' and therefore fell within s.18, Rule 4. The property had passed to the defendants because it had not been returned within a reasonable amount of time and the Court was particularly concerned with the depreciation of a 1956 car between September and October when the market was declining. The defendants must pay the contract price as agreed.

Although s.18, Rule 4 will not apply if the parties have expressed a contrary intention, that will not necessarily prevent the buyer from giving a good title if he sells goods held on sale or return.

(309) *Weiner* v *Harris* [1910] 1 K.B. 285

The plaintiff was a jeweller and he entrusted certain goods to one Fisher who was a traveller in the jewellery trade. The terms of the agreement were that Fisher had the goods on 'sale or return' and that they were to remain the property of the plaintiff until sold or paid for. The defendant was a moneylender and he advanced money to Fisher on the security of the goods. The plaintiff now sued to recover the goods from the moneylender. *Held*—The defendant had a good title in spite of the terms of the contract between the plaintiff and Fisher. Fisher was a mercantile agent for the purposes of s.1 of the Factors Act 1889, and therefore had power to pledge the goods under s.2 of the Factors Act 1889.

The relationship between s.16 and s.18, Rule 5(1) is a difficult one. It would seem that the court may take the view that the property has passed where part of a larger quantity is sold leaving what is left belonging to the buyer, even though there is no unconditional appropriation of that balance within the terms of s.18, Rule 5(1) if the court thinks that it was the intention of the parties that ascertainment should also be appropriation.

(310) *Laurie and Morewood* v *Dudin & Sons* [1926] 1 K.B. 223

On 2 February 1925, Messrs Alcock and Sons sold to John Wilkes & Sons 200 quarters of maize from 618 quarters belonging to Alcock and Sons and lying in the defendants' warehouse. Wilkes & Sons were given a delivery note which they sent to the defendants who were therefore on notice of the sale. On 18 February, Wilkes & Sons sold the 200 quarters of maize to the plaintiffs and gave them a delivery note which the plaintiffs sent to the defendants on 19 February. On both occasions when they received delivery notes the defendants merely made entries in their books and no attempt was made to appropriate the goods to the contract. Wilkes & Sons failed to pay Alcock and Sons for the maize and Alcock and Sons instructed the defendants to withhold delivery. The plaintiffs now sued the defendants in detinue, claiming that the property in the maize had passed to them. *Held*—The plaintiffs' action failed. The maize did not belong to them because there had been no appropriation of the goods and therefore the property in the maize had not passed either to Wilkes & Sons or to the plaintiffs.

(311) *Wait and James* v *Midland Bank* (1926) 31 Com. Cas. 172

The sellers sold 1250 quarters of wheat on credit from a larger cargo lying in a warehouse. The buyers were given delivery orders which were acceptable to the warehouseman for purposes of delivery when required. The buyers did not ask for delivery but pledged the delivery orders to a bank as security. At this time no severance of the buyers' wheat had taken place. Later the sellers sold and delivered the remainder of the wheat leaving the buyers' share of the cargo in the warehouse. It was *held*—by Roche, J.,—that the second sale had the effect of passing the property in the remaining wheat to the first buyers and the bank's security was good against the 1250 quarters left.

Comment. (i) Roche, J., appears to have assumed that ascertainment was enough to pass the property. There had been no unconditional appropriation as required by s.18, Rule 5.

(ii) This case was applied in *Karlshamns Oljefabriker* v *Eastport Navigation* [1982] 1 All E.R. 208. The buyer purchased 6000 tons of copra under four contracts. 22,000 tons of copra was loaded on to the vessel *Elafi* which belonged to the defendants. It was to be shipped from the Phillipines to Sweden. 16,000 tons were off-loaded at Hamburg and Rotterdam. The remaining 6000 tons went on to Sweden. On arrival in Sweden it was discovered that the copra had been damaged by water. The *Elafi* was allegedly not seaworthy. The buyers said the goods were not theirs because the property had not passed. It was *held* in the High Court that it had. Mr Justice Mustill in applying the *Wait* case, referred to the judgment of Roche, J., and noted that it omitted any mention of s.18, Rule 5, He then went on to say: 'In my judgment, this objection adds nothing to the argument in relation to ascertainment. It is true that in some cases the ascertainment of goods may not be the same as the unconditional appropriation of them, although the distinction would usually be difficult, if not impossible to draw. But here I cannot see any difference. . . . Before leaving the question of appropriation I should draw attention to one other factor, namely that the want of an unconditional approrpriation is not an absolute bar to the passing of the property but merely one of the factors to be taken into account when ascertaining the presumed intentions of the parties.'

Assent to appropriation may be express or implied and be given either before or after appropriation is made. Under s.20(1) risk passes with the property. The person who has the risk is not necessarily in possession of the goods.

(312) *Pignataro* v *Gilroy & Son* [1919] 1 K.B. 459

By a contract made on 12 February 1918, the defendants sold to the plaintiff 148 bags of rice, the plaintiff to take delivery within 14 days. The rice was unascertained when the contract was made. On 27 February, the plaintiff sent a cheque for the rice and asked for a delivery order. On 28 February the defendants sent a delivery order for 125 bags which were lying at a place called Chambers' Wharf. A letter accompanying the delivery order said that the remaining 15 bags were at the defendants' place of business at 50 Long Acre, and requested the plaintiff to collect them there. The plaintiff did not send for the 15 bags until 25 March when it was found that they had been stolen without negligence on the part of the defendants. *Held*—The goods were at the plaintiff's risk. He had not dissented from the appropriation made by the defendants, and his assent to it must therefore be implied.

The property in identical goods destined for different owners or yet to be weighed, measured, or tested, to ascertain price, does not pass on delivery to a carrier.

(313) *Healey* v *Howlett & Sons* [1917] 1 K.B. 337

Howlett & Sons were fish dealers in Ireland and they supplied fish to English customers. They had an agent at Holyhead, all fish being sent to the agent who selected parcels of fish for dispatch to customers in England. The appellant was a fish saleman in London and he ordered 20 boxes of mackerel from the respondents. The respondents dispatched 122 boxes of mackerel to their agent in Holyhead to fulful the appellant's order and others. The agent selected 20 boxes for dispatch to the appellant, but because of delays in getting the fish to Holyhead, the fish was found to be bad on arrival in London. The delay in getting the fish to Holyhead was not the respondents' fault. The appellant refused to pay the respondents and the respondents sued in the City of London Court for the full price on the ground that the dispatch of 122 boxes of fish to their agent was sufficient appropriation to pass the property to Healey in respect of his 20 boxes. Howlett succeeded in the City of London Court at first instance and Healey now appealed from that decision. *Held*—There was no appropriation until the agent at Holyhead earmarked the 20 boxes for the appellant. The fish had deteriorated before arrival at Holyhead and was at the respondents' risk under s.16 when it did deteriorate. The appellant was therefore not liable to pay for the fish.

Comment. A puts 100 boxes of fish on a train from Holyhead to London. No appropriation is made but 25 boxes are for B at Colwyn Bay, 25 for C at Crewe, 25 for D at Rugby, and 25 for E at London. Appropriation is made at each station. The goods are damaged in an accident at Watford. Do the goods belong to E? *Wait* and *Karlshamns* (see above) would suggest that they might.

(314) *National Coal Board* v *Gamble* [1958] 3 All E.R. 203

The Coal Board supplied coal to a buyer at a colliery by loading from a hopper into the buyer's lorry. The lorry was then driven to a weighbridge so that the weight of the coal could be ascertained and a weight-ticket, as required by statute, issued. The Court held that the property did not pass until the coal had been weighed and the ticket given to and accepted by the buyer. The Court was also of opinion that under the system in operation at the colliery any coal in excess of the buyer's requirement could have been unloaded before the weight-ticket was issued and accepted. It would seem, therefore, that the Court was assuming that although appropriation took place when the coal was loaded on to the lorry, it was not unconditional until it was weighed and the weight-ticket accepted by the buyer.

An agreement that the risk shall not pass with the property and *vice versa* may be inferred from the circumstances of the case.

(315) *Sterns Ltd* v *Vickers Ltd* [1923] 1 K.B. 78

On 3 January 1920, the Admiralty sold to Vickers Ltd, 120,000 gallons of white spirit out of a larger quantity of 200,000 gallons then lying at Thames Haven in Tank No. 78. The tank belonged to a storage company called London and Thames Haven Oil Wharves Company. Vickers Ltd sold the spirit to Sterns Ltd, who did not take delivery for some months. When they did take delivery, the specific gravity of the spirit had changed by deterioration over time. Sterns Ltd claimed damages for breach of warranty against the sellers. *Held*—Whether or not the property in the oil had passed at the time of sale (the goods being unascertained), the oil was at the plaintiffs' risk from the time of sale and the defendants were not liable for breach of warranty.

(316) *Head* v *Tattersall* (1870) L.R. 7 Ex. 7

Tattersall sold a horse to Head warranting that it had hunted with the Bicester Hounds, and giving Head the right to return the horse by a certain date if it did not comply with the warranty. Head discovered that the horse had not hunted with the Bicester Hounds and returned it to Tattersall within the time stipulated. However, whilst the horse was in Head's possession, it was injured, though without negligence on his part. *Held*—In the circumstances it was possible to take the view that the property had passed but not the risk, and Tattersall was obliged to accept the injured horse.

Comment. The general rule is that where goods are delivered on approval or on sale or return the property in them remains with the seller until the buyer adopts the transaction. However, this case shows that it is possible to enter into a transaction which has a similar purpose but under which the property passes immediately to the buyer subject to his right to return the goods.

Under s.20 where the seller has in pursuance of the contract set aside goods to await instructions as to their delivery and they perish because the buyer fails to give these instructions, the risk is with the buyer.

(317) *Demby, Hamilton & Co. Ltd* v *Barden* [1949] 1 All E.R. 435

The plaintiffs were sellers of apple juice, and on 8 November 1945 they entered into a contract with the defendants who were wine merchants. Under the contract the plaintiffs were to supply and the defendants were to buy 30 tons of apple juice to be delivered by lorry in weekly instalments, the contract to be completed by the end of February 1946. The plaintiffs crushed a quantity of apples and put the juice into casks, but the property did not pass at that stage since the casks were not specifically appropriated to the contract. $20\frac{1}{2}$ tons of apple juice were delivered and at that stage the buyers said that they could not take the other instalments until further notice. The last delivery was made on 4 April 1946. The plaintiffs repeatedly asked for delivery instructions, and on 7 November 1946 they informed the defendants that the contents of the remaining casks had gone putrid and had been thrown away. The plaintiffs now sued for the price of the goods sold and delivered, and for damages in respect of the apple juice which had been thrown away. *Held*—Under the proviso to s.20 the goods were at the buyer's risk because he was responsible for the delay. If the sellers could have sold the remainder of the apple juice elsewhere, the loss might have fallen on them, but their contract with the defendants obliged the plaintiffs to hold the goods available for delivery as and when required by the defendants. The plaintiff's action for the price of the goods sold and for damages succeeded.

Where the owner of goods, by his words or conduct, represents to the buyer that the seller is the true owner, the owner is unable to deny the title of the buyer.

(318) *Henderson & Co.* v *Williams* [1895] 1 Q.B. 521

The plaintiffs were sugar merchants at Hull. The defendant was a warehouseman at Hull and Goole. On 3 June 1894, a fraudulent person named Fletcher, posing as the agent of one Robinson, negotiated a purchase of sugar from Messrs Grey & Co., who were Liverpool merchants. The sugar was lying in the defendant's warehouse at Goole, and Messrs Grey & Co. sent a telegram and later a letter advising the defendant that the sugar was to be held to the order of Fletcher, and the defendant entered the order in his books. Robinson was a reputable dealer and a customer of Messrs Grey & Co., and of course Fletcher had no right to act on Robinson's behalf. Fletcher sold the goods to the plaintiffs who, before paying the price, got a statement from the defendant that the goods were held to the order of Fletcher. The defendant later discovered Fletcher's fraud and refused to release the sugar to the plaintiffs who now sued in conversion. *Held*—The defendant was estopped from denying Fletcher's title and was liable in damages based on the market price of the goods at the date of refusal to deliver. Further the true owners, Messrs Grey & Co., could not set up their title to the sugar against that of the plaintiffs, since they had allowed Fletcher to hold himself out as the true owner.

In order that s.21(1) shall apply to estop the true owner from denying the authority of the seller to sell, there must be a representation by statement or conduct by the original owner that the seller was entitled to sell the goods.

(319) *Eastern Distributors Ltd* v *Goldring* [1957] 2 Q.B. 600

A person named Murphy was the owner of a Bedford van and wished to buy a Chrysler car from one Coker who was a car dealer. Murphy could not find the money to pay the hire-purchase deposit on the Chrysler. Coker suggested that Murphy authorize him to sell the van to a finance company and get an agreement from the finance company under which they agreed to sell the van to Murphy on hire-purchase terms and then Murphy could apply the proceeds of the sale of his van in putting down deposits on the van and the Chrysler.

Murphy gave Coke authority, but limited it to selling the van and arranging the hire purchase of the van and the Chrysler. Under the authority given to him Coker was bound to effect *both* transactions and not one only. Murphy then signed the necessary documents leaving Coker to fill them in. In the proposal form for the hire purchase of the van Coker described himself as owner of the vehicle and without authority from Murphy sold the van to the plaintiffs, who were the finance company, as if it was his own. The plaintiffs then hired it out to Murphy and sent him a copy of the agreement. The hire purchase of the Chrysler was not carried out and later Coker told Murphy that the whole deal had fallen through, and was cancelled. Murphy then sold the van which he believed to be his own to Goldring, who bought in good faith and without knowledge of Murphy's previous dealings. Murphy made no payments under the hire-purchase agreement, and the plaintiffs terminated it and claimed the van or its value from the defendant. *Held*—by the Court of Appeal—

(1) Coker had no actual authority to sell the van separately to the plaintiffs but only as part of a double transaction. However, Murphy, by providing Coker with documents which enabled him to represent himself to the plaintiffs as entitled to the van, had clothed Coker with apparent authority to sell and was prevented by s.21(1) of the Sale of Goods Act from denying that authority. The plaintiffs had obtained a good title and Murphy had no title to give Goldring.

(2) Section 25(1) of the Sale of Goods Act did not make the sale to Goldring valid, because Murphy was, after the hire-purchase agreement, not in possession as a seller but as a bailee by virtue of the agreement.

Comment. If Goldring was a private purchaser he would now obtain a good title under the Hire-Purchase Act 1964, Part III, as substituted by s.192 and Sch.4, para. 22 of the Consumer Credit Act 1974.

In order to obtain a good title in market overt the sale must take place openly in the City of London or other market overt; be according to the usage of the market concerned, and the buyer must act in good faith and be unaware of the seller's lack of title.

(320) *Reid* v *Commr of Police of the Metropolis*, [1973] 2 All E.R. 97

In December 1969 a pair of Adam candelabra were stolen from the plaintiff's home in Chelsea. In February 1970 between 7 a.m. and 8.15 a.m., a Mr Cocks bought them at a stall in a statutory market in Southwark, the permitted hour for the opening of which was 7 a.m. When the goods were purchased the sun had not risen and it was still only half light. The plaintiff discovered the whereabouts of the goods and informed the police who took them into custody. The plaintiff claimed their return and the Court of Appeal decided that in order to establish that a sale of goods had taken place in market overt so as to convey a good title to the goods even against the true owner, it must be shown that the goods were sold between sunrise and sunset. Seeing that this sale was made before sunrise, Mr Cocks did not get a good title. The plaintiff, the true owner, was entitled to have the pair of Adam candelabra returned to him.

Comment. Usage of the market is illustrated by *Bishopgate Motor Finance Corporation* v *Transport Brakes Ltd* [1949] 1 All E.R. 37. In that case a person who had a car on hire purchase put it up for sale at an auction in Maidstone market. It was not sold at auction but by a private agreement later. Maidstone market was established in 1747 by Royal Charter and was therefore a market overt. The innocent buyer could not get a good title unless the sale was according to the usage of the market. It was held that it was because it was customary in the Maidstone market for goods not sold at auction to be sold privately in the market after the auction.

(321) *Clayton* v *Le Roy* [1911] 2 K.B. 1031

In 1902 Mrs Clayton, the plaintiff's wife, bought a gold watch from the defendant for £100 and gave it to her husband. In 1908 the watch was stolen from Major Clayton whilst he was on the Riviera and shortly afterwards the watch was pawned with a firm of pawnbrokers. In 1909 the watch was sold as an unredeemed pledge by public auction at the auctioneer's auction rooms, No. 38, Gracechurch Street in the City of London. The watch was bought at the auction by a *bona fide* purchaser for £26 and eventually came into the hands of a Mr Bennett who bought it for £44. In May 1910, Mr Bennett brought the watch to the defendant for examination in order to find out if it was a genuine gold watch. Mrs Clayton had told the defendant that the watch had been stolen and now the defendant recognized it, and wrote to Bennett telling him that the watch was stolen and asking him how much he wanted for it. Bennett said he would let the true owner have it back, the price being what Bennett gave for it. The defendant then wrote to Mrs Clayton telling her he had found the stolen watch and of Bennett's proposals. The Claytons instructed their solicitor to act and he went to the defendant's shop and demanded the return of the watch. The defendant refused to give it up and this action was commenced. It was held by Scrutton, J., after inspecting the auctioneer's sale rooms, that the defence of sale in market overt failed. The city auction rooms were not a shop, and because passers-by could not see the sale taking place, the sale was not open in the sense required by the custom. The ground floor windows of the premises were ordinary office windows, and nothing could be seen from the street of what took place on the ground floor. The first floor also had office windows only and, although the sales of jewellery were advertised, a passer-by could not see them actually taking place. Because of this decision on the defence of market overt, the purchaser at the auction did not get a good title, the goods being stolen, and Bennett had derived his title from the original purchaser. The plaintiff was therefore entitled to the watch and had no need to pay Bennett anything.

Comment. Sales by a member of the public to a trader in the market will not normally be sales in market overt because the member of the public will not have displayed the goods for sale. (*Ardath Tobacco* v *Ocker* (1930) 47 T.L.R. 177.)

If the original owner of the goods sold in circumstances of fraud or misrepresentation wishes to avoid the contract he should inform the buyer who misled him. If he cannot find him the contract is avoided when the original owner has done everything he can in the circumstances to avoid the contract.

(322) *Car & Universal Finance Co. Ltd* v *Caldwell* [1964] 2 All E.R. 547

On 12 January 1960, Mr Caldwell sold a motor car to a firm called Dunn's Transport, receiving a cheque signed 'for and on behalf of Dunn's Transport, W. Foster, F. Norris'. Caldwell presented the cheque to the bank but it was dishonoured, and so he went to see the police and asked them to recover the car. He also saw officials of the Automobile Association and asked them to trace the car by their patrols. The car was found on 20 January 1960, in the possession of a director of a firm of car dealers called Motobella & Co. Ltd. The company claimed to have bought it on 15 January from Norris and to have a good title, though the director concerned was on notice of the defect in Norris's title. On 29 January, the defendant's solicitors demanded the car from Motobella and at the same time Norris was arrested and pleaded guilty to obtaining the car by false pretences. The defendant sued Motobella & Co. Ltd for the return of the car and obtained judgment, but when he tried to repossess the car, a finance house, Car & Universal Finance Co. Ltd, claimed that it belonged to them. It appeared that Motobella had transferred the ownership to a finance house called G. & C. Finance on 15 January 1960, and they had transferred it to the plaintiffs on 3 August 1960, the latter company taking the vehicle in good faith. In this action the plaintiffs claimed the car. It was *held* that Caldwell was entitled to it because amongst other things, he had avoided the contract of sale to Norris when he asked the police to get the car back for him so that later sales of the car to Motobella and to G. & C. Finance did not pass the property.

Comment. This case is now of little practical importance since although it decides that a contract of sale induced by fraud can be rescinded without actually communicating with the fraudulent person, the third party can still keep the property by relying on s.25(1) of the Sale of Goods Act 1979. This happened in *Newtons of Wembley Ltd* v *Williams* [1964] 3 All E.R. 532. In that case the seller had rescinded a contract under which the buyer obtained goods by fraud but it was held that as the buyer had bought the goods and was in possession with the seller's consent, he could still pass a good title under what is now s.25(1) of the Sale of Goods Act 1979 to a third party buyer who acted in good faith. The *Car and Universal Finance* case was distinguished on the grounds that there the person who bought from the seller with a voidable title had notice of the defect in his title and so could not be protected by s.25(1).

If the seller has agreed to deliver the goods to the buyer delivery is effected in law when he or his carrier hands them over to a person who might reasonably be regarded as having authority to receive them.

(323) *Galbraith & Grant Ltd* v *Block* [1922] 2 K.B. 155

The plaintiffs were wine merchants and they sued the defendants for £16 2s 11d being the price of a case of champagne delivered to the defendant who was licensed victualler. The defendant admitted the contract but said that the champagne had never been delivered to him. Evidence showed that the defendant asked the plaintiffs to deliver the goods and they employed a carrier who delivered them to the defendant's premises and obtained a receipt signed in the defendant's name by a person on the defendant's premises who seemed to the carrier to have authority to receive them. In fact the person to whom the goods were delivered had no authority to receive them and did not hand them over the defendant. It was *held* that, where a vendor had been told to deliver goods at the buyer's premises, he fulfils his obligation if he delivers them to those premises and without negligence gives them over to a person apparently having authority to receive them. The trial judge had not taken sufficient evidence on the care taken by the carriers so that it was not possible to say whether they were negligent or not, and the case was sent back for a new trial on this point.

Where delivery is by instalments whether a breach in respect of one instalment amounts to repudiation is a question of fact depending on the quantative ratio of the instalment to the whole and the likelihood of repetition.

(324) *Maple Flock Co. Ltd* v *Universal Furniture Products (Wembley) Ltd* [1934] 1 K.B. 148

The plaintiffs agreed to sell to the defendants 100 tons of black linsey flock at £15 2s 6d per ton to be delivered three loads a week, $1\frac{1}{2}$ tons per load, as required. The plaintiffs guaranteed that the flock should not contain more than 30 parts of chlorine to 100,000 parts of flock. The sixteenth delivery contained 250 parts of chlorine to 100,000 parts of flock. The buyers repudiated the contract and refused to take further deliveries. The sellers sued for breach of contract. Evidence showed that the first 15 deliveries were as per contract, and the plaintiffs' plant and equipment was good so that there was little chance of subsequent deliveries being affected. *Held*—The matter was covered by s.31(2) of the Sale of Goods Act and the main tests to be applied in cases falling under that section were—(1) The ratio quantitatively which the breach bears to the contract as a whole, and (2) The degree of probability or improbability that such a breach will be repeated.

In this case a delivery of $1\frac{1}{2}$ tons was defective out of a contract to supply 100 tons and there was little chance of the breach being repeated. The buyers were not, therefore, entitled to repudiate the contract and were liable for breach. They could have recovered damages in respect of the defects in the sixteenth delivery but did not claim any because the delivery had been used in the manufacture of bedding and furniture before the sample was tested and found defective.

Comment. (i) In *Munro (Robert A.) & Co. Ltd* v *Meyer* [1930] 2 K.B. 312, where the contract was for the sale of 1500 tons of bone meal and 611 tons were found to be defective, it was *held* that the buyers were entitled to repudiate the contract.

(ii) In *Regent OHG Aisenstadt und Barig* v *Francesco of Jermyn Street Ltd* [1981] 3 All E.R. 327 the plaintiffs were delivering suits to the defendants by instalments. In one consignment there was one suit short. The defendants, who wished to cancel the arrangement, repudiated the contract under s.30(1). Mustill, J., found that the contract was divisible and s.31 applied. The defendants were liable in damages for non-acceptance of the instalment and repudiation of the contract.

In regard to stoppage *in transitu*, s. 45(3) provides that if after the arrival of the goods at the appointed destination the carrier acknowledges to the buyer or his agent that he holds the goods on his behalf and continues in possession of them as bailee for the buyer or his agent, the transit is at an end and it is immaterial that a further destination for the goods may have been indicated.

(325) *Kendall* v *Marshall, Stevens & Co.* (1883) 11 Q.B.D. 356

This was an action to recover damages for conversion of 55 bales of waste cotton. The plaintiff was the liquidator of one Leoffer, trading as Higginbottom & Co. The defendants were shipping agents and carriers, and the second defendants were Peter Ward & Son of Bolton, who sold the bales of cotton. It appeared that on 9 November 1880, Ward & Son sold the cotton to Leoffer and on 12 November Leoffer asked the vendors to send the goods to Marshall, Stevens & Co. at Garston. He also informed Marshall, Stevens & Co. that they were to ship the goods as soon as possible to Durend & Co. at Rouen, France. The actual transit of the goods was therefore from Bolton to Rouen. On 13 November, the goods were sent by the vendors to Marshall, Stevens & Co. and they arrived at Garston on 15 November. The railway company's advice note which accompanied the goods gave Marshall Stevens & Co. notice that unless the goods were collected by a certain time, the company would hold them as warehousemen at owner's risk and not as common carriers. On 18 November, Leoffer filed a petition for the liquidation of his estate, and on 22 November, Ward & Son telegraphed Marshall, Stevens & Co. to stop the goods. This was done and they were returned to Bolton on 24 November. The liquidator sued in conversion to recover the value of the goods for the benefit of the estate. *Held*—The right to stop the goods expired when they arrived at Garston *and* when the railway company's notice had expired, which it had in this case. Once the railway company held the goods as warehousemen the goods were in the constructive possession of the buyer, Leoffer, and the defendants were liable in conversion.

Section 47(2) provides that if a document of title to goods has been transferred lawfully to a person as buyer or owner of the goods and then that person transfers the document to someone else who takes it in good faith and for valuable consideration, then if the transfer was by way of sale the unpaid seller's right of stoppage *in transitu* is defeated, and where the transfer was by way of pledge for value the unpaid seller's right of stoppage *in transitu* is in effect postponed to the rights of the person who has taken the document of title under pledge.

(326) *Leask* v *Scott Bros* (1887), 2 Q.B.D. 376

Green & Co., who were merchants, were indebted to the plaintiff, who was a broker, and asked him for a further advance of £2000. The plaintiff agreed to make the further advance but wanted some security. Green & Co. gave him a bill of lading which they had received from the defendants for goods shipped to Green & Co. Two days later Green & Co. became insolvent and the defendants stopped the goods in transit. The jury found that the plaintiff took the bill of lading honestly and fairly and that he gave valuable consideration on the understanding that he was being given a security. *Held*—The plaintiff was entitled to the goods as against the defendants.

When a seller exercises his rights of resale under s.48(3) the contract with the original buyer is rescinded.

(327) *R.V. Ward Ltd* v *Bignall* [1967] 2 All E.R. 449

The defendant bought a Ford Zodiac and a Vanguard from the plaintiffs for a total price of £850, paying a deposit of £25 and leaving both cars with the plaintiffs until payment of the balance. The defendant refused to pay the balance, alleging that he had been misled as to the date of manufacture of the Vanguard, although he did offer to take the Zodiac but his offer was refused. Eventually the plaintiffs resold the Vanguard for £350 and brought an action against the defendant, claiming £497 10s, being the balance of the total purchase price less £350 in the addition of £22 10s for expenses incurred in advertising in order to resell the cars. *Held*—by the Court of Appeal—that when an unpaid seller exercised his right to resell the whole or part of the goods under s.48 (3) of the Sale of Goods Act, he could no longer perform his contract which must therefore be regarded as rescinded. Accordingly the plaintiffs' proper claim was for damages for non-acceptance. Sellers, L.J., said '. . . the plaintiffs cannot recover the price of the Zodiac, which is in the circumstances their property. They can, however, recover any loss which they have sustained by the buyer's default. The parties have sensibly agreed that the value of the Zodiac in May 1965 was £450. The total contract price was £850, against which the plaintiffs have received £25 in cash and £350 in respect of the Vanguard, and have to give credit for £450 for the Zodiac. To the loss of £25 must be added the sum for advertising, which was admittedly reasonably incurred—£22 10s 0d. The plaintiffs loss was, therefore, £47 10s 0d.

I would allow the appeal and enter judgment for £47 10s 0d in favour of the plaintiffs . . . .'.

Section 50(3) provides that where there is an available market for the goods in question, the measure of damages is *prima facie* to be ascertained by the difference between the contract price and the market or current price at the time or times when the goods ought to have been accepted, or (if no time was fixed for acceptance) at the time of the refusal to accept. However, this measure of damages will apply only if it represents the seller's loss but not otherwise.

(328) *Thompson (W.L.) Ltd* v *Robinson (Gunmakers) Ltd* [1955] 1 All E.R. 154

On 4 March 1954, the defendants agreed in writing with the plaintiffs who were motor car dealers to purchase from them a Standard Vanguard car. On 5 March 1954, the defendants said they were not prepared to take delivery. The plaintiffs returned the car to their supplies who did not ask for any compensation. The plaintiffs now sued for damages for breach of contract. The selling price of a standard vanguard was fixed by the manufacturers and the plaintiffs' profit would have been £61 1s 9d. When the agreement was made there was not sufficient demand for Vanguards in the locality as would absorb all such cars available for sale in the area, but evidence did not show that there was no available market in the widest sense, i.e. in the sense of the country as a whole. *Held*—The plaintiffs were entitled to compensation for loss of their bargain, i.e. the profit they would have made being £61 1s 9d because they had sold one car less than they would have sold. Even if the 'available market' concept as used in s.50(3) of the Sale of Goods Act, meant taking in the whole of the country, it would not be just to apply s.50(3) in this case, and therefore s.50(3) was no defence to the plaintiffs' claim. Section 50(3) need not be applied if the court thinks it would be unjust in the circumstances.

(329) *Charter* v *Sullivan* [1957] 1 All E.R. 809

The plaintiffs who were motor dealers agreed to sell a Hillman Minx car to the defendant for £773 17s 0d which was the retail price fixed by the manufacturer. The defendant refused to complete the purchase and the plaintiffs resold the car a few days later to another purchaser at the same price. The plaintiffs sued for breach of contract, the measure of damages claimed being £97 15s 0d, the profit the plaintiffs would have made on the sale to the defendant if it had gone through. Evidence showed that the plaintiffs could have sold the second purchaser another Hillman Minx which would have been ordered from the manufacturers' stock had the defendant taken the first Hillman Minx as agreed. The plaintiffs' sales manager said in his evidence, 'We can sell all the Hillman Minx cars we can get'. This evidence was accepted by the trial judge. The plaintiffs were really suggesting that, but for the defendant's refusal to complete, they would have sold two cars and not one and in so doing would have made two lots of profit. *Held*—Section 50(3) of the Sale of Goods Act did not apply here because the language of the subsection postulates that in the case to which it applies there will or may be a difference between the contract price and the market or current price which cannot be the case where the goods are, as here, saleable only at a fixed retail price. Having discarded s.50(3), the Court of Appeal applied s.50(2) which provides that damages should be the loss directly and naturally resulting in the ordinary course of events from the buyer's breach of contract. This was in the view of the court nominal damages of 40s only, because, as the plaintiffs' sales manager said, the plaintiffs could always find a purchaser for every Hillman Minx car they could get from the manufacturers and so the plaintiffs must have sold the same number of cars and made the same number of fixed profits as they would have sold and made if the defendant had duly carried out his promise.

(330) *Lazenby Garages* v *Wright* [1976] 2 All E.R. 770

The plaintiffs were dealers in new and secondhand cars. They bought a secondhand BMW for £1325. The defendant agreed in writing to buy it for £1670 but before taking delivery he changed his mind and refused to purchase the car. Six weeks later the plaintiffs sold the same car for £1770 to someone else but claimed damages from the defendant in the sum of £345, being the loss of profit on the agreed sale to him. The defendant contended that the plaintiffs had suffered no loss. The judge found that there was no 'available market' within s.50(3) of the Sale of Goods Act, but applying s.50(2) awarded the plaintiffs £172.50 on the basis that they would have had a 50/50 chance of selling an additional car had they sold the BMW to the defendant. On appeal it was *held*—by the Court of Appeal—allowing the appeal, that a secondhand car was a unique article, unlike new cars which are much the same and sell at fixed retail prices. Since the plaintiffs had sold the car at a higher price they had suffered no loss on the transaction and their action failed.

Comment. Since each secondhand car is unique, no two being in the same condition, there is no available market for them. There is no group of people interested in buying the same secondhand car. No group of people would be looking for, e.g. a Ford Escort which had done 20,000 miles having two good and two worn tyres. In these circumstances the seller has to find a specific market.

As regards damages against the seller where goods are in breach of warranty, e.g. as to quality, the fact that the buyer has sold some of the goods is not normally taken into account as mitigating his loss.

(331) *Slater* v *Hoyle and Smith Ltd* [1920] 2 K.B. 11

The plaintiffs, who were manufacturers of cotton cloth, sued for damages for the refusal of the defendants to accept 1375 pieces of unbleached cotton cloth, being the balance of 3000 pieces which the defendants agreed to purchase from the plaintiffs. The defence was that the 1625 pieces delivered and paid for were unmerchantable, and the defendants counter-claimed for damages in respect of this. The defendants had contracted to sell *bleached* cloth to other persons, and had bleached and sold 691 pieces of the cloth bought from the plaintiffs for this purpose. The plaintiffs took the view that the defendants should not recover on their counter-claim damages for 1625 pieces of cloth as unmerchantable but, 1625 less the 691 pieces actually sold. *Held*—The subcontract should not be taken into account and the defendants should recover on their counter-claim for the reduced value of the 1625 pieces of cloth delivered to them. The subcontracts were not known to the plaintiffs, and a subsale cannot be relied upon in mitigation of damages unless the subsale is of the identical article bought. Here what was bought was unbleached cloth and what was sold was bleached.

Losses on subsales may be recovered if the seller has actual or constructive notice that such sales will take place.

(332) *Pinnock Brothers* v *Lewis and Peat Ltd* [1923] 1 K.B. 690

The plaintiffs bought from the defendants some East African Copra Cake which, to the defendants' knowledge, was to be used for feeding cattle. The cake was adulterated with castor oil and was poisonous. The plaintiffs resold the cake to other dealers, who in turn sold it to farmers, who used it for feeding cattle. Cattle fed on the cake died, and claims were made by the various buyers against their sellers, the whole liability resting eventually on the plaintiffs. In this action the plaintiffs sued for the damages and costs which they had been required to pay. Two major defences were raised, the first being an exemption clause saying that the goods were not warranted free from defects, and the other that the damage was too remote. The Court dismissed the exemption clause and *held* that, when a substance is quite different from that contracted for, it cannot merely be defective. Further the damage was not too remote, since it was in the implied contemplation of the defendants that the cake would at some time be fed to cattle.

Specific performance will not in general be granted to enforce a contract for the sale of goods. However, the granting of an injunction may in some cases have an almost identical effect.

(333) *Sky Petroleum* v *V.I.P. Petroleum* [1974] 1 All E.R. 954

In March 1970 the plaintiffs agreed to buy from the defendants all the petrol they required at their filling stations. The agreement was for 10 years. In December 1973, when the petrol crisis was at its height, the defendants said they would terminate the agreement on the grounds that the plaintiffs were in breach of contract, having exceeded the credit provisions. This would have meant that the plaintiffs would lose their only source of petrol supplies and they applied for an injunction to restrain the defendants from withholding the supply. It was *held*—by Goulding, J.,—that the injunction would be granted, even though it was in this case tantamount to specific performance.

When a sale is expressly made subject to a reserve the auctioneer cannot be made liable for breach of warranty if he will not sell below the reserve, nor is the owner liable for breach of contract since the auctioneer has no apparent authority to sell except at or above the reserve.

(334) *McManus* v *Fortescue* [1903] 2 K.B. 1

The defendants were auctioneers and offered for sale certain property on the terms of a printed catalogue and conditions of sale. Condition No. 2 was as follows—

> 'Each lot will be offered subject to a reserve price, and the vendors reserve the right of bidding up to such reserve price. The highest bidder for each lot shall be the purchaser. If any dispute arise concerning a bidding, the lot in question shall be put up again and re-sold, or the auctioneer may determine the dispute.

The lot in question was a corrugated iron building for which the plaintiff made a bid of £85. This was the highest bid and the auctioneer knocked the lot down to the plaintiff. Before the memorandum of sale was made and signed by the auctioneer, he opened a sealed envelope containing the reserve price and discovered that it was £200. The auctioneer then withdrew the lot and would not sign the memorandum of sale or accept the plaintiff's deposit. The plaintiff now sued the auctioneer for breach of his duty to sign the memorandum of sale. *Held*—When the hammer falls on a bid at an auction sale of property subject to a reserve, the auctioneer agreeds on behalf of the vendor to sell at the amount of the last bid *provided* that such bid is equal to the reserve that has been made. The plaintiff's action failed.

In a c.i.f. contract stipulations as to time and place of shipment must be complied with and are usually treated as conditions.

(335) *Aruna Mills* v *Dhanrajmal Gobindram* [1968] 1 All E.R. 113

A contract for sale of cotton provided for a variation in price if the prevailing rate of exchange should vary between the contract date and the date when the price was payable. The sellers, in breach of contract, failed to ship the cotton until 27 June 1966, although the last permitted date for shipment was 31 May 1966. The rupee was devalued on 6 June 1966, and the buyers paid the additional price on receipt of the shipping documents which were received *after* 6 June 1966. They now sued to recover that additional price by way of damages for late shipment, alleging that if the goods had been shipped on or before 31 May 1966, they would have received the shipping documents and made payment on or before 5 June 1966, i.e. before devaluation. *Held*—by Donaldson, J.,—that the loss flowing from the devaluation was not too remote, for the parties had contemplated it as likely to result from late shipment. The case was remitted to the arbitrators to decide whether, as a matter of fact, if shipment had been made on or before 31 May 1966, the documents would in the ordinary course of events have been tendered and the price paid before 5 June 1966.

Hire purchase and consumer credit

Section 75 of the Consumer Credit Act 1974 provides the consumer with an additional or alternative defendant, i.e. the supplier of credit, in respect of misdescriptions of the goods made to the consumer by the supplier of those goods.

(336) *United Dominions Trust* v *Taylor*, 1980 S.L.T. 28

Mr Taylor entered into a credit agreement for the purchase of a second-hand car. The finance was supplied by United Dominions Trust in a connected transaction with the dealer. The suppliers said that the car was in good roadworthy condition but Mr Taylor soon found that it was almost unroadworthy. He made efforts to get the supplier to remedy the faults but eventually had to return the car to Parkway Cars. He did not feel bound to pay back any of the loan from UDT and stopped payments immediately. He was sued by UDT for the balance of the loan plus interest. Mr Taylor said that he had rescinded his contract with the suppliers on the grounds of their misrepresentation and declared that under s.75(1) of the Consumer Credit Act 1974 he was entitled to ask the Court to rescind the contract of loan on the same grounds. The Scottish Court decided that he could rescind on the basis that s.75(1) said that the debtor has a 'like claim against the creditor' as he has against the supplier. Since the contract could be rescinded against Parkway Cars there was no reason why a 'like claim' should not be brought against the finance company so that rescission was possible against both of these parties.

Comment. In *Porter* v *General Guarantee Corp.* [1982] R.T.R. 384, the plaintiff had a car on hire purchase from the defendants. The car was purchased as a minicab. It was misdescribed, the supplier saying it had been chauffeur-driven and also that it was in excellent mechanical condition. The finance company had to pay damages to the plaintiff because the car was not worth what he paid for it. The finance company also got an indemnity from the dealer, supposedly under s.75(2) of the 1974 Act. However, s.75 does not apply to hire-purchase transactions. Nevertheless, the decision was correct because the finance company was entitled to an indemnity under the contract of supply with the dealer. The finance company was liable under the hiring contract for the misdescription and could turn to the dealer for an indemnity under their contract with him, much like a retailer who sells misdescribed goods under the Sale of Goods Act 1979 can turn to the manufacturer for an indemnity if the manufacturer has misdescribed them.

If a debtor exercises a contractual right to terminate the contract, the money, if any, which the contract requires him to pay in that event, is not damages and is not, therefore, subject to the penalties rule. If, however, the debtor terminates his contract by breach, any sum mentioned as payable on termination of the contract is then of the nature of liquidated damages and the penalty rules apply.

(337) *Bridge* v *Campbell Discount Co. Ltd* [1962] 1 All E.R. 385

A contract of hire purchase of a Bedford Dormobile required the debtor to pay on termination (1) arrears of payments due before termination, plus (2) an amount to which together with payments made and due before termination amounted to two-thirds of the hire-purchase price. This was in addition to the fact that the creditor was entitled to the return of the goods. After paying the deposit and one instalment the hirer wrote to the owners saying: 'Owing to unforeseen personal circumstances I shall be unable to pay any more payments on the Bedford.' The owner repossessed the vehicle and sued for £206 3s 4d under the clause. The Court of Appeal held that the hirer was exercising his option to determine the contract, the 'fee' for which was £206 3s 4d, under the clause. Since this sum was never intended as damages it was not subject to the rules regarding penalties. The House of Lords reversed this decision, *holding* that from the general tone of the letter the hirer was in breach of the contract and was not exercising his option. On this view the sum of £206 3s 4d could be regarded as liquidated damages and was subject to the rules regarding penalties. Accordingly the sum was irrecoverable because it was in the nature of a penalty. The £206 3s 4d was not a genuine pre-estimate of the owner's loss, because if one included the value of the returned goods the clause would in nearly all cases give the creditor more than 100 per cent of the purchase price.

In order to obtain a good title under Part III of the Hire Purchase Act 1964 the purchaser must be a private purchaser and not a dealer or finance house carrying on business in the motor trade. He must act in good faith and not be aware that the vehicle is the subject of a hire-purchase or conditional sale agreement.

(338) *Barker* v *Bell (Ness, Third Party)* [1971] 2 All E.R. 867

A man called Hudson had a Morris Mini on hire purchase from Auto Finances (Hallamshire) Ltd. He sold it to Mr Ness, who was not a dealer in cars, after telling him that the car had formerly been on hire purchase but that the last instalment had been paid. Hudson produced a receipt for £6 across which was written 'Final Payment'. This receipt was in fact from Bowmakers Ltd and had no connection with the hire arrangements with Auto Finances, though Mr Ness had no way of knowing this. Mr Ness resold the vehicle and eventually the car was purchased by a dealer, Mr Barker. The vehicle was repossessed by Auto Finances from Mr. Barker who then sued the dealer from whom he bought the car, Mr Bell. Mr Bell brought in Mr Ness as third party. It was *held*—by the Court of Appeal—that Mr Ness had obtained a good title from Hudson and that in consquence Barker and Bell had good titles even though they were dealers. Mr Ness was a *bona fide* purchaser without notice of a hire-purchase agreement as required by s.27(2) of the Hire Purchase Act 1964. 'Notice' meant notice of a relevant existing agreement. A hire-purchase agreement which had supposedly been paid off was irrelevant for this purpose.

(339) *Stevenson* v *Beverley Bentinck* [1976] 2 All E.R. 606

The plaintiff was a tool inspector who dealt in motor cars in his spare time. He bought a Jaguar for his own use without enquiring as to whether or not it was subject to any hire-purchase agreement. The car was subject to a hire-purchase agreement between the defendants and the seller. The latter having defaulted on his monthly instalments, the defendants repossessed the car. The plaintiff claimed the return of the car or damages for conversion. It was *held*—by the Court of Appeal—that the plaintiff was not protected because his part-time business brought him within the definition of 'trade or finance purchaser' and judgment was given for the defendants.

Section 51 of the 1974 Act makes illegal the giving of credit tokens unless these are requested by the recipient.

(340) *Elliott* v *Director General of Fair Trading, The Times*, 17 May 1980

In an attempt to boost their sales, Elliott & Sons, shoe retailers, mailed to selected members of the public an envelope containing advertising literature relating to the Elliott Credit Account Card and a card which had the appearance of a bank credit card. The front of the card said: 'Elliott Shoe Account', and on the back there was a box for the holder's signature and the words: 'This credit card is valid for immediate use. The sole requirement is your signature and means of identification. Credit is immediately available if you have a bank account.' The Director General of Fair Trading instituted proceedings against the company alleging that the cards were sent contrary to s.51(1) of the 1974 Act. The central issue in the case was whether the cards were credit tokens within the meaning of the Act. In the Magistrates Court the company was found guilty of a contravention of s.51(1) and appealed to the Divisional Court. In the Divisional Court counsel for the company argued that the word 'undertakes' in s.14(1) implied that there was a need for a contractual agreement, i.e. making an offer capable of being accepted so as to impose upon the trader a legally binding obligation to supply to the consumer goods on offer. Taking this one step further counsel argued that since the production of the card did not entitle the customer to a supply of goods on credit, but only to apply for a credit card when he signed an agreement, the card was not a credit card; the card was not valid for immediate use, the sole requirement was not a signature, and credit was not immediately available since, in order to get credit, a customer would have to fill in a direct debiting mandate to his bank.

However, the Divisional Court did not accept these arguments. There was no need, they said, for a contractual agreement to exist. One looked at the card and asked, whether on its face or its back, the company undertook on the production of it that cash or goods would be supplied. The fact that none of the statements on the card were true did not prevent it being a credit token within the Act. The Court found that the card in this case did fall within the meaning of s.51(1) and that the company was guilty of a contravention of that subsection.

Partnership (*Section references are to the Partnership Act, 1890 unless otherwise indicated.*)

There may be a partnership in regard to one transaction only if that appears to be the intention of the parties concerned.

(341) *Reid* v *Hollinshead* (1825) 4 B. & C. 867

The plaintiff, who was a London merchant, wrote to a firm called Davison & Co., who were Liverpool brokers, asking them to buy 1000 bales of cotton for him and to take a third interest in the proceeds of the sale of the cotton instead of a commission. Davison & Co. agreed and purchased the cotton. In subsequent letters the relationship between the plaintiff and Davison & Co. was referred to as a joint account; a joint venture; a joint concern; a joint speculation; a joint purchase; and a joint cotton adventure. Davison & Co. also insured the cotton and warehoused it, and pledged the cotton as security for a loan to the defendant. The plaintiff now sued the defendant for conversion of the cotton alleging that Davison & Co. had no authority to pledge it. *Held*—The defendant had a good title as against the plaintiff because Davison & Co. must be deemed partners of the plaintiff and in the circumstances they had authority to bind the plaintiff by the pledge.

Comment. (i) The parties were sharing gross returns. However, the letters which passed between them were regarded as evidence of partnership. There can be a partnership sharing gross returns if there is other evidence of partnership. Section 2(2) says merely that the sharing of gross returns does not 'of itself' create a partnership.

(ii) Section 32(*b*) recognizes the possibility of a partnership for one project. It provides that subject to any agreement between the partners, a partnership is dissolved if entered into for a *single* adventure or undertaking, by the termination of that adventure or undertaking. (See p. 250.)

(iii) The Court construed an intention of partnership in this case but it seems unlikely that the partners had ever thought themselves to be.

There will not be a partnership if it is shown that the persons concerned were preparing to carry on business as a company as soon as possible.

(342) *Keith Spicer Ltd* v *Mansell* [1970] 1 All E.R. 462

The defendant and a Mr Bishop having lost their jobs decided to go into business together and to form a limited company. Before incorporation of the company Mr Bishop ordered goods from the plaintiffs which were intended for the use of the company. In addition Mr Mansell and Mr Bishop opened a bank account in the name of the proposed company but without the word 'limited'. The company was not formed and Mr Bishop went bankrupt before any payment had been made to the plaintiffs in respect of the goods they had supplied. The plaintiffs sued Mr Mansel on the basis that he was a partner with Mr Bishop and was therefore liable to pay for the goods. *Held*—by the Court of Appeal—that Mr Mansell was not liable. There was no partnership under s.1(1). The defendant and Mr Bishop were not carrying on a business together in partnership. They were preparing to carry on business as a company as soon as they could. This negatived the suggestion that they were partners.

Creditors who are paid their debts out of the profits of their debtor's business are not for that reason partners.

(343) *Cox* v *Hickman* (1860) 8 H.L.Cas. 268

The Stanton Iron Company carrying on business as a partnership near to Derby was in financial difficulties and the partners assigned the business to trustees who were also creditors of the firm. The trustees were to supervise the management of the business in the name of the firm until the firm's debts were paid by instalments out of profits. The deed was entered into for the benefit of creditors and with their consent. Under the deed the creditors had power to appoint new trustees, to alter the trust instrument, and to direct that the company be discontinued. The business was carried on and an agent of the trustees accepted a bill of exchange as follows: 'Per pro Stanton Iron Co.' Hickman, who was the drawer of the bill, brought this action against Cox, who was a creditor of Stanton Iron Company and a retired trustee, for the amount of the bill, since the firm could not pay. The plaintiff was really suggesting that the arrangement which the creditors of the firm had entered into made them partners in the Stanton Iron Company. *Held*—It did not. The real relationship was that of debtor and creditor.

Comment. (i) The creditors were not carrying on business 'in common' with the partners of Stanton. But, creditors must not assume control of the business or give the impression that they are partners otherwise s.14 (partnership by estoppel) may apply. (See further p. 213.)

(ii) A more modern approach would be for the creditors to ask for the appointment of a receiver to run the business. He would obviously not be regarded as a partner.

By reason of s.2(2) the sharing of gross returns does not of itself create a partnership.

(344) *Cox* v *Coulson* [1916] 2 K.B. 177

The defendant was the lessee of a theatre and he made an agreement with a Mr Mill, who was the manager of a travelling company of players, to present a play called 'In Time of War'. The arrangement was that the defendant was to provide the theatre and pay for the lighting and advertising and receive 60 per cent of the *gross* takings. Mill paid the players and provided the scenery for the play and got 40 per cent of the *gross* takings. The plaintiff purchased a 9d seat in the dress circle to see the play and during the performance she was shot by a defective cartridge which should have been blank. She now sued the defendant as the person liable. One aspect of the defendant's liability was whether the servant who discharged the pistol was the defendant's servant for whose conduct the defendant would be vicariously liable. It was held that the actor was not the defendant's servant but was employed solely by Mill. On the question whether the defendant was liable as a partner of Mill, the Court decided that the sharing of gross returns did not give rise to a partnership because of s.2(2). The defendant might have been liable as an occupier of premises and the Court of Appeal ordered a new trial to ascertain whether the defendant exercised proper supervision over the loading of the firearms used in the play.

Comment: There may be a partnership where the partners share gross returns if the agreement so provides. If there is no agreement or other evidence this is not so. The sharing of profits seems to show a partner-like concern with the management and expenses of the business. The sharing of gross returns does not.

By reason of s.2(3)(*b*) a contract under which an employee or agent is remunerated by a share of profits does not give rise to a presumption of partnership.

(345) *Walker* v *Hirsch* (1884) 27 Ch.D. 460

The plaintiff made an agreement with the defendant firm of tea merchants under which the plaintiff was to receive £180 per annum plus an eighth share of the net profits. He was also to bear an eighth share of any losses. The plaintiff also agreed to advance £1500 to the business. The agreement was at four months' notice on either side. The plaintiff had previously been the defendants' clerk, and after the agreement he continued his duties as before and was never introduced to the firm's customers. The defendants gave the plaintiff notice, being dissatisfied with his services, and he brought this action, claiming to be a partner and asking for an order to wind up the firm. *Held*—After looking at all the circumstances he was not a partner but a servant, and as such was not entitled to the order claimed; but in refusing the order the Court did require the defendants to pay into Court for the plaintiff the sum of £1500 which the firm had received from him.

Comment. Section 2(3)(*b*) is required because a capital contribution is not necessary for a partnership. A labour contribution will suffice. (Per Jessel, M.R., in *Pooley* v *Driver* (1876) 5 Ch.D. 455 at p. 472.) The subsection ensures that the court will investigate *all* the circumstances of the case and not jump to a conclusion of partnership merely because of profit-sharing by an employee or agent. The matter has been complicated in modern times by the introduction of salaried partners. (See case 348 below.)

An agreement for the sale of a business under which the goodwill is to be paid for by a share of profits does not by reason of s.2(3)(*e*) of itself create a partnership.

(346) *Pratt* v *Strick* (1932) 17 Tax Cas. 459

A medical practitioner assigned his medical practice, including goodwill, by deed to a purchaser on terms that he would for three months reside in the house from which the practice was carried on and introduce patients, being entitled to half the profits and liable for half the expenses. It was *held* that there was no partnership; the practice was the purchaser's from the date of assignment.

Comment. (i) Strick was an Inspector of Taxes who, under the law as it then was, had assessed the vendor doctor to tax as a partner to 3/12ths of the annual profit, not merely the profit he took during the three months he was introducing patients. Strick's assessment was not sustained, there being no partnership.

(ii) This was an agreement to accept the purchase price of the goodwill out of the future profits the vendor claimed it would create. The 1890 Act provides that the receipt of such profits by way of an annuity or otherwise (as here) does not raise a presumption of partnership. This was a contract of sale, not a partnership.

(iii) Although it does not affect the ruling in this case, National Health Service legislation prevents doctors from selling the goodwill of NHS practices.

An annuity in payment of goodwill will not make the recipient a partner, nor a deferred creditor under s.3 if it is a fixed annuity and not one varying with profits.

(347) *Re Gieve, Ex parte Shaw* (1899) 80 L.T. 737

John Shaw was a stock and share dealer and died leaving his widow his sole legatee. In 1892 she assigned the business and goodwill to Gieve and Willis under an agreement by which, amongst other things, she was to receive an annuity of £2650 from the buyers. Gieve and Willis carried on the business until Willis died. Gieve carried it on by himself until 1898 when he became bankrupt. Mrs. Shaw then claimed to prove in the bankruptcy for the capitalized value of the annuity but the trustee in bankruptcy said that her claim was postponed under s.3 of the Partnership Act 1890. It was *held*—by the Court of Appeal—that her claim was not postponed for she was not 'a person receiving by way of annuity or otherwise a portion of the profits of the business in consideration of the sale of the goodwill of the business', since she was simply stipulating that a certain annuity should be paid to her. There was no question that it would vary with profits.

A salaried partner is by reason of s.14 clearly liable for the debts of the firm. In addition, it is unlikely that the court will dissolve a partnership on his request because he would not normally have put capital into the business. Therefore he can have no interest in the dissolution in the sense that there is no capital coming to him.

(348) *Stekel* v *Ellice* [1973] 1 All E.R. 465

Ellice, a chartered accountant and sole proprietor of a practice took in Stekel as a salaried partner under an agreement for a fixed remuneration. Ellice provided the capital and took all the profits. No steps were taken towards a full partnership agreement and in August 1970 the agreement was dissolved by mutual consent, so that Stekel was no longer a salaried partner. However, the business continued exactly as before, Stekel receiving only his salary. Stekel claimed that there was a partnership at will under s.24 of the Partnership Act 1890 and asked for an order winding up the firm. *Held*—there was no partnership at will under s.24 so that Stekel was not entitled under s.24(1) to 'share equally in the capital and profits of the business'. Section 27 applied and therefore the original agreement continued in force. Although Stekel was a partner under this agreement, he could not seek a dissolution because he had no interest in the capital. Although the point was not argued, Megarry, J., was of the opinion that a salaried partner would be liable for the debts of the firm as if he were a full partner.

Comment. (i) There may be circumstances in which a salaried partner could ask for a dissolution. For example, if a salaried partner had a fixed term contract with some years to run and the firm was running at a loss so that his potential personal liability for the debts of the firm was increasing, he might ask for a dissolution rather than leave the firm in breach of his contract before that contract had expired. This assumes, of course, that he is liable for the firm's debts, which seems likely. Section 24(1) provides that in the absence of any special agreement, all partners are entitled to share equally in the capital and profits of the business. However, here there was a special agreement, i.e. a salaried partnership, and in that situation s.27 applies and provides that when a fixed-term partnership ends but the business is carried on there is a partnership at will on the terms of the previous fixed-term partnership.

(ii) The definition of a partnership in s.1 does not refer to division of profits. Thus a person would not seem to be prevented from being a partner by reason only that he is paid a salary and does not share in any other way in the division of profits. Neither is the contribution of capital an essential requirement. A labour contribution is enough. However, s.44(*b*)4—which oddly enough was not brought into issue in *Stekel*—suggests that a person may be a partner but unless he has a profit share will not be able to participate in surplus assets on a winding up. The provision states in relation to the assets of the firm on dissolution that after payments of debts, etc. 'the ultimate residue if any, shall be divided among the partners in the proportion in which the profits are divisible'.

Firm name: passing off at common law: effect of using an assumed name.

(349) *Jay's Ltd* v *Jacobi* [1933] All E.R. Rep. 690

The plaintiffs were ladies' costumiers in Regent Street, London, and ran a high-class business. They asked for an injunction to restrain the defendants from carrying on a business in Brighton under the name of 'Jays'. The defendant, Mrs Fay Jacobi, had for some 15 years prior to 1931 been in the employ of a company known as 'Lafayettes (Brighton) Ltd', also ladies' outfitters, and she was always known to the customers as Miss Jay. Her contract with Lafayettes terminated when the company was liquidated in 1931 and so Miss Jacobi took a partner, a Miss Limburg, and they set up in business in Hove under the firm name of 'Jays'. It was agreed that the defendants had acted innocently in the matter. *Held*—Mrs Jacobi had acquired the name 'Jay' by reputation, and had a right to trade under that name. She and Miss Limburg could not be restrained from trading under the name, even though there might occasionally be confusion, although this was doubtful since the two businesses catered for different kinds of customers.

Comment. A person may acquire a surname by reputation, as was done in this case by Mrs Jacobi. Where this has been done a person will not be restrained from using the second name honestly, no more than he or she would if they used the surname they were born with honestly.

Partners' power to bind the firm generally: s.5: the acts of every partner, who does any act for carrying on in the usual way the business carried on by the firm, binds the firm and his partners.

(350) *Mercantile Credit Co. Ltd* v *Garrod* [1962] 3 All E.R. 1103

Parkin and Garrod had entered into an agreement for the letting of garages and the execution of motor repairs, but expressly excluded the buying and selling of cars. Parkin, without Garrod's knowledge, purported to sell a car to a hire-purchase company for the sum of £700, which was paid into the partnership account, the owner of the car not having consented to the sale. Mocatta, J., in holding that the firm was accountable for the £700 to the hire-purchase company, dismissed the argument that the transaction was not binding because of the exclusion of buying and selling in the partnership deed, looking at the matter instead from 'what was apparent to the outside world in general'. Parkin was doing an act of a like kind to the business carried on by persons trading as a garage.

Comment. It will be noted that although the buying and selling of cars was expressly forbidden by the partnership agreement, the firm was bound. This is obviously a correct application of s.8 which provides that internal restrictions on the authority of partners have effect only if the outsider deals with a partner but with *actual* notice of the restrictions. Obviously this would not have been the case if the hire-purchase company had been aware of the prohibition. There is, however, no constructive notice of the contents of partnership agreements. It should also be noted that although Garrod was a sleeping partner, the agent of Mercantile actually knew he was a partner.

(351) *Mann* v *D'Arcy* [1968] 2 All E.R. 172

D'Arcy and Co. carried on business as a partnership dealing with produce in a wholesale vegetable business. The managing partner agreed on behalf of the partnership to enter into a joint venture with Mann for the purchase and resale of a part cargo of potatoes. The venture was to be under the practical management of D'Arcy and Co. and profits and liabilities were to be shared between the firm and Mann. D'Arcy and Co. failed to share with Mann the profit made on the sale of the potatoes and he sued the firm. *Held*—by Megarry, J.—that in the circumstances the venture was 'in the usual way business of the kind was carried on by' D'Arcy and Co. within the meaning of s.5 of the Partnership Act 1890. In consequence the partner concerned had implied authority to bind the firm to the venture and Mann was entitled to his share. The firm as a whole, and not merely the managing partner, was subject to the liabilities which the joint venture entailed.

Comment. (i) By reason of s.24(8) no partner has implied authority to commit his co-partners to a partnership *in any other business*. However, here Megarry, J., was obviously of opinion that the same business was being carried on, but in a different way. Indeed, he says in his judgment: '. . . the arrangement was merely one mode of buying and selling what he was authorized to buy and sell on behalf of a partnership; and he was mitigating the risk at the expense of reducing the profits.'

(ii) Megarry, J., also said in this case that a partner had an insurable interest in the property of the firm and could insure it. Compare *Macaura v Northern Assurance Co Ltd* 1925 (see p. 574) which decides that a shareholder has not got an insurable interest in the assets of a company.

(iii) This arrangement was a joint venture with Mann and a partnership. By s.24(7) a partner has no usual authority to bring an outsider like Mann into the firm as a partner, and yet Megarry, J., held it was within the managing partner's usual authority. A very wide interpretation of s.5 indeed.

(iv) In view of the frequent use of arbitration proceedings in modern times, and the wide interpretation of 'usual authority' in this case, it may be that the rule forbidding a partner to submit a dispute to arbitration would not be followed today.

Partner's power to bind the firm: cheques: s.23 of the Bills of Exchange Act 1882 states that 'no person is liable as drawer, endorser or acceptor of a bill who has not signed it as such; provided that the signature of the name of a firm is equivalent to the signature by the person so signing of the names of all persons liable as partners in that firm.'

(352) *Ringham* v *Hackett, The Times* 9 February 1980

In July 1977 a partnership in the entertainment business, Hackett/Walmsley Promotions, was set up by Messrs Hackett and Walmsley. A bank account was opened in the firm's name and two cheque books were issued with 'Hackett/Walmsley Promotions' printed on each cheque. It was also agreed that the bank would pass any cheque signed by one partner.

Without Mr Walmsley's authority Mr Hackett wrote and signed a crossed partnership cheque for £500 in favour of Paul Ringham as payment for stage appearances. Mr Hackett then disappeared and Mr Walmsley instructed the bank not to honour any cheques which had been drawn by Mr Hackett. When Mr Ringham presented the cheque to the bank he was told that the bank had orders not to pay. The County Court judge at first instance held that Mr Walmsley was liable to Mr Ringham for £500 under s.23(2) of the Bills of Exchange Act 1882 and the Court of Appeal unanimously dismissed Mr Walmsley's appeal.

Counsel for Mr Walmsley submitted that although it might be banking practice under s.23(2) of the 1882 Act that a signature of one partner on a cheque with the partnership name printed on it bound the other partner, that was not the true legal position. He argued that the other partner would only be liable if the firm 'signed' the cheque, and if that was to occur there had to be some link on the face of the cheque between the signature and the printed name of the firm, such as 'pp' before the printed word. The Court of Appeal *held* that no such link was required. It was a necessary inference that a partner who signed his name under the printed name was making a cheque on the firm and all its partners. Thus the cheque was binding on the firm and Mr Ringham was entitled to payment.

Comment. Regardless of whether s.23(2) of the 1882 Act applies, it was held in *Central Motors (Birmingham) Ltd* v *P.A. & S.N.P. Wadsworth*, (1983) 133 N.L.J. 555 that s.91(1) of the 1882 Act combined with s.5 of the Partnership Act 1890 would make a partnership cheque binding on the firm. The former section provides that a person may be bound by the signature of his authorized agent, and the latter section states that 'every partner is an agent of the firm and his other partners for the purpose of the business of the partnership; and the acts of every partner who does any act for carrying on in the usual way business of the kind carried on by the firm . . . bind the firm and his partners.'

The opening words of s.23 of the 1882 Act do not therefore prevent a partner who has not signed a cheque from being liable on it even under ordinary principles of agency and partnership law.

Liability of the firm for wrongs. By s.10 the firm is liable for the wrongful acts of a partner provided he is acting in the ordinary course of business of the firm.

(353) *Hamlyn* v *Houston & Co* [1903] 1 K.B. 81

The plaintiff was a merchant carrying on a business in London buying grain. The defendant firm ran a similar business also in London. There were two partners in the defendant firm, Houston and Strong, and it appeared that Houston bribed the plaintiff's clerk to give information to the defendants which enabled them to compete more favourably with the plaintiff. *Held*—Both partners were liable in damages to the plaintiff on the grounds that Houston's tortious act was within the general scope of his authority as a partner.

(354) *Arbuckle* v *Taylor* (1815) 3 Dow 160

One partner of a firm instituted a criminal prosecution against the plaintiff for alleged theft of certain of the partnership property. The plaintiff now sued for malicious prosecution and wrongful imprisonment and the question of the liability of the other partners arose. *Held*—The partner instituting the proceedings was alone liable. It was not within the general scope of the firm's activities to institute criminal proceedings, and the other partners were not liable simply because the property alleged to have been stolen was partnership property.

Under s.14 a person who either represents or allows himself to be represented as a partner, will be estopped from denying this when an outsider tries to make him liable for the debts of the firm. However, he must know and consent to the representation. This liability can continue after retirement unless the procedures of s.36 are complied with.

(355) *Tower Cabinet Co. Ltd* v *Ingram* [1949] 2 K.B. 397

In January 1946, Ingram and a person named Christmas began to carry on business in partnership as household furnishers under the name of 'Merry's' at Silver Street, Edmonton. The partnership lasted until April 1947, when it was dissolved by mutual agreement. Ingram gave notice of the dissolution to the firm's bankers, and arranged with Christmas to notify those dealing with the firm that Ingram was no longer connected with it. There was no advertisement to this effect in the *London Gazette*. After the dissolution of the partnership, Christmas continued to run 'Merry's' and had new notepaper printed on which Ingram's name did not appear. In January 1948, Christmas was approached by the plaintiffs' representative and eventually ordered furniture from the plaintiffs who had not had previous dealings with 'Merry's'. The order was confirmed on notepaper which had been in use before the dissolution and which bore Ingram's name as well as that of Christmas. Ingram had no knowledge of this and it was contrary to the arrangement between him and Christmas. The company obtained a judgment for the price of the goods against 'Merry's' and now applied for leave to issue execution against Ingram as a former member of the firm. *Held*—Ingram had not knowingly allowed himself to be represented as a partner in 'Merry's' within s.14 of the Partnership Act 1890. Further the plaintiffs did not know Ingram *as a partner before the dissolution*; therefore s.36(3) applied, and Ingram was not liable for debts contracted after the partnership was dissolved.

An s.14 partner does not acquire rights against or have a partner's duties towards the other partners.

(356) *Floydd* v *Cheney* [1970] 1 All E.R. 446

Mr Floydd was in practice as an architect and in 1963 he employed

Mr Cheney as an assistant with a view to partnership, though at a later stage Cheney entered into an agreement which made him an associate but expressly negatived partnership. In 1968 there were further discussions as to partnerships and although no agreement was made an insertion was put in the Journal of the Royal Institute of British Architects to the effect that Cheney had become a full partner. While Floydd was away on holiday Cheney made copies of various drawings and papers belonging to the firm and refused to return them. Floydd then sought, among other things, an injunction to prevent Cheney from making copies of documents and to compel him to return all originals and copies alleging that such acts were in breach of his duty of good faith as a partner. *Held*—by Megarry, J.—

(1) There was probably no partnership in spite of the holding out. It did not appear that a partnership agreement had superseded the initial master and servant relationship.

(2) Nevertheless Floydd was entitled to the injunction because Cheney's acts were in breach of his duty of good faith as a servant. It was not necessary to establish a partnership.

Comment. Here the judge was able to give a suitable remedy to Mr Floydd because the relationship of employer and employee gives rise to a duty of fidelity similar to that of a partner. However, if Mr Floydd had been attempting, e.g. to restrain Mr Cheney from competing with him, then the judge would have been obliged to find a partnership before he could have granted any remedy to restrain competition. The relationship of employer and employee is not one which gives rise to a duty in the employee not to compete, whereas s.30 provides that it is the duty of partners not to compete with the business of the firm.

(ii) The reason why an s.14 holding out did not make Mr Cheney a partner is surely that Mr Floydd *knew* that Mr Cheney was not a partner. Mr Floydd could hardly rely on his own representation that Mr Cheney was a partner when he knew it was not so.

A retiring partner may be discharged from debts incurred before retirement by a novation express or implied.

(357) *Thompson* v *Percival* (1834) 5 B. & Ad. 935

James and Charles Percival were in partnership, but Charles later retired from the firm. A notice was placed in the *London Gazette* regarding the dissolution and saying also that James would carry on the business and receive and pay the debts of the firm. The plaintiffs, who were creditors of the firm, applied to James for the sum due to them for goods sold to the firm and were told that Charles had retired and that James alone was responsible for payment. The plaintiffs thereupon drew a bill for the amount of the sum due to them on James Percival alone. *Held*—This amounted to an implied discharge of Charles Percival by the plaintiffs.

Comment. (i) A novation is the same as any other contract in the sense that it requires consideration. This is essential if the creditor is to enforce his debt against the new firm, and if the retiring partner is to take advantage of it.

If there is a replacement partner, the transfer of the creditor's legal rights from the retiring partner to the new partner is enough. If there is no replacement partner, there would appear to be no consideration at common law. Presumably it is a case of equitable promissory estoppel, as in the *High Trees* case[47] because the old partner has retired in reliance on the creditor's promise not to sue him.

(ii) In general terms, novation is not a practical solution in a firm with many creditors, though it may, perhaps, be used with a large creditor. There must be an express contract or a dealing with the creditor, as in this case. The mere fact that existing customers continue to deal with the newly constituted firm as if no change had been made will not of itself effect a novation.

Section 19 provides that there may be variation by consent of the terms of the partnership agreement. Even where the original agreement is written, the partners may, either orally, or by course of dealing vary the agreement.

(358) *Pilling* v *Pilling* (1865) 3 De G. J. & Sm. 162

A father took his two sons into partnership with him. The articles provided that the business was to be carried on with the father's capital which should remain his, and that the partners should share profits and losses in thirds. Each son was to have, in addition to a third share of the profits, £150 per annum out of the father's share of profit, and repairs and expenses were to be paid out of profits. It was also agreed that the father should have 4 per cent on his capital per annum and that depreciation of the mill and machinery was to be deducted before the profit was calculated. The partnership existed for 10 years and no depreciation was charged on the mill and machinery. £150 per annum was paid to the sons but it was charged against the profits of the business and not against the father's share. Each partner was credited with interest on capital, not merely the father, and the profit was divided in thirds. *Held*—This mode of dealing evidenced a new agreement, and in the action brought by one partner for an account as to his interest, the mill and machinery were deemed to be partnership property even though the articles said that the capital brought in by the father was to remain his.

Comment. The major change here was to allow each partner interest on capital. Thus the presumption was made that the father's capital had become partnership property and had not remained his personal property as was the original intention.

Partnership property is jointly owned by the partners as tenants in common. Even so, it can be stolen by one partner, on the grounds that under the Theft Act 1968 he dishonestly appropriates his co-owner's share.

(359) *R.* v *Bonner* [1972] 2 All E.R. 97

Bonner was convicted of stealing metal from W. His defence was that he and W had been partners, that the metal was partnership property and he though he had a right to it. W denied that they had been partners but on appeal there was produced an application for the registration of a firm with Bonner and W as partners. Bonner was convicted under s.1(1) of the Theft Act 1968 which provides: 'A person is guilty of theft if he dishonestly appropriates property belonging to another with the intention of permanently depriving the other of it; and "thief" and "steal" shall be construed accordingly.' Bonner appealed on the question whether the judge gave a proper direction on the law relating to theft by a partner of partnership property. It was *held*—by the Court of Appeal—that the direction was unsatisfactory and the conviction was quashed on that ground. However, in the view of the Court of Appeal a partner could steal partnership property under s.1(1) of the Theft Act 1968.

Section 20 provides that all property and interests in property originally brought into partnership stock or acquired on account of the firm, or for the purposes of and in the course of the partnership business, is partnership property unless a contrary agreement appears. It is thus a rebuttable presumption. Furthermore, mere use of the asset in the business will not necessarily bring it in. It is a matter of intention of the partners which may be inferred from their conduct.

(360) *Miles* v *Clark* [1953] 1 All E.R. 779

The defendant wished to start a photography business and he took a lease of premises for the purpose. He was not a skilled photographer and employed other persons to do photography. The business made a considerable loss, but after some negotiations, the plaintiff, who was a successful freelance photographer, decided to join in with the defendant. The plaintiff brought in his business connection which was considerable. The agreement made between the plaintiff and the defendant merely provided that the profits be shared equally, and the plaintiff was to draw £125 per month on account of his share in the business. The business prospered, but the plaintiff and the defendant quarrelled and the business had to be wound up. In this action the court was being asked to decide the ownership of the assets, and the plaintiff, Miles, was claiming a share in all the assets of the business. *Held*—There was no agreement except as to the division of profits and so the stock-in-trade of the firm, and other consumable items such as films, must be considered as part of the partnership assets, even though they were brought in by Clark. However, the lease and other plant and equipment should be treated as belonging to the partner who brought them in, i.e. Clark. The personal goodwill belonged to the person who brought it in, so Miles retained the value of his connection and Clark retained the value of his.

(361) *Waterer* v *Waterer* (1873) L.R. 15 Eq. 402

A nurseryman on his death left his real property to his three sons F, M and J as tenants in common. The nursery business was operated on part of this land. The sons carried on the business and bought more land out of the money left by their father. This new land was also employed in the business, F and J bought M's share of the land and the business and paid (1) out of money in their father's estate, and (2) out of money borrowed on the security of the land. F died intestate, and the question arose as to whether his share in the real property was a share in the partnership property or not, because this would affect the inheritance of it since partnership land is personalty and not realty. *Held*—Both the land left by will and the land later purchased were partnership property and converted into personalty.

Comment. (i) The basis of the decision seems to have been that in nursery gardening it is impossible to separate the land from the business. As Vice-Chancellor James said: 'It is, in fact, in nursery gardening, practically impossible to separate the use of the soil for the trees and shrubs, from the trees and shrubs themselves, which are part of the freehold, and at the same time constitute the substantial stock in trade'. We have seen from the decision in *Miles* above that items of stock in trade are generally brought in by use in the business because they are either sold or consumed and it cannot be expected that the partner who brought them in can ever have thought that he would take them out.

(ii) In addition, when F and J bought M's share of the land and business they paid *one* price for both. There was no division of the price into so much for the land and so much for the business. This also evidenced an intention to regard the land as partnership property.

Section 21 provides that property bought with money belonging the firm is deemed to have been bought on account of the firm. Section 21 applies if land is acquired from profits as well as from capital. It does not apply to land acquired with profits arising from a mere co-ownership. (S.20(3).)

(362) *Davis* v *Davis* [1894] 1 Ch. 393

A testator, who was a fan maker, left his two sons his business and three freehold houses in equal shares as tenants in common. The sons let one of the houses and employed the rents in enlarging the workshops in which the business was conducted. One of the sons died intestate and letters of administration were granted to his widow. The question whether the additional property was partnership land or not arose. *Held*—the Partnership Act 1890, s.20(3) applied and the additional property acquired to expand the workshop was not partnership land and so on the death of the son his share did not descend as personality but as realty.

Under s.28 partners are bound to render true accounts and full information of all things affecting the partnership to any partner or his legal representatives. Thus if a partner sells his share in the firm to another partner and the purchaser has a greater knowledge of the accounts of the business than the vendor has, then the purchaser must disclose that knowledge, and if he fails to do so the transaction is voidable.

(363) *Law* v *Law* [1905] 1 Ch. 140

Two brothers, William Law and James Law, were partners in a woollen manufacturers' business at Halifax. William lived in London and did not take a very active part in the business, and James offered to buy William's share for £10,000. After the sale William discovered that certain partnership assets, i.e. money lent on mortgage, had not been disclosed to him by James. William brought an action against James for misrepresentation. *Held*—There was a duty of disclosure in this sort of case and the action was settled by the payment of £3550 to William, which he accepted in discharge of all claims between him and his brother.

Comment. If the parties had not agreed to settle the claim in the way they did the Court would have rescinded the agreement by William to sell his share.

Under s.29(1) every partner must account to the firm for any benefit derived by him without the consent of the other partners from any transaction concerning the partnership, or from any use by him of the partnership property, name, or business connection. Under s.42 an outgoing partner may in certain cases have a right to share in profit made after dissolution.

(364) *Bentley* v *Craven* (1853) 18 Beav. 75

The plaintiff carried on business in partnership with the defendants, Craven, Prest and Younge, as sugar refiners at Southampton. Craven was the firm's buyer and because of this he was able to buy sugar at great advantage as to price. He bought supplies of sugar cheaply and sold it to the firm at the market price. The other partners did not realise that he was selling on his own account and Bentley, when he found out, brought this action, claiming for the firm the profit of £853 17s 3d made by Craven. *Held*—The firm was entitled to it.

(365) *Pathirana* v *Pathirana* [1966] 3 W.L.R. 666

Robert and Ariya Pathirana were partners in selling petrol at a service station in Ceylon. Robert gave notice determining the partnership but before the date of termination he obtained new agreements with the Caltex Company supplying the petrol, giving himself the sole agency for its sale. He continued to trade on the same premises under his own name. Ariya discovered the new agreements and claimed a share of the profits. *Held*—by the Privy Council—that Ariya was entitled to such a share because—

(1) Robert had continued to carry on the business on the premises using Ariya's share of the capital and profits without accounting for them, and Ariya was accordingly entitled under s.42(1) to a share of the profits made since the dissolution:

(2) that s.29(1), which provided for the accountability of a partner deriving any benefit from the use by him of partnership property without the consent of other partners, also applied.

In addition to being accountable for private profits under s.29, a partner has a duty under s.30 not to compete with the firm. However, there must be real competition.

(366) *Aas* v *Benham* [1891] 2 Ch. 244

The defendant was a member of a firm of shipbrokers, the firm dealing with the chartering of vessels and not with the building of ships. The defendant gave considerable assistance in the formation of a company whose object was the building of ships. The information and experience he had obtained as a shipbroker greatly assisted him in the work of promoting the company. He also used the firm's notepaper from time to time in correspondence about the promotion of the company. The defendant was paid for his promotion services and was made a director of the company at its formation, being paid a salary. He also threatened to go into business as a shipowner, using the firm name. The other partners in the firm of shipbrokers brought this action to obtain an injunction to restrain the defendant from using the firm's name, and also to claim an account of his salary and promotion fees in connection with the new company. *Held*—The defendant must be restrained from using the firm name in the business of ship owner since that was a business carried on by him on his own account. However, there could be no account of salary and fees as requested by the plaintiffs, because the business of the company which the defendant had assisted in promoting was beyond the scope of and did not compete with the partnership business. The mere use of the firm's notepaper was not itself enough to show that the defendant regarded his company promotion activities as within the scope of the firm's business.

A potential partner is accountable to the other potential partners of the firm when it comes into being for profits made during the negotiations leading up to the formation of the firm, if the transaction out of which the profit was made would have affected the firm had it been in existence.

(367) *Fawcett* v *Whitehouse* (1829) 1 Russ. & M. 132

Messrs Knight & Co. were lessees for a long term of land and other property at Varteg in Monmouth and they carried on business as iron-masters. They wished to get rid of the lease and the business, and Whitehouse agreed to find others to take over the business as partners with him. He obtained the interest of a Mr Fawcett and a Mr Shand, and later the three of them, Whitehouse, Fawcett and Shand, formed a partnership to take over the lease and the business. It later emerged that Whitehouse had received a bribe of £12,000 from Knight & Co. for his part in procuring Fawcett and Shand to enter into these engagements. *Held*—Whitehouse must account for two-thirds of the £12,000 to the firm since he held it as a trustee for his fellow-partners.

Section 31(1) provides that an assignment by a partner of his share in the partnership does not entitle the assignee so long as the partnership continues to interfere in the management or administration of the firm. The assignee is therefore obliged to accept a *bona fide* agreement as to partners' salaries.

(368) *Re Garwood's Trusts, Garwood* v *Paynter* [1903] 1 Ch. 236

Three partners carried on a colliery business, and the partnership articles provided that they should share the profits equally. No provision was made for the payment of salaries to the partners. One of the partners, J.T. Garwood, separated from his wife and in February 1889, he made a settlement in connection with the separation under which he charged his share in the partnership business and assets with payment to the trustees of the settlement of £10,000, and he also agreed to pay to the trustees two-thirds of his annual share of the profits. After the settlement had been made the partners began to take turns to supervise the loading of coal at the pit head because they suspected theft. Since this involved them in extra work they paid themselves salaries out of profits, thus reducing the share of the profit accruing to J.T. Garwood, and reducing also the amount of money going to his wife. The wife objected to the payment of salaries. *Held*—It having been proved that the partners acted *bona fide* in the matter and did genuinely work for their salaries, the payment of such salaries was part of the management or administration of the business within s.31(1) of the Partnership Act and was binding on the assignees under the settlement, namely the trustees of the settlement made on J.T. Garwood's separation.

The general rule is that specific performance will not be granted of partnership agreements, though in rare cases a decree may be made.

(369) *England* v *Curling* (1844) 8 Beav. 129

The plaintiff and two of the defendants agreed to become partners as ship agents and they signed their initials to an agreement to that effect. A deed was prepared to carry out the agreement but it was never executed and differed somewhat from the less formal arrangement. The parties carried on business as partners and then began to quarrel. Curling gave notice to dissolve the partnership and in order that the other partners should have the rights which the partnership deed gave them, the Court made an order of specific performance requiring Curling to sign it.

Where no fixed period has been agreed for the duration of a partnership, or where the partners carry on the business after the expiration of a fixed term without any express new agreement, the partnership is regarded as a partnership at will and in both cases can be terminated by any partner at any time.

(370) *Firth* v *Armslake* (1964) 108 S.J. 198

In 1948 two medical practitioners, Dr Firth and Dr Armslake, entered into a partnership which was to be for their joint lives under a written partnership deed. In 1958 they agreed with another doctor that all three would go into partnership, sharing profits and losses equally. It was also agreed that they would obtain a lease of the premises where Dr Firth and Dr Armslake had their joint surgery, make a clinic there and equip it at their joint expense. In 1959 a lease was granted to the three doctors who were described as the lessees who would carry on the business of medical practitioners in partnership. Dr Armslake instructed solicitors to draft a deed of partnership which it was agreed would be signed. In the event the deed was not signed because Dr Firth objected to the seniority and holiday provisions in it. However, from May 1959, all three doctors had their surgeries at the clinic and also practised at their respective private addresses. In October 1959, Dr Firth and the other doctor wrote to Dr Armslake saying that since agreement could not be reached on the issues mentioned above the partnership ought to be dissolved as from 30 November 1959. In proceedings for dissolution of the partnership, it was *held*—by Plowman, J.—that the effect of the partnership between the three doctors was to supersede the partnership between Dr Firth and Dr Armslake. However, where there was no express agreement about the duration of a partnership, s.26 of the Partnership Act 1890 applied, rendering the partnership a partnership at will which could be dissolved by notice of any partner. Therefore the partnership between the three doctors was dissolved on 30 November 1959.

Hostility between the partners is a circumstance in which the court may dissolve a partnership under s.35, i.e. the just and equitable ground.

(371) *Re Yenidje Tobacco Co. Ltd* [1916] 2 Ch. 426

In 1914 Weinberg and Rothman amalgamated their cigarette and tobacco businesses, forming a private limited company in which they were the only shareholders and directors. They had equal voting powers, one director was to form a quorum, and disputes were to be referred to arbitration. Up to June 1915, things went well, but differences then arose, one of which was a dispute on the appointment of a manager which was submitted to arbitration, the costs of which were over £1000 of which Rothman was to pay two-thirds which he never did. Disputes continued, although the firm continued to make substantial profits. Rothman brought an action against Weinberg for fraudulent misrepresentation, and the directors were so hostile that they refused to speak to each other, and communicated, even at directors' meetings, by means of notes passed through the agency of the secretary. Weinberg presented a petition for winding up, alleging that complete deadlock had arisen, that the substratum of the company had gone, and that it was just and equitable that an order be made. *Held*—by the Court of Appeal—affirming the decision of Astbury, J., that the position amounted to deadlock and it was 'just and equitable' that the company be wound up. Points made were that a private company is analogous to a partnership, and in a case of partnership there would be grounds for dissolution. Although there was provision for disputes to be settled by arbitration, it was not envisaged that the parties, who were at loggerheads, should be continually using such an expensive procedure. When one person is suing another, who is tantamount to a partner, for fraud, they cannot be expected to work together. The fact that the company was making larger profits was accountable by the growth of the tobacco trade generally, and was no bar to the making of a winding-up order.

Comment. The company was treated as a partnership in order to wind it up because although there was at that time a provision in company law for winding up companies on the ground that it was just and equitable, it was thought that the jurisdiction was limited in the case of companies to instances where the substratum has gone, i.e. where the main object has failed and cannot be pursued.

Section 37 confirms previous judicial decisions under which a partner who wishes to advertise the dissolution of the firm in the *London Gazette* may compel his other partners to co-operate to achieve this.

(372) *Troughton* v *Hunter* (1854) 18 Beav. 470

In an action to dissolve a partnership the plaintiff asked the court to order the defendant to concur in procuring the insertion of a notice of dissolution in the *London Gazette*. It appeared that by the practice of the *London Gazette* no advertisement of the dissolution of a partnership was inserted unless signed by both partners. *Held*—The Court would make such an order requiring the defendant to do all acts necessary to procure notice of the dissolution of the firm.

Section 38 provides that after the firm has been dissolved the authority of the partners to bind the firm continues despite the dissolution so far as is necessary to wind up the firm's affairs.

(373) *Re Bourne* [1906] 2 Ch. 427

W.T. Bourne and G. Grove carried on business in partnership under the name of Bourne and Grove. Grove died and at the time the firm was indebted to its bankers, Messrs Bernick & Co., to the amount of £6476 9s 6d. Bourne continued the business in the firm name for 18 months and continued the bank account. He deposited the title deeds of certain real estate forming part of the partnership assets to secure the overdraft in order to wind up the business and later died insolvent, the bank overdraft being £4463 12s 4d. The partnership articles gave the personal representatives of a partner who died whilst a member of the firm the right to his capital plus interest at 5 per cent. The executors of Grove alleged in this case that they had a lien on the partnership assets, including the realty mortgaged by Bourne, for £3000, the value of Grove's capital. They alleged that Bourne had no authority to mortgage the realty. The bank claimed that its equitable mortgage took priority over the executors lien. *Held*—In the absence of evidence to the contrary, the bank was entitled to assume that the dealings with the account by Bourne were for the purpose of winding up the partnership, and the mortgage was a valid security and took priorty over the lien of Grove's executors.

If there are insufficient assets to repay partners' capital then the partners must make a payment to swell the assets of the firm in the profit-sharing ratio. If a partner cannot make such a payment the Act does not require the partners to contribute more to satisfy the insolvent partner's capital requirements. So repayment is ratable, i.e. in effect the ratio of contributed capital. Thus the solvent partners pay in their share of the loss in profit-sharing ratio and receive back whatever capital is then amassed in proportion to their last agreed capitals.

(374) *Garner* v *Murray* [1904] 1 Ch. 57

A firm had three partners, the plaintiff Garner, and the defendants Murray and Wilkins. Articles of partnership had been drawn up but the deed had never been executed. The partnership was carried on, the terms being that capital was to be provided by the partners in unequal shares but the net profits were to be divided equally. Later the partnership was dissolved and a receiver was appointed. The plaintiff had originally contributed £2500 of which £1300 had been repaid, leaving a balance of £1200 due to him and £314 3s 4d was due to the defendant Murray. Wilkins was indebted to the firm in the sum of £263 3s 1d which in his financial position was taken as irrecoverable. After payment of all debts and liabilities due from the firm there was a fund in Court to the credit of the firm amounting to £764 9s 4d which was not enough to meet the deficiency of capital. The question before the Court was how the fund of £764 9s 4d was to be distributed in the circumstances, having regard to s.44 of the Partnership Act 1890. *Held*—The true principle of division of assets under s.44 was for each partner to be treated as liable to contribute an equal third of the deficiency (i.e. the proportion in which the partners shared profits) and then apply the assets in paying each partner rateably what was due to him in respect of capital. Thus, solvent partners must make up all deficiency so far as is necessary to pay creditors' and partners' advances, but if there is only a loss of capital, as in this case, and one of the partners is unable to contribute his share of the loss, the solvent partners are not bound to contribute for him.

An increase in the value of the firm's assets between dissolution and winding up is not profit under s.42

(375) *Barclays Bank Trust Co Ltd* v *Bluff* [1981] 3 All E.R. 232

A father and son carried on a partnership at will in the business of farming. The partnership was dissolved when the father died. The son continued the business pending the final settlement of accounts. The father's executor wished to elect under s.42(1) for the estate to receive interest at 5 per cent instead of a share of profit made by the use of the father's share of assets for the period from the date of his death until the sale of those assets. During this period the value of the partnership assets had substantially increased. It was contended for the defence that the executor's election deprived the estate of the right to receive a share of the increase of value of the assets since the father's death on the grounds that this increase was in the nature of 'profit'. It was *held* by Judge Francis, sitting as a deputy judge of the High Court, that on a proper construction of s.42(1) the term 'profit' referred only to profit occuring in the ordinary course of business pending realization of the assets. Thus even though the executors had elected to take 5 per cent the estate was still entitled to a share in the increase of the assets.

Comment. (i) If the increase in value of the assets had been regarded as profit the executor's claim would have failed.

(ii) The Court also made clear that when electing whether to take interest at 5 per cent or profit, the personal representatives of a deceased partner must, by reason of a fiduciary duty, get the best deal they can for the estate. They should certainly not make any election until they have seen and evaluated the partnership accounts.

Section 42(1) provides that if on the death of a partner the surviving partners carry on the business, then the deceased partner's estate can claim such share of the profits since dissolution as the court finds attributable to his share of the partnership assets.

(376) *Manley* v *Sartori* [1927] 1 Ch. 157

At his death on 19 October 1913, Charles Calder was carrying on the business of timber merchants in partnership with his son James Calder. Charles Calder left part of his share in the business to the plaintiff, Manley, and the business was continued by James Calder, Manley and Sartori, the last two being also the trustees of the will of Charles Calder. This state of affairs lasted until James Calder died in 1919, Manley then becoming the surviving partner. The Court made an order that the partnership had been dissolved by the death of James Calder and directed Manley to wind up the partnership business. In the course of the winding up, the question of the rights of the partners in respect of profits earned since the death of James Calder arose. Manley had been actively engaged in the supervision and general management of the business during that time. *Held*—Before the parties concerned were entitled to share in the profits earned since the death of James Calder by the use of the assets of the firm, an inquiry must be made to see what extra sum should be paid to Manley for his part in the management during that time, since some of the profit made must be attributed to his skilful management of the firm.

The law relating to cheques (*Section references are to the Bills of Exchange Act 1882 unless otherwise indicated.*)

A cheque, being a species of bill of exchange, must be an unconditional order. The form of a receipt may render a cheque conditional or not depending upon the wording.

(377) *Bavins* v *London and South Western Bank Ltd* [1900] 1 Q.B. 270

In the course of this action, the Court of Appeal had to deal with an instrument in the form of a cheque given to the plaintiffs by the Great Northern Railway Co. for work done. The instrument read as follows. 'The Great Northern Railway Company No. 1 Accountants drawing account London, 7 July 1898, the Union Bank of London Limited . . . Pay to J. Bavins Jnr and Sims the sum of Sixty-nine Pounds Seven Shillings, Provided the receipt form at the foot hereof is duly signed, stamped, and dated £69 7s.'. *Held*—That the instrument was not a cheque within the definition given by the Bills of Exchange Act 1882, because it was not an unconditional order. The bank was not to pay the instrument unless the receipt was signed.

(378) *Nathan* v *Ogdens Ltd* (1906) 94 L.T. 126

In the course of this action the Court of Appeal was dealing with an instrument on the face of which were printed the words 'The receipt at the back hereof must be signed, which signature will be taken as an endorsement of the cheque.' *Held*—The order to pay was unconditional and therefore the cheque was valid. The words could be taken as addressed to the payee and not to the bank.

An instrument made payable to 'cash or order' is not a cheque. However, it is a mandate to the banker to make a payment from the account.

(379) *Orbit Mining and Trading Co. Ltd* v *Westminster Bank* [1962] 3 All E.R. 565

The plaintiff company had an account with the Midland Bank, and the cheques drawn on this account had to be signed by two directors. One of these directors, A, was often abroad and had been in the habit of signing cheque forms in blank before going abroad, assuming that the other director authorized to sign, B, would use the cheques only for trading purposes.

B added his signature to three cheque forms and inserted the word 'cash' between the printed words 'Pay' and 'or order' and passed cheques for collection to the Westminster Bank Ltd, where he had a private account. The Westminster Bank collected the sums due on the cheques and B used the money for his private purposes. The Westminster Bank did not know that B was connected with the plaintiff company and his signature on the cheques was, in any case, illegible. Each cheque form was crossed generally and was stamped 'for and on behalf of' the company under which appeared the signatures of A and B. *Held*—The three instruments in this case were not cheques, but were documents issued by a customer of a banker intended to enable a person to obtain payment from the banker within s.4(2) of the Cheques Act 1957, and since the bank had acted without negligence it was entitled to the protection of the Act in respect of the collection of an instrument to which the customer had no title.

Comment. This case decides that there is no duty upon a bank to continually keep itself up to date as to the identity of a customer's employers. In addition, the case is somewhat unusual in that the normal use of 'pay cash or order' instruments is to obtain cash over the counter. They are rarely, if ever, paid into an account for collection. Nevertheless the Court seems to have regarded the bankers as not being negligent in dealing with such a cheque in the way that it did.

The meaning of a non-existent payee under s.7(3) is a payee who does not exist in the mind of the drawer of the instrument as a person to whom he might owe money. As a payee he is fictitious, but not necessarily as a person.

(380) *Vinden* v *Hughes* [1950] 1 K.B. 795

A clerk persuaded the plaintiff, his employer, to draw cheques in favour of his actual customers by saying the employer owed money to them which he did not. The clerk then forged the customers' endorsements and negotiated the cheques to an innocent third party, who obtained payment from the firm's bankers. *Held*—These were existing payees and therefore order cheques and the defendants had no title because of the forged endorsements of the clerk.

(381) *Clutton* v *Attenborough & Son* [1879] A.C. 90

A clerk persuaded his employers, Cluttons, the land agents, to draw cheques in favour of a person called Brett by telling them that Brett had done work for the firm. The employers had never heard of Brett.

The clerk then forged the endorsements and transferred the cheques to Attenboroughs who obtained payment on them. Cluttons sued Attenboroughs for the money they had received and it was *held* that since Brett was a non-existent payee the cheques were bearer cheques and Attenboroughs had received a good title to them and were not obliged to compensate Cluttons.

Under s.27(1)(*a*) any consideration sufficient to support a simple contract will support a cheque. Thus the consideration need not be money or goods but may consist of conferring benefits or suffering detriments.

(382) *Pollway Ltd* v *Abdullah* [1974] 2 All E.R. 381

D contracted at an auction to purchase land from V. P, the auctioneer acting for V in the sale, signed the memorandum of the contract and, as agent for V, accepted D's cheque in payment of the ten per cent deposit. The payee named in the cheque was P. D wrongfully stopped the cheque and refused to pay the deposit, whereupon V exercised his right to treat the contract as repudiated. Was P a holder for value and able to enforce the cheque against D?

It was *held* by the Court of Appeal that P was the holder of the cheque within the Bills of Exchange Act 1882, s.2. The consideration for the cheque was sufficient to support a simple contract, *viz.* either (1) P's warranty of his authority to sign the memorandum on V's behalf and to receive the cheque, or (2) P's acceptance of a cheque in place of legal tender. Valuable consideration within the Bills of Exchange Act 1882, s.27(1) having been given, P could enforce payment against D.

Comment. (i) In this case the vendors had not supplied consideration to the defendant because they had not gone on with the sale. The defendant had forfeited his deposit and the plaintiffs were the only ones who might have been in a position to claim consideration sufficient to enforce the cheque, which, in the event, the Court *held* they had done. The cheque was, of course, also in the plaintiffs' name but if they had endorsed it over to the vendors this would not have enabled the vendors to sue because, as we have seen, they had not supplied consideration to the defendant.

(ii) The decision was vital to auction practice, Roskill, J., said that if the purchaser had not been liable to the auctioneer, no auctioneer could safely accept cheques at an auction.

Under s.27(2) consideration for a cheque need not move from the promisee. The doctrine of privity of contract does not apply. Thus although consideration must exist it need not have passed between one party to a cheque to another party to the same cheque.

(383) *Diamond* v *Graham* [1968] 2 All E.R. 909

A Mr Herman was anxious to borrow the sum of £1650 for immediate commitments and he asked a Mr Diamond whether he would lend him that sum. Diamond agreed provided Herman could repay by the following Monday the sum of £1665. Herman said that he would have a cheque from a Mr Graham by that time which he would ask to be made payable to Diamond. Diamond then drew a cheque for £1650 in favour of Herman. Herman could not get a cheque from Graham on the following Monday because he was not available on that day. However, Herman presented the cheque for payment but Diamond countermanded payment and told the bank manager not to pay it until authorized by Diamond. Some days later Herman obtained a cheque from Graham in favour of Diamond. Graham asked who was providing Herman with temporary relief and was told it was the plaintiff. Mr Hermann gave the cheque to Diamond who paid it into his bank and authorized payment of his cheque to Herman. However, the cheque drawn by Graham was dishonoured. Herman had also drawn a cheque in favour of Graham and this also was dishonoured, Diamond's cheque being the only one paid. Diamoned now sued Graham on his unpaid cheque. The defendant argued that the plaintiff was not a holder for value within s.27(2) of the Bills of Exchange Act 1882, because no value had passed between him and Graham. It was held by Danckwerts, L.J., that there was nothing in s.27(2) which required value to be given by the holder of a cheque to the drawer so long as value had been given by someone. Here value had been given by Diamond when he released his cheque to Herman.

Thus, Diamond was a holder for value of the cheque and was entitled to judgment and the appeal must be dismissed. Diplock and Sachs, L.JJ., also dismissed the appeal.

Comment. The plaintiff in this case gave consideration after the defendant's cheque was issued, i.e. he released his cheque to Herman.

Consideration must have passed between one party to a cheque to another party to the same cheque where the holder relies on a past consideration.

(384) *Oliver* v *Davis and Another* [1949] 2 All E.R. 353

On 18 July 1947, the plaintiff lent £350 to William Davis and received from him a cheque for £400, post-dated to 8 August 1947. This was presented on 19 August 1947, and Davis was not able to meet it. Davis persuaded a Miss Marjorie Woodcock (he was 'engaged' to her sister although he was married) to draw a cheque for £400 in favour of the plaintiff, and an envelope containing this cheque, but without any covering letter, was left at the plaintiff's house.

The plaintiff was away at the time and returned on 22 August when he received Miss Woodcock's cheque but did not know who had sent it. Miss Woodcock, however, had discovered that Davis was a rogue and she informed the plaintiff within a hour or two of his receiving the cheque why she had sent it and also that she had stopped payment of it. On 23 August, the plaintiff presented Davis's cheque which was dishonoured and later presented Miss Woodcock's cheque which was returned marked, 'Stopped by order of the drawer'. In an action by the plaintiff against Miss Woodcock, suing her on the cheque, the plaintiff relied *inter alia* on s.27(1)(*b*) of the Bills of Exchange Act 1882. Miss Woodcock contended that there was no consideration for the cheque. *Held*—An antecedent debt or liability within the meaning of s.27(1)(*b*) was a debt or liability due from the maker or negotiator of the instrument and not from a third party. The plaintiff, therefore, could not rely on s.27(1)(*b*) but must show consideration sufficient to satisfy a simple contract under s.27(1)(*a*). This he could not do because he had not given her any promise, express or implied, to forbear in respect of any remedy he might have against Davis, nor had he changed his position for the worse in regard to his claim on Davis's cheque. There was no evidence of any consideration and the plaintiff's action failed.

Comment. In this case the plaintiff did nothing after Miss Woodcock's cheque was issued which could be regarded as amounting to consideration to Davis or Miss Woodcock. If, for example, he had said after receiving Miss Woodcock's cheque that he would not sue Davis, he might have provided consideration sufficient to enable him to enforce Miss Woodcock's cheque since forbearance to sue can amount to consideration.

A holder in due course is a person who satisfies the definition in s.29(1) or a person who has taken from a holder in due course under s.29(3). A s.29(3) holder in due course need not satisfy the definition in s.29(1) and may even be aware of the defect. However, if the defect is fraud or illegality he must not be a party to it.

(385) *Jade International Steel* v *Robert Nicholas (Steels)* [1978] 3 All E.R. 104

Jade sold steel to Nicholas and drew a bill of exchange on Nicholas payable after 120 days. Nicholas accepted the bill and returned it to Jade. Jade discounted it with their bankers who became holders in due course. The bank presented the bill to Nicholas who dishonoured it because they said the steel supplied by Jade was sub-standard. The bank then debited Jade's account and passed the bill to Jade. Jade were not holders in due course when they received the bill from the bank because they took the bill after dishonour and with notice of same, but they were holders in due course under s.29(3) of the Bills of Exchange Act 1882 because they took from a holder in due course, i.e. the bank, and so judgment was given for Jade on the bill and the counter-claim by Nicholas could not be admitted against Jade in this action because Jade were holders in due course who had overcome defects on the bill. Nicholas would have to pursue a separate action for a reduction of price in a subsequent claim.

In order to satisfy the definition of a holder in due course the plaintiff

must have taken the cheque complete and regular on the face of it.

(386) *Arab Bank Ltd* v *Ross* [1952] 1 All E.R. 709

The plaintiffs claimed to be holders in due course of two promissory notes made by Ross and payable to 'Fathi and Faysal Nabulsy Company', a firm of which the two men named were the only partners. Ross alleged that he had been induced to make the notes by the fraud of the payees, and attempted unsuccessfully to show that the plaintiffs had knowledge of this fraud and had not taken the notes in good faith. The plaintiffs claimed to be holders in due course, but the point was taken that the endorsement on the notes was simply 'Fathi and Faysal Nabulsy' with the omission of the word 'Company'. *Held*—by the Court of Appeal—that an endorsement could be valid to pass the property without being regular on the face of it. Regularity is different from validity. The Arab Bank were not holders in due course, because the endorsement was not regular, but were holders for value. Although the endorsers were in fact the only two partners, the word Company did not imply this, and therefore the endorsement was not manifestly regular by reference only to the instrument. The circumstances under which an endorsement gives rise to doubt is a practical matter and is best answered by the practice of bankers. This practice insists that the endorsement shall correspond exactly with the payee as named.

In order to satisfy the definition of a holder in due course the plaintiff must take the cheque in good faith and without notice of defects, if any. Actual notice is not essential. A plaintiff may be put on enquiry.

(387) *Sheffield (Earl)* v *London Joint Stock Bank* (1888) 13 App. Cas. 333

A moneylender advanced money to clients on the security of negotiable instruments. The moneylender deposited these instruments with the defendant bank as security for the loan of a higher amount than he himself had advanced to his clients. The bank knew the nature of the moneylender's business and that he was in the habit of lending money on such securities. The moneylender became bankrupt. The House of Lords *held* that the bank was not a holder in due course of the instruments because it had knowledge of facts which were calculated to be had on enquiry as to the moneylender's authority to deal with the instruments. In the result the bank had no better title to the instruments than the moneylender, and upon payment to the bank by the moneylender's clients of the money he had lent them the bank had to give up the instruments.

The original payee of a cheque cannot be a holder in due course. The cheque is issued to him and not negotiated to him.

(388) *Jones (R.E.) Ltd* v *Waring and Gillow* [1926] A.C. 670

A fraudulent person named Bodenham was indebted to Waring and Gillow in the sum of £5000 which he could not pay. He went to the plaintiffs and said that he was an agent for International Motors' new car the Roma, but they would have to take 500 cars and pay a deposit of £5000. The plaintiffs were interested in the deal but did not wish to pay Bodenham or International Motors because they did not know these parties. Bodenham then said that Waring and Gillow were the real backers and asked the plaintiffs to make out a cheque for £5000 to them, which the plaintiffs did. Waring and Gillow received payment of the cheque and when the fraud was discovered the plaintiffs sought to recover their money from Waring and Gillow. The House of Lords held that the plaintiffs succeeded because the money was paid under a mistake of fact and that the original payee of a bill of exchange is not a holder in due course.

Notice of dishonour of a bill may be given as soon as the bill is dishonoured (but not before) or within a reasonable time thereafter.

(389) *Eaglehill Ltd* v *J. Needham (Builders) Ltd* [1972] 3 All E.R. 895

The plaintiffs were holders for value of a bill of exchange for £7660 drawn by the defendants and accepted by Fir View Furniture Co. payable at a certain bank. The bill became due and payable on 31 December 1970 but prior to that date Fir View Furniture Co. went into liquidation. By mistake the plaintiffs posted their notice if dishonour dated 1 January 1971 on 30 December 1970 and it arrived at Fir View Furniture Co.'s office on 31 December. The Court of Appeal *held* that the notice was not subsequent to the dishonour within the Bills of Exchange Act 1882 and was therefore invalid. On appeal by the plaintiffs it was *held*—by the House of Lords allowing the appeal—that a notice of dishonour was given when it was received, i.e. when it was opened in the ordinary course of business, or would have been if the ordinary course of business had been followed. Provided that notice is received after dishonour it is valid regardless of when it is sent off. The notice was valid and the plaintiff's action succeeded.

A banker must obey his customer's mandate. He does not do this if he accepts one signature when two are required.

(390) *Ligget (Liverpool) Ltd* v *Barclays Bank* [1928] 1 K.B. 48

In this case a bank which had been mandated by a company to pay cheques when drawn by two directors, paid a cheque drawn by one director only. It was *held* that the bank had exceeded its mandate and was entitled to debit the company's account only because the cheque was issued to pay a genuine debt of the company and so in equity the bank was entitled to be subrogated, i.e. stand in the shoes of the creditor whose debt had been discharged.

A customer owes a duty of care to the banker to draw his cheques in such a way as not to facilitate fraud. This is particularly so where the drawing is such as to allow an alteration to the amount.

(391) *London Joint Stock Bank Ltd* v *Macmillan and Arthur* [1918] A.C. 777

Macmillan and Arthur were customers of the bank and entrusted their clerk with the duty of filling in cheques for signature. The clerk presented a cheque to a partner for signature, drawn in favour of the firm or bearer, and made out for £2 0s 0d in figures but with no sum written in words. The clerk then easily altered the figures to £120 0s 0d and wrote 'one hundred and twenty pounds' in words, presenting the cheque to the bank and obtaining £120 in cash. The firm contended that the bank could only debit them with £2; the bank alleged negligence on the part of the firm. *Held*—by the House of Lords—that the relationship of banker and customer imposes a special duty of care on the customer in drawing cheques. A cheque is a mandate to the banker to pay according to the tenor. The customer must exercise reasonable care to prevent the banker being misled. If he draws a cheque in a manner which facilitates fraud, he is guilty of a breach of duty as between himself and the banker, and he will be responsible to the banker for any loss sustained by the banker as a natural and direct consequence of this breach of duty. If the cheque is drawn in such a way as to facilitate or almost to invite an increase in the amount by forgery if the cheque should get into the hands of a dishonest person, forgery is not a remote but a very natural consequence of such negligence. The bank could, therefore, debit Macmillan and Arthur with the full £120 0s 0d.

Because alterations other than to amount are less usual, the drawer of a cheque may not be required to protect himself and the banker against them.

(392) *Slingsby* v *District Bank* [1931] All E.R. Rep. 147

The executors of an estate drew a cheque payable to John Prust & Co. but left a space between the payee's name and the printed words 'or order'. A fraudulent solicitor named Cumberbirch wrote 'per Cumberbirch and Potts' after the payee's name. He then endorsed the cheque and received payment. *Held*—There was no negligence on the part of the executors; it was not a usual precaution to draw lines before or after the name of the payee and the executors were entitled to recover the amount of the cheque from the bank.

Comment. If the precaution of filling in the gap after the payee's name is more usual now than in 1931, then a present-day court may not follow *Slingsby* because the question of what is usual is purely one of evidence.

Notice to a bank of countermand must be actual, not constructive.

(393) *Curtice* v *London, City & Midland Bank Ltd* [1908] 1 K.B. 293

The plaintiff drew a cheque for £63 in favour of a Mr Jones to pay for some horses. When the horses were not delivered he stopped the cheque by a telegram to the bank which was delivered into the bank's letter box at 6.15 p.m. The telegram was not noticed on the next day and the bank paid the cheque, only to find on the following day both the telegram which had been overlooked and a written confirmation of countermand which had been posted. The plaintiff was notified that the countermand was received too late to be effective, and he retorted by drawing a cheque on the bank for the whole of his funds, including the £63, which the bank naturally enough dishonoured. The plaintiff brought an action for money had and received. The County Court gave judgment for the plaintiff; the Divisional Court dismissed the bank's appeal; but it was held by the Court of Appeal that there had been no effective countermand of payment and the bank was not liable for money had and received. The bank might have been held liable in negligence, but the damages would not then have been the same. Cozens-Hardy, M.R., said: 'There is no such thing as a constructive countermand in a commercial transaction of this kind.'

Comment. (i) Although damages would have been available in negligence, they would have been based upon the loss which the bank's negligence had caused and this would not necessarily have amounted to the full sum in the plaintiff's account. The Court would have had to investigate what the real value of the horses was set against the amount which Mr Curtice was eventually made to pay for them by reason of the bank's negligence.

(ii) In practice a bank will normally act upon a customer's instructions in order to countermand an instrument, but require written confirmation immediately. There can be no stopping of a cheque accepted against a cheque guarantee card. Where a customer has lost his cheque book and tells the bank they will put a stop on the remaining cheques. If a bank pays a stopped cheque it is liable to the customer and cannot recover from the payee, but it seems where the cheque has been used to pay for goods the bank can claim the goods.

A countermand must addressed to the branch of the bank upon which the cheque is drawn.

(394) *Burnett* v *Westminster Bank* [1965] 3 All E.R. 81

B had for some years accounts at both the Borough and the Bromley branches of the Bank and eventually, because the Borough branch had introduced computer accounting, his cheque book on that branch for the first time included a notice that 'The cheques in this book will be applied to the account for which they have been prepared'. B drew a Borough branch cheque for £2300 but altered the branch in ink to Bromley and later instructed Bromley branch to stop payment; but the cheque, as the computer could not read the ink of the alteration, was sent to Borough branch where no action was taken on the alteration and the cheque was paid because no 'stop' had been received at that branch. It was *held* that although in the ordinary course of events a countermand must be sent to the branch on which the cheque was drawn, B could recover the £2300 from the bank in this case. The cheque book cover fell within a class of documents which recipients would normally assume did not contain conditions varying existing contractual arrangements between themselves and their bank and as the plaintiff had long had accounts with the bank he was not bound by the notice on the cheque book cover as to the restricted use of the cheque forms for only one account.

Comment. It is not certain how this decision would be applied if the same circumstances occurred today. For one thing, the Court said that if B had been a new customer it might have been reasonable to expect him to read the instruction in the cheque book. In addition, of course, customers of banks are normally aware these days that sorting is done by computer and might therefore be deemed to know that an ink alteration would not be read by the computer.

It is a term of the implied contract between a customer and the bank that the bank shall not disclose information concerning the customer's affairs unless the customer consents expressly or by implication.

(395) *Tournier* v *National Provincial and Union Bank of England* [1924] 1 K.B. 461

Tournier banked with the defendants and, being overdrawn by £9 6s 8d, signed an agreement to pay this off at the rate of £1 a week, disclosing the name and address of his employer, Kenyon & Co., with whom he had a three months' contact as a traveller. The agreement to repay was not observed and the bank also discovered, through another banker, that Tournier had endorsed a cheque for £45 over to a bookmaker. The manager of the bank thereupon telephoned Kenyon & Co. to find out Tournier's private address and told them that Tournier was betting heavily. Kenyon & Co., as a result of this conversation, refused to renew Tournier's contract of employment. Tournier sued the bank for slander and for breach of an implied contract not to disclose the state of his account or his transactions. Judgment was entered for the defendants but the Court of Appeal allowed Tournier's appeal and ordered a new trial. Bankes, L.J., laid down four qualifications to the duty of non-disclosure: (1) where the disclosure is under compulsion of law; (2) where there is a duty to the public to disclose; (3) where the interests of the bank require disclosure; (4) where the disclosure is made by the express or implied consent of the customer. Atkin, L.J., said 'I do not desire to express a final opinion on the practice of bankers to give one another information as to the affairs of their respective customers, except to say it appears to me that if it is justified it must be upon the basis of an implied consent of the customer'.

(396) *Sunderland* v *Barclays Bank Ltd, The Times*, 25 November 1938

Mrs Sunderland had drawn a cheque in favour of her dressmaker on an account containing insufficient funds. The cheque was returned because the bank knew she indulged in gambling and thought it unwise to grant her an overdraft. Mrs Sunderland complained to her husband and the manager of the bank informed him, over the 'phone, of the wife's transactions with bookmakers. Mrs Sunderland regarded this as a breach of the bank's duty of secrecy, but in fact the husband's telephone conversation was a continuation of one of her own in which she requested the bank to give an explanation to the husband concerning the return of the cheque. The bank pleaded implied authority to disclose. Du Parcq, L.J., gave judgment for the defendants and affirmed the criteria relating to disclosure laid down in *Tournier* v *National Provincial and Union Bank of England.* 1924[395] However, each case must depend on its own facts. The relationship of husband and wife was a special one. The demand by Dr Sunderland for an explanation required an account of why the bank had done what it had done. It might be said that the disclosure was with the implied consent of the customer and the interests of the bank required disclosure. Since the husband had taken over conduct of the matter, the manager was justified in thinking that the wife did not object to the offer of an explanation. If judgment had been for the plaintiff, the damages were assessed at £2—nominal damages.

The negligence of a banker under s.4 of the Cheques Act 1957 has occurred in the operation of an existing account and in the opening of a new one.

(397) *Lloyds Bank Ltd* v *E.B. Savory & Co.* [1933] A.C. 201

Two clerks, Perkins and Smith, stole bearer cheques from Savory & Co., their employers, who were stockbrokers, and paid them into branches of Lloyds Bank—Perkins into an account at Wallington, and Smith into his wife's account at Redhill and subsequently at Weybridge. The clerks paid in the cheques at other branches, using the 'branch credit' system, with the result that the branches in which the accounts were kept did not receive particulars of the cheques. Neither bank made inquiries concerning the employers of Smith and Perkins. The frauds were discovered and Savory & Co. brought an action against the bank for conversion. The bank pleaded s.82 of the Bills of Exchange Act, and denied negligence, since the 'branch credit' system was in common use by bankers. At first instance judgment was given for the bank, but this was reversed on appeal and the bank then appealed to the House of Lords. *Held*—The appeal should be dismissed as the bank had not been able to rebut the charge of negligence. With regard to the defence under s.82, the court held that, although the branch credit system had been in use for 40 years, it had 'an inherent and obvious defect which no reasonable banker could fail to observe'. Lord Wright said: 'Where a new customer is employed in some position which involves his handling, and having the opportunity of stealing, his employer's cheques, the bankers fail in taking adequate precautions if they do not ask the name of his employers. . . . Otherwise they cannot guard against the danger known to them of his paying in cheques stolen from his employer.' This was not the ordinary practice of bankers but that did not acquit them of negligence. Such inquiries should be made on the opening of an account even though they could turn out to be useless if the customer changed his employment immediately afterwards.

(398) *Bute (Marquis)* v *Barclays Bank Ltd* [1954] 3 All E.R. 365

A Mr McGaw in his capacity as Manager of farms belonging to the Marquis of Bute made applications to the Department of Agriculture for Scotland for Sheep Hill Subsidies. McGaw left the Marquis's employment and subsequently warrants drawn by the Department (similar in effect to cheques) were sent to McGaw in satisfaction of his applications. Each warrant was payable to 'D. McGaw (for the Marquis of Bute)'. McGaw applied to a branch of the defendant bank for permission to open a personal account with the warrants and the bank did so, collecting the amounts of the warrants for McGaw's newly opened personal account. The Court *held* that the defendant bank was liable in conversion to the Marquis and could not claim statutory protection because it had not discharged the onus of proving that it had acted without negligence. McNair, J., pointed out that the warrants clearly indicated that McGaw was to receive the money as an agent and it is elementary banking practice that such documents should not be credited to the personal account of the named payee without inquiry.

Comment. There was obvious negligence here because there was an agent paying cheques clearly intended for his principal into his own account. Some have argued that he could be regarded as an agent for collection, but this would still have involved negligence because he was paying into a private, and not an agency, account.

(399) *Underwood* v *Bank of Liverpool* [1924] 1 K.B. 775

A cheque was made payable to a one-man company and it was held negligent for a bank to collect it for the private account of the 'one man' who was also the managing director.

(400) *Marfani & Co.* v *Midland Bank* [1968] 2 All E.R. 573

The managing director of the plaintiff company signed a cheque for £3000 drawn by the office manager Kureshy payable to Eliaszade and gave it to Kureshy for despatch. However, Kureshy opened an account with the cheque at the Midland Bank by falsely representing that he was Eliaszade and that he was about to set up a restaurant business.

The bank asked for references and Kureshy gave the names of two satisfactory customers of the bank, and one of these references indicated, while on a visit to the bank, that Kureshy, whom he knew as Eliaszade, would be a satisfactory customer. The second referee did not reply to the bank's inquiry. Kureshy then drew a cheque for £2950 on the account and absconded. It appeared that the bank did not ask to see Kureshy's passport and his spelling of Eliaszade was inconsistent with the spelling on the cheque. Further the bank officials did not notice the similarity in handwriting between the cheque and the endorsement. The plaintiff company sued the bank for conversion and it was held that the bank had not fallen short of the standard of ordinary practice of careful bankers and was protected by s.4 of the Cheques Act 1957.

The collecting banker as a holder for value or holder in due course. The effect of s.2 of the Cheques Act 1957.

(401) *Westminster Bank Ltd* v *Zang* [1965] 1 All E.R. 1023

Mr Zang, having lost heavily at seven-card rummy, drew a cheque for £1000 payable to 'J. Tilley or order', receiving from Mr Tilley £1000 in cash to pay part of his gambling debts. The £1000 cash belonged to Tilley's Autos Ltd, a company of which Tilley was managing director. Tilley took Zang's cheque to his bank, asking them to credit the account of the company, which was overdrawn. Tilley did not endorse the cheque before paying it in. The cheque was dishonoured and the bank returned it to Tilley so that he could sue Zang. The action was commenced but discontinued and the cheque was returned to the bank who sued Zang as holder in due course or holder for value of the cheque. The bank failed in its claim. The reasons given in the Court of Appeal were—

(1) As the payee (Tilley) had asked the bank to credit the cheque to the account of a third party (Tilley's Autos), the cheque had not been received for collection within the meaning of s.2, and as the cheque was not endorsed the bank were not 'holders'. (Per Denning, M.R.)

(2) The cheque had been received for collection but the bank had not given value, so that s.2 did not apply. (Per Salmon, L.J.)

(3) The cheque had been received for collection but the bank in returning the cheque to Tilley lost their lien and consequently the protection of s.2 (Per Danckwerts, L.J.)

In the House of Lords (see [1966] 1 All E.R. 114) their Lordships unanimously *held* that the cheque had been received for collection, but the bank had not given value.

The company's account was overdrawn, but it was hard to see how, by crediting the cheque to the account and reducing the overdraft, the bank gave value for it, because in fact interest had been charged on the original amount of the overdraft unreduced by the cheque. There was no agreement express or implied to honour the cheques of Tilley's

Autos before they had been cleared, and consideration could not, therefore, be established in this way.

(402) *Barclays Bank Ltd* v *The Astley Industrial Trust Ltd* [1970] 1 All E.R. 719

Mabons Garage Ltd were motor dealers who banked with the plaintiffs and arranged hire-purchase transactions with the defendants. In November 1964, the plaintiffs gave Mabons a temporary overdraft up to £2000 and on the 18 November when the account was £1910 overdrawn cheques for £2673 drawn by Mabons were presented for payment. The bank manager agreed to pay them only after receiving an assurance from the directors of Mabons that cheques for £2850 in favour of Mabons and drawn by the defendants would be paid into the account the next day. On 19 November when Mabons' overdraft stood at £4673 two further cheques for £345 drawn by Mabons were presented for payment and bank manager refused to pay these until he had received the defendants' cheques for £2850. On the 20 November the defendants stopped their cheques which it appeared they had been induced to draw by the fraud of Mabons' directors. In an action by the bank claiming to be holders in due course of the cheques the defendants alleged that the bank had not taken them for value. *Held*—by Milmo, J.—that the bank was a holder in due course since—

(1) A banker who takes a cheque as agent for collection can also be a holder in due course under s.2 of the Cheques Act 1957.

(2) The bank was a holder in due course. they were holders because they had a lien on the cheques and were entitled to hold them pending payment of the overdraft. The value was the overdraft of £4763. An antecedent debt would support a bill of exchange.

The bank was entitled to recover the amount of the cheques from the defendants.

Regarding the decision in *Westminster Bank Ltd* v *Zang* 1965[401] Milmo, J., said 'I should mention that *Westminster Bank Ltd* v *Zang* was strongly relied upon by the defendants, but I do not consider that it established their contentions. The facts were materially different from those in the present case and in particular there was no question of the bank having a lien such as there admittedly was in the present case'.

Comment. The bank appears to have obtained the benefit of the antecedent overdraft by virtue of their banker's lien.

General principles of insurance law

Duty of disclosure. Materiality. The proposer must reveal that another insurance company has refused to insure him. Failure to do so allows the insurance company to rescind the contract. A statement, though

true in itself, may not tell the whole truth and thereby give a false impression.

(403) *London Assurance* v *Mansel* (1879) 11 Ch.D. 363

Mansel completed a proposal for a life assurance of £10,000 with London Assurance. He was asked on the form if he had made a proposal on his life at any other office, and whether it was accepted at the ordinary or an increased premium, or declined. His reply was: 'Insured now in two offices for £16,000 at ordinary rates. Policies effected last year.' He signed a declaration that the particulars were true and formed the basis of the contract. He paid the premium and received a certificate of assurance. London Assurance then discovered that, although the statement was true so far as it went, Mansel had tried to increase a policy he held for £6000 and the company had refused his request, and other proposals to other companies had been declined. London Assurance therefore refused to go on with the assurance and returned the cheque for the premium to Mansel, who sent it back to the company. The plaintiffs now asked for declaration that the contract was void because the defendant had failed in his duty of disclosure. *Held*—The defendant had a duty to disclose and the contract was void. In cases of insurance to conceal anything material is a fraud, and to conceal anything which may influence the rate of premium vitiates the policy, even if the proposer does not know it would have that effect.

Duty of disclosure. The test of materiality is objective so that it is irrelevant that the assured thought a fact to be immaterial.

(404) *Roselodge Ltd* v *Castle* [1966] 2 Lloyd's Rep. 105

The plaintiffs, who were diamond merchants, claimed under an indemnity policy after a director of the company had been robbed of £300,000 worth of diamonds. It appeared that when taking out the policy with the defendant underwriter the diamond merchants had not disclosed that their sales manager had been convicted eight years before in the United States for smuggling diamonds into that country. The diamond merchants thought that fact to be immaterial. *Held*—The sales manager's conviction was a material fact which should have been disclosed and the claim under the policy failed.

The agent of an insurance company who completes a proposal form for the proposer is normally regarded as the agent of the proposer and not of the insurance company.

(405) *Newsholme Bros* v *Road Transport and General Insurance Co.* [1929] 2 K.B. 356

Newsholme Bros wished to insure a motor bus and Willey, an agent of the insurance company, filled in the proposal form and handed it to A. Newsholme, a partner in the firm, who signed it without reading it. Newsholme had given Willey correct oral answers to the questions, but the latter, whether in error or intentionally in order to earn a commission he would not otherwise have got, put down three incorrect answers. The proposals contained a warranty that the answers were true and should be the basis of the contract. A policy was issued and a premium paid. An accident occurred, the plaintiffs claimed indemnity and the company denied liability. *Held*—The agent was not authorized by the company to fill in the proposal and must be regarded as the agent of the proposer. Knowledge of the untruth of the answers by the agent was not, therefore, notice to the company. The written contract alone could be looked at, and therefore the company was not liable. Scrutton, L.J., said: 'I have great difficulty in understanding how a man who has signed, without reading it, a document which he knows to be a proposal of insurance, and which contains statements in fact untrue, and a promise that they are true and the basis of the contract, can escape from the consequences of his negligence by saying that the person he asked to fill it up for him is the agent of the person to whom the proposal is addressed.'

(406) *O'Connor* v *B.D.B. Kirby & Co. (A Firm)* [1971] 2 W.L.R. 1233

The plaintiff consulted the defendants, who were insurance brokers, with regard to insuring his car. The brokers filled in the proposal form incorrectly saying that the car was garaged at night, whereas it was parked in the road outside the plaintiff's house. The plaintiff had read the proposal form and signed it. Some time later the plaintiff's car was damaged while parked in the road and the insurance company repudiated liability. *Held*—by the Court of Appeal—that it was the proposer's duty to see that the information given in the proposal form was correct. There was no negligence on the part of the defendants who could reasonably rely on the plaintiff to correct errors on the form.

The knowledge of the agent completing the proposal form for the proposer is imputed to the insurance company.

(407) *Stone* v *Reliance Mutual Insurance Society Ltd, The Times* 15 March 1972

The plaintiff signed a proposal form for burglary insurance. The form contained a clause stating 'I further declare in so far as any part of this proposal is not written by me the person who has written the same has done so by my instructions and as my agent for that purpose. I agree that the above proposal and this declaration shall be the basis of the contract of insurance between the society and myself.'

The defendant's district inspector put questions to the plaintiff and wrote down the answers and later asked the plaintiff's wife to sign the completed forms which she did without reading them. During the currency of the policy a burglary took place and the plaintiff made a claim on the defendants. They repudiated liability on the ground that the following questions had been answered incorrectly—

Ques. 5: 'State policy numbers of insurances held by you and whether lapsed or in force.' Answer—'None.'

Ques. 6: 'Give particulars of any claims you have made in respect of any risks hereby proposed to be insured.' Answer—'None.'

It appeared that the plaintiff had taken out another policy with the defendants which had lapsed and had not disclosed a claim made under the earlier policy in respect of a loss by fire. *Held*—by the Court of Appeal distinguishing *Newsholme*[405]—that the plaintiff's claim succeeded. The mistakes were those of the district inspector because in spite of the agency clause it was obviously the defendant's practice to rely on the answers the district inspector arrived at with the proposer and—

(1) The inspector must have known that there had been an earlier policy which had lapsed for he only called on those whose policies had lapsed.

(2) The inspector might have forgotten or never known about the fire. Thus there was no misrepresentation or non-disclosure to defeat the policy.

(408) *Woolcott* v *Excess Insurance Co.* No. 2 [1979] 2 Lloyd's Rep. 210

The plaintiff wished to insure his house and its contents for £32,500 under a fire policy. A policy was issued by X Ltd, insurance brokers, acting on behalf of Excess Insurance. In the proposal form the plaintiff failed to disclose a previous conviction for robbery in 1960. This fact, however, was known by X Ltd. A loss by fire occurred in 1974 and the plaintiff claimed under the policy. However, the insurance company refused to pay on the ground that there had been non-disclosure of a material fact. It was *held* in the High Court that there would be judgment for the plaintiff. Since X Ltd knew of his criminal record such knowledge was imputed to the insurance company and liability on the policy could not be avoided.

A contract of insurance is one of utmost good faith. If utmost good faith is not observed by either of the parties in the sense that material facts are not disclosed, the contract can be avoided by the other.

(409) *March Cabaret Club and Casino* v *London Assurance* [1975] 1 Lloyd's Rep. 169

A and his wife were the proprietors of the Cabaret Club which was insured against loss or damage by fire by the defendants. A fire occurred and a claim for £27,024 was made against the defendants. They contended that the policy should be avoided on the ground, among others, that A had not disclosed that he had been convicted of handling stolen goods. It was *held* that since A had committed a criminal offence this was material to the contract of insurance, and the duty to disclose imposed by the Marine Insurance Act 1906 applied to non-maritime insurance as well as maritime. Judgment was given for the defendants.

Comment. See also *Woolcott* v *Sun Alliance and London Insurance* [1978] 1 All E.R. 1253, see p. 297.

(410) *Mutual Life Insurance Company of New York* v *Ontario Metal Products Co. Ltd* [1925] A.C. 344

The managing director of the respondent company, F.J. Schuch, took out a life policy with the appellants when he was aged 44 and apparently in good health. In the application for the policy. Schuch was asked to give details of illnesses, diseases or surgical operations since childhood, and the physicians consulted in the preceding five years. He failed to mention that on several occasions during that time he had obtained from his own doctor a tonic when he was feeling overworked or run down. Schuch died less than 18 months after the issue of the policy from a disease (cancer) which was not present when he made his proposal. The interest under the policy became vested in the respondent company and when they tried to enforce it the appellants claimed to avoid it on the grounds of non-disclosure. *Held*—by the Judicial Committee of the Privy Council—The omission was not material and the policy was enforceable.

In deciding whether a material misrepresentation has been made in an insurance contract, the court will not regard as material matters which the representative of the insurer has failed to notice, provided the matters concerned were not concealed.

(411) *Re Universal Non-Tariff Fire Insurance Co., Forbes & Co.'s Claim* (1875) L.R. 19 Eq. 485

Forbes & Co. entered into a fire policy through one William Donald, who was an agent of the insurance company. Donald inspected the premises before the policy was made. One of the conditions of the policy was that any material misdescription of any of the property insured should render the policy void. The policy stated that the property was built of brick and slate but when a fire occurred, it was discovered that part of the building was roofed with tarred felt. The insurance company went into liquidation and Forbes & Co. claimed £1350 under the policy. The liquidator of the insurance company resisted the claim on the grounds of misdescription and that Donald was not the agent of the company. Evidence showed that Donald was truly the agent of the company and it was *held* that the misdescription did not render the policy void because (1) it was not material; and (2) even if material, the knowledge of Donald was imputed to the insurance company.

It is a question of fact whether a circumstance which has not been disclosed is material or not.

(412) *Ionides* v *Pender* (1874) L.R. 9 Q.B. 531

A cargo of goods worth £8000 was shipped to Russia and, because the adventure was expected to be very profitable, was insured for £20,000. The ship was lost in suspicious circumstances in mid-ocean in fair weather without any known cause. *Held*—An insurance of profits must be taken to imply possible profits. Where the assured does not disclose to the underwriters the fact that the goods are largely overvalued, it is a question of fact for the court whether the concealment is material in the light of the reasonable practice of underwriters. The court was in this case justified in finding that the overvaluation was a material fact which ought to have been disclosed, and the claim under the policy failed.

The duty to disclose material facts continues up to the time the contract of insurance is made.

(413) *Looker* v *Law Union and Rock Insurance Co. Ltd* [1928] 1 K.B. 554

Looker made a proposal to insure his life which the company accepted, conditions being that he remained in good health until the first premium was paid and that no risk should attach until then. Looker became ill with pneumonia but he did not notify the company and sent off a cheque for the first premium three days before he died of the disease. The company then accepted the proposal and promised to send a policy. *Held*—Looker's executors could not claim under the policy. Looker had a duty to inform the insurance company of the change in risk arising from his illness, and this duty existed independently of the company's stipulation that he should do so.

A statement made in a proposal form may be construed as a description of the risk and not as a warranty.

(414) *Farr* v *Motor Traders' Mutual Insurance Society* [1920] 3 K.B. 669

The plaintiff was the owner of two taxi cabs and insured them with the defendants in February 1918, for one year against accidental damage. In the proposal form the plaintiff, in answering a question, said that each of the cabs was to be driven for one shift in every 24 hours. The policy provided that all statements in the proposal form were to be the basis of the contract. In August 1918, while one of the cabs was being repaired, the other cab was driven for two shifts in 24 hours for a short time, and then went back to the original pattern of one shift in 24 hours. In November 1918, the cab that had been driven in two shifts in August was damaged in an accident, being driven for one shift in 24 hours when this accident occurred. In an action on the policy, the defendants contended that the policy was avoided because the vehicle had for a short time been used for two shifts in a day. *Held*—The statement was not a warranty (this term in insurance means a condition) but merely described the sort of risk involved, i.e. that the cab would be covered only if an accident occurred whilst it was being used for one shift in 24 hours. This having happened, the plaintiff could recover.

Where the peril insured against is fire, a claim can be made even though the fire and loss are due to the negligence of the insured. In addition, there can be loss by 'fire' even where the fire is in a domestic grate.

(415) *Harris* v *Poland* [1941] 1 K.B. 462

The plaintiff, who lived in a flat at 4 Chartfield Avenue, London, took out in January 1939, at Lloyd's a comprehensive insurance policy against fire, burglary and housebreaking. There was an attempted burglary at her flat during the summer and, being nervous concerning the safety of her jewellery, worth £500, she hid it, together with £100 in banknotes, under the Coalite on the fire in her sitting-room on an occasion when she would be out all day. She wrapped the money and jewellery in a newspaper and mixed it with newspaper already there. Returning home later in the afternoon and feeling cold, the plaintiff lit the fire and only remembered the hiding of the notes and valuables next morning when the notes and most of the jewellery were completely destroyed. She claimed under her policy which insured her 'from loss or damage caused by fire'. The underwriters did not allege negligence or that the loss was the result of her own act, but alleged that the loss was not covered because the fire was where it was intended to be and had not broken bounds, and although it was a loss which might be covered by an all risks policy, it was not a loss by fire within the meaning of the policy. It was claimed that there must be ignition where no ignition ought to be in order to create liability. Atkinson, J., applied three rules of construction: (1) construction depends on the meaning of the words and not the intention of the parties; (2) the court has no right to imply terms into a written contract; (3) under the *contra proferentem* rule the policy must be construed most strongly against the underwriters who had prepared it. It did not expressly exclude the circumstances of this case. *Held*—The fire came within the terms of the policy and the plaintiff was awarded £460 and costs.

A voidable insurance policy is sufficient to satisfy the compulsory insurance requirements of the Road Traffic Act 1972.

(416) *Adams* v *Dunne* [1978] Crim. L.R. 365

The insured was disqualified from driving and failed to disclose this fact which vitiated his motor insurance policy. The insured deliberately hid the fact of the disqualification and was later prosecuted, amongst other things, for driving uninsured and for a road traffic offence of withholding material information from the insurer under s.170(6)(*a*) of the Road Traffic Act 1972. The prosecution contended on appeal to the Divisional Court that the insurance policy was void from the beginning because it was illegal. The Divisional Court *held*, however, that since the insurers had been misled by the defendant's concealment, the contract was voidable, not void. The insurers had taken no steps up to the relevant time to avoid the policy, so for the purposes of the driving uninsured charge, the defendant was not guilty because had a current policy of insurance.

The owner of a parked vehicle which, owing to its condition, cannot be driven but can be moved, must nevertheless maintain insurance on the vehicle for the compulsory road traffic risks.

(417) *Elliott* v *Grey* [1960] 1 Q.B. 367

On 7 February 1959, the appellant's car, which was parked outside his house in Belloc Avenue, South Shields, was run into by another motor car. This attracted the attention of the police and it appeared that the appellant's car had broken down on 20 December 1958, and could not be driven, so he placed it outside his house and left it there until 7 February when the accident occurred. He had jacked up the car and removed the battery and, since he did not intend to drive the car until it was repaired, had terminated his insurance cover. On the very day, 7 February, he had turned his attention to the car and had unjacked it and done some work on it, although at the time in question the engine would still not work, nor had the appellant any intention of driving or removing it. He was charged with unlawfully using on the road a motor car without the statutory insurance cover. The South Shields justices convicted him and the matter came before the Queen's Bench Division by way of a case stated. *Held*—To 'use a motor vehicle on the road' means to 'have the use of a motor vehicle on the road', and, as the car could be moved, the appellant had the use of it, even if it could not be driven, and there might be a risk to third parties.

Comment. In *Hewer* v *Cutler* [1974] R.T.R. 155 the above case was distinguished where the owner of a vehicle had disconnected the gearbox linkage, thus locking the rear wheels and rendering the car totally immobile in the sense that it could not even be moved. It was held that such a vehicle is not 'used' on a road within the meaning of s.143(1) of the Road Traffic Act 1972.

Failure to comply with the requirements of road traffic legislation is a criminal offence but also a breach of statutory duty on which an action for civil law damages may be based.

(418) *Monk* v *Warbey and Others* [1935] 1 K.B. 75

Albert Warbey, the owner of a Morris car which was properly insured in accordance with the provisions of the Road Traffic Act 1930, while he himself or members of his family were driving, was not covered if some other person were allowed to drive. He lent the car out of kindness of heart to Knowles, one of the defendants, in the expectation that the car would be driven by another defendant, Frank May. An accident occurred owing to the admitted negligence of Frank May, and Monk, who was injured, brought the action not only against Knowles and May, but also against Warbey. Warbey was clearly in breach of the road traffic legislation then in force (now s.143 of the Road Traffic Act 1972) (the offence of causing or permitting a person to 'drive whilst uninsured'). *Held*—A person damaged as a result of a breach of statute has a right to recover damages from the person who has broken the provisions of the statute, unless it can be established by looking at the whole of the Act that it was not the intention that he should have such a right. The statute was not designed to limit civil remedies and the plaintiff was entitled to damages on the grounds that (1) Warbey had committed a breach of a statutory duty; and (2) the damage resulting to the plaintiff was not too remote.

Comment. Of course, it might well have paid the plaintiff these days to have sued the driver because a judgment against him would be enforceable against the Motor Insurers Bureau. If a person does sue in this way and the driver personally or the Motor Insurers Bureau pays all the claims in full, then the owner of the vehicle would be liable to pay nominal damages only.

A person who has been permitted to drive an insured car and who causes injury to the person insured is entitled to an indemnity from the insurance company.

(419) *Digby* v *General Accident Fire and Life Assurance Corporation* [1943] A.C. 121

Under a motor policy taken out by Merle Oberon, the actress, the insurers agreed to indemnify her against claims by 'any person', and the policy covered persons driving with her consent. Her car was involved in an accident, owing to her chauffeur's negligence, and she was injured. Miss Oberon then recovered damages against her chauffeur and the question of the payment of an indemnity to the chauffeur arose. *Held*—by the House of Lords—that an indemnity was payable because—

(1) the policy covered claims by 'any person' thus including a claim by Miss Oberon herself;

(2) as the chauffeur was driving with Miss Oberon's consent he was covered against the risk of accident and could claim an indemnity from the insurers under the Road Traffic legislation then in force.

Comment. The relevant provision is now s.148(4), Road Traffic Act 1972.

Policies of motor insurance may in addition to covering a specified vehicle, extend cover to the person insured when driving another vehicle not owned by him. A policy is not effective, however, if the person insured ceases to have an interest in the vehicle specified.

(420) *Tattersall* v *Drysdale* [1935] 2 K.B. 174

A comprehensive motor policy was issued covering a specific vehicle and extending cover to the insured while driving other cars. The insured drove another vehicle after having sold the specific car. *Held*—That when he sold the specific vehicle the policy ceased to have effect.

(421) *Boss* v *Kingston* [1963] 1 All E.R. 177

In this case the prosecution alleged that the defendant was guilty of driving an uninsured motor cycle. It appeared that the defendant had owned a Triumph motor cycle and had taken out a policy which covered his legal liability to third parties while riding the Triumph and also purported to cover him while riding other motor cycles not owned or hired by him. The policy in this case seemed to be an insurance of the defendant personally rather than of the Triumph motor cycle, though it did require him to keep the Triumph in good condition and give the insurers access to it. The defendant sold the Triumph and while riding a motor cycle belonging to a friend was prosecuted for using an uninsured vehicle. *Held*—As a matter of construction the insurance was effective only while the defendant retained the Triumph, because the conditions regarding maintenance and access could not be complied with after sale. Therefore the defendant was guilty of the offence with which he was charged.

Where a journey is made for two purposes, one permitted by the policy and the other not, the court must consider what was the primary purpose of the journey. If the non-permitted purpose predominates a claim will be defeated.

(422) *Seddon* v *Binions, Zurich Insurance Co. (Third Party); Stork* v *Binions Zurich Insurance (Third Party)* [1978] R.T.R. 163

A father who was assisting his son in the son's business agreed to drive, in his son's car, the son's employee who was suffering from toothache, to a dentist and/or home on his way home from lunch. On the way the car was involved in an accident in which one person died and another was injured. Judgment was awarded against both father and son for some £45,000 and the father in third-party proceedings unsuccessfully claimed an indemnity from his own insurers who insured him to drive any car 'for social, domestic and pleasure purposes.' It was *held* by the Court of Appeal, dismissing the father's appeal, that the primary purpose of the journey was a business purpose of the son and was therefore not covered by the policy; alternatively, the fact that one of the purposes for which the car was being driven was a business purpose sufficed to defeat the claim.

(423) *D.H.R. Moody (Chemists)* v *Iron Trades Mutual Insurance Co.*, (1970) 115 S.J. 16

A motor car which was lent by a member of Clacton-on-Sea Urban District Council to take French guests from Valence (with which Clacton was twinned) to Heathrow Airport was involved in an accident when it was being driven back by Mr Ramsden, the Clerk of the Council. The car was covered by an insurance policy covering only use for 'social, domestic and pleasure purposes and use for the business of the insured'. The defendant insurance company repudiated liability on the ground that the car was being used otherwise than in accordance with the terms of the policy. *Held*—by Wrangham, J.—that at the material time the car was being used for 'social purposes' within the terms of the policy. The activities of an individual could be divided into those which he pursued because he had to in order to earn a living, which would be business, and those which he pursued of his own free will, such as social or domestic pleasures. The activities of a local authority could also be so divided into those duties that they were compelled by statute or convention to carry out, and voluntary activities which might be, and probably were, of a social character. There was no reason why the council's activities in trying to arrange contact with Valence should not be regarded as social. Cars being used in the course of those activities were being used for a social purpose. There remained the defence argument that at the time of the accident the car was being used by Ramsden, the clerk, to enable him to carry out his council duties, in other words for a business purpose. But the car had not been lent to Ramsden but to the local authority for it was the social duty of the local authority to convey their visitors to the airport. And the fact that the actual driver of a car was fulfilling his duty to his employer by driving it, did not prevent its use from being for a social purpose.

In the case of life assurance, where the premium is paid during the period of grace it is regarded as having been paid on the due date and, if a person so insured dies after the due date of the premium, but before the expiry of the days of grace, his representatives can pay the premium and claim the benefit of the policy.

(424) *Stuart* v *Freeman* [1903] 1 K.B. 47

The plaintiff had taken an assignment of a policy on another person's life. The policy was for a year, the premium being payable quarterly and the first of such premiums having been paid at the date of the policy. The policy provided that if at the time of the death of the assured any quarterly premium should be more than 30 days in arrear, the policy should be of no effect. The life assured died during the year—after one of the dates laid down for payment of a quarterly premium, but before the 30 days of grace had expired. The premium was paid by the plaintiff after the death of the assured but within the days of grace. The plaintiff now sued to recover the amount of the policy. *Held*—The policy was prevented from lapsing by the plaintiff's payment and he was entitled to recover.

Where it is shown that a loss has been caused by fire, the person insured has a *prima facie* presumption in his favour that it was not caused by him. The insurer must show on a balance of probabilities that the insurer caused the fire.

(425) *Slattery* v *Mance* [1962] 1 All E.R. 525

The plaintiff brought an action claiming £4500 under a Lloyd's policy for the loss by fire of his vessel, the *Treworval Light.* The defendant disclaimed liability on the ground that, although the vessel was lost by fire, the plaintiff wilfully caused or connived at the destruction of the vessel. The defendant argued that the onus of proof was on the plaintiff to prove that the fire was caused other than by his own act. Salmon, J., said in the course of his judgment. 'On the law as it now stands, when a plaintiff claims for loss under a policy of marine insurance, asserting that the loss was caused by perils of the sea, the onus is on him to prove that the loss was accidental.' In the case of fire the onus of proof is different and it is for the defendant to prove that, on the balance of probability, the plaintiff destroyed the ship.

Comment. The decision is of general application and not confined to marine situations.

A beneficiary or his assignee under a life policy cannot recover under that policy if he murdered the person insured. In cases of unlawful killing the court may authorise a claim under the Forfeiture Act 1982.

(426) *Cleaver* v *Mutual Reserve Fund Life Association* [1892] 1 Q.B. 147

James Maybrick insured his life for £2000 with the defendants on 3 October 1888, and died on 11 May 1889, being murdered by his wife, Florence Maybrick, who was convicted in August 1889, although sentence of death was commuted to penal servitude for life. The policy moneys were to be payable to the wife, if living at the time of Maybrick's death. Before her trial Mrs Maybrick assigned the policy by deed to the plaintiff, Cleaver. James Maybrick had appointed as his executors, Thomas and Michael Maybrick, also plaintiffs in the action. The insurers refused to pay the £2000. *Held*—The contract of insurance was made between the husband on the one side and the defendants on the other. The husband died by the criminal act of the wife. Upon his death the right to sue went to his executors. The rule of public policy prevents the wife or anyone claiming through her from recovering and reaping the fruits of her crime. The executors were suing for the estate of he husband and would hold it as trustees for the estate, available for the deceased's creditors or his children (if any). Children are not shut out since they claim through the father and not the mother. Therefore the insurers must pay the money to T. and M. Maybrick as executors.

An insured person who becomes liable to pay damages for injury or death caused to any other person cannot claim an indemnity under a householder's comprehensive insurance policy where the person insured is guilty of deliberate, intentional, or unlawful violence.

(427) *Gray* v *Barr, Prudential Assurance Co. (Third Party)* [1971] 2 All E.R. 949

Mr Barr went to seek his wife at the house of Mr Gray, her paramour, carrying a loaded shotgun to frighten him. Barr threatened Gray, there was a scuffle during which Barr fell and the gun went off accidently killing Gray. Barr was tried and acquitted of murder and manslaughter. Gray's administrators brought an action against Barr for damages and Barr joined the Assurance Company in order to claim an indemnity from them under an accident insurance policy which he had taken out with them. *Held*—by Geoffrey Lane, J., on the matter of the insurance claim—on the grounds of public policy a person who is guilty of another's death by deliberate, intentional and unlawful violence or threats of violence, may not avail himself of an insurance indemnity however unintentional the death itself may be.

Although an insured person who commits suicide no longer commits a crime in so doing, the concept of risk in insurance does not include loss due to the wilful act of the insured unless there is an express provision to this effect in the policy. Thus insurers may still be able to reject a claim in the absence of an express provision to the contrary where the insured commits suicide. If the insured commits suicide while insane his act will not be regarded as wilful and the insurers will be liable unless the policy provides to the contrary.

(428) *Beresford* v *Royal Insurance Co. ltd* [1938] A.C. 586

Major Rowlandson took out a policy on his life with the Royal Insurance Co. in 1925. The policy provided that—

If the life assured shall die by his own hand whether sane or insane within one year from the commencement of the insurance the policy shall be void as against any person claiming the amount hereby assured or any part therof.

Major Rowlandson paid the premiums regularly until 3 August 1934. At about 2.57 p.m. on that day he shot himself being in debt to the extent of £60,000. It was found as a fact by the jury that Major Rowlandson was sane at the time of his death. *Held*—by the House of Lords—that the condition in the policy implied an undertaking by an insurance company to pay if the assured died by his own hand sane or insane after the expiry of one year from the commencement of the policy. However, it was contrary to public policy that either a person who had committed a crime, or his personal representatives, should be allowed to benefit from that crime. Therefore the policy was unenforceable.

The term 'accident' in a policy can include a wilful murder.

(429) *Trim and Joint District School Board of Management* v *Kelly* [1914] A.C. 667

Kelly was a dependant of an assistant master at an industrial school. Whilst the master was engaged in the performance of his duties, two of the pupils of the school attacked and killed him. The boys were unruly and badly disposed towards the master. Kelly claimed compensation from the managers of the school on the grounds that the assistant master met his death by accident in the course of his employment. *Held*—by the Judicial Committee of the Privy Council—that although the master was murdered, his death was nevertheless caused by an accident and, being in the course of his employment, compensation was recoverable under the relevant industrial legislation.

The insured person can claim a refund of premiums even if the contract is illegal and void, provided the insured is not *in pari delicto* (in equal wrong).

(430) *Hughes* v *Liverpool Victoria Legal Friendly Society* [1916] 2 K.B. 482

John Henry Thomas, a grocer, had originally taken out five policies on customers who owed him money. It was agreed that Thomas had an insurable interest in the customers because they were his debtors. Thomas let the policies drop and an agent of the defendant company persuaded a Mrs Hughes to take them up, assuring her that she had an insurable interest which she had not. She now brought this action to recover the premiums paid. *Held*—The contract was illegal but the plaintiff could recover the premiums. She had been induced to take up the policies by the fraud of the defendants' agent.

It is a matter of fact for the court to decide in each case whether a condition in a policy requiring the insured or his representatives to give notice of loss within a specified times has been complied with.

(431) *Verelst's Administratrix* v *Motor Union Insurance Co. Ltd* [1925] 2 K.B. 137

The plaintiff was the administratrix of a lady who had been killed in a motor accident in India. The policy of insurance covered the death of the insured by an accident of the type in question but it contained the following condition: 'In case of any accident, injury, damage, or loss . . . the insured, or the insured's representatives for the time being, shall give notice . . . in writing to the head office of the company of such accident, injury, damage, or loss as soon as possible after it has come to knowledge of the insured, or of the insured's representatives for the time being.' The accident which killed the insured took place on 14 January 1923, and the plaintiff heard of the death within a month afterwards but she only discovered the existence of the policy in January 1924.

She then gave notice to the insurance company as soon as possible, but the insurance company denied liability on the ground that notice had not been given as soon as possible within the meaning of the condition in the policy. The dispute was submitted to arbitration and the arbitrator found for the plaintiff. On appeal it was *held* that, taking into account all the circumstances, the plaintiff had given notice as soon as she possibly could and the arbitrator's decision was right.

Where the contract of insurance stipulates the time and method in which the insured person must notify the event upon which loss may be caused, the insurance company may turn down a claim where the rules have not been followed even though there was no real fault on the part of the insured.

(432) *Cassel* v *Lancashire & Yorkshire Accident Insurance Co. Ltd* (1885) 1 T.L.R. 495

The plaintiff had an accident while paddling a canoe but did not feel the effects until some months later. He had an accident policy with the defendants which required notice of an accident within 14 days together with medical certificates describing the injuries received. He did not notify the accident until he felt the effects and it was *held* that he was not entitled to recover because of the delay and non-compliance with the terms of the policy.

An insurance company may waive a breach of condition or warranty relating to the notification of a claim in the policy. Such a waiver will not, however, be deemed to have taken effect by mere lapse of time on the part of the insurance company unless there is prejudice to the insured or others.

(433) *Allen* v *Robles (Compagnie Parisienne de Guarantie Third Party)* [1969] 3 All E.R. 154

The defendant, Mr Robles, drove his car in a negligent fashion and ran into the plaintiff's house. In an action at Nottingham Assizes the judge awarded the plaintiff damages against Robles, and the question arose as to whether Robles could claim on his insurance policy with the French insurance company which was joined as third party in this action. Robles was in breach of his contract of insurance because that contract provided that he must notify the insurance company of any claim made against him within five days of the claim. This he had not done. In fact he failed to inform the insurance company of the claim by the plaintiff until two months after he knew it had been made. On the other hand the insurance company did not repudiate their liability until some four months after Robles informed them of the claim. It was *held*—by the Court of Appeal—that the insurance company had not lost its right to repudiate the contract. The delay was not so long as to indicate that they had accepted liability and it had in no way changed the circumstances of the case. It had not, for example, increased Allen's loss or altered Robles' liability. There was thus no prejudice to those concerned.

Not all statements in a proposal form are in the nature of conditions or warranties but may be merely descriptive of the risk.

(434) *Provincial Insurance Co.* v *Morgan and Foxon* [1933] A.C. 240

In a proposal form for insurance of a lorry against damage and third party claims, the proposal form asked the proposer to state the purposes in full for which the vehicle would be used, and the nature of the goods to be carried. His answers were: 'Delivery of Coal' and 'Coal' respectively. He agreed that the answers in the proposal should form the 'basis' of the contract. The lorry did carry on one occasion both coal and timber, but it collided with a car while loaded with coal only. *Held*—The questions and answers were a mere description of the risk covered. The lorry was only carrying coal when the accident occurred and was, therefore, covered. The term 'purposes in full' did not mean 'exclusive purposes'. The clause, being drafted by the insurers, was construed in favour of the insured, using the *contra proferentem* rule.

Where the policy is a valued one, the insured recovers the agreed value even if it is more than his loss unless the difference in the actual and the agreed value is so great as to make an illegal wager. In the case of a partial loss with no reinstatement, the insured is entitled to be indemnified in respect of depreciation which was caused by the fire and that percentage is a percentage of the agreed, not the actual, value.

(435) *Elcock* v *Thomson* [1949] 2 All E.R. 381

In 1940 a mansion at Easthampstead Park, near Wokingham, was insured against fire. The value was agreed at £106,850. The mansion was damaged by fire in 1947 when it was found that the true value of the premises was £18,000 before the fire, and the actual value was £12,600 after the fire, i.e. the depreciation in value was 30 per cent. *Held*—In assessing the claim this percentage of depreciation should be applied to the agreed value and the insured was entitled to 30 per cent of £106,850, namely £32,055.

The risks which will be met through the Motor Insurers Bureau are only those for which a motorist must insure.

(436) *Lees* v *Motor Insurers Bureau* [1952] 2 All E.R. 511

By an agreement between the Ministry of Transport and the Motor Insurers Bureau, the bureau undertook to satisfy any judgment not satisfied within seven days in respect of 'any liability which is required to be covered by a policy of insurance . . . under Part II of the Road Traffic Act 1930' (as it then was). An employer had a policy which 'excluded liability in respect of death arising out of and in the course of his employment of a person in the employment of the insured'. One employee killed another by the negligent driving of a lorry, and the latter's widow obtained judgment against the lorry driver which was unsatisfied. She claimed on the Motor Insurers Bureau under the agreement. *Held*—The Road Traffic Act 1930 did not require cover for liability of the type set out in the exclusion clause, and therefore the bureau was not liable.

Section 143 of the Road Traffic Act 1972 does not embrace in 'compulsory risk' the liability of a vehicle owner to a permitted driver in respect of the defective state of the vehicle.

(437) *Cooper* v *Motor Insurers' Bureau* [1983] 1 All E.R. 353

The owner of a motor cycle asked the plaintiff to give the cycle a road test. The brakes failed and the plaintiff was seriously injured. Later he obtained a judgment for damages against the owner of the motor cycle for the latter's negligence in failing to warn him that the brakes were defective. The owner of the motor cycle had no third party insurance and could not meet the judgment from his own funds. The plaintiff then brought an action against the MIB contending that it was liable to meet the judgment by reason of its undertaking to the Secretary of State that it would satisfy judgments in regard to liabilities required by the Road Traffic Act 1972 to be covered by insurance. Section 145(3)(*a*) of the 1972 Act requires that to satisfy the legislation a motor policy must—'insure such person, persons or classes of persons as may be specified in the policy in respect of any liability which may be incurred by him or them in respect of the death of or bodily injury to any person caused by or arising out of, the use of the vehicle on a road in Great Britain. . . .' The plaintiff's argument was that the words 'any person' should be given their ordinary meaning so as to include the plaintiff, it being immaterial that he was driving the vehicle and that 'third party risks' covered by the section did not relate to those outside the vehicle but could include those in or on it. There was some validity in this argument because liability to passengers must now be covered. However, it was *held* by Barry Chedlow, Q.C., sitting as a Deputy Judge of the High Court, that the motor cycle owner's liability to the plaintiff was not a compulsory risk within the scope of the Act. On a true construction of the section the only liabilities required to be covered were liabilities to persons other than the insured or his permitted driver. In consequence, the liability of the insured to a permitted driver himself when the latter is using the vehicle is not a compulsory risk and not a liability which the Motor Insurers' Bureau has agreed to satisfy.

Subject to the Life Assurance Act 1774, a person without an insurable interest can insure a risk so long as he agrees to hold the proceeds of the policy as a trustee for a person(s) having an insurable interest.

(438) *Prudential Staff Union* v *Hall* [1947] K.B. 685

The plaintiff in this case was a union of the employees of an insurance company. The employees concerned were agents and collectors and often held sums of money on behalf of the company. The union took out a policy with Lloyd's underwriters to cover loss by its members of such moneys by burglary and housebreaking. The policy described the union as 'the assured' and under the provisions of the policy the underwriters agreed to pay the union in respect of losses occurring by reason of the perils mentioned above. The union received 3s from each member in respect of the premium, and paid 2s 6d per member to the insurers. Claims were made at various times and were met by the insurers, but on one occasion, when the union made a claim in respect of loss by burglary of moneys held by two of its members, one of the underwriters, Hall, refused to pay the claim, pleading that the union had no cause of action, having no insurable interest. *Held*—The union had no insurable interest in the moneys insured, since liability for losses of money was in the members themselves and not the union. Nor did such an interest arise out of the union's general concern for the welfare of its members. However, the union was entitled to recover the money because the underwriters had contracted to pay the union, and the union was in the position of trustee for the members concerned in respect of the money received.

Comment. The Life Assurance Act of 1774 did not render the contract void since, for the purposes of the policy, moneys were 'goods' within that Act, and insurances on goods were excepted from it.

A fire insurance contract is one of indemnity and under the rule of subrogation the insured person cannot recover more than an indemnity.

(439) *Castellain* v *Preston* (1883) 11 Q.B.D. 380

In March 1878, the defendants insured their premises against fire, and in July 1878 they agreed to sell the premises for £3100, took a deposit, and arranged for the contract to be completed on a day within two years to be named by them. A fire damaged the premises in August and the insurers paid the defendants £330, not knowing of the sale. The purchasers completed the sale in December 1879, and paid the full agreed price to the defendants. The insurers claimed (1) a refund of the £330 on the ground that, because of the sale, the defendants had suffered no loss; and (2) the right to be subrogated to the rights of the defendants to the proceeds of the sale, up to £330. *Held*—by the Court of Appeal—that the insurers be given judgment for £330. Brett, L.J., made the following points: (*a*) a contract of marine or fire insurance is a contract of indemnity and the assured shall be fully, but never more than fully, indemnified; (*b*) as between the underwriter and the assured, the underwriter is entitled to the advantage of every right of the assured, whether in contract or tort, or any other right legal or equitable, by exercising or acquiring that by which the loss insured against can or has been diminished.

An insured person may not profit from his misfortune but will only be indemnified in regard to his actual loss, valued policies apart.

(440) *Leppard* v *Excess Insurance Co. Ltd* [1979] 2 All E.R. 668

Mr Leppard bought a house in 1972 with the sole intention of selling it. At first the asking price was £12,500, but at the time of the fire he was willing to sell for £4500. The house was insured against fire for £10,000, Mr Leppard having signed a declaration to the effect that the sum insured represented not less than the 'full value', value being defined as the amount which it would cost to replace in existing form should it be destroyed. The house was totally destroyed by fire in 1975 and liability was accepted by the insurance company, though the amount payable was contested. Mr Leppard argued that where a property was completely destroyed loss of the full value was incurred, thus entitling him to recover the loss of reinstatement even though it exceeded the amount of the actual loss suffered. In the insurance company's view Mr Leppard was entitled only to the market value of the house at the time of the fire. The Court of Appeal *held* that Mr Leppard could only recover the market value at the date of the fire. The company had agreed to indemnify him in respect of loss or damage by fire. The maximum amount recoverable under the policy, £10,000, was not recoverable if it exceeded the actual loss. Since Mr Leppard was willing to sell the property at the time of the fire for £4500 or less, that was its actual value at that time, and so his actual loss was £4500 less the site value and the company was ordered to pay him £3000.

Sometimes the court may take the view that a bailee of goods has assumed the interest of the owner in those goods. Where this is so the bailee may claim upon a policy and holds the insurance money in trust for the bailor.

(441) *A. Tomlinson (Hauliers) Ltd* v *Hepburn* [1966] A.C. 451

The plaintiffs, who were carriers, were required by their contract with tobacco owners to 'insure and keep insured with a full comprehensive cover against loss of goods in transit or otherwise'. The plaintiffs insured the tobacco owners' goods with the defendant, who was an underwriter, the policy being a Lloyd's Goods in Transit Policy. The policy provided for insurance for the goods 'in transit . . . including loading and unloading' and also for 'all risks of loss or damage however arising'. The plaintiffs' vehicles carried tobacco to the owners' depot but arrived after working hours so that the lorries were left in the depot but not unloaded. The same evening the lorries and tobacco were stolen without negligence on the part of the plaintiffs. The plaintiffs claimed on the policy and the defence was that the goods were 'off risk' because the transit had ended; that the policy covered the carriers in respect of their negligence, if any, but did not cover the owners' proprietary interest; that the carriers had no insurable interest outside of their charges. *Held*—by the House of Lords—that as transit was defined as including loading and unloading, the goods were on risk until loading was completed; this was a policy on goods and was not solely concerned with the bailees' negligence; that the carriers had an insurable interest in the tobacco, the value of which was recoverable under the policy, though the bailees must account to the bailor for his share of the loss after deducting what was owing to them.

A shareholder has no insurable interest in the assets of the company. The latter is a separate entity and owns its own property.

(442) *Macaura* v *Northern Assurance Co. Ltd* [1925] A.C. 619

Macaura agreed to sell timber to a company of which he was the major shareholder for £42,000, which was paid for by allotting him 42,000 fully-paid shares in the company of £1 each. He also financed the company and was an unsecured creditor for £19,000, its other debts being trifling. He insured the timber against fire, and on 23 February 1922 most of the timber was destroyed by fire. Macaura claimed under his policies, but he was *held* not to have an insurable interest. Macaura could only be insuring either as a creditor or as a shareholder of the company, and neither a simple creditor nor a shareholder has any insurable interest in a *particular* asset which the company holds.

Comment. Unlike a shareholder, a debenture holder can insure the property of the company on which his debenture is secured. (*Westminster Fire Office* v *Glasgow Provident Investment Society* (1888) 13 App Cas 699.) The difference in the debenture holder's position is justifiable since, as a secured creditor he has an interest in the company's property which, of course the shareholder does not have, at least in the legal sense.

Double insurance occurs when the policies cover the same adventure, the same risk, and the same interest in the same subject-matter. Where the interests covered by the policies are different there is no double insurance.

(443) *North British & Mercantile Insurance Co.* v *London, Liverpool & Globe Insurance Co.* (1877) 5 Ch.D 569

Wharfingers insured grain and seed stored with them against loss or damage by fire. The policy was subject to the following condition: 'If at any time of any loss or damage by fire happening to any property hereby insured there be any other subsisting insurance or insurances, whether effected by the insured or by any other person, covering the same property, the company shall not be liable to pay or contribute more than its rateable proportion of such loss or damage'. The grain and seed in question were also insured by the merchant who had an interest in it. The merchant's policy, however, also covered grain stored elsewhere. The policy contained a similar clause to the one set out above. While both policies were subsisting, a fire destroyed the grain stored with the wharfingers. The wharfingers were paid in full by their own insurers, and this action was brought by the insurers concerned to determine the liability of the insurers as between themselves. *Held*—The merchant's insurers were not liable to contribute. The condition as to double insurance only applied to a case where the same property was the subject-matter of the contract and the interests were the same. Here the merhant's policy covered other goods in addition to those destroyed, and the merchant's interest was that of owners, while that of the wharfingers was that of bailee.

It is a general principle of indemnity insurance that a person suffering loss under an insurance policy cannot claim to be indemnified by a sum of money larger than his actual loss. Under the doctrine of subrogation the insurers acquire a right as against third parties to all the rights which the insured person had and this is particularly important in the case of tortious damage.

(444) *Darrell* v *Tibbitts* (1880) 5 Q.B.D. 560

The defendant leased certain premises, taking a covenant from the tenant to repair them if the premises should be damaged by gas. The defendant also insured the premises under a fire policy. The premises were damaged by an explosion of gas caused by the negligence of the local authority. The defendant obtained payment of £750 from the insurer; the tenant, who was obliged to repair and did so, recovered damages against the local authority. In this action the insurer sought to recover from the defendant the money paid under the policy. *Held*—Since the policy was a contract of indemnity, the insurer could recover the £750, otherwise the landlord would have received, in effect, £1500 for damage amounting to £750.

(445) *Goole & Hull Steam Towing Co.* v *Ocean Marine Insurance Co.* [1928] 1 K.B. 589

The defendants were the insurers of the plaintiffs' ship against the usual marine risks. The steamer, which was valued at £4000, was in collision with another vessel. The plaintiffs paid for the repair of the ship and then sued the owners of the other vessel. The action was settled by payment to the plaintiffs of £2500, which sum represented half the actual damage. The plaintiffs now sued the insurers to recover the balance of the loss, i.e. £2500, claiming that they were entitled to that sum in full since they had insured the ship for £4000. *Held*—The defendants need only pay £1500, as representing the difference between the value of the policy, £4000, and the £2500 which the plaintiffs had already recovered from the owners of the other vessel.

Because of the right of the insurers to subrogation, the insured person must not settle or compromise claims with third parties without the consent of the insurers.

(446) *Phoenix Assurance Co.* v *Spooner* [1905] 2 K.B. 753

The defendant took out a fire policy with the plaintiff company in respect of her buildings. While the policy was in force, the Plymouth Corporation served her with a notice to acquire the buildings under the Lands Clauses Consolidation Act 1845. Before the corporation had taken any further steps under the notice, the buildings were destroyed by fire. The plaintiffs paid to the defendant the agreed sum representing the loss she had incurred. When the corporation actually came to take over the property, the price they were to pay was agreed between them and the defendant, and was reduced by the amount which the defendant had received from the insurance company, the corporation agreeing to indemnify the defendant against any claim which the insurance company might make against her. *Held*—The insurance contract was one of indemnity, and when the plaintiffs paid the agreed amount under the policy, they became entitled to all the rights of the defendant. These included the right to be paid by the corporation the full value of the property as it existed at the date of service of the notice to acquire. The defendant had no right to deprive the plaintiffs of that right by compromising with the corporation. Therefore the plaintiffs were entitled to recover from the defendant the amount paid to her under the policy.

Comment. Under the agreement with the corporation, the defendant would be able to claim an indemnity in respect of the money paid back to the insurers.

If there is a 'knock for knock' agreement between two insurers under which they agree not to exercise their rights against each other, then in the absence of some express provision in the policy, this agreement does not affect the insured person.

(447) *Morley* v *Moore* [1936] 2 All E.R. 79

Moore, a motorist, negligently damaged the car of Morley, another motorist, in a collision. Moore and Morley were both insured with companies who had a 'knock for knock' agreement whereby Moore's insurer paid for Moore's damage and Morley's insurer paid for Morley's. Morley's insurer paid Morley £28 2s 8d. The actual damage was £33 2s 8d. but under the policy Morley was to bear the first £5 of any claim. Since the object of the 'knock for knock' agreement was to obviate litigation, Morley's insurers strongly dissuaded him from pursuing action against Moore. However, Morley persisted and claimed £33 2s 8d. Moore admitted liability but only for £5, since Morley had already received the balance under his insurance. *Held*—Morley could recover the full amount. Although his insurance company did not want him to sue, they could not prevent him from so doing. Nor could Moore refuse to pay the £28 2s 8d on the grounds that Morley's insurers had paid it. He had no rights to the benefits of Morley's insurance. Morley would be liable to refund the £28 2s 8d to the insurance company. They had said they did not desire this in the hope that he would not sue. If they chose to make Morley a gift of this sum, that was their affair. It in no way impaired his legal right to claim it from Moore.

Law of Employment Protection

Sex discrimination: genuine occupational qualification: requirement of decency.

(448) *Sisley* v *Britannia Security Systems* [1983] I.C.R. 628

The defendants employed women to work in a security control station. The plaintiff applied for a vacant job but was refused employment. It appeared that the women worked 12-hour shifts with rest periods and that beds were provided for their use during such breaks. The women undressed to their underwear during these rest breaks. The plaintiff complained that by advertising for women the defendants were contravening the Sex Discrimination Act 1975. The defendants pleaded genuine occupational qualification, i.e. that women were required because of the removal of uniform during rest periods was incidental to the employment. The Employment Appeal Tribunal accepted that defence. The defence of preservation of decency was, in the circumstances, a good one. It was reasonably incidental to the women's work that they should remove their clothing during rest periods.

A man and a woman will be regarded as engaged in 'like work' even though there may be some differences between the jobs, but not if these differences are 'material'.

(449) *Capper Pass* v *Lawton* [1976] I.R.L.R. 366

A female cook who worked a 40-hour week preparing lunches for the directors of Capper was paid a lower rate than two male assistant chefs who worked a 45-hour week preparing some 350 meals a day in Cappers' works canteen. The female cook claimed that by reason of the EPA (as amended) she should be paid at the same rate as the assistant chefs since she was employed on work of a broadly similar nature.

It was held by the EAT that if the work done by a female applicant was of a broadly similar nature to that done by a male colleague it should be regarded as being like work for the purposes of the EPA unless there were some practical differences of detail between the two types of job. In this case the EAT decided that the work done by the female cook was broadly similar to the work of the assistant chefs and that the differences of detail were not of practical importance in relation to the terms and conditions of employment. Consequently, the female cook was entitled to be paid at the same rate as her male colleagues.

(450) *Navy, Army and Air Force Institutes* v *Varley* [1977] 1 All E.R. 840.

Miss Varley worked as a Grade E clerical worker in the accounts office of NAAFI in Nottingham. NAAFI conceded that her work was like that of Grade E male clerical workers employed in NAAFI's London Office. However, the Grade E workers in Nottingham worked a 37-hour week, while the male Grade E clerical workers in the London office worked a 36½-hour week. Miss Varley applied to an industrial tribunal under the EPA for a declaration that she was less favourably treated as regards hours worked than the male clerical workers in London and that her contract term as to hours be modified so as to reduce it to 36½ hours a week. The industrial tribunal granted that declaration and NAAFI appealed.

It was *held* by the EAT that the variation in hours was genuinely due to a material difference other than the difference of sex. It was due to a real difference in that the male employees worked in London where there was a custom to work shorter hours. Accordingly NAAFI's appeal was allowed and Miss Varley was held not to be entitled to the declaration.

'. . . There is a geographical distinction between the conditions operated by NAAFI in respect of their employees in London and those outside London. That is by no means a unique situation; it is common to the Civil Service and to all sorts of other employment. . . . In other words, the variation between her contract and a man's contract is due really to the fact that she works in Nottingham and he works in London. It seems to us that it is quite plain that that is the difference between her case and his case, namely that she works in Nottingham where this old custom operates and he works in London where the custom of a shorter working week operates.' (Per Phillips, J.)

Sexual and racial discrimination. Indirect discrimination: requirements or conditions applied to all workers but the ability of some persons to comply because of sex or race is considerably smaller and cannot be justified.

(451) *Price* v *The Civil Service Commission* [1977] I.R.L.R. 291

The Civil Service required candidates for the position of executive officer to be between 17½ and 28 years. Belinda Price complained that this age bar constituted indirect sex discrimination against women because women between those ages were more likely than men to be temporarily out of the labour market having children or caring for children at home. It was *held* by the Employment Appeal Tribunal that the age bar was indirect discrimination against women. The Court held that the words 'can comply' must not be construed narrowly. It could be said that any female applicant could comply with the condition in the sense that she was not obliged to marry or to have children or to look after them—indeed she may find someone else to look after them or, as a last resort, put them into care. If the legislation was construed in that way it was no doubt right to say that any female applicant could comply with the condition. However, in the view of the Court to construe the legislation in that way appeared to be wholly out of sympathy with the spirit and intention of the Act. A person should not be deemed to be able to do something merely because it was theoretically possible, it was necessary to decide whether it was possible for the person to do so in practice, as distinct from theory.

Constructive dismissal. What type of conduct by the employer will entitle the employee to end the contract?

(452) *Western Excavating Ltd* v *Sharp* [1978] 1 All E.R. 713

Under the terms of his employment if Mr Sharp worked extra time he could have time off in lieu. In February 1976 he asked for three hours off to play cards for a team. He was told that he could not have the time off that afternoon as there was too much work; nevertheless he went to play cards. The next day he was dismissed. The disciplinary panel set up by the employers substituted five days' suspension without pay for the dismissal. That left Mr Sharp in financial difficulties and he asked his employer for an advance on his accrued holiday pay. This was refused, as was a request for a loan of £40, and he then left his employment in order to obtain his holiday pay and brought a claim for unfair dismissal. That claim was upheld by an industrial tribunal and the Employment Appeal Tribunal and the matter came before the Court of Appeal.

The Court of Appeal decided that in order to establish constructive dismissal is must be shown that the employer was guilty of conduct which was sufficiently serious to amount to a breach of the contract of service. If it was, then the employee could be regarded as unfairly dismissed even though it was the employee who left the employment. The other approach which had been adopted in cases before tribunals, i.e. that if the employer acted 'unreasonably' an employee might leave and yet be regarded as having been unfairly dismissed, was wrong.

'The present case is a good illustration of a "whimsical decision". Applying the test of 'unreasonable conduct', the Industrial Tribunal decided by a majority of two to one in favour of the man. The Employment Appeal Tribunal would, all three of them, have decided in favour of the employer, but felt that it was a matter of fact on which they could not reverse the Industrial Tribunal. So, counting heads, it was four to two in favour of the employers, but yet the case was decided against them, because of the test of 'unreasonable conduct'.

'If the 'contract test' had been applied, the result would have been plain. There was no dismissal, constructive or otherwise, by the company. The company were not in breach at all. Nor had they repudiated the contract at all. Mr Sharp left of his own accord without anything wrong done by the company. His claim should have been rejected. The decision against the company was most unjust to them. I would allow the appeal accordingly.' (Per Lord Denning, MR.)

Comment. In spite of the decision of the Court of Appeal that unreasonable conduct in the employer was not enough, there have been cases since *Sharp* where the court has decided that unreasonable conduct may be enough to amount to a repudiatory dismissal. Thus in *Palmanor* v *Cedron* [1978] I.C.R. 1008, an employee barman was held to have been constructively dismissed when he left because the manager swore at him. Again in *Robinson* v *Crompton Parkinson* [1978] I.C.R. 401, an employee of good character was falsely accused of theft and the police were called and he eventually resigned after being promised a written apology which he did not get. He applied for compensation for unfair dismissal, but the Industrial Tribunal held that he had not proved that the employer's action was such as to bring the contract of employment to an end. On appeal to the EAT it was held that the situation did amount to repudiation of the contract of employment, though they sent the case to another Industrial Tribunal for rehearing in case the employer could show some background knowledge to justify his suspicion of the employee. If there had been reasonable grounds for the allegations, however false, the employer may not have appeared quite so unreasonable.

Conduct justifying dismissal may be the way in which an employee dresses.

(453) *Boychuk* v *H.J. Symons (Holdings) Ltd* [1977] I.R.L.R. 375

Miss B was employed by S Ltd as an accounts audit clerk but her duties involved contact with the public from time to time. Miss B insisted on wearing badges which proclaimed the fact that she was a lesbian and from May 1976 she wore one or other of the following:

(*a*) a lesbian symbol consisting of two circles with crosses (indicating women) joined together;
(*b*) badges with the legends 'Gays Against Fascism' and 'Gay Power';
(*c*) a badge with the legend 'Gay Switchboard' with a telephone number on it and the words 'Information Service for Homosexual Men and Women'.
(*d*) a badge with the word 'Dyke' on it, indicating to the initiated that she was a lesbian.

These were eventually superseded by a white badge with the words 'Lesbians Ignite' written in large letters on it. Nothing much had happened in regard to the wearing of the earlier badges but when she began wearing the 'Lesbians Ignite' badge there were discussions about it between her and her employers. She was told she must remove it—which she was not willing to do—and if she did not she would be dismissed. She would not remove the badge and was dismissed on 16 August 1976, and then made a claim for compensation for unfair dismissal.

No complaint was made regarding the manner of her dismissal in terms, e.g. of proper warning. The straight question was whether her employers were entitled to dismiss her because she insisted on wearing the badge. An Industrial Tribunal had *held* that in all the circumstances the dismissal was fair because it was within an employer's discretion to instruct an employee not to wear a particular sign or symbol which could cause offence to customers and fellow-employees. Miss B appealed to the Employment Appeal Tribunal.

The Employment Appeal Tribunal dismissed her appeal and affirmed that her dismissal was fair. The judgment of the Court was read by Mr Justice Phillips who made the following points:

(*a*) There was no question of Miss B having been dismissed because she was a lesbian or because of anything to do with her private life or private behaviour. Such a case would be entirely different and raise different questions. This was only a case where she had been dismissed because of her conduct at work—that, the judge said, must be clearly understood;

(*b*) The decision did not mean that an employer by a foolish or unreasonable judgment of what could be expected to be offensive could impose some unreasonable restriction on an employee. However, the decision did mean that a reasonable employer, who was after all ultimately responsible for the interests of the business, could be allowed to decide what upon reflection or mature consideration could be offensive to customers and fellow-employees, and he need not wait to see whether the business will in fact be damaged before he takes steps in the matter.

Dismissal on a transfer of business.

(454) *Meikle* v *McPhail (Charleston Arms)* [1983] I.R.L.R. 351

After contracting to take over a public house and its employees, the new management decided that economies were essential, and dismissed the barmaid. She complained to an Industrial Tribunal on the grounds of unfair dismissal.

Her case was based on Reg. 8(1) of the Transfer of Undertakings (Protection of Employment) Regulations 1981. This states that a dismissal is to be treated as unfair if the transfer of a business or a reason connected with it, is the reason or principal reason for the dismissal. The pub's new management defended the claim under Reg. 8(2). This states that a dismissal following a transfer of business is not to be regarded as automatically unfair where there was, as in this case, an economic reason for making changes in the workforce. If there is such a reason unfairness must be established on grounds other than the mere transfer of business.

The Employment Appeal Tribunal *held* that the reason for dismissal was an economic one under Reg. 8(2) and that the management had acted reasonably in the circumstances. The barmaid's claim failed. The EAT also decided that for dismissals on economic grounds on a transfer of business, under Reg. 8(2) the fairness standards for redundancy should be applied. These were laid down in *Williams* v *Compair Maxam* [1982] I.R.L. 83. The standards require the giving of maximum notice; consultation with unions, if any; the taking of the views of more than one person as to who should be dismissed; the following of any laid down procedure; ie last in, first out; and finally, an effort to find employees concerned alternative work within the organisation.

Redundancy—change in work is sufficient.

(455) *Murphy* v *Epsom College* [1983] I.R.L.R. 395

The College employed two plumbers, one of whom was Mr Murphy. The other, Mr Williams, had longer service with the College.

During a period when the College was carrying out improvements and modifications to its buildings, Mr Murphy was asked to deal with the necessary changes in the heating and hot-water systems and to maintain them for the future. Mr Murphy felt that this heavy concentration on heating work was outside the normal range of a plumber's activities. He wrote to his employers telling them so. His letter made them wonder whether they had employed the right person in Mr Murphy. It looked as if they needed one plumber and one fully-trained heating technician. They made Mr Murphy redundant, and proposed to replace him with a heating technician. Mr Murphy did not agree that he was redundant. He thought that he had been unfairly dismissed, and made a claim against his employers for this. He appeared at first sight to have a good case. Could a redundancy situation exist when the need of the College for a given amount of work remained unchanged, and the number of employees required to do it to remained the same, i.e. two?

The Employment Appeal Tribunal decided that there was a redundancy situation in Mr Murphy's case under s.81(2)(*b*) of the EPCA. This states:

> For the purposes of this Act an employee who is dismissed shall be taken to be dismissed by reason of redundancy if the dismissal is attributable wholly or mainly to; (b) the fact that the requirements of that business for employees to carry out work of a particular kind, or for employees to carry out work of a particular kind in the place where he was so employed, have ceased or diminished or are expected to cease or diminish.'

The particular kind of work required by the College from the plumbers had changed. Such a change was within the redundancy law. The ETA in its judgment says: 'It is nowadays a common occurrence that employers need to reorganize so as to reallocate functions between employees. If, for example, some new technology requires the introduction into the workforce of an employee with a new skill, it may be a prudent and necessary management decision to include in the job of the new employee all or some of the functions previously performed by existing employees. In consequence, although there is no reduction in the overall work requirements of the business, or in the overall number of the employees of the business doing such work, the employer no longer requires the services of the employee who formerly carried out the functions which have been added to those of the new employee. In our judgment the employee so dismissed may in come circumstances be dismissed by reason of redundancy following from that reorganizaton'.

Redundancy—two redundancies following abolition of one post.

(456) *Robinson* v *British Island Airways* [1977] I.R.L.R. 477

BIA carried out a genuine reorganization of their workforce and as part of this eliminated the post of Flight Operations Manager held by Captain Robinson. His duties and those of another employee, the General Manager Operations and Traffic, were absorbed into a new post entitled Operations Manager. BIA alleged that Captain Robinson and the General Manager Operations and Traffic did not have the qualities suitable for the new post and both were made redundant. Captain Robinson then claimed that he had been unfairly dismissed on the ground that if only one post was abolished there could not be two redundancies arising from that abolition.

The Employment Appeal Tribunal found that Captain Robinson was in fact redundant. His dismissal was attributable to the fact that the requirements of BIA's business for employees to carry out work of a particular kind had ceased or diminished and Captain Robinson and his fellow-employee were redundant.

Appendix B
Graded questions and tutorial problems

Law of contract

TEST 1 OFFER AND ACCEPTANCE

Question 1

Eric wants to sell his house and advertises it in a local newspaper at £50,000, giving his telephone number. Fred sees the advertisement and being interested in buying a house at about that price rings Eric and makes an appointment to see the house. Fred likes the property but cannot agree a price with Eric, his highest offer being £49,000, while Eric insists on £50,000.

On the following Monday Fred receives a letter from Eric offering him the house for £49,500 and saying that Fred can have until noon on Friday to think about it.

On Wednesday evening Fred meets his brother Tom in the local. Tom tells him that Eric's son-in-law has bought the house earlier that day for £49,800. Fred gulps down his pint, goes straight home and writes a letter to Eric accepting his offer to sell the house at £49,500. He posts the letter immediately at the main post office in the town. Eric receives Fred's letter on Thursday morning but replies by return 'You are too late. I have sold the house to my son-in-law'.

Fred thinks that Eric is in breach of contract and proposes to sue him for damages.

Advise Fred.

Question 2

The Barchester Corporation wished to make arrangements for the supply of black gloss paint to its Building Department for the year commencing 1 January 1985. In November 1984 the Chief Executive placed an advertisement in the Barchester Argus inviting would-be suppliers to complete and return a form of tender issued by the Corporation. The advertisement went on to state that the Corporation did not bind itself to accept the lowest or any tender.

A local builders' merchant, Artemus Bodge, completed and returned one of the Corporation's forms in which he agreed to supply black gloss paint to the Building Department at £6 per five litres 'in such quantities as the Corporation may order from time to time'. In December 1984 Bodge was notified that his tender had been accepted.

In the first six months of 1985 Bodge did not receive any orders from the Corporation but learned that the Building Department was obtaining supplies of black gloss paint from a merchant in the nearby town of Westchester. In July 1985 the Corporation placed an order with Bodge for 100 litres of black gloss paint. Bodge, incensed by the fact that the Corporation had not placed orders with him in the first half of the year, refused to supply the paint. He was told in a letter from the Chief Executive that he would be sued for damages if he did not. Bodge replied saying 'I have no intention of meeting your orders either now or in the future. You cannot sue me for damages—that's just an empty threat'.

Advise Bodge.

Question 3

Smart, a young salesman employed by Speedytype Ltd, a company manufacturing electric typewriters, visits Wiley, a partner in Wiley and Fox, solicitors, with a view to selling a new electric typewriter to the firm.

In the course of conversation Smart, being desperate to make his first sale for several days, offers the machine at £50 less than the normal selling price. Wiley says that he will consult Miss Dragon, the head of the typing pool, and let Smart have an answer by letter in a few days.

On returning to the area sales office Smart realizes that although he has authority to give special prices he might have been unduly generous in his offer to Wiley. Accordingly he consults Allick, the area sales manager, who is not prepared to sell the typewriter at the price at which Smart has offered it. Smart rings Wiley immediately but is unable to speak to him or any of the other partners in the firm—even Miss Dragon is not available. Smart therefore writes a letter to Wiley revoking the offer and posts it immediately by first class mail.

When Wiley arrives at his office on the following day he notices that among the incoming mail is a franked envelope bearing the slogan 'Speedytype Ltd for Electric Typewriters'. It occurs to him that the envelope might contain a retraction of the offer made by Smart and decides not to open it immediately. Instead he dictates a letter to his secretary accepting the offer and tells her to post it before lunch. After lunch Wiley, having ascertained that his secretary has posted his letter, opens the letters from Smart and discovers that it is indeed a revocation of the offer made the previous day. Nevertheless Wiley rings Allick, the area sales manager of Speedytype Ltd, and asks for delivery of the typewriter. Allick replies 'We cannot possibly sell at that price. Surely you received our letter this morning?' 'Yes' says Wiley, 'it came first delivery but I had already posted my acceptance before I had chance to open all my mail'.

Wiley intends to sue Speedytype for breach of contract. Will he succeed?

Question 4

On 1 November Adder, an accountant, receives through the post a large volume entitled 'Tax Made Easy'. Accompanying the volume is a note from the publishers, Messrs Galley & Co., stating that the volume will greatly assist Adder in his work and that if he does not reply within seven days Messrs Gallery & Co. will assume that he wishes to purchase the volume and they will expect to receive a remittance of £12.

Adder does not wish to purchase the book but forgets to reply to Gallery & Co. At the end of the month he receives an invoice for £12 from the publishers.

Is Adder obliged to pay for the book?

TEST 2 CONSIDERATION

Question 1

In December 1984 Mr Smith, who owned a number of unfurnished houses, decided to give his son John a start in his married life by granting him a lease of one of the houses which had recently been vacated by a previous tenant. Under the agreement John received a lease for two years at a rent of £1 per annum and he and his wife took possession.

Mr Smith died in March 1985 leaving all his houses to his wife Vera and appointing two of the partners in a firm of accountants as his executors. Unfortunately Vera had never approved of her son's marriage and she and John were not on speaking terms. Vera now refuses to honour the agreement made by her husband with John and threatens to bring a court action in order to have John and his wife evicted from the house. She claims that the agreement to pay the rent of only £1 annually was manifestly inadequate and no real consideration at all.

Advise John.

(*Note*: Matters relating to security of tenure under legislation concerning landlord and tenant can be ignored.)

Question 2

On 1 October 1984, Mr Golightly, the office manager of Twitchett Ltd, was authorized to purchase a calculating machine for the accounts department. On 5 October 1984, he saw Sharp, a sales representative of Addom Ltd, who manufacturered what Mr Golightly regarded as a suitable machine. After some discussion Mr Golightly selected an Addom Mark 1 and delivery was arranged for 1 November 1984.

On 12 October 1984, Sharp rang Mr Golightly and said 'We have just received an export order for 100 Addom Mark II machines. This is an important order for us and I wondered whether you would be prepared to accept a delivery of your machine on 1 December 1984. I am asking a number of people who have placed small orders to help our production side out in this way'. Mr Golightly agreed to delivery on 1 December 1984.

On 12 November 1984, Mr Golightly attended a sale of office machinery and bought a second-hand Addom Mark I for his company. On the same day he rang Sharp saying 'I have bought a good second-hand machine and shall not require the new one. I am very sorry about this but it is your fault in a way because you could not delivery on time'. Sharp replied: 'But you agreed to take delivery later. I am afraid that we altered our production arrangements on the strength of promises from customers like yourself and we shall sue you for damages if you do not accept the machine'. Mr Golightly replied: 'But you gave us nothing for the promise so we are not bound to accept'.

The machine was delivered on 1 December 1984, but was returned by Mr Golightly.

What is the legal position?

Question 3

Lucre, the managing director of a manufacturing company, arranges for a party of overseas buyers to spend the weekend at his country estate in the hope of obtaining export orders for the company. As part of the entertainment Lucre makes an agreement with Rodger under which Rodger is to give the guests a two-hour trip in his private plane on the Saturday afternoon. A fee of £1000 is agreed by Rodger and the arrangement regarding the air trip is mentioned by Lucre in all the letters of invitation.

On the preceding Thursday Rodger tells Lucre that the fee which has been agreed is not enough and that he will not turn up on the Saturday. Lucre discusses the matter with his sales manager, Sellars, and both agree that it is too late to make other arrangements and that Rodger must somehow be persuaded to carry out the contract.

Later that day Sellars rings Rodger saying 'I will give you £200 of my own money if you agree to show up on Saturday'. Rodger agrees to do so and Sellars leaves immediately for a weekend business trip to the Continent without discussing the matter with Lucre.

On Friday morning Lucre rings Rodger saying 'I think I can afford to pay you a little more. Would an extra £100 be all right?' Rodger replies 'Yes that's enough. See you Saturday'. Rodger turns up on Saturday and carries out a two-hour flight as agreed.

Lucre returns to the office on Monday and in the course of conversation with Sellars learns of the extra payment which Sellars has promised to Rodger. Lucre and Sellars are furious at being treated in this way and Lucre sends Rodger a cheque for £1000 with a note saying 'Sellars and I are disgusted by your behaviour in this matter. The enclosed cheque is in final settlement. You will get no more from either of us'.

Two weeks later Lucre and Sellars each receive a letter from Rodger stating that unless he receives £200 from them both he will sue for the money. What is the legal position?

Question 4

John Smith died in 1978 leaving all his property to his wife, Mary, for life and after her death to their children, Matthew, Margaret and Luke in equal shares. The property included a dwelling house at 4 Acacia Avenue where John Smith and his wife had lived for some years.

Some months after John Smith's death Matthew and his wife, Ruth, decide that in view of Mary Smith's indifferent health they would live at 4 Acacia Avenue from Monday to Friday of each week, returning to their own home for the weekend, Matthew's sister Margaret looking after her mother on Saturdays, and Luke spending every Sunday at Acacia Avenue.

In 1980 Ruth decided that she could not continue to live during the week with her mother-in-law at Acacia Avenue unless the house was modernized, and accordingly she spent £1000 of her own money during 1981 in carrying out modifications to the property which enhanced its value. Matthew, Margaret and Luke, realizing that a third share in the house would come to each of them on Mary Smith's death, signed a document addressed to Ruth stating 'In consideration of your carrying out certain alterations and improvements to 4 Acacia Avenue, Barchester, we, the beneficiaries under the will of John Smith, hereby agree that the executors, the National Bank Ltd, shall repay to you from the said estate when distributed the sum of £1000 in settlement of the amount spent on such improvements.'

Mary Smith died on October 1984 and Margaret and Luke now refuse to authorize payment to Ruth. Matthew writes to the National Bank informing them of the agreement to pay the money and asks that Ruth be paid from the proceeds of the sale of 4 Acacia Avenue. An official of the Bank replies stating 'I am afraid your wife has no claim on the estate. The agreement to which you refer was not supported by any valid consideration and is unenforceable.'

What is the legal position?

TEST 3 FORMALITIES

Question 1

Jasper owns a number of terraced houses which are rented to various tenants. One of the tenants recently bought a house of his own and gave up his tenancy. Jasper decides to sell the property with vacant possession on completion. He advertises in the local newspaper and as a result Simon comes to see the house and agrees to buy it for £40,000 promising to send a deposit by post the next day. Two days later Jasper receives a cheque for £4000 from Simon along with the following letter:

4 Heath Road
Barfield

15 December 1984

Dear Sir
I am enclosing a cheque for £4000 as a deposit on number 4 Wilson Terrace, Barfield, which I purchased yesterday for £40,000. I will be seeing my solicitor tomorrow regarding the legal formalities.
yours faithfully

Simon

Jasper pays the cheque into the bank and it is duly cleared and the sum of £4000 is credited to his account.

On 17 December 1984 Simon agrees to buy a semi-detached house in Thorpe Gardens and rings Jasper saying 'I have seen a better property and have agreed to buy it. Sorry to have put you to this trouble. No doubt you will return my deposit'.

Jasper refuses to return the deposit and is intending to bring an action against Simon for specific performance of the contract. Simon intends to counter-claim for the return of the deposit.

What is the legal position?

Question 2

Compost Ltd, who are manufacturers of various kinds of health foods, are anxious to expand the export side of the business. Some years ago the company initiated a similar sales drive abroad but unfortunately incurred a number of bad debts which were not recovered because of the difficulties experienced by the company in bringing actions in foreign courts.

Vend, the sales manager of Compost, decides to enter into negotiations with Schloss, who is a general agent with branches in England and Boravia. Schloss agrees for an extra commission to introduce Compost's products in Boravia on terms that he will reimburse Compost if any of the customers he introduces fails to pay for goods received. This agreement is made on the telephone and Schloss agrees to send written confirmation as soon as possible. Shortly afterwards Braunbrot, who is the buyer for Gesundheit, a chain of health food shops in Boravia, rings up Vend and says 'Schloss tells me that you are prepared to supply us with some items at a very competitive price. You will be receiving our order this week.' A large order from Gesundheit arrives and the goods are despatched by Compost. Unfortunately Braunbrot does not regard the packaging as sufficiently attractive and complains to Schloss. As a result of this complaint, Schloss rings Vend and says 'Braunbrot does not think much of your packaging and for that matter neither do I. You will get no more orders from him and what is more I will no longer act as your agent here. There is no point now in writing to you regarding our agreement.'

Three months later, Vend learns that Gesundheit have become insolvent and cannot pay for the goods which they received. Vend rings Schloss immediately and asks him to pay Gesundheit's debt as agreed. Schloss refuses to make any payment and Compost are intending to sue him and claim against his assets in England.

What is the legal position?

Question 3

Some two years after his wife's death Arthur, a widower aged 72, orally agreed with Mabel a widow of 67 that if she would move into his house and look after him for the rest of his life, she should have the house and the contents on his death. It was also agreed that Mabel should pay her own board and buy her own coal.

Mabel gave up her Council flat, moved into Arthur's house and looked after him as agreed, paying for her board and coal. Arthur died in November 1984 without leaving Mabel anything in his will. Arthur's executors wish to sell the house with vacant possession but Mabel has refused to leave claiming that she is now the owner of the property.

What is the legal position?

TEST 4 CAPACITY

Question 1

Dabbler, who was training to be a commercial artist, left art school on his seventeenth birthday without having completed the course and decided to go into business as a dealer in antiques and bric-a-brac. For this purpose he entered into an agreement with Jasper to rent for one year a small shop and obtained £1000 worth of stock on credit from another dealer, Peddler, with whom he was friendly.

After trading for two months Dabbler found that because of inexperience he was unable to buy articles at a price which would give a reasonable margin of profit, and he therefore decided to give up his business and informed Jasper that he would no longer require the shop. Dabbler has not paid any rent to Jasper and still owes Peddler £1000; he also refuses to hand over the remainder of the original stock on the ground that he might start another business.

Dabbler also received £100 from Gauder for a cameo brooch which he said he could obtain. Gauder has not received a brooch nor has his money be returned.

What legal obligations, if any, has Dabbler in respect of the various contracts he has made?

Question 2

The Chartered Institute of Hod Carriers was incorporated by Royal Charter for the purpose of advancing the science of hod-carrying and promoting a uniform system of education of those who should practise the same. The Institute has announced a scheme under which it intends to set up a chain of launderettes in the hope that the profits will render an increase in subscriptions unnecessary.

Peregrine, who is a member of the Institute, is outraged by the Council's scheme which he regards as seriously affecting the image of the profession. He asks your advice in regard to ways in which he might prevent the Council from carrying out its intention.

Question 3

In 1984 the directors of Cosmetico & Co. Ltd, a small private company manufacturing toiletries, decided to begin a programme of diversification. For this purpose they took a lease of a small factory on a local trading estate at which they intended to make reproduction antique furniture. Unfortunately this venture turned out to be highly unprofitable and in 1985 the company went into liquidation.

The company's memorandum of association, which was drafted in 1905, has a short objects clause containing only two paragraphs, neither of which gives the company power to make furniture of any kind.

Among the claims outstanding against the company are the following—

(1) an account for £1000 from Lumber & Co. Ltd, who had supplied various kinds of woods for use in making the furniture after inspecting the memorandum; and

(2) an account for £500 from Mammoth Oil Co. Ltd, who had supplied oil to the furniture factory for heating purposes without having inspected the memorandum.

It appears that the wood was ordered by telephone and the oil by means of letterheading describing Cosmetico & Co. Ltd as 'Specialist Manufacturers of Reproduction Antique Furniture'.

Are the claims of Lumber & Co. Ltd and Mammoth Oil Co. Ltd valid?

Question 4

Lord Seaworthy is 95 years of age and a wealthy retired Rear Admiral. He suffers from periods of mental incapacity and his family has been advised to place his property and affairs under the management of a receiver but no steps have been taken to achieve this.

Lord Seaworthy recently visited London with his grandson but during the visit managed to slip away on his own for three hours. He was subsequently found standing under one of the fountains in Trafalgar Square re-enacting a naval battle with a number of paper boats. It now appears that he had visited the Boat Show and purchased a cabin cruiser worth £125,000 after telling the salesman it would look well on his mantelpiece. He had also bought a new suit worth £270 after telling the tailor that he wanted it for a cocktail party to celebrate Lord Nelson's recent return from the Nile.

The manufacturers of the cabin cruiser and the tailor, having delivered Lord Seaworthy's purchases, are now pressing for payment. Lady Seaworthy is resisting both claims on the ground of her husband's mental incapacity and asks the family solicitor for advice.

What advice should Lady Seaworthy receive, bearing in mind that Lord Seaworthy already has a cabin cruiser but only one reasonable suit?

TEST 5 REALITY OF CONSENT

Question 1

Fusty, an antique dealer, discovered that he was a beneficiary under the will of his deceased maiden aunt, Virginia. She left him the contents of her house including an oil painting of a dog signed 'J. Hargreaves' which he knew she had received as a gift from the Hargreaves family in the 1930s. John Hargreaves was a minor Victorian artist specializing in animal studies whose paintings began to increase in value during the 1960s. Knowing this, Fusty put the painting up for sale in his shop at £700. In September 1984 Garner saw the painting and offered £600 for it. Fusty refused stating that the painting was by John Hargreaves and had belonged to his aunt Virginia who had received it as a gift from the Hargreaves family in the 1930s. On the basis of this assurance Garner paid £700 for the painting and took delivery of it.

In February 1985 Garner held a party at his house at which Dabster, who was an expert on Victorian oil paintings employed by Christby's, was a guest. Dabster told Garner that the painting was a copy valued at £200 and executed in the 1920s, probably by the painter's son, Joseph Hargreaves, who was a good amateur artist.

Garner intends to sue Fusty and wishes to know what remedies might be available to him. Advise him.

Question 2

In October 1984 Jake, the son of a restaurant owner, Purvey, was in financial difficulties. Knowing that his father had consistently refused to help him pay his debts, Jake asked Dibbs plc, a finance company, for a loan of £1000 without security. Dibbs plc were prepared to lend Jake the money provided that Purvey gave an indemnity in respect of the loan and Jake agreed that a form of indemnity should be sent to Purvey for his signature.

Jake managed to intercept all the mail received by Purvey during the following week and extracted the form of indemnity from an envelope franked in the name of Dibbs plc. Jake placed the form on Purvey's desk along with a number of other business documents, marking the place for signature with a cross. Later that day Purvey, who was running late for a luncheon appointment, signed all the documents without bothering to read any of them. Jake then extracted the indemnity and posted it to Dibbs plc, and later Purvey's secretary posted the rest of the mail. In due course Jake received the loan from Dibbs plc and used it to take a holiday in France.

Jake and his father have now been adjudicated bankrupt and Dibbs plc approach you in your capacity as Purvey's trustee in bankruptcy asking your advice as the liability of his estate with regard to the indemnity. What advice would you give?

Question 3

Carter, the transport manager of N.O. Body Ltd, has been instructed by the board to sell one of the company's cars. He inserts an appropriate advertisement in the local paper and on the following day Crook arrives at Carter's Office with a view to buying the vehicle.

After some discussion Carter offers the car to Crook for £3000. Crook accepts the offer and starts to write a cheque. Carter refuses to accept the cheque until Crook convinces him that he is in fact Sterling, a director of Boodle Ltd, a well-known finance house with which Carter has had dealings in the past. On this understanding Carter lets Crook have the car. A few days later the bank tells Carter that the cheque is worthless.

Meanwhile Crook has sold the car to Greenhorn who bought it in good faith and without knowledge of the way in which the transaction between Carter and Crook was conducted.

Carter manages, with the help of the police, to trace the car to Greenhorn and now wishes to take the car away from him.

What is the legal position?

TEST 6 CONTRACTUAL TERMS INCLUDING EXEMPTION CLAUSES

Question 1

Booker, the accountant of Bloggs Ltd, a small manufacturing company, wished to appoint a successor to Scribe, a clerk in charge of wages and salaries who was leaving to take up another appointment. After interviewing a number of applicants Booker decided to appoint Dodger who had some 10 years' previous experience in a similar post.

Dodger agreed to accept the appointment with effect from 1 February and gave his employer two months' notice. He also undertook as part of the agreement to spend up to four Saturday mornings during his period of notice at the offices of Bloggs Ltd so that Scribe, who was leaving on 31 January, could introduce him to the company's procedures. Two dates in December and two in January were agreed between Scribe and Dodger but by the end of December Dodger had presented himself on only one occasion.

On 1 January Booker rang Dodger and asked him why he had not attended at the company's offices as agreed. Dodger replied that Saturday was inconvenient because he played for a local football team which always trained for one hour on Saturday morning prior to an afternoon match. Dodger did however agree to attend on the first date in January but said that he could not make the second, adding 'I have been doing similar work for 10 years and I already understand most of your procedures from my visit in December'. Booker replied that this arrangement was not suitable and concluded 'You need not bother to turn up on 1 February. I would not dream of taking an unreliable person such as yourself into employment here'.

Dodger's employer refused to accept the withdrawal of his resignation and he was out of work for two months.

What is the legal position?

(*Note*: Statute law relating to unfair dismissal is not relevant here and should be ignored.)

Question 2

Steward, the manager of Westchester Motels Ltd, wished to have all the spare uniforms of his staff dry-cleaned and placed the contracts with two firms of dry cleaners, Beautician Ltd and Cleanwell Ltd.

On the following Monday Beauticlean Ltd's vandriver collected some uniforms from Steward's office at 9.00 a.m. and before taking them away asked Steward to sign a duplicate copy of an order form which contained the following clause: 'The company is not liable for damage howsoever arising'. Steward signed the form without reading it or questioning the driver as to its purpose. Cleanwell Ltd's vandriver collected the remainder of the uniforms at 11.00 a.m. and asked Steward to sign a similar order form containing the following clause: 'The company is not liable for damage howsoever caused'. Before signing Steward asked the driver to explain the effect of the order form. He was told that in addition to its function as a record of the transaction, the form also exempted Cleanwell from liability from certain kinds of damage to clothing, and in the case of this contract the motel would have to take the risk of damage to the gold braid on the uniforms. Having received this explanation Steward signed the form without reading it.

The uniforms were returned one week later by both companies and Steward discovered that of those cleaned by Beautician Ltd the gold braid on four had been badly damaged by the chemicals used and would have to be replaced. Of those cleaned by Cleanwell Ltd, five were badly stained, though the gold braid was not affected in any way.

Can the Motel make a successful claim against either or both of the dry-cleaning companies?

Question 3

In January 1985 Quick, a dealer in secondhand office equipment, took delivery of a consignment of electric typewriters and calculating machines. In view of the shortage of storage space at his own premises, Quick decided that the consignment should be stored with Stow & Co. who were warehousemen. The contract for storage which Quick signed, but did not read, consisted of a standard form supplied by Stow & Co. A duplicate copy of the form was given to Quick and the terms of the contract required him to produce the form before the goods could be released. A few days after depositing the goods Quick met Coveter, a rival dealer, and boasted of his recent purchase and the growth of the business which had caused him to take up storage space with Stow & Co.

The following day Coveter, being jealous of Quick's success, sent an assistant, Tricker, to the warehouse in order fraudulently to persuade the clerk in charge to release some of Quick's goods. Tricker, who was not in possession of the necessary document, told the clerk that he had been sent by Quick to collect four crates of equipment. Tricker was allowed to take the crates and the clerk instructed two of his workmen to help load them. Coveter then sold the goods to a dealer in the North of England.

Quick, being unaware of Coveter's involvement in the matter, is intending to sue Stow & Co. for breach of contract. Stow & Co. are refusing to accept liability on the ground that the standard form signed by Quick contains the following clause: 'The company is not liable for loss, misdelivery, or damage to any articles where the value is in excess of £10 unless at the time of deposit the true value and nature of the goods is declared by the depositor and an extra charge paid.' No such declaration had been made by Quick.

What is the legal position?

TEST 7 CONTRACTS AND PUBLIC POLICY

Question 1

Upon entering the service of Pans plc (who manufacture kitchenware) as sales manager, Egon undertook by his contract that if, for any reason, he should leave that service he would never—

—by Clause (a) solicit any of the company's customers;

—by Clause (b) divulge to anyone details of certain secret processes;

—by Clause (c) set up in competition with the company.

Egon, who is now considering leaving Pans' employment, shows you a copy of the contract and wishes to know to what extent if he does leave he will be bound by the terms set out in (a) to (c) above.

Advise Egon.

Question 2

Leach and Nostrum are doctors in general practice at Bloxborough under a partnership deed of 1970. The partnership income is derived solely from the National Health Service capitation fees of Leech and Nostrum, Leach's list being 2800 patients and Nostrum's 2400. Either of the partners has the right to expel the other for improper behaviour and either of them has the right to give six months' notice of retirement to the other expiring on 1 October in any year. Clause 21 of the partnership deed reads as follows: 'If any partner shall retire or be expelled from the partnership he shall not for a period of five years immediately following such retirement or expulsion engage in practice as a medical practitioner including consultancy either alone or jointly with any other person within a radius of 10 miles of the Town hall in Bloxborough.'

Friction has arisen between Leach and Nostrum. They had to leave their surgery premises by the end of September 1984 because their tenancy came to an end at that time. Leach found new premises in Bloxborough but Nostrum did not approve of them and gave notice of his retirement on 1 March 1985. Nostrum told Leach that he would disregard Clause 21 and set up in partnership with a rival group of doctors at Oaktown, which is two miles from Bloxborough, keeping his National Health Service patients who, although on his list, are patients of the practice of Leach and Nostrum.

What action, if any, can Leach take at law to prevent Nostrum from carrying out his intention, bearing in mind that within a 10-mile radius of Bloxborough are several areas of population which have grown substantially in size since 1970 and from which Leach and Nostrum's practice has never drawn any patients, and that the practice has always limited itself to general medical work?

Question 3

Victor Vendor, the sole proprietor of a television sales and rental business, sold the business, including the shop premises, goodwill and sound and merchantable stock in trade to Peter Purchaser who already owned an electrical goods shop in the same town. Vendor agreed as part of the sale of his business not, for one year after completion of the transaction, to carry on the business of television sales and rental and the sale of electrical goods with two miles of the premises he had sold. Shortly afterwards Vendor opened two shops; one next door selling electrical goods and another one mile away selling television sets.

What is the legal position?

TEST 8 DISCHARGE OF CONTRACT

Question 1

Hatcher, an interior designer specializing in offices, was employed by Tally Ltd to design the interior of a small branch accounts office at Grantchester. The terms of payment were contained in a letter from Hatcher to Tally Ltd which set out the work to be done and concluded:

> 'The foregoing, complete, for the sum of £15,000 net. Terms of payment are net cash as the work proceeds; and balance on completion.'

Hatcher commenced work in December 1983 and received £5000 from Tally Ltd in February 1984 and a similar sum in April 1984. The work was completed on 30 June 1984 and Tally Ltd moved staff and equipment into the new office on 1 July 1984 and full use was made of all the facilities provided by Hatcher. On 10 July 1984 Hatcher asked for payment of the balance of £5000 but Tally Ltd replied complaining of bad workmanship, but sent a further £500 saying that no more would be paid until the work had been completed to their satisfaction. In fact two doors were badly warped and will have to be replaced and a row of bookshelves which are shorter than specified will have to be remade. These defects can be put right for about £500 but Hatcher cannot do the work since he has now gone to America to carry out another contract. Nevertheless he is demanding payment of £5000.

What is the legal position?

Question 2

For some years past it has been the practice of Pathfinders Ltd, travel agents, to advertise their package tours on the screens of certain cinemas in London and the Midlands during January and February. The necessary contracts have been made annually by local branch managers on receipt of a letter from head office describing the particular tour to be advertised in their areas. Having considered its advertising policy for

1984 Pathfinders Ltd decided to abandon cinema advertising in favour of an increased television campaign and during September 1983 letters were sent to branch managers outlining the new policy and instructing them not to make advertising contracts with local cinemas for 1984.

However, in July 1984 Earlybird, the manager of Pathfinder's Midchester branch, had entered into contracts on behalf on his company with the managers of certain cinemas belonging to a large chain and also with Luxor Cinemas, a small but successful chain operating only in the Midlands. The contracts were to run a series of advertisements on package holidays in France, Italy and Germany which Earlybird understood to be his company's policy for 1984, his information having been received unofficially from Clara his girlfriend who worked at head office.

As soon as he received the offical letter from head office Earlybird rang Stoney, the manager of the local Luxor cinema and told him to cancel the contract. Stoney refused saying that he had already prepared the necessary frames of film in accordance with Earlybird's specification and that these would be run as agreed in January and February 1984. Earlybird wrote to head office informing them of the situation and they wrote to Luxor Cinemas saying that they did not regard themselves as bround by the unauthorized arrangements mady by Earlybird, and would not pay for the advertising which they did not now require. Luxor Cinemas refused to accept this arrangement and ran the advertisements as agreed. They have now submitted an invoice for the agreed charge and Pathfinders Ltd are refusing to pay.

What is the legal position?

Question 3

Mine Host plc, a company which owns a number of hotels, entered into a contract with Hypocaust Ltd under which Hypocaust Ltd were to carry out improvements in the central heating system at the Grand Hotel, Westcove. The work, which was expected to last for about six months, did not involve the installation of new equipment but consisted entirely of moving existing radiators to new and more advantageous positions. The price agreed between the parties was £20,000.

Hypocaust Ltd moved workmen into the Grand Hotel on 1 October 1984 and had completed about half of the work by 23 December 1984. Over the Christmas holiday the Grand Hotel was totally destroyed by fire, the precise cause of which is still unknown, though it does not appear to have been caused by any negligence on the part of Mine Host plc, nor Hypocaust Ltd, or their employees. Although there is no provision for such an eventuality in the contract itself, Hypocaust Ltd are intending to sue Mine Host plc for damages for breach of contract in that they cannot now complete the work and in the alternative for the value of work completed up to 23 December 1984. Mine Host plc have not paid and are refusing to pay any money to Hypocaust Ltd.

What is the legal position?

TEST 9 REMEDIES FOR BREACH OF CONTRACT

Question 1

Kitchener Ltd agreed to supply and fit an electric cooking range in a new restaurant belonging to Cook and situated near a major junction on the M99. The contract provided that the range should be delivered and fitted during the period 29 to 30 May so that the restaurant could open on Saturday 3 June 1984. Cook has provided restaurant facilities from older premises on the site since 1975 serving an average 750 meals a week. These premises were to the knowledge of Kitchener Ltd to be demolished during the week ending 27 May 1984.

Unknown to Kitchener Ltd Cook had organized as part of the opening ceremony of the new restaurant a beauty contest which was to take place on the forecourt of the restaurant, and had also entered into a contract to supply meals to the canteen of a local factory from Monday 5 June 1984.

Kitchener Ltd, who had taken orders in excess of production capacity, were unable to supply and fit the range until 27 June 1984. Cook opened the restaurant on Saturday 1 July 1984 and the beauty contest which was held on that date was won by Gloria who received a prize of £500. Unfortunately Freda, who was one of the eight girls entered for the contest, did not attend, Cook having failed to notify her of the revised date. The supply of meals to the factory commenced on 3 July 1984.

Cook intends to sue Kitchener Ltd for damages for loss of profit and Freda is suing Cook for damages for his breach of contract in failing to notify her of the revised date of the contest.

What is the legal position?

Question 2

In April 1984 Replica Ltd, a small company manufacturing reproduction furniture, decided to purchase a generator of sufficient capacity to provide the power necessary to drive a variety of electrical tools used in the business. The decision was reached in view of production difficulties experienced in previous years as a result of power failures arising from industrial disputes.

The type of equipment required by Replica Ltd was rather specialized, the power needed being somewhat above that supplied by a domestic generator but considerably less than that provided by equipment available to larger concerns.

After consultation with representatives of Electripower Ltd, who were wholesalers dealing in a variety of electrical equipment, it was decided that the right level of power could be supplied by a particular type of

Japanese generator provided that there was some conversion which Electripower Ltd agreed to carry out.

Electripower Ltd purchased the generator and made certain modifications to it. In June 1984 they notified Replica Ltd that it was ready for delivery at the agreed price of £3000. By this time the two directors of Replica Ltd had seen the company's accounts for the period 1983/84 and it appeared that the power cuts had not had the serious effect upon profits which they had thought. In the light of this information, and faced with a bill of £3000 for the generator, the directors refused to accept delivery of it.

Electripower Ltd tried to resell the generator knowing that the market was limited and chancy. In addition Electripower Ltd were short of liquid capital and realized that they would soon have to pay the Japanese manufacturers. Accordingly after several efforts they sold the generator to a domestic user who had regarded it as too large and expensive for his purposes but was eventually prepared to pay £2400 for it.

Electripower Ltd are now bringing an action against Replica Ltd for damages of £600. Replica Ltd denies liability for that amount of loss claiming that if Electripower Ltd had not been so impecunious they could have waited a little longer before selling in order to get a better price.

What is the legal position?

Question 3

Layouts Ltd agreed to design and install new equipment at a factory belonging to Bloggo Ltd within 20 weeks from the receipt of the final approval of drawings. A clause in the contract provided that if this period was exceeded Layouts Ltd would pay to Bloggo Ltd the sum of £200 per week for every week in excess of the twenty weeks.

In the event Layouts Ltd, who had made a number of similar contracts with other companies, found that they were unable to carry out the work in time and the installation of the equipment designed for Bloggo Ltd was eventually completed 30 weeks after final approval of drawings.

The 10-week delay has in fact resulted in a loss of profit to Bloggo Ltd of £4000 and Bloggo Ltd are now claiming this sum by way of damages. Layouts Ltd are standing by the contractual arrangement under which they see their liability as limited to £2000.

What is the legal position?

Question 4

In 1981 a group of four musicians who called themselves The Bards appointed Trendy to manage their professional careers for a period of five years. The contract was made primarily because the members of the group had no business experience and were told by their solicitor that they were unlikely to succeed in the entertainment business without the services of an experienced manager.

In the contract, which was to operate world-wide, Trendy agreed to use all his resources of knowledge and experience to advance The Bards' careers and the contract also provided that The Bards would not engage any other person to act as manager or agent for them and that they would not act themselves in such a capacity. Trendy was to receive 20 per cent of all money earned by The Bards during the period of the contract.

By 1982 The Bards had become a well established group earning as much as £2000 a night, but in May 1984 they repudiated the management contract with Trendy and began to arrange their bookings and conduct their business affairs through the agency of Boodle, a retired bank manager who was the uncle of one of them. Since May 1984 The Bards have refused to pay any money to Trendy in spite of the fact that prior to May 1984 he had supported them in the fullest possible way and had to a large extent been responsible for the success which the group had achieved. Trendy is intending to bring an action against The Bards in order to prevent them from engaging any corporation, firm, or person other than Trendy as their manager.

What is the legal position?

TUTORIAL PROBLEMS

1. Going, Going, Gone & Co., who were well-known auctioneers in East Anglia, were asked by the liquidator of Carter Ltd, a company which until liquidation had operated haulage and van rental business, to sell a number of vehicles by auction.

Going, Going, Gone & Co. advertised the sale, which was to take place at Norwich, in a number of trade journals and invited those interested to apply for a catalogue. Renter and Charter who conducted van rental businesses in Cornwall and London, respectively, applied for a catalogue and on reading it decided to attend the sale which was stated to be without reserve. Renter was interested solely in two Ford Transit vans which were listed as Lots 10 and 11. Charter was interested in a number of the vehicles listed, provided he could obtain them at what he regarded as a reasonable price.

Renter travelled by train to Norwich on the day before the sale and stayed overnight at a four-star hotel. Charter travelled by car on the day of the sale, arriving some 20 minutes before it commenced.

Charter joined in the bidding for Lot 6 which was a 1981 Transit Van and his rivals dropped out when Charter made his final bid for £1500. The auctioneer, feeling that the van should fetch more, refused to accept Charter's bid and withdrew the van from the sale.

When Lot 9 had been sold the auctioneer announced that Lots 10 and 11 had been withdrawn and would not be put up for sale so that Renter had no chance to bid.

Both Renter and Charter are intending to sue the auctioneer.

What is the legal position?

2. Swinger, a promoter of jazz concerts, made an agreement in January under which Bopper and his band were to visit England from America in order to play concents in London, Birmingham and Manchester, on 4, 6 and 8 June, respectively. Carol, a famous American jazz singer, was also booked to appear in the concerts.

Swinger booked concert halls in each of these cities and also made a contract with Setter Ltd under which they were to print the publicity material, including posters and programmes.

Both the band and Carol were due to arrive in England on 1 June in order to play the first concert in London on 4 June as agreed. However, on 1 April, Bopper sent a cable to Swinger saying that he would not be bringing his band to England since he had obtained a more highly paid concert tour in the States for the whole month of June. Carol was apparently to accompany the band on the American tour and on 2 April she, too, cabled Swinger saying that she would not make the English tour.

Swinger rang Setter Ltd immediately to cancel the order for the publicity material and programmes. However, the company's manager refused to accept the cancellation stating that although he had not issued instructions for the printing, he had given up other orders so as to cope with Swinger's requirements, and in these circumstances intended to carry out Swinger's order and send him a bill for the agreed price. Swinger told the manager that he could not accept this arrangement and that printing should not commence.

Swinger then cabled Bopper and Carol as follows—

> 'Arrangements for tour so advanced that cannot cancel without serious loss. Will wait until 15 May before taking further action in the matter.'

Bopper and Carol replied stating yet again that they had no intention of cancelling the American tour.

On 1 May Carol was imprisoned in America on what turned out to be a false accusation of drug-taking. She was released on 10 June and joined Bopper and the band on the American tour. On 2 May, Setter Ltd delivered all the publicity and other material as agreed and followed this with a bill for their charges.

Swinger is refusing to pay Setter Ltd and is also intending to sue Bopper and Carol for breach of contract.

Examine the legal position.

3. Rover was a baker's roundsman and had been employed for one year by Crusty Ltd, who were bakers and confectioners. Crusty Ltd was taken over by Tucker plc, who were bakers but had recently diversified, primarily by purchasing restaurants in various parts of the country, and Rover was asked to enter into a new contract of employment. The contract consisted of a printed form of agreement, certain clauses of which dealt with wages, holidays, hours of work, and pension. Clause 8 provided as follows—

> 'The employee expressly agrees not at any time during the period of one year after the termination of his employment under this agreement, either on his own account or as representative or agent of any person or company to serve or sell bread or bakery produce to any person or company who at any time during the last six months of employment shall have been a customer of the employer and served by the employee in the course of his employment.'

Clause 9 was couched in similar general terms but was restricted to engagement in the business of restaurant keeper and omitted reference to the bakery business. Rover signed the contract and worked for Tucker plc as a baker's roundsman for a further five years. He then left the service of the company and almost immediately began to serve the same bread round in the capacity as baker's roundsman employed by Bestbread plc, which was a rival concern.

Tucker plc is bringing an action against Rover for an injunction and damages for Rover's breach of his former contract of employment.

What is the legal position?

4. Fuller is the owner of a launderette in Midchester. Although the business is successful, Fuller has had numerous requests from his customers to install a dry-cleaning machine and accordingly approached Beauticlean plc, who manufacture a suitable machine, with regard to the possibility of their installing one in his launderette.

Fuller enters into a contract with Beauticlean plc under which they are to install a machine by 3 July. Fuller then embarks upon a local advertising campaign which states that dry-cleaning facilities will be available at the Midchester launderette from Monday 10 July.

Two days after the publication of the advertisement Fuller receives a telephone call from Chapman, the manager of a large local supermarket, commenting on the usefulness of the dry-cleaning facility and asking whether he can book the machine every Friday morning in order to dry-clean staff uniforms and other protective clothing. Fuller agrees to this arrangement, which is to commence on 14 July.

After speaking to Chapman, Fuller rings up the managers of three other supermarkets in Midchester asking whether they would be interestested in booking the dry-cleaning machine on a regular basis and inviting them to see it in operation on 14 July before making up their minds.

In the event, Beauticlean Ltd, who have taken orders in excess of production capacity, are unable to deliver and install the machine until 7 August and in consequence Fuller's regular customers are unable to dry-clean their clothes until then. Fuller has managed to persuade Chapman to carry on with his regular Friday morning order, though this did not start until 11 August.

The other supermarket managers have now lost interest and Fuller cannot persuade them even to look at the machine in operation. Fuller intends to sue Beauticlean plc for damages for breach of contract and will claim for loss of profit on ordinary customers and on the supermarket contract made by Chapman. Fuller is also claiming damages for possible loss of contracts with the other three supermarkets.

How far will he succeed with the various parts of his claim?

Agency

Question 1

Alan went on holiday to the South of France without leaving an address at which he could be contacted. Two days after Alan had left, his neighbour Bill noticed that there was a slate missing from the roof of Alan's house. At lunch-time on the same day Bill heard a weather forecast which predicted heavy rain and thunderstorms for the next two days. Bill rang up Cyril, a jobbing builder, and asked him to come at once and replace the slate. Cyril completed the job just before the start of a violent thunderstorm.

Alan returned home last week and is refusing to pay Cyril for his work on the grounds that he had already arranged for his brother, David, to replace the slate without charge when he had time.

What is the legal position?

Question 2

Arthur, a well-known philanthropist who is concerned regarding the rise in house prices, put one of his properties on the market at £24,000, though its true market value was in the region of £26,000. He engaged Bob, an estate agent, to deal with the sale. Bob made an arrangement with his brother-in-law, Charles, under which the house was to be purchased in Charles' name and later conveyed to Bob. After signing the contract of sale Arthur learned of the arrangement between Bob and Charles and now refuses to complete.

What is the legal position?

Question 3

Albert, a coal merchant, supplied coal during the whole of 1984 to Bloggs Ltd. Under an arrangement with Cecil, who was Bloggs Ltd's purchasing officer, Albert was required, in order to obtain the contract, to put an extra 10p a ton on the tender and pay this additional sum to Cecil. The managing director of Bloggs Ltd has recently learned of the arrangement between Albert and Cecil under which Cecil received £250 during 1984. Cecil has repaid £250 and Bloggs Ltd is now suing Albert to recover what is regarded as a secret commission. The action is for £250.

Will the company succeed?

Question 4

Toby, who lives in Lancashire, asked Bertrand, a London property agent, to find him suitable premises in London in which to set up a restaurant. Two weeks later, when Toby was in London, he called at Bertrand's office and asked whether suitable premises had been found. Bertrand said that certain premises which were now empty in Kensington might suit Toby but he wished to make certain enquiries before giving Toby the exact address.

Christopher, a client of Bertrand's who was also seeking premises for a restaurant, was in Bertrand's waiting room and overheard the conversation with Toby. Christopher went straight to Kensington and within two hours found some empty premises which he thought might be suitable. He read the agent's notice on a board outside, went to his office and later entered into a lease at £20,000 per annum.

It appears that the premises concerned were those which Bertrand had in mind for Toby.

Can Bertrand recover commission from Christopher?

Question 5

Glass, a wealthy drunkard, wished to attend a dinner-dance provided monthly by the management of the Barchester Towers Hotel, Barchester. Knowing, however, that the manager, Damper, had given instructions to his staff that Glass should not be admitted because of his disorderly conduct in the past, Glass asked his friend, Wiley, to order a ticket in his own name for Glass's use.

Wiley received a ticket and passed it to Glass. When Glass arrived for the dinner-dance, Damper, who was at the entrance, refused to admit him. Glass now intends to sue Damper for maliciously procuring the hotel company to break its contract with him.

What is the legal position?

Question 6

Sweeting was employed by Loot plc, a multi-million enterprise, for 10 years as an agent to purchase sugar. During that time Sweeting had made purchases on Loot plc's behalf from Cane. On Monday, Loot plc informed Sweeting that they no longer wished him to act as their agent.

On Wednesday, Sweeting, in order to maintain his prestige in the sugar market, purchased sugar from Cane on behalf of Loot plc. Cane did not know that Sweeting was no longer Loot plc's agent. Loot plc are now refusing to take delivery of the sugar and Cane is intending to sue them for damages.

Will he succeed?

Question 7

On Saturday, Alexander, an estate agent, sold William's house to John for £30,000 'subject to contract', under an agreement between himself and William providing for commission at 2 per cent. The following Tuesday, Alexander received an offer of £31,000 for William's house from Donald. Alexander said the house was sold and the sale to John has now be completed. William is now suing Alexander for damages and has refused to pay commission.

What is the legal position?

TUTORIAL PROBLEMS

1. An estate agent, A, convinced one of his clients to accept an offer by a company to purchase his farm property. When the contract had been signed, but before all the paperwork had been completed and the transaction concluded, it appeared that the company would be unable to raise the sum of money necessary to complete the transaction. A therefore entered into an agreement with the company, by which he invested money in it which was later used to complete the transaction involving the purchase of the farm. Three years later, the company resold the farm property at eight times the amount they had originally paid for it. The client who first sold the farm brought an action against A claiming that he had no right both to obtain a commission and to be one of the buyers of the property. The client also claimed that any profits made on the resale of the property should be turned over to him on the grounds that an agent cannot make a profit from a transaction involving one of his clients.

What is the legal position?

2. John approaches a local estate agent, Peter, and asks him to find a buyer for his house. Peter introduces Gullible who is willing and able to buy the house and signs a contract. John then decides that he will sell the house to a friend of his and this sale goes to completion. No agent is involved in the introduction of John's friend.

Consider the principles which will decide whether Peter is entitled to any commission.

Sale of Goods

Question 1

Seed, who owned a chain of gardening shops in England, ordered 600 tonnes of garden peat from O'Turf, who lived in Co. Kerry, Eire. O'Turf agreed to ship the peat during the month of March. On 15 February, Seed received a letter from O'Turf saying that the peat would be shipped on 16 February. The next day, Seed received a business circular from Cunnane, who lived in Co. Mayo, offering to sell garden peat at a much lower price. Seed placed an order for 600 tonnes of peat with Cunnane and refused to take delivery of the peat supplied by O'Turf when it arrived at Liverpool on 17 February.

What is the legal position?

Question 2

Rich bought a second-hand Daimler for £5000 from Sharp, who was a dealer in motor vehicles. Two months later, after Rich had driven the car for some 3000 miles, the police took possession of it. It appears that the car was stolen from Boodle's home by a person unknown, and that it was the thief who sold it to Sharp.

What is the legal position?

Question 3

Feather agreed to sell to Fur, the proprietor of a number of pet shops, 4000 packets of bird seed to be sent to Fur's warehouse in boxes containing 40 packets each. Two days later, Fur received a better offer from Grain, but decided to honour his contract with Feather. Fur arranged for the redistribution of 10 boxes to each of his 10 branches. Feather delivered 4000 packets of first-class quality seed, but one half of the boxes contained only 30 packets. This upset Fur's redistribution arrangements; he flew into a rage and refused to take delivery, placing an order with Grain instead.

Advise Feather.

Question 4

Trendy asked Valve, a dealer in television, radio and stereo, to recommend suitable equipment for use in a new discotheque which Trendy was about to set up. After seeing the premises to be used by Trendy, Valve consulted a number of manufacturers' brochures and recommended equipment made by Discequipment Ltd, although he had never sold any of their products before. Valve purchased the equipment and delivered it to Trendy's premises. Trendy now discovers that the amplification is inadequate in terms of the volume expected by his customers, though the reproduction is perfect.

Trendy has been advised that he cannot make a successful claim against Valve under Sale of Goods legislation because Valve is not a dealer in Discequipment's products, never having sold them before.

Explain the legal position to Trendy.

Question 5

Fast wished to buy a secondhand sports car from Connor, a dealer. Connor told Fast that the clutch was defective and offered either to put it right and sell it for £1975, or leave Fast to put it right and sell for £1950. Fast said that he would see to the clutch and bought the car for £1950. Fast then found that the defect was more serious than he had anticipated, and the repair cost him £80. Fast wishes to claim £55 from Connor.

Advise Fast.

Question 6

On 1 July Digger, who owned several gardening shops, asked Sward to supply him with a quantity of best quality Cumberland grass seed. The order form which Digger signed, contained to his knowledge a clause excluding all conditions and warranties express or implied. When the seed arrived, Digger's employees packed it into bags labelled 'Best quality Cumberland grass seed' and the bags were dispatched to and displayed in Digger's shops. On the front of each bag was a notice saying: 'The sellers give no condition or warranty express or implied as to the growth description or any other matters or the fitness for the purpose of any seed sold by them or its freedom from injurious quality or from latent defect.'

Proud, a householder, bought several bags in order to grow a lawn at his new home and was aware of the notice appearing on the front of the bag.

The seed has now grown, and is obviously of very poor quality, so that Proud will have to resow the lawn.

What is the legal position?

Question 7

Glitter, a jeweller, entrusted some items of jewellery to Roamer, who was a traveller in the jewellery trade. The arrangement between Glitter and Roamer provided that Roamer had the goods 'on sale or return' and that they were to remain the property of Glitter until paid for. Roamer pledged the jewellery with Pawn, a moneylender, as security for a loan and has absconded. Glitter intends to bring an action against Pawn to recover the jewellery.

Advise Glitter.

Question 8

Alice owned a Georgian silver teapot of unusual design. Bert stole the teapot from Alice's flat and took it to the home of Cecil, a dealer, who gave him £500 for it. Cecil had a stall in an open-air market set up by statute in London which opened for business at 7.00 a.m. Cecil took the teapot to his stall, arriving at 7.05 a.m., while it was still dark. Donald saw Cecil setting up his stall, using the headlights of his van, and bought the teapot for £1000. Donald sold it to Edgar, a West End antique dealer for £1200, and Edgar displayed it in his window. Alice saw it in Edgar's window and is asking that it be returned to her.

What is the legal position?

Question 9

Alf, a car dealer, sold a secondhand car to Bob for £1600, which was the agreed market price. Bob left a part-payment of £20, promising to return later in the day and pick it up. Before taking the car away, Bob had another look at it and said he thought it was older than Alf alleged, and refused to accept it. Alf wrote to Bob, giving him one week to pay for the car and take delivery, otherwise he would sell it. Bob did not pay, and Alf sold the vehicle to Charlie for £1550 after advertising it again at a cost of £20. Bob has told Alf he can keep the £20 part-payment. Alf is not satisfied.

Tell Alf how much he would receive if he sued Bob for damages, and give him your reasons.

TUTORIAL PROBLEMS

1. John, who deals in carpet, wrote to Swordminster & Co., who were wholesalers, saying that he was interested in a certain type of shag pile carpet. The manager of Swordminster told John that they could supply that type of carpet in various widths and any length.

John ordered 1000 square metres of the carpet in various specified widths. When the carpet was delivered John opened the end of each package to see whether the carpet was of the shag pile type which he had ordered. Having done this he signed the form of acceptance of the goods which read: 'The purchaser has examined the goods which are in accordance with the contract'.

When John opened the packages he found that they consisted entirely of offcuts of various sizes which could be resold but only after considerable wastage.

Advise John.

2. Joe sells John 1000 gallons of spirit out of a larger quantity in a tank on Joe's wharf. A delivery note is issued to John but no appropriation to the contract is made. The delivery note is not acted upon for some months and during that time the spirit deteriorates.

Does the loss fall on Joe or John?

The supply of goods and services

Question 1

Mrs Smith wanted a new fitted kitchen. She eventually agreed with a company called Boxo Ltd to carry out the work. The materials and labour were supplied by Boxo Ltd but Mrs Smith did ask them to fit a 'Whoosh' extractor fan. After being used normally for two months the motor stopped and could not be put right. Mrs Smith could not contact the company which made the fan because it had been wound up. She therefore contacted Boxo Ltd saying that it was their responsibility. Boxo's representative said: 'Oh, no it's not. You told us to get a "Whoosh". Actually, if you had left it to us we would have fitted a "Zoom"'.

Advise Mrs Smith. Would your answer have been different if Mrs Smith's complaint about the 'Whoosh' had been that it was not powerful enough to extract air sufficiently quickly?

Question 2

John Speed crashed his estate car which he used in his job as a plumber and in which he carried tools and materials. He took it to Bloggs Garage and they said they would repair it for him. In fact they took six weeks to do the job and John had to hire another vehicle to carry out his work. This broke down three times causing John loss of business. John has now been told by Snooks Garage, from which he hired the car, that the repairs on his own estate car could have been done in two weeks at the most. This seems to be the true position and Bloggs Garage are not claiming to have been held up by difficulties in getting parts. It appears that they were short of staff and had given preference to the vehicles of a bakery company for which they had the service contract.

Advise John.

Question 3

Mrs Mopp's electric pop-up toaster would not toast because she could not push the handle down fully. She took it to a small electrical shop owned by Fred Sparks for repair. Fred said: 'Leave it with me. I'll fix it. Call back in a couple of hours'. Mrs Mopp returned some two hours later and Fred said: 'Its fine now, that'll be £10.' Mrs Mopp was a bit shocked and asked what was wrong with the toaster. Fred said: 'Not much; we had to bend the handle straight and oil it, that's all.' Mrs Mopp said: 'But surely you cannot charge me £10 for that.' 'Sorry, Madam,' said Fred, 'Its our minimum charge; labour costs, you know.'

Advise Mrs Mopp. Would your advice have been different if Fred had a notice in large letters in his window saying: 'Repairs undertaken—minimum charge £10'?

Question 4

Anthony took his car to Bernard's garage for a service as laid down by the maker's manual, the cost of which was normally £70. When he collected the car he was told that the bill was £200. Bernard said: 'That slight knock you said you could hear was a major bearing. We have had to replace it. That's what has bumped the bill up.'

Advise Anthony whether he must pay £200. Would Anthony have had to pay £200 if he had said to Bernard: 'Find out what is causing that knock and put it right'?

TUTORIAL PROBLEMS

1. Arthur hired Bertram, an experienced forester to fell one of his garden trees for him. Bertram felled the tree but, because of his carelessness, it dropped on to Arthur's car which was standing in the drive. Some of the larger branches fell on to Eric's delivery van which was parked in the street adjoining Arthur's house.

Advise Arthur and Eric as to the source of their rights (if any) in respect of the damage.

2. Angela Jones was getting married. Her father and mother agreed with Posh Caterers Ltd to provide the wedding reception. The Jones family agreed the menu, drinks, and the price. They were angry to find that on the day the food was of poor quality and the drinks were cheap brands, particularly the champagne. Nevertheless, Posh are demanding the agreed price.

Advise Mr and Mrs Jones.

Hire purchase and consumer credit

Question 1

Snooks had a 1983 BL Mini on hire purchase from Motor Finance Ltd. In January, when returning from a party, he scraped the vehicle on the wall of a hump-backed bridge causing considerable damage to the near-side wing and door.

The following day when Snooks was surveying the damage outside his lodgings he was approached by Sharp, a student, who said it would 'cost a bomb' to repair the car and that he would take it off Snooks' hands for £1000. Snooks agreed to sell and Sharp asked him whether the car was on hire purchase. Snooks said it wasn't. To prove the point Snooks went to his room and produced a receipt from Vehicle Finance Ltd for £50 dated some three months earlier. Across the receipt was written 'Final Payment'. This receipt related to an earlier hire-purchase transaction in respect of another vehicle which Snooks had owned.

Later the same day Sharp gave Snooks £1000 for the car and was given a receipt in the following terms:

> 'I, Snooks, hereby confirm the said vehicle, BL Mini DDP 757Y is not covered by any HP agreement whatsoever, and I accept the sum of £1000 from Mr Sharp in absolute payment for the above-named vehicle.'

Sharp repaired the car and in February sold it to a dealer, Pedlar, who later in the month sold it to another dealer, Hawker.

On 1 March, while the vehicle was in Hawker's possession, an agent on Motor Finance Ltd saw it and on 4 March the company sent men to claim it from Hawker. They brought with them a letter from the company in the following terms:

> 'You have purported to acquire the above vehicle which is the property of this company under a rental agreement with one J. Snooks of Barchester. The bearer of this letter has instructions to collect our property forthwitch, and legal proceedings will be taken against any person attempting to prevent him from carrying out these instructions.'

Hawker let the men take the car and intends to sue Pedlar for damages. Pedlar has said that he will bring Sharp into the action and claim damages from him. Snooks has left his lodgings and cannot be found.

Examine the legal position.

Question 2

Yesterday Rev. Mupp took delivery of a vacuum cleaner under a regulated agreement. The agreement was made by a door-to-door salesman representing Electrics Ltd, a large local store. Rev. Mupp signed the agreement in the vestry. Today, having checked his finances, he is not sure that he can pay for it.

Advise Rev. Mupp as to his legal position.

Question 3

On 1 August, Brick, a builder, took delivery of a small generator worth £2000 for use in his business. On the same day Manfred took delivery of a similar generator to provide electricity for his country cottage, which had no mains supply. Both generators were bought from the manufacturer, Portapower Ltd, on hire-purchase terms. In each case the hire-purchase agreements contained a clause stating that the owners, Portapower, gave no condition or warranty express or implied as regards the quality or fitness for the purpose of the generators. Both generators broke down within one month of delivery and Brick and Manfred are intending to make a claim against Portapower.

Advise Brick and Manfred.

Question 4

Alf took delivery of a car on hire purchase terms, the total credit being £2000. Later when Alf had paid, by deposit and instalments, £1000, he lost his job and was unable to meet the instalments. He informed the finance company of this fact by telephone at 10.00 a.m. prior to leaving home for the Job Centre. When he returned home for lunch his wife told him that two men from the finance company had taken the car away.

Advise Alf.

TUTORIAL PROBLEMS

1. John is a retailer in hi-fi equipment and provides credit facilities for his customers through Fred's Finance Ltd.

Advise the parties as to their rights and liabilities in the following cases—

(1) Mark takes hi-fi equipment to the value of £800 on credit under an agreement with Fred's Finance which excludes that company's liability if the goods are not merchantable, and also for any misstatement by John as to the quality of the goods. The equipment is constantly breaking down although John assured Mark that the equipment was in first-class condition and entirely suitable to his requirements. However, certain parts of the equipment were included at Mark's request.

(2) Norman signs one of Fred's Finance Ltd's forms for goods worth £500 on John's premises and two days later tells John that he does not want to go on with the transaction. John does not inform Fred's Finance of this and seven days later the finance company writes to Norman accepting his offer.

2. Alan, Bert, and Cyril each purchase a television set on credit through Cheetham Ltd, a finance company, the total credit being £240 and the instalments being £20 per month. Alan terminates his agreement when he has paid two instalments but before the third is due. Bert terminates his agreement when he has paid seven instalments but before the eighth is due. Cyril terminates his agreement when he has paid seven instalments but after the date on which the eighth instalment became due.

All three return the sets in good condition to Cheetham Ltd on terminating the agreement.

How much is each of them liable to pay to Cheetham Ltd?

Partnerships

Question 1

Able and Baker are solicitors in partnership in Barchester. Charles is a solicitor employed by Able and Baker at a salary of £15,000 per annum. Charles does not take a share of profits or a payment contingent on or varying with profits, though his name appears with his consent, on the firm's stationery along with the names of Able and Baker.

Advise Charles as to his liability for the debts of the firm.

Question 2

Alan became 17 on 1 January 1984 and on that day entered into partnership on equal terms with Basil and Cecil who were 19 and 20, respectively. The object of the partnership was the setting up of a hairdressing business called 'Manstyles'. Alan's father gave him £500 for investment in the firm as capital and Basil and Cecil put up £500 each. During the first six months the firm prospered and all the trading debts were paid. However, a rival firm set up in business nearby and profits diminished. Towards the end of Alan's first year as a partner the firm became unable to pay its debts and on 3 January 1985, Alan left the firm and took up employment, in a neighbouring town. Basil and Cecil struggled on until 1 April 1985 before dissolving the business at a time when cash at the bank was £1500.

The following debts remain unpaid—

(1) £150 for supplies ordered and received in November/December 1984;

(2) £150 for supplies ordered and delivered in February/March 1985 by a firm which had not previously done business with 'Manstyles'.

Advise Alan as to his liability for these debts and as to the amount of capital which he may recover.

Question 3

Adam was a farmer and the tenant under a 99-year lease of land adjacent to the main farm. Adam entered into partnership with his son Jack, the deed stating that the partnership capital was to consist of the stock, machinery and other assets of the business. From then on the partnership paid the rent under the lease and Adam and Jack farmed the land which was the subject matter of the lease as well as the freehold land forming the main farm.

One year later Adam and Jack quarrelled and the partnership was dissolved. The assets of the business are now being sold. Adam is claiming all the proceeds of sale of the lease, which had 90 years to run, because he maintains that it was not transferred to the partnership and is not therefore one of the assets of the firm but belongs to him.

What is the legal position?

Question 4

Wyre and Watt were in partnership for 20 years dealing in electrical goods under the firm name of 'Sparks Electrical Supplies'. The partnership was dissolved by agreement on 1 January when Wyre retired. No announcement of the dissolution was made either in the *London Gazette* or in any other way. Watt carried on the business under the name of 'Sparks Electrical Supplies' as agreed and new letter-heading, order forms and invoices were prepared showing Watt as the sole proprietor of the business. Four months after Wyre had left the firm, a new typist ordered goods from Super Electrics (who had supplied goods to the old firm) and Modern Electrics (who had not supplied goods to 'Sparks' before and did not know or believe Wyre to be a partner) on old order forms showing the names of Wyre and Watt as proprietors. The goods were supplied but before payment was made Watt, who had always been a gambling man, went bankrupt and both Super Electrics and Modern Electrics obtained a judgment against Sparks Electrical Supplies. The firm's assets are not sufficient to pay the judgment and Super Electrics and Modern Electrics are intending to enforce the judgment against Wyre as a partner in 'Sparks'.

Advise Wyre.

Question 5

Arthur, Bernard and Cuthbert are partners who share profits and losses equally, their capitals being £6000, £4000 and £700, respectively. They have also advanced money to the firm as follows: Arthur—£1000; Bernard—£500; Cuthbert—£500. The firm has recently been dissolved. Assume that after all creditors and partners' advances have been paid, there is a fund of £8000 left and Cuthbert is insolvent.

How much will each partner receive?

Question 6

Bill and Ben were partners in a business venture which failed. On dissolution the firm had debts of £1000 and assets totalling £650. Bill has private assets of £400 and debts of £700 and is bankrupt. In addition he owes £100 to Ben, being the balance of the purchase price of a car which was purchased by Bill from Ben for private use.

Ignoring the £100 which Bill owes him, Ben has private assets of £500 and debts of £400.

Can Ben prove in Bill's bankruptcy for £100? How much will Bill's private creditors receive as a dividend in Bill's bankruptcy? How much will the firm's creditors receive as a dividend on dissolution? Give reasons for your answers.

Question 7

Hemming, Button and Cutter were in business as dress manufacturers and Cutter was the firm's buyer. Cutter managed to make a purchase of material for £3000, being £200 below the normal market price. Unknown to Hemming and Button, the material was charged to the firm at £3200 and Cutter retained £200 for himself.

Can Cutter be made to account to the firm for the £200? Would your answer have been different if Cutter had purchased the material two days after the partnership had been dissolved by the death of Button?

Question 8

Sugar and Spicer were partners in a grocery business. They employed a boy, Joe, on a casual basis to make deliveries on the firm's bicycle. While making a delivery to a local housing estate, Joe took a corner too fast, mounted a pavement and injured Ethel. The firm had no insurance policy covering the injury to Ethel and, since Spicer died two days after the accident, Ethel sued Sugar and has obtained a judgment for £1000 against him. Sugar cannot pay but Spicer's estate is solvent and his executors have sent Ethel a cheque for £1000.

If Ethel had sued Spicer's estate, would she have succeeded? Since Spicer's executors have paid Ethel, is Sugar's liability at an end? Give reasons for your answer.

TUTORIAL PROBLEMS

1. Joe Soap was a car dealer. He died in 1979 leaving his widow his sole legatee. In 1980 she assigned the business and the goodwill to Jones and Brown under an agreement by which she was paid an annuity of £4000 by the buyers. Jones and Brown carried on the business until Brown died. Jones carried on alone until 1985 when he became bankrupt. Mrs Soap is proving in the bankruptcy for the capitalized value of the annuity but the trustee in bankruptcy contends that her claim is postponed until the claims of other creditors have been met.

Advise Mrs Soap.

2. In 1981 Bill and Ben entered into a partnership for a term of 15 years selling men's clothing under the registered name of 'Trend'. In 1985 Bill, without consulting Ben, set up a ladies' boutique under the registered name of 'Fashion Girl', while retaining his partnership in 'Trend'. This action gave rise to acrimonious quarrels between Bill and Ben. Ben has now refused Bill admission to the firm's premises and will not discuss the position with him.

Ben wishes to dissolve the partnership and would like Bill to account for the profits he has derived from 'Fashion Girl'.

Advise him.

Cheques and banking law

Question 1

On 1 August Arthur lent Bruce £120 to be repaid by monthly instalments of £20 each and received a cheque from Bruce for £20 post-dated to 1 September. Arthur presented the cheque for payment on 11 September but it was returned by the bank since there was no money in Bruce's account and he had no permission to overdraw.

Bruce then persuaded his fiancée's sister Catherine to draw an open cheque for £20 in favour of Arthur dated 14 September. Bruce took the cheque to Arthur's home, but he was away on business so Bruce left it with Arthur's wife, together with a note which said: 'This one is okay.'

Arthur returned on 17 September and found Catherine's cheque and the note. In the meantime, Bruce and his fiancée had quarrelled and broken off their engagement with the result that on 18 September, before Arthur had presented Catherine's cheque for payment, Catherine telephoned Arthur and told him that she intended to stop payment of it immediately.

Arthur thereupon altered Catherine's cheque to £120, the cheque being drawn in such a way as to enable this to be done without detection. Arthur then presented the cheque for payment at Catherine's bank and received the money before Catherine managed to inform the bank that the cheque should be stopped.

Catherine's bank has debited her account with £120 and she is wondering what right, if any, the bank has to do this. She is also interested to know what right, if any, she might have to recover the money from Arthur.

What is the legal position?

Question 2

Section 27(2) of the Bills of Exchange Act 1882 provides that, where value has at any time been given for a bill, the holder of it is deemed to be a holder for value as regards the acceptor and all parties to the bill who became parties before value was given.

Explain the effect of this section.

Question 3

John, a minor, buys necessary goods from Jones and uses a cheque to pay for them. Jones endorses the cheque to a wholesaler Brown, who on presenting it for payment finds that it is dishonoured.

Advise Brown and Jones.

Question 4

X gives Y a blank cheque so that Y can purchase for X a lawnmower. Y fills in the cheque for £50 and inserts his own name. He then negotiates it to Z, a holder in due course.

What is the legal position?

Question 5

When is the payee of a cheque considered to be non-existing? How does the law treat a cheque which is made payable to a non-existing payee?

Question 6

William Brown is in business as 'William Brown & Co.' and he endorses a cheque made out in favour of the business by signing 'Brown'. He then delivers the cheque to Green. Brown's title is defective but Green claims a good title as a holder in due course.

State, with reasons, whether Green is correct.

Question 7

X, who is a customer of the Y Bank Ltd, has a deposit of £400 with no permission to overdraw. X draws up a cheque payable to Z for £600.

How will the bank deal with this situation?

Question 8

X draws a cheque on the Y Bank Ltd payable to Z. Z, on receipt of the cheque, crosses it generally. The cheque is then stolen by T who opens an account at the U Bank Ltd in the name of Z. The U Bank presents the cheque to the Y Bank Ltd which pays in good faith and without negligence.

Advise Z in regard to a possible action against the bank and against X.

Question 9

'Under the Cheques Act 1957 a payee who presents an uncrossed cheque for payment over the counter must endorse it.'

State, with reasons, whether or not this statement is correct.

TUTORIAL PROBLEMS

1. Body was indebted under a credit agreement to Globe Motors in the sum of £6000 which he could not pay. He went to Agricultural Supplies

and said he was an agent for International Tractors and that Agricultural Supplies could be the sole agents in Midshires for International Tractors if they would agree to take 40 tractors and pay a deposit of £6000.

Agricultural Supplies were not prepared to do business until Body told them that Globe Motors were backing the deal and that the cheque should be made payable to them. Agricultural Supplies thereupon gave Body a cheque for £6000 made payable to Globe Motors which Body used to pay his debt. Agricultural Supplies are now seeking to recover the money from Globe Motors.

What is the legal position?

2. John stole two cheques from his employer, Bloggs. One, which was payable to bearer, he cashed immediately at the Barchester Bank on which it was drawn. The other cheque was made payable to Charles, but John forged Charles' endorsement on the cheque and negotiated it to Ernest as payment for a record player. The bank paid Ernest on the cheque. Bloggs is intending to sue the Barchester Bank for paying the two cheques.

What defences, if any, might the bank be able to raise?

General principles of insurance law

Question 1

In 1983 Wise insured his home with the Foresight Insurance Co. The premiums were collected weekly until 1984 when there was a fire at Wise's house. Wise received an indemnity of £3000 under the policy and thereafter no premiums were collected and the policy lapsed.

In January 1985 Seller, the insurance company's district inspector, who visited only those whose policies had lapsed, called at Wise's house with a view of getting Wise to revive the lapsed policy and take out new ones. Seller saw Wise and produced two proposal forms, one for fire and one for burglary. Seller filled in the forms himself without asking Wise to give the answers to the questions posed and Wise signed as 'proposer' without reading the forms. Seller also left a proposal form for life assurance with Wise. Wise later completed this and was accepted by the insurance company without a medical examination.

In June 1985 there was a burglary at Wise's house and Wise wished to claim. Seller brought a claim form round to Wise's house and found that Wise was off work with hypertension. Seller was told by Wise he had been in hospital in 1983 with hypertension and had since that time received continuous medical treatment for high blood pressure. Wise then filled in the claim form which required him to answer the question: 'Have you ever before sustained loss by fire, burglary or theft?' Wise answered: 'Yes. Fire damages £3000.' Seller went on collecting premiums on all the policies, but reported the fact of Wise's illness to head office.

Head office has recently rejected the claim for an indemnity in respect of the burglary because the form which Wise signed after Seller had filled it in contained an incorrect answer as follows: 'State policy numbers of insurances held by you with the company and whether lapsed or in force'. Answer: 'None'.

The final clause of the proposal form signed by Wise was as follows: 'I further declare in so far as any part of this proposal is not written by me the person who has written same has done so by my instructions and as my agent for that purpose. I agree that the above proposal and this declaration shall be the basis of the contract of insurance between the company and myself.'

Head office is also seeking to rescind the life assurance policy because Wise did not declare the fact that he had hypertension. Wise says he thought that his illness was not important and, therefore, did not disclose it.

What is the legal position?

Question 2

John's house is worth £80,000, but is only insured for £60,000. Fire has recently caused £20,000 worth of damage to the property. The policy contains an average clause.

State, with reasons, what John will recover.

Question 3

Being afraid of burglary Mary hid money and jewellery under paper and coal in the sitting-room fireplace. Later, having forgotten she had done this she lit the fire and the notes and most of the jewellery were destroyed. Mary has a policy which insures her against 'loss or damage caused by fire'.

State, with reasons, whether or not Mary can make a successful claim under the policy.

Question 4

Alan took out an insurance policy with Bloggs Ltd under which Bloggs Ltd agreed to indemnify Alan for any liability in defamation arising from material contained in a magazine produced by Alan.

Alan's magazine has recently included material which Alan knew to be libellous and Alan has been successfully sued for damages.

State, with reasons, whether or not Alan is entitled to an indemnity from Bloggs Ltd.

Question 5

The common-law rule relating to insurances on property is that the person insured is not required to use any of the money payable under a policy on reinstating the property. There is, however, an Act of Parliament which requires reinstatement in some cases.

What is the name of the Act and what are its major provisions?

Question 6

Alan signed a contract to buy Bert's house on Monday. On the following Wednesday the house was badly damaged by fire. Alan has not insured the property. Is any insurance available to him in these circumstances?

Question 7

Arthur has not used his car for three months. It is standing in the road outside his flat with the battery removed so that it cannot be mechanically propelled.

State, with reasons, whether in these circumstances Arthur needs compulsory insurance.

TUTORIAL PROBLEMS

Mrs Mopp had an 'All-Risks' insurance policy to cover her own and her husband's jewellery. She signed a proposal form in 1971 but gave no information about previous convictions, although her husband to her knowledge had been convicted some years earlier of receiving 2000 cigarettes knowing them to have been stolen and had been fined £25. No specific question about previous convictions was asked.

Her husband was convicted for a second time in 1984 of two offences of dishonesty and was sentenced to 15 months' imprisonment. The policy was renewed in 1985, the conviction not having been disclosed although again, Mrs Mopp knew about it.

Later in 1985 several items of the insured jewellery which were valued at £300 were stolen.

Mrs Mopp is intending to claim on the policy, but the insurance company is disputing her claim, having discovered the previous convictions of her husband.

Advise Mrs Mopp.

2. Joe, a retired bank manager, was to be employed by his son, John for seven years at a salary of £6000 per annum. Joe insured John's life for £5000. After Joe had been employed for two years, John died. The insurance company is now disputing Joe's claim on the grounds that he had no insurable interest in his son's life.

Advise Joe.

Principles of employment law

Question 1

Maurice is the owner of a biscuit factory at Stoneford. He employs 50 women and 10 men. Stoneford's population contains a considerable number of immigrants, some of whom are employed by Maurice. He feels that he has not paid sufficient attention to the provisions of legislation relating to discrimination.

Write a report for Maurice explaining the basic provisions of current legislation on the subject, dividing your report into two parts, the first to be concerned with discrimination in recruitment, and the second with discrimination in regard to those already employed by Maurice.

Question 2

(*a*) Albert suffers with rheumatism and during the winter months he is often away from work. Bill, his employer feels that Albert's absences are such that he can no longer employ him. Bill dismisses Albert on the grounds that he is unreliable.

(*b*) Jane works on the checkout at John's supermarket. John has discovered that Jane stole a fur coat from a friend's house where she had been for a party. John has now dismissed Jane.

Advise Albert and Jane who wish to take these various matters before an industrial tribunal.

Question 3

Boxo Ltd is a company which manufacturers washing machines. Sales are badly down and the board has instructed the managing director to dispense with the services of 150 workers over the next eight weeks.

The managing director seeks your advice as to the procedures and legal requirements which must be followed in regard to the selection and compensation of those who are to be dismissed.

TUTORIAL PROBLEM

Arthur, a plumber, who works mainly in the domestic field, thinks that his employer, Bertram, would like him to resign. Over the past months Bertram has been giving Arthur work in industrial heating situations which are outside his usual range. Bertram is also these days highly critical of Arthur's work. Arthur feels he will have to resign.

What will the legal position be if he does?

General Index